THE ROMAN AQABA PROJECT
FINAL REPORT
VOLUME 1

AMERICAN SCHOOLS OF ORIENTAL RESEARCH
ARCHEOLOGICAL REPORTS

Kevin M. McGeough, Editor

Number 19

The Roman Aqaba Project. Final Report, Volume 1
The Regional Environment and the Regional Survey

THE ROMAN AQABA PROJECT
FINAL REPORT

VOLUME 1 – THE REGIONAL ENVIRONMENT AND THE REGIONAL SURVEY

By

S. THOMAS PARKER *and* ANDREW M. SMITH II

With Contributions by

CASSANDRA BURNS, MARNI COCHRANE, DAVID F. GRAF,

DONALD O. HENRY, TINA M. NIEMI, JOHN D. RUCKER,

AND TRAVIS TAVERNA

AMERICAN SCHOOLS OF ORIENTAL RESEARCH • BOSTON, MA

The Roman Aqaba Project. Final Report, Volume 1

The Regional Environment and the Regional Survey

by

S. Thomas Parker and Andrew M. Smith II

Publication of this book has been aided by a grant from the von Bothmer Publication Fund of the Archaeological Institute of America.

Cover: Petroglyph of a male ibex and what appears to be a female hunter preparing to throw a spear, carved on a boulder at SAAS Site 167.

The American Schools of Oriental Research © 2014

ISBN 978-0-89757-042-8

Library of Congress Cataloging-in-Publication Data

Roman Aqaba Project.
   The Roman Aqaba Project : final report / by S. Thomas Parker and Andrew M. Smith II ; with
       contributions by Cassandra Burns, Marni Cochrane, David F. Graf, Donald O.Henry, Tina
       M. Niemi, John D. Rucker, and Travis Taverna.
    volumes cm. -- (Archeological reports ; number 19)
Includes bibliographical references and index.
ISBN 978-0-89757-042-8
1. 'Aqabah (Jordan)--Antiquities, Roman. 2. Excavations (Archaeology)--Jordan--'Aqabah. 3.
       Romans--Jordan--'Aqabah. 4. Roman Aqaba Project. I. Parker, S. Thomas (Samuel Thomas)
       II. Smith, Andrew M. (Andrew Michael), 1967- III. Title.
DS154.9.A62R64 2014
939.4'8--dc23
                2013049234

Printed in the United States of America on acid-free paper.

Contents

List of Illustrations

List of Tables

Abbreviations

AASOR	*Annual of the American Schools of Oriental Research*
ADAJ	*Annual of the Department of Antiquities of Jordan*
AJA	*American Journal of Archaeology*
BA	*Biblical Archaeologist*
BAR	*British Archaeological Reports*
BASOR	*Bulletin of the American Schools of Oriental Research*
CIK	W. Caskel, ed., 1966. *Ǧamharat an-Nasab. Das genealogische Werk des Hišam ibn Muḥammad al-Kalbī.* Leiden: Brill.
CIS	*Corpus Inscriptionum Semiticarum* (1881–)
HIn	G. L. Harding, ed., 1971. *An Index and Concordance of Pre-Islamic Arabian Names and Inscriptions.* Near and Middle East Series 8. Toronto: University of Toronto.
IEJ	*Israel Exploration Journal*
JAS	*Journal of Archaeological Science*
JFA	*Journal of Field Archaeology*
JNES	*Journal of Near Eastern Studies*
JRA	*Journal of Roman Archaeology*
JRS	*Journal of Roman Studies*
NEA	*Near Eastern Archaeology*
NEAEHL	E. Stern, A. Lewinson-Gilboa, J. Aviram, eds., 1993. *New Encyclopedia of Archaeological Excavations in the Holy Land.* 4 vols. New York: Simon & Schuster.
PEQ	*Palestine Exploration Quarterly*
QDAP	*Quarterly of the Department of Antiquities in Palestine*
RB	*Revue Biblique*
SHAJ	*Studies in the History and Archaeology of Jordan*
ZDPV	*Zeitschrift des deutschen Palästina-Vereins*
ZPE	*Zeitschrift für Papyrologie und Epigraphik*

Chapter 1

Introduction

by S. Thomas Parker

I. INTRODUCTION

This chapter introduces the Roman Aqaba Project. It begins with an overview of the project: its purpose, research design, project history, sponsorship, and personnel. The chapter then turns to the purpose and scope of the final report and an overview of the natural environment. Next is a discussion of the relevant documentary sources and a review of previous archaeological research in the region. The chapter concludes with some acknowledgments.

II. BACKGROUND

Scholars have long debated the nature of the Roman Empire's economy. Understanding this economy is admittedly a daunting task. Rarely has quantitative documentary evidence survived on such fundamental aspects as levels of production, trade, taxation, or budgets. Contemporary writers were usually little interested in such matters and official documents rarely survive. Archaeological evidence can be valuable but must be considered cautiously.

Renewed scholarly interest in the ancient Mediterranean economy must be credited above all to M. I. Finley (1973), who strongly countered long-established "modernist" views of earlier scholars such as M. Rostovtzeff (1957). Finley attacked earlier notions about such key economic issues as the

economic purpose of coinage and the presumed preeminent role of cities in the imperial economy as simplistic equations drawn from modern parallels. Finley claimed that the ancient evidence suggested the absence of mass markets and thus the overwhelming predominance of a near-subsistence agricultural economy. The small agricultural surplus available was mostly consumed locally. Trade was therefore limited in quantity, quality, and geographical extent. Except in a few special situations, such as supplying the city of Rome or the armies on the frontiers, trade was largely a local affair. Long distance trade, due to the absence of mass markets and high cost of transport, was confined mostly to luxury items. Even the apparent abundance of Roman coinage was minimized as largely for fiscal needs rather than for economic exchange. Many found these "minimalist" views persuasive. Later work modified Finley's salient conclusions to some degree. Hopkins (1978; 1983), for example, accepted Finley's basic views, but still suggested that real economic growth occurred in the Roman Empire during the last few centuries BC and first two centuries AD. In fact, a new edition of Finley's work (1999, including a review of subsequent scholarship by Ian Morris), several monographs (e.g., Young 2001), many articles (e.g., Harris 1994; Morris 1994), and published collections of papers devoted to these issues (e.g., Kingsley and Decker 2001; Scheidel and von Reden 2002; Manning and

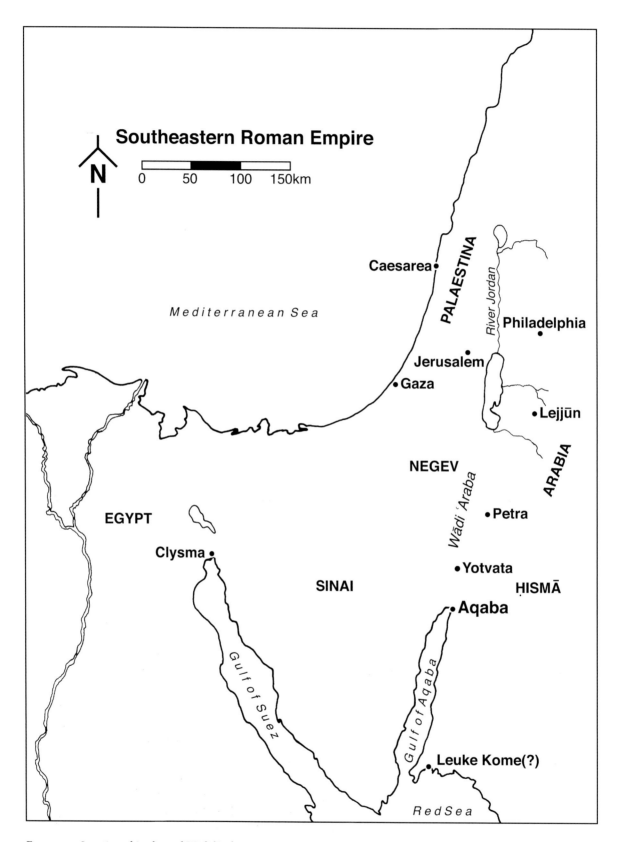

FIG. 1.1 *Location of Aqaba and Wādī ʿAraba.*

Morris 2005) all illustrate the continued vibrancy of this debate. The editors of one such collection reasonably concluded that Finley's view of cities as essentially "parasitic" was too simplistic and that a variety of models may be applicable for these urban economies (Mattingly and Salmon 2001). Although attempts at quantification of available documentary data produced some useful insights (Duncan-Jones 1982; 1990), scholars increasingly turned to archaeology for new evidence about the Roman economy. Recent syntheses of archaeological evidence have challenged minimalist views about the nature of this economy. Greene, for example, argued that analysis of agriculture, trade, coins, industry, and settlement patterns suggests a more complex Roman economy than others have advanced (Greene 1986). Study of Roman coinage, especially quantitative analysis of hoards and dies, have refuted Finley's minimalist notion of the role of coinage and suggest that the empire's economy was largely monetized (Harl 1996). Another influential work has stressed the importance of micro-environments in the development of economic networks throughout the Mediterranean World (Horden and Purcell 2000). The debate has even attracted economists. One concluded that "Finley was wrong, ancient Rome had an economic system that was an enormous conglomeration of interdependent markets" (Temin 2001: 181).

Clearly, further study of trade in the Roman Empire is needed. One method of approach is to examine sites that served as major nodules of trade. Research into such cities as Carthage (Fulford and Peacock 1984), Corinth (Engels 1990), and Caesarea Maritima (Holum 1999; 2008) offers insights into trade. This evidence can be subjected to quantitative analysis in elucidating patterns of long distance trade (Tomber 1993).

Roman Trade with the East

A key region for international trade was the empire's eastern frontier, stretching from the Black Sea to the Red Sea. This trade was so extensive that, according to controversial statements by the Elder Pliny (*Natural History* 6.26; 12.41) in the 1st century AD, the empire suffered a serious drain of hard currency to pay for eastern imports. There

are important studies of documentary evidence for Rome's eastern trade (Raschke 1978; Sidebotham 1986; Young 2001). One major avenue was the Red Sea, for which written sources, such as the *Periplus of the Red Sea* (Casson 1989), reveal something of this trade. Excavated Roman sites on the Egyptian coast have yielded important insights (Whitcomb and Johnson 1979; 1982; Sidebotham 1994; 2011; Sidebotham and Wendrich 1995–1999; Peacock and Blue 2006), as well as ports farther south beyond the Roman Empire (Tomber 2008), such as Adulis (Peacock and Blue 2007), Qana (Sedov 1995; Salles and Sedov 2010) and Khor Rori (Avanzini 2008). But, before the current project, no ports on the Arabian side of the Red Sea had been excavated, despite their importance as suggested by literary evidence. Therefore, the author was drawn to Aqaba, ancient Aila, now in modern Jordan at the north end of the Gulf of Aqaba, an arm of the Red Sea.

III.   THE ROMAN AQABA PROJECT

Purpose

Various documentary sources reveal that Aila was a port city on the southeastern frontier of the Roman Empire (fig. 1.1). Aila is first mentioned as an urban center in the early first century AD within the Nabataean kingdom, a Roman client state. The sources assert that Aila handled trade between the Empire and south Arabia, east Africa, and India. It continued to flourish as a port under direct Roman rule from the early 2nd century AD into the early 7th century, when the region fell under Islamic rule.

Therefore, the Roman Aqaba Project was launched to reconstruct the economy of Aila and produce new evidence about the imperial Roman economy. The project sought to answer two principal historical questions. What was the role of Aila in the economy of the Roman Empire and how did this role evolve over time? How does the evidence from Aila relate to the debate about the nature of the Roman Empire's economy?

From these primary questions came several subsidiary questions: What was Aila's role in international trade? What specific products passed through the port? Where were their origins and destinations? What were the principal routes of access?

Tell Maqass
ca. 3500 B.C.

AQABA

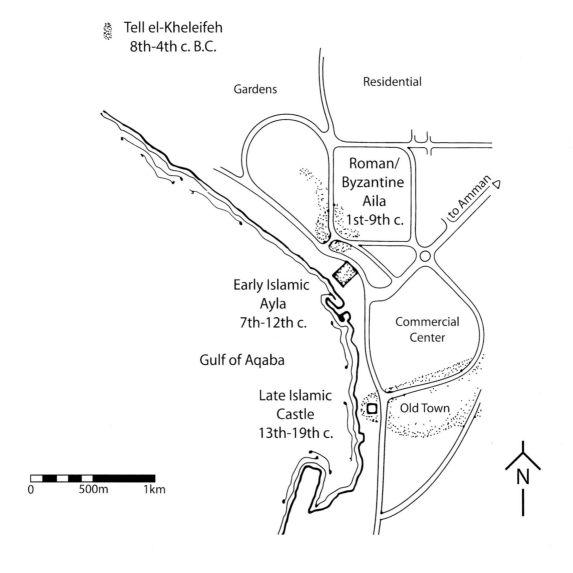

Tell el-Kheleifeh
8th-4th c. B.C.

Gardens

Residential

Roman/
Byzantine
Aila
1st-9th c.

to Amman

Early Islamic
Ayla
7th-12th c.

Commercial
Center

Gulf of Aqaba

Late Islamic
Castle
13th-19th c.

Old Town

0   500m   1km

N

FIG. 1.2   *Map of the modern city of Aqaba, with ancient and medieval archaeological sites.*

Further, what was the impact of the regional environment on the urban economy and how did human activity impact the environment? Most Roman cities controlled a *territorium* or rural hinterland to provide food and raw materials. Was Aila's hinterland adequate for self-sufficiency in these necessities, or were imports necessary?

Moreover, how was economic and other human activity organized within and around the urban space? How did the physical plan of the city evolve? Could areas of specific activities be identified, e.g., residential, industrial, commercial, cultic, or military?

Finally, would the evidence from Aila lend support to the so-called "primitivist" view of long distance trade confined largely to luxury items, the so-called "modernist" view of mass markets served by long distance trade in bulk commodities, or another economic model?

Research Design

In order to address the research question posed above, the research design of the project was formulated around three components: 1) a regional archaeological and environmental survey of the environs of Aila, focusing especially on Wādī 'Araba north of the city, 2) excavation of extensive areas within the ancient city, and 3) analysis of artifacts and other material relevant to Aila's economy.

The Regional Survey

The economy of Aila obviously could only be fully assessed by examining its regional context. The site lies at the southern end of Wādī 'Araba, a linear valley extending 165 km north from Aqaba to the Dead Sea. Wādī 'Araba in turn is part of the Great Rift in the earth's surface that extends far to the north and south, including the Red Sea and as far as east Africa. When the project began fieldwork in 1994, the western side of Wādī 'Araba in modern Israel had already witnessed surveys and excavations by several scholars. But the eastern side in Jordan, particularly north of Aqaba, was largely *terra incognita* in archaeological terms. Therefore the southeastern Wādī 'Araba became the principal target of the project's regional survey, conducted

through a reconnaissance in 1993 and then over three seasons in 1994, 1996, and 1998. The primary goal of the survey was to explore both the hinterland of Aila and, in the SE Wādī 'Araba, one of the city's principal trade routes. The survey studied the natural environment (including geomorphology, hydrology, climate, flora, and fauna) and evidence for past human activity by recording archaeological sites. All sites of all periods (including prehistoric sites) encountered were recorded. The boundaries of the survey extended 70 km NNE from Aqaba to the 'Araba's watershed, to the east by an escarpment of mountains, and to the west by the modern Israeli border. Some 330 sites were recorded, nearly all new additions to the archaeological map of Jordan.

Detailed discussion of the goals, methodology, and results of the survey are presented in Chapter 4 in this volume.

Excavation of Aqaba

It must be stressed that selection of excavation areas within the modern city of Aqaba (fig. 1.2) was complicated by several factors. First and above all, the presence of the modern city severely limited the areas available for excavation. The project was limited essentially to undeveloped open areas, particularly in the so-called "Circular Area," northeast of the line of hotels along the beach and west of the Radwan housing district (fig. 1.3). Therefore, access to the modern shoreline, where one might reasonably search for ancient harbor facilities, for example, was prohibited by modern structures and a military area. Second, there were no visible surface ruins prior to excavation. The sheer size of the "Circular Area," the one large sector available for excavation, necessitated a strategy of sampling. Therefore, many widely scattered excavation areas were opened as suggested by concentrations of artifacts on the surface, analysis of aerial photographs, and remote sensing. In the first season in 1994 some forty trenches in thirteen separate excavation areas were opened. Some areas, particularly in the northern "Circular Area," were devoid of ancient remains while others proved productive. Third, excavation revealed that Early Islamic Ayla, previously excavated by the University of Chicago, extended well beyond the walled settlement and covered much of Roman and

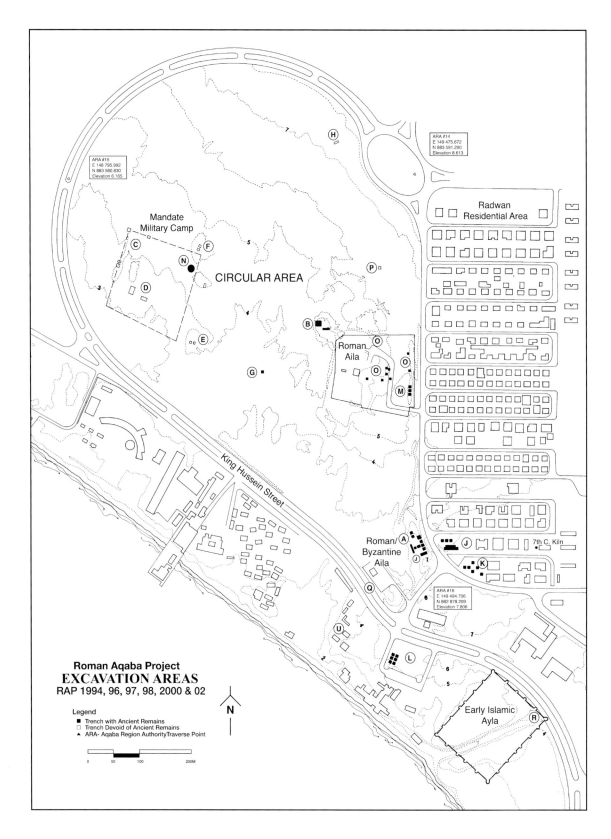

FIG. 1.3   *Excavation Areas of the Roman Aqaba Project, 1994–2002.*

Byzantine Aila. Therefore, in some areas substantial Early Islamic strata overlaid the pre-Islamic remains. Fourth, there was a great sense of urgency to the excavation. Imminent development threatened the ancient site. It occupied what was then the last large undeveloped tract of land within downtown Aqaba, which was developing rapidly. But as the project revealed significant remains of the ancient city, local authorities responded by reserving some areas for permanent protection within an archaeological park. This includes the Nabataean/Late Roman domestic complex in Area M, the putative Late Roman church and a long segment of the Byzantine city wall in Area J, and the Early Byzantine cemetery and Late Byzantine/Early Islamic domestic complex in Area A. Unfortunately, other areas judged to be of lesser significance could not be saved and have since been lost to modern development.

Excavation areas that proved productive were subsequently expanded to expose large horizontal areas, including portions of six domestic complexes (in Areas A, B, K, L, M, O), a dump (Area O), a monumental public building (probably a church, Area J), an extensive segment of the city's fortifications (Area J), a clay mine (Area N), and two cemeteries (Areas A and M). Several excavation areas yielded complete vertical profiles stretching over several centuries. In short, the excavations exposed significant portions of Aila and produced stratigraphic profiles that together span nearly its entire history from the 1st to the 10th centuries AD. Area R was excavated in 2000 and 2003 in order to date the curtain wall of Early Islamic Ayla. This operation had the full support of Donald Whitcomb, the previous excavator of this site.

A number of excavation areas, mostly opened during the initial season, proved to be largely sterile of archaeological deposits (Areas C, D, E, F, G, H, P, Q). Because all these areas faced the prospect of imminent destruction by modern development, mechanical equipment was employed in some cases to excavate more rapidly and deeply to confirm the absence of archaeological deposits.

Soundings of Qasr el-Kithara

In 2002 five small scattered trenches were opened at this site, a small Roman fort about one day's march northeast of Aqaba in Wādī Yutum on the *Via Nova Traiana*. Although the basic sequence of occupation had previously been established by surface survey (Parker 1986: 108–11, 177–78), the soundings (Area T) were intended to date the extant fort and recover evidence about the nature of trade entering or leaving Aila through one of its main land arteries.

Excavation Methods

The project employed a modified version of the "Wheeler-Kenyon" method of stratigraphic excavation. A grid of rectangular excavation trenches was laid out by surveyors and designated as an excavation "area," identified by a capital Roman letter. As excavation proceeded in each trench (identified by an Arabic number), identifiable stratigraphic features, called "loci" (such as soil layers, floors, and architectural structures, also identified by an Arabic number), were exposed, recorded, and sometimes removed in their reverse chronological order of deposition. Thus, "A.6:57" refers to Area A, trench 6, locus 57. All associated artifacts were retrieved and sorted from each locus. Due to the imminent threat by modern development, deposits were generally not sieved, although sieving was employed occasionally, particularly in some critical contexts. Soil samples were taken for froth flotation to retrieve botanical remains. Great care was exercised in identification, recording, and interpretation of each distinctive stratigraphic feature or locus. The vertical walls ("balks") exposed on the sides of each trench were drawn. Top plans of each significant locus were drawn and often photographed. Groups of chronologically related loci were then grouped into "phases," which in turn were grouped into broader units called "strata." All stratigraphic data recovered were entered into a computer database, discussed below. All this allowed the stratigraphic history of each excavated area to be reconstructed. The stratigraphic history of each area provided the evidence for reconstructing the history of the entire site.

Artifact Analysis

The methods employed in the analysis of artifacts and other material recovered from excavation and survey varied according to the nature of the material. But in general the following methods were employed. Each artifact or other material cultural sample was labeled and registered according to its find context (excavation locus or survey site number). It then was analyzed by an appropriate specialist, either in the field or after shipment to the US. The specialist made a preliminary analysis which was then offered to the director and field staff to aid in interpretation of their own excavation areas or survey sites. The specialists entered their data into a specific database linked to the project's general database. In particular, the specialists considered the economic implications of their specific materials, such as evidence of agriculture, industry, trade, and the regional environment. Reports on the chipped stone artifacts, Nabataean inscriptions, and pottery from the regional survey are included in this volume of the project's final report. Reports on other materials will appear in subsequent volumes.

Computer Software

Given the enormous amount of data from the fieldwork, the project's computer software package facilitated access to and manipulation of the data. A package of three integrated Microsoft software programs is employed: Word (word-processor), Access (database manager), and Excel (spreadsheet). Several interrelated databases have been designed, including those devoted to excavation (by individual locus), survey (by individual sites), and most categories of artifacts. A separate database contains a registry of all photographs taken. The location of excavation areas and other features was entered into an Autocad database. Field drawings of architecture and artifacts were scanned into a computer graphics program (Corel Draw) for ease in manipulation and reconstruction.

History of the Project

The author made a brief visit to Aqaba in April 1992 at the suggestion of and accompanied by Donald Whitcomb, who was then engaged in excavation of Early Islamic Ayla. He pointed out to the author the so-called "Circular Area," a large undeveloped sector northwest of the Early Islamic site where a survey had found possible evidence of a pre-Islamic site (Meloy 1991). In June 1993 the author and Mary Mattocks conducted a week-long reconnaissance in Aqaba, looking especially at this "Circular Area." The results of these visits persuaded the author to proceed with a full-fledged project, made more urgent by the rapid pace of development in and around Aqaba. The author also encouraged one of his graduate students at NCSU, Andrew W. Smith II, and Tina Niemi to conduct a preliminary reconnaissance of the southern portion of Wādī ʿAraba that summer as preparation for organizing the survey component of the proposed project (Smith and Niemi 1994).

The project formally began fieldwork in 1994, with a field season conducted between May 15 and July 6. A staff of 15 professionals, 35 students, and up to 70 local workers conducted excavations in thirteen widely scattered areas (Areas A–M) around the modern city but focusing especially on the "Circular Area." Many of these areas, especially those in the northern sector of the "Circular Area," yielded little or no evidence of ancient remains. But some of the southern areas, especially Areas A, B, J, K, L, and M, began yielding rich remains immediately below the modern ground surface. Meanwhile the project's regional survey (the Southeast ʿAraba Archaeological Survey, or SAAS), under the direction of Andrew Smith, began its work both in the environs of Aqaba and farther north in Wādī ʿAraba. A brief summary of results (Parker 1995b) and more detailed preliminary reports of this season were subsequently published (Parker 1995b; 1997a; Smith, Niemi, and Stevens 1997), as well as an article on site migration in the Aqaba region (Parker 1997b). Brief notices on the first season were published in several popular and semi-popular venues (Parker 1994a; 1994b; 1996a).

The second season was conducted from May 16 to July 4, 1996. A team of 16 staff, 32 students, and

75 local workers continued excavation primarily in those areas which had proven productive in 1994 (i.e., Areas A, B, J, K, L, and M). Tina Niemi also bored a number of geologic cores in and around the "Circular Area" and did limited excavation in one new area (Area N). The survey also continued its work in Wādī ʿAraba. The author published a short notice (Parker 1997c), a detailed preliminary report (Parker 1998a), and two popular articles (Parker 1996b; 1996c). Niemi and Smith published a preliminary study of climate history based on their research in the region (Niemi and Smith 1999).

At the request of the then Director-General of the Department of Antiquities, Dr. Ghazi Bisheh, a smaller excavation was conducted from May 16 to June 30, 1997. A team of 25 staff and students plus 20 local workers under the field direction of Mary-Louise Mussell confined excavation to the putative church in Area J. Short notices on this season were subsequently published (Mussell 1997; 1998), but more detailed results of this season were incorporated into the preliminary reports of the next season in 1998.

The project's fourth field season extended from May 20 to July 4, 1998, with a team of 18 staff, 35 students, and 70 local workers. Large-scale excavation continued in Areas A, B, J, K, and M. Two new areas (O and P) were opened, although only the former yielded significant ancient evidence. The regional survey conducted its final season of field work in Wādī ʿAraba. A short notice (Parker 1999b), a more detailed preliminary report (Parker 2000a), and several popular articles (Parker 1998b; 1999c) soon appeared, as well as articles devoted specifically to the putative church (Parker 1999a; Mussell 2000a). A preliminary review of the glass from the site also appeared after this season (Jones 2000). The announcement about the early date of the possible church spurred much interest in the popular media, including short reports in *Archaeology* (Rose 1998) and *National Geographic* (Weintraub 1999).

The fifth field season was from May 24 to July 9, 2000, with a team of 15 staff, 37 students, and 70 local workers. With the regional survey now completed, research was confined to excavation within Aqaba itself, in Areas A, J, K, M, O, and in one new area (R). This last area conducted soundings of the curtain wall of Early Islamic Ayla, with the support of this site's original excavator, Donald Whitcomb. An abnormally dry winter in 1999–2000 had lowered the groundwater table, raising the possibility of reaching the foundations of the curtain wall. It was hoped that such soundings might yield conclusive evidence for dating its construction, which had been controversial. This effort, with the help of a water pump, proved successful. Both short notices (Parker 2000b; 2001) and a detailed preliminary report (Parker 2002) on the 2000 season soon appeared. An article on a notable glass find was also published after this season (Jones 2002), as well as a detailed study of the Nabataean–Roman domestic complex in Area M (Retzleff 2003).

The sixth field season extended from May 22 to July 10, 2002, with a team of 14 staff, 18 students, and up to 60 local workers. Excavation at Aqaba continued in three existing areas (J, K, and M) and one new area (U), the latter an ultimately successful attempt to trace the Byzantine city wall farther southwest towards the beach. In addition, limited soundings were conducted at the Roman road fort of Qasr el-Kithara, the first road station north of Aqaba on the *Via Nova Traiana*. A brief notice on the 2002 season was soon published (Parker 2003a), with a more detailed preliminary report to follow (Parker 2003b).

A brief, small-scale effort in RAP Areas J and R was led by Tina Niemi in the summer of 2003, assisted by four staff and a handful of workers. The main goal was to elucidate features that might assist in reconstructing the tectonic history of the region. A report on this work was also subsequently published (Thomas, Niemi, and Parker 2007). This completed the project's fieldwork.

The years after the conclusion of fieldwork in 2003 witnessed a steady stream of publications on various aspects of the project as analysis of the evidence continued. These included a monograph on the Nabataean pottery from the site (Dolinka 2003), further study of the glass (Jones 2003), an article on fish sauce (van Neer and Parker 2007), and a series of conference papers (Parker 2005; 2006; 2007; 2009a; 2009b; Tomber 2005). Several graduate student master's theses and doctoral dissertations were based largely or partly on the evidence from this project (Smith 1995; Dolinka 1999;

Grubisha 2000; Ward 2001; Perry 2002; Williams 2009). Smith's thesis (2005), heavily revised and updated with results of more recent fieldwork, has also now been published (Smith 2010).

Sponsorship

Throughout the decade of fieldwork in 1994–2003, the project worked under permits issued by and with the full support of the Jordanian Department of Antiquities during the tenure of three successive Director-Generals of Antiquities: Dr. Safwan et-Tell, Dr. Ghazi Bisheh, and Dr. Fawwaz al-Khrayseh. We also benefited greatly from the unstinting and enthusiastic support of Dr. Sawsan Fakhiry, Inspector for the DOA of the Aqaba District,who served as departmental representative for all field seasons of the project.

North Carolina State University, in Raleigh, North Carolina, was the institutional sponsor of the project throughout its history. It also provided significant financial support for the project through faculty research grants. In 1998 NCSU created the Archaeological Laboratory and Repository within the Department of History for analysis and permanent storage of the artifacts, records, and other materials from both the current project and the director's earlier *Limes Arabicus* Project.

The project was also affiliated with the American Center of Oriental Research (ACOR) in Amman and with the American Schools of Oriental Research (ASOR). ACOR and particularly its then Director, Pierre Bikai, provided crucial logistical and administrative support. Project staff presented many papers of research in progress, including several project workshops, during the annual meetings of ASOR.

Financial support for the project derived from a number of sources. Funding for the 1994 season was provided by grants from the National Endowment for the Humanities, National Geographic Society, Samuel H. Kress Foundation, the Institute of Classics of the University of Helsinki, IBM Corporation, and private donors. In addition, four students received travel fellowships to permit their participation: Elizabeth Ann Pollard and Elizabeth Stephens both received Jennifer C. Groot Fellowships in the Archaeology of Jordan

funded by ACOR. Kirsten Anderson received a fellowship from the Kyle-Kelso Foundation, and Jennifer Blakeslee received a travel grant from the Endowment for Biblical Research.

The 1996 season was funded by grants from the National Geographic Society, Joukowsky Family Foundation, Samuel H. Kress Foundation, Lockheed Martin Corporation Foundation, the Institute of Classics of the University of Helsinki, and private donors. Fellowships enabled three students to participate on the project. Carol Frey was a Jennifer C. Groot Fellow from ACOR. Elizabeth Ann Pollard and Chaffee Viets received fellowships from the Endowment for Biblical Research.

Funding for the 1998 season was provided by grants from the National Geographic Society, Joukowsky Family Foundation, Samuel H. Kress Foundation, and private donors. Fellowships permitted two students to participate in the project. Robin Armstrong was a Jennifer C. Groot Fellow, funded by ACOR. Valerie Johnson received a fellowship from the Endowment for Biblical Research.

The 2000 season was funded by grants from the National Geographic Society, Joukowsky Family Foundation, Samuel H. Kress Foundation, Foundation for Biblical Archaeology and private donors. Walter Ward received a Jennifer C. Groot Fellowship from ACOR.

Funding for the 2002 campaign was provided by grants from the National Geographic Society, Joukowsky Family Foundation, Foundation for Biblical Archaeology, and private donors. The participation of two students, Joanne Whitmore and Jenny Spruill, was facilitated by Jennifer C. Groot Fellowships in the Archaeology of Jordan, awarded by ACOR.

In the years after the completion of fieldwork, the project continued to benefit from continued annual support from the Joukowsky Family Foundation, Foundation for Biblical Archaeology, and private donors, as well as two gifts from the North Carolina Community Foundation. Finally, the project enjoyed consistent and generous financial support from North Carolina State University through several faculty research grants and other awards.

Personnel

The senior staff of the 1994 campaign included Vincent A. Clark as Semitic epigrapher, Dorianne Gould as pottery and small finds registrar, Nelson Harris as assistant camp manager, Mary Mattocks as landscape architect and draftsperson, Tina M. Niemi as geologist, Erick S. Parker as surveyor, S. Thomas Parker as director, stratigrapher, and ceramicist, Andrew M. Smith II as director of the survey, Michael P. Speidel as classical epigrapher and project advisor, Michelle Stevens as lithics specialist and survey archaeologist, Jonathan Tedder as photographer and videographer, and Peter Warnock as archaeobotanist and camp manager. Area supervisors were Vincent A. Clark (Areas C and L), Dorianne Gould (Areas E, F, H, and K), Mary-Louise Mussell (Areas D and J), Joanne Ryan (Areas B, G, and M), and James Terry (Area A). Senior staff not in the field in 1994 included John Wilson Betlyon as numismatist, Janet Jones as glass specialist, Andrea Lain as human osteologist, Michael P. Speidel as classical epigrapher and project advisor, and Michael R. Toplyn as faunal analyst.

Student staff serving as trench supervisors in 1994 included Kirsten Anderson, Heather Beckman, Jennifer Blakeslee, Ghida El-Osman, Mark Friedrich, Susan Dana Gelb, Christopher Groves, Jane Ann Hanck, Sherry Hardin, Nancy Hulbert, Bradley Kurtz, Anne McClanan, Sarah Morgan, Matti Mustonen, Brian Overton, Charles Parker, Megan Perry, Elizabeth Ann Pollard, Christopher Port, Alexandra Retzleff, David Simpson, Elizabeth Stephens, Joseph Stumpf, Lennart Sundelin, Will Tally, Laurent Tholbecq, Mary Turner, Jan Vihonen, Brian A. Wade, Joel Walker, Kristi Jo Warren, and Michele Zaparanick. Marie Barnett and Mary Ann Schumpert were architects/surveyors. John Rucker served on the survey. Heather Beckman, Jennifer Blakeslee, and Elizabeth Ann Pollard Lisi were assistant registrars. Elizabeth Stephens supervised field processing of faunal and human osteological remains.

In 1996, the senior staff included Christopher Gregg as assistant small finds specialist, Nelson Harris as assistant camp manager, Mary Mattocks as landscape architect, Joann McDaniel as small finds specialist and registrar, Tina M. Niemi as ge-ologist, S. Thomas Parker as director, stratigrapher, and ceramicist, Megan Perry as human osteologist, John Rucker as camp manager, Colleen Shannon as architect and surveyor, Andrew M. Smith II as director of the survey, Jonathan Tedder as photographer, and Peter Warnock as archaeobotanist. Area supervisors were Jeff Blakely (Area B), Mary-Louise Mussell (Area J), Megan Perry (Area A), Alexandra Retzleff (Area M), and Joseph Stumpf (Area K). Senior staff not in the field in 1996 included John Betlyon as numismatist, Vincent A. Clark as Semitic epigrapher, Janet Jones as glass specialist, David Reece as shell specialist, Michael P. Speidel as classical epigrapher, Michelle Stevens as lithics specialist, and Michael R. Toplyn as faunal analyst. Blakely also offered invaluable assistance in the field analysis of the ceramics.

Student staff serving as trench supervisors included Jennifer Beaver, Claudia Christen, Nathan Craig, Elena Dodge, Susan Gelb, Catherine Goodman, Geri Greenspan, John Haynick, Susan Hull, Kristine Johnson, Ellen Kenney, Klaus Krohn, Joanne Laird, Christopher Lambert, Elizabeth Ann Pollard, Kimberly Mastenbrook, Linda McRae, Shannon McCormick, Erko Mikkola, Sarah Morgan, Kim Nguyen, Jane Oltmann, Brian Overton, Michael Orr, Kenyon Reed, Angela Roskop, and Chaffee Viets. Sabina Mirabelli was assistant architect/surveyor. Carol Frey, James Christian Giercke, and Heather Walters served on the survey. Elizabeth Ann Pollard was pottery registrar. Claudia Christen supervised field processing of faunal remains, including shell. Elena Dodge and Joseph Stumpf supervised field processing of glass.

In 1997, the field staff consisted of Connie Gleason as architect, Joanne Laird as camp manager, Mary-Louise Mussell as field director and area supervisor, S. Thomas Parker as director, stratigrapher, and ceramicist, Gia Spina as photographer, and Rene Young as surveyor. Student staff included James Campbell, Sarah Campbell, Stephanie Carles, Kim Cavanagh, Catherine Goodman, Alexandra Graham, John Haynik, Alexander Holmes, Susan Johnston, Alen Katic, Amanda Lawes, Carl Martel, Tracey Sharman, Ehab Shanti, Angela Sinn, Brett Todd, Carrie Tremblay, and Julie Wieland.

In 1998, senior staff in the field included Kim Cavanagh as photographer, Christopher Gregg as small finds specialist, Eric Lapp as ceramic lamp specialist, metallurgy specialist, and assistant small finds registrar, Nasser Mansour as assistant geologist, Mary Mattocks as landscape architect, Tina M. Niemi as geologist, S. Thomas Parker as director, stratigrapher, and ceramicist, Megan Perry as human osteologist, John Rucker as camp manager, Wayne Sawtell as architect and surveyor, and Andrew M. Smith II as director of the survey. Area supervisors were Susan Gelb (Areas O and P), Sarah Morgan Harvey (Area B), Mary-Louise Mussell (Area J-east), Megan Perry (Area A), Alexandra Retzleff (Area M), Joseph Stumpf (Area K), and James Terry (Areas J-west and Q). Senior staff not in the field in 1998 included John Betlyon as numismatist, Vincent A. Clark as Semitic epigrapher, William Grantham as faunal analyst, Janet Jones as glass specialist, David Reece as shell specialist, Michelle Stevens as lithics specialist, and Peter Warnock as archaeobotanist.

Student staff serving as trench supervisors in 1998 included Jennifer Beaver, Meg Butler, Rod Constantineau, Sarah Campbell, Stephanie Carles, David Dawood, Benjamin Dolinka, William Ellwood, Flint Foster, Mital Gondha, Catherine Goodman, Geri Greenspan, Tony Hartley , Valerie Johnson, Susan Johnston, Christina Kahrl, Rebecca Kerster, Joanne Laird, Amanda Lawes, Carl Martel, Tim Miles, Michael Orr, Mark Robbescheuten, Robert Slusser, Jennifer Swimmer, Suzanne Tiefenbeck, Walter Ward, Julie Wieland, and Cheri Williams. Eric Domeier, Nader Husseini, and Hannah Threndyle were assistant architects/surveyors. Karen Kumeiga, Eric Lapp, and Michael Decker served on the survey. Susan Gelb was pottery registrar and Sarah Campbell was assistant pottery registrar. Tony Hartley supervised field processing of faunal remains, including shell. Joseph Stumpf supervised field processing of glass.

In 2000, senior field staff in the field included Kim Cavanagh as photographer, David Clark as consultant for the church, Christina Kahrl as conservator, Joann McDaniel as small finds specialist, Nasser Mansour as assistant geologist, S. Thomas Parker as director, stratigrapher, and ceramicist, Megan Perry as human osteologist, Alexandra Retzleff as assistant director, John Rucker as camp manager, and Wayne Sawtell as architect and sur-

veyor. Area supervisors were Susan Gelb (Areas O and P), Mary-Louise Mussell (Area J-east), Megan Perry (Area A), Alexandra Retzleff (Area M), Joseph Stumpf (Area K), and James Terry (Area J-west and Area T). Sarah Morgan Harvey served as assistant area supervisor for Area J-east. Senior staff not in the field in 2000 included John Betlyon as numismatist, Vincent A. Clark as Semitic epigrapher, William Grantham as faunal analyst, Christopher Gregg as small finds specialist, Janet Jones as glass specialist, Eric Lapp as ceramic lamp specialist and metallurgy specialist, Mary Mattocks as draftsperson, Tina M. Niemi as geologist, David Reece as shell specialist, Andrew M. Smith II as director of the survey, Michelle Stevens as lithics specialist, and Peter Warnock as archaeobotanist.

Student staff serving as trench supervisors in 2000 included Jennifer Armstrong, Stephanie Bowers, Matthew Breznai, Meredith Campbell, Sarah Campbell, Jennifer Cunningham, Collier de Butts, Elena Dodge, Benjamin Dolinka, Catherine Goodman, Diane Grubisha, Tony Hartley, Rebecca Hunter, Thomas Johnson, Christina Kahrl, Alison Kooistra, Eric Lamb, Kris Larson, Amanda Lawes, Carl Martel, Tim Miles, Robert Patterson, Kenyon Reed, Marie Sanka, Jordan Somers, Jennifer Swimmer, James Sutton, Nancy Teeple, Suzanne Tiefenbeck, Genevieve Trottier, Amanda Vellia, Jessica Watkins, Walter Ward, Heather Whitman, Cheri Williams, and Bonnie Wright. Tom Bonhomme and Tracy McKenney were assistant architects/surveyors. Susan Gelb was pottery registrar and Sarah Campbell was assistant pottery registrar. Tony Hartley supervised field processing of faunal remains, including shell. Elena Dodge and Joseph Stumpf supervised field processing of glass.

In 2002, senior field staff in the field included Kim Cavanagh as photographer, David Clark as consultant for the church, Nasser Mansour as assistant geologist, Tracy McKenney as architect and surveyor, Tina M. Niemi as geologist, S. Thomas Parker as director, stratigrapher, and ceramicist, Alexandra Retzleff as assistant director, and John Rucker as camp manager. Area supervisors were Diane Grubisha (Area T-Qasr al-Kithara), Mary-Louise Mussell (Area J-east), Alexandra Retzleff (Area M), Joseph Stumpf (Area K), and James Terry (Area J-west and Area U). Sharon Penton and Kenyon Reed served as assistant area supervisors for Area J-east. Senior staff who were not in the field in 2002 included John Wilson Betlyon as numismatist, Vincent A. Clark as Semitic epigrapher, William Grantham as faunal analyst, Janet Jones as glass specialist, Christina Kahrl as conservator, Eric Lapp as ceramic lamp specialist and metallurgy specialist, Mary Mattocks as draftsperson, Joann McDaniel as small finds specialist, Megan Perry as human osteologist, David Reece as shell specialist, Andrew M. Smith II as director of the survey, and Peter Warnock as archaeobotanist. Kenyon Reed supervised field processing of faunal remains, including shell. Joseph Stumpf supervised field processing of glass. Sharon Penton and Diane Grubisha supervised field processing of small finds.

Student staff serving as trench supervisors in 2002 included Stephanie Bowers, Marilyn Brooks, Sarah Campbell, Elizabeth Colistro, Andrea Covington, Danielle Godard, Catherine Goodman, Carl Martel, Caroline Raynor, Jennifer Marie Sanka, Michael Smith, Jenny Spruill, Ross Thomas, Genevieve Trottier, Walter Ward, Joanne Whitmore, and Cheri Williams. Hannah Lippard was the assistant architect/surveyor. Cheri Williams was pottery registrar and Sarah Campbell was assistant pottery registrar.

The small team in 2003 was led by Tina M. Niemi and also included Alivia Allison, John Rucker, and Ross Thomas.

The years after conclusion of fieldwork also witnessed some changes in personnel in terms of publication for the final report. Jennifer Ramsay assumed responsibility for the paleobotanical material and Christopher Gregg for the small finds. Above all, the tragic death of Mary-Louise Mussell in 2005 necessitated the transfer of responsibility for publication of the putative church to Ross Thomas and the author.

Purpose and Scope of the Final Report

The purpose of this report is twofold. The first is to present in final form the results of all field seasons conducted by the project, including the regional survey, the excavations, and the material cultural evidence. The second goal is to offer a historical synthesis of all this material that relates to the principal and subsidiary research questions posed above.

The final report will consist of three volumes. The first volume includes this introduction and a detailed report on the results of the regional survey, including a catalogue of sites, reports on related material culture recovered by the survey (i.e., chipped stone tools, pottery, and epigraphic evidence), and interpretation of the survey evidence. The second volume will be devoted to the results from most excavation areas at Aqaba, the soundings at Qasr el-Kithara, and some material cultural evidence. The third and final volume will include a few additional excavation areas from Aqaba, other material cultural evidence, and a historical synthesis. Specific decisions on which excavation areas and material cultural evidence to include in volumes two and three are based largely on when authors completed and submitted their chapters to the editor.

Obviously this "final report" does not mean the end of analysis and interpretation of this evidence. All project records and many artifacts are in the archaeological laboratory and repository at North Carolina State University and available for study to qualified scholars. One expects that in the future this precious corpus of material will be subjected to further scrutiny by future generations of scholars, who may question, refine, or revise the interpretations offered here.

The historical and archaeological periodization used in this report follows the most widely used convention, slightly modified, among archaeologists and historians working in Jordan. Thus the transition from "Early Roman" to "Late Roman" occurs with the Roman annexation of Nabataea in AD 106 and the beginning of direct Roman rule in the region. The transition from "Late Roman" to "Early Byzantine" occurs in the early fourth century, when Constantine I gained control of the East in 324. The Byzantine period in the southern Levant (ca. 324–636) is conventionally subdivided into "Early Byzantine" and "Late Byzantine" periods, with the transition at ca. 500, i.e., during the reign of Anastasius (491–518). The Byzantine period at Aila naturally terminates with the submission of the city to Islamic forces in 630.

All scholars working in this region wrestle with the inconsistencies posed by the transliteration of Arabic names, especially place names. An entirely consistent system might have been advisable, but this requires spelling many place names differently from their long accepted form. The usual practice followed here is to transliterate Arabic names either according to the authoritative list published by the Department of Antiquities of Jordan or the most authoritative or current publication on the particular site or region. This compromise solution avoids potential confusion for the reader caused by the difference between a previously published and thus familiar name versus a consistent system of transliteration. In some cases alternative spellings are offered in parentheses, particularly if the current official spelling differs from a long accepted spelling. By agreement with Donald Whitcomb it was decided to refer to the classical (i.e., Nabataean, Roman, and Byzantine) site as "Aila" and the adjacent Early Islamic site as "Ayla."

IV.   AILA IN ANCIENT AND MEDIEVAL SOURCES

A number of documentary sources refer to Aqaba and its immediate region. These may be divided chronologically into ancient (i.e., pre-classical and classical) and medieval (i.e., Islamic). Because the focus of the project is on the classical period, the sources from this period are obviously of more importance, but sources of the preceding and following periods may also offer some useful insights. All such sources naturally require critical analysis when exploited as possible historical evidence.

Pre-classical Sources

Several passages from the Hebrew Bible refer to the predecessor site of classical Aila, variously called "Elath" or "Ezion-geber." The authors of the Hebrew Bible clearly regarded this region as within the kingdom of Edom. King David of Israel, who is usually dated to the 10th century BC, allegedly conquered the Edomites (2 Samuel 8:13–14; 1 Chronicles 18:12–13) and garrisoned their territory. This allowed his successor, Solomon, to build a fleet of ships at Ezion-geber, "which is near Eloth on the shore of the Red Sea, in the land of Edom" in order to trade with Ophir. The location of Ophir is unknown but perhaps was thought to be in the Horn of Africa or located in the southern Arabian peninsula. Solomon's ships supposedly returned with gold, "algum wood" (sandal wood?), and precious stones (1 Kings 9:26; 2 Chronicles 8:17). As seen below, although the site of Tell el-Kheleifeh was long associated with Solomon's port, reinterpretation of the old excavations there casts considerable doubt on the historicity of these accounts. The more grandiose claims of a large and powerful Israelite United Monarchy advanced by biblical writers are now widely perceived as greatly exaggerated, if not largely fictional.

Other biblical passages assert that a 9th-century king of Judah, Jehoshaphat, controlled Edom during the Divided Monarchy and constructed "ships of Tarshish" to sail to Ophir for gold. But "the ships were wrecked at Eziongeber" (1 Kings 22:48–49; cf. 2 Chronicles 20:36–37). The biblical sources also claim that control of Ezion-geber/ Elath changed hands several times between Judah and Edom. During the reign of Joram, the son of Jehoshaphat, Edom successfully revolted (2 Kings 8:21–22), implying the loss of Ezion-geber/Elath to Judah. But a later king of Judah, Amaziah (early 8th century), again defeated the Edomites (2 Kings 14:7). This gave an opportunity to his son Uzziah, who allegedly "built Elath and restored it to Judah" (2 Kings 14:22; 2 Chronicles 26:2).

The biblical writers assert that Elath was permanently lost to Judah during the reign of King Ahaz (late 8th century). With Jerusalem under siege by the kings of Syria and Israel, "at that time the king of Edom recovered Elath for Edom and drove the men of Judah from Elath; and the Edomites came to Elath, where they dwell to this day" (2 Kings 16:5; cf. Josephus, AJ 9.12.1; 9.245).

Although the excavations of Tell el-Kheleifeh document continued occupation of the site through the later Iron Age and Persian periods (539–332 BC), there appear to be no further documentary sources about this region until the Hellenistic period.

Classical Sources

Perhaps the earliest source of the classical period is Diodorus Siculus, who wrote his history between ca. 60–30 BC, but often depended on earlier Hellenistic writers. In book 3, after describing the Arabian coast, he states that

> After one has sailed past this country the Laeanites Gulf comes next, about which are many inhabited villages of Arabs who are known as Nabataeans. This tribe occupies a large part of the coast and not a little of the country which stretches inland, and it has a people numerous beyond telling and flocks and herds in multitude beyond belief. Now in ancient times these men observed justice and were content with the food which they received from their flocks, but later, after the kings in Alexandria had made the ways of the sea navigable for their merchants, these Arabs not only attacked the shipwrecked, but fitting out pirate ships preyed upon the voyagers, imitating in their practices the savage and lawless ways of the Tauri of the Pontus; some time afterward, however, they were caught on the high seas by some quadriremes and punished as they deserved (3.43.4).

Diodorus appears to be relying here on Agatharchides of Cnidus, who was active in the mid-2nd century BC at the Library of Alexandria and thus was presumably well-informed from Ptolemaic sources. If the passage does in fact reflect mid-2nd century BC conditions, one may note several points. There is no mention of a permanent settlement at the head of the Gulf in this period. This is in accord with the regional archaeological evidence. Tell el-Kheleifeh seems to have been abandoned no later than the late Persian or early Hellenistic period, and the successor settlement, Aila, appears not to have been founded until the late 1st century BC. The region is dominated by pastoral nomads, the Nabataeans, who are described as numerous. Perhaps their population began to exceed the carrying capacity of their land, encouraging attempts at piracy. A firm response to such piracy by Ptol-

emaic naval power perhaps discouraged further piracy on the Red Sea. By the end of the Hellenistic period the Nabataeans were developing agriculture throughout much of their kingdom, including intensive exploitation of marginal lands through advanced hydrological technology.

The first explicit mention of Aila itself is by Strabo in his *Geography*, completed early in the reign of Tiberius (AD 14–37) but again relying in part on earlier Hellenistic sources. When discussing the port of Gaza and its trade routes, Strabo notes that the distance from Gaza

> is said to be an overland passage of 1,260 stadia to Aila, a city situated on the head of the Arabian Gulf. This head consists of two recesses: one extending into the region of Arabia and Gaza, which is called Ailanites, after the city situated on it, and the other, extending to the region near Egypt in the neighborhood of the City of Heroes to which the overland passage from Pelusium is shorter; and the overland journeys are made on camels through desert and sandy places (16.2.30).

In a subsequent passage, Strabo mentions that frankincense and myrrh from the southern Arabian peninsula was sold there to merchants, who arrive "in 70 days from Ailana (Ailana is a city on the other recess of the Arabian Gulf, the recess near Gaza called Ailanites)" (16.4.4).

Thus Strabo claims that by the early 1st century AD there was already a "city" ("polis") called Aila at the head of the "Arabian Gulf" (i.e., Gulf of Aqaba) connected by a trade route via camel caravans to Gaza on the Mediterranean coast. Further, merchants from Aila itself traveled via camels to south Arabia to obtain frankincense and myrrh, the main products of this trade, and presumably north to Gaza.

However, in other passages in his *Geography*, Strabo mentions other routes for transport of the aromatics, including another port on the Arabian coast called Leuke Kome ("White Village"), whence to Petra and then to the Mediterranean coast at Rhinocolura, southwest of Gaza (16.4.24; cf. 16.4.18). But he also claims in this passage that the bulk of this trade had moved by his day to the opposite side of the Red Sea, to the Egyptian port of Myos Hormos, and from there overland to the Nile and thence to Alexandria (16.4.24).

The Elder Pliny (died AD 79) mentions the site in his *Natural History* (5.12). When discussing the two gulfs at the head of the Red Sea, Pliny names "Aelana" on the "Aelanitic Gulf" and Gaza on "our sea" as two "towns" ("*oppida*") some 150 miles apart, very close to the actual distance as the crow flies. Again, it is important to note the connection between Gaza and Aila.

The Jewish historian Josephus, writing in the late 1st century AD and recounting the reign of Solomon in the *Antiquities of the Jews*, mentions that "The king also built many ships in the Egyptian gulf of the Red Sea at a certain place called Gasiongabel not far from the city (*polis*) of Ailane, which is now called Berenike" (*AJ* 8.6.4; 8.163).

Why Josephus thought that Aila was called in his time Berenike, the name of several Ptolemaic queens, is unclear but is certainly an error. Perhaps Josephus confused Aila with the actual city of Berenike, a port far to the south on the Egyptian coast of the Red Sea, apparently founded in the 3rd century BC. The recent excavations at Aqaba yielded no evidence whatsoever of any Ptolemaic presence.

Soon after the Roman annexation of the Nabataean kingdom as their new province of Arabia in AD 106, the Romans constructed a major trunk road, the *Via Nova Traiana*, which ran north–south through this new province, now called Arabia. Various milestone inscriptions describe the road as extending *a finibus Syriae usque ad mare rubrum* ("from the borders of Syria to the Red Sea;" Thomsen 1917: nos. 71, 87, 90). Thus it is widely assumed that Aila was the southern terminus of this road, which was completed between AD 111 and 114. Such an inscribed milestone dated to 111/112 was in fact recovered by the Chicago team, reused in Early Islamic Ayla (MacAdam 1989: 172). It is noteworthy that the segment of this road immediately north of Aqaba was the first portion to be completed.

Ptolemy, writing in the early 2nd century AD, lists "Elana" as a "village" (*komé*) in his *Geography* (5.17.1). This is notable in that he is the only source to describe Aila as a "village" rather than a "city."

The Peutinger Table, essentially a road map of the Roman Empire, perhaps composed in the 2nd century and revised in the 4th century (Talbert 2010), places "Haila" at the junction of several routes. It places Aila 170 Roman miles from *Clysma* (modern Suez), 50 miles from *Phara* (in Sinai), 16 miles from *ad Dianam* (presumably a site in Wādī 'Araba), and 20 miles from *Praesidio* (probably on the *Via Nova Traiana*, perhaps the site of Khirbet el-Khalde, cf. Parker 1986: 108–09).

The provincial reorganization of Diocletian (284–305) included the partition of provincial Arabia, resulting in the transfer of southern Jordan, including Aila, and the Negev to the province of *Palaestina*. Subsequent subdivisions of Palestine resulted in Aila falling within *Palaestina Salutaris*, later styled *Palaestina Tertia* by the early 5th century.

The church historian Eusebius of Caesarea lists Aila among the biblical sites in his *Onomasticon*, usually dated to the end of the 3rd or early 4th century: "Ailam. It is in Palestine on the border between the desert to the south and the Red Sea, whence they sail to Egypt and India. Based there is the Tenth Roman Unit. Now it is called Aila" (6.17–21). In another passage, Eusebius describes the site of Pharan (probably the Phara of the Peutinger Table) in Sinai as being three days distant from Aila (166.12–15). The former passage provides several bits of crucial evidence. Aila is described as a port regularly visited by ships from Egypt and India, although what Eusebius actually means by "India" in this period is debatable. As will be seen, there is abundant archaeological evidence for Egyptian artifacts at Aila. Second, this is the first evidence for the presence of *Legio X Fretensis* at Aila. This famous legion was based at Jerusalem from AD 70 until at least the mid-3rd century, implying that it was transferred from Jerusalem to Aila in the late 3rd century. Various lines of circumstantial evidence suggest that this occurred during the reign of Diocletian (284–305), who redeployed the legions of the eastern frontier (Parker 2009c).

Jerome (Hieronymus), writing in the late 4th and early 5th centuries, produced a Latin translation of Eusebius' *Onomasticon*. In his passage on Aila (Freeman-Grenville 2003: 7.25–28) he essentially repeats the information from Eusebius but does add that the "Tenth Roman Unit" is in fact a legion ("*legio*"). In his *Commentary on Ezekiel* (*CCSL* 75: 724), dated ca. 410–415, he describes a "tongue of the Red Sea, on which coast is situated Ahila, where now is based a Roman legion and garrison ("*legio et praesidium Romanorum*). Finally, in his *Vita Hilarionis*, Jerome describes how Hilarion in ca. 320 exorcised a legion of demons from a certain Orion, one of the most prominent and richest men in Aila. Orion later returned to Hilarion's monastery in Gaza "bringing numerous gifts as thanks," but Hilarion urged him to give these to the poor (Jerome 1893: 306–07).

The Chicago team recovered fragments of a Latin inscription reused in Early Islamic Ayla. The text can be dated within the reign of Constantine (ca. 317–326). Although the portion of the text which may have mentioned a specific construction is not preserved, the form of the letters and use of Latin itself in this period almost certainly implies an official character, most likely a monumental building inscription perhaps associated with the legion (MacAdam 1989).

The latest mention of the legion at Aila is in the *Notitia Dignitatum* (Seeck 1876: *Oriens* 34.30), dating to ca. 400, which lists among the garrison of *Palaestina* the "*Praefectus legionis decimae Fretensis, Ailae.*" How long the legion remained garrisoned at Aila after this date is unknown.

The documentary sources also provide the names of several bishops of Aila. The first attested bishop appears in the early 4th century. Peter, bishop of Aila, attended the Council of Nicaea in 325. The mention of a bishop of Aila in 325 surely implies a significant Christian population in the city by that date, when the structure excavated by the current project and interpreted as an early church was in use. Beryllus, "bishop of Aila in *Palaestina Tertia*," attended the Council of Chalcedon in 451 and Paul, bishop of Aila, attended the Synod of Jerusalem in 536 (Abel 1967: v. 2: 201). Another bishop of Aila, named Moses, sent a letter to a certain Victor, son of Sergius, at Nessana via a Saracen messenger. This document is preserved among the Nessana papyri (Kraemer 1958: 146, no. 51).

From the late 4th century (ca. 375) is a reference to Aila by Epiphanius of Salamis, "For there are different ports on the Red Sea which in their several locations give access to the Roman Empire.

One of them is at Aela, which in the sacred scriptures is Elath. Here Solomon's ships would come every three years bringing gold and ivory, spices and peacocks and other things" (Williams 1994: *Panarion* 66.19–10).

Theodoret, an early to mid-5th century ecclesiastical source, in his commentary on Jeremiah states that Aila was a city on the Red Sea trading with India and Egypt (Schertl 1936: 41–42).

Timotheus of Gaza, who wrote his work *On Animals* during the reign of Anastasius (491–518), mentions a merchant from Aila who dealt in products from "India" (in fact perhaps meaning east Africa or south Arabia). He passed through Gaza, bringing two giraffes and an elephant as gifts to the emperor, reaching Constantinople with his animals in 496 (Bodenheimer and Rabinowitz 1949). Since this merchant hailed from Aila and was likely bringing his exotic cargo from India or Africa to the imperial capital via Gaza, he probably passed through Aila en route to Gaza.

The Emperor Justin I (518–527) in 522 ordered ships to be provided in support of his allies, the Axumites in east Africa, against the Himyarites in south Arabia. Aila was to provide twenty such ships, Clysma (Suez) in Egypt was to furnish ten ships, and Iotabe (location uncertain but somewhere on the Gulf of Aqaba) seven ships. It is perhaps notable that Aila was expected to provide twice as many ships as Clysma, by now a major rival port on the Red Sea. The historian Procopius of Caesarea, writing in the mid-6th century, makes several references in passing to Aila, describing it as a city on a narrow gulf on the border of Roman territory (*Bellum Persicum* 1.19.3; 1.19.19) and that Roman vessels sailed from Aila on the Red Sea (*Bellum Persicum* 1.19.23).

Of greater interest is the work of the so-called Cosmas Indicopleustes, an anonymous early 6th-century merchant of Alexandria who traveled from Egypt via Adulis on the east coast of Africa ultimately to India and Ceylon. He later became a monk, writing the *Christian Topography*. He reports that "On the coast of Ethiopia, two miles from the shore, is a town called Adulis, which forms the port of the Axumites and is much frequented by traders who come from Alexandria and Ela (Aila)" (2.54; Wolska-Conus 1968: 54). Thus it is striking that a recent archaeological investigation of Adulis, now in modern Eritrea, reports that the surface of this site is littered with Byzantine pottery from Aila (Peacock and Blue 2007: 95).

Other 6th-century sources mention Aila as a staging post for pilgrims traveling to Mount Sinai. Theodosius, for example, who describes routes from Jerusalem to Mount Sinai in the early 6th century, describes a route from Jerusalem to Elusa (in the northern Negev) in three stages (*mansiones*), from Elusa to Aila in seven stages, and from Aila to Mount Sinai in eight more stages, or a total of eighteen stages "if you choose the short way across the desert, but twenty-five if you go through Egypt" (Schertl 1936: 53; cf. Wilkinson 1977: 70).

The itinerary of Antoninus Placentius (ca. 570), notes that after visiting Mount Sinai some pilgrims chose "to return to the Holy City through Egypt and others by way of Arabia. From Mount Sinai it is eight staging posts to Arabia, and the city (*civitas*) called Aila (emended from "Abila"). Shipping from India comes into a port at Aila, bringing a variety of spices" (Antoninus Placentius 1965: v. 175, ch. 40, p. 149; cf. Wilkinson 1977: 87–88).

One final source about pilgrimage is recounted by Anastasius the Sinaite. Writing in the mid-7th century, he mentions a group of almost 800 Armenian pilgrims who had come to Mt. Sinai 20 years earlier (i.e., in the early 7th century), as had been their regular custom before the disruptions of the Persian occupation of the Levant in 614–628 (*OC2* 1902: 81–82). In other words, Armenian pilgrims had frequented Mount Sinai in the 6th century. The discovery of numerous Armenian graffiti west of Aila along the route towards Mount Sinai lends support to this account (Mayerson 1982).

The evidence for such pilgrimage via Aila seems well-attested, especially in the 6th century, but its economic impact on the city is difficult to assess. However, the passage from Antoninus Placentius suggests that sea-borne trade in aromatics between Aila and "India" (perhaps east Africa or south Arabia) continued in the late 6th century.

There is further documentary evidence for this traffic around the turn of the 7th century. Sophronius, who was later patriarch of Jerusalem, was in Egypt with a certain monk named Joseph. A man from Aila, clearly a merchant or ship-owner, offered to pay Joseph 3 *nomismata* to pray for the successful return of a ship he had sent to Ethiopia (Regnault 1966–78: 191–93).

Arabic sources refer to a monastery in Aila itself, called "Dayr al-Qunfud" (monastery of the hedgehog"). Shahîd argues that it was founded in the 5th century by a Christian Arab tribe, the Balī, who lived in the vicinity (Shahîd 1989: 309, 313, 446). Also at the Synod of Jerusalem in 535, mentioned above, was a certain "John, priest and monk through God's mercy," who signed "for all the monks of Aila in *Palaestina Tertia*" (Schertl 1936: 47).

John Moschos, a monk from the late 6th/early 7th century, provides details in *The Spiritual Meadow* about "the monastery of Ailiotes" in Sinai. He relates several anecdotes about the "abbot Stephen, a presbyter of the monastery of the Aeliotes" (*PG* 87 part 3 #62–65: 2913–16). John himself lived for ten years at this monastery, which was founded by a certain Antonius (*PG* 87 part 3 #66–68: 2917–20). Although it seems clear from the name that the monastery was founded by Christians from Aila, it is unknown how many of the monks in residence were actually from Aila.

Epigraphic evidence about Aila includes a few texts from the site itself, as well as inscriptions from elsewhere in the region. Among the former, the Latin inscription from the reign of Constantine I has been cited above. Other important inscriptions from the site itself include a capital from an engaged column with half figures of two saints carved on both worked sides. The accompanying Greek texts identify these as Saints George and Isidore (Wooley and Lawrence 1936: 144). A few years later, Glueck reported finding two sandstone capitals that depicted two warrior saints, identified in Greek inscriptions as Saints Theodore and Longinus (Glueck 1939: 1–3; Zayadine 1994: 488–89, figs. 2–5). Such artifacts presumably derived from a church or churches at Aila. The site has also yielded a Christian funerary inscription of AD 555 (Schwabe 1953). Finally, in 1991, a limestone lintel inscribed with an abbreviated Christian Greek inscription was recovered from a secondary context in Early Islamic Ayla. Zayadine observed that the formulaic text is paralleled elsewhere in the region and is likely to have been originally associated with a church (Zayadine 1994: 489–94, figs. 9–10).

The project's own excavations have produced a few scraps of epigraphic evidence, mostly in Greek. These will be published in a subsequent volume of the final report.

Several inscriptions found elsewhere also reference Aila. These are mostly Christian funerary texts inscribed in Greek and include two tombstones found at Beersheba (Bir es-Saba); one dated to 543 memorializes a certain "Kaimous of Aila" (Alt 1921: 18, no. 19) and the other, also of the mid-6th century, references "Nonna, daughter of Stephen of Aila" (Alt 1921: 23, no. 36; cf. Schertl 1936: 53). Another inscription from Sinai, undated but marked with a cross, mentions "Ababios, son of Sabinos, of Aila" (Euting 1891: pl. 4, no. 57).

Also of interest is a Greek Christian text inscribed on a roof beam in the basilica at St. Catherine's monastery in Sinai dated 548–556. It reads "Lord God, who revealed yourself in this place, save and have mercy on Your servant Stephanus, son of Martyrius, builder and architect of Aila, and Nonna; and give peace to the souls of their children George, Sergius, and Theodore." (Šenčenko 1966: 257, 262). It is unknown whether the Stephen and Nonna of this text are the same individuals mentioned in the Beer-Sheba inscription of approximately the same date referenced above. But in any case this text provides more evidence for the close connections between Aila and the monastic community at Mount Sinai.

Medieval Sources

A few medieval sources also provide evidence relevant to the chronological focus of the current project.

There are several accounts in Arabic sources about the surrender of Aila to the Muslims in 630. The account of Ibn Hisham (*Sirat Rasul Allah,* 902), for example, contains some details of interest. The surrender of Aila was actually negotiated by a certain Yuhanna b. Ruʻba (possibly the bishop of Aila) with the Prophet himself at Tabuk (now in northwestern Saudi Arabia). Ibn Hisham describes the

> guarantee from God and Muhammed the prophet, the apostle of God, to Yuhanna b. Ruʻba and the people of Ayla, for their

ships and their caravans by land and sea. They and all that are with them, men of Syria, and the Yaman, and seamen, all have the protection of God and the protection of Muhammed the prophet. Should any one of them break the treaty by introducing some new factor then his wealth shall not save him; it is the fair prize of him who takes it. It is not permitted that they shall be restrained from going down to their wells or using their roads by land or sea. (Zayadine 1994: 499)

It is notable that the ancient site is dotted with wells, which were the principal means of obtaining water at Aqaba until the 20th century. The source also implies that Aila was still heavily dependent on trade by both land and sea in this period.

Soon after, the Muslims founded a new walled town less than 1 km to the southeast. Recent excavations, discussed below, have revealed that this Early Islamic Ayla flourished from the mid-7th to 12th centuries. When the Arab geographer Shams ad-Din Muqaddasi visited Early Islamic Ayla in the 10th century, he reported that the city "is usually called Ayla, but [the true] Ayla is in ruins nearby." (Khouri and Whitcomb 1988: 11). It has reasonably been supposed that Muqaddasi was looking from the Early Islamic town northwest to the ruins of the Roman/Byzantine town, by then abandoned and in ruins (Khouri and Whitcomb 1988: 12). The new evidence obtained by the current project further substantiates this interpretation. A 15th-century Arab chronicler, al-Maqrizi, mentions an arched gate at the site attributed to the Romans (Zayadine 1994: 488).

The early Islamic town was abandoned ca. 1200. A new settlement appeared ca. 1 km farther south down the coast around the present Hashemite castle. This Late Islamic settlement included the castle, date palm plantations, and fishing village reported by various Arab and western travelers (Khouri 1988: 140–41; Whitcomb 1994: 7; Zayadine 1994: 501). Inscriptions from the castle suggest construction around 1514/1515 (Glidden 1952). Recent excavations in and around the castle, discussed below, have revealed much new evidence about this site in the Late Islamic period.

In sum, the rather limited and fragmentary ancient documentary sources suggest that Aila was founded as a Nabataean city no later than the early 1st century AD, with an economy based on pastoralism and long distance trade between the Mediterranean and the Red Sea littoral. A number of sources in the 1st century AD explicitly identify Aila as a "polis" or city. Nabataean merchants from Aila traveled to south Arabia to engage in the aromatics trade. Following the Roman annexation of the Nabataean Kingdom in 106 as the new province of Arabia, a great trunk road, the *Via Nova Traiana*, was constructed from southern Syria to its southern terminus at Aila. The strategic importance of Aila is suggested by the transfer of *Legio X Fretensis* from Jerusalem to Aila at the end of the third century, when ships were sailing from Aila to Egypt and "India." There was a significant Christian population in the city by at least the early 4th century and a Christian monastic presence by the early 6th century, if not earlier. Byzantine Aila was also a frequent stop for Christian pilgrims en route to Mount Sinai. Merchants from Aila traveled the length of the Red Sea to Adulis, the port of Axum in east Africa, in the 6th century. Various sources suggest that Aila remained an active commercial port through the Byzantine period until the Muslim conquest in the early 7th century.

V.   PREVIOUS ARCHAEOLOGICAL RESEARCH

The region of Aqaba was until recently little known archaeologically. Some useful information may be gleaned from various western travelers who visited the site in the 19th and early 20th centuries and from scholars who subsequently conducted research in the region. The following discussion of earlier western travelers does not pretend to be exhaustive but focuses on the more significant reports from these visitors. The next section does attempt a comprehensive review of prior archaeological research in and around Aqaba.

On May 8, 1816, Burckhardt approached Aqaba along the coast of Sinai via Wādī Tāba but failed to reach the site. He nevertheless provided some valuable information about current conditions in the region, especially the local Bedouin. He also noted an "ancient wall" blocking the mouth of Wādī Yutum north of the site (Burckhardt 1822: 507).

Among the earliest westerners to actually visit Aqaba in the modern era was Eduard Rüppell in 1822. He reported seeing an "old settlement recognizable among many heaps of debris" and suggested these were "perhaps the remains of ancient Ailat" (Rüppell 1829: 248). He was followed by Léon de Laborde in 1828 (Laborde 1838: 131), Edward Robinson in 1838, and E. Joy Morris in 1840. The latter two explorers reported extensive mounds of ruins near the sea (Robinson 1841: 241; Morris 1842: 262). Morris also reported that "near the mouth of this valley (i.e., Wādī Yutum) I observed the remains of a wall that had once been built across it" (Morris 1842: 265). Presumably this was the structure also seen by Burckhardt.

Among the more important early visitors was Richard Burton, who reached Aqaba in 1878:

> Inland and to the north rise the mounds and tumuli, the sole remains of ancient Elath, once the port of Petra, which is distant only two dromedary marches. During rain-floods the site is an island: to the west flows the surface-water of the Wady el-ʿArabah, and eastward the drainage of the Wady Yitm has dug a well defined bed. A line of larger heaps to the north shows where, according to the people, ran the city wall: finding it thickly strewn with scoriae, old and new, I decided this was the Siyàghah or "smith's quarters." Between it and the sea the surface is scattered with glass, shards, and slag (Burton 1879: 240).

Among several valuable observations are the supposed line of a city wall on the northern side of the site and the quantity of slag and "scoriae" on the surface. Recent excavations have revealed Late Byzantine/Early Islamic pottery kilns near the Byzantine city wall, the latter exposed in the current project's Area J, which roughly corresponds with Burton's observations. Also notable is Burton's remark about the problems posed by surface water flowing around the site. He later notes that the locals had constructed earthen dams to divert water away from the town and its date palm plantation (Burton 1879: 241).

Morris, Burton, and Charles Doughty, who visited Aqaba ca. 1876, all reported seeing a wall or crude masonry dam built across the mouth of "Wādī Lithm," i.e., Wādī Yutum (Morris 1842: 265; Burton 1879: 241; Doughty 1936: 84–85). These early reports are important, for they preclude the possibility that this structure was erected by the Turks to protect Aqaba from the Arab attack via Wādī Yutum in 1917.

T. E. Lawrence visited Aqaba in 1913. It now seems clear that he correctly located the Early Islamic settlement of Ayla. Of special interest is his observation that "There are remains a little farther inland, and these probably represent a small village outside the gates of the larger place" (Woolley and Lawrence 1936: 144). Recent work now suggests that these remains are in fact portions of Nabataean, Roman, and Byzantine Aila.

Fritz Frank visited the region during his survey of Wādī ʿAraba in 1933. He apparently was the first scholar to notice the low-lying mound of Tell el-Kheleifeh, ca. 550 m north of the modern shoreline, ca. 2 km northwest of Aila, and ca. 3.5 km northwest of the Late Islamic castle at Aqaba. He suggested that Kheleifeh, which appeared to be pre-Classical in date from its surface pottery, was in fact Solomon's port of Elath/Ezion-geber (Frank 1934: 243–45).

Nelson Glueck surveyed the Aqaba region in 1934 and 1936 and directed extensive excavations of Tell el-Kheleifeh in 1938–40. Several observations from his initial visit to Aqaba are noteworthy:

> About a kilometre west-northwest of ʿAqabah (i.e., the Late Islamic castle) we came upon a very large site, thickly strewn with sherds, which has been correctly identified with the Roman Aila. The site was, however, originally Nabataean, being covered with large quantities of Nabataean sherds of all kinds. In addition there were large quantities of Roman, Byzantine, and mediaeval Arabic sherds. Some fragments of glass were found, which are probably Roman in origin…. No sherds earlier than Nabataean were found at Aila (Glueck 1935: 46–47).

In 1936, Glueck confirmed the absence of pre-classical pottery at this site and recorded two Byzantine

capitals with bas-reliefs, perhaps from a Byzantine church of Aila, cited above (Glueck 1939a: 1–3).

Glueck's subsequent excavation of Tell el-Kheleifeh yielded important evidence of the Iron Age II and Persian periods. He initially dated the foundation of the site to the 10th century BC and accepted Frank's identification with biblical Elath/Ezion-geber. Finds of imported Greek pottery and Aramaic *ostraca* pushed the terminus of the site into the 4th century BC. Although he reported "a few Nabataean sherds" from the surface of the site (Glueck 1939a: 3), no Nabataean remains were ever reported from the excavations. He also stressed the importance of copper processing in the site's economy. Glueck produced an admirable record of promptly published preliminary reports (Glueck 1935; 1938a; 1938b; 1939a; 1939b; 1940; 1967), but no final report. In one of his last published statements about the site, Glueck expressed more caution about his initial interpretations, but continued to assert that Kheleifeh could have been Elath/Ezion-geber or "a fortified industrial, maritime, storage and caravanserai for both" (Glueck 1965: 71).

A detailed reappraisal of Glueck's work has cast serious doubt on his proposed identification of Tell el-Kheleifeh as Solomon's port of Elath/Ezion-geber. Pratico's reinterpretation of the pottery now suggests that occupation began no earlier than the 8th century BC and continued into the 5th or perhaps 4th century BC (Pratico 1985; 1993). A stamped Rhodian jar handle dated ca. 200 BC, an isolated surface find, was his only evidence for later occupation (Pratico 1993: 62). An intensive ceramic survey by the present project in 1996, presented elsewhere in this volume, generally supported Pratico's conclusions. Limited soundings, conducted in 1999 by Mary-Louise Mussell but still mostly unpublished, recovered 7th- and 6th-century BC material (Mussell 2000b).

Aurel Stein reached Aqaba in 1939. He noted that the "ancient name of Aila clings to a mound stretching for about half a mile [ca. 800 m] at a short distance from the northern extremity of the Gulf of ʿAqaba" (Gregory and Kennedy 1985: 304).

With the site of Aila seemingly well-located by these early travelers and scholars, it seems surprising that its exact location was soon lost. Only a few years after Stein's visit, Kirkbride and Harding visited the modern site known as "Aileh" and reported no sherds of the classical period (Kirkbride and Harding 1947: 24). The first archaeological excavation of Aqaba was conducted in 1954 by Salim Saad, apparently adjacent to the beach and east of the former Aqaba Hotel. He "uncovered what was thought to be a section of a city rampart, along with Nabataean lamps and pottery sherds" (Khouri 1988: 138). Unfortunately, nothing about this brief excavation was ever published (Salim Saad, personal communication, July 8, 1994).

The years after World War II witnessed the growth of Aqaba as Jordan's only seaport and as a tourist resort. The modern city rapidly expanded from its old center around the Late Islamic castle northward over the archaeological site. By the 1980s it could truthfully be stated that "The site of Roman Aila is unknown" (Gregory and Kennedy 1985: 429).

Although the precise location of the Classical Aila was now a mystery, excavations in the 1980s revealed important evidence from both the pre- and post-Classical periods. In 1985 excavations began at Tell Maqaṣṣ, a small mound ca. 4 km north of the present coastline near the modern airport. The site dated from the late Chalcolithic to the beginning of the Early Bronze Age (mid- to late 4th millennium BC) and yielded evidence of copper-processing (Khalil 1987; 1988; 1992; Khalil, Eichmann, and Schmidt 2003). The rediscovery of early Islamic Ayla began in 1986. Whitcomb located a walled, rectangular town founded on the beach in the mid-7th century and which flourished until the 12th century (figs. 1.2–3; Whitcomb 1986; 1987; 1988; 1989a; 1989b; 1989c; 1993; 1994; 1995; 1997; 1998; 2006a; 2006b; 2009; Khouri and Whitcomb 1988; Melkawi, 'Amr, and Whitcomb 1994). A suggestion that the walled Early Islamic town in fact represents the reused Roman legionary fortress of *Legio X Fretensis* (Knauf and Brooker 1988) was rejected by the excavator himself (Whitcomb 1990). This suggestion has since been disproven by the current project's own soundings of the walls, which support the excavator's proposed date of a mid-7th-century foundation (Parker 2002: 421). The Chicago excavations yielded some pre-Islamic artifacts mixed with later material. Among the most significant artifacts were fragments of a Latin building inscription of

317–326 (MacAdam 1989) and the Byzantine lintel inscribed with Christian symbols and a Christian Greek inscription mentioned above (Zayadine 1994: 489). All this suggested that the pre-Islamic Aila might lie somewhere in the immediate vicinity.

Meloy offered some suggestions about the location of pre-Islamic Aila in 1991. He surveyed the region northwest of the Early Islamic town. This largely flat-lying area was then covered partly by modern buildings and sand dunes, mostly within 500 m of the modern shoreline. The portion within the modern ring road, designated the "Circular Area," encompassed about 40 ha. Here Meloy identified several mounds, traces of mudbrick walls, and scatters of surface artifacts. The surface pottery, largely dated from the 1st century BC to the 6th century AD, suggested that this area could have been part of the classical Aila (Meloy 1991). This survey and the encouragement of Donald Whitcomb encouraged the author to excavate in this area to locate classical Aila. The current project's fieldwork did in fact subsequently reveal significant portions of the classical city in this and adjacent areas.

Recent archaeological research on the Late Islamic castle and its environs in Aqaba, directed by Johnny De Meulemeester, Denys Pringle, and Reem al-Shqour, began in 2000 (Al-Shqour et al. 2009).

Finally, excavations on the Early Islamic site were resumed by Kristoffer Damgaard in 2008 (Damgaard 2009).

VI. ACKNOWLEDGMENTS

I have long looked forward to writing this portion of the final report, because any undertaking of the size and duration of Roman Aqaba Project required the support of an enormous number of people and organizations. All are deserving of my heart-felt thanks.

Obviously, the project was only possible with significant and sustained funding. Above all, I wish to thank the National Geographic Society, which funded all five major seasons of fieldwork, and the Joukowsky Family Foundation, which generously supported both the field work and post-field analysis towards publication, for their sustained support. Other financial sponsors included the National Endowment for the Humanities (an independent federal agency), Samuel H. Kress Foundation, Foundation for Biblical Archaeology, North Carolina Community Foundation, Lockheed Martin Corporation Foundation, and IBM Corporation. NEH supported the project both through a grant from its Division of Collaborative Research as well as a fellowship provided to the author.

A number of agencies offered financial support to enable students to work on the project, including ACOR (the Jennifer C. Groot Fellowship in the Archaeology of Jordan), the Institute of Classics of the University of Helsinki, the Endowment for Biblical Research, and the Kyle-Kelso Foundation.

My own institution, North Carolina State University, supported the project in innumerable ways: several faculty research grants, two sabbatical leaves, and other financial support. Several Heads of the History Department, including John Riddle and Jonathan Ocko, were strong supporters of my research. Above all, in 1998 with the crucial support of Dr. Margaret Zahn, then Dean of the College of Humanities and Social Sciences (CHASS), the university provided permanent space for an archaeological laboratory and repository on campus, which enormously facilitated this research. Two subsequent Deans of CHASS, Linda Brady and Jeffrey Braden, also provided important support. Finally, among the NCSU administration, Philip Stiles, then Provost of the university, offered some much needed financial support in the early stages of the project.

My work in Raleigh was also aided over the years by a long list of student research assistants, both graduates and undergraduates. Among these were Anna Adams, Marie Barnett, Heather Beckman, Stephanie Brown, Benjamin Dolinka, Elizabeth Ericksen, Russell Gentry, Anna Hendrick, Lindsay Holman, Nader Husseini, Valerie Johnson, Tiffany Key, Pamela Koulianos, Carrie McMillan, Elizabeth Ann Pollard, Andrew M. Smith II, Elizabeth Stephens, Chaffee Viets, Walter Ward, and Cheri Williams.

In Jordan the project was also assisted by many individuals and organizations. Three successive Director-Generals of Antiquities, Dr. Safwan et-Tell, Dr. Ghazi Bisheh, and Dr. Fawwaz al-Khrayseh, generously issued permits for the field work, loan agreements for the export of finds, and various other kinds of support. At Aqaba itself I am especially grateful to Dr. Sawsan al-Fakhiry, Inspector of the Aqaba District and our departmental representative for all field seasons of the project. She helped the project in innumerable ways, from assisting in the excavation to lining up the many local workers for each season. Sawsan is dedicated to the preservation of the precious antiquities of this region, and I am proud to call her my friend.

In Aqaba our team enjoyed the hospitality of the Showkini Center apartment building throughout all seasons of fieldwork. The manager of the building, Fuad Showkini, was always helpful during each of our stays. The center provided plenty of living and working space, including use of their roof for pottery processing, as well as spectacular views of the Gulf of Aqaba and the surrounding landscape. The city of Aqaba and the surrounding areas also provided dozens of workers for our project each season. These men, numbering several hundred over the course of the project and thus too numerous to name individually, worked diligently and were valued members of our team.

ACOR, our home away from home, always played a significant role in assisting our work. The institute was blessed to have an outstanding Director, Pierre Bikai, throughout the entire phase of RAP's fieldwork as well as most of the following years of analysis towards publication. I am also grateful to ACOR's then Associate Director, Patricia Bikai, and to several Assistant Directors, Glen Peterman, Kurt Zamora, and Chris Tuttle, for their assistance. ACOR's current director, Barbara Porter, also provided valuable assistance in the publication phase of our work.

Above all I wish to express my deepest and sincerest thanks to the staff of the Roman Aqaba Project. They spent six summers working hard and in good spirits in the blazing sun and oppressive heat and humidity of Aqaba. Altogether, some 170 individuals, including 32 senior staff and 138 students, served on the project. A major reason for the success of the project was continuity among its senior staff. Most of these colleagues either joined the team from the beginning and remained throughout the fieldwork and publication or began the project as students and were subsequently promoted to the senior staff. Several of these team members have since gone on to direct their own projects. All this has been especially gratifying to me.

Finally, it is important to acknowledge the contribution of Mary-Louise Mussell, who joined the project at its inception and served during every subsequent field season. Mary-Louise supervised Area J (East) and uncovered a major portion of the Byzantine city wall and, above all, the putative Late Roman church in this area. In fact, she was the first team member to suggest that this monumental mud-brick structure might in fact be a church and argued strenuously for this interpretation. Unfortunately, she was only able to publish a preliminary analysis of this structure (Mussell 2000a). She was a loyal and dedicated team member who brought many excellent students from Canada to the project. She also served as field director for the limited excavation season in 1997. Tragically, Mary-Louise was already ill during the 2002 field season and died of cancer on January 23, 2005, just 45 years old and with her final report on this structure unfinished. Therefore, I and other team members have undertaken this key responsibility, which will appear in a subsequent volume of the final report. Mary-Louise will be listed as a posthumous co-author, a well-deserved distinction.

REFERENCES

Abel, F. M.
1967 *Geographie de la Palestine.* 2 vols. Paris: Lecoffre.

Al-Shqour, R.; De Meulemeester, J.; and Herremans, D.
2009 The Aqaba Islamic Project. *SHAJ* X: 641–55.

Alt, A.
1921 *Die griechischen Inschriften der Palaestina Tertia westlich der 'Araba.* Berlin: Wissenschaftliche Veröffentlichungen des deutschtürkischen Denkmalschutzkommandos.

Avanzini, A.
2008 *A Port in Arabia Between Rome and the Indian Ocean, 3rd C. BC–5th C. AD: Khor Rori Report 2.* Rome: L'Erma di Bretschneider.

Bodenheimer, F. S., and Rabinowitz, A.
1949 *Timotheus of Gaza on Animals* (Perizoon). *Fragments of a Byzantine Paraphrase of an Animal-Book of the 5th century A.D. Translation, Commentary and Introduction.* Leiden: Brill.

Burckhardt, J. L.
1822 *Travels in Syria and the Holy Land.* London: Murray. Reprint New York: AMS, 1983.

Burton, R.
1879 *The Land of Midian (revisited).* 2 vols. London: Kegan Paul. Reprint New York: Oleander, 1984.

Casson, L.
1989 *The Periplus Maris Erythraei. Text with Introduction, Text, and Commentary.* Princeton, NJ: Princeton University.

Damgaard, K.
2009 A Palestinian Red Sea Port on the Egyptian Road to Arabia: Early Islamic Aqaba and its Many Hinterlands. Pp. 85–97 in *Red Sea IV: Connected Hinterlands, held at the University of Southampton 2008.* Oxford: Archaeopress.

Diodorus Siculus
1933–67 *Library of History.* 12 vols. Loeb Classical Library. Trans. C. H. Oldfather et al. Cambridge, MA: Harvard University.

Dolinka, B.
1999 Towards a Socio-Economic History of Nabataean Aila (Aqaba, Jordan) from the 1st Century BC through the early 2nd Century AD: Ceramic Evidence from the Roman Aqaba Project. M.A. thesis. North Carolina State University.

2003   *Nabataean Aila from a Ceramic Perspec-
        tive.* British Archaeological Reports, In-
        ternational Series 1116. Oxford: British
        Archaeological Reports.

Doughty, C. M.
1936   *Travels in Arabia Deserta.* 2 vols. 3rd ed.
        London: Jonathan Cape. Reprint New York:
        Dover, 1979.

Duncan-Jones. R.
1982   *The Economy of the Roman Empire: Quan-
        titative Studies.* Cambridge: Cambridge
        University.
1990   *Structure and Scale in the Roman Economy.*
        Cambridge: Cambridge University.

Engels, D. W.
1990   *Roman Corinth: An Alternative Model for
        the Classical City.* Chicago, IL: University
        of Chicago.

Eusebius
1904   *Onomasticon der Biblischen Ortsnamen.* Ed.
        E. Klostermann. Leipzip: Hinrichs.

Euting, J.
1891   *Sinaitische Inschriften.* Berlin: Reimer.

Finley, M. I.
1973   *The Ancient Economy.* Berkeley, CA: Uni-
        versity of California.
1999   *The Ancient Economy: Updated with a new
        foreword by Ian Morris.* Berkeley, CA: Uni-
        versity of California.

Frank, F.
1934   Aus der ʿAraba. *ZDPV* 57: 191–280.

Freeman-Grenville, G. S. P.
2003   *The Onomasticon: Palestine in the Fourth
        Century A.D.* Jerusalem: Carta.

Fulford, M. G., and Peacock, D. P. S.
1984   *The Avenue du President Habib Bourgiba,
        Salammbo: The Pottery and Other Ceramic
        Objects from the Site. Excavations at Car-
        thage: The British Mission.* V . I, 2. Sheffield:
        University of Sheffield.

Glidden, H. W.
1952   The Mamluke Origin of the Fortified Khan
        at al-ʿAqabah, Jordan. Pp. 116–18 in *Ar-
        chaeologica Orientalia in Memoriam Ernst
        Herzfeld.* G. C. Miles, ed. Locust Valley, NY:
        Augustin.

Glueck, N.
1935   *Explorations in Eastern Palestine II. AASOR*
        15. New Haven, CT: American Schools of
        Oriental Research. Pp. 46–53.
1938a   The First Campaign at Tell el-Kheleifeh.
        BASOR 71: 3–17.
1938b   The Topography and History of Ezion-
        geber and Elath. *BASOR* 72: 2–13.
1939a   *Explorations in Eastern Palestine III.
        AASOR* 18–19. New Haven, CT: American
        Schools of Oriental Research.
1939b   The Second Campaign at Tell el-Kheleifeh
        (Ezion-geber: Elath). *BASOR* 75: 8–22.
1940   The Third Season at Tell el-Kheleifeh.
        BASOR 79: 2–18.
1965   Ezion-geber. *Biblical Archaeologist* 28:
        70–87.
1967   Some Edomite Pottery from Tell el-Khel-
        eifeh. *BASOR* 188: 8–38.

Greene, K.
1986   *The Archaeology of the Roman Economy.*
        Berkeley, CA: University of California.

Gregory, S., and Kennedy, D.
1985   *Sir Aurel Stein's Limes Report.* BAR Interna-
        tional Series 272. Oxford: British Archaeo-
        logical Reports.

Grubisha, D.
2000   An Analysis of the Steatite Artifacts from
        the Archaeological Site of Aila, Jordan.
        M.A. thesis, University of Wisconsin at
        Milwaukee.

Harl, K. W.
1996   *Coinage in the Roman economy, 300 B.C. to
        A.D. 700.* Baltimore, MD: Johns Hopkins
        University.

Harris, W. V.
1994   Between Archaic and Modern: Some Cur-
        rent Problems in the History of the Roman
        Economy. Pp. 11–29 in W. V. Harris, ed. *The
        Inscribed Economy: Production and Distri-
        bution in the Roman Empire in the Light of
        instrumentum domesticum: The Proceed-*

ings of a Conference held at the American Academy in Rome on 10–11 January, 1992. JRA Supplementary Series 6. Ann Arbor, MI: Journal of Roman Archaeology.

Holum, K. G. (ed.)
1999   *Caesarea Papers 2: Herod's Temple, the Provincial Governor's Praetorium and Granaries, the Later Harbor, a Gold Coin Hoard, and Other Studies*. JRA Supplementary Series 35. Portsmouth, RI: Journal of Roman Archaeology.
2008   *Caesarea Reports and Studies: Excavations 1995–2007 within the Old City and the Ancient Harbor*. BAR International Series 1784. Oxford: Archaeopress.

Hopkins, K.
1978   Economic Growth and Towns in Classical Antiquity. Pp. 35–79 in P. Abrams and E. A. Wrigley, eds., *Towns in Societies: Essays in Economic History and Historical Sociology*. Cambridge: Cambridge University.
1980   Taxes and Trade in the Roman Empire (200 BC–AD 400). *JRS* 70: 101–25.

Horden. P., and Purcell, N.
2000   *The Corrupting Sea: A Study of Mediterranean History*. Oxford: Blackwell.

Jerome (Hieronymus)
1893   *Vita Hilarionis*. Pp. 303–15 in W. H. Fremantle, ed., *Nicene and Post-Nicene Fathers*, 2nd series, vol. 6. New York: Christian Literature.
1964   *Commentariurum in Hiezechielem libri XIV*. CCSL 75. Turnhout: Brepols.

Jones, J. D.
2000   Roman Export Glass at Aila (Aqaba). Pp. 147–150 in *Annales du 14e Congrès de l'Association Internationale pour l'Histoire du Verre*. Lochem: Association Internationale pour l'Histoire du Verre.
2002   Recently Discovered Cage Cup Fragments from Aqaba. *Journal of Glass Studies*. 45: 180–82.
2003   Glass Vessel Finds from a Possible Early Fourth-Century CE Church at Aila (Aqaba), Jordan. Pp. 139–43 in *Annales du 15e*

Congrès de l'Association Internationale pour l'Histoire de Verre. Lochem: Association Internationale pour l'Histoire du Verre.

Josephus
1926–65   *Jewish Antiquities*. 7 vols. Loeb Classical Library. Trans. H. St. J. Thackery, R. Marcus, A. Wikgren, and L. H. Feldman. Cambridge, MA: Harvard University.

Khalil, L.
1987   Preliminary Report on the 1985 Season of Excavation at el-Maqaṣṣ-ʿAqaba. *ADAJ* 31: 481–83.
1988   Excavation at Maqaṣṣ-ʿAqaba, 1985. *Dirasat* 15.7: 71–117.
1992   Some Technological Features from a Chalcolithic Site at Magaṣṣ-ʿAqaba. Pp. 143–48 in *SHAJ IV*. Amman: Department of Antiquities.

Khalil, L.; Eichmann, R.; and Schmidt, K.
2003   Archaeological Survey and Excavations at the Wādī al-Yutum and al-Magaṣṣ Area - al-ʿAqaba (ASEYM): A preliminary Report on the Third and Fourth Seasons Excavations at Tall Hujayrat al-Ghuzlan in 2002 and 2003 Wādī al-Yutum. *ADAJ* 47: 159–183.

Khouri, R. G.
1988   *The Antiquities of the Jordan Rift Valley*. Amman: Al Kutba.

Khouri, R. G., and Whitcomb, D. S.
1988   *Aqaba: "Port of Palestine on the China Sea."* Amman: Al-Kutba.

Kingsley, S. A., and Decker, M.
2001   *Economy and Exchange in the East Mediterranean During Late Antiquity: Proceedings of a Conference at Somerville College, Oxford, 29th May, 1999*. Oxford: Oxbow.

Kirkbride, A. S., and Harding, G. L.
1947   Hasma. *PEQ* 79: 7–26.

Kraemer, C. J.
1958   *Excavations at Nessana*. Volume III: *Non-literary Papyri*. Princeton, NJ: Princeton University.

Laborde, L. de
1836 *Journey through Arabia Petraea, to Mount Sinai and the Excavated City of Petra, the Edom of the Prophecies.* London: Murray.

MacAdam, H. I.
1989 Fragments of a Latin Building Inscription from Aqaba, Jordan. *ZPE* 79: 163–72.

Manning, J. G., and Morris, I. (eds.)
2005 *The Ancient Economy: Evidence and Models.* Stanford, CA: Stanford University.

Mattingly, D. J., and Salmon, J.
2001 *Economies beyond Agriculture in the Classical World.* New York: Routledge.

Mayerson, P.
1982 The Pilgrim Routes to Mount Sinai and the Armenians. *IEJ* 32: 44–57.

Melkawi, A.; ʿAmr, K.; and Whitcomb, D.S.
1994 The Excavation of Two Seventh Century Pottery Kilns at Aqaba. *ADAJ* 38: 447–68.

Meloy, J. L.
1991 Results of an Archaeological Reconnaissance in West Aqaba: Evidence of the Pre-Islamic Settlement. *ADAJ* 35: 397–414.

Morris, E. J.
1842 *Notes of a Tour through Turkey, Greece, Egypt, and Arabia Petraea, to the Holy Land: Including a Visit to Athens, Sparta, Delphi, Cairo, Thebes, Mount Sinai, Petra, etc.* Philadelphia, PA: Carey and Hart.

Morris, I.
1994 The Ancient Economy Twenty Years after *The Ancient Economy. Classical Philology* 89: 351–66.

Mussell, M.-L.
1997 Roman Aqaba Project. *ACOR Newsletter* 9.1: 10–11.
1998 The Roman Aqaba Project. *AJA* 102: 600–601.
2000a The Oldest Known Christian Chuches: Dura Europos and Aqaba. Pp. 189–99 in *Recherches canadiennes sur la Syrie antique/ Canadian Research on Ancient Syria.* Québec: Musée de la civilisation à Québec.

2000b Tell el-Kheleifeh. *AJA* 104: 577–78.

Niemi, T. M., and Smith, A. M., II
1999 Initial Results from the Southeastern Wādī ʿAraba, Jordan Geoarchaeological Study: Implications for Shifts in Late Quartenary Aridity. *Geoarchaeology* 14 (8): 791–820.

Parker, S. T.
1986 *Romans and Saracens: A History of the Arabian Frontier.* Winona Lake, IN: American Schools of Oriental Research.
1994a The Roman ʿAqaba Project: Aila Rediscovered. *BA* 57.3: 172.
1994b The Roman ʿAqaba Project. *ACOR Newsletter* 6.2: 8–9.
1995a The Roman ʿAqaba Project: The 1994 Campaign. *ADAJ* 40: 231–57.
1995b The Roman ʿAqaba Project. *AJA* 99: 522–23.
1996a The Roman ʿAqaba Project. *Old World Archaeology Newsletter* 19.2: 9–11.
1996b The Roman ʿAqaba Project: The Economy of Aila on the Red Sea. *BA* 59.3: 182.
1996c Roman Aqaba. *ACOR Newsletter* 8.1: 7–8.
1997a Preliminary Report on the 1994 Season of the Roman ʿAqaba Project. *BASOR* 305: 19–44.
1997b Human Settlement at the Northern Head of the Gulf of Aqaba: Evidence of Site Migration. Pp. 189–93 in *SHAJ VI*, eds. G. Bisheh, M. Zaghloul, and I. Kehrberg. Amman: Department of Antiquities of Jordan.
1997c The Roman ʿAqaba Project. *AJA* 101: 525–26.
1998a The Roman ʿAqaba Project: The 1996 Campaign. *ADAJ* 42: 375–94.
1998b An Early Church, Perhaps the Oldest in the World, Found at Aqaba. *NEA* 61.4: 254.
1999a Brief Notice on a Possible Fourth Century Church at Aqaba, Jordan. *JRA* 12: 372–76.
1999b The Roman ʿAqaba Project. *AJA* 103: 511–13.
1999c Roman ʿAqaba Project. *ACOR Newsletter* 12.1: 4–5.
2000a The Roman ʿAqaba Project: The 1997 and 1998 Campaigns. *ADAJ* 44: 373–94.
2000b The Roman ʿAqaba Project. *ACOR Newsletter* 14.1: 11–12.
2001 Roman ʿAqaba Project. *AJA* 105: 457–58.

2002 The Roman 'Aqaba Project: The 2000 Campaign. *ADAJ* 46: 409–28.

2003a The Roman 'Aqaba Project. *AJA* 107: 473–75.

2003b The Roman 'Aqaba Project: The 2002 Campaign. *ADAJ* 47: 321–33.

2005 Supplying the Roman Army on the Arabian Frontier. Pp. 415–25 in Z. Visy, ed. *Limes XIX: Proceedings of the XIXth International Congress of Roman Frontier Studies, Pécs. Hungary, September 2003.* Pécs: University of Pécs.

2006 Roman Aila and Wādī 'Arabah: An Economic Relationship. Pp. 227–34 in P. Bienkowski and K. Galor, eds., *Crossing the Rift: Resources, Routes, Settlement Patterns, and Interaction in the Wādī 'Arabah.* British Academy Monographs in Archaeology. Oxford: Oxford University.

2007 Beyond Frankincense and Myrrh: Reconstructing the Economy of Roman Aqaba. Pp. 359–366 in T. E. Levy, P. M. M. Daviau, and M. Shaer, eds. *Crossing Jordan: North American Contributions to the Archaeology of Jordan.* London: Equinox.

2009a The Foundation of Aila: A Nabataean Port on the Red Sea. Pp. 685–90 in *SHAJ X: Crossing Jordan.* Amman: Department of Antiquities of Jordan.

2009b The Roman Port of Aila: Economic Connections with the Red Sea Littoral. Pp. 79–84 in *Red Sea IV: Connected Hinterlands.* Society for Arabian Studies Monographs. British Archaeological Reports, International Series. Oxford: British Archaeological Reports.

2009c *Arabia Adquisita*: The Roman Annexation of Arabia Reconsidered. Pp. 1585–92 in A. Morillo, N. Hanel, and E. Martín, eds., in *Limes XX: Roman Frontier Studies. XXth International Congress of Roman Frontier Studies.* 3 vols. Madrid: Consejo Superior de Investigaciones Científicas.

Peacock, D., and Blue, L. (eds.)
2006 *Myos Hormos-Quseir Al-Qadim: Roman and Islamic ports on the Red Sea.* Oxford: Oxbow.

2007 *The Ancient Red Sea Port of Adulis, Eritrea: Results of the Eritro-British Expedition, 2004–5.* Oxford: Oxbow.

Perry, M. A.
2002 Health, Labor, and Political Economy: A Bioarchaeological Analysis of Three Communities in Provincia Arabia. Ph.D. dissertation. University of New Mexico.

Pliny the Elder
1938–62 *Natural History.* 10 vols. Loeb Classical Library. Trans. H. Rackham, W. H. S. Jones, and D. E. Eichholz. Cambridge, MA: Harvard University.

Pratico, G. D.
1985 Nelson Glueck's 1938–1940 Excavations at Tell el-Kheleifeh: A Reappraisal. *BASOR* 259: 1–32.

1993 *Nelson Glueck's 1938–1940 Excavations at Tell el-Kheleifeh: A Reappraisal.* American Schools of Oriental Research Archaeological Reports 3. Atlanta: Scholar's.

Procopius
1914 *The Persian War.* Vol. 1. Loeb Classical Library. Trans. H. B. Dewing. Cambridge, MA: Harvard University.

Ptolemy
1843–45 *Geographia.* C. F. A. Nobbe, ed. Leipzig: Tuebner (Reprint Hildesheim 1966).

Raschke, M.
1978 New Studies in Roman Commerce with the East. *Aufstieg und Niedergang der römischen Welt*, II.9: 604–1361. Berlin: de Gruyter.

Regnault, L. (ed.)
1966–78 *Les sentences des pères du désert: Nouveau recueil. Evergentinos.* Sablé-sur-Sarthes: Solesmes.

Retzleff, A.
2003 A Nabataean/Roman Domestic Complex at the Red Sea Port of Aila. *BASOR* 331: 45–65.

Robinson, E.
1841 *Biblical Researches in Palestine, Mount Sinai, and Arabia Petraea: A Journal of Travels in*

the Year 1838. Boston, MA: Crocker and Brewster.

Rose, M.
1998 Early Church at Aqaba. *Archaeology* 51.6: 18.

Rostovtzeff, M.
1957 *The Social and Economic History of the Roman Empire.* Oxford: Oxford University.

Rüppel, E.
1829 *Reise in Nubien, Kordofan und dem peträischen Arabien vorzüglich in geographischee-statistischer Hinsicht.* Frankfurt: Wilmans.

Salles, J.-F., and Sedov A. V.
2010 *Qāni': Le port du Hadramawt entre la Méditerranée, l'Afrique et l'Indie.* Indicopleustoi: Archeologies of the Indian Ocean 6. Turnhout: Brepols.

Scheidel, W., and von Reden, S. (eds.)
2002 *The Ancient Economy.* New York: Routledge.

Schertl, P.
1936 Ela-Akaba. *Orientalia Christiana Periodica* 2: 33–77.

Schwabe, M.
1953 A Greco-Christian Inscription from Aila. *Harvard Theological Review* 46: 49–55.

Sedov, A. V.
1995 Qana' (Yemen) and the Indian Ocean and the Archaeological Evidence. Pp. 11–35 in H. P Ray and J.-E Salles, eds., *Tradition and Archaeology: Early Maritime Contacts in the Indian Ocean.* New Delhi: Manohar.

Seeck, O.
1876 *Notitia Dignitatum.* Berlin: Weidmann.

Šenčenko, I.
1966 The Early Period of the Sinai Monastery in the Light of its Inscriptions. *DOP* 20: 255–64.

Shahîd, I.
1989 *Byzantium and the Arabs in the Fifth Century.* Washington, DC: Dumbarton Oaks.

Sidebotham, S. E.
1986 *Roman Economic Policy in the Erythra Thalassa, 30 B.C.–A.D. 217.* Leiden: Brill.
1994 Preliminary Report on the 1990–1991 Seasons of Fieldwork at 'Abu Sha'ar (Red Sea Coast). *Journal of the American Research Center in Egypt.* 31: 133–58.
2011 *Berenike and the Ancient Maritime Spice Route.* Berkeley, CA: University of California.

Sidebotham, S. E., and Wendrich, W. Z. (eds.)
1995 *Berenike 1994: Preliminary Report of the 1994 Season Excavations at Berenike (Egyptian Red Sea Coast) and Survey of the Eastern Desert.* Leiden: Research School of Asian, African, and Amerindian Studies.
1996 *Berenike '95: Preliminary Report of the Excavations at Berenike (Egyptian Red Sea Coast) and the Survey of the Eastern Desert.* Leiden: Research School of Asian, African, and Amerindian Studies.
1998 *Berenike '96: Report of the Excavations at Berenike (Egyptian Red Sea Coast) and the Survey of the Eastern Desert.* Leiden: Research School of Asian, African, and Amerindian Studies.
1999 *Report of the 1997 Excavations at Berenike and the Survey of the Egyptian Eastern Desert, including Excavations at Shenshef.* Leiden: Research School of Asian, African, and Amerindian Studies.

Smith, A. M., II
2002 An Historical Geography of Wādī 'Araba. M.A. thesis. North Carolina State University.
2005 Pathways, Roadways and Highways: Networks of Communication and Exchange in the Wādī 'Araba. *NEA* 68: 180–89.
2010 *Wādī 'Araba in Classical and Late Antiquity: An Historical Geography.* BAR International Series 2173. Oxford: Archaeopress.

Smith, A. M., II, and Niemi, T. M.
1994 Results of the Southeast 'Araba Archaeological Reconnaissance. *ADAJ* 38: 469–83.

Smith, A. M., II; Niemi T.M.; and Stevens, M.
2003 The Southeast 'Araba Archaeological Survey: A Preliminary Report of the 1994 Season. *BASOR* 305: 45–71.

Strabo
1930 *Geography.* 8 vols. Loeb Classical Library. Trans. H. L. Jones. Cambridge, MA: Harvard University.

Talbert, R. J. A.
2010 *Rome's World: The Peutinger Map Reconsidered.* Cambridge: Cambridge University.

Temin, P.
2001 A Market Economy in the Early Roman Empire. *JRS* 91: 169–81.

Thomas, R.; Niemi, T. M.; and Parker, S. T.
2007 Structural Damage from Earthquakes in the 2nd–9th Century A.D. at the Archaeological Site of Aila in Aqaba, Jordan. *BASOR* 346: 59–77.

Thomsen, P.
1917 Die römischen Meilensteine der Provinzen Syria, Arabia, und Palaestina. *ZDPV* 40: 1–103.

Tomber, R.
1993 Quantitative Approaches to the Investigation of Long-distance Exchange. *JRA* 6: 142–66.
2005 Troglodites and Trogodites: Exploring Interaction on the Red Sea during the Roman Period. Pp. 41–49 in J. C. M. Starkey, ed., *People of the Red Sea. Proceedings of the Red Sea Project II Held at the British Museum, October 2004.* Society for Arabian Studies Monograph 3. BAR International Series 1395. Oxford: British Archaeological Reports.
2008 *Indo-Roman Trade: From Pots to Pepper.* London: Duckworth.

Van Neer, W., and Parker, S. T.
2007 The First Archaeological Evidence for Haimation, the Invisible Garum. *JAS* 35: 1821–27.

Ward, W. D.
2004 Roman Red Sea Ports: Benenike, Myos Hormos, Clysma, Leuke Kome, and Aila from Augustus to Diocletian. M.A. thesis, North Carolina State University.

Weintraub, B.
1999 Unearthing a Pioneer Church. *National Geographic* (Feb. 1999).

Whitcomb, D. S.
1986 Excavations in Aqaba: Preliminary Report on the 1986 Season. Unpublished field report.
1987 Excavations in Aqaba: First Preliminary Report. *ADAJ* 31: 247–66.
1988a A Fatimid Residence in Aqaba, Jordan. *ADAJ* 32: 207–24.
1988b *Aqaba: "Port of Palestine on the China Sea."* Amman: Al Kutba.
1989a Evidence of the Umayyad Period from the Aqaba Excavations. Pp. 164–84 in M. Adnan Bakhit and Robert Schick, eds., *The Fourth International Conference on the History of Bilād al-Shām during the Umayyad Period. Proceedings of the Third Symposium,* v. 2. Amman: University of Jordan.
1989b Coptic Glazed Ceramics from the Excavations at Aqaba, Jordan. *Journal of the American Research Center in Egypt* 26: 167–82.
1989c Mahesh Ware: Evidence of Early Abbasid Occupation from Southern Jordan. *ADAJ* 33: 269–85.
1990 'Diocletian's' *misr* at 'Aqaba. *ZDPV* 106: 156–61.
1990–91 Glazed Ceramics from the Abassid period from the Aqaba Excavations. *Transactions of the Oriental Ceramic Society* 55: 43–65.
1993 The Fourth Gate at Ayla: A Report on the 1992 Excavations at Aqaba. *ADAJ* 37: 533–47.
1995 The *Misr* of Ayla: The Evidence for the Islamic City. Pp. 277–88 in M. Zaghloul, K. 'Amr, F. Zayadine, and R. Nabeel, eds., *SHAJ IV.* Amman: Department of Antiquities.
1997 The Town and Name of 'Aqaba: An Inquiry into the Settlement History from an Archaeological Perspective. Pp. 359–63 in G.

Bisheh, ed., *SHAJ VI*. Amman: Department of Antiquities of Jordan.

1998   Out of Arabia: Early Islamic Aqaba in its Regional Context. Pp. 403–18 in R-P. Gayraud, ed., *Colloque international d'archéologie islamique*. Cairo: Institut Français d'Archéologie Orientale.

2006a The Walls of Early Islamic Ayla: Defense or Symbol? Pp. 61–74 in H. Kennedy, ed., *Muslim Military Architecture in Greater Syria*. Leiden: Brill.

2006b Land behind Aqaba: the Wādī ʿArabah during the Early Islamic Period. Pp. 239–42 in P. Bienkowski and K. Galor, eds., *Crossing the Rift: Resources, Routes, Settlement Patterns, and Interaction in the Wādī ʿArabah*. British Academy Monographs in Archaeology. Oxford: Oxford University.

2009   Ayla at the Millennium: Archaeology and History. Pp. 123–32 in *SHAJ 10: Crossing Jordan*. Amman: Department of Antiquities of Jordan.

Whitcomb, D. S., and Johnson, J. H. (eds.)

1979   *Quseir al-Qadim 1978 Preliminary Report*. Malibu, CA: Undena.

1982   *Quseir al-Qadim 1980 Preliminary Report*. Malibu, CA: Undena.

Wilkinson, J.

1977   *Jerusalem Pilgrims before the Crusades*. Warminster: Aris and Phillips.

Williams, C. L.

2009   Egyptian Red Slip Pottery at Aila. M.A. thesis. North Carolina State University.

Williams, F.

1994   *The Panarion of Epiphanius of Salamis, Volume 2*. Leiden: Brill.

Wolska-Conus, W.

1968–73 *Cosmas Indicopleustès. Topographie Chrétienne*. 3 vols. Sources Chrétiennes 141. Paris: Les Éditions du Cerf.

Woolley, L., and Lawrence, T. E.

1936   *The Wilderness of Zin*. New York: Scribner.

Young, G.

2001   *Rome's Eastern Trade: International Commerce and Imperial Policy, 31 BC – AD 305*. New York: Routledge.

Zayadine, F.

1994   Ayla-ʿAqaba in the Light of Recent Excavations. *ADAJ* 38: 485–505.

Chapter 2

Regional Environmental Setting, Seismic History, and Natural Resources of Aqaba, Jordan

by Tina M. Niemi

I. INTRODUCTION

Aqaba lies on the coast of the Gulf of Aqaba at the southern end of the Wādī ʿAraba valley in a hyperarid climate. This chapter summarizes various aspects of the environmental setting of the southern Wādī ʿAraba including the climate, geography, geologic history, and Quaternary alluvial fan deposition and soil pedogenesis. Of particular importance in understanding the distribution of archaeological survey data is the age of geological surfaces and documentation of the processes that can bury or erode archaeological sites. Of equal importance for understanding the history of Roman-Byzantine Aila and the Aqaba region in general is how and why the landscape may have changed over time. Chapter 3 presents human modification of the region and a history of early 20th-century land use practices, based on air photo interpretation and interviews with local inhabitants about life in Aqaba before recent urbanization.

Excavations of the Roman Aqaba Project (henceforth RAP) revealed that the site of Roman-Byzantine Aila sits across an active fault of the complex Dead Sea transform fault, part of the tectonic boundary that separates the Sinai Plate from the Arabian Plate (fig. 2.1). Earthquakes have

ruptured this fault system numerous times in antiquity, leading to the potential reorganization of structures and occupation patterns. This chapter summarizes the evidence for active faulting both offshore in the Gulf of Aqaba and the extension of these faults on land. The evidence of earthquake damage at archaeological sites in Aqaba is also discussed in the context of historical accounts collected in published earthquake catalogues.

Finally, questions abound as to what resources were available to the inhabitants of ancient Aqaba. Key among these resources for a port such as Aqaba are building materials, products for export including raw materials and agricultural products, and clay for the production of shipping containers. This chapter briefly reviews the agricultural potential of soils on the alluvial and aeolian surfaces in the Aqaba region. It also discusses the availability of natural resources, including ground water, dimension stone, metals and other raw minerals, and potential clay deposits.

Various resources utilized in this study include early travel accounts, aerial photography and other imagery, previous geologic data and maps, and my own field research, carried out predominately in Jordan and supplemented with information from trips to Israel. The first reconnaissance survey for

33

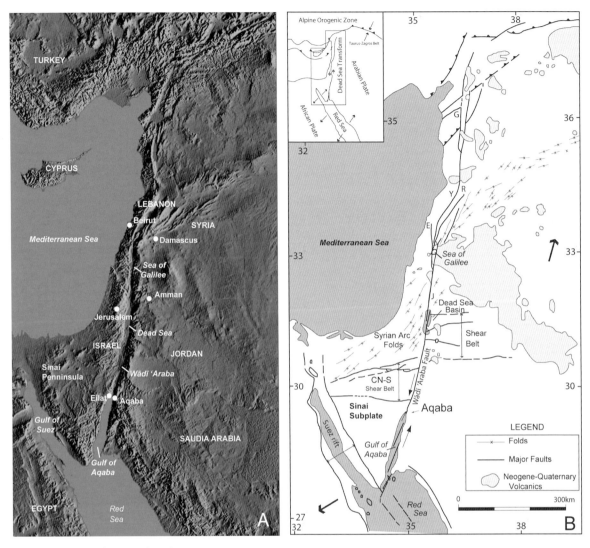

FIG. 2.1   *Regional setting of Aqaba.*

this study was in 1993 (Smith and Niemi 1994), and geological mapping was largely accomplished during the RAP field survey in 1994 (Smith et al. 1997; Niemi and Smith 1999). There were additional geoarchaeological, archaeoseismic, and geological studies of the environs of Aila during the RAP seasons of 1996, 1998, and 2002. The author has also directed the Wādī ʿAraba Earthquake Project (WAEP) since 1996. The objective of WAEP is to collect stratigraphic, geomorphic, and geophysical data preserved in the geologic and archaeological record that will help us better understand the history of past earthquakes and their societal impact and to characterize the future earthquake potential in the region. Therefore, significant overlap exists

between the goals of RAP and WAEP. Important geological data were collected in Aqaba during WAEP field seasons in 1999, 2001, 2003, 2009, and 2010. Invaluable contributions to the understanding of the paleoseismology and paleoenvironmental setting of Aqaba were made through M.S. thesis work by several students at the University of Missouri-Kansas City: Nasser Mansoor (2002; Mansoor et al. 2004), Abdel-Rahmen Abueladas (2005), and Alivia Allison (2007; Allison and Niemi 2010). In addition to the above field research, the author participated between 2006 and 2012 on a Middle East Regional Cooperation project to understand the seismic hazard of the Aqaba-Eilat region through collection and interpretation of

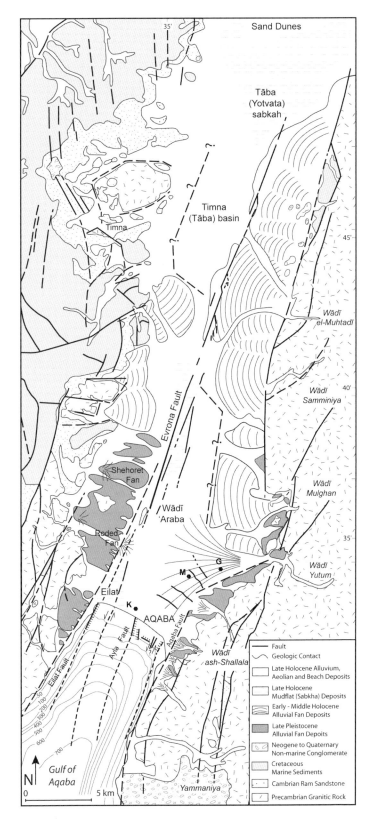

FIG. 2.2   *Geologic map of the Aqaba region.*

marine geophysics data, offshore sediment coring, and onshore geophysical and geological mapping.

II. REGIONAL ENVIRONMENTAL SETTING

Physiography and Climate

The northern shore of the Gulf of Aqaba is characterized by a straight, northwest-trending coast composed of sand and gravel beaches (fig. 2.2). The modern and ancient cities of Aqaba lie at the NE corner of this shoreline. Modern coral reefs presently grow only along the west and east shores of the gulf. These coastlines are also lined with elevated fossil coral reefs (e.g., Friedman 1965; al-Rifaiy and Cherif 1988; Shaked et al. 2004). Water depths in the gulf exceed 1500 m. Water flow into the 180-km-long Gulf of Aqaba from the Red Sea is restricted at the southern end by the Straits of Tiran (fig. 2.1). Surrounded by arid lands, the sea is characterized by high temperatures and salinities due to very low freshwater input, high evaporation, and strong winds (e.g., Morcos 1970). The tidal range at the north end of the gulf is less than a meter. Summer monthly average temperatures exceed 30°C, while winter mean temperatures range from 15°C to 17.5°C.

The morphology of the northern Gulf of Aqaba seafloor has recently been mapped based on multibeam and side-scan sonar data (Tibor et al. 2010). The broad flat NE shelf extends 1.3–1.8 km seaward from the shore along a 3–4° gradient to the shelf-slope break in 80–100 m water depths (fig. 2.2). The deepest water in the northern gulf is about 900 m in the offshore Eilat basin. The submarine Aqaba fault system forms a steep escarpment with a very narrow shelf and deep water adjacent to the eastern shore of the gulf. A less precipitous slope and

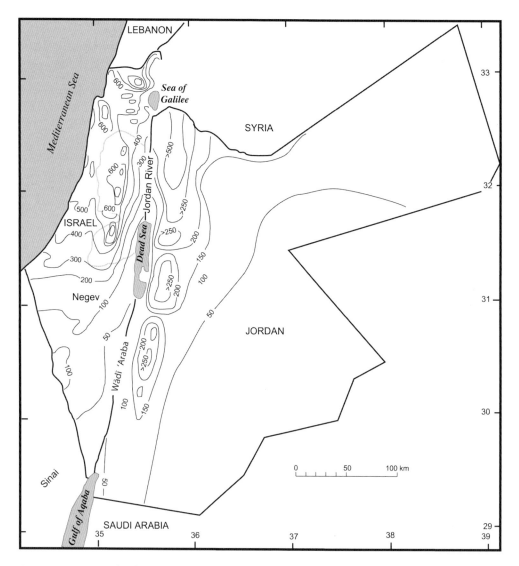

FIG. 2.3   *Present-day distribution of mean annual precipitation in mm.*

a broader shelf mark the western shore along the Eilat fault system.

Rainfall in Aqaba occurs sporadically during the winter months between November and March. Aqaba and the whole of Wādī ʿAraba, along with parts of the Negev desert and SE Jordan, are hyper-arid and fall within the zone that receives less than 50 mm of annual precipitation (fig. 2.3). Rainfall shows a high spatial and annual variability in the region. Daily rainfall data for Eilat and Aqaba for three years in the mid-1960s (Bruins 2006) show how individual storms can deliver twenty times more rain to one city compared to the other over a distance of less than 6 km. Precipitation to the

Levantine coast and Jordan including the Aqaba region is modulated by two different weather systems: the mid-latitude cyclone (the Cyprus Low) that brings moisture from the eastern Mediterranean and the Red Sea trough (low pressure), an extension of the tropical monsoon system from the south (e.g., Black et al. 2011). Most precipitation from the cyclonic systems falls north of Aqaba in the Judean Mountains and northern Jordan, creating the dry deserts of Wādī ʿAraba, the Negev, and southern Jordan. By analyzing historical rainfall records from Jerusalem, Enzel et al. (2003) concluded that wet years are associated with an increase in the number of frontal systems and a 1° latitudinal

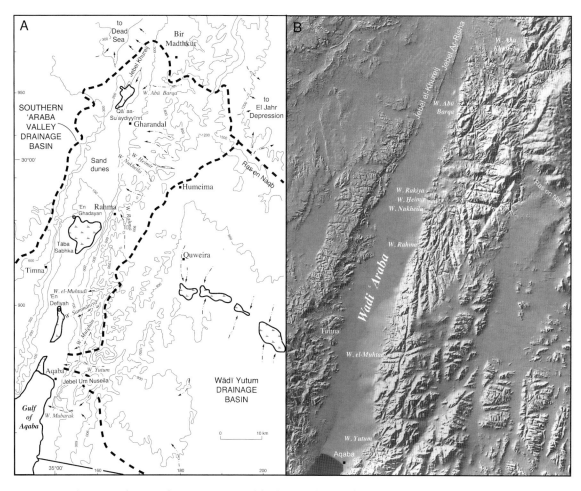

FIG. 2.4   A) Topographic map showing a portion of the drainage basins of the Southern Wādī ʿAraba and the Wādī Yutum.
B) Digital elevation model of the Wādī ʿAraba.

shift south of the storm tracks. Prolonged drought periods were also associated with a drop in the water level of the Dead Sea.

Precipitation that falls on the valley and adjacent highlands feeds the drainage networks and groundwater. The drainage basin of the southern ʿAraba valley extends from the Gulf of Aqaba 80 km NE to Jebel el-Khureij and Jebel Ar-Risha that lie in the middle of the valley (fig. 2.4). North of Jebel Ar-Risha and the divide at 250 m elevation, drainage is toward the Dead Sea in a channel of Wādī ʿAraba. Short drainages flow into the southern Wādī ʿAraba from its flanking mountain ranges. The granitic rock on the eastern side forms a very steep escarpment rising to elevations near 1200 m over a short distance (fig. 2.4). The mountains along the western side of the valley are much

lower, reaching an average elevation of only 600 m. There are no perennial streams in the southern Wādī ʿAraba drainage. Flash floods from torrential winter storms carry sediment through steep gorges eroded into the mountains that flank the valley. At the mouths of drainages, large alluvial fans accumulate sediment and radiate into the ʿAraba valley. The active channels of these alluvial fans flow into four seasonal *sabkhas,* or mudflats, along the valley floor: Eilat, ʿEn Defiya (Evrona), Tāba (Yotvata), and Qāʿ as-Suʾaydiyyīn (fig. 2.4). The Wādī el-Muhtadī alluvial fan extends far westward, restricting the width of the ʿAraba valley and separating the ʿEn Defiya and Tāba depressions. Low annual rainfall and high evaporation rates lead to precipitation of salts in these *sabkhas* (e.g., Amiel and Friedman 1971; Abed 2002).

Extensive sand dune fields lie between Gharandal-Tāba and Qaʿ as-Suʾaydiyyīn. These are two of four dune fields covering ca. 16% of Wādī ʿAraba (Saqqa and Atallah 2004). The dunes developed in this hyperarid environment where sandstone bedrock to the east provides an ample source of sand. Two predominant winds patterns prevail. The northern "*Shamal*" wind and the southern "*Khamsin*" or hot winds from the Red Sea trough weather pattern have created barchanoid and linear dune fields. Dunes also climb the bedrock escarpment near Wādī Nukheila. The dune fields are actively migrating. Sand storms are a common feature in Wādī ʿAraba, especially between April and July (Saqqa and Atallah 2004).

The drainage basin of Wādī Yutum (variously transliterated as Yutim, Yitum, Yitm, and Yutm) reaches far into the eastern plateau (fig. 2.4) with a catchment area of 4,545 km² (Foote et al. 2011). The size of the drainage system, including areas with higher annual precipitation than Wādī ʿAraba, promotes high discharge flash flood events as well as ground water recharge. Wādī Yutum is by far the largest drainage system in the southern ʿAraba. Several branches of Wādī Yutum flow SW towards the Gulf of Aqaba.

Bedrock Geology

The geology of the rock units in the Aqaba region is summarized from published geologic maps and reports. Burdon (1959) published the first synthesis of the geology of Jordan. He provided detailed descriptions and explanation of the accompanying 1:250,000-scale geologic maps by Quennell (1959). Although these publications predate the advent of the plate tectonic theory, Burdon accepted Quennell's 1956 interpretation that the Dead Sea-Jordan Rift valley was a fault system that accommodated over 100 km of lateral motion. Bender (1974) summarized the geology of Jordan along with a series of geologic maps at a scale of 1:100,000. The Jordan Natural Resources Authority geological mapping project provides maps at a scale of 1:50,000. For southern Wādī ʿAraba, these include the following map sheets, from south to north: Ayn Al Hashim, Jabal Al Mubarak and Al Yamaniyya (Abdelhamid et al. 1994), Wādī ʿAraba/Al ʿAqaba (Rashdan

1988), Rahma (Ibrahim 1991), and Wādī Gharandal (Ibrahim 1993). Also useful were geologic maps for areas farther north, including the Faynan area (al-Qurayqira map sheet by Rabbʾa 1994) and the Fifa map sheet (Tarawneh 1992). I also utilized the 1:200,000-scale Elat geologic map (Sneh et al. 1998) and the mapping of Garfunkel (1970).

Israel, Jordan, and the wider Levant share a similar tectonic history. Garfunkel (1988) synthesized the regional geologic data and divided the tectonic history into three main phases. The first is the late Precambrian Pan-African Orogeny, marked by emplacement of plutons and consolidation of the continental crust. High temperature/low pressure metamorphism is associated with this tectonic convergence. Radiometric dating of the rocks indicates the Pan-African orogenic phase ended ca. 550–540 million years ago (Ma). The plutonic phase was immediately followed by intense tectonic uplift, erosion, and development of a peneplain surface. A long period of continental and marine sedimentation, lasting from the early Cambrian to the mid-Cenozoic, defines the Platform Phase. This phase is divided into four major depositional groups punctuated by long periods of non-deposition or erosion. The Platform Phase is marked by deposition of sandstone in the lower two rock groups and carbonates in the upper two rock groups. There was only minor magmatism during this phase. The third or Continental Breakup Phase began in the Oligocene to Miocene, with rifting of the Arabian plate away from the Africa plate along the Red Sea and the initiation of the Syrian-African rift system known as the Dead Sea-Jordan transform fault zone. This phase is also characterized by distinct pulses of volcanic extrusion, uplift, faulting, and folding (fig. 2.1). Sedimentation is localized along new basins formed along the main fault lines, including the pull-apart basins forming the Gulf of Aqaba, the Dead Sea, the Sea of Galilee, and the Wādī ʿAraba and Jordan Valleys that lie between the deeper basins.

The continental breakup phase of tectonic motion created the linear valley that defines the Wādī ʿAraba (Arava) valley. Tectonic motion along this fault zone has subsided the valley floor and elevated the flanking mountains. An accumulative left-lateral offset of 107 km along the Dead

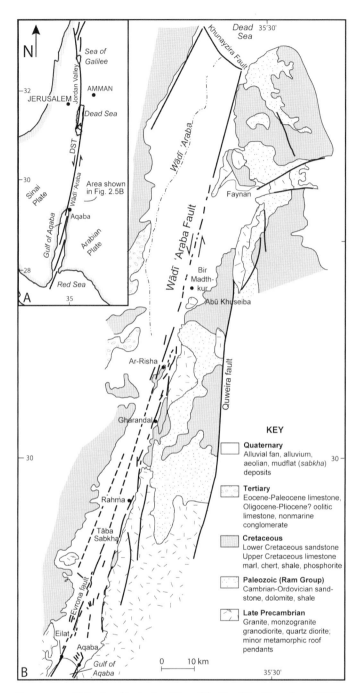

FIG. 2.5   A) Regional tectonic setting of the Dead Sea Transform (DST).
           B) Generalized geologic map of the Wādī ʿAraba valley.

alized stratigraphic section of the rocks exposed along the eastern side of Wādī ʿAraba is shown in figure 2.6.

Extending east of Aqaba for 50 km NE are outcrops of Precambrian igneous rocks of the Aqaba Granite Complex (e.g., Quennell 1956; Bender 1974; Rashdan 1987; Ibrahim 1991; 1993). Plutonic rocks of this age are also exposed west of Aqaba in the mountains of Eilat and down the Gulf of Aqaba coast of the Sinai Peninsula. These igneous rocks are composed mainly of granite, monzogranite, granodiorite, and diorite. Isolated occurrences of Precambrian metamorphic rocks, mainly gneiss and schist, are found around Wādī Abū Barqa (Ibrahim 1993) and along the west shore of the Gulf of Aqaba (Bentor et al. 1965). The field relationship of the metamorphic rocks to the granitic intrusions and U-Pb zircon ages indicate that they must date to >600 Ma (McCourt and Ibrahim 1990). A series of aphanitic dikes with widely varying rhyolitic to mafic compositions cross cut the plutonic and metamorphic rocks of the Aqaba Complex. Dikes and faults trend strongly in the NE–SW and E–W directions similar to the regional extensional fracture (joint) directions (Ibrahim 1991). Minor NW–SE dikes and fractures are also present. Faults trend predominantly NNE–SSW, cutting the structural grain of the older rocks. These regional fracture patterns are readily discerned on the digital elevation model map shown in figures 2.1 and 2.4. Together the Late Precambrian metamorphic rocks, the Aqaba Complex intrusions dating to ca. 550 Ma (McCourt and Ibrahim 1990), the overlying, isolated Safi Group rocks (conglomerate and volcaniclastic rocks of the Saramuj and Hayyala formations), and the ʿAraba Complex extrusions are part of the Pan African Orogenic tectonic phase.

Unconformably overlying the Aqaba Granite Complex is the Cambrian to Ordovician Ram

Sea-Jordan transform fault (e.g., Quennell 1959; Freund et al. 1970) juxtaposes different bedrock types across the valley. Thus, along southern Wādī ʿAraba the mountains to the east are composed of granitic rock and sandstone, while the mountains to the west are mostly limestone (fig. 2.5). A gener-

Era	Period	Age	Group	Formation	Rocks	Notes	
Cenozoic	Quaternary	Holocene		Aeolian/coastal sand Sabkha / mudflats Wadi sediments Lacustrine marl		Lisan-like marl	CONTINENTAL BREAK-UP PHASE
		Pleistocene		Alluvium fans			
	Tertiary	Pliocene Miocene Oligocene?		Dana Conglomerate		Halite and Marl in the Dead Sea; Interbedded sandstone, conglomerate with bedded chert and limestone in the lower section	
Mesozoic		Eocene	Belqa	Wadi Shallala Umm Rijam Chert Limestone		Marl; Nummulitic limestone; Gypsum; Chalk and chert beds;	PLATFORM PHASE
		Paleocene		Muwaqqar Chalk Marl		Chert beds; Traces of bitumen; Gypsum veins	
	Cretaceous	Maastrichten Campanian Santonian		Al Hisa Phosporite Amman Silicified Limestone Wadi Umm Ghudran		Phosphate mined on the plateau; Chert beds;	
		Coniacian				Interbedded chalk and sandstone;	
		L. Turt./Con.	Ajlun	Khuraij Limestone		Oolitic limestone quarry in valley;	
		Turtonian (Late)		Wadi As Sir Limestone		Massive micrite (ooids, chalk, dolomite); Chert; Dimension stone	
		Cenomanian		Shu'ayb Formation Hummar Formation Fuheis Formation		Upper brown dolomite; Interbedded limestone, siltstone, and mudstone; Traces of bitumen and some gypsum;	
				Na'ur Limestone		Upper nodular fossilerous limestone; Lower sandstone, siltstone w/ some gypsum	
		Albian Aptian Neocomian (Early)	Kurnub	Kurnub Sandstone		Friable quartz arenite; Suitable for glass production; Major aquifer; reservoir rock;	
Paleozoic	Ordovician	Late?	Ram	Disi Sandstone		Friable quartz arenite; Suitable for glass production; Major aquifer; reservoir rock;	
	Cambrian	Middle		Umm Ishrin Sandstone		Multicolored sandstone with some siltstone (Petra)	
		Early to Mid.		Abu Khusheiba Sandstone Burj Dolomite-Shale		Units often absent from section; Fe, Cu and Mn mineralization;	
		Early		Salib Arkosic Sandstone		Above a peneplain surface; Clasts mostly quartz; Fe, Cu and Mn mineralization;	
Precambrian	Precambrian	Late		Araba Complex		Dikes; Aheimir volcanic suite; Rhyolite; Gold	PAN AFRICAN OROGENY
		Late	Safi	Hayyala Volcaniclastic Saramuj Conglomerate		Exposed in Wadi Abu Barqa; Angular unconformity with Ram Group;	
		Late		Aqaba Complex Wadi Abu Barqa and other metamorphic rocks		Granite, Granodiorite, Quartz monzogranite, Diorite, Two-Mica granite; Quartzdiorite; Leucocratic granite; Aplite; Schist, Gneiss, Mylonites; Metarhyolite (Gold)	

FIG. 2.6   *Lithostratigraphic and chronostratratigraphic chart of rocks exposed in the southern Wādī.*

Group that comprises the base of the Platform Phase sedimentation (fig. 2.6). The basal contact between the Aqaba Complex and the Ram Group is a vast, flat, erosional surface or peneplain that is structurally tilted to the east. Several resistant rocks of the Aqaba Complex protrude above the peneplain and stand as *inselbergs,* including mountains in the Timna and Wādī Abū Barqa region (Garfunkel 1988; Ibrahim 1993). The overlying Salib Arkosic Sandstone was deposited in a braided stream environment and contains clasts of angular rhyolite, quartz, and feldspar derived from erosion of the weathered granitic and volcanic rocks. These rocks grade into the cross-stratified quartzose sandstones of Abū Khusheiba, Umm Ishrin, and Disi Sandstones deposited in fluvial and shallow marine environments. The Abū Khusheiba Sandstone is sometimes missing from the section, especially south of Gharandal. This sandstone appears correlative to the Burj Dolomite-Shale in Timna and Faynan, and both units host copper ore deposits. The Umm Ishrin Sandstone is interbedded with siltstone and is characterized by variegated bands of ferruginous and manganiferous color banding that are prevalently exposed in Petra. The Disi Sandstone is recognized in the field by its rounded weathering, widely spaced joints, and white color.

The Ram Group is unconformably overlain by the Kurnub Sandstone of Early Cretaceous age. Ram and Kurnub sandstones have frequently been correlated to the regionally extensive "Nubian sandstone" that is both a groundwater aquifer and hydrocarbon reservoir rock across North Africa and Arabia. The contact between the Ram and Kurnub sandstones represents a long hiatus of non-deposition and/or erosion including all the upper Paleozoic and lower Mesozoic rocks. Sedimentary layers thicken NNW toward the developing passive margin along the present Levant Mediterranean coast (Garfunkel 1988). In southern Wādī ʿAraba, outcrops of Kurnub Sandstone are similar in lithology to the underlying quartzose sandstones of the Ram Group. About 50 km NE of Aqaba along the eastern mountain range, erosion of the Kurnub Sandstone and Ram Group sandstones supply the sand that has formed the extensive dune fields in Wādī ʿAraba between the Tāba and Qaʿ as-Suʾaydiyyīn mudflats (figs. 2.2 and 2.4).

Upper Cretaceous to Eocene limestones of the Ajlun and Belqa Groups represent high eustatic sea level flooding of the platform and deposition of hundreds of meters of carbonate sediment across the Levant and Jordan (fig. 2.6). Whereas the Ajlun Group represents mostly shallow marine and lagoonal environments, the Belqa Group limestones were deposited predominantly on the shelf in a pelagic marine environment, although there are many variations in the environment, including brackish shallow water conditions (Ibrahim 1993; Garfunkel 1988). A disconformity separates the two groups. The mountains west of the ʿAraba are composed predominately of these Cretaceous limestone formations that in Israel are called the Judean Group and the Mt. Scopus/Avdat Group (Garfunkel 1988). North of Ras an-Naqab on the Jordan Plateau, the upper Cretaceous limestones also predominate. The Ajlun Group in southern Wādī ʿAraba contains the Naʾur, Fuheis, Hummar, Shuʾayb, Wādī As Sir, and Khuraij limestone formations. The Ajlun Group contains shallow marine fossiliferous limestones and dolostones interbedded with oolites, sandstone, siltstone, and mudstone (Ibrahim 1993). The Belqa Group contains chalky, marly limestones with chert beds and phosphate concentrations largely in the form of bones, teeth, and pellets. The uppermost layer of the Belqa group extends into the Eocene and contains a distinct nummulitic limestone that outcrops in the Wādī Gharandal area.

In the late Eocene, the Tethys Sea regressed and drained off the platform. The tectonic regime of the region dramatically changed with the onset of the Continental Break-up Phase. By the end of the Oligocene or early Miocene (ca. 25–20 Ma), the Red Sea and Suez rift had started to open as the Arabian plate rotated NE away from Africa (fig. 2.1). The rift opening caused the formation of the Dead Sea transform fault that accommodates the NE translation of Arabia along a strike-slip fault. This tectonic phase produced the Syrian arc fold belt, broad uplift, and extrusive basaltic magmatism predominantly east of the Dead Sea fault zone. Sedimentation was localized along fault-bound basins, including Wādī ʿAraba. The Dana Conglomerate is an early manifestation of this tectonic phase marking tectonic uplift and erosion. It consists of

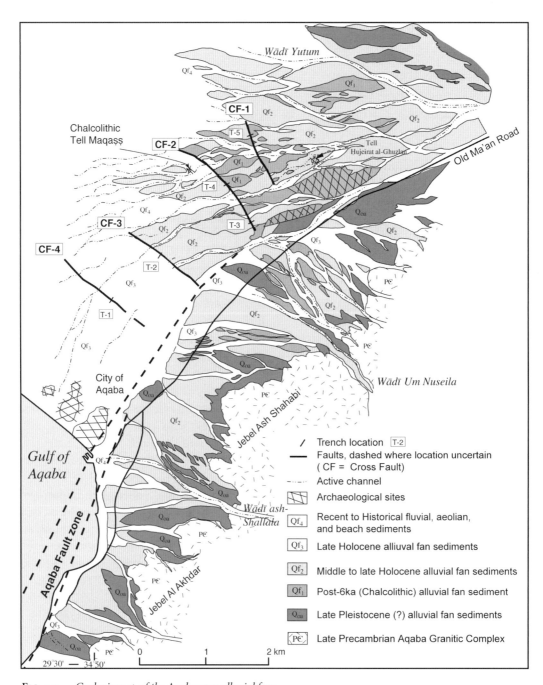

FIG. 2.7   *Geologic map of the Aqaba area alluvial fans.*

interbedded sandstone, conglomerate with bedded chert, and limestone in the lower section. Clasts in the conglomerates are derived from the Ajlun and Belqa Group formations. The Dana conglomerate has an erosional base. The age of the formation ranges from Oligocene(?) to Early Pleistocene. The formation is overlain farther north by Pleistocene and younger basalts (Ibrahim 1993).

Quaternary Geology

Bender (1974) defined five stratigraphic units for Quaternary-aged sediment. Three generations of alluvial deposits were mapped: a Pleistocene "fluviatile gravel," "alluvial fans, talus," and "wadi deposits and weathering mantle." Also included on the geological map are mudflat sediment and aeolian sand. On the 1:50,000-scale Jordanian Natural Resources Authority geologic map of the Aqaba sheet, Rashdan (1987) follows a similar mapping pattern for the Quaternary deposits.

Based predominantly on interpretation of the 1:25,000-scale black-and-white aerial photographs of Aqaba from 1953 (Royal Geographic Center of Jordan 1953), Niemi and Smith (1999) divided the surficial deposits of Wādī Yutum near Aqaba into four fan units (Qf1, Qf2, Qf3, and Qf4). The oldest fan unit was defined based on a well-developed desert pavement and dark patina or desert varnish on surface gravel recognized in air photos. Based on additional field investigations and analyses of 1:10,000 scale black-and-white air photos (Royal Geographic Center of Jordan 1978), the Qf1 surface was shown to be younger in places and incised into the older alluvial fan deposits. Thus, Slater and Niemi (2003) placed the older and presumably Pleistocene-age alluvial fans into a new map unit, Qoa. The Qf1 became designated as the Chalcolithic fans and Qf2 as middle to late Holocene. The Qf3 and Qf4 sedimentary units remained as mapped, i.e., late Holocene and recent deposition, respectively (fig. 2.7).

Remnants of a Pleistocene alluvial fan sequence in Aqaba, designated Qoa, lie near the mountain front where the fan apex is topographically higher than younger Holocene fans. The distal portions of the Qoa deposits are often difficult to distinguish from Qf1 surface. The Qoa is deeply dissected. There may be multiple cycles of deposition of the older alluvium. No chronological data exist for the Qoa deposits in Aqaba. The Qoa deposits may correlate in part to the Upper Pleistocene fan surfaces mapped on the Shehoret alluvial fan sequence on the west side of Wādī ʿAraba, 7 km north of Eilat (fig. 2.2). The oldest Shehoret fan surface has a late Pleistocene age (70.7 ± 9.6, 57.9 ± 3, 55.7 ± 4.3, and 56.0 ± 10.8 ka) based on the infrared optically stimulated luminescence (IRSL) age of alkali feldspars from the uppermost sediments (Amit et al. 1995; 1996; Enzel et al. 1996) or 62 ± 5 ka (Porat et al. 2010). The Qoa fan also likely correlates to the oldest fan mapped across the Wādī el-Muhtadī fan complex north of Aqaba. Le Béon et al. (2010), using [10]Be cosmogenic radionuclide dating of cobbles embedded in the surface, derived an average age of 56 ± 14 ka for the oldest surface.

The oldest Holocene alluvial fan surface (Qf1) of Wādī Yutum is distinguished by a moderately developed desert varnish. Two late Chalcolithic tells (Tell Maqaṣṣ and Tell Ḥujeirat al-Ghuzlan, e.g., Khalil 1995; Khalil and Schmidt 2009) and the associated agricultural field system are associated with the Qf1 deposits (figs. 2.2 and 2.7). The field system includes water diversion walls, stone alignments, channels that parallel the channel courses and some that cross the channels and extend onto the interfluves (Siegel 2009; Heemeier et al. 2009). A moderate coating of desert varnish has developed on these Chalcolithic rock alignments and rocks exposed on the tells. Multiple radiocarbon dates of wooden beams, seeds, and other organic material excavated from Tell Ḥujeirat al-Ghuzlan and Tell Maqaṣṣ date occupation at the sites to 4000–3500 BC (Klimscha 2009). Thus, the Qf1 fan developed after 6 ka as the deposits buried portions of the agricultural and water management systems. A similar sequence of fill terraces was mapped in the Wādī Ḥeimir drainage located 55 km north of Aqaba (Niemi and Smith 1999). The late Chalcolithic field system does not appear to have been utilized in later periods, given the desert varnish on the wall alignments in both the Ḥeimir and Yutum areas indicates the surfaces remain undisturbed.

The Qf2 fan surface is slightly inset into or buries the Qf1 and likely the Qoa surfaces. Borehole data across the Wādī Yutum alluvial fan indicate that the basement lies ca. 24–50 m below ground level near the mouth of the wadi and deepens significantly toward the gulf head (Farajat 2002). Modeling of gravity data also shows that the shallow Aqaba basin deepens toward the Gulf of Aqaba (ten Brink et al. 1999). It appears that tectonic subsidence controlled by faulting is minimal at the fan head and strong along the western side of the valley. Thus, the fan head is characterized by lateral migration of channels and cut-and-fill sedimentation and the distal fan by thick sediment accumulation into tectonically controlled accommodation space.

The Qf2 alluvium is constrained to be younger than the Qf1 surface or <6 ka. There is a gradation between Qf1 and Qf2, probably due to partial burial of the Qf1 deposits. A slight desert varnish has also developed on the Qf2 surface. The Qf1 and Qf2 deposits probably correlate with the Shehoret

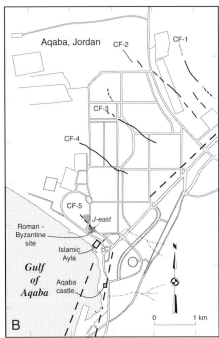

FIG. 2.8   A) Aerial photograph of Aqaba from ca. 1982. B) Map of Aqaba showing the three archaeological sites near the coast,
some major roads, and location of cross faults and possible Aqaba fault strands.

Qa2–3 fan deposits which are considered early to middle Holocene based on soil development criteria (4–7 ka, Amit et al. 1996) and an IRSL date of 13.6 ± 2.3 ka at the base of the fan sediments (Amit et al. 1996). The middle and lower Muhtadī fan has an average age of 11.1 ± 4.3 and 4.6 ± 0.7 ka, respectively (Le Béon et al. 2010).

Qf3 deposits are very limited. On aerial images the Qf3 surface is found only south of two prominent fault scarps (fig. 2.8, CF-3 and CF-4, see below) and appears smoother in tonal texture than the Qf4 surface. It is uncertain why Qf3 deposits are localized along the east side of the valley. The cross fan faults are also only preserved along this area. There may be a structural reason, as inferred from the location of offshore faults east of the Ayla fault system (Tibor et al. 2010) or the construction of a dam in antiquity at the mouth of the Wādī Yutum canyon, the remains of which were noted by several 19th- and early 20th-century western travelers (Parker 1997a: 22). A dam at the mouth of the Yutum canyon may have directed the flow westward away from the settlements on the NE corner of the Gulf of Aqaba. The Qf3 deposits are a mixture of fluvial and aeolian deposition and form the substrate for archaeological deposits in

RAP excavation areas. Very weak pedogenesis and dated artifacts indicate a <2 ka age of the surface.

A large area of recent alluvium is concentrated north of the older fan deposits, in the middle of the valley, and along the coastal zone. The area is notable on air photos by the scrub vegetation that dots the landscape. One of the main active channels of Wādī Yutum flows to the west, although numerous small channels incise and braid through the Qf1, Qf2, and Qf3 deposits. Areas of recently active Wādī Yutum fan channels are mapped as Qf4. Cobble- to boulder-sized clasts indicate a high flow regime in the channels. Sediment size within the channels decreases from the fan head to sand and gravel in the lower reaches of the fan. Recent fan deposits grade into the mudflats of Eilat *sabkha* along the Jordanian–Israeli border and aeolian dunes and beach deposits near the shoreline. The aeolian deposits are also mapped as Qf4. Stratigraphic sections of the distal portion of the Wādī Yutum fan were exposed in existing bulldozer pits, geologic probes, and archaeological excavations in the Aqaba coastal zone.

A sequence of erosion-aggradation-soil formation can be modeled for the SE Wādī ʿAraba as follows. First, episodic entrenchment phases mark destabilizations of the fluvial system that may be triggered by increased discharge, perhaps near the end of a regional drier period as precipitation increased in the watershed. Changes in the amount of rainfall over the catchment basin, in seasonality of storms, or mean average temperature variations over the large watershed may help to explain the sedimentologic and geomorphic changes seen in the alluvial fan sequences. Secondly, as more humid conditions prevailed on a regional scale, continuous sediment concentration in a stream flow resulted in channel or valley alluviation. And finally, aggradation stopped or slowed as soil formation processes stabilized the landscape. This cycle can be seen in three phases of Wādī Yutum fan aggradation: Qoa (ca. 60 ka?), Qf1–2 (ca. 6 ka), and Qf3 (<2 ka), followed by surface stabilization and incipient soil formation. Niemi and Smith (1999) also showed that surface cultural remains apparently peaked during the same time periods: Middle Palaeolithic, Late Chalcolithic–Early Bronze, and Roman-Byzantine. Survey and excavation data from the Eilat region and Aqaba indicate that late Umayyad to Abbasid (late 8th to 9th centuries AD) occupation is also strongly represented, at least locally (Avner and Magness 1998; Whitcomb 2006).

Quaternary surfaces older than 59–70 ka are apparently absent in the southern valley based on available data. In the Aqaba region, older Quaternary alluvium (Qoa) deposits have not been dated. They are relatively limited and located along the mountain front and on isolated spurs preserved at a higher topographic elevation than the Holocene alluvium. These older fan deposits have different distributions along the fans of Wādī ʿAraba. Although the dynamics of sedimentation can be generalized, deposition is controlled by the geological structure of the adjacent subsurface basins. Ten Brink et al. (1999) defined three major continental basins (Aqaba, Timna/Tāba, and Gharandal or Qāʿ as-Suʾaydiyyīn) along this section of the Dead Sea transform fault based on modeling of gravity data. Tectonic subsidence of these basins controls base level of the channels flowing to them. Furthermore, discharge of the drainage is dependent on the size of the catchment basin and the amount of precipitation and rates of evapo-transpiration over

the catchment that has fluctuated on various scales throughout the Quaternary.

It is likely that evidence of older cultural remains are buried beneath younger sedimentary deposits within the lower reaches of the alluvial systems along the southern Wādī ʿAraba valley, A significant portion of the fan systems (Mulghān, Sammāniya, Muhtadī, Qattar) has the appearance of Early to Middle Holocene-aged Qf1–2 fans (fig. 2.2; Garfunkel 1970). This suggests that alluvial fan aggradation was likely driven by regional climate variation. These surfaces thus would have high potential for preserving sites from the Chalcolithic period to the present. In Aqaba, the eastern side of the valley is mapped as older Qf1–3. This area has been isolated from the recent Qf4 alluvial deposition. Either tectonics or human occupation and constructions may have altered the natural sequence of deposition in this area. Winds have reworked distal fluvial deposits into sand sheets and dunes.

Soils

The soils developed on the Aqaba fan are typical young Reg soils, i.e., a soil developed on coarse parent materials (sands and gravels) in a hyperarid environment (J. B. J. Harrison, 2011, pers. comm.). The evolution of a Reg soil is characterized by the following features: salt-shattered clasts at the average depth of water infiltration into the profile, accumulation of silts and clays resulting in gravel-free upper A and B horizons, and accumulation of gypsum and halite in the C-horizon (Amit and Gerson 1986). Amit and Gerson found that the development of a surface pavement and the amount of fine clay in the soil profile were the most reliable features to differentiate soils of different ages and pedogenic development. With the continual accumulation of silt and clays, the depth of infiltrating water decreases in older soils and the zone of salt-shattered clasts moves closer to the surface.

Several soils of the Wādī Yutum fan complex were studied in soil pits and paleoseismic trenches (shown as T-1 through T-5 on fig. 2.7). The profile mass of silt, clay, carbonate, and soluble salts was measured. Analyses of the soil profile data show that the soils are very porous. Infiltrating water

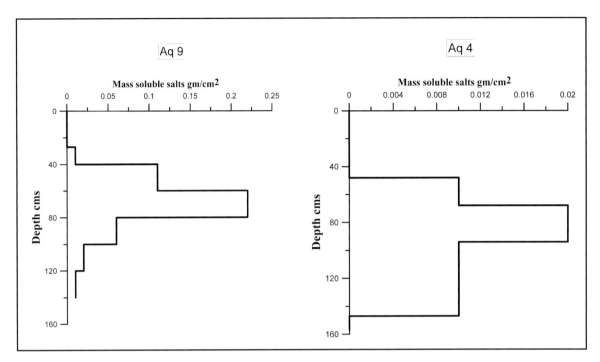

FIG. 2.9   *Soluble salt measurements from two soils on the Wādī Yutum alluvial fan complex.*

can reach depths of 80 cm as is seen in the depth of soluble salts and salt-shattered clasts (fig. 2.9). Although four Holocene fan surfaces were identified on the basis of rock varnish development on surface clasts, as described above and by Slater and Niemi (2003), the analyzed soil properties do not reflect these different ages. This is primarily due to the short duration and slow rate of pedogenesis in the hyperarid environment of Aqaba. There is little to distinguish the soils forming on the Qf2, Qf3, and Qf4 surfaces. Only the soil forming on Qf1 is clearly different. This soil was described on part of the Qf1 surface within Chalcolithic agricultural fields or gardens.

Soil properties are determined by the hydrological characteristics of the soil, which in these young soils is determined by the fluvial stratigraphy in the soil profile. The dominant texture in the soils is loamy sand in the upper horizon and interbedded gravelly fine sand to cobbly sand units lower in the profile. The changes in stratigraphy determine how quickly and to what depth infiltrating water moves thorough the soil. All the soils measured on the Wādī Yutum alluvial fan sequence have high, unsaturated conductivity, except for sample

site AQ 9, which formed part of the Chalcolithic garden structure found on the Qf1 surface (fig. 2.7).

The young coarse textured fan soils have low agricultural potential due to their free draining nature and low natural fertility, generally a consequence of the coarse textured sediments in the soil profile. The biggest impediment to agriculture in this area is the lack of water. Precipitation is primarily in the form of localized, short but intense rainstorms, which generate high volumes of runoff from the rocky hill slopes onto the fan surfaces.

To develop an area for agriculture the Chalcolithic gardeners built dams across the fan surface that slowed the runoff and allowed for greater infiltration of water into the underlying soils. It also caused the suspended sediment in the runoff to be deposited behind the dam walls. This type of floodplain farming was also utilized by Chalcolithic settlements in the Jordan Valley (e.g., Mabry 1992). Over time the fine sediments accumulated, resulting in the typical deep fine-textured agricultural soil AQ9. The fine sediments have a high moisture-holding capacity that keeps infiltrating water closer to the surface than is typical in the coarse textured non-agricultural soils. They also have a higher cation exchange capacity and natural fertility, making them more suitable for agriculture. However, as soil moisture is close to the surface, the high evaporative flux results in accumulation of salts, principally gypsum ($CaSO_4$) and halite (NaCl), usually detrimental to plant growth. Constant irrigation is required to flush the salts deeper into the soil profile and beyond the rooting depth of the plants (J. B. J. Harrison, pers. comm., 2011).

III. GEOLOGIC CONTEXT OF ARCHAEOLOGICAL DEPOSITS

Within 500 m of the present coastline, isolated mounds or small tells suggest the presence of buried antiquities. In the study area, once known locally as the "Circular Area" and now the site of the Saraya development, the surface topography can be divided into two distinct geomorphologic areas (fig. 2.10). The northern area slopes from 8 m to 5 m elevation along NW–SE contour lines and is the distal part of the southwest drainage of the Wādī Yutum alluvial fan. The southern area is characterized by several low, isolated mounds aligned in a NNE direction with intervening topographic depressions. Several of these tells were excavated. The walled Islamic city of Ayla (7th–12th centuries) is a large and prominent tell rising more than 8 m asl (fig. 2.10). Included in the region with Islamic Ayla are RAP Areas A, K, and L.

In order to understand the subsurface geology and the distribution of antiquities in this area and given the imminent threat from modern development, twenty-five backhoe trenches were excavated here during RAP excavation seasons (fig. 2.10). Within and adjacent to the Circular Area eighteen backhoe test pits (BH 1–BH 18) were excavated during the 1994 campaign. Five additional trenches (BH 19–23) were excavated in 1996. BH 24 was excavated in 1998 and BH 25 in 2002. Stratigraphic information of the topographic highs within the Circular Area was also obtained from a hand-dug 4-m section in the large "G-8" mound (so-called from the survey grid of Meloy 1991), in RAP excavations areas (Areas A, B, G, and M), and within an existing bulldozer pit designated Area N. The following is a geologic interpretation of stratigraphic information from these subsurface exposures.

In the northern Circular Area, existing bulldozed exposures and 1.6 m deep backhoe trench (BH4) show similar natural, fluvial deposition. The surface of this area that extends from 5–8 m elevation is covered with gravel and sand. Meloy (1991: 406–7) identified this area as a surface of "hard pavement of sand and gravel" covered "with a substantial amount of pottery slag." The upper 20-cm gravelly horizon contained sherds above a 1.4 m section of culturally sterile deposits. The sediment is composed of poorly-sorted subangular-to-angular granitic and mafic-to-rhyolitic dike rock detritus deposited as the distal portion of the Wādī Yutum alluvial fan. Several thick (ca. 0.5 m) fining-upwards sequences with cobble-filled channel thalweg deposits grading to clayey silt beds suggest that deposition is episodic and characterized by flood events. These fluvial sediments were also encountered at the base of the Area B excavation trenches and at the base of the G8 mound and Area N (fig. 2.11). Although these alluvial fan sediments are apparently sterile of human occupational material, it is possible that pre-Roman antiquities lie at greater depth beneath the fluvial gravels.

Area N was a pre-existing large pit located 500 m from the modern shoreline, where a ca. 2.5 m section of sediment was exposed at surface elevations between 4 and 5.5 m (fig. 2.11). A portion of the exposure crossed a small topographic mound. Similar stratigraphic sequences of the upper 2 m of section were documented in BH 2, 3, 5, and 9. The stratigraphic section consisted of thin strata of pebbly sand that grade upward into fine-grained sand, silt, and clay, indicating fluvial deposition. Above the alluvium were two levels of mudbrick walls and associated floors and deteriorated mudbrick horizons. These structures were associated with Roman-Nabataean sherds. There was fine-grained well-sorted aeolian sand with planar cross-beds between the mudbrick layers. Laterally, the level of the deteriorated lower mudbrick horizon correlates to a buried soil with a cambic B-horizon. The soil was overlain by a sequence of fine- to medium-grained sand that contained occasional freshwater gastropods. The sand was very loose in places. The uppermost section was marked by wavy laminae, floating pebbles, and poorly-sorted bioturbated sand that apparently represented wet-

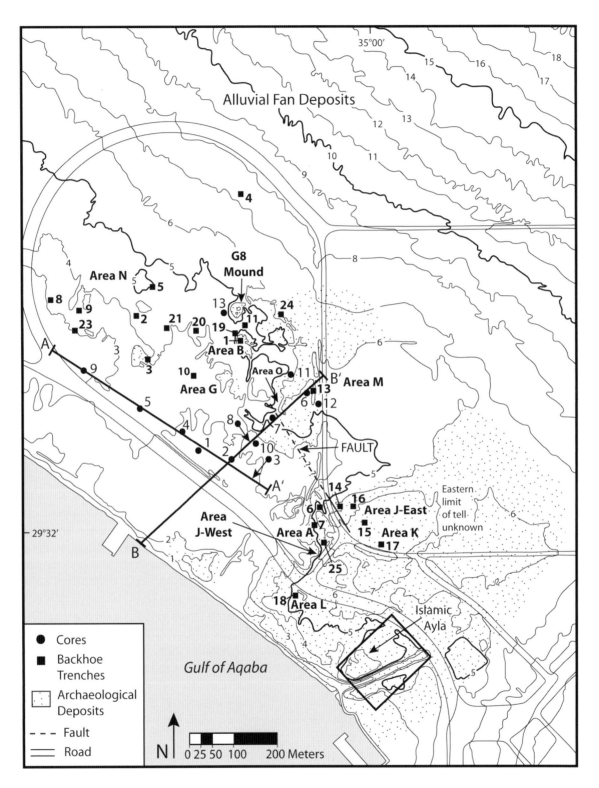

FIG. 2.10 *Topographic map of a portion of coastal zone of Aqaba.*

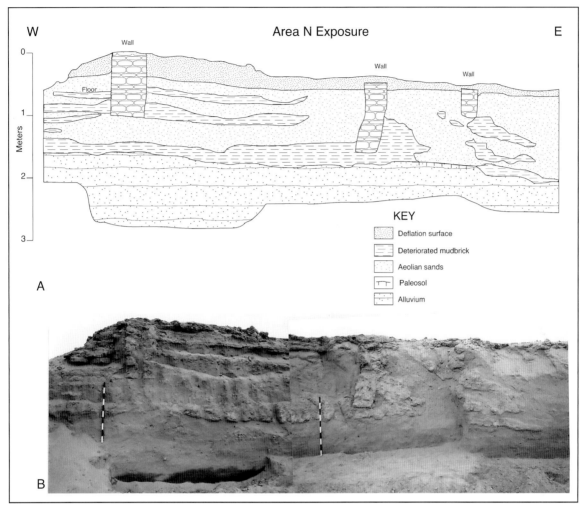

FIG. 2.11 *Sketch (A) and photograph (B) of the north wall exposure of Roman period ruins exposed in a trash pit in the western section of the city of Aqaba*

ting and desiccation cycles. The mudbrick walls were eroded and the core of the wall was exposed on the ground surface. The ground surface was covered by a pebble and sherd lag that demonstrates active deflation and a shift from a previous aggradation phase. Together these data suggest that the ground surface is quite old. Furthermore, in Area N and in backhoe trenches BH 20–22 was evidence of cultural modification of the landscape (fig. 2.12). This included excavation of pits, possible extraction of clay, and a soil horizon possibly used for agriculture.

The highest of all isolated mounds in the Circular Area was G8 at an elevation of 8.4 m. Its upper layer was modern fill associated with the emplacement of 20th-century stone- and concrete-lined

military trenches. Beneath the fill was an unstratified layer of fine- to medium-grained sand with a random scatter of angular pebbles. A mudbrick debris layer sloped eastward from 1 to 1.5 m below the surface of the mound. The base of this layer contained well-defined mudbrick whose tumble thickened toward the crest of the mound. Two additional mudbrick detritus layers lay beneath this horizon, separated by layers of fine-grained aeolian sand. The sherd from the earliest context was collected at an elevation of ca. 4.5 m, directly above a 1.25-m-thick layer of fluvial sands and gravels. The base of the section consisted of medium- to coarse-grained sand.

Backhoe trenches were also excavated near the crest of an 8-m-high mound (BH 1) and along its

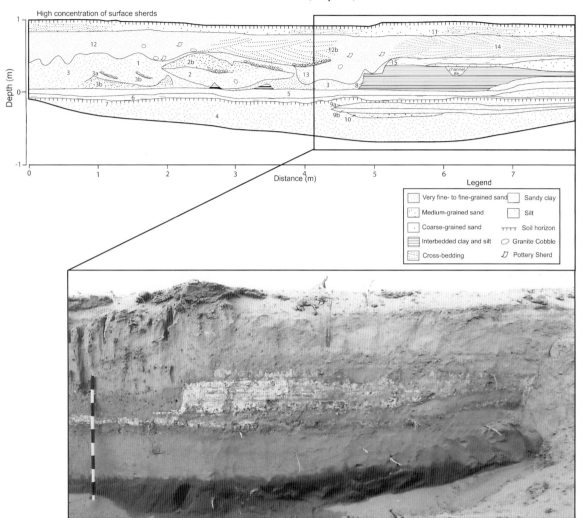

FIG. 2.12 *Exposure of Backhoe Trench 21 showing an interbedded clayey silt to silty clay layer with intrusive pit.*

flanks (BH 11, 19, and 24) in what became Area B. The exposure in BH 19 revealed mudbrick walls standing to a height of over 2 m. The walls were founded on either alluvial gravel or sand. A 40-cm probe beneath the sand and gravel recovered a lower occupation debris layer. An auger core at the lowest excavated point in this area suggests that cultural layers may extend to an elevation of 2.7 m and rest on alluvial gravel. Wind-blown sands rapidly filled the abandoned mudbrick structure. This phase of sand infilling was a key element in preserving the 2-m-high walls and in producing the mound topography. Later structures were founded both on the aeolian sand and the earlier

walls. This part of the coastal zone appears to have been devoid of permanent structures between the early 4th century AD and the 20th century military trenches.

A 2.2-m-deep backhoe trench (BH 13) was excavated in what became Area M. The upper 0.9 m of the stratigraphic section contained a silty-rich fill layer with ash layers and pottery. No overburden covered the archaeological deposits, suggesting that the area was mechanically leveled in the 20th century prior to construction of the military base that occupied the site prior to 1994. Between 0.9–1.6 m was a sandy interval that contained large fragments of pottery vessels. The sand was sterile below 1.6 m. This was confirmed in a probe, Trench M.4, beneath the lowest cultural levels that revealed 1 m of sand without artifacts to an elevation of about 3 m.

Area G was laid out on the northern portion of a mound with a surface elevation of 5.3 m. The mound was disrupted by military emplacements along its east and south sides. Archaeological excavation in a 5 × 5 m trench (G.1) on the north end of the mound revealed mudbrick tumble with individual well-defined bricks at a subsurface depth of 0.2 m in the east (Ryan 1995). The dip slope of the deteriorated mudbrick extended to a depth of 2.0 m in the western part of the square. Balk sections showed the mudbrick resting on sand similar to the lower section of the G8 mound. A few sherds were found at the base of the trench on a slightly-cemented sand. No walls were discovered, but the mudbrick was associated with a few Byzantine and Early Islamic sherds (ca. AD 500–800). Fine windblown sand also covered the mudbrick collapse and was largely devoid of cultural artifacts from later periods.

The subsurface stratigraphy of the low-lying region between 3 and 4 m elevation in the Circular Area (BH 8–10 and 23) was devoid of significant cultural material. Three layers were identified in these 2- to 2.5-m deep trenches. The upper 0.50 m of sediment was a bioturbated sand layer mixed with rock fragments and other debris. The interval between 0.5–2.0 m in depth was aeolian sand. The base of the section near the water table was a silty sand layer. The trenches were completely sterile of cultural material. However, microscopic analysis of the sediment revealed charcoal fragments, shells, bones, and possible mudbrick fragments that suggest that deposition of sediments was influenced by human occupation. This may be interpreted as redeposition or coeval deposition of cultural material.

Other backhoe test pits searched for subsurface antiquities later excavated as part of RAP. These included BH 6 and 7 in Area A, BH 14–16 in Area J-East, BH 17 in Area K, and BH 18 near Area L. These excavations showed a similar stratigraphic sequence as seen in Area N and BH 19 with successive mudbrick and stone structures founded on sand and later filled by windblown sand. One additional backhoe trench, BH 25 in Area J-West,

was excavated to investigate whether an active fault crossed the area. None was found in the sand section exposed, although sand is not likely to preserve such a feature.

In summary, the northern portion of the study area above 5 m elevation is part of the distal Wādī Yutum fan and is dominated by fluvial sedimentation. The topographic area below 5 m elevation is characterized by isolated mounds or tells, cored by the remnants of ancient houses and other structures that rise 1–3 m above the surrounding coastal plain. In this area, the upper 1 m of the subsurface sediment is aeolian sand. In the low-lying areas away from the mounds at depths of 1 m below the surface, layers of interbedded clay and silt indicate standing pools of water. The clayey layers are discontinuous. In places they show signs of being excavated and removed in antiquity and are crosscut by ashy pits.

The structure of the mounds was elucidated in backhoe and archaeological excavation. Meloy (1991) originally proposed that the isolated mounds were remains of ancient structures. Excavated exposures of the G8 mound, Area N, and BH 19 clearly showed that mudbrick walls standing 2m in height or layers of deteriorated mudbrick from collapse horizons were interbedded with aeolian sand. The structures appeared to be rapidly infilled, which both preserved the structures and led to the aggradation of the land surface. Continued occupation and construction of mudbrick and other structures further helped to build up the mounds.

The surface of the Circular Area west of the main occupation in Areas B, O, and M and adjacent to and inside the Byzantine city wall (Areas A, J, and K) appears to have aggraded to its present elevation by the 5th century (i.e., Early Byzantine). The surface was largely devoid of later-period artifacts. Construction of 20th-century military trenches and other installations across the area has in some areas inverted the stratigraphy. Buried sherds have been brought to the surface by these activities. This is an important factor in understanding modern distribution of artifacts across the surface.

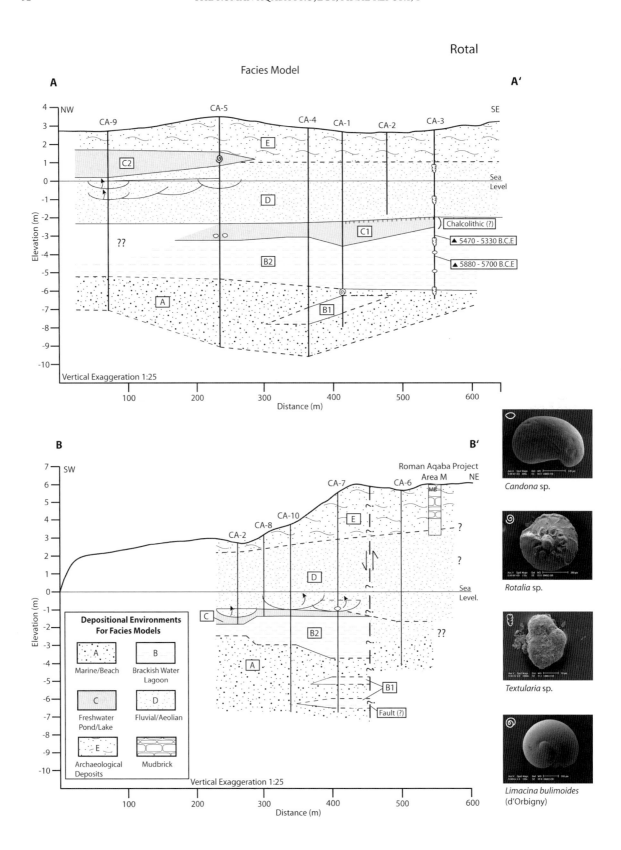

FIG. 2.13   *Cross sections.*

IV. PALEOENVIRONMENT
AND PALEOCLIMATE

Allison and Niemi (2010) reported on the paleoenvironmental interpretation of the coastal area of Aqaba adjacent to the Early Roman/Nabataean to Byzantine-period archaeological remains based on analyses of thirteen cores (fig. 2.10). The sediment cores with a maximum depth of 12.5 m were extruded from a rig-mounted hollow-stem rotary auger (see Allison 2007 for details). The sedimentological properties and microfossil identifications were used to define five depositional environments: A. marine/beach, B. brackish water lagoon, C. freshwater pond/lake, D. fluvial and aeolian, and E. archaeological deposits (shown in fig. 2.13).

Interpretation of the stratigraphic data indicates a basal marine transgression overlain by a regressive sequence of coastal lagoon deposits and backshore lake, sand dune, and distal alluvial fan (Allison and Niemi 2010). The marine sediments are older than 5700–5900 bc, with an inland transgression of at least 400 m north of the present shoreline. Additionally, to the east of RAP Areas J and K and 150 m from the modern shoreline, Brückner (1999) and Brückner et al. (2002) reported on a core with a 6-m-thick alluvial sequence that overlies littoral sands encountered at 1.35 m below sea level (mbsl). Three factors — a slowing rate of sea-level rise, slow subsidence of the coastal zone, and an increased sediment supply either from increased runoff due to higher precipitation or human modification of the watershed — likely all acted to drive the stratigraphic changes seen in the Aqaba cores.

A similar stratigraphic sequence was found along a core transect adjacent to the Tell el-Kheleifeh archaeological site (see fig. 2.8 for location) on the east side of the Eilat *sabkha* on the distal Wādī Yutum fan complex (Brückner 1999; Brückner et al. 2002). In that study, a transgressive-regressive sedimentary sequence was identified beneath the tell and in five other cores recovered from 340 to 770 m north of the shoreline. Marine sand, to a maximum depth of 4.5 mbsl, is overlain by beach gravel and backshore sand dunes interbedded with alluvium. Radiocarbon dating of a shell within the littoral sands from 2.6 mbsl and 600 m inland

yielded a marine reservoir corrected age of 6200 ± 60 BP (2 sigma, 4810–4535 BC). A second radiocarbon date on marine shells only 340 m from the shore and 1.4 mbsl yielded an age of 3,740 ± 50 (2 sigma, 1840–1575 BC). With these data, Brückner calculated a shoreline progradation rate of 9–11 m per century. Tell el-Kheleifeh rises about 3 m above the surrounding coastal plain. Pratico (1993), reviewing Nelson Glueck's 1938–1940 excavation of the site, reported that the elevation of the top of the tell was 6.83 m and the maximum thickness of archaeological deposits was 4.37 m. These data suggest that at the founding of the site in the 8th century BC, the surface elevation was at ca. 2.5 m, with the shoreline located south of the site.

Lagoonal sediments were not documented in the subsurface sediment adjacent to Tell el-Kheleifeh. Allison and Niemi (2010) report that lagoonal deposits above the basal marine layer near Roman-Byzantine Aila represent a low-energy, slightly brackish environment (fig. 2.13). Due to the fine-grained nature of deposits, the body of water in which these particles were suspended must have been largely protected by a beach barrier from the wave action of the Gulf of Aqaba. Several freshwater ostracods, all identified as *Candona* sp., were also collected within the lagoonal sediment and from backshore lakes, ponds, or swamp facies. Weathered and abraded ostracods indicate that coastal ponds and swamps probably extended farther inland. The freshwater ostracods were likely washed into the shoreline embayment by fluvial processes.

Archaeological surveys and excavations in and around the Aqaba coastal zone suggest that a considerable amount of migration and human settlement has taken place since late prehistoric times. This is exemplified by the fact that occupation is not concentrated on one tell but found at several sites at different locations across the area. According to Parker (1997a), this migration has generally trended north to south and ranges from the Chalcolithic to the Late Islamic periods. Whitcomb (1997) describes a seaward and southeastern movement of settlements in the Aqaba region, as does Brückner et al. (2002). Brückner et al. (2002), based on the location of archaeological sites in the region, concluded that the coastline was further to the north from at least the 6th to the 2nd millennium BC. The general southward human migration trend could also result from changing availability of freshwater resources (Parker 1997a; Brückner et al. 2002).

An alternative explanation for the lack of early settlement along the coast presented by Allison and Niemi (2010) is that the coastal zone was swampy or contained lagoons. Habitation of the Aqaba coastal zone did not occur until after the 8th century BC, when the lagoons and coastal wetlands and lakes were dried and covered with sand dunes. The migration of humans across the coastal plain as evidenced by the change in location of archaeological sites in later periods could have simply been an attempt by ancient peoples to avoid the heavy flood waters that periodically came rushing through rapidly shifting channels of the distal Wādī Yutum alluvial fan. The Iron Age to Persian period occupation at Tell el-Kheleifeh and the Nabataean period sites, for example, are situated at roughly the same distance from the present shoreline. Thus, it seems that instead of human migration patterns following the location of the shoreline, migration may have been an attempt to avoid the changing course of Wādī Yutum. Archaeological sites tend to move from the middle of the valley, near Tell el-Kheleifeh, to the southeast, away from Wādī Yutum. These findings suggest that the concentration of Chalcolithic settlements situated several kilometers inland from the present-day shoreline and located higher on the alluvial fan could be a result of higher discharge that would produce more frequent torrential flash floods through the wadi and coastal wetlands and brackish water lagoons along the shore. These swamps may also have formed in response to a 0.5 to 2 m higher-than-present sea level at ca. 6.5 to 4.5 ka that has been documented from exposed coral reef terraces (Friedman 1965; al-Rifaiy and Cherif 1988; Gvirtzman et al. 1992; Gvirtzman 1994) and analyses of cores and geomorphic features such as wave-cut notches at the Red Sea Pharaonic harbor of Mersa/Wādī Gawais (Hein et al. 2011). Analyses of coral dating to about 5.7 to 4.4 ka suggest a higher input of terrigenous sediment due perhaps to more humid climatic conditions (Moustafa et al. 2000). Migration of sites may also be due to possible flood control implementations put in place during the

Nabataean, Roman, or Byzantine periods to divert water westward and away from the eastern Aqaba coastal plain. Alternatively, changing technology of maritime shipping, vessel construction, and methods of docking ships may have played a significant role in the location of the establishments of ports, harbors, and settlements in Aqaba.

Fluctuations in climate across the Near East over the past 10,000 years have been documented using various proxies. An early- to mid-Holocene period of expanded lakes and vegetation in North Africa and Arabia, known as the African Humid period between 9 to 6 ka, correlates with intensification of the African monsoon in response to high Northern Hemisphere summer insolation values (e.g., deMenocal et al. 2000). In the Aqaba region over the past 6 ka, data on the regional climate variability are sparse. Records on precipitation from Jerusalem gleaned from stable isotope speleothem data from the Soreq cave in Israel suggest two dry climatic periods at the end of the Chalcolithic period (5.7–5.6 ka) and during 4.2–4.05 ka (Bar Matthews and Ayalon 2011).

Levels of the Dead Sea also provide a measure for climate variability across the region. Although the Dead Sea region has remained very arid over most of the past 10,000 years (the Holocene geologic epoch), changes in its water level indicate climatic fluctuations. The Dead Sea itself receives very little direct precipitation. Most of the inflow is water derived from the large drainage basin of the Jordan River that reaches up to the snow-covered peaks of Mount Hermon in the north and from the eastern plateau in Jordan. The level of the Dead Sea has risen in wetter times and lowered during drier times throughout the Holocene. The elevation of archaeological sites on the Dead Sea shore, geological studies of sediment exposed in channel incisions, and other methods have been used to construct a curve of the fluctuations in Dead Sea level (fig. 2.14; Bookman et al. 2006; Migowski et al. 2006). As the Wādī Araba itself has not likely witnessed dramatic changes in rainfall over most of the Holocene, given synoptic weather patterns and orographic constraints (Enzel et al. 2008), small-scale fluctuations in climate such as the frequency of storm events probably were distributed across the larger drainage basin.

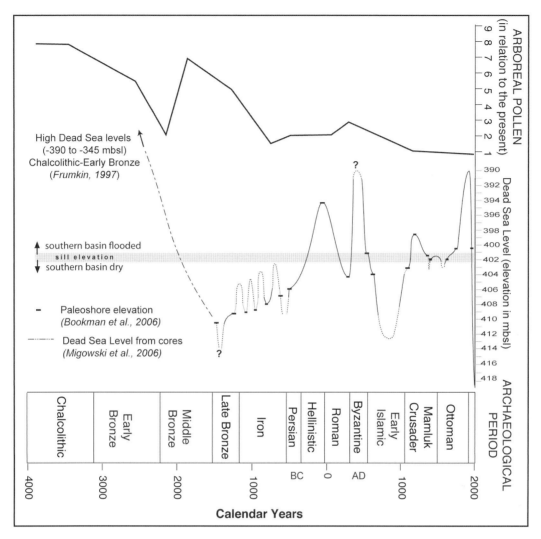

FIG. 2.14 *Dead Sea level curves.*

Four archaeological periods — the Chalcolithic–Early Bronze (4500–2500 BC), the Late Hellenistic to Early Roman (1st century BC to 1st century AD), the Byzantine (4th–early 6th centuries AD), and the Crusader (11–13th century AD) periods — are marked by high Dead Sea levels. Figure 2.14 compares high Dead Sea levels with a curve for arboreal pollen from different archaeological sites of varying ages in the arid regions of Israel (Horowitz 1992). Subsurface sedimentologic data in the southern Dead Sea basin support a highstand of the lake ca. 5.5–4.3 ka during the Chalcolithic period, as does the elevation of cave outlets of Mt. Sedom (Frumkin et al. 1991; 1997). Chalcolithic farming, with the cultivation of flax, wheat, and barley, the use of poplar and willow wood beams in construction, and the raising of cattle at Tell Ḥujeirat al-Ghuzlan also suggest a more humid climate (Khalil and Schmidt 2009). During the Late Hellenistic to Early Roman periods, the Dead Sea was about as high as in the beginning of the 20th century (Bookman et al. 2006; Migowski et al. 2006). The climate was apparently regionally wetter and more runoff was delivered to the Dead Sea. Carbon and oxygen isotopic analyses of the wood within the Roman siege ramp at Masada provide evidence of a moister climate (Yakir et al. 1994). During the Crusades and the Medieval Warm climatic period (mid-11th–13th centuries), Dead Sea levels were high.

In summary, alluvial fan aggradation of the Wādī Yutum fan complex, coastal lagoons or swamps evidenced in sediment cores, and botanical evidence at Tell Ḥujeirat al-Ghuzlan appear to correlate with regional data that suggest a more humid climate and a 0.5–2 m-high stand of sea level during the Chalcolithic period. Sea level likely fell to present levels by 2200 BC during a regression and 500 m progradation of the shoreline. Over the past 3,000 years, climate records especially from the Dead Sea levels suggest more favorable climatic conditions during the Late Hellenistic to Early Roman, 4th–6th century Byzantine, and Medieval periods.

V.   SEISMIC HISTORY

Earthquakes in the southern Wādī ʿAraba and Gulf of Aqaba are created by motion along the Dead Sea-Jordan transform fault system. The Mw 7.2 Nuweiba earthquake of November 22, 1995, that ruptured a submarine fault in the Gulf of Aqaba was the largest earthquake in the modern instrumented era (Hofstetter et al. 2003). Most of the significant damage was concentrated in cities in the Sinai Peninsula near the epicenter, but damage was also reported from the Saudi Arabian coastline and at Aqaba and Eilat, 70 km north of the epicenter.

Historical earthquake data reported in recent catalogues (Guidoboni 1994; Guidoboni and Comastri 2005; Ambraseys 2009) suggest that seismic events in AD 110–114, 363, 749, 1068, 1212, 1458, and 1588 likely caused damage in the region of southern Jordan and Aqaba. It is unclear whether events recorded in the Dead Sea region or Jerusalem, such as the earthquakes of AD 419, 597, 634, 659, 1293, and 1546, could have caused damage in Aqaba. Data from earlier catalogues (Kallner 1950–51; Ben Menahem 1979; 1991; Ghawanmeh 1992; Ambraseys et al. 1994; Amiran et al. 1994) have largely been superseded by the more recent catalogue compilations.

Aqaba lies along the transition from the marine to the continental Eilat/Aqaba sedimentary basin. Faults controlling the structural dynamics of sedimentation as well as seismic activity lie both onshore and offshore. In order to understand the history of earthquakes in the region, an under-

standing of the seismogenic faults is essential. The next section reviews evidence for the location and activity of faults as well as evidence for earthquake damage at archaeological sites in Aqaba.

Faults

Offshore geophysical surveys have recently identified four submarine fault zones in the northern Gulf of Aqaba (Tibor et al. 2010). Two fault zones flank the margins of the gulf (the Eilat fault and Aqaba fault) and continue as faults on land, where they truncate the distal portions of alluvial fan systems. Both the onshore and offshore Eilat marginal faults have normal fault displacement (e.g., Garfunkel 1970; Ben-Avraham et al. 1979; Ben-Avraham 1985; Bowman and Gerson 1986; Reches et al. 1987; Ben-Avraham and Tibor 1993). Along the eastern margin of the gulf lie the Aqaba and west Aqaba fault zones. The very steep bathymetric escarpment with granitic bedrock truncated at the eastern shoreline indicates that a significant amount of vertical offset is accommodated on faults of the Aqaba fault zone. The zone is wide with three offshore strands. Hartman (2011) mapped strands of a "West Aqaba" fault that may also accommodate strike-slip motion. In the middle of the basin, the Ayla fault zone that appears to bound subsidence across a localized basin was apparently active in the early Holocene. The main offshore strike-slip fault continues northward into Wādī ʿAraba and is called the Evrona fault in Israel. This fault extends into Jordan, where it crosses the Wādī el-Muhtadī alluvial fan and continues northward to the Dead Sea. In Jordan this is called the Wādī ʿAraba fault. Faulting in the 1068 earthquake has been documented on this fault in the Evrona sabkha (Amit et al. 1999; 2002; Zilberman et al. 2005).

In Aqaba a concerted effort has been made to map the onshore continuation of the Aqaba fault zone. Because of dense urbanization, mapping the northward continuation of faults has been difficult. Air photo interpretation of the Aqaba regional surficial geology suggests that the Aqaba fault emerges from the gulf and that slip is transferred to northwest-trending cross faults (fig. 2.8; Niemi and Smith 1999; Mansoor 2002; Slater and Niemi 2003; Mansoor et al. 2004). Because the cross faults are linear and not offset, this geometry constrains the location of the Aqaba fault to lie south and/or east of the cross faults and west of alluvial fan surfaces. A ground-penetrating radar survey in the city confirmed the location of a portion of one strand of the Aqaba fault (Slater and Niemi 2003). However, recent analyses of newly acquired aerial photographs from 1918 and 1947 reveal that the toe of the alluvial fan systems of the Um Nuseila and Shallala drainages have anomalous linear topographic ridges that appear to be offset alluvial fan segments. From the surface desert varnish, these fan segments are likely to be Qf1 or Qoa. Unfortunately, these features are now completely built over and buried under the city.

The Aqaba fault zone apparently bends NE with increasing curvature as it dies out. This bending NE of the eastern bounding fault of a pull-apart has been noted for other large pull-apart basins along the Dead Sea Transform, including the Dead Sea and the Sea of Galilee (Garfunkel et al. 1981; Garfunkel 1981). Reches (1987) used clay model experiments to show that the faults initially bend away from each other at a dilational jog in ductile materials. The Aqaba fault should therefore have a reverse component to its motion.

Geological trenches (T-1 through T-5) were excavated across four of the NW-trending cross-faults (CF-1 to C-4; fig. 2.8) that produce active tectonic subsidence at the head of the Gulf (Mansoor 2002; Slater and Niemi 2003). Mapping of alluvial fan and buried soil horizons in the trenches reveal multiple fault ruptures on the highest scarps and fewer distinct ruptures on the lowest scarp (Mansoor 2002). The scarp heights range from 25 cm across the youngest Qf3 surface to 1.3 m across the older Qf1 and Qf2 surfaces. These data indicate that scarp heights reflect cumulative slip events. The most recent scarp-forming event fault occurred after AD 1045–1278 based on a corrected, calibrated radiocarbon age from charcoal collected from a buried campfire at the base of the scarp in Trench T-1. This likely represents fault motion in one of the historical earthquakes affecting southern Jordan (e.g., 1068, 1212, 1458, or 1588).

Archaeoseismology

Based on both historical accounts and the excavations of Roman and Byzantine Aila (Thomas et al. 2007), Early Islamic Ayla (Whitcomb (1994), and Late Islamic Aqaba (De Meulemeester and al-Shqour 2008), it is clear that earthquakes have played a significant role in the history of the region. Major earthquake damage in Aqaba is likely to occur by either a rupture of the Aqaba fault in the Gulf of Aqaba or the Evrona/Wādī ʿAraba fault on land.

Excavations in and around the Aqaba castle from 2000 to 2008 revealed three different phases in the "khan," or castle, from the late 12th to 16th centuries (fig. 2.8; De Meulemeester and al-Shqour 2008). The extant castle was built in 1515 and rebuilt in 1587/8, probably after the Gulf of Aqaba earthquake of January 4, 1588, which, based on historical accounts, was felt in NW Arabia, Aqaba, and Sinai (Guidoboni and Comastri 2005; Ambraseys 2009). The archaeological data from the Aqaba castle (De Meulemeester and al-Shqour 2008) also appear to support rupture of the Gulf of Aqaba fault segment in the earthquake of 1212 and possibly of a Wādī ʿAraba fault segment in 1458.

The early Islamic (8th–11th centuries AD) site of Ayla was excavated in 1986–1995 (fig. 2.8). Whitcomb (1993) hypothesized that the wadi running through the ancient site originated in erosion along the structural weakness of a fault and placed such a fault on his site plan (Whitcomb 1994). However, excavations by Rucker and Niemi (2005) of the NE corner tower of the walled city in the wadi and interpretation of 1918, 1945, and 1953 air photos (see chapter 3) indicate the wadi is man-made. There is evidence at Islamic Ayla for damage as a result of the 749 (or 746 or 756? Cf. Ambraseys 2005; 2009) earthquake followed by extensive reconstruction at the beginning of the Abbasid period. Major damage occurred in the town of Ayla in the March 18, 1068, earthquake. One contemporary source living in Baghdad, Ibn al-Banna, wrote: "As for Aila, its inhabitants all perished except for 12 persons who had gone fishing at sea, thus escaping death" (Guidoboni and Comastri 2005: 53). The site of Early Islamic Ayla was apparently never reoccupied to any significant degree after this earthquake.

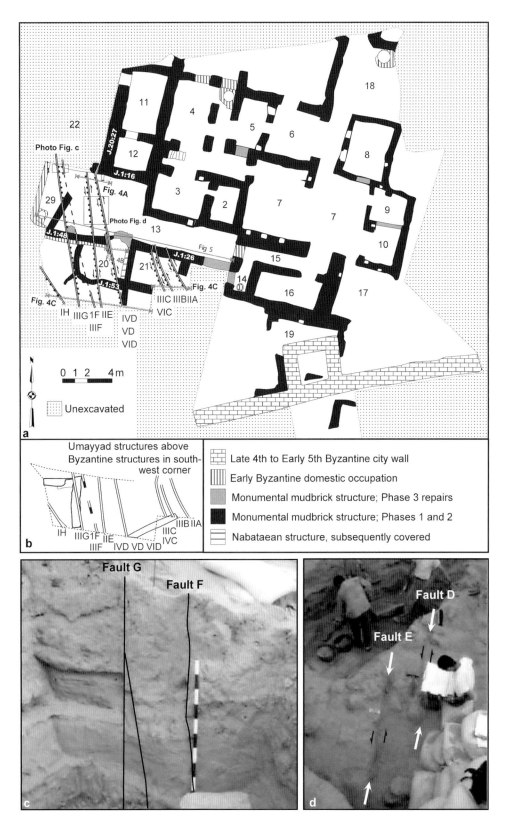

FIG. 2.15   *Faults exposed in the Roman Aqaba Project excavation Area J-East.*

Al-Hamoud and Tal (1998) conducted geo-technical investigations using three boreholes to a depth of 12m on the tell of Early Islamic Ayla. Archaeological deposits overlie sand and gravels. They noted tilting and sinking of exterior walls, interpreted as slumping due to horizontal ground acceleration in an earthquake. Al-Tarazi and Korjenkov (2007) reported similar conclusions. Ayla lies in an area of high liquefaction suscep-tibility due to the presence of saturated sands at shallow depth (Mansoor et al. 2004). This means that during seismic shaking, the substrate may lose its ability to bear weight, resulting in the collapse of structures. Areas along the beach zone near the ancient Ayla in modern Aqaba experienced subsid-ence in the Nuweiba earthquake of 1995 (Malkawi et al. 1999; al-Tarazi 2000).

The RAP and WAEP 2003 excavations within Area J-East identified a sequence of seven earth-quakes that ruptured faults across the site since the 2nd century AD (fig. 2.15; Thomas et al. 2007). Evidence for the oldest earthquake in Area J-East is based on a 1-m-thick mudbrick collapse horizon of an early 2nd-century AD Nabataean structure. Whole and partial bricks apparently indented the surfaces beneath, indicating a violent fall. No rupture was documented because of the limited excavated area. This evidence may correlate to an earthquake ca. 110–114 AD. Ambraseys (2009) lists a possible earthquake ca. 110–114 in Jordan based largely on archaeological data (Russell 1985). Struc-tural damage, destruction horizons, and rebuilding phases in the early 2nd century are reported across a wide zone from Caesarea on the Mediterranean coast to Jerash in the NE, in the Negev (Avdat, Mampsis), the Dead Sea (Masada), and Petra, among other locations (Russell 1985). Korjenkov and Erickson-Gini (2003) attribute archaeoseismic damage at the site of Metzad 'En Raḥel in Wādī 'Araba to this early-2nd-century earthquake. The houses at Ez-Zantur in Petra show extensive fire damage (Stucky 1996) that has been interpreted as the result of the conquest and annexation of Ara-bia to the Roman Empire (Schmid 1997; cf. Parker 2009). Whether the damage found at all these sites is seismic in origin and contemporaneous remains unclear. There is no known primary textual evi-dence attesting an early-2nd-century earthquake.

The earthquake of May 19, 363, is evidenced at Aila by the partial collapse of the monumental mudbrick structure (church) exposed in the J-East excavation area. Over 100 coins of Constantius II (337–361) were found beneath a thick layer of col-lapsed mudbrick walls. Our detailed mapping of the excavated Early Byzantine walls revealed an-cient repair work over seismically-induced struc-tural wall failures prior to the 363 collapse (Thomas et al. 2007). The structural repairs of the church walls indicate that the SW corner of the building subsided. This damage may have occurred in a minor earthquake (perhaps a significant foreshock) prior to the major 363 earthquake that collapsed the structure. After 363, surviving portions of the monumental structure were converted to domestic use in the late 4th century (Parker 2003: 326).

A widespread and destructive earthquake sequence that affected an area from north of the Sea of Galilee south to Petra occurred in 363. An important textual reference for this earthquake is an extant document, *Harvard Syriac 99*, a letter attributed to Cyril, Bishop of Jerusalem in ca. 350-388 (Brock 1977). *Harvard Syriac 99* describes two earthquake shocks that occurred six hours apart on the night of May 18–19, 363. The letter lists the cities or regions affected and the amount of damage sus-tained in the earthquake. Russell (1980) provides a comprehensive discussion of earthquake evidence from both the historical texts and from Byzantine archaeological sites excavated up to that date.

Excavations since 1980 have added further information about the 363 earthquake. The excava-tion of the Ez-Zantur domestic complex at Petra uncovered two earthquake victims — a woman and child — caught under the rubble. Both the latest and the vast majority (60 of 65) of the coins found with the skeletons date to 351–363, confirm-ing severe damage in Petra from this earthquake. Other excavations at Petra have also documented mid-4th-century earthquake destruction horizons (e.g., Bedal et al. 2007). Three Christian tombstones recovered from Ghor es-Safi (ancient Zoara), SE of the Dead Sea, document four more victims of the earthquake (Meimaris and Kritikakou-Nikolaro-poulou 2005). One burial contained a daughter and her father. The Greek epitaphs date the earthquake to May 18, 363. Other sites in Wādī 'Araba and the

Negev show evidence of this earthquake, including Ḥazeva (SW of the Dead Sea), Avdat and Mampsis in the Negev, and Yotvata near Aqaba (Erickson-Gini 1999; 2004; pers. comm., 2006).

There is also evidence for primary ground-rupture for at least four earthquakes that post-date 363 and that transect the ruins in Area J-East (Thomas et al. 2007). Primary fault rupture is documented in stratigraphic sections and plans of walls of various construction ages (fig. 2.15). Two earthquakes occurred during the Late Byzantine to Umayyad periods (6th to 8th centuries). There was a hiatus of occupation in this area between the Umayyad and modern periods. The two most recent earthquakes, with 42 and 35 cm of dip slip, occurred sometime after the 8th century and may correlate to the historical earthquakes of 1068, 1212, 1458, or 1588. No stratified materials were found in this area to refine the dating (Thomas et al. 2007).

VI. NATURAL RESOURCES

Water

Potable water for human consumption and water for husbandry and industry are basic necessities of life. Therefore, any settlement, whether ancient or modern, needs to develop a successful strategy to secure and maintain water resources. Wells are boreholes or vertical shafts dug to the water table. They differ from springs, which are the natural seepage of subsurface groundwater where the water table intersects the ground surface. The flow or discharge rate of a spring or the depth of water in a well is dependent on infiltration recharge to the aquifer feeding the groundwater. In addition to wells and springs, people have constructed various structures to divert and/or impound surface water behind dams or into built reservoirs (*birkeh* in Arabic).

Modern Aqaba has seen a transition in its source of water. Wells drilled into the Wādī Yutum aquifer supplied Aqaba with water throughout the 1950s–1970s. Because of the large catchment area of Wādī Yutum, recharge to the subsurface aquifer is strong. MacDonald (1966) calculated a discharge of 3–5 million m³/yr (MCM/yr) for the subsurface groundwater flow of Wādī Yutum.

Table 2.1   Distribution of Surface Water in the Southern Wādī ʿAraba and Wādī Yutum in MCM or millions of cubic meters per year (from Bilbeise 1992).

Basin	Flood flow MCM/yr	Spring flow MCM/yr
Southern ʿAraba	3.16	2.44
Inter-catchment	0.80	1.84
Abū Barqa	0.37	0.60
Rakiya	0.19	0.00
Wādī Yutum	1.80	0.00

However, extensive over-pumping caused saltwater intrusion in some of the wells. Also, with the expansion of the national border 17 km to the south in an agreement with Saudi Arabia, the demands for water in Aqaba grew as the country began to develop export markets for potash and phosphate. Population in Aqaba surged after each regional conflict (1948, 1967, 1980s Iran–Iraq war, and the Gulf Wars). In the late 1970s to early 1980s, a ca. 60 km-long pipeline was completed to bring Disi aquifer water from a well field east of the city to Aqaba. The Disi formation is part of the Cambrian sandstone that makes up the rocks on the plateau east of Aqaba and northward to Wādī Rum and Petra. The Disi aquifer is considered nonrenewal or fossil water that was recharged during wetter climatic periods in the Pleistocene compared to the slow present-day recharge (Lloyd and Pim 1990).

Ample early 20th-century evidence indicates that both wells and springs continued to be utilized in Wādī ʿAraba. Table 2.1 lists the annual discharge of these water sources. In the Aqaba coastal area and along the internally drained mudflats or *sabkhas* within Wādī ʿAraba, as in Tāba, wells are or were within the historically recent past hand-dug and often lined with rocks. Glueck, in his excavation of Tell el-Kheleifeh as presented in Pratico (1993), shows a garden and well between the archaeological site and the coast. Whitcomb's excavations of Early Islamic Ayla encountered a number of wells dating to the latest phases of occupation.

Likewise, excavations of the Mamluk to Ottoman era castle of Aqaba uncovered a number of wells.

In Wādī 'Araba, the springs ('Ain in Arabic, 'En in Hebrew) form oases with lush vegetation within the desert environment and have largely determined the location of settlements and travel routes across this desolate terrain. Several springs are well-known within the southern part of the valley. These include springs on the west side: 'En Defiya in the Evrona *sabkha* and 'Ain Ghadayan in Yotvata/Tāba *sabkha*. The *sabkhas* have a high water table that, coupled with high evaporation rates, leads to the precipitation of salts. Thus, the water in the *sabkha* wells tends to be brackish. Today water for villages in Jordan adjacent to these *sabkhas* is supplied by wells from local aquifers. Two desalination plants at Qattar and Ar-Risha remove the salts because of the high salinity of the Wādī 'Araba aquifers. Other springs lie along the drainages within the adjacent bedrock mountains where faults and other geological structures impede subsurface flow, leading to ground water discharge, such as at Gharandal.

Water management remains a long-standing concern for the Aqaba region. Various modern diversion walls and channels have been constructed to direct floodwater away from inhabited areas. There is substantial evidence of an extensive system of diversion walls to channel the flow of water, impound water, and redirect flow and sediment to agricultural fields in the late Chalcolithic period around Tell Ḥujeirat al-Ghuzlan (Niemi and Smith 1999; Brückner et al. 2002; Heemeier et al. 2009; Siegel 2009). In the late Umayyad and Abbasid period, there were *qanats,* or *foggara,* an elaborate system of underground tunnels, vertical shafts, and irrigation channels, to bring water to agricultural plots in the mudflats of Evrona and Yotvata (west side of Tāba *sabkha*; Avner and Magness 1998). It is likely that similar strategies of water management were also implemented during the Roman and Byzantine eras.

Building Stone

Examination of archaeological structures in excavation areas of Roman/Byzantine Aqaba, Early Islamic Ayla, and the Aqaba castle reveals four general types of building stones used as foundations and walls: igneous rocks, variegated sandstone with siltstone interbeds, limestone, and coral fragments. There are rectangularly-cut sandstone and limestone building blocks in both primary and secondary use. Primary use is stone cut for the structure in which it was found. Secondary use is stone fabricated for an earlier building but reused in a later structure. There are ample examples of secondary use of building elements in Byzantine and later-period structures.

In Byzantine Aila most building stones are unhewn blocks of the Aqaba Complex (fig. 2.6), granitic rocks outcropping locally in the mountains to the east and west. Because the rocks appear undressed, it is unlikely that they were quarried directly from outcrops. The building stones were probably collected from Wādī Yutum and other drainages where the streams deliver a large quantity of cobbles and boulders into the valley and spread out into alluvial fans. Older alluvial fan deposits may also have been a convenient source of cobble-sized granitic building stones.

Although the Wādī Yutum drainage basin reaches far eastward into the region of the Ram Group sandstone bedrock, particularly into the Umm 'Ishrin and Disi Formations on the plateau, large clasts in the Wādī Yutum alluvium are composed almost exclusively of Aqaba Complex rocks. The Ram Group sandstones crop out ca. 25 km east of Aqaba and 55 km NE of Aqaba in the Wādī Nukheila region. The lower Cretaceous Kurnub sandstone is also exposed 30 km north of Eilat on the west side of the valley and north of Wādī Nukheila. Along the west side of Wādī 'Araba near Timna are three ancient sandstone quarries (Avner and Magness 1998). Isolated outcrops of the Ram Group sandstone at the north end of the Al Yamaniyya Pleistocene gravels and late Cretaceous Kurnub Sandstone in Wādī Mubarak are exposed 10 km south of Aqaba (Khatib 1987).

North of the Muhtadī fan, there is a unique occurrence of Cretaceous sandstone and limestone that forms low hills west of the main mountain front. In the middle of the valley is a limestone ridge forming Jebel el-Khureij and Jebel ar-Risha. Ibrahim (1993) defined these rocks as a new formation in the upper part of the Ajlun Group (Khureij

FIG. 2.16   *A) View west across the Qāʿ as-Suʿaydiyyīn mudflat. B) Blocks of the oolitic Khureij limestone used as a stone quarry.*

Formation). On the 1:50,000 scale map and in the "Economic Geology" section of the accompanying report, Ibrahim (1993: 65) notes that the oolitic Khureij limestone "was extensively used for building purposes in the Nabataean and Roman" times. Jebel el-Khureij was clearly utilized as a stone quarry, as partially shaped Roman milestones (figs. 2.16, 4.22) were discovered at the site (Smith et al. 1997). A limestone quarry was also reported in Naḥal Roded (Avner and Magness 1998). Ajlun Group limestone crops out in the western Wādī ʿAraba just south of Timna. Cut, dressed, and sometimes decorated blocks of this rock appear in Roman-Byzantine Aila and Early Islamic Ayla. Geotechnical research at Early Islamic Ayla concluded that the building blocks are weakened by structural loading and chemical weathering (al-Homoud and Tal 1998). The weathering is enhanced by the salt spray from the sea and otherwise saline soils due to high evaporation rates.

Basalt and Schist

Ancient querns, mortars, and pestles recovered in the RAP excavation are often shaped from vesicular olivine alkaline basalt. There is no local source of basalt in the Aqaba area. Miocene to Pliocene basalts outcrop as sills, dikes, and flows ca. 30 km north of Maʾan and extend in isolated occurrences northward along the highland plateau east of the rift valley and the Dead Sea. Linear basaltic dikes lie 50 km SE of Quweira and in the mountains that flank the west shore of the Gulf of Aqaba and the

north shore of the Red Sea. There is an extensive area of Pliocene to Quaternary flood basalts in Zerka Maʾin east of the Dead Sea, the Hauran plateau in NE Jordan and southern Syria, and SW of the Sea of Galilee.

Local sources of schist include biotite schist from the Wādī Abū Barqa region (Ibrahim 1993) and "crystalline schist" from the NW shore of the Gulf of Aqaba (Bentor et al. 1965). Metasedimentary and metavolcanic rocks crop out over an 8-km distance along the Jordanian–Saudi Arabian border, 9 km east of the shore of the gulf (Khatib 1987). However none of these sources appear to match the soft, easily sculpted chlorite and graphite schist ("steatite") recovered in the RAP excavations. Analysis of these schist artifacts suggests a possible origin in Hejaz of NW Saudi Arabia (Grubisha 2000).

Flint (Chert)

Cretaceous limestones outcrop in the southern ʿAraba ca. 10 km north of the gulf along the western side of the valley just south of Timna (Bender 1975) and cap the western highland mountains 5–7 km inland of the range front. These rocks contain "limestone, sandy limestone, dolomite, nodular limestone, shale, and gypsum" (Bender 1975) that correlate to the Ajlun Group in Jordan. Chert is found in limestone either as nodules or as beds. A single, 22-m-thick outcrop of late Cretaceous limestone is exposed in Wādī Mubarak, south of Aqaba. The lithology is a "nodular shelly limestone and dolomitic limestone" (Khatib 1987). Chert-bearing limestones are also found in the central plateau of Jordan.

Chert appears in the stratigraphic section in the upper Ajlun Groun (Wādī As Sir and Khureij limestones) but becomes abundant in the deep-water Belqa Group limestones. Chert-bearing rocks include the Amman Silicified limestone and the Eocene Umm Rijam formation. Exposures of the Umm Rijam along the northern rim of the Al Jafr basin contain 20-cm-thick chert beds that have been mined and exported since at least the Early Bronze Age (Abu-Jaber et al. 2009).

Detrital chert sources include the late Teritary Dana Conglomerate Formation. A single isolated outcrop of Dana Conglomerate overlies Cretaceous limestone in Wādī Mubarak, south of Aqaba. The 15-m-thick conglomerate contains "boulders of limestone, phosphatic limestone, phosphatic chert and chert" (Khatib 1987). Other outcrops of the Dana Conglomerate appear as isolated knolls along the mountain front of Wādī el-Muhtadī and Wādī Abū Barqa. Chert in cobble detrital, nodular, and bedded forms, used for flint tool-making, thus appears in ample supply locally.

Copper and Other Metals

The closest source for copper ore is the Timna district (including Timna Valley, Nahal Shehoret, and Wādī Amram) along the west side of the southern ʿAraba, ca. 20 km north of Aqaba. Additional sites of copper mineralization occur along the east side of Wādī ʿAraba in Wādī Abū Khusheiba and Wādī Faynan, 90 and 125 km NE of Aqaba, respectively. Lateral fault offset of 107 km along the Dead Sea-Jordan transform has separated what was once a single copper region. The ore is mainly in the form of small malachite nodules and chrysocolla hosted in sedimentary rocks. Layers or veins of the copper-rich deposits are found predominantly in the Cambrian Burj Dolomite-Shale and Abū Khusheiba sandstone. The copper ore is associated with iron at Timna and with manganese at Faynan. The Timna copper deposit was actively mined in the 20th century. Both the Timna and Faynan districts have ample evidence of copper mining and processing in antiquity from as early as the

Chalcolithic period (Hauptmann 2006; Hauptmann et al. 2009).

Gold mines mentioned in Deuteronomy and described by Eusebius in the *Onomasticon* as an "eleven day" trek from Mount Horeb in the Sinai suggest that gold was likely associated with the copper mineralization in the Faynan and Timna areas (Meshel 2006). Okour et al. (2006) describe traces of gold up to 5–8 parts per million (ppm) in heavy metal concentrations of placer deposits in wadi sediment. Traces of gold were detected in quartz veins associated with the Ḥeimir rhyolitic volcanic suite of rocks that crop out in isolated areas around the Wādī Abū Khusheiba area, 90 km north of Aqaba. The gold is sometimes visible in the veins, with nuggets up to 1 mm in length (Okour et al. 2006). These authors also report gold occurrences in "metarhyolite rocks in Jebel al Mubarak and Enn El-Hasheem (Aqaba Complex) in extreme southern Jordan near the Saudi Arabia border."

It is uncertain whether these gold resources in Jordan were exploited in antiquity. In Israel, in a tributary of Nahal Roded NW of Eilat, a gold production site was in operation from the 8th to 10th centuries, based on radiocarbon dating and ceramic analysis (Avner and Magness 1998). Wādī Tawahin means "millstone drainage" in Arabic. Gilat et al. (1993) describe rooms with large rectangular or square quartz diorite millstone blocks, hammer stones, and anvils at the site. They suggest that the ore was probably mined locally from ferrugineous quartz veins that contain up to 9 ppm gold. Analyses of the powder at the site yielded mostly quartz and gold concentrations of 29 ppm. The very fine size of the gold particles in the sample (5–20 microns) suggests that the gold was not visible to the naked eye in the ore deposit (Gilat et al. 1993).

Gypsum, Bitumen, Salt, and Sulfur

Gypsum, hydrated calcium sulfate, is a sedimentary mineral found in primary and secondary context in carbonate or evaporitic rocks. In Jordan the thickest accumulation of gypsum is a 60-m-thick bed of gypsum of Triassic age in the Zarqa River area (Tarawneh et al. 2006). There is also bedded gypsum between 1 and 7 m thick in the Fuhesis/Hummar/Shuʾayib formations in the Ajlun Group on the plateau (Tarawneh et al. 2006). In Wādī 'Araba, gypsum appears in the middle Ajlun beds and in the carbonate rocks of the Belqa Group in the Gharandal area (fig. 2.6; Ibrahim 1993). The RAP survey recovered large gypsum crystals in Wādī Abū Barqa (Site 302). Primary gypsum also appears in beds up to 60 cm thick within sediment of the Tāba *sabkha* (Amiel and Friedman 1971) and the Lisan marl unit found around the Dead Sea and Jordan Valley.

Gypsum is used to make plaster and is sometimes mixed in cement or mortar. Various samples of raw gypsum appeared in excavated contexts from most RAP excavation areas. Four different types were recovered. The majority of gypsum samples are satinspar, an acicular, needle-like or fibrous mass of crystals. This type of sedimentary gypsum is prevalent in upper Cretaceous chalk and marl units that outcrop near Gharandal and to the north and on the plateau to the NE. Outcrops of the Muwaqqar Chalk-Marl formation west of Jebel Muhtadī also contain common gypsum veins, 25 km north of Aqaba. Next in abundance from the excavation are selenite crystals of gypsum. In the geologic setting, these clear euhedral crystals form during the process of diagenesis when the host rock is buried and lithified. One sample may be associated with bitumen. Two samples, one pink-colored and rather dense and another of banded gypsum and calcite, may be imported alabaster. Several dozen alabaster artifacts were recovered by the RAP excavation.

The excavations also yielded several bitumen samples. These are solid vitreous refined bitumen or tar. Ibrahim (1993) reported traces of bitumen in the Hummar Formation, part of the Ajlun Group Upper Cretaceous rocks near Gharandal. The most likely source of the bitumen is the Dead Sea, well-known for asphalt seeps and blocks floating in its waters. Greeks and Romans referred to the Dead Sea as the Asphalt Lake. The Nabataeans harvested floating blocks of bitumen (Hammond 1959). These blocks are likely produced when seismic shifting of the faults below the Dead Sea loosen and provide conduits for the heavy oil to be liberated from deeper reservoirs. The appearance and disappearance of floating bitumen may be related to earthquake cycles in which periods of increased seismic activity

are followed by periods of earthquake quiescence. Reflecting the seismic activity of the 1st century AD, Josephus reported that the sea "in many places casts up black masses of asphalt, which float on the surface, in their shape and size resembling decapitated bulls" (*BJ* 4.8.4). In antiquity, bitumen (asphalt or pitch) was used as a sealant for waterproofing, as well as for medicinal and agricultural purposes. It was also traded to Egypt for use in the embalming process (Nissenbaum 1993).

The most common occurrence of bitumen is asphalt that seeps especially along the southern Dead Sea (Nissenbaum 1993). This asphalt is not pure but mixed with sand and gravel. Philby (1925) described bituminous soaked rocks used to fuel cooking fires on his trek around the northern Dead Sea in 1923. He also claimed that the quantity of bitumen in the Dead Sea rocks was not viable for commercial exploitation, in contrast to the mining of similar rocks in the Yarmouk River valley that was used to fuel trains on the Hejaz Railway.

The Dead Sea is also referred to as the Salt Sea. Evaporation of Dead Sea water precipitates large quantities of halite. Salt, the mineral halite, can be collected from the shore of the hypersaline lake or from special evaporation ponds. In the modern evaporation ponds of the Dead Sea Works (Israel) and the Arab Potash Company (Jordan) in the south basin of the Dead Sea, halite is the first salt precipitated in the process of concentrating carnellite, the potash mineral. Alternatively, rock salt may also have been mined in antiquity from Mount Sedom, an 11 km-long by 2 km-wide diapir of salt along the SW shore of the Dead Sea. Halite is also locally present in several Wādī 'Araba *sabkhas* (Ibrahim 1991). Salt collection in Aqaba may also have been produced by evaporating Red Sea waters, which are slightly elevated in salinity compared to normal marine water.

Finally, another resource likely exploited from the Dead Sea is sulfur. Three samples were collected by RAP. Native sulfur today accumulates along the thermal springs on the east side of Dead Sea near Zerka Ma'in. Evaporation of hot spring water enriched in sulfate ions can precipitate sulfur near the spring conduit. In antiquity, sulfur was used in medicines, fumigation, and bleaching cloth (Pliny the Elder, *HN* 35.50).

FIG. 2.17 *Mudbrick house in the Circular Area (1994).*

Quartz for Glass

Both the Disi and Kurnub Sandstones are friable quartz arenite units. The pure quartz composition of these rocks makes them an exceptional good source rock for glass production. Disi Sandstone is exposed on the Jordanian plateau east and north of Aqaba. The Kurnub Sandstone has isolated outcrops in the Gharandal area and further north. However, the RAP excavation yielded no evidence for ancient local production of glass. The substantial amount of glass recovered from the RAP excavations was all apparently imported.

Clay

Clay is an important resource both as a basic raw material for buildings, especially in the production of mudbricks, and for pottery. The economic value of this natural resource cannot be overstated. Mudbrick was widely used regionally for millennia in the construction of buildings in Aqaba. The city walls of Byzantine Aila and Early Islamic Ayla

were apparently constructed entirely of masonry, as is the extant Mamluk-Ottoman castle of Aqaba. The superstructure of most other ancient buildings excavated in Aqaba appears to have been of poured mud or of coursed mudbrick — a sun-dried mixture of clay and coarser inclusions, sometimes mixed with organic matter to reduce shrinking. The predominance of mudbrick must largely be a function of the lack of easily hewn rocks as is common in alluvial valley settings. Sedimentary rock quarries lie 10 km to the west (Avner and Magness 1998). The locally exposed granitic bedrock on the east side of the valley is difficult to quarry and shape. Thus, a local inexpensive mud must have been available for construction in ancient Aqaba. Extant mudbrick buildings in the Aqaba Old Town near the castle and the RAP excavations (fig. 2.17) show that the tradition of mudbrick building lasted well into the 20th century until the introduction of mass manufactured cinder block.

Furthermore, as a port city, ancient Aqaba needed to load and unload ships laden with trade goods and thus required a substantial supply of shipping containers. Amphorae served this purpose. Ample evidence of the local production of amphorae in kilns is documented for Aqaba (Melkawi et al. 1994) and for the Eilat area (Avner and Magness 1998). There is also evidence of some local pottery production, as evidenced by stratified kiln wasters and ceramic slag, through the site's history at least through the 7th century. Thus, clay to feed these kilns must have been available, if not abundant.

Where did the people of Aqaba get their clay? Is the mudbrick clay different from the pottery clay? These are fundamental questions. As noted above, the region is characterized by coarse clastic sedimentation eroded from the Aqaba Granitic complex by streams that enter the valley from the east. Fine-grained sediments are relatively rare at the surface in present-day Aqaba. There are several potential local sources of clay in the Aqaba region and southern Wādī ʿAraba. These include Pleistocence clay beds south of Aqaba, mudflats or *sabkhas* along the low-lying axis of Wādī ʿAraba, and flood slack water deposits from Wādī Yutum and other local drainages.

The Al Yamaniyya deposit is an interbedded sequence of Pleistocene sand, silt, and clay located about 10 km south of the Aqaba port. Three clay-bearing layers with thicknesses ranging from 20 cm to 3 m were reported to be "gray, green, and light brown in color, soft, plastic, and fissile" (Ibrahim and Abdelhamid 1990: 3). The composition of the clay is predominately kaolinite and montmorillonite with traces of illite and chlorite (Ibrahim and Abdelhamid 1990). It is unclear whether these beds were mined in antiquity.

Along the low-lying axis of the southern Wādī ʿAraba valley is a series of mudflats and *sabkhas* where floodwater runoff collects and ponds during high rainfall events. Abed (2002) makes the distinction between a mudflat (*Qaa'* in Arabic) and an inland (as opposed to a coastal) *sabkha*. A *qaa'* drains easily, lacks evaporates, and thus can be cultivated in rainy years as is the case with Qāʿ as-Suʾaydiyyīn (fig. 2.16). The ephemeral standing water settles out silt and clay. High temperatures and evaporation cause precipitation of gypsum, halite, dolomite, and the rare magnesium mineral, sepiolite (Abed 2002; Khalil 1991). Analyses of

the red-brown-colored muds of the Tāba *sabhka* sediment indicate that, in addition to the evaporite suite, are the minerals kaolinite, smectite, and palygorskite (Khalil 1991). Thus, the *sabkha* sediment appears to be an important supply of clay.

The floodwaters of the southern ʿAraba valley and Wādī Yutum pond in the Eilat *sabkha*. In cores recovered near Tell el-Kheleifeh, Brückner (1999) described alluvial layers of clayey silt and silty clay at the surface and buried >2 m in depth. The stratigraphic sequence of a 10 m-long core from the ʿEn Defiya *sabkha*, 12 km north of Aqaba, was composed of "monotonous yellowish brown silty clay to clayey silt" interbedded with sand and distinct layers with large gypsum crystals (Brückner et al. 2002: 226). Halite was not mentioned but may also have been present. These alluvial sediments sampled at the periphery of the *sabkha* contain more silt than those described in the central part of Tāba *sabkha*.

The third possible clay source is the purposive direction of ephemeral stream flow into natural or artificial depressions in order to settle out the fine-grained sediment. Alternatively, when constructed water reservoirs or *birkehs* are periodically cleaned out, their by-product of silt and clay settled on the bottom of the reservoir may have been utilized for mudbrick production.

Stratigraphic sections exposed in a ca. 20 m-square bulldozer excavation (apparently dug as a modern trash disposal pit) and designated as RAP Area N and in backhoe trench BH 21 show evidence of natural deposition of thin-bedded mud and possible reservoir clean-out mud piles. Area N and BH 21 were ca. 500 m from the shoreline and ca. 250 and 150 m NW of Area B, respectively. The mud layers appear to be natural deposited sediment in the distal portion of the alluvial fan, where low-lying areas caused ponding. Figure 2.18 shows two stratigraphic sections within the Area N exposure. The mud layer is of limited thickness and pinches out laterally. In places the mud layers appear to be modified by human activity. At one stratigraphic section in Area N (fig. 2.19), blocks of mud appear in a jumbled pile. This exposure is adjacent to pits in the mud layer.

In Trench BH 21 mud layers overlie a basal, 50-cm-thick layer of cross-bedded, fine-to-medium-grained sand (fig. 2.12). The top of the sand may

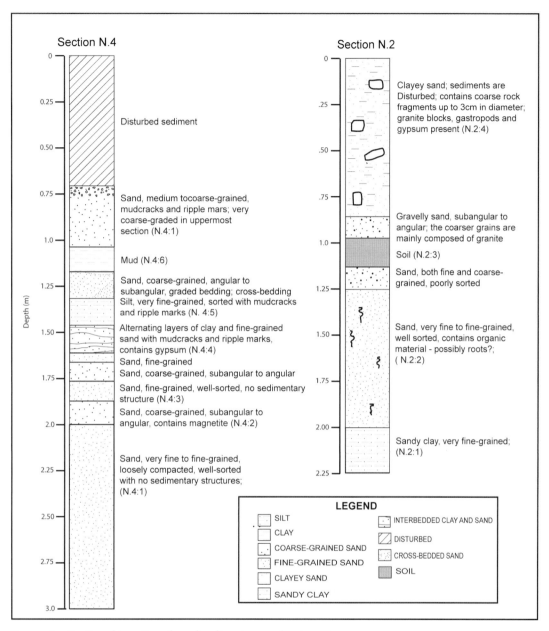

FIG. 2.18   *Stratigraphic sections through sediment exposed in Area N.*

have been modified by pedogenesis. Overlying the sand is a 50-cm-thick, flat-lying layer of interbedded clayey silt and silty clay. The interbeds vary in thickness from 2 to 10 cm. The top of the clay layer is irregular with evidence of having been cut and removed. In places the edge of the clay layer has a vertical face and appears to be the boundary of a pit. The mud layer thins toward the west and appears to onlap and interfinger with sand. It is unclear whether this is a natural boundary or a

purposively built berm to temporarily impound water. The pits above the mud layer were filled with poorly sorted sand, ash, and occupational debris. Early Roman/Nabataean potsherds were associated with these deposits and the surface (Parker 1998: 378; 2000: 375).

Grain-size analyses on the fine-grained layers in Area N show that they are only 3–8 weight percentages within the clay-size fraction. X-ray diffraction (XRD) analyses of the clay layers (fig.

FIG. 2.19   *Pile of clay chips in Area N.*

2.20) reveals only minor amounts of kaolinite. The main clay in Tāba *sabkha* samples near the eastern margin is chlorocline. Abundant minerals with all the samples include quartz, feldspar, gypsum, and calcite. XRD analyses of "clay" deposits recovered from various archaeological contexts show that the mineralogy is very similar to compositions recorded from the naturally deposited muds in Area N. Elemental analyses on the mud layers using ICPMS show Al, Mg, Ti, Fe, and Pb elevated above the values for the more sandy layers. Together these data suggest that the mud from Area N does not contain ceramic quality clay, contrary to the suggestion offered in the preliminary reports (Parker 1998: 378; 2000: 375). The deposits may instead have been used to make mudbrick. The exact source of the ceramic-quality clay is not known at this time but might be buried deeper in the Eilat *sabkha*.

VII.   CONCLUSIONS

The city of Aqaba lies at the northern end of the Gulf of Aqaba along the southern part of the Dead Sea Transform fault system that separates the Sinai and Arabian tectonic plates. Furthermore, Aqaba lies along the transition from the marine to the continental Eilat/Aqaba sedimentary basins. Faults controlling the structural dynamics of sedimentation as well as the seismic activity lie both onshore and offshore. Based on historical accounts as well as archaeological and geological excavations, it is clear that earthquakes have played a significant role in the history of the region. Detailed investigation of the stratigraphy at the Roman-Byzantine archaeological site of Aila reveals evidence for seven earthquakes. Based on subsidence across the fault, changes in floor elevations, offset and repaired walls, and layers of collapsed mudbrick, the archaeological data suggest that the site was ruptured by earthquakes in the early 2nd century, early 4th century, and in AD 363. In addition, two earthquakes occurred between the 6th and 8th centuries. The most recent earthquakes occurred sometime after the 8th century. These latter earthquakes likely affected the Islamic city of Ayla that was founded around 650, suffered some damage but extensive reconstruction ca. 750 (the beginning of the Abbasid period), and experienced

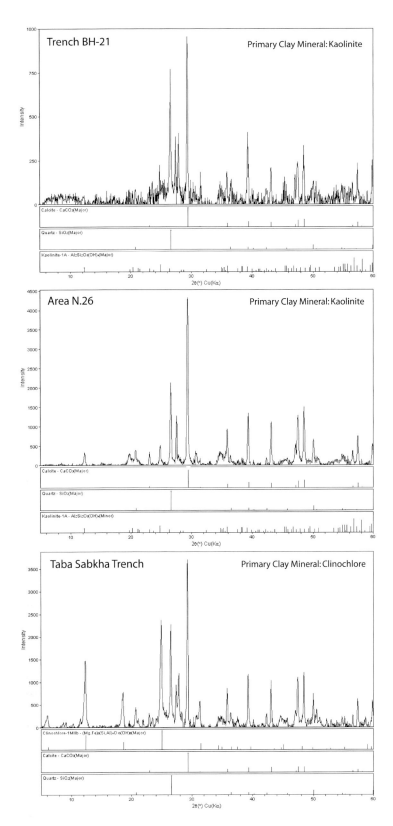

FIG. 2.20 *X-Ray diffraction analyses of mud from Area N, Backhoe Trench 21 and the Tāba sabkha.*

collapse in the 1068 AD earthquake. Later earthquakes likely affected the Aqaba castle in 1212 and 1588. These data suggest significant periods of active seismicity in the 4th, 7th–8th, 11th–13th, and 15–16th centuries and a recurrence of faulting and damaging earthquakes at intervals of every three to four centuries. It is interesting to note that some earthquakes have coincided with major political transitions in the region. Seismic activity thus possibly played a significant role in these political shifts.

The climate of Aqaba today is hyperarid with temperatures often exceeding 40° C in the summer months, with a mean annual precipitation of less than 50 mm. Several lines of evidence from marine cores, Dead Sea levels, speleothem data, and floral and faunal materials from the Late Chalcolithic tells in Aqaba suggest wetter-than-present conditions about 6000–4000 BC, and possibly during the Hellenistic-Roman, Byzantine, and Crusader periods in the region. This record is punctuated by periods of marked aridity that may be characterized by a rapid onset.

Sediment coring in the coastal zone of Aqaba indicates that the environment has changed from coastal lagoons, swamp, or embayment during the Neolithic to Chalcolithic periods to one dominated by fluvial deposits and aeolian sand dunes. The shoreline has prograded at least 400 m since the 6th millennium BC. Fossil coral reef data suggest that sea level may have been slightly higher than present during the Neolithic and Chalcolithic periods. Fluvial runoff from the large Wādī Yutum that drains the Jordanian Plateau to the east caused the siltation of the Aqaba embayment. Late Chalcolithic sites are located higher on the alluvial fan and away from the shoreline. Tectonic subsidence of the region coupled with subsequent climate and human-induced siltation probably have driven the major environmental changes. By the 8th century BC, when the site of Tell el-Kheleifeh was founded in the middle of the coastal plain of the Gulf of Aqaba, the shoreline had prograded seaward and the environment was dominated by fluvial and aeolian processes. Later coastal settlements from the Nabataean through the Islamic periods (1st century BC through the 20th century AD) lie along the NE margin of the gulf.

The internal stratigraphy of the mounds within the coastal zone clearly demonstrates that they are constructional and formed by the aeolian infilling of mudbrick structures. The age of the structures dating to Nabataean/Roman periods shows that the mounds have been part of the landscape for the past 2000 years. In the Aqaba area the burial of these Nabataean/Roman structures by aeolian sand dunes suggests that arid conditions have prevailed since then. Incipient soil development on alluvial deposits of Roman date in the region may be attributed to changes in the seasonal delivery of moisture, to changes in temperature, or to changes in land use practices during this period.

The groundwater table in Aqaba is fed by the large watershed of Wādī Yutum and has provided the site with readily available potable water from wells dug into the aquifer. Structures built in antiquity were largely constructed of mudbrick founded on lower walls of coursed stone. The stones are mostly local granitic boulders collected from the wadi and alluvial fan deposits. Some hewn blocks were quarried on the west side of the valley or farther north in Wādī 'Araba. Inhabitants exploited the copper and gold resources. It is evident from examples of import items (e.g., Parker 2003; Whitcomb 1994) that Aqaba was a vibrant port during several periods in history. Kilns, ceramic wasters, and locally made amphorae all indicate that clay must have been locally available to facilitate exportation. The results of mineralogical analyses of clays from the coastal zone using x-ray diffraction and other methods, however, do not definitely identify a source for the local production of pottery.

VIII. ACKNOWLEDGEMENTS

Sources of funding for the Roman Aqaba Project are acknowledged in Chapter 1. Funding for the Wādī 'Araba Earthquake Project was provided by a University of Missouri Research Board grant and two grants from the Committee for Research and Exploration of the National Geographic Society. Dr. Fawwaz al-Khraysheh, former General-Director of the Department of Antiquities of Jordan, granted permission to work in Aqaba and supported the sediment coring conducted by the Jordan Natural Resource Authority. The assistance of Richard Gentile on faunal analyses, James Murowchick with geochemical analyses, Vladimir M. Dusevich for SEM photographs, and Alivia Allison for drafting is gratefully acknowledged.

REFERENCES

Abdelhamid, G.; Ibrahim, K.; and Mortimer, C.
1994 *The Geology of Ayn Al Hashim, Jabal Al Mubarak, and Al Yamaniyya: Map sheets 3048 I, 3048 IV, and 2948 I*, Bulletin 27, Geology Directorate, Geological Mapping Division, Hashemite Kingdom of Jordan, Ministry of Energy and Mineral Resources, Natural Resources Authority.

Abed, A. M.
2002 An Overview of an Inland Sabkha in Jordan: The Tāba Sabkha, Southern Wādī 'Araba. Pp. 83-97 in H.-J. Barth and B. Boër, eds., *Sabkha Ecosystems:* Volume I: *The Arabian Peninsula and Adjacent Countries*. Dordrecht: Kluwer Academic.

Abed, A. M.; Jarrar, G.; and Atalla, M.
1998 Geology of Jordan – An Overview. Paper delivered to the 6th Jordanian Geological Conference, 5–8 October 1998. Amman: University of Jordan.

Abu-Jaber, N.; Al Saad, Z.; and Al Quday, M.
2009 Geomorphological and Geological Constraints on the Development of Early Bronze Chert Industries at the Northern Rim of the Al Jafr Basin, Southern Jordan. *Mediterranean Archaeology and Archaeometry* 9.1: 17–27.

Abueladas, A.
2005 Ground-penetrating Radar Investigation of Active Faults and Antiquities along the Dead Sea Transform in Aqaba and the Tāba Sabkha, Jordan. Unpublished Master's thesis, University of Missouri–Kansas City.

al-Farajat, M.
2002 Hydrogeo-Eco-Systems in Aqaba/Jordan – Coasts and Region; Natural Settings, Impacts of Land Use, Spatial Vulnerability to Pollution and Sustainable Management. Dissertation, Julius-Maximilians-University of Würzburg.

al-Homoud, A. S, and Tal, A. B.
1998 Geotechnical Study for Evaluating Stability and Restoration Work at the 1,000 Year Old Archaeological Site of Ayla, Gulf of Aqaba, Kingdom of Jordan. *Environmental Engineering Geoscience* 4: 103–14.

al-Qudah, A.
2011 Floods as Water Resource and as a Hazard in Arid Regions: A Case Study in Southern Jordan. *Jordan Journal of Civil Engineering* 5.1: 148–61.

al-Rifaiy, I., and Cherif, O.
1988 The Fossil Coral Reefs of al-Aqaba, Jordan. *Facies* 18.1: 219–29.

al-Tarazi, E.
2000 The Major Gulf of Aqaba Earthquake, 22 November 1995–Maximum Intensity Distribution. *Natural Hazards* 22: 17–27.

al-Tarazi, E., and Korjenov, A. M.
2007 Archaeoseismological Investigation of the Ancient Ayla Site in the City of Aqaba, Jordan. *Natural Hazards* 42.1: 47–66.

Allison, A. J.
2007 Paleoenvironmental Reconstruction of Late Holocene Coastal Sediments Along the Southern Dead Sea Transform in Aqaba, Jordan. Unpublished Master's thesis. University of Missouri–Kansas City.

Allison, A. J., and Niemi, T. M.
2010 Paleoenvironmental Reconstruction of Holocene Coastal Sediments Adjacent to Archaeological Ruins in Aqaba, Jordan. *Geoarchaeology* 25.5: 602–25.

Ambraseys, N. N.
2009 *Earthquakes in the Mediterranean and Middle East: A Multidisciplinary Study of Seismicity up to 1900.* Cambridge: Cambridge University.
2005 The Seismic Activity in Syria and Palestine During the middle of the 8th century; An Amalgamation of Historical Earthquakes. *Journal of Seismology* 9: 115–25.

Ambraseys N. N.; Melville, C. P.; and Adams, R. D.
1994 *The Seismicity of Egypt, Arabia, and the Red Sea.* Cambridge: Cambridge University.

Amiel, A. I., and Friedman, G. M.
1971 Continental Sabkha in Arava Valley Between Red Sea and Dead Sea: Significance for the Origin of Evaporates. *Bulletin of the American Association of Petroleum Geologists* 55: 582–92.

Amiran D. H. K.; Arieh, E.; and Turcotte, T.
1994 Earthquakes in Israel and Adjacent Areas – Macroseismic Observations Since 100 B.C.E. *IEJ* 44: 260–305.

Amit, R., and Gerson, R.
1986 The Evolution of Holocene REG (gravelly) Soils in Deserts—An Example from the Dead Sea Region. *Catena* 13: 59–79.

Amit, R.; Harrison, J. B. J.; and Enzel, Y.
1995   Use of Soils and Colluvial Deposits in Analyzing Tectonic Events—The Southern Arava Rift, Israel. *Geomorphology* 12: 91–107.

Amit, R.; Harrison, J. B. J.; Enzel, Y.; and Porat, N.
1996   Soils as a Tool for Estimating Ages of Quaternary Fault Scarps in a Hyperarid Environment—The Southern Arava Valley, the Dead Sea Rift, Israel. *Catena* 28: 21–45.

Amit, R.; Zilberman, E.; Porat, N.; and Enzel, Y.
1999   Relief Inversion in the Avrona Playa as Evidence of Large-Magnitude Historical Earthquakes, Southern Arava Valley, Dead Sea Rift. *Quaternary Research* 52.1: 76–91.

Amit, R.; Zilberman, E.; Enzel, Y.; and Porat, N.
2002   Paleoseismic Evidence for Time Dependency of Seismic Response on a Fault System in the Southern Arava Valley, Dead Sea Rift, Israel. *Geological Society of America Bulletin* 114.2: 192–206.

Avner, U., and Magness, J.
1998   Early Islamic Settlement in the Southern Negev. *BASOR* 310: 39–57.

Bar Matthews M.; Ayalon, A.; and Kaufman, A.
1997   Late Quaternary Paleoclimate in the Eastern Mediterranean Region from Stable Isotope Analysis of Speleothems at Soreq Cave, Israel. *Quaternary Research* 47: 155–68.

Bar Matthews M., and Ayalon, A.
2011   Mid-Holocene Climate Variations Revealed by High-Resolution Speleothem Records From Soreq Cave, Israel and their Correlation with Cultural Changes. *The Holocene* 21.1: 163–71.

Bedal, L.-A.; Gleason, K. L.; and Schryver, J. G.
2007   The Petra Garden and Pool Complex, 2003–2005. *ADAJ* 51: 151–76.

Begin, Z. B.; Broecker, W.; Buchbinder, B.; Druckman, Y.; Kaufman, A.; Magaritz, M.; and Neev, D.
1985   Dead Sea and Lake Lisan levels in the Last 30,000 years. *Geological Survey of Israel.* Preliminary report GSI/29/85.

Ben-Avraham, Z.; Almagor, G.; and Garfunkel, Z.
1979   Sediments and Structure of the Gulf of Eilat (Aqaba)—Northern Red Sea. *Sedimentary Geology* 23: 239–67.

Ben-Avraham, Z.
1985   Structural Framework of the Gulf of Eilat (Aqaba), Northern Red Sea. *Journal of Geophysical Research* 90: 703–26.

Ben-Avraham, Z., and Tibor, G.
1993   The Northern Edge of the Gulf of Eilat. *Tectonophysics* 226: 319–31.

Bender, F.
1974   *Geology of Jordan*. Berlin: Borntraeger.

Ben-Menaham, A.
1979   Earthquake Catalogue for the Middle East (92 B.C. - 1980 A.D.). *Bollettino di Geofisica Teorica ed Applicata* 21: 245–310.
1991   Four Thousand Years of Seismicity Along the Dead Sea Rift. *Journal of Geophysical Research* 96: 20,195–216.

Bentor, Y. K.; Vroman, A.; and Zak, I.
1965   *Geological Map of Israel*. Survey of Israel, Southern Sheet scale 1:250,000.

Black, E.; Hoskins, C.; Slingo, J.; and Brayshaw, D.
2011   The Present-Day Climate of the Middle East. Pp. 13–24 in S. Mithen and B. Black, B., eds., *Water, Life and Civilisation: Climate, Environment and Society in the Jordan Valley*. Cambridge: Cambridge University.

Bienkowski, P.
2006   The Wādī ʿArabah: Meanings in a Contested Landscape. Pp. 7–28 in P. Bienkowski and K. Galor, eds., *Crossing the Rift: Resources, Routes, Settlement Patterns and Interaction in the Wādī ʿArabah*. Levant Supplementary Series 3. Oxford: Oxbow.

Bilbesisi, M.
1992   Jordan's Water Resources and the Expected Domestic Demand by the Years 2009 and 2010, Detailed according to Area. Pp. 7–29 in A. Gärber and E. Salameh, eds., *Jordan's Water Resources and Their Future Potential*. Amman: Ebert.

Bookman, R.; Bartov, Y.; Enzel, Y.; and Stein, M.,
2006 Quaternary Lake Levels in the Dead Sea Basin: Two Centuries of Research. Pp. 155–70 in Y. Enzel, A. Agnon, and M. Stein, eds., *New Frontiers in Dead Sea Paleoenvironmental Research*. Geological Society of America Special Paper 401. Denver: Geological Society of America.

Bowman, D., and Gerson, R.
1986 Morphology of the Latest Quaternary Surface-Faulting in the Gulf of Elat Region, Eastern Sinai. *Tectonophysics* 128: 97–119.

Brock, S. P.
1977 A Letter Attributed to Cyril of Jerusalem on the Rebuilding of the Temple. *Bulletin of the School of Oriental and African Studies* 40: 267–86.

Brückner, H.
1999 Paläogeographische Küstenforschung am Golf van Aqaba im Bereich des Tell el-Kheleifeh, Jordanien. *Frankfurter Gewissenschaftliche Arbeiten, Series D, Physische Geographie* 25: 25–41.

Brückner, H.; Eichmann, R.; Herling, L.; Kallweit, H.; Kerner, S.; Khalil, L.; and Miqdadi, R.
2002 Chalcolithic and Early Bronze Age Sites Near Aqaba, Jordan. Pp. 217–331 in R. Eichmann, ed., *Ausgrabungen und Surveys im vorderen Orient I*. Orient-Archäologie 5. Rahden: Leidorf.

Bruins, H. J.
2006 Desert Environments and Geoarchaeology of the Wādī ʿArabah. Pp. 29-43 in P. Bienkowski and K. Galor, eds., *Crossing the Rift: Resources, Routes, Settlement Patterns and Interaction in the Wādī ʿArabah*. Levant Supplementary Series 3. Oxford: Oxbow.

Burdon, D. J.
1959 *Handbook of the Geology of Jordan*. Amman: Hashemite Kingdom of Jordan.

deMenocal, P.; Ortiz, J.; Guilderson, T.; and Sarnthein, M.,
2000 Abrupt Onset and Termination of the African Humid Period: Rapid Climate Responses to Gradual Insolation Forcing. *Quaternary Science Reviews* 19: 347–61.

De Meulemeester, J., and al-Shqour, R.
2008 Islamic Aqaba Project 2008: Unpublished Preliminary Report to the Department of Antiquities of Jordan.

Enzel, Y.; Amit, R.; Zilberman, E.; Harrison, J. B. J.; and Porat, N.
1996 Estimating the Ages of Fault Scarps in the Arava, Israel. *Tectonophysics* 253: 305–17.

Enzel, Y.; Bookman, R.; Sharon, D.; Gvirtzman, H.; Dayan, U.; Ziv, B.; and Stein, M.
2003 Late Holocene Climates of the Near East Deduced from Dead Sea Level Variations and Modern Regional Winter Rainfall. *Quaternary Research* 60: 263–73.

Enzel Y.; Amit, R.; Dayan, U.; Crouvi, O.; Kahana, R.; Ziv, B.; and Sharon, D.,
2008 The Climatic and Physiographic Controls of the Eastern Mediterranean over the Late Pleistocene Climates in the Southern Levant and its Neighboring Deserts. *Global and Planetary Change* 60.3–4: 165–92.

Erickson-Gini, T.
1999 Mampsis: A Nabataean Roman Settlement in the Central Negev Highlands in Light of the Ceramic and Architectural Evidence Found in Archaeological Excavations During 1993–1994, Unpublished M.A. dissertation, Tel Aviv University.
2004 Crisis and Renewal – Settlement in the Central Negev in the Third and Fourth Centuries C.E., With an Emphasis on the Finds from Recent Excavations in Mampsis, Oboda and Mezad ʿEn Hazeva. Unpublished Ph.D. dissertation, The Hebrew University in Jerusalem.

Fleitmann D.; Burns, S. J.; Mangini, A.; Mudelsee, M.; Kramers, J.; Villa, I.; Neff, U.; al-Subbarye, A. A.; Buettner, A.; Hippler, D.; and Matter. A.
2007 Holocene ITCZ and Indian Monsoon Dynamics Recorded in Stalagmites from Oman and Yemen (Socotra). *Quaternary Science Reviews* 26: 170–88.

Foote, R.; Wade, A.; El Bastawesy, M.; Oleson, J. P.;
and Mithen, S.
2011   A Millennium of Rainfall, Settlement and
        Water Management at Humayma, Southern
        Jordan, c. 2,050–1,150 BP (100 BC to AD
        800). Pp. 302–34 in S. Mithen and E. Black,
        eds., *Water, Life and Civilisation—Climate,
        Environment and Society in the Jordan Val-
        ley.* Cambridge: Cambridge University.

Frank, F.
1934   Aus der Araba I: Reiseberichte. *ZDPV* 57:
        191–280.

Freund, R.; Garfunkel, Z.; Zak, I.; Goldberg, M.;
Weissbro, T.; and Derin, B.
1970   The Shear Along the Dead Sea Rift. *Philo-
        sophical Transactions of the Royal Society
        of London, Series a - Mathematical and
        Physical Sciences* 267.1181: 107–30.

Friedman, G. M.
1965   A Fossil Shoreline Reef in the Gulf of Elat
        (Aqaba). *Israeli Journal of Earth Sciences* 14:
        86–90.

Frumkin, A.; Magaritz, M.; Carmi, I.; and Zak, I.
1991   The Holocene Climatic Record of the Salt
        Caves of Mount Sedom, Israel. *The Holo-
        cene* 1.3: 191–200.

Frumkin, A.
1997   The Holocene History of Dead Sea Lev-
        els. Pp. 237–48 in T. M. Niemi, Z. Ben-
        Avraham, and J. Gat, eds., *The Dead Sea:
        The Lake and Its Setting.* Oxford: Oxford
        University.

Garfunkel, Z.
1970   The Tectonics of the Western Margins of the
        Southern Arava: A Contribution to the Un-
        derstanding of Rifting. Unpublished Ph.D.
        Dissertation. Jerusalem, Hebrew University.
1981   Internal Structure of the Dead Sea Leaky
        Transform (rift) in Relation to Plate Kine-
        matics. *Tectonophysics* 80: 81–108.
1988   The pre-Quaternary Geology of Israel. Pp.
        7–24 in E. Yom-Tov and E. Tchernov, eds.,
        The Zoogeography of Israel. Dordrecht:
        Junk.

Garfunkel, Z.; Zak, I.; and Freund, R.
1981   Active Faulting in the Dead Sea Rift.
        Tectonophysics 80: 1–26.

Garfunkel, Z., and Ben-Avraham, Z.
1996   The Structure of the Dead Sea Basin.
        Tectonophysics 266: 155–76.

Ghawanmeh, Y. H.
1992   Earthquake Effects on Bilad Ash-Sham
        Settlements. Pp. 53–59 in *SHAJ* IV. Amman:
        Department of Antiquities of Jordan.

Gilat, A.; Shirav, M.; Bogoch, R.; Haliez, L.;
Avner, U.; and Nahlieli, D.
1993   Significance of Gold Exploitation in the
        Early Islamic Period. *JAS* 20: 429–37.

Grubisha, D.
1999   An Analysis of the Steatite Artifacts from
        the Archaeological Site of Aila, Jordan.
        Unpublished M.A.thesis, University of
        Wisconsin at Milwaukee.

Guidoboni, E.
1994   *Catalogue of Ancient Earthquakes in the
        Mediterranean Area up to the 10th Century.*
        Rome: Istituto Nazionale di Geofisica.

Guidoboni, E., and Comastri, A.
2005   *Catalogue of Ancient Earthquakes in the
        Mediterranean Area up to the 10th Century.*
        Rome: Istituto Nazionale di Geofisica.

Gvirtzman, G.
1994   Fluctuations of Sea Level During the past
        400,000 Years: The Records of Sinai, Egypt
        (Northern Red Sea). *Coral Reefs* 13: 203–14.

Gvirtzman, G.; Kronfeld, J.; and Buchbinder, B.
1992   Dated Coral Reefs of Southern Sinai (Red
        Sea) and Their Implication to Late Quater-
        nary Sea Levels. *Marine Geology* 108: 29–37.

Gupta, A. K.; Anderson, D. M.; and Overpeck, J. T.
2003   Abrupt Changes in the Asian Southwest
        Monsoon During the Holocene and Their
        Links to the North Atlantic Ocean. *Nature*
        421: 354–57.

Hamiel, Y.; Amit, R.; Begin, Z. B.; Marco, S.; Katz, O.; Salamon, A.; Zilberman, Z.; and Porat, N.
2009 The Seismicity Along the Dead Sea Fault During the Last 60,000 Years. *Bulletin of the Seismological Society of America* 99.3: 2020–26.

Hammond, P. C.
1959 The Nabataean Bitumen Industry at the Dead Sea. *BA* 22: 40–48.
1980 New Evidence for the 4th Century A.D. Destruction of Petra. *BASOR* 238: 65–67.

Hartman, G.
2011 Quaternary Evolution of a Transform Basin: The Northern Gulf of Eilat/Aqaba. Unpublished Ph.D. dissertation, Tel-Aviv University.

Hashemite Kingdom of Jordan
1956 Wādī ʿAraba topographic map, sheet 135/885, scale 1:25,000.
1956 ʿAqaba topographic map, sheet 135/875, scale 1:25,000.
1956 Jebel Abū Ridman topographic map, sheet 150/875, scale 1:25,000.
1982 Archaeological map: Amman, Jordan, Maʾan sheet 3, scale 1: 250,000.

Hauptmann, A.
2006 Mining Archaeology and Archaeometallurgy in the Wādī ʿArabah: The Mining District of Faynan and Timna. Pp. 125–33 in P. Bienkowski and K. Galor, eds., *Crossing the Rift: Resources, Routes, Settlement Patterns and Interaction in the Wādī ʿArabah.* Levant Supplementary Series 3. Oxford: Oxbow.

Hauptmann, A.; Khalil, L.; and Schmitt-Strecker, S.
2009 Evidence of Late Chalcolithic/Early Bronze Age I Copper Production from Timna Ores at Tall al-Magass, ʿAqaba. Pp. 295–304 in L. Khalil and K. Schmidt, eds., *Prehistoric ʿAqaba I.* Orient-Archäologie Band 23, Rahden: Leidorf.

Heemeier, B.; Rauen, A.; Waldhör, M.; and Grottker, M.
2009 Water Management at Tell Huyayrat al-Ghuzlan. Pp. 247-71 in L. Khalil and K.

Schmidt, eds., *Prehistoric ʿAqaba I.* Orient-Archäologie Band 23, Rahden: Leidorf.

Hein, C. J.; FitzGerald, D. M.; Milne, G. A.; Bard, K.; and Fattovich, R.
2011 Evolution of a Pharaonic Harbor on the Red Sea: Implications for Coastal Response to Changes in Sea Level and Climate. *Geology* 39.7: 687–90.

Hofstetter, R.; Gitterman, Y.; Pinksy, V.; Kraeva, N.; and Feldman, L.
2008 Seismological Observations of the Northern Dead Sea Basin Earthquake on 11 February 2004 and its Associated Activity. *Israel Journal of Earth Sciences* 57.2: 101–24.

Horowitz, A.
1992 *Palynology of Arid Lands.* Amsterdam: Elsevier.

Ibrahim, K. M
1991 *The Geology of the Wādī Rahma Map Sheet No. 3049 IV.* Bulletin 15, Geology Directorate, Geological Mapping Division, Hashemite Kingdom of Jordan, Ministry of Energy and Mineral Resources, Natural Resources Authority.
1993 *The Geology of the Wādī Gharandal Area Map Sheet No. 3050 II.* Bulletin 24, Geology Directorate, Geological Mapping Division, Hashemite Kingdom of Jordan, Ministry of Energy and Mineral Resources, Natural Resources Authority.

Ibrahim, K. M., and Abdelhamid, G. A.
1990 *Al Yamaniyya Clay Deposits.* Amman: Ministry of Energy and Mineral Resources, Natural Resources Authority, Geology Directorate.

Kallner, D. H.
1950–51 A Revised Earthquake-Catalogue of Palestine. *IEJ* 1.4: 223–46.

Kedar, B. Z.
1999 *The Changing Land Between the Jordan and the Sea: Aerial Photographs from 1917 to the Present.* Jerusalem: Yad Ben-Zvi.

Khalil, L.
1995   The Second Season of Excavation at al-Magass-'Aqaba, 1990. *ADAJ* 39: 65–79.

Khalil, L., and Schmidt, K.
2009   *Prehistoric 'Aqaba I.* Orient-Archäologie Band 23, Rahden: Leidorf.

Khatib, F.
1987   *Geologic map of Al Yamaniyya and Jabal Al Mubarak: Map sheet 2948 I and 3048 IV.* Bulletin 27, Geology Directorate, Geological Mapping Division, Hashemite Kingdom of Jordan, Ministry of Energy and Mineral Resources, Natural Resources Authority.

Klimscha.F.
2009   Radiocarbon Dates from Prehistoric 'Aqaba and Other Related Sites from the Chalcolithic Period. Pp. 363–401 in L. Khalil and K. Schmidt, eds., *Prehistoric 'Aqaba I.* Orient-Archäologie Band 23, Rahden: Leidorf.

Korjenkov, A. M., and Erickson-Gini, T.
2003   The Seismic Origin of the Destruction of the Nabataean Forts of Ein Erga and Ein Rahel, Arava Valley, Israel. *Archäologischer Anzeiger* 2: 39–50.

Le Béon, M.; Klinger, Y.; al-Qaryouti, M.; Mériaux, A.-S.; Finkel, R. C.; Elias, A.; Mayyas, O.; Ryerson, F. J.; and Tapponnier, P.
2010   Holocene and Late Pleistocene Slip Rate of the Southern Dead Sea Transform Determined from [10]Be Cosmogenic Dating of Offset Alluvial fans. *Journal of Geophysical Research* 115, B11414, doi:10.1029/2009JB007198.

Lloyd, J. W., and Pim, R. H.
1990   The Hydrogeology and Groundwater Resources Development of the Cambro-Ordovician Sandstone Aquifer in Saudi Arabia and Jordan. *Journal of Hydrology* 121.1–4: 1–20.

MacDonald, M.
1966   *Report on the Water Supply Potential of the Wādī Yutm.* London: Hunting Geology and Geophysics Ltd.

Malkawi, A. H.; Numayr, K.;S.; and Barakat, A. B.
1999   The Aqaba Earthquake of November 22, 1995. *Earthquake Spectra* 15.3: 397–415.

Mansoor, N.
2002   A GIS-based Assessment of Active Faults and Liquefaction Potential of the City of Aqaba, Jordan. Unpublished Master's thesis. University of Missouri-Kansas City.

Mansoor, N.; Niemi, T. M.; and Misra, A.
2004   A GIS-based Assessment of the Liquefaction Potential of the City of Aqaba, Jordan. *Environmental and Engineering Geoscience* 10.4: 297–320.

Mabry, J. B.
1992   Alluvial Cycles and Early Agricultural Settlement Phases in the Jordan Valley. Unpublished Doctoral Dissertation, University of Arizona.

McClure, H. A.
1976   Radiocarbon Chronology of Late Quaternary Lakes in the Arabian Desert. *Nature* 263: 755–56.

McCourt, W. J. and Ibrahim, K.
1990   *The Geology, Geochemistry and Tectonic Settig of the Granitic and Associated Rocks in the Aqaba and Araba Compleses of Southwest Jordan.* Bulletin 10, Geology Directorate, Geological Mapping Division, Hashemite Kingdom of Jordan, Ministry of Energy and Mineral Resources, Natural Resources Authority.

Meimaris, Y. E., and Kritikakou-Nikolaropoulou, K. I.
2005   *Inscriptions from Palaestina Tertia,* Vol. Ia: *The Greek Inscriptions from Ghor es-Safi (Byzantine Zoora).* Athens: The National Hellenic Research Foundation.

Melkawi, A.; 'Amr, K.; and Whitcomb, D. S.
1994   The Excavation of Two Seventh Century Pottery Kilns at Aqaba. *ADAJ* 38: 447–68.

Meloy J. L.
1991   Results of Archaeological Reconnaissance in West Aqaba: Evidence of Pre-Islamic Settlement. *ADAJ* 35: 397–414.

Meshel, Z.
2006 Were There Gold Mines in the Eastern 'Arabah? Pp 231-38 in P. Bienkowski and K. Galor, eds., *Crossing the Rift: Resources, Routes, Settlement Patterns and Interaction in the Wādī 'Arabah.* Levant Supplementary Series 3. Oxford: Oxbow.

Migowski, C.; Stein, M.; Prasad, S.;
Negendank, J. F. W.; and Agnon, A.
2006 Holocene Climate Variability and Cultural Evolution in the Near East from the Dead Sea Sedimentary Record. *Quaternary Research* 66.3: 421–31.

Morcos, S. A.
1970 Physical and Chemical Oceanography of the Red Sea. *Oceanography Marine Biology Annual Review* 8: 73–202.

Moustafa, Y. A.; Patzold, J.; Loya, Y.; and Wefer, G.
2000 Mid-Holocene Stable Isotope Record of Corals from the Northern Red Sea. *International Journal of Earth Sciences* 88: 742–51.

Niemi, T. M., and Smith, A. M., II
1999 Initial Results of the Southeastern Wādī 'Araba, Jordan Geoarchaeological Study: Implications for Shifts in Late Quaternary Aridity. *Geoarchaeology* 14.8: 791–820.

Nissenbaum, A.
1993 The Dead Sea–An Economic Resource for 10,000 Years. *Hydrobiologia* 267: 127–41.

Okour, M. A.; Abu Laila, J.; and Qararraa', M. E.
2006 *Mineral Status and Future Opportunity – Gold.* Geological Survey Administration, Hashemite Kingdom of Jordan, Ministry of Energy and Mineral Resources, Natural Resources Authority.

Parker, S. T.
1997a Human Settlement at the Northern Head of the Gulf of al-'Aqaba: Evidence of Site Migration. Pp. 189–93 in G. Bisheh, M. Zaghloul, and I. Kehrberg, eds., *SHAJ* VI. Amman: Department of Antiquities of Jordan.
1997b Preliminary Report on the 1994 Season of the Roman Aqaba Project. *BASOR* 305: 19–44.

1998 The Roman 'Aqaba Project: The 1996 Campaign. *ADAJ* 42: 375–94.
2000 The Roman 'Aqaba Project: The 1997 and 1998 Campaigns. *ADAJ* 44: 373–94.
2003 The Roman 'Aqaba Project: The 2002 Campaign. *ADAJ* 47: 321–33.
2009 *Arabia Adquisita:* The Roman Annexation of Arabia Reconsidered. Pp. 1585–92 in A. Morillo, N. Hanel, and E. Martín, eds., *Limes XX: Roman Frontier Studies. XXth International Congress of Roman Frontier Studies.* 3 vols. Madrid: Consejo Superior de Investigaciones Científicas.

Philby, H. St. J. B.
1925 The Dead Sea to 'Aqaba. *The Geographical Journal* 66.2: 134–55.

Poirier, J. P., and Taher, M. A.
1980 Historical Seismicity in the Near and Middle East, North Africa and Spain from Arabic Documents (VIIth–XVIIIth Century). *Bulletin of the Seismological Society of America* 70: 2185–201.

Porat, N.; Amit, R.; Enzel, Y.; Zilberman, E.;
Avni, Y.; Ginat, H.; and Gluck, D.
2010 Abandonment Ages of Alluvial Landforms in the Hyperarid Negev Determined by Luminescence. *Journal of Arid Environments* 74: 861–69.

Pratico, G. D.
1993 *Nelson Glueck's 1938–1940 Excavations at Tell el-Kheleifeh: A Reappraisal.* American Schools of Oriental Research Archaeological Reports 3. Atlanta: Scholars.

Quennell, A. M.
1956 *Geological Map of Jordan (East of the Rift Valley):* Ma'an map sheet 3, scale 1:250,000, Department of Lands and Surveys of Jordan.
1959 Tectonics of the Dead Sea Rift. Pp. 385–405 in *Proceedings of the 20th International Geological Congress, Mexico, 1956.* Mexico City: Associacion de Servicos Geologicos Africanos.

Rabb'a, I.
1994 *The Geology of the Al Qurayqira (Jabal Hamra Faddan). Map Sheet No. 3051 II.*

Geology Directorate, Geological Mapping Division, Hashemite Kingdom of Jordan, Ministry of Energy and Mineral Resources, Natural Resources Authority.

Rashdan, M.
1988 *The Regional Geology of the Aqaba-Wādī 'Araba Area, Map Sheets 3049 III, 2949 II.* Ministry of Energy and Mineral Resources, Natural Resources Authority, Geology Directorate, Amman, Jordan, Bulletin 7.

Reches, Z.
1987 Mechanical Aspects of Pull-apart Basins and Push-up Swells with Application to the Dead Sea Transform. *Tectonophysics* 141: 75–88.

Reches, Z.; Erez, J.; Garfunkel, Z.
1987 Sedimentary and Tectonic Features in the Northwestern Gulf of Eilat, Israel. *Tectonophysics* 141: 169–80.

Rucker, J. D., and Niemi, T. M.
2005 New Excavations of the City Wall at Islamic Ayla in Aqaba, Jordan. *ADAJ* 49: 501–8.

Russell, K. W.
1980 The Earthquake of May 19, A.D. 363. *BASOR* 238: 47–64.
1985 The Earthquake Chronology of Palestine and Northwest Arabia from the 2nd Through the mid-8th Century A.D. *BASOR* 260: 37–59.

Ryan, J.
1995 Roman Aqaba Project Area G: Field Report. Unpublished report.

Saqqa, W., and Atallah, M.
2004 Characterization of the Aeolian Terrain Facies in Wādī 'Araba Desert, Southwest Jordan. *Geomophology* 62.1–2: 63–87.

Schmid, S. G.
1997 Nabataean Fine Ware Pottery and the Destruction of Petra in the Late First and Early Second Century AD. Pp. 413–20 in G. Bisheh, M. Zaghloul, and I. Kehrberg, eds., *SHAJ* VI. Amman: Department of Antiquities of Jordan.

Shaked, Y.; Agnon, A.; Lazar, B.; Marcio, S.; Avner, U.; and Stein, M.
2004 Large Earthquakes Kill Coral Reefs at the North-west Gulf of Aqaba. *Terra Nova* 16: 133–38.

Siegel, U.
2009 Hydrological Structures in the Wādī al-Yutum Fan in the Vicinity of Tell Ḥujeirat al-Ghuzlan. Pp. 273–94 in L. Khalil and K. Schmidt, eds., *Prehistoric 'Aqaba I.* Orient-Archäologie Band 23, Rahden: Leidorf.

Slater, L., and Niemi, T. M.
2003 Detection of Active Faults Along the Dead Sea Transform Using Ground Penetrating Radar and Implications for Seismic Hazards Within the City of Aqaba, Jordan. *Tectonophysics* 368: 33–50.

Smith, A. M., II, and Niemi, T. M.
1994 Results of the Southeast Araba Reconnaissance. *ADAJ* 38: 1–15.

Smith, A. M., II; Stevens, M.; and Niemi, T. M.
1997 Southeast Araba Archaeological Survey: A Preliminary Report of the 1994 Season. *BASOR* 305: 45–71.

Sneh, A.; Bartov, Y.; Weissbrod, T.; and Rosensaft, M.,
1998 *Geological Map of Israel, 1:200,000.* Israel Geological Survev. (4 sheets).

Staubwasser M.; Sirocko, F.; Grootes, P. M.; and Segl, M.
2003 Climate Change at the 4.2 ka BP Termination of the Indus Valley Civilization and Holocene South Asian Monsoon Variability. *Geophysical Research Letters* 30: 1425. Doi:10.1029/2002GLo16822

Stucky, R. A.
1996 Die Nabatäischen Bauten. Pp. 13–50 in A. M. Bignasca et al., eds., *Petra ez Zantur, I, Ergebnisse der Schweizerisch-Liechtensteinischen Ausgrabungen 1988–1992.* Terra Archaeologica 2. Mainz: von Zabern.

Stucky, R. A., et al.
1990   Schweizer Ausgrabungen in Ez Zantur, Pe-
        tra: Vorbericht der Kampagne 1988. *ADAJ*
        34: 249–83.

Tarawneh, B.
1992   *The Geology of the Fifa Area Map Sheet No.
        3051 I.* Bulletin 20, Geology Directorate,
        Geological Mapping Division, Hashemite
        Kingdom of Jordan, Ministry of Energy
        and Mineral Resources, Natural Resources
        Authority.

Tarawneh, B.; Yasin, S.; Madanat, M.; Mehyar, N.;
and al-Omari, Y.
2006   *Mineral Status and Future Opportunity
        – Gypsum.* Geological Survey Adminis-
        tration, Hashemite Kingdom of Jordan,
        Ministry of Energy and Mineral Resources,
        Natural Resources Authority, 2 Maps.

ten Brink, U. S.; Rybakov, M.; al-Zoubi, A. S.;
Hassouneh, M.; Frieslander, U.; Batayneh, A. T.;
Goldschmidt, V.; Daoud, M. N.; Rotstein, Y.;
and Hall, J. K.
1999   Anatomy of the Dead Sea Transform; Does
        it Reflect Continuous Changes in Plate
        Motion? *Geology* 27.10: 887–90.

Thomas, R.; Niemi, T. M.; and Parker, S. T.
2007   Structural Damage from Earthquakes in
        the 2nd–9th Century at the Archaeological
        Site of Aila in Aqaba, Jordan. *BASOR* 346:
        59–77.

Tibor, G.; Niemi, T. M.; Ben-Avraham, Z.; al-Zoubi,
A.; Sade, R. A.; Hall, J. K.; Hartman, G.; Akawwi,
E.; Abueladas, A.; and al-Ruzouq, R.
2010   Active Tectonic Morphology and Subma-
        rine Deformation of the Northern Gulf of
        Eilat/Aqaba from Analyses of Multibeam
        data. *Geo-Marine Letters* 30: 561–73.

Whitcomb, D. S.
1993   Earthquakes in Aqaba. Unpublished Manu-
        script.
1994   *Ayla: Art and Industry in the Islamic Port
        of Aqaba.* Chicago: University of Chicago,
        Oriental Institute.
1997   The Town and Name of 'Aqaba: An In-
        quiry into the Settlement History from an
        Archaeological Perspective. Pp. 359–63 in
        G. Bisheh, M. Zaghloul, and I. Kehrberg,
        eds., *SHAJ* VI. Amman: Department of
        Antiquities of Jordan.
2006   Land Behind Aqaba: The Wādī 'Arabah
        During the Early Islamic Period. Pp 239–42
        in P. Bienkowski and K. Galor, eds., *Cross-
        ing the Rift: Resources, Routes, Settlement
        Patterns and Interaction in the Wādī 'Arabah.*
        Levant Supplementary Series 3. Oxford:
        Oxbow.

Yakir, D.; Issar, A.; Gat, J.; Adar, E.; Trimborn, P.;
and Lipp, J.
1994 ^{13}C and ^{18}O of Wood from the Roman Siege
        Rampart in Masada, Israel (AD 70–73):
        Evidence for a Less Arid Climate for the
        Region. *Geochimica et Cosmochimica Acta*
        58: 3535–39.

Zilberman, E.; Amit, R.; Porat, N.; Enzel, Y.;
and Avner, U.
2005   Surface Ruptures Induced by the Devastat-
        ing 1068 AD Earthquake in the Southern
        Arava Valley, Dead Sea Rift, Israel. *Tecto-
        nophysics* 408.1–4: 79–99.

Chapter 3

Fish, Dates and Flying Machines: Ethno-History and Aerial Photography in the Investigation of Aqaba, Jordan

by John D. Rucker and Tina M. Niemi

I. INTRODUCTION

The modern city of Aqaba (population ca. 100,000) lies at the northern end of the Gulf of Aqaba (fig. 3.1), the easternmost of the two branches of the Red Sea that extend north on both the east and the west sides of the Sinai Peninsula. The Gulf of Aqaba is a part of the same tectonic system that extends from the great African Rift Valley in East Africa, through the Red Sea, and into the Wādī 'Araba to the Dead Sea. Aqaba lies on the eastern side of the end of the Gulf, on Jordan's ca. 26 km of coastline. As such, it is the country's only seaport and thus is an invaluable center for international trade and commerce. Aqaba today is a lovely oasis of palm trees, luxury hotels, and blue ocean water — when viewed from the north. However, to the east dramatic pinkish granitic mountains, cut by dark igneous dykes, provide a striking vista, but limit both the view and the local environment. To the west is the modern border with Israel and that country's port on the Red Sea, Eilat. Extending north beyond the urban sprawl of Eilat are similar mountains that form the western boundary of Wādī 'Araba. Just as the Gulf of Aqaba extends south from Aqaba, Aqaba itself sits at the southern end of Wādī 'Araba — the other major element in its environment. This valley,

extending 166 km from the Gulf of Aqaba to the Dead Sea, is one of the hottest and driest places on earth with a mean annual temperature of 24–25° Centigrade and annual rainfall of under 50 mm per year.

In 2004, the Jordanian Administrative District of Wādī 'Araba contained only 4175 inhabitants, excluding the city of Aqaba itself (Jordan Department of Statistics, 2004 census). In contrast to the sparsely populated valley, modern Aqaba is a bustling port and tourist destination, nestled into the shadow of forbidding mountains in a very unforgiving environment, with one exception. Historically, groundwater in Aqaba has been fresh, abundant, and accessible only a few meters below the surface in most areas. This water until quite recently was adequate for its population, although there has been some infiltration of brackish water into the aquifer. This resource makes Aqaba a coastal oasis as reflected by its vegetation, including the date palm plantation noted by early European visitors (e.g., Burton 1879: 241; fig. 3.2). Even with abundant groundwater in the immediate vicinity, the date palms seem to be the only agriculture practiced on a large scale around the city in recent times.

At different times in the 20th century both the Turks and the British maintained significant

FIG. 3.1   *Google Earth image of Aqaba region from June 6, 2010.*

garrisons in Aqaba, although apparently with little interaction with local residents. Within the last 50 years, Aqaba began to remake itself with some success into a major tourist destination and a duty free special economic zone.

This chapter has several goals. First and foremost is to understand the chronology of the complex manmade structures and human-influenced landforms from a variety of periods, all extant in the environs of Aqaba. Since the desert environment tends to prevent the building of deep stratigraphy, in some cases somewhat deflating sites (excluding tells), a desert surface may contain a Neolithic rock alignment, a Nabataean stone wall, and the foundation of a hut from the British Mandate — with no stratigraphy to provide dating evidence. Therefore the ethno-historical approach is an important tool in elucidating at least one of the above. Aqaba in particular is rife with modern military trenches and structures (fig. 3.3). Many contain corrugated metal, modern concrete, or other tell-tale signs of modernity. Unfortunately, many others are not so clear, especially absent excavation. Thus the memories of local residents are of prime importance.

A secondary goal of the ethno-historical approach in this project is to involve the local community in the project, to give them a sense of ownership or, in some cases, even awareness over what is, after all, their cultural heritage. Thus, ideally, this research will be beneficial to both subject and researcher, as both gain new understanding of the culture and history of the area. It was obviously vital to record these memories before they were lost forever. Further, the rapid development of Aqaba is destroying the archaeological record nearly as rapidly as the march of time is winnowing the population of those who remember the events and lifestyles of the past. These folk informed us as to which sites or structures are in fact modern and in many cases their memories were the only record of now lost antiquities and ancient sites.

FIG. 3.2 *Images of the area around the Aqaba Castle. A) Roberts' lithograph of the exterior of the castle. B) Alois Musil's 1910 photograph of Aqaba with the castle. C) Photograph of the "custom house and fort" or castle of Aqaba.*

II. SPECIFIC RESEARCH QUESTIONS AND METHODS

With the above larger goals in mind, we hoped to gain some insight into four specific topics about the history and archaeology of Aqaba:

1. *Origins of Wādī Ayla:* The wadi cutting through the corner of the early Islamic site of Ayla was

tentatively identified as a fault line (Whitcomb 1994). More recent excavations (Rucker and Niemi 2005) revealed no significant fault offset of structures in the wadi channel. Our informants stated that the British, in fact, cut the wadi as a diversion channel to keep runoff from the Wādī Yutum away from the area which today is the Yacht Club harbor (fig. 3.4).

2. *Origins of walls and enigmatic structures north of Aqaba:* Numerous walls and enigmatic structures exist on the alluvial fan north of Aqaba in the Wādī Yutum drainage, presumably for flood diversion or water catchment. Some may be related to the maintenance of a small British air strip in the area, but others may be ancient and, thus, may shed light on hydrological engineering of the region in antiquity.

3. *Folk knowledge of antiquities:* It is well-known amongst survey archaeologists that local residents are generally aware of significant and, in some cases, rather obscure archaeological sites and antiquities. This knowledge is rarely accurate as to date and type but often quite accurate as to location. Loose cooperation between local residents (for location) and archaeologists (for explication) of archaeological sites is common in North American and British archaeology, and is becoming more common elsewhere in the world. This study uses local knowledge to enhance understanding of ancient ruins in Aqaba.

4. *Explication of modern military features:* By accident or the providence of strategy and settlement patterns (i.e., a convenient or strategic location tends to maintain its desirability over time) many archaeological sites in and around Aqaba are covered with modern military installations. These range from extensive trenches and bunkers to small structures of all kinds. Large walls and water channels also may be modern military construction.

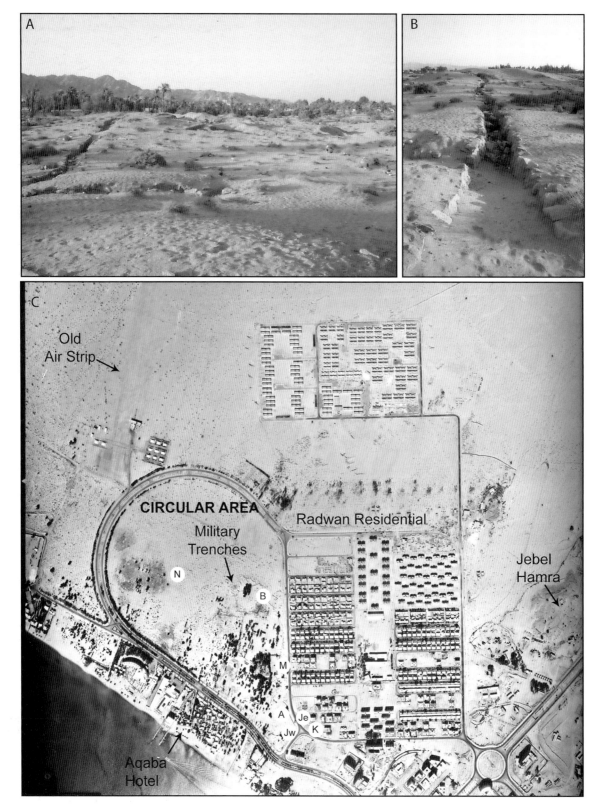

FIG. 3.3   *The circular area of Aqaba showing WWII military trenches and excavation areas. A) View toward the south. B) View north along a trench to the G-8 Mound area. C) Aerial photograph of the Circular Area of Aqaba from 1978.*

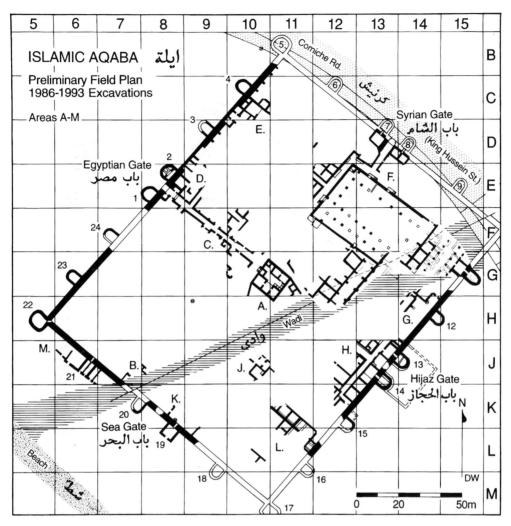

FIG. 3.4   *Plan of the Islamic site of Ayla, excavated by Whitcomb, illustrating the wadi cut by the British (reprinted from Whitcomb 2009: 124, fig.1, with permission).*

While it is vital to separate these from the underlying antiquities, one must also remember that these are an important part of the archaeological and historical record of modern Aqaba and worthy of explication in their own right. Obviously any light that could be shed by local residents on their construction would be significant.

This study is only the beginning of exploration of this subject in the Aqaba region. It makes no pretense of randomness or statistical validity. In some sense this research could be considered "salvage" ethnology, as local knowledge dies along with the generation of people who remember it. With the assistance of various locals, we made contact with three elderly local residents who had lived in the Aqaba region all their lives, and who were willing to be interviewed about their lives and the history of Aqaba as they experienced it. In all three cases the subject was an elderly family member of a local Aqaba resident known to the authors, who was present and sometimes acted as an Arabic/English translator. Each interview was recorded on cassette tape in May 2004 and transcribed immediately following the interview. Contact was later made with the fourth subject, a British soldier from New Zealand who was stationed in Aqaba in 1949. He answered questions and shared his memories of Aqaba via email.

III. INTERVIEWS

Interview 1

Adel Mohammad Fakhri

Born 1929 (aged 75 when interviewed);
lived in Aqaba entire life.
Shahima Kabariti (his wife, 61 years old);
lived in Aqaba entire life

Mr. Fakhri began by describing some aspects of life in Aqaba in his father's and grandfather's time during the Turkish occupation, which ended in 1917. Before then Aqaba was considered part of Saudi Arabia; in fact, it was called "little Hejaz." His family originally came from the Hejaz. His grandfather owned a large house near that of Sharif Hussein (the current Aqaba Museum), who stayed there when he came from Hejaz (fig 3.2). Later Emir Feisal stayed in Mr. Fakhri's grandfather's house for one year after Feisal (assisted by T. E. Lawrence) took Aqaba in 1917 during the Arab revolt. This house was torn down by the city in the 1960s. Mr. Fakhri's father, Mohammad Hassan Fakhri, was a soldier in the Turkish army before 1917. The Turks lived in mudbrick buildings around the castle during their occupation of Aqaba and also built a watchtower at or near the current location of Gate #4 of the modern port of Aqaba. This site was called Tell el Braij ('tower'?) and its purpose was to observe shipping activity in the gulf, specifically British ships. At this time Aqaba consisted only of the settlement around and upslope from the castle. This was the settlement pattern until about 1940.

Mr. Fakhri continued the discussion with some reminiscences from his youth. The main well for all of Aqaba was just west of the castle. The water was only 2 m below the surface and very sweet. Another well was inside the castle, but apparently the only source of water for the general population was the exterior one. Other water sources were apparently not sweet/potable. He described cranking a windlass to raise the bucket of water to fill containers on donkey-back for transport to his house. The people subsisted primarily on fish and dates (from the ubiquitous date palms to the north and south of the old city). Fish was apparently the ubiquitous food

in Aqaba, as implied by such quotes as "too much fish," "everyday- fish," "the sea is like an icebox" (i.e., you can just reach in and grab a fish whenever you want one). Apparently fish was only eaten fresh and was not a significant trade item. He did also point out that the current scarcity of sharks in the Gulf is a recent phenomenon. He also mentioned some small-scale farming/gardening but not any trade in produce. There was also no emphasis on herding whatsoever — "maybe some Bedouin have some sheep." Aqaba residents apparently differentiated themselves from the Bedouin. Mr. Fakhri did not offer any personal tribal affiliation. Every 15 days, a car came from the town of Ma'an to the north with flour, sugar, and other staples. These products came from Amman to Ma'an by train and were then transported to Aqaba. Some were consumed locally, while the rest were sold for further trade into Saudi Arabia. A major source of money for Aqaba families at this time was the salaries of young men serving in the army. In 1940 the population of Aqaba was no more than 500.

Mr. Fakhri then described the activities of the British during their occupation of Aqaba between 1940 and 1951. He described several separate British encampments: a "big barracks" west of the old city, housing for the British families (our other informants did not mention dependents with the British militay) in the area now occupied by the Princess Haya Hospital, Tell al-Hamra, and the British airstrip. The British also built the road from Aqaba north to Ras an-Naqab and the protected harbor now used by the Royal Yacht Club. (Mr. Fakhri's daughter, Sawson Fakhri, Inspector of the Aqaba region of the Department of Antiquities, reported finding two Roman milestones in the construction debris of the Yacht Club harbor.) He said that the British forces here were not less than 2000 men and included tanks, which were unloaded at the Yacht Club harbor from "a big ship with a big mouth" (clearly a description of some kind of landing craft). The British encampments consisted of two kinds of structures. The barracks for the soldiers were of concrete blocks with corrugated sheet metal roofs. Structures housing the families were more substantial, of metal and concrete (perhaps in a Quonset hut style). The British also engaged in significant hydrological engineering in 1940, with two major projects affecting the drainage system in the Aqaba area. The first was a diversion wall or berm to direct runoff from the Wādī Yutum to the southwest, around the British encampments to reach the Gulf near the former Coral Beach Hotel and current Royal Palace. The second was the cutting of the wadi that currently bisects Islamic Ayla and enters the Gulf between the Yacht Club and the Mövenpick Hotel. The purpose for this channel is less immediately clear. Mr. Fakhri remembered the British using heavy equipment, especially bulldozers, for both these projects. The Aqaba airstrip was apparently not overly busy at this time. He told of one plane arriving per day carrying 6 people. The fare from Amman to Aqaba was 3 Jordanian Dinars (JD) and it was possible to charter a plane for 21 JD.

Mr. Fakhri then described some of his own activities as a young man just before, during, and immediately after the British occupation. He remembered Nelson Glueck's work at Tell el-Kheleifeh (in 1938–1940). His cousin worked for Glueck at a rate of 100 *fils* (10% of 1 JD) per day. He himself claims to have had the first private car in Aqaba in 1952, a 1948 Dodge, which he bought in Amman for 250 JD and used as a taxi. He charged British soldiers 1 shilling for a ride from their camp to the beach. At this time, there was little west of Aqaba (what is now the modern city of Eilat across the Israeli border), apart from Umm Rashrash, a small mudbrick hut with 6 Jordanian soldiers. Mr. Fakhri was tasked with riding a donkey to take them both mail and water. Apparently there was no good source of potable water on what is now the Israeli side.

Mr. Fakhri had little to say about the period of the various Arab/Israeli conflicts. Glubb Pasha was peaceful here with the Israelis. "Nothing happened here in 1949 or 1967." The translation of the interview was somewhat problematic at this point, but it was generally clear that Mr. Fakhri felt that there had been no significant conflict here. He did mention that it was during this period that Aqaba first got electrical power in 1952 (the British military installations had it much earlier).

With regard to the local antiquities, Mr. Fakhri was somewhat more illuminating. He recalled that there was some evidence of ancient material on Tell al-Hamra, but was not able to elaborate

further. The most significant information relating to antiquities he recalled was the existence of an additional (previously unreported?) tell in Aqaba. "Tell Jermi" was described as a very high tell located under what is now the Moon Beach Hotel and the Maltrans building, NW of the castle. The Turks used this tell as a cemetery; the name is apparently derived from a "*sheik kabir*" ("big sheikh") who had a tomb there. The government removed it when the Corniche Road was built in the 1960s. Mr. Fakhri had no other knowledge of antiquities in the area. He was unaware when questioned about the "Roman arch" and other extant ruins mentioned by certain early explorers,

When questioned about earthquakes, Mr. Fakhri could only recall the November 1995 Nuweiba quake, which made his whole house rock back and forth in a dramatic fashion (this was acted out).

Interview 2

Shafia'ah al Badhri

Born 1924 (aged 80 when interviewed); lived in Aqaba entire life

Mrs. Al Badhri was interviewed in company with and with the assistance of her son, Dr. Mohammad al Badhri, M.P. Her maiden name was Abu Unif, and her mother and grandmother were also from Aqaba. In fact, she said "family always from Aqaba." Her son was of the opinion that the family may have originated from the Hejaz.

She offered some reminiscences about her early life in Aqaba, before the arrival of the British military. Her family lived in the old city of Aqaba, near the sea, around the castle. Aqaba was a small place, with roughly 200–300 families. They lived in a house of mudbrick with two rooms and a terrace, although houses built of local stone were not unknown. There was no cement, just mud and stones. People lived a simple life with some small-scale gardening and farming, particularly of tomatoes and watermelons. There was no other work, except fishing. There was some grazing of sheep and goats, but apparently only for local use, not for trade. Fishing was apparently the main occupation; she said,

"Everybody has a (fishing) boat." Other goods came from Egypt in boats, which were drawn up on the beach to unload. There was some small-scale trade in fish, fruit, and vegetables, but the main trade item seems to have been dried dates. There were many more date palms then than now. The people of Aqaba dried dates both for their own use in the winter months and for trade. She recalled that some boats also came from Saudi Arabia to trade as well. The money used was the Palestinian pound. Water was obtained almost entirely from the well near the castle, which was called the 'sit' well. Water was drawn up with a bucket on a wire and then carried home in a *zir* (ceramic jar) or in a yoke with two buckets. She recalled that the water at the castle was not good, saying it was only "half and half" sweet.

Mrs. Al Badhri also shared some more personal details of her life in Aqaba. She had two sisters and two brothers, all now deceased. One of her brothers served in the British army. She was the first of her husband's two wives. She had six girls, so her husband married another woman in an attempt to have a son. Mrs. Al Badhri then had four boys, three of whom were present at the interview. The second wife had three girls and four boys. She stated that there was little tension between the wives and their respective offspring "because they lived in two houses." Her husband died in 1973. She shed some light on the status of women in Aqaba prior to the British occupation. In those days women rarely ("never") left the house. They spent their time cooking, cleaning, washing, etc. Women sometimes went swimming, but only fully dressed. Some women smoked the *arghileh*. There was no doctor in Aqaba, but all the women helped each other in childbirth. Women knew which herbs to use for sick children (*maramia, babaunage*).

Mrs. al Badhri's memories about the British occupation were less detailed than those of other interviewees. One of her sons attributed this to "women not leaving the house in those days." She did remember the British army presence, but did not recall numbers, except to say, "Too many British come." She recalls the British building a hospital and generally good relations with the British soldiers. They gave the people of Aqaba goods such as sugar. Before this, small boats brought these goods (including tea) from Egypt.

Mrs. Al Badhri had some memories about overland travel. She has never left Aqaba, except to go to Ma'an, which she did not do until it was possible by truck. Her parents' generation had to make the same trip by camel, which took one week. One of the Hajj routes, especially for pilgrims from North Africa before 1948, came through Aqaba. There was a Hajj camp near the King Hussein mosque in the old city. From Aqaba some Hajj pilgrims apparently took ships to Saudi Arabia.

Mrs. Al Badhri had relatively little knowledge of either antiquities or stories about events before she was born. She was vaguely aware of the Turkish tower near the Turkish port and the cemetery on Tell Jermi, but also said "the government took all the antiquities."

She remembered the first Arab/Israeli conflict mainly in terms of the refugees who came here. In 1948–49 many, many Palestinians came here, "too many thousand." They moved into the old city, where they were apparently made welcome. Every family kept some Palestinians as guests in their home because they came with nothing and had no food. Most of them came from Beersheba. The Palestinians mostly became businessmen (this possibly hints at a more difficult social interaction than expressed here).

Mrs. Al Badhri had some other reminiscences that do not fit easily into the above categories. She remembers flooding that destroyed houses and roads in the old city, when "people died." This happened many times. There were apparently many big sharks here, "somebody here, the sharks, they eat the hand." Her husband, who was taught to read by a private tutor, had the first library in Aqaba. Before 1948, there was no radio in Aqaba. Electricity came to Aqaba in 1950 and the city water system became operational in 1958. Before 1948, Ma'an was a much more important place than Aqaba. She also recalled earthquakes near the castle, with cracks, but nobody died. Her husband owned land in the Circular Area, which was otherwise empty at the time (though she also mentioned that the well in their current house in the Circular Area was 120 years old).

Interview 3

Fu'ad Hillawi

Born 1935 (aged 69 when interviewed);
lived in Aqaba all his life

Mr. Hillawi was interviewed in the Hillawi souvenir shop with his cousin Khamel acting as interpreter, although he often used English himself. His father and his two brothers lived within a family complex in the old city. His father was Hassan Hillawi, who worked for the British as a guard at the harbor. His grandfather came to Aqaba from Ma'an. Neither his father nor his grandfather could read. The three families lived in a complex of three houses in the old city, on the seaside near the castle. The three families, totaling 26 people, cooked and ate together.

Mr. Hillawi stated that at that time it was not unusual for several families to live together in one house. The main produce of Aqaba was fish and dates. He and his cousin Khamel (54) remembered carrying water from the well near the castle, which was known for its sweet water, which they attributed to its depth. In 1948 his family moved to a house on the beach between the current Mövenpick Hotel and the Aqaba Hotel.

Mr. Hillawi was particularly loquacious on the subject of fish and water-borne trade. He said that fish were so plentiful you could walk along the beach and pick them up (where they had beached themselves fleeing larger fish). He also said that there were many sharks but there was not any trouble with them. He described fishing trips lasting only one day until ice became available. Before the British army came, a man named "Spinney" [sp?] built an ice and a soda factory near the old [Turkish] harbor. When ice was available, fishing trips lasting up to six days farther down both sides of the Gulf were possible. (Interpretation: it is interesting to note that prior to the British arrival and construction in the Aqaba area, there were no long fishing trips. This implies either more fish consumption, the introduction of new technologies that allowed preservation of a larger harvest, or a reduction in the local fish supply, i.e., overfishing.) He also described the process of fish-

ing with "bombs." These explosives must have been acquired from the British. There was a famous local incident where a fisherman blew off his hands with these. When asked about the vessels that came to port in Aqaba before the British military arrived, Mr. Hillawi described ships from Egypt laden with staples such as sugar, rice, and tea. According to his recollection, these vessels had two sails and were manned by around six sailors. A ship arrived about every two or three months. He said that one of these vessels can still be seen onshore near the Yacht Club (fig. 3.5; there is a traditional wooden ship preserved onshore, currently on the jetty of the Yacht Club, but more recently another example has been placed in an artificial pool in the Aqaba Gateway development). The local boats were all small dinghies with one mast and main sail. Mr. Hillawi said that he didn't know how to sail a boat but liked riding on them as a boy. Khamel Hillawi stated that his father owned a boat with one sail.

Mr. Hillawi painted a vivid picture of an area in old Aqaba called "Tell Jermi." This was a large hill north of the castle that possibly contained one or two tombs. He claimed that this site was somewhere by the Housing Bank and the Naur 2 Hotel (not the Moon Beach Hotel as claimed by another source). The slopes of this "tell" were described as "very steep" on the side facing the beach, whereas the northward slope was not steep. Mr. Hillawi remembered a large hill of sand that he used to slide down as a child. He could not remember when asked specifically about an arch standing in the vicinity. He was apparently unaware of other antiquities in the area, saying, "Nobody here knows anything about antiquities." He did provide the information that when the Aqaba Hotel and the Coral Beach Hotel (now both demolished) were built in 1963, there were no antiquities revealed by the excavation, only a lot of soft sand and specifically no *fukhar* (pot sherds).

His uncle, Mr. Khalil Hillawi (Kamel's father) had a general store in old Aqaba. Before the arrival of the British military there were only three or four shops in the village. The goods sometimes arrived from Ma'an by truck or from Egypt by ship. Other times, Fu'ad Hillawi's father, along with a group of other men, would each take a camel and make the trek to Yafo to pick up goods for the store.

With regard to the British presence in Aqaba, Mr. Hillawi had several things to say. His father worked for the British when they were building their harbor, constructed by New Zealand units of the British army. They apparently brought in all their equipment by ship. He recalled that the British army did all construction by hand, with no heavy equipment, and that "everybody" worked for them. The pay was 7 JD per month. The British army got their water from a well in the Hillawi garden. Mr. Hillawi had a job as a child cleaning tents for the British soldiers. He remembers the British building a big barracks with a steel roof, as well as encampments on Tell al-Hamra.

FIG. 3.5   *Traditional Arab Dhow, preserved on the jetty at the Royal Yacht Club, Aqaba.*

He remembered walking along the beach to Umm Rashrash, where there was nothing but some Bedouin tents and five or six police with camels. He said, "I could go over to Egypt, no one speak to me." Palestinians came to Aqaba after 1948 — all of the people in the Negev came to Aqaba. He stated that nothing militarily significant happened at Aqaba in the 1948–49 war.

His family did not get a car until 1962, but there was one taxi in Aqaba before then, operated by the Kabariti family. During the interview Fu'ad Hillawi was wearing a Palestinian *khefiyeh* and stated it was simply because he liked the color better. It is notable that this family (like others in Aqaba) do not consider themselves Bedouin.

Interview 4

Eric Moore (New Zealand)

Stationed at Aqaba in 1949; British Royal Marines

From the "Britain's Small Wars" website:

> "Ah Aqaba! 45 Cdo was camped at Hodgson Camp at Port Foud wondering what

we were going to do next, when on the 1st March 1949 we had to pack up and move to the dock area at Adabiya, just south of Port Suez, where we boarded HMS LST Reginald Kerr and headed down the Gulf of Suez. We thought that we were going to Aden, but when we sailed past Sharm Al Shaykh on our port side, we worked out that we were heading for somewhere else. We entered the Gulf of Aqaba and finally landed on the beach of the town between Aqaba and the border with Israel.

Setting up camp in a set of old mudbrick buildings with no roofs about 4 miles inland from Aqaba town, we covered the roofs with our tent tops to make life easier. Over the next few days we dug deep slit trenches facing the Israeli border and manned them night and day. Across the border was one mud hut in Elat, the city that is there now but was not there in 1949. Some armed Israelis, who we kept a watch on, occupied the mud hut.

One day we received automatic machine gun fire from the Israelis across the border and we all stood to in the slit trenches. Over the next few days these attacks happened again and again. Colonel Palmer

RM our Commanding Officer decided that he had had enough of this so he had all of the Bren guns in 45 Commando line up just inside of the Jordanian border facing the mud building in Elat. When we received automatic fire from the Israelis again, the order was given to open fire on the mud building and all the Bren guns fired at once (about 30 of them). Whether we killed any of the Israelis we don't know but we were not fired on again.

45 Commando RM was in Aqaba till about the 19th June 1949. During that time I visited the 'Red Rose City of Petra,' which was a great experience for me, as I love visiting old ruins of the Greek and Roman era and it made my stay in Jordan worthwhile. I also was attached to the Arab Legion at a fort somewhere in the Jordanian Desert for two weeks as a signalman. The Jordanian soldiers were very smart in their uniforms and when on their camels. Of course at that time their Commanding Officer was the English officer "Glubb Pasha."

I never went into Aqaba and I don't think anybody else did either. We did go swimming but we had to be very careful of the sharks and barracuda that were in the Gulf. The heat there was very high and at one point it topped 140F. When you had a shower using cold water, it was hot. Opening a bottle of beer from the NAAFI meant you lost half the contents foaming out of the bottle. The heat haze was always about eight feet high and it was a very uncomfortable place to live. We were all very pleased when we finally left there.

The mountain behind Aqaba will probably still have the 'Union Jack' on its summit where one of our climbing teams placed it. We arrived back at Hodgson Camp on the 21st July 1949. On the 26th August 1949, we boarded the MV Georgic and sailed for Hong Kong with the rest of the 3rd Commando Brigade RM, to protect the colony against the Communist Chinese Army if they tried to invade the territory." (Moore 2000)

Further email communication with Mr. Moore elicited the following:

"I was based at Port Suez, a member of 45 Commando Royal Marines, when on about the 15th March 1949, we boarded a Royal Naval LST ship. We were not told where we were going, and sailed down the Red Sea, sailing left as we reached the base of the Sinai peninsula, when we finally found out where we were going. I had the pleasure of going ashore at Sharm el Sheikh to visit the Coptic monastery there, then we sailed up the Gulf of Aqaba. Finally beaching at Aqaba, we moved inland for about two to three miles to a lot of ruined mudbrick buildings which we used as our barracks, how long they had been there or what they had been used for I don't know.

Aqaba village was a mixture of small mudbrick buildings — not very many of them. I never even saw a fishing boat there. It was a very desolate place. And strange to say we never got to seeing or meeting any of the Arabs living there. Maybe they were told to stay away from us, who knows?

The whole area was barren and not the area I would usually live in, the only trees growing in that area were down just off the beach, there were none anywhere else. The road leading to Amman was rough and patchy, and the railway line from Amman ended about 10 miles from Aqaba. The Israeli side of the border was just as barren, Eilat was just a one room mudbrick single story building, which was used by the Israeli border guards. There was hardly any vehicle movement in that area, nor down that side of the Gulf, there was not a road down there, also no towns or cities, not like now.

Because we were between the Sinai and Jebel Ram mountain range, we had a lot of "*giblis*" (sand storms), making life very uncomfortable…We always tried, if it was possible, to stop work at eleven in the morning, and start work again at

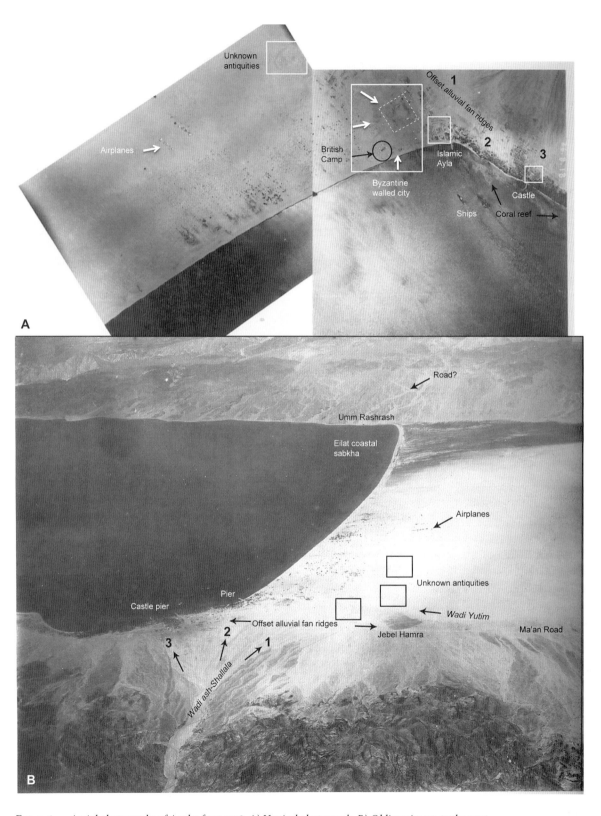

FIG. 3.6   *Aerial photographs of Aqaba from 1918. A) Vertical photograph. B) Oblique image to the west.*

five in the afternoon, so we were not out in the sun too much, unless we were on duty watching the Israelis, which was for 24 hours a day. They had been shooting across the border, at what, I don't know, but this stopped when we gave them a military gun barrage one day. They got the message — Don't do it!

I never saw or came across any ancient sites in that area, some rocks that may have been a wall over near Jebel Ram mountain, but that was all, there were also groups of rocks around here and there, but nothing you could say was an ancient site, but I was not an expert on that anyway. We left Aqaba after about 2 months there, the Israelis had stopped their shooting, and we went back to Port Suez."

IV. INTERPRETATION OF AERIAL PHOTOGRAPHS

This ethnohistorical information, while interesting on its own, is much more important as a source of corroboration for other lines (archaeological, geological, etc.) of evidence. In particular, it can in this case corroborate both evidence from archaeological excavation (Rucker and Niemi 2005) and from interpretation of aerial photography. Thus it is an important element in understanding recent cultural modification of the landscape and the local environment.

The use of aerial photography for archaeological and geological research dates almost to the origins of human flight itself. In the present study, topographic maps and aerial photographs of Aqaba and southern Wādī 'Araba from various years were analyzed and compared to identify changes over time in the landscape. The earliest known aerial photographs of Aqaba date from World War I (WWI). Kedar (1999) published historical accounts and aerial photographs taken over Palestine during WWI and compares these to present-day images. For Aqaba, Kedar (1999: 42–45) describes the WWI German Air Squadron flights over the area and compares 1918 photographs to ones from 1945, 1956, and 1995. In addition to these images, we analyzed a series of 1:25,000-scale aerial photographs

of Aqaba from 1953 (Royal Geographic Center of Jordan [RGCJ] 1953) and 1:10,000-scale from 1978 (RGCJ 1978). We also used topographic maps of the Aqaba region at a scale of 1:25,000 (RGCJ 1956) and 1:5,000 compiled from survey data in 1986 from the Aqaba Regional Authority (now Aqaba Special Economic Zone Authority, ASEZA).

The aerial photographs include both vertical and oblique views at various scales. The resolution of features that can be detected depends on the scale; small objects cannot be discerned from large-scale images. Because of the regional nature of the oblique images, only generalized information about landscape changes can be noted. The highest resolution images are the 1:10,000-scale 1978 black-and-white air photos.

Several very distinct cultural features appear on the 1918 aerial photographs. Two straight piers extended from the coast of Aqaba: one at the Late Islamic (Mamluk/Ottoman) castle and the other farther north along the coast near the present-day Yacht Club (fig. 3.6). Two ships appear to be steaming toward the northern pier. The end of a natural ground airstrip, with airplanes lining the east and west side, lies 650 m from the shoreline and west of town. The town of Aqaba is concentrated along the north side of the castle and east up the Wādī ash-Shallala alluvial fan. Other structures are clustered adjacent to the northern pier. The white tents of the British camp are seen along the northern shore (fig. 3.6).

The area of the Early Islamic walled site of Ayla is readily discerned on the vertical 1918 photograph. The northern wall appears as a prominent and continuous wall marked by two parallel black lines. No interruption or wadi drainage transects the wall. This observation supports the interpretation that the drainage that crosses Islamic Ayla post-dates World War I and that it is man-made, as described in the interview and excavations (Rucker and Niemi 2005). The Byzantine walled city of Aila is also detectable on the photograph as a change from a lighter tone to a smoother, darker-toned area. White arrows point to the location of the city wall in fig. 3.6. This area is larger than the Early Islamic walled Ayla, as suggested by analysis of historical texts (Whitcomb 1997) and excavation (Parker 2002). A faint rectangular outline of a possible

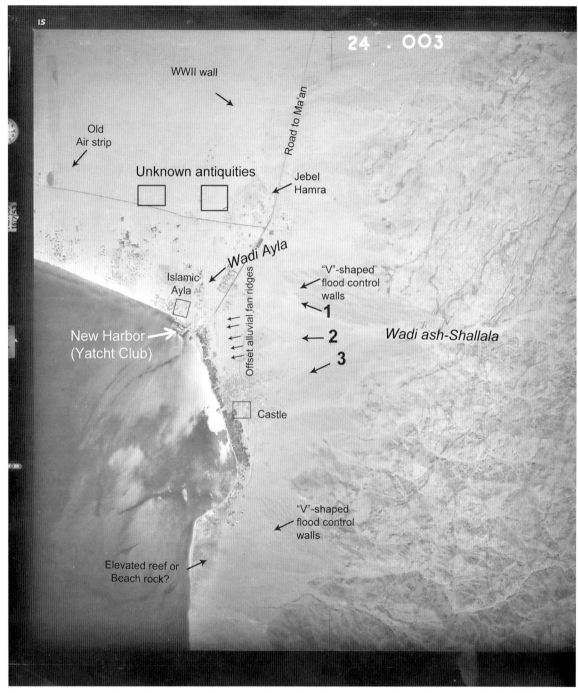

FIG. 3.7   *Aerial photography from July 16, 1953 of the Aqaba region.*

structure also appears in this area. Finally, there are three roughly rectangular areas of unusual raised topography. These areas of possible unknown antiquities are roughly equal in size to Early Islamic Ayla. Two of these same areas can be also identified on the 1953 photographs (fig. 3.7).

Several geomorphic observations, including vegetation, landforms, and drainages, can be interpreted from both the 1918 and the 1953 aerial photographs. While the northern shore has only isolated pockets of vegetation, extensive cultivation, noted by the dark tree cover, is localized from the pier to south of the castle along this north-trending section of the coastline. A photograph published in Philby (1925) of the area around the Castle pier indicates that these are date palms (fig. 3.2). The palm trees appear to be dense and extend ca. 125 m inland, especially south of the castle. It is likely that the understory was planted with legumes, cereals, and other crops, as in the present gardens at this location. The vegetation stops where the coastline bends west at the edge of the Wādī ash-Shallala alluvial fan. A flat promontory gives the eastern shoreline its unusual shape. The morphology of the point suggests that it may be an elevated coral reef or beachrock. As this area is underneath the modern port, it is not possible to interpret the geology at this location.

Coral reefs are likely to have significantly limited where ancient seafarers could harbor or beach a vessel. Of all the archaeological ruins in Aqaba, only the castle is known to be located along the east shore where modern coral fringe reefs can be seen in the shallow waters. The fringe reef does not extend across the northern shore. The northern shoreline of the Gulf of Aqaba is smooth and slightly arcuate in shape across the entire gulf head. Here, a sandy beach appears to be built up to a width of ca. 50–100 m.

The Wādī ash-Shallala drains from the Jebel Um Nuseila (elev. 560 m) and the mountains to the east. The three most recently active courses of the wadi are shown as bright tones on the images and labeled 1–3 in figures 3.6 and 3.7. Channel 1 is a west-flowing active drainage that joins a south-flowing branch of the Wādī Yutum drainage. The outlet of this flow was likely east and/or west of Early Islamic Ayla. This may be the origin of the observation that when it rains, "Ayla is an island" with water flowing by it (Burton 1879: 240). However, the flow path is difficult to trace in the 1918 photos. Flow diversion walls constructed by the time of the 1953 photos show V-shaped control walls directing the flow south. Channel 2 flows WSW to the coast to form a small delta. Channel 3 flows SW into the old town and clearly was a flood hazard to Aqaba. These flows caused disasters and casualties in the town as described by one of the interviewees. T. E. Lawrence wrote that "the village lies at the foot of the slopes of the Arabian hills and wady after wady

descends from them each pointing directly at the town; a flood from any one of these would sweep away every building in the place" (Woolley and Lawrence 1936: 128). By 1978, a dam and diversion channel had been constructed along the south side of the Wādī ash-Shallala alluvial fan, directing the flow to the south, and the city had expanded up the fan surface.

Whitcomb (1997) suggested that although one interpretation of the name "Aqaba" is that it means a mountain pass, it may also be derived from "hillock" or "slopes." He postulated that the founding of the 12th-century fort of "Aqabat Ayla" may have been on a prominence or hill within the Wādī ash-Shallala drainage and that the morphology of the hill was lost by buildup of fluvial sediments. The 1918 photos show a set of linear hills at the foot of the Shallala alluvial fan slope oriented perpendicular to the stream flow and nearly parallel to the beach (figs. 3.6–7). These linear ridges and Jebel Hamra to the north appear to be older alluvial fan deposits that have been displaced by faulting on the Aqaba fault system (fig. 3.8). Lawrence described "a huge bank, 100 to 200 yards from the beach and parallel to it; this was 10–30 feet high toward the sea, and 3–10 feet towards the land and presumably constructed to deflect water from the hills away from the town" (Woolley and Lawrence 1936: 128). An alternative geological interpretation of this north-trending "bank" is that it is a scarp formed along a portion of the alluvial fan offset by the fault. The lithograph of Roberts (1828) and photograph by Musil (1910) both view the castle from the north (fig. 3.2). In these images hillocks and ridges are prominent in the foreground. The detail within the mounds is bedded similar to natural fluvial deposits. Recent road excavations in this region confirm natural gravelly alluvium.

A major change along the shore, prior to the 1945 photograph (Kedar 1999) and also seen on the 1953 aerial photograph (fig. 3.7), was the development of new harbor facilities. The construction of an L-shaped protected harbor with a northwest entry must date to the WWII military build-up as confirmed by our interviews. Also noted at this time is the bisection of the wall of the Early Islamic Ayla site with a constructed drainage. In the 1945 aerial image published by Kedar, one of

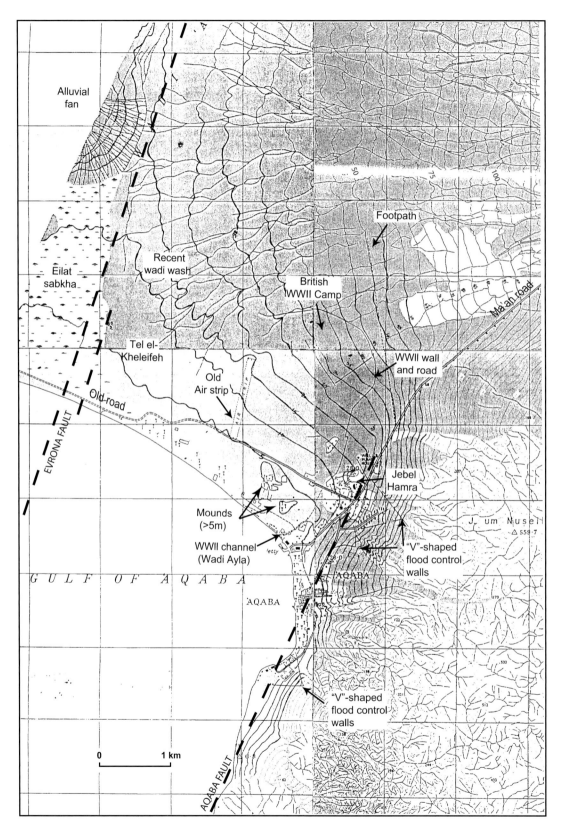

FIG. 3.8 *The 1956 topographic map of the Aqaba region was compiled from the 1953 air photos.*

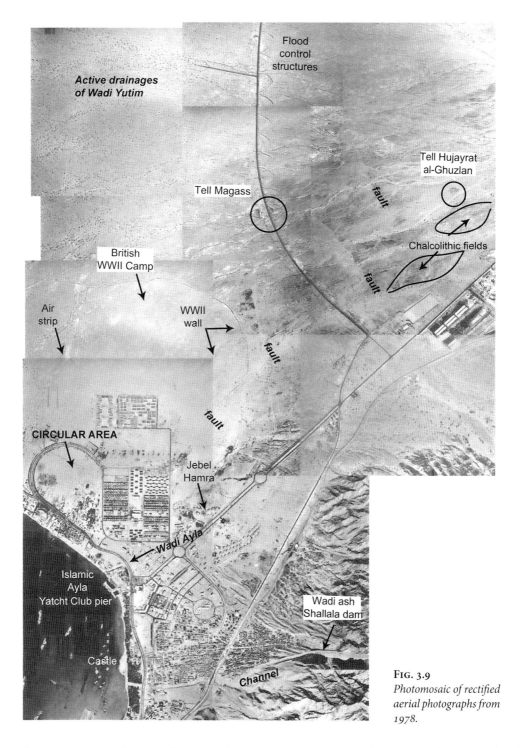

FIG. 3.9
Photomosaic of rectified aerial photographs from 1978.

the British army camps 2 km north of the shore is clearly visible as regularly spaced structures. A second camp lies just south of Jebel Hamra. By 1953 these sites had been cleared of military buildings, but the foundations are still clearly visible even on the 1978 photographs (fig. 3.9).

The topographic maps of the Aqaba region at a scale of 1:25,000 were compiled from 1953 air photos. These maps are contoured at a 5 m interval. A comparison of the topographic maps and aerial images with 1978 air photos and later maps reveals several common features. To register the maps and images the following cultural features were located: 1) the old road to the air strip, 2) the abandoned air strip, 3) the jetty by the castle and present-day museum, 4) archaeological tells (Kheleifeh, Maqaṣṣ, Ghuzlan), and 5) the main road leading into Aqaba from the north. In addition to these built structures, clusters of trees, the shape of the coastline, and prominent alluvial fan surfaces were traced from image to image.

Three topographic mounds appear on the 1956 topographic map (fig. 3.8). There are two closed topographic highs between the beach and the 5 m contour. The NW one measures 150 × 400 m and the southern one is 250 × 150 m. These artificial mounds or tells were excavated by the Roman Aqaba Project as Areas B, M, O, and G in the north, and Areas A, J, K, L, and U in the south (fig. 3.3). The contours on the 1956 map suggest that the northern mound is larger. No closed topographic high was identified over Early Islamic Ayla on the 1956 map. This is puzzling, because the pre-excavation elevation of the site exceeded 5 m (Whitcomb 1997). There is a third topographic high at the intersection of the old airstrip road and the main road to Ma'an at the edge of the alluvial fan surface; it lies ca. 1.4 km northeast of the jetty and west of the boulevard that leads into Aqaba from the north. This is the site of Jebel Hamra — one of the offset older alluvial fan surfaces.

The 1953 and 1978 aerial images show that west of the Ma'an road and the older alluvial fan sediments that flank the mountain front is an area of relatively smooth topography (appearing as an even gray tone on black and white aerial photographs) with fewer recent wadi washes and flash floods crossing it. This area includes the region from the British WWII camp to the coastline. The 5–20 m contour lines on the 1956 topographic map are straight and parallel to the shoreline for a distance of ca. 2 km west of the old Ma'an Road (fig. 3.8). The smooth topography is anomalous from the surrounding landscape and is likely due to two factors: 1) sand dune deposition, and 2) diversion of the wadi drainages away from the east coastal zone. A broadly curved wall with a long segment that extends along the east side connects with the channel cut across the site of Early Islamic Ayla. The earthen wall appears to have been dug from the outside and mounded inward with the exterior used as a road. There are two overlapping openings: one toward the NE, and the other midway down the east side. From the NE opening and inside the protected area is an additional road extending south that bisects the old military camp. The association of this wall with the WWII camp suggests that the wall is contemporary with it. It also cannot be discerned on the 1918 oblique air photo.

If the arcuate wall 2 km from the shoreline is modern, it does not explain the smoother topography and the hydrogeologic isolation of the area. One possible explanation is that there were pre-existing ancient diversion structures at the site or farther up the Wādī Yutum alluvial fan. Philby's detailed account and photographs of his journey from "The Dead Sea to 'Aqaba" along Wādī 'Araba during December 1923 notes that "A little lower down and practically at the point where the valley debouches into Wādī 'Araba are numerous evidences of human handiwork, including an enormous masonry dam (Masadd) now largely demolished, which apparently stretched at one time right across the valley, and of which the purpose did not seem to me at all clear" (Philby 1925: 153). He then suggested, based on his reading of Burton (1879), that the dam was part of a gold placer mining operation. Several other early European travelers also mention a large dam at or near the mouth of the Wādī Yutum (Morris 1842: 265; Burton 1879: 241; Doughty 1936: 84–85). A large dam at the mouth of the Wādī Yutum canyon would have changed the pattern of sedimentation, perhaps significantly, on the alluvial fan system down-gradient. But the location, date, and nature of such a structure are not yet known.

The area west of the abandoned air strip has a more youthful geomorphic surface than the east side of the valley (fig. 3.8). It is characterized by irregular, rough topography due to very young wadi channels and wash. The wadi cut across the air strip indicates flooding after 1918. This young wash from the Wādī Yutum masks evidence of shoreline changes. The wadi wash ends abruptly in the coastal Eilat *sabkha*. This area slopes gently southward (10 m over 2.3 km). Contour lines suggest that this was once an embayment, probably filled with sea water and then brackish water. The

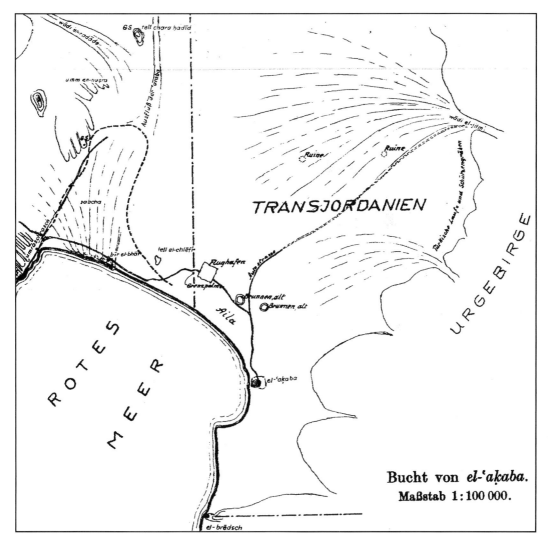

FIG. 3.10 *The 1934 sketch map of Fritz Frank of the Aqaba region.*

mound of Tell el-Kheleifeh lies at the edge of the mudflat, 1 km from the modern shoreline at an elevation of ca. 7 m.

During the early 20th century, water for the fishing village of Aqaba was satisfied by hand-dug shallow wells. The small population lived near the castle in the "Old Town" within the drainage of Wādī ash-Shallala. The interviewees noted that citizens pulled water from the well near the castle. The Shallala aquifer also seeps out at the beach south of the castle. Frank's sketch map from his 1933 visit to Aqaba depicts two "Brunnen, alt" ("old well" or "water hole;" Eichmann et al. 2009: 19). Several features on this map (fig. 3.10), such as the road to the old airstrip, allow fairly accurate location of

the wells. The western well lies within the so-called Circular Area east of RAP excavation Area M and was still visible in 1994. It was a circular structure ca. 2.5 m in diameter and 3 m in depth constructed of fieldstones cemented into the wall lining the well. A ladder descended on one side of the well. The well apparently by then was a privately-owned water source to irrigate a local garden and residential area of the family interviewed. The eastern "Brunnen, alt" was not relocated. Also noted on Frank's map is a *bir el-bhar,* or "sea well," west of Tell el-Kheleifeh. Frank makes a distinction between the German *Brunnen* and the Arabic *bir.* He does not use the Arabic word *ain* for spring. Also clear from Frank's map is the placement of the name "Aila" in the area of the future RAP excavations and Early Islamic Ayla NW of the modern town. The Chalcolithic sites appear on the Wādī Yutum fan as "ruins."

The 1978 aerial images of Aqaba (fig. 3.9) show that the city had grown extensively up the Wādī ash-Shallala alluvial fan, but large areas west of the Ma'an road remained undeveloped. This latter region is now intensely urbanized (fig. 3.1). The photomosaic of the aerial images in figure 3.9 shows several features not previously discussed north of the old town. The Aqaba Regional Authority constructed several flood control measures to divert water into culverts under the road and into channels. Two Chalcolithic tells (Tell Maqaṣṣ and Tell Ḥujeirat al-Ghuzlan) and agricultural terraces lie on the alluvial fan surfaces (figs. 3.7–8). These terraces include stone alignments parallel to wadi courses; some cross the wadi and extend onto the interfluve. A moderate coating of desert varnish has developed on these Chalcolithic rock alignments.

Changes observed in the gradient of the Wādī Yutum fan originate in tectonics as well as climatic-driven shifts in sedimentation. Four zones of distinct lineaments cross the fan normal to southwestward flow lines. These lineaments are approximately parallel to the present coastline. Bender (1974) interpreted the lineaments as "ancient shorelines." The lineaments consistently separate older fan deposits on the northeast from younger fan deposits on the southwest (fig. 3.9). The NW and SE extension of these lineaments has been eroded by recent wadi wash. Subsurface investigations across these lineaments (Mansoor 2002; Mansoor et al. 2004; Slater and Niemi 2003; Niemi 2009) conclusively show that these lineaments are active fault scarps.

V. CONCLUSIONS

Analysis of all this varied evidence permits some larger conclusions about human occupation and modification of the landscape of Aqaba. The site has undergone exponential growth within living memory from a sleepy fishing village to a major port city. As a result, many unrecorded ancient sites have been permanently lost. Local inhabitants in the last 70 years produced and ate a lot of dates and fish with relatively little other agriculture

or animal husbandry. Subsistence gardening was practiced. Apparently, both substantial fish stocks and large predators (sharks and large barracuda) have sharply declined in the northern Gulf of Aqaba. This is possibly due to either overfishing or environmental effects of development. Both the facility and quality of the local aquifer has declined within living human memory as more and more pressure has been placed on it.

The aerial photographs, several early travelers' accounts, and modern experience all attest to the seriousness of flooding in and around Aqaba. From the Chalcolithic to the present, considerable effort has been spent to control and channel the occasional major floods from Wādī Yutum and Wādī ash-Shallala. Some success has been achieved at different times but the danger remains, as attested by casualties in a 2006 flood. In stark contrast to other settlements in the region, relatively little effort is discernable in any period to contain and reserve the floodwaters for later use. Major cisterns, water canalization systems, and other water catchment structures are curiously absent in and around Aqaba (Tell el-Kheleifeh, Tell Maqaṣṣ, Roman/Byzantine Aila, and early Islamic Ayla). While hydrological installations are not totally absent from these sites, they are nowhere near as prominent a feature here compared to such sites as Humayma and Petra. It is notable that the Chalcolithic water management system was seemingly set up for extensive farming irrigation and soil enhancement (Khalil and Schmidt 2009). Apparently, the local aquifer, problems with salt water infiltration notwithstanding, was sufficient for the population.

It is possible, as Whitcomb suggested, that the name "Aqaba" derives from the small rise on which the extant Aqaba Castle was constructed, rather than from the passes to the north or south. This is supported by our interpretation of the aerial photographs. It is likely that both Tell Jermi and Tell/Jebel Hamra are remnant fragments of older alluvial fans, separated and shifted by fault movement.

Local witnesses, analysis of air photos, and archaeological excavation show conclusively that the wadi cutting across Early Islamic Ayla was constructed by the British using bulldozers. While our informants were able to shed much light on the arrival of British troops, the location of their encampments, and some of their activities in the region, they were not very informative about the many military trenches and bunkers scattered throughout the Circular Area and the southern part of Early Islamic Ayla. Comparison of the 1953 and 1978 aerial photographs seems to reveal that these trenches were constructed between these two dates.

REFERENCES

Bender, F.
1974   *Geology of Jordan*. Berlin: Borntraeger.

Burton, R. F.
1879   *The Land of Midian (revisited)*. 2 vols. London: Kegan Paul (Reprint New York: Oleander, 1984).

Doughty, C. M.
1936   *Travel in Arabia Deserta*. 2 vols. 3rd ed. London: Jonathan Cap (Reprint New York: Dover, 1979).

Eichmann, R.; Khalil, L.; and Schmidt, K.
2009   Excavations at Tell Ḥujeirat al-Ghuzlan ('Aqaba/Jordan). Excavations 1998–2005 and Stratigraphy. Pp. 17–77 in L. Khalil and K. Schmidt, eds., *Prehistoric 'Aqaba I*. Orient-Archäologie Band 23, Rahden: Leidorf.

Kedar, B. Z.
1999   *The Changing Land Between the Jordan and the Sea: Aerial Photographs from 1917 to the Present*. Jerusalem: Yad Ben-Zvi.

Khalil, L., and Schmidt, K. (eds.)
2009   *Prehistoric 'Aqaba I*. Orient-Abteilung des Deutschen Archäologischen Instituts, Orient-Archäologie Band 23, Rahden: Leidorf.

Mansoor, N. M.
2002   A GIS-based assessment of active faults and liquefaction potential of the city of Aqaba, Jordan. M.S. Thesis, University of Missouri at Kansas City.

Mansoor, N. M.; Niemi, T. M.; and Misra, A.
2004   A GIS-based assessment of liquefaction potential of the city of Aqaba, Jordan. *Environmental and Engineering Geoscience* 10.4: 297–320.

Moore, E.
2000   Four Five take on the Israelis, Aqaba 1949, Britain's Small Wars. Http://www.britains-smallwars.com/RRGP/Aqaba.htm.

Morris, E. J.
1842   *Notes of a Tour through Turkey, Greece, Egypt, and Arabia Petraea, to the Holy Land: Including a Visit to Athens, Sparta, Delphi, Cairo, Thebes, Mount Sinai, Petra, etc.* Philadelphia: Carey and Hart.

Niemi, T. M.
2009   Paleoseismology and Archaeoseismology of Sites in Aqaba and Petra, Jordan: Field guidebook. Http://www.gsi.gov.il/Eng/Index.asp?CategoryID=175.

Parker, S. T.
2002   The Roman Aqaba Project: Preliminary Report of the 2000 Season. *ADAJ* 46: 409–28.

Philby, H. St. J. B.
1925   The Dead Sea to 'Aqaba. *The Geographical Journal* 66.2: 134–55.

Pratico, G. D.
1993   *Nelson Glueck's 1938-1940 Excavations at Tell el-Kheleifeh: A Reappraisal*. American Schools of Oriental Research Archaeological Reports 3. Atlanta, GA: Scholars.

Roberts, D.
1842–49   *The Holy Land, Syria, Idumea, Arabia, Egypt & Nubia*. 3 vols. London: Moon.

Rucker, J. D., and Niemi, T. M.
2005   New Excavations of the City Wall at Islamic Ayla in Aqaba, Jordan. *ADAJ* 49: 501–8.

Slater, L., and Niemi, T. M.
2003   Detection of active faults along the Dead Sea transform using ground penetrating

radar and implications for seismic hazards within the city of Aqaba, Jordan. *Tectonophysics* 368: 33–50.

Whitcomb, D. S.
1994 *Ayla—Art and Industry in the Islamic Port of Aqaba.* Chicago, IL: Oriental Institute, University of Chicago.
1997 The Town and Name of 'Aqaba: An Inquiry into the Settlement History from an Archaeological Perspective. *SHAJ* 6: 359–63.

2009 Ayla at the Millennium: Archaeology and History. Pp. 123–32 in *SHAJ* 10: *Crossing Jordan.* Amman: Department of Antiquities of Jordan.

Woolley, C. L., and Lawrence, T .E.
1936 *The Wilderness of Zin.* New York: Palestine Exploration Fund.

Chapter 4

The Southeast 'Araba Archaeological Survey

by Andrew M. Smith II

I. INTRODUCTION

The Southeast 'Araba Archaeological Survey (SAAS) was a regional study of the Jordanian sector of the southern Wādī 'Araba.[1] The SAAS, a unit of the Roman Aqaba Project (RAP), conducted its fieldwork in 1994, 1996, and 1998 (Smith and Niemi 1994; Smith 1994; Smith et al. 1997). While RAP investigated the role of the ancient city of Aila (Aqaba) in the broader economy of the Roman Empire, the SAAS placed this investigation into a broader regional context (Parker 1996; 1997a; 1997b; 1998; 2000). The primary objective of the survey was to elucidate the hinterland of Roman Aqaba through the discovery and documentation of archaeological sites contemporary with the classical period occupation of Aila. But the SAAS recorded all sites of all periods encountered in the study area, providing evidence of the settlement history of the region in a much broader range of periods.

This chapter will outline the geographic parameters of the study area and review previous archaeological exploration of the region. The chapter next turns to the survey itself, including methodological considerations imposed by the regional environment, political restrictions, time, equipment, and personnel. Then the chapter will present the survey's goals and methods (including what is considered a "site"). Finally, the results of the survey will be presented diachronically. Wider historical conclusions about the results of the survey as seen through both wider regional trends and the results from the excavations at Aqaba itself appear in the final chapter of this volume.

II. STUDY AREA

Wādī 'Araba is part of the Syrian-African rift that extends ca. 165 km north from the Gulf of Aqaba to the escarpment overlooking the Southern Ghor of the Dead Sea (fig. 4.1). The projected targeted the SE sector of Wādī 'Araba, which extends ca. 80 km N–NE from Aqaba to the watershed of the valley, a distinct geomorphological boundary, ca. 12 km north of Gharandal in the vicinity of Qā' as-Su'aydiyyīn (fig. 4.2). The rugged, mountainous escarpment of the Aqaba Granite Complex, rising to 1200 m over a short distance, bounds the study area to the east. The modern Jordanian–Israeli border formed the western boundary. The actual E–W dimensions of the region surveyed varied from south to north. In the southern region, the actual surveyed area averaged 12 km N–S × 6.50 km E–W; in the central region, the area averaged 42 km N–S × 1.50 km E–W; and in the northern region, the area averaged 26 km N–S × 7.50 km E–W.[2] Thus the total area of the region surveyed,

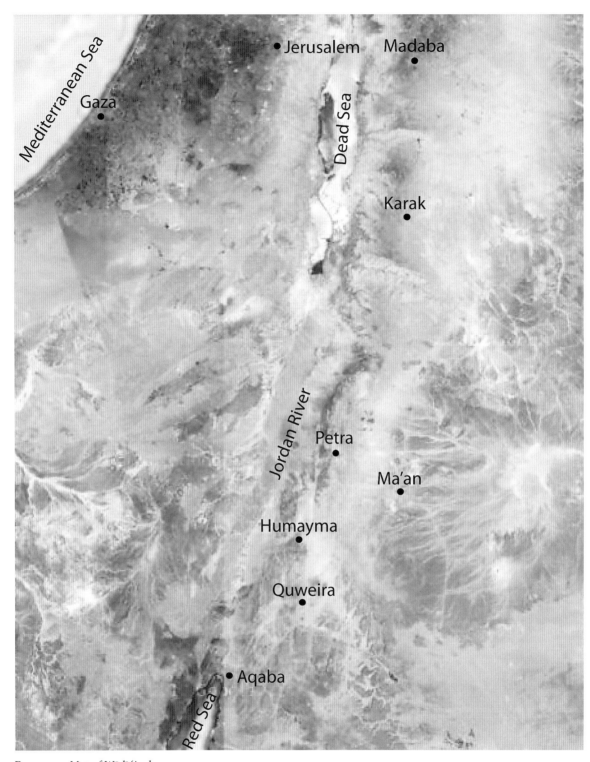

FIG. 4.1   *Map of Wādī ʿAraba.*

though not all with the same intensity, was ca. 336 square km — just over half of the total area of the SE sector of Wādī ʿAraba, as defined above, which is at least 570 square km. The physical and natural environment of the study area is discussed at length in Chapter 2.

III.   PREVIOUS EXPLORATIONS

Before 1993, most of Wādī 'Araba — and especially its SE sector — was mostly unexplored archaeologically. Nineteenth-century explorers largely neglected its archaeological landscape, though many ventured into the valley and provided us with significant ethnographic data of the indigenous population. Not until the early 20th century was this deficiency addressed. In the 1930s, Fritz Frank and Nelson Glueck recorded in detail some of the chief archaeological sites of the 'Araba (Frank 1934; Glueck 1935). Their focus, however, was limited to the few sites with impressive architectural features. In the SE 'Araba this included, among other sites, Bir Madhkur and Gharandal. Nevertheless, Frank and Glueck put the 'Araba on the map — as it were — by drawing attention to the valley's rich cultural resources. Within three years of his ground survey, Glueck revisited Wādī 'Araba from the air, and in 1938–40 excavated the Iron Age site of Tell el-Kheleifeh near Aqaba (Glueck 1935; 1938a; 1938b; 1939a; 1939b; 1940; 1965). Glueck never published a final report of this excavation. Nearly fifty years later, Glueck's evidence from at Tell el-Kheleifeh was re-examined and published in more definitive form (Pratico 1985; 1993).

In 1948, Wādī 'Araba became an international political boundary between Israel and Jordan. This discouraged further exploration of the region, especially on the eastern side, throughout most of the later 20th century. Thus the few subsequent investigations in the southeastern 'Araba made only a limited contribution to knowledge of the region's archaeology. Brief surveys by David McCreery (unpublished report) and David Graf (unpublished report), for example, were purposive in nature and recorded only a few archaeological sites in the area. Thomas Raikes, a British engineer who surveyed the alignment of the new 'Araba highway in the late 1960s, also advanced knowledge of the region's archaeological resources. Though not an archaeologist, Raikes made many acute observations regarding the archaeological landscape and suggested that the valley was rich in undocumented cultural resources (Raikes 1980; 1985). In 1982, G. R. D. King cursorily surveyed many of the known forts and caravanserais in the valley (King

et al. 1989). All this suggested that more intensive survey of the southern 'Araba would be rewarding.

In 1993, the Southeast 'Araba Archaeological Reconnaissance (SAAR), which became the Southeast 'Araba Archaeological Survey (SAAS) the following year, addressed the gap in knowledge of the cultural history of the study area. The results of this survey form the basis of this report.

Several other projects have focused on the SE Wādī 'Araba over the past decade. Most notable is the excavation of the Chalcolithic/Early Bronze Age sites of Ḥujeirat al-Ghuzlan and Tell Maqaṣṣ near Aqaba (Khalil 1987; 1988; 1992; 1995). Khalil excavated these sites in 1985 and 1990, then began collaborating with Ricardo Eichmann in 1998. The joint Jordanian-German project continued work at Ḥujeirat al-Ghuzlan and Tell Maqaṣṣ and began new investigations at contemporary sites in the vicinity (Eichmann and Khalil 1998; Khalil and Eichmann 1999; 2001). Further north in the valley, Donald O. Henry surveyed prehistoric sites along Wādī Nukheila (Henry et al. 2001) and in the vicinity of Gharandal. Benjamin Dolinka surveyed the Nabataean settlement of Rujm aṭ-Ṭāba (Dolinka 2002; Dolinka et al. 2002). Research at Aqaba itself is discussed in the first chapter of this volume.

Archaeological explorations of Wādī 'Araba beyond the study area provide an important contextual framework for the data presented here. Burton MacDonald's Southern Ghors and Northeast 'Araba Archaeological Survey (MacDonald 1986; 1992; MacDonald et al. 1987; 1988), for example, which recorded evidence of all prehistoric and historic periods, has provided an important model for survey strategy and design to which the present project is indebted. Also, British, German, and American teams have conducted extensive fieldwork in Wādī Fidan and the copper mining district of Faynan, especially between the Neolithic and Iron Age (Adams 1991; Adams and Genz 1995; Bachmann and Hauptmann 1984; Barker et al. 1997; 1998; 1999; 2000; Hauptmann 1986; Hauptmann, Weisgerber, and Knauf 1985; Hauptmann and Weisgerber 1987; Hauptmann et al. 1992; Kind 1965; Levy et al. 1999). There has also been much research on the Israeli side of Wādī 'Araba, mostly focused on such principal settlements as Yotvata (Meshel 1989; 1993), Moyat 'Awad (Cohen 1993b),

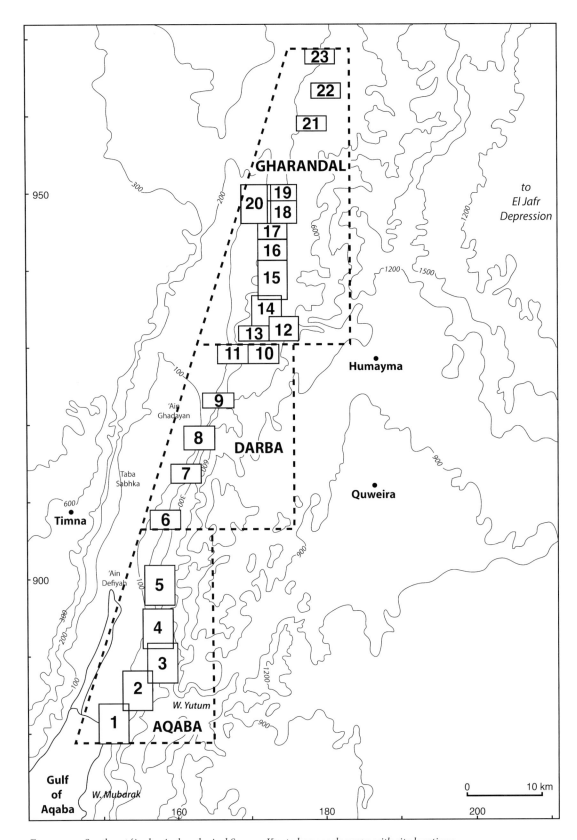

Fig. 4.2   *Southeast 'Araba Archaeological Survey: Key to large scale maps with site locations.*

and H̱aẕeva (Cohen 1993a; 1993b; 1994; Cohen and Yisrael 1995; 1996), mostly from the Iron Age to the early Islamic periods. Moreover, among several purposive surveys of the western ʿAraba (e.g., Avner 1984; 1990; Avner, Carmi, and Segal 1994; Avner and Roll 1997), Beno Rothenberg's work in the 1960s may be the most comprehensive (Rothenberg 1962; 1971). Rothenberg's extensive work at Timna complements that in the eastern ʿAraba in Wādī Fidan and has illuminated the history of the valley from the Chalcolithic period onward. The author himself has continued research in the region (Smith 2005a; 2005b; 2010).

IV. THE SOUTHEAST ʿARABA ARCHAEOLOGICAL SURVEY

In short, despite all this fieldwork, prior to 1993 exploration of the SE Wādī ʿAraba had been mostly limited to a handful of sites with substantial remains. This region was largely *terra incognita* archaeologically. Therefore in 1993, with planning underway for the Roman Aqaba Project, an archaeological reconnaissance was conducted from June 12 to June 22 in the SE ʿAraba (Smith and Niemi 1994). The reconnaissance was in essence a feasibility study with four specific objectives: 1) to study the natural environment, including the geomorphology, hydrology, climate, flora, and fauna of the region; 2) to assess the cultural landscape by visiting the few known archaeological sites in the region; 3) to document new archaeological sites in the area based on accounts of past explorers; 4) to assess the feasibility of a more intensive survey of the southern ʿAraba as a component of the Roman Aqaba Project. The results of this reconnaissance exceeded expectations and indicated that a more comprehensive survey of the SE ʿAraba was both warranted and feasible.

The SAAS commenced in 1994, with additional seasons in 1996 and 1998 (Smith et al. 1997; Parker 1998: 375–76; 2000: 374–75). As a unit of the Roman Aqaba Project, the SAAS was formulated to study the hinterland of Roman Aila, including one of the principal land routes extending north from the city. The primary goal was to reconstruct the cultural landscape through discovery and documentation of ancient sites in the region and by study of the natural environment. The goal was to gain greater understanding of human history in the valley and place the history of Aila in a broader regional context. Above all, it was hoped that the survey would aid in reconstructing the economic relationship between Aila and its hinterland.

To sum up, a key impetus for the archaeological survey of Wādī ʿAraba was to re-examine earlier views, e.g., that the valley was throughout history a desolate wilderness nearly void of human habitation. Such views are easily sustained when there is no conflicting evidence. But it seemed possible that this resulted primarily from a lack of sufficient archaeological exploration of the ʿAraba, particularly the SE sector. Rothenberg, whose knowledge of the western ʿAraba may surpass most, has been adept in expounding this minimalist view. While discussing the difficulties of interpreting various site types from his research and establishing a corpus of comparative material evidence with neighboring regions, Rothenberg argued that such difficulties are due to "the unusual character of the Arabah as an arid no-man's-land between North Africa, Palestine, Arabia and the Red Sea, the population of which had remained cut off from the mainstream developments in the neighboring, more fertile regions" (Rothenberg and Glass 1992: 141). In his preface to Rothenberg's *Timna*, Sir Mortimer Wheeler went so far as to characterize the ʿAraba as the "abomination of desolation" (Rothenberg 1972: 8). Based on the new evidence from the current project, this report will reconsider such views.

V. METHODOLOGICAL CONSIDERATIONS

The first step in designing the survey was to address the fundamental question of what constitutes a successful survey strategy (Binford 1964; Cherry 1984; Banning 2001; 2002). Responses to this vexed question tend to vary significantly among researchers (Cherry 1983; Barker 1991; Mattingly 1992). Various factors, including the project's research goals, the archaeologist's professional training, perception of the environment, available financial and human resources, and the many natural and cultural processes that affect the landscape all form a unique perspective on how best to investigate a specific region. Moreover, as regional variations abound, so do the various techniques and methods viewed as appropriate or feasible within a given landscape.

Schiffer, Sullivan, and Klinger have noted that "archaeological survey is the application of a set of techniques for varying the discovery probabilities of archaeological materials in order to estimate parameters of the regional archaeological record" (Schiffer, Sullivan, and Klinger 1978: 2). Survey design therefore is the process by which these techniques are selected. With the obvious provision that an unbiased or representative sample is obtained, attention must also be given to cost-effectiveness as an integral component of survey design. Schiffer, Sullivan, and Klinger also define several important factors that must be considered when selecting techniques and strategies for survey. These are: 1) abundance and clustering, which is the frequency or prevalence of a specific type of site or artifact and the degree to which these are spatially aggregated; 2) obtrusiveness, which is "the probability that particular archaeological materials can be discovered by a specific technique;" 3) visibility, which is the "variability in the extent to which an observer can detect the presence of archaeological materials at or below a given place;" 4) accessibility, or the "constraints of observer mobility" (Schiffer, Sullivan, and Klinger 1978: 4–10). Clearly, the archaeologist cannot directly control all of these factors, but he or she must nonetheless consider each in survey design.

The archaeologist can directly control the methods of survey, i.e., the techniques and strategies selected for the study area. Since project goals largely determine the methods employed, it is essential that these be specific and feasible. Goals and methods, however, rarely remain static. Ongoing results from fieldwork, for instance, often warrant modification of the original goals and methods to comply with overall research objectives. In other words, within certain parameters, goals and methods must be formulated (and altered if necessary) to ensure that the project's specific research questions are answered. Such parameters that affect decisions include (but are not limited to) financial resources, equipment, staff, and time. The methodology of the SAAS itself differed somewhat each season, due in part to better understanding of the study area from year to year,

logistical constraints imposed by limited financial resources, time, equipment, manpower, and restrictions of local authorities.

The survey methodology presented here relates to the specific goals established (or modified) for each season (see below). Given the great geophysical differentiation of the landscape throughout the study area, the following discussion of survey methodology details the strategies and techniques deemed most suitable to and applied in specific landscapes.

Geophysical Variations

For practical purposes, the SAAS arbitrarily partitioned the study area into three regions on the basis of the Jordan Series K737 1:50,000 scale maps (fig. 4.2; Rashdan 1988; Ibrahim 1991). The southern area (Area I: Aqaba region) extends ca. 22 km north from Aqaba to the alluvial fan of Wādī el-Muhtadī. Within this area lies "greater Aqaba," defined as the densely populated region extending ca. 7 km north from the Gulf of Aqaba. The central sector (Area II: Ḍarba region) lies between Wādī el-Muhtadī and Jibāl Um Nukheila. The northern area (Area III: Gharandal region) extends from Jibāl Um Nukheila to just north of Wādī Abū Barqa.

The SAAS identified several discrete geographical zones based on the range of distinct geophysical features that characterize the southern 'Araba. These were alluvial fans and alluvial plains, sabkhas (usually dry mudflats), sand dunes and sand fields, ridges and mountainous zones, wadi floors and wadi terraces, and beaches (Bender 1975). With the exception of the beaches along the seacoast, each of these zones appears in varying degrees within each of the three survey regions defined by the project. Because site formation processes vary in different geophysical contexts (Rapp and Hill 1998), the following sections present an overview of these zones and the survey strategies and techniques applied in each.

Alluvial Fans and Alluvial Plains

Alluvial fans and alluvial plains constitute the predominant land forms throughout the study area, especially in the south (Cooke and Warren 1973;

Brown 1997). Since the eastern escarpment is of bold relief, with an elevation change of hundreds of meters over a short distance in most areas, Wādī 'Araba serves as a catchment basin for detrital materials discharged from its tributary wadi systems. These tributary wadis each have catchment zones of varying size that govern the rate of discharge, which may occur as torrential floods or less forceful stream flows, depending on the amount of rainfall in the highlands. This discharge emerges from the escarpment at the apex of the alluvial fan, which then radiates in a conical shape down the slope toward the valley bottom. These deposits are of clay- to boulder-size particles. The coarser gravels predominate near the apex of the fan, with intermediate size particles concentrated across the mid-fan, and silts and clays along the base (Blissenbach 1954: 182). In many areas compound alluvial fans have formed by the lateral coalescence of the primary fan systems.

The drainage patterns within these fan systems affected the survey strategy significantly. Cooke and Warren (1973: 175–77) classified channel flows across an alluvial fan into two distinct groups. The first is the primary output channel originating at the apex of the fan and its tributaries. The second consists of channels that originate on the fan itself, which usually result from local rather than regional runoff. These secondary channels themselves erode much of the alluvial surface and what remain are vestiges of the older fan surfaces. These may best be described as "islands of preservation," randomly interspersed across the alluvial fans. When located, such areas make excellent targets for survey and are often the only viable areas for the preservation of cultural remains.

The most extensive fan system in the southern 'Araba is that of Wādī Yutum. The apex of the wadi is situated ca. 8 km N–NE of the Gulf of Aqaba. It has a radius of ca. 5–7 km, which spans most of the floor of the valley where it assumes the character of an alluvial plain due to the low angle of deposition. Further north, expansive alluvial fans radiate from each of the major and tributary wadis that debouch into the 'Araba. Most prominent among these is that of Wādī el-Muhtadī, which also has a radius that spans most of the valley floor. In the south, where the relief of the eastern escarpment

is greatest, these alluvial fans appear largely as formidable boulder and gravel fields from the mid-fan to the apex. With limited resources, survey is not viable within these areas due to the difficulty of the terrain.

A vast amount of time and energy would be required to survey these fan complexes intensively. The most feasible approach would be to plot out beforehand and then survey the areas where older alluvial fan surfaces remain intact and unaffected by the drainage flows discharging from the wadis. These "islands of preservation" are easily distinguished in aerial photographs due to the dark patination of the stones along the surface. For the most part, however, these are widely dispersed and not easily accessible, and a great deal of time would be lost crossing sterile drainages of wadi outwash between preserved remnants of the alluvial fans. In order to avoid these difficulties, the SAAS limited its coverage to areas along the escarpment and at the apex of the primary fan systems where pedestrian transects proved most viable.

Sabkhas *or Mudflats*

Two major *sabkhas,* or mudflats, are situated in the study area. These are Qā' aṭ-Ṭāba, which is bounded along its southern edge by the alluvial fan complex of Wādī el-Muhtadī, and Qā' as-Su'aydiyyīn, which lies in the extreme north of the study area (the 'En Defiya *sabhka* lies just south of the Wādī el-Muhtadī fan system and outside of the study area). These are topographic depressions with variably high levels of saline groundwater. Near the eastern escarpment, the modern 'Araba highway winds along the edge of Qā' aṭ-Ṭāba just south of Wādī Ḍarba and the village of Rama. Here lie the ruins of the Nabataean settlement of Rujm aṭ-Ṭāba (Sites 152–53) and what may have been a popular crossing of the valley along the flat plain of the *sabkha.* The high level of the groundwater at the east edge of the mudflat makes it convenient to access water by means of shallow wells excavated into the alluvial surface. This is practiced by the bedouin today, who herd large numbers of sheep and camels in this sector of the valley. Also, limited agricultural activity can be supported along the edge of the *sabkha,* where the groundwater is less saline than in the center due to the slightly higher elevation.

The most extensively cultivated area in the SE 'Araba is that of Qāʿ as-Suʾaydiyyīn, where wheat is produced today in great quantities. It is a relatively flat plain situated at the watershed of the valley. The eastern edge of the *sabhka* is characterized by a narrow band of sand dunes, which lie just below the modest alluvial fan complexes projecting from the eastern escarpment. An expansive sand dune field bounds the *sabhka* to the south, and the mountain range of Jebel el-Khureij, which rises abruptly near the center of the valley and trends roughly N–S, lies west of the *sabkha*. Because wells can tap groundwater at fairly shallow levels, the area could have been extensively cultivated in antiquity. Direct evidence of agricultural activity in the region may be found at Site 316, perhaps an agricultural settlement.

These *sabkhas* may be easily surveyed with standard techniques, such as the employment of pedestrian transects. Both visibility and accessibility are generally good, and artifact frequency tends to be high where sites are found. When artificial restrictions are placed on what areas may be accessed, however, more purposive methods must be employed with predetermined objectives. These may be determined based on prior knowledge of site location or the potential of site discovery. Analyses of low altitude aerial photographs of the region informed the survey considerably. However, Jordanian military authorities sharply curtailed the SAAS access west of the modern highway, which happens to be most of the area spanned by the mudflats (see below).

Sand Dunes and Sand Fields

Sand dunes and sand fields are the predominant landforms in the northern sector of the study area. These bound the Qaʿ as-Suʾaydiyyīn to the east and south, where they extend as far south as Qāʿ aṭ-Ṭāba. Although often characterized as impenetrable, this is not true. Whereas the sand dunes themselves present formidable obstacles to overland movement, the sand fields interspersed among the dune fields can be easily navigated and there are indications of land routes in various direc-

tions across the valley. Such land routes, which may range from formal roads to simple tracks, can be identified in aerial photographs, but they are not always detectable on the ground or even datable when found.

Areas of sand dunes and sand fields require significant time and energy to survey and the negative results typically outweigh the resources expended. It is generally difficult to estimate how much of the surface is covered by the dune fields, and what narrow portions are exposed frequently are covered again by the shifting sands (for discussion of sand dune formation and movement, see Cooke and Warren 1973: 267–328). In areas along the escarpment where the dunes blanket the mountain ridges (a characteristic feature of the valley between Gharandal and Rama), sand coverage is usually total. With limited resources, the best survey strategy would incorporate both selective and purposive techniques, although more intensive survey may be applicable in some cases. The areas selected for survey should be limited to those with a high probability of locating sites based on analysis of aerial photographs of the region.

The SAAS did not survey large sectors of the valley between Gharandal and Rama. This was due primarily to the sand coverage, rough topography, and inadequacies of time, staff, and equipment.

Ridges and Mountainous Zones

As mentioned above, the mountains bordering the 'Araba to the east are of high relief and quite rugged. In only a few cases did the SAAS attempt any exploration of the mountainous zones, with preference placed on areas of low relief and nearer to resources that might explain or sustain human presence. The SAAS selected areas for survey in the mountains based on previously known archaeological sites, locations offering good vantage points, and the presence of natural resources. The SAAS also targeted hillocks and low ridges along the escarpment in addition to portions of Jebel el-Khureij near the center of the valley. Pedestrian transects that followed the topography generally proved the best method of survey in these areas.

Wadi Beds and Wadi Terraces

The terraces within each of the major wadis that debouch into Wādī ʿAraba proved fruitful archaeologically, above all because of proximity to water resources. Groundwater is generally high and easily accessible along the wadi beds and the runoff from the infrequent winter rainfall also moves along the wadi bottoms as streams or as torrential floods. Occasionally, hydraulic installations can be found that illuminate the methods employed for harvesting water resources. Less durable but still effective are shallow pits that local bedouin excavate in the wadi beds to tap the groundwater.

The most effective and feasible means of surveying the wadi beds and terraces is by foot. Pedestrian transects along the course of the wadis permit fairly easy identification of hydraulic installations such as dams and miscellaneous wall alignments, otherwise difficult to identify in aerial photographs. The same holds true for the wadi terraces, where such unobtrusive sites as small campsites and sherd scatters may be recovered. Accessibility, time, and energy dictate the extent to which wadi beds and wadi terraces can be explored.

The SAAS lacked the resources to explore every wadi system. Only those with clear and easy access to the eastern plateau were targeted for evidence of sites and as lines of communication. These included Wādī Ḥeimir, Wādī el-Quṣeib, and Wādī Museimīr.

Beaches

The beaches along the coast of the Gulf of Aqaba were, for the most part, eliminated from the survey design. Results from a preliminary reconnaissance showed that the impact of modern development was too serious to warrant an intensive survey along the coast.

VI.   GENERAL SURVEY RESTRICTIONS

The SAAS surveyed each of the environmental zones outlined above at varying levels of intensity, based on the specific goals for each season of the project (discussed below). The methods of survey applied within each zone varied, with decisions based largely on such considerations as topography, accessibility, and assessments of the probability of site location. Artificial boundaries transposed over these areas also affected the methods of survey, which includes zones not surveyed due to security restrictions imposed on the project.

The SAAS, for example, was not allowed to investigate any area west of the ʿAraba highway for security reasons, with the exception of some areas around Qāʿ as-Suʾaydiyyīn in the north. Elsewhere, some limited survey was conducted around the principal architectural sites north of Area I while these sites were being recorded. Since many recorded sites lie outside of Area I and are geographically dispersed, systematic or intensive coverage was not possible. In fact, local authorities carefully monitored the survey, and areas targeted had to be approved in advance. This obviously necessitated detailed analyses of aerial photographs beforehand to identify archaeological remains that might be verified on the ground in unrestricted zones.

In the central sector of the study area, the highway winds around the eastern fringe of Qāʿ aṭ-Ṭāba nearly adjacent to the escarpment. Since access was restricted west of the highway, the SAAS had to exclude the entire *sabkha* region. Potential sites identified in this region, which could not be verified on the ground though all were visible in aerial photographs, included numerous corral-type structures, routes through the valley, and what may have been a caravanserai or way station near the center of Qāʿ aṭ-Ṭāba. The SAAS was also not permitted to survey the region west of Gharandal, although the SAAS did identify archaeological features in aerial photographs that could not be verified on the ground, including presumed land routes and architectural remains. Immediately north of Aqaba itself, the SAAS had to limit its coverage to the region east and SE of the airport, areas most modified by modern development.

The authorities also warned SAAS to avoid other zones of unspecified danger (probably from landmines) intermittently spread across the valley. Thus it is prudent to repeat the caution offered to the survey team that pedestrians are ill-advised to stroll randomly through the valley without a military escort. In order to ensure the safety of the survey team, the Jordan military daily assigned such escorts to the SAAS. Finally, the SAAS team was excluded from areas that were militarily sensitive. These obviously abound in the 'Araba, particularly until the peace treaty between Jordan and Israel was signed soon after the 1994 season. Despite these constraints, however, the SAAS carried out purposive survey in those areas where there were no restrictions, in order that the survey data be comparable across geographical zones.

VII. TIME, EQUIPMENT, AND PERSONNEL

The only maps available for the SE Wādī 'Araba north of Wādī Yutum were those at a scale of 1:50,000, and, as noted, the three map sheets that cover the region provided the basis for the initial partition of the study area. Sheets at this scale were prepared by the Ministry of Economy and the United States Agency for International Development in Jordan. Their compilation was based on photogrammetric methods from aerial photography in 1961 and from existing data provided by the Jordan Department of Lands and Surveys. They are among the Series K737, Tranverse Mercator Projection, Zone 36, International Spheroid. Sheets used at this scale were: Sheet 3049 III (Aqaba); Sheet 3049 IV (Wādī Ḍarba); and Sheet 3050 III (Gharandal). Maps at a scale of 1:10,000 and 1:5,000 were available for the region south of Wādī Yutum to the Gulf of Aqaba. The latter were produced by the Royal Jordanian Geographic Centre and printed in 1987. Their compilation was based on photogrammetric methods from aerial photography dated 1981, with a field compilation dated 1986. These then provided the basis for the compilation of the 1:10,000 map sheets, also produced by the Royal Jordanian Geographic Centre.

Aerial photographs at a scale of 1:10,000 (Series IGN-78-JOR-12/100) were also used by the project. These, however, were not obtained until 1995, i.e., after the 1994 season. Analyses of aerial photographs provided the basis for the survey methodology employed in 1996 and 1998, when the SAAS used more purposive techniques for site discovery (see below).

Other logistical factors that influenced the survey methodology included time and the size and composition of the staff. Six weeks were projected for each season, but in 1996 this devolved into an actual field presence of no more than four weeks due to complications with the survey vehicle. Also, the project reduced the field staff in 1996 to three individuals (the survey director and two students), whereas the field staff for the 1994 and 1998 seasons consisted of four individuals (mostly senior staff). Furthermore, much time was spent simply driving from the project base at Aqaba to the areas intended for survey, because local officials forbade camping in the valley. Under optimal conditions, the SAAS spent roughly six or seven hours per day on active survey. The rising summer heat index, when temperatures peaked in the early afternoon, dictated the time limit of each day's fieldwork.

VIII. SURVEY GOALS AND METHODS

The 1994 Season

The 1994 season of the survey had four specific goals. First, the survey team returned to Area III in order to survey an ancient stone-paved road discovered in 1993 (Smith and Niemi 1994: 479; Smith 1994). The SAAS recorded the extent and alignment of this road and associated sites. The second goal was to study the immediate hinterland of Roman Aila by conducting an intensive regional study of Wādī 'Araba immediately north of Aqaba to the north branch of the Wādī Yutum alluvial fan. The third goal was to investigate the upper portions of the alluvial fans and the apexes of the principal wadis north of Wādī Yutum within Area I. This served as a less intensive continuation of the survey immediately north of Aqaba. The fourth goal was to survey the principal archaeological sites previously known within Areas I–III. The SAAS focused on the main caravanserais or forts and their immediate environs as far north as Bir Madhkur to suggest how these sites might relate to Roman Aila.

The survey methods applied to achieve the goals in the 1994 season were both intensive and purposive. The SAAS recorded the sites discovered during transects in the following manner: first, the basic information concerning the site was recorded on a standard form (figs. 4.3–4); second, both black

Roman Aqaba Project
SOUTHEAST ARABA ARCHAEOLOGICAL SURVEY
Site Record Form

Site #: _____ Site Name: _____ Recorder(s):_____

Date: _____ Time: _____ Time Spent Recording (min.):_____

Site Size (m): NS _____ EW _____   **How Measured:** ☐ Est. ☐ Pace ☐ Tape

Elevation: _____ **Mapsheet:** _____   **Air Photo Ref:** _____

Site Composition: (choose one)   **UTM:** N _____

☐ **(1)** Artifact Scatter (No other visible features)   E _____

☐ **(2)** Features w/ associated artifacts   **Pal. Grid:** N _____

☐ **(3)** Features w/ NO associated artifacts   E _____

Do features consist of walls or structures? ☐ Yes ☐ No

Specific Codes for Site Type:_____ _____ _____ _____ _____ _____ _____

Site Condition: ☐ **(0)** No Information ☐ **(1)** Excellent ☐ **(2)** Good ☐ **(3)** Fair

☐ **(4)** Poor ☐ **(5)** Inundated ☐ **(6)** Destroyed

Inventory Rating (see Codes): _____   **Disturbance** (see Codes): _____ _____ _____ _____

Is there threat of Destruction? ☐ Y ☐ N (If yes, indicate type/level): _____ / ☐ Low ☐ Med. ☐ High

---

Topographic Setting (Location):_____

Codes for Topographic Setting (see Codes): _____ _____ _____

Present Surface (Geology/Soils): _____

Vegetation:_____

Assemblage Composition:			Type	Collection			Count	Density
Pottery:	☐ Yes	☐ No	_____	☐ Purp. /	☐ Random /	☐ N/A	_____	_____ m²
Lithics:	☐ Yes	☐ No	_____	☐ Purp. /	☐ Random /	☐ N/A	_____	_____ m²
Ground Stone:	☐ Yes	☐ No	_____	☐ Purp. /	☐ Random /	☐ N/A	_____	_____ m²
Shell:	☐ Yes	☐ No	_____	☐ Purp. /	☐ Random /	☐ N/A	_____	_____ m²
Slag:	☐ Yes	☐ No	_____	☐ Purp. /	☐ Random /	☐ N/A	_____	_____ m²
Minerals (ore):	☐ Yes	☐ No	_____	☐ Purp. /	☐ Random /	☐ N/A	_____	_____ m²
Bone:	☐ Yes	☐ No	_____	☐ Purp. /	☐ Random /	☐ N/A	_____	_____ m²
Other (specify):			_____	☐ Purp. /	☐ Random /	☐ N/A	_____	_____ m²

Were Photographs Taken? ☐ Yes ☐ No (If yes, indicate type): ☐ B/W ☐ Color Slide ☐ Color Print

---

Codes: Topographic Setting		Codes: Disturbance		Codes: Inv. Rating	Selected Codes for Site Type	
00 - Unknown	16 - Plateau	00 - No Information	21 - Bulldozing	0 - Site destroyed:	01 - Sherd or lithic scatter	58 - Road
01 - Alluvial Fan	21 - Slope	01 - Archaeological	22 - Trench	No excavation possible	02 - as above (uncertain	60 - Kite
02 - Alluvial Plain	22 - Upper Slope	Excavation	(pipeline, aqueduct)	1 - Site damaged or very	presence)	62 - Animal pen
03 - Valley Bottom	23 - Middle Slope	02 - Clandestine	23 - Trench (canals)	disturbed:	03 - as above (main presence)	63 - Hut circle
04 - Wadi Terrace	24 - Lower Slope	Excavation/ Vandalism	24 - Road Work	excavation not advisable	04 - as above (one-period site)	65 - Cairn
05 - Cutbank	25 - Terrace on	03 - Deflation	25 - Quarry	2 - Excavation not essential:	05 - Mat. cult.	67 - Stone fences
06 - Gully	Hill Side	04 - Erosion	26 - Mining	low priority	(w/ no structures)	/enclosures
11 - Hilltop	26 - Cliff Top	11 - Agricultural Use	27 - Construction	3 - Excavation recommended:	21 - Nomadic Camp	71 - Quarry
12 - Ridge	27 - Cliff Face	(general)	28 - Modern Houses	medium priority	22 - Cave/Shelter	72 - Mine
13 - High Spur	28 - Cliff Bottom	12 - Plowing	29 - Bedouin Camp	4 - Excavation imperative:	24 - Isolated structure/house	73 - Smelting site /
14 - Low Spur	29 - Beach	13 - Deep Plowing	30 - Modern Tombs	high priority	25 - Other/unsp. structures or	slag heap
15 - Saddle	30 - Summit	14 - Grazing	31 - Structural Decay	5 - Preservation recommended	walls	75 - Kiln
	31 - Dune Field	15 - Terracing	32 - Reuse of ancient	6 - Preservation imperative	26 - Domestic installation	81 - Cemetery
		16 - Reforestation	masonry	9 - Site already under	36 - Stone circle	88 - Grave
		17 - Fruit/Olive Grove	33 - Reuse of ancient	protection	37 - Menhir	89 - Burial cairn /
		18 - Threshing Floor	structures		41 - Hamlet/Farmstead	tumulus
		19 - Animal Pen/Shelter	98 - Other disturbance		44 - Agricultural Terrace	
			99 - No Disturbances			

FIG. 4.3   *SAAS Site Record Form, front side.*

General Site Description / Interpretation (Include relationships between features):

Main Feature Data:

Site # _____   Feature # _____   **Feature Type(s)** (see Codes): _____ _____ _____

Area (m): NS _____ EW _____   **Is there a plan of Feature(s)?**   ☐ Y   ☐ N

Description: _____

FIG. 4.4   *SAAS Site Record Form, back side.*

and white photographs and color slides were taken at most sites; third, all architectural features at each site were drawn; fourth, if present, artifacts were collected at all sites. Initially, the site was zoned so that different structures or features of the same site were given distinct "feature" numbers in addition to a common "site" number. Then, artifacts were collected separately from each distinct feature of the same site. During the collection process, the SAAS employed both random and purposive procedures. Although surface artifacts were used to date sites from the survey, it must be stressed that this type of data is necessarily limited and must be supplemented and tested by stratified excavations.

Pedestrian transects were the preferred means of sampling the greater Aqaba region, from the urban center to the north branch of the Wādī Yutum alluvial fan. Generally, each walker was spaced 50 m apart, though the gap was lessened to 25 m in some areas. This allowed for the documentation of the more obtrusive sites in a given area — highly unobtrusive sites (e.g., isolated graves) were probably missed. Within the urban zone of Aqaba itself, the methods of survey shifted into a more selective sampling of vacant lots and other "open" areas where the survey team was permitted access. The intent was to establish the possible boundaries of Roman Aila. Accordingly, the SAAS surveyed within the modern city using the "Circular Area" as a focal point. Most of the sites recorded in this area were light to dense sherd scatters recorded in heavily disturbed areas (see fig. 4.38: map 1 of Aqaba region). Thus it proved difficult to determine whether the disturbed material was brought in from other areas as fill or if the disturbance was localized. If the latter is true, then some cultural materials may lie *in situ* below the disturbed contexts. This may be the case for those sites that lie nearest to Roman Aila.

Further north in the valley, where the landscape is characterized by immense alluvial fans (the largest being that of Wādī el-Muhtadī), the SAAS initially planned to sample these areas by conducting pedestrian transects along the length of each fan complex. While this would have permitted the best sample of archaeological sites present, it took little time to recognize that this method was not at all feasible with the resources at hand. As noted,

these expansive alluvial fans in Area I may best be characterized as formidable boulder fields cut randomly by shallow and deep drainages. Accessibility is extremely limited. Accordingly, and as an alternative, the SAAS focused its efforts with pedestrian transects along the base of the escarpment and at the apexes of the fan complexes. The SAAS also targeted older alluvial fan surfaces, with areas selected for survey based on visibly heavy patination. Further, the SAAS made periodic excursions into the wadi systems proper, but only when and where the probability of site discovery seemed highest. For the most part, the SAAS noticed that sites generally concentrated along the tops of the alluvial fans, and more densely along their bases. Since the latter extend west of the modern highway (and in some cases nearly across the entire width of the valley), these areas were omitted. Only in the region of Qā' as-Su'aydiyyīn was the survey permitted limited access west of the highway.

Survey farther north in the valley was even more purposive. With respect to the possible ancient road discovered the prior year, the SAAS followed its course north to Gharandal. Its extension further north was not discovered until 1998. While surveying along the road, one team member walked on the road itself while the others were spaced 50 m and then 100 m on either side. The SAAS recorded several features associated with the road but found nothing that might supply a definitive date for its construction or use.

The SAAS also returned to the Early Bronze Age sites in Wādī Ḥeimir that were first discovered in 1993. The goal was to record these sites properly and collect artifacts. The SAAS also sought out evidence to suggest occupation in the wadi system in other periods, to illuminate the wadi system itself as a major land-route linking the 'Araba with the eastern plateau.

Visits to the principal architectural sites were also purposive and of short duration. Generally, these are all situated at or near the major water sources in the valley, which accounts for their *raison d'être* and continued significance up to the present day. The SAAS targeted five sites. These are, from north to south, Bir Madhkur, Qasr Wādī eṭ-Ṭayyiba, Qasr Qā' as-Su'aydiyyīn, Gharandal, and Rujm aṭ-Ṭāba. With the exception of the survey around Qasr Wādī eṭ-Ṭayyiba and Qasr Qaʿ as-Suʾaydiyyīn, the survey team was under keen observation and instructed not to proceed far beyond the ruins themselves. Where the survey was permitted to extend its coverage, a number of important discoveries were made, as discussed below.

The 1996 and 1998 Seasons

The SAAS made significant changes to the goals and methods of survey during the 1996 and 1998 field seasons, prompted by the project's acquisition of aerial photographs of the region and because of logistical constraints in 1996. Preliminary analyses of the aerial photographs were initiated and mostly completed in 1995. Beginning in 1996, because the survey was under tighter constraints to utilize its resources to maximum effect, each day the survey team targeted specific areas and features of interest pre-selected from aerials. For example, many archaeological sites with architectural features were identified in the aerial photographs, and it seemed prudent to target these as possibly contemporary with Roman Aila and associated with the trade and transport networks in the valley. Though many unobtrusive sites were sure to be missed, this new approach permitted the survey to achieve its research objectives and to address the specific research questions posed by the Roman Aqaba Project more effectively. More importantly, the SAAS spent less time engaged in pedestrian transects across less productive landscapes where the opportunities for site detection were limited.

In order to record sites identified beforehand in aerial photographs, the survey team often drove directly to them. At times, however, the terrain prevented vehicular access to the sites. When this happened, in order to sample a larger area, at times across different geographical zones, pedestrian transects were plotted that would cross the site. This sort of random sampling proved beneficial in terms of placing the more obtrusive sites visible in the aerials into a broader framework. When the number of architectural features appeared particularly dense in a given area, the transects were extended to examine broader areas and interrelationships between features. The SAAS accomplished this chiefly in the northern sector of the study area. In the region north of Gharandal, the survey worked along the base of the whole escarpment and sampled an old alluvial fan surface north and west of Wādī Abū Barqa. The latter was conducted more thoroughly than elsewhere because the fan complex appeared much older than the surrounding terrain, which suggested a broader range of settlement activity and, as suggested by aerial photographs, a greater diversity of site types. Intensive survey of the entire fan complex utilizing pedestrian transects spaced 30 m apart confirmed these suggestions. In this example then the SAAS documented those sites that appeared in the aerial photographs as well as several unobtrusive sites.

Some objectives and methods, however, continued from the 1994 season. Methods of recording sites, for example, continued from the previous season. Also, in terms of coverage, the SAAS completed its intensive pedestrian survey of the Wādī Yutum alluvial fan north of Aqaba in 1996 — at least in those areas where access was granted; and in 1998, the SAAS explored several major wadi systems where the probability of site discovery appeared particularly high despite a lack of visible evidence from aerial photographs (e.g., in Wādī el-Quṣeib and Wādī Museimīr).

IX.   SITE DEFINITION

What constitutes an archaeological site? Unfortunately, this is a contested matter and there are no simple definitions. Two essential factors must be evaluated and debated before a site can be defined: its key elements and its limits. On one end of the spectrum: how many stray artifacts comprise a site when no other archaeological features are present? At the other end: when artifacts or other cultural features are consistently distributed over an expansive area, where does one site end and another begin? Few would doubt, for example, that Petra is an archaeological site of great regional importance, but what are its limits? How far must the archaeological surveyor go from the urban center to document archaeological sites that are sufficiently isolated not to be interpreted as just another feature of the larger settlement? Decisions may be very subjective and any catalog of archaeological sites may or may not have any statistical merit in regional contexts.

The SAAS defined as a site all artifact scatters (e.g., pottery and lithics) and all man-made or architectural features that appeared to be pre-modern (dating before AD 1918; see MacDonald 1992: 9; Banning 1988: 15–17). This included modern features only when ancient remains were present. In some instances, however, it was difficult to determine whether a man-made feature was pre-modern, when no artifacts were present. Only when such features were not in current use or, based on proximity, not associated with areas of modern use, did the SAAS regard them as sites. Field walls, enclosures, and stone circles, for example, were recorded as sites when there was little question as to whether they were ancient, whether artifacts were present or not, and when there was no indication of recent use. In many instances, the patination of the surfaces negated the question of the antiquity of a particular site. Pot-busts — obvious evidence of human activity in the region — were also regarded as sites. Since it was a key objective to explore the 'Araba as a major land route in which Aqaba was a nexus, such data helped to determine areas of human traffic.

Site delineation, as noted, is another methodological issue that affects site definition. In most cases, the SAAS was able to determine the extent of archaeological sites due to their relative isolation, since there was usually sufficient distance between sites not to confuse their association. However, difficulties arose periodically that hindered site delineation. In some cases, over a large area several temporally distinct sites were evenly distributed, and no clear boundaries could be identified between them. The SAAS then arbitrarily zoned these areas using natural features such as ridges or drainages as divisions between sites (e.g., Sites 33–37). Otherwise, the SAAS delineated the area itself according to the decline in the number of sites across the landscape. For example, at least 50 m between disassociated features was necessary when there was no continuous distribution of artifacts across the surface, a requirement which proved most applicable along alluvial fans and in alluvial plains, due to their expansive nature. Instances in which the SAAS made such arbitrary site delineations, however, were few. Generally, the aim was to identify such large areas as single sites

and to designate archaeological remains within them as specific features of the site (e.g., along wadi terraces).

X. SCOPE OF THE PRESENT REPORT

The evidence discovered during our survey of the SE Wādī 'Araba and presented here illustrates the complex history of human settlement activity in the region. Although the study area was not surveyed in its entirety or intensively in all areas, there was sufficient coverage to project a range of activity over time. The data does serve a functional purpose in that it reveals to historians and archaeologists that the 'Araba is more than a simple no-man's land and certainly not the "abomination of desolation" once described. Within the parameters of the objectives of the Roman Aqaba Project, the data also illuminate the nature of the hinterland of a Roman port city on the Gulf of Aqaba.

The SAAS recorded 330 sites in three field seasons. Pottery was collected at 186 (56.36%) sites, lithics at 154 (46.67%) sites, and among these both pottery and lithics at 100 (30.30%) sites. No datable artifacts could be found at 90 (27.27%) of the sites surveyed, some of which exhibited architectural features. At sites where the SAAS collected pottery, 45 sites yielded five or less sherds; 27 sites yielded between six and 10 sherds; 32 sites yielded between 11 and 20 sherds; and 82 sites yielded more than 20 sherds. The sites recorded range in date from prehistoric to modern periods, although some periods are not represented in the surveyed area. Importantly, because only about a quarter of all sites (82 of 330, or 24.85%) yielded more than 20 sherds, the dating of many sites with fewer sherds must be regarded as tentative, at least for ceramic period sites, and should be confirmed through stratified excavation.

The following section presents the survey data according to the periods represented by the ceramic evidence. An analysis of the 154 sites where the SAAS collected lithics (Sites 29, 33, 38, 43, 48, 52, 54, 56–63, 66, 68–70, 76, 79–80, 123–24, 131–32, 134, 143–44, 148, 155, 157–68, 171–75, 180–82, 184, 186, 188–91, 193–95, 197–99, 201–4, 207–12, 216–21, 223–30, 232–34, 237–38, 240–42, 244, 247–63, 265–74, 276–77, 279–80, 283, 287, 290–91, 300,

303–7, 312–25, 327–28, 330) is provided in Chapter 5. Also, while all sherds were re-examined during the post-season to confirm or to update preliminary field identifications, because the vast majority recovered were small body sherds that were often sandblasted by exposure to the elements, the analysis of this material proved especially difficult (see Chapter 6). Again, excavation would be required to confirm the dating of many of the ceramic period sites discussed here. There is a complete catalog of all 330 sites as well as maps appended to this chapter. Selected pottery from some surveyed sites is presented in Chapter six and a small group of Nabataean inscriptions recorded at Site 225 is presented in Chapter seven.

XI.   RESULTS BY HISTORICAL PERIOD

Chalcolithic – Chalcolithic/Early Bronze Age

The earliest ceramic period sites recorded belong to the Chalcolithic (Table 4.1) or the Chalcolithic/Early Bronze Age (Table 4.2). Except for the Early Roman/Nabataean period, the Chalcolithic/Early Bronze Age was the best represented in the surveyed area, with a total of 61 sites (or 18.49% of all sites recorded). From Chalcolithic/Early Bronze Age sites the SAAS collected a total of 1078 sherds, or 14.22% of all sherds collected in the region,[3] which included five sherds or less at 25 sites and 20 or more sherds at only 14 sites.

The Chalcolithic and the Chalcolithic/Early Bronze Age sites are located near Aqaba (Sites 49–50, 52–60, 62–63, and 70), along the north bank of Wādī Yutum (78–80), near Wādī es-Sammāniya (Site 132), and near Wādī el-Muhtadī (Site 142) in Area I.[4] In Area II, Chalcolithic or Chalcolithic/Early Bronze Age sites are located on the slopes to the east of Sīḥ Duḥayla (Site 147), near Wādī Ḍarba (Site 155), in Wādī Ḥeimir (Site 163), and near Wādī Nukheila (Site 169 and 172). In Area III, Chalcolithic or Chalcolithic/Early Bronze Age sites are located just to the south of Wādī es-Sīq (Site 178), within a secondary drainage system to the north of Wādī Gharandal (Sites 180, 189, and 191), in Wādī el-Quṣeib (Sites 199, 203–4, and 208), Wādī Museimīr (Sites 221 and 226), along the escarpment between Wādī Museimīr and Wādī

Table 4.1   Chalcolithic Period Sites.

Site No.	Field Site No.	No. of Chalcolithic Sherds	% of Total Sherds from Site
54	72	13	72.22
56	66	69	100.00
57	73	24	85.71
58	71	20	33.33
60	76	11	64.71
132	94	4	100.00
142	128	7	100.00
242	142	20	95.24
243	141	46	57.50

Abū Barqa (Sites 234 and 238), and at the mouth of Wādī Abū Barqa (Sites 242 and 243). The greatest concentration of Chalcolithic or Chalcolithic/Early Bronze Age sites lies along the escarpment north of Wādī Abū Barqa, which includes Sites 244, 249–50, 255–58, 262–63, 265, 267, 270, 273, 279–80, 286–87, 290, 294–95, 297, and 299–300, in addition to those at Wādī Um Saiyāla (Sites 312–13). Also, Chalcolithic or Chalcolithic/Early Bronze Age sherds were recovered in the vicinity of Jebel el-Khureij (Sites 277, 314, and 316–17) and in the far northern part of the study area near Qasr Wādī eṭ-Ṭayyiba (Site 321).

In the Aqaba region, settlements of the Chalcolithic or Chalcolithic/Early Bronze Age concentrate in two areas. These are on the alluvial fan of Wādī Yutum, where the two excavated sites of Tell Maqaṣṣ (Site 56) and Ḥujeirat al-Ghuzlan (Site 63; fig. 4.5) are situated, and on high alluvial spurs along the north bank of Wādī Yutum where it debouches into the ʿAraba. On these alluvial spurs the SAAS documented three settlements in 1996 (Sites 78–80; fig. 4.6) with ceramic material similar to that recovered from Tell Maqaṣṣ and Ḥujeirat al-Ghuzlan.

Lutfi Khalil partially excavated both Tell Maqaṣṣ (Khalil 1987; 1988; 1992; 1995) and Ḥujeirat al-Ghuzlan (Eichmann, Khalil, and Schmid 2009).

Table 4.2   Chalcolithic/Early Bronze Age Sites.

Site No.	Field Site No.	No. of Chalco/EB Sherds	% of Total Sherds from Site	Site No.	Field Site No.	No. of Chalco/EB Sherds	% of Total Sherds from Site
49	195	1	50.00	249	255	3	100.00
50	230	18	21.18	250	261	11	100.00
52	231	71	94.67	255	236	4	100.00
53	232	2	50.00	256	259	22	75.86
55	233	8	88.89	257	254	20	95.24
58	71	34	56.67	262	242	3	5.36
59	75	12	100.00	263	240	24	100.00
62	70	19	54.29	264	257	1	11.11
63	74	55	93.22	265	241	1	100.00
70	169	8	25.00	267	245	6	85.71
78	192	33	100.00	270	249	18	100.00
79	193	5	100.00	273	247	1	50.00
80	164	126	99.21	277	132	3	60.00
147	334	6	100.00	279	223	15	93.75
155	328	4	100.00	280	218	3	100.00
163	110	80	96.39	286	216	2	66.67
169	101	1	11.11	287	222	47	73.44
172	107	12	48.00	290	205	5	8.20
178	327	13	100.00	294	215	9	60.00
180	321	2	15.39	295	214	11	100.00
189	319	7	100.00	297	210	3	100.00
191	317	19	100.00	299	208	7	87.50
199	309	5	18.52	300	207	49	69.01
203	302	7	8.54	304	185	14	46.67
204	305	1	11.11	312	196	13	19.40
208	299	1	25.00	313	191	101	95.28
221	291	5	13.51	314	234	2	2.99
226	281	30	18.87	316	187	6	7.79
234	272	5	62.50	317	188	64	100.00
238	268	4	18.18	321	160	2	5.88
244	264	14	100.00				

The joint Jordanian-German project in the area, however, has added considerable knowledge to our understanding of the history of these sites (Eichmann and Khalil 1998; Khalil and Eichmann 1999; 2001). Tell Maqaṣṣ, according to Khalil (1992), was primarily an industrial center where copper, shell, and stone were worked, decorated, and traded, and Ḥujeirat al-Ghuzlan probably served as a local market. In 1994 and 1996, the SAAS carried out pedestrian transects of the area east of Tell Maqaṣṣ and SW and east of Ḥujeirat al-Ghuzlan and recorded Sites 46, 48–55, and 57–62. Ceramics and lithic material collected at most of these sites dated to the Chalcolithic period or Chalcolithic/Early Bronze Age (Smith et al. 1997: 51–56). Only Sites 46 and 51 yielded no artifacts, but the nature of these sites suggests their close association (probably with the terracing of the fan complex). Exposed wall alignments at all of these sites may be remnants of domestic, agricultural, or industrial installations.

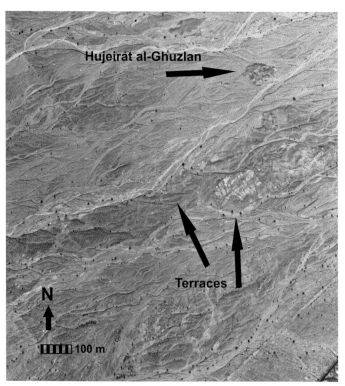

FIG. 4.5   *Aerial view of Wādī Yutum alluvial fan showing agricultural terracing. Ḥujeirat al-Ghuzlan (Site 63) is visible to the north of the terraces.*

Smith et al. (1997: 52) first suggested that Ḥujeirat al-Ghuzlan provided the agricultural basis that sustained settlement in the area during the Chalcolithic period, based on the extensive terracing of the fan and other water management installations discovered along the Wādī Yutum alluvial fan (fig. 4.5) — a suggestion recently supported by the joint Jordanian-German survey and excavations in the region (Brückner et al. 2002: 233). Site 54, for example, which consists of two large curvilinear stone alignments that parallel each other, several linear rock alignments that join a trapezoidal enclosure, a stone ring within this enclosure, and a sherd and lithic scatter, lies at the head of a series of agricultural terraces that extends more than 225 m to the SW (these stone terrace walls are over 100 m in length and divided from each other by ca. 15 m). The SAAS collected 13 Chalcolithic sherds from Site 54. Site 58, which yielded 54 Chalcolithic and Chalcolithic/Early Bronze Age sherds and some lithics, also consists of a series of rock alignments or terraces, some of

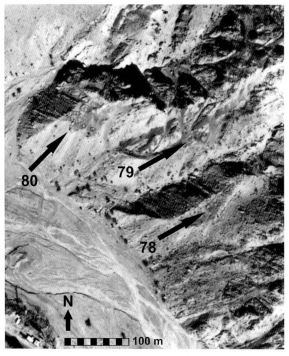

FIG. 4.6   *Aerial view of settlements (Sites 78–80) in Wādī Yutum.*

FIG. 4.7   *SAAS Site 55, massive wall alignment, looking northeast.*

another massive wall alignment, oriented E–W and extending along the middle portion of the alluvial fan in two distinct, lengthy segments, that may also have deflected discharge from the Wādī Yutum (fig. 4.7). The eastern wall segment is 68 m long; then, after a gap of 55 m, the western segment continues another 52 m. Both wall segments appear as linear mounds of stone and alluvial deposits. Finally, as noted, all the pottery collected near these installations (Sites 49, 51–52, 54–55, 58, and 60) dated predominately to the Chalcolithic or Chalcolithic/Early Bronze Age (158 of 181 sherds, or 87.29%); the remainder ranged in date from the Early Bronze Age to the Early Islamic period. All sherds, seemingly, were detritus washed there from nearby sites.

In addition to the aforementioned sites near Ḥujeirat al-Ghuzlan that illuminate agricultural or water management practices, other enigmatic sites in the area further reveal a broad range of settlement activity in the same period. Site 59, for example, is a massive stone wall spanning ca. 28 m N–S, which appears distinct from Sites 55 and 60 discussed above. Large pits (excavation trenches?) have been dug before the west face of the wall revealing the foundations and exposing its height at almost two meters. Two curvilinear walls project from the west face, both of which resemble bastions but their true function remains enigmatic; they may well be secondary appendages. An additional wall alignment lies exposed to the south. Unfortunately, the nature of Site 59 remains unclear, though the SAAS collected exclusively Chalcolithic/Early Bronze Age pottery (12 sherds) from the site and few lithics. SE of Ḥujeirat al-Ghuzlan and spread over a large area (ca. 150 m N–S × 200 m E–W), Site 62 consists of several stone rings and semicircular rock alignments, a massive stone wall (some stones are over a meter wide), and an associated scatter of ground stone, ceramics (19 Chalcolithic/Early Bronze Age sherds), lithics, mudbricks, and copper slag, all of which would indicate some industrial activity. SW of Ḥujeirat al-Ghuzlan, Site 57 is a small mound or tell with various exposed wall

which enclose relatively large areas. Further terracing of the alluvial fan defines the wall alignments that comprise Sites 49 and 51–52, where the SAAS collected a total of 77 sherds from which 72 were of the Chalcolithic/Early Bronze Age (only Site 52 yielded lithics). In addition to the terracing, there may also have been other means of managing the discharge from Wādī Yutum. Site 60, for example, a massive stone wall extending ca. 20 m across the alluvial fan, may have served as a diversion wall or deflection dam against the seasonal floods. Although the wall itself cannot be dated, it seems to be associated with the Chalcolithic agricultural activity that predominates in the area (e.g., 11 of 17 sherds from the site were Chalcolithic and some lithics were present). Similarly, Site 55, which yielded 8 Chalcolithic/Early Bronze Age sherds, is alignments indicating a complex structure buried beneath it. The surface of the mound, from which the SAAS collected lithics and 24 Chalcolithic sherds, is covered in rubble. SW of the mound are a series of seven elongated rock alignments, all of which trend roughly NW–SE. The best-preserved alignment is two courses wide with a rubble fill, and a small, rectilinear structure appears attached to the westernmost one. There is also a smaller mound ca. 260 m to the NW of the larger one, with what appear to be circular wall alignments around its edge. Further SW of Ḥujeirat al-Ghuzlan, Site 53, which may be a burial, consists of a large mounded stone alignment and three stone circles, one of which was back-filled with a mixture of cobbles and large stones and smoothed to create an evenly paved surface on the top. The SAAS collected only two Chalcolithic/Early Bronze Age sherds from Site 53. Still further to the SW, Site 48 is a circular stone mound, perhaps a large burial cairn, comparable to Site 61, a much larger mound or cairn to the east of Ḥujeirat al-Ghuzlan. At both sites the SAAS found no pottery, although bone fragments and lithics were present.

Site 50, presumably a small settlement consisting of numerous wall alignments, structures, rectilinear enclosures, stone mounds, and stone rings (possibly circular huts), covers an area of ca. 50 m N–S × 100 m E–W and is the most significant among the sites near Ḥujeirat al-Ghuzlan. Some of the rectilinear enclosures, with walls comprised of tightly packed stones a single course high and wide, may in fact be terrace walls. Also, across the entire site are numerous stone mounds or burial cairns. Among finds from various periods (Early Roman/ Nabataean, Roman/Byzantine, and Early Byzantine), especially Early Islamic (possibly Umayyad), the SAAS collected 18 Chalcolithic/Early Bronze Age sherds from the site.

Another small settlement, Site 70, lies on a spur bisected by the railroad near the mouth of Wādī Yutum. The site consists of a large double stone circle or enclosure on an alluvial spur (fig. 4.6). There is also a smaller semicircular stone alignment nearby and a small stone ring to the west and down the slope from the large enclosure. Two further enclosures or stone rings lie to the SE. The site yielded lithics and pottery (19 Chalcolithic/Early Bronze

Age sherds, plus two Early Roman/Nabataean sherds and 14 unidentified sherds regarded as early in date). Furthermore, sites nearby where the SAAS collected no pottery may all be associated with the Chalcolithic or Early Bronze Age occupation of the area, generally, and perhaps related to Site 70, specifically based on proximity and similarity of archaeological remains. These are Site 68, a lithic scatter; Site 66, a series of wall alignments S–SE of Site 70, which yielded some lithics; and Site 69, a series of stone rings, possibly circular huts, with associated lithics. Perhaps Site 77, a semicircular stone structure in the alluvial plain below Site 70 to the north, also belongs to this period.

In 1996, the SAAS recorded a series of Chalcolithic/Early Bronze Age settlements set high on top of alluvial spurs near the mouth of Wādī Yutum (Sites 78–80; fig. 4.6); some of these sites were later excavated by a joint Jordanian-German team (Brückner et al. 2002: 241–43). Site 78 consists of a complex of stone structures, which includes both large and small stone rings and rectilinear structures. There are also apparent courtyards, large enclosures, and possible corridors providing access between structures. One stone ring, perhaps a circular hut, contains an obvious entranceway marked by two large boulders set upright on either side. These stone rings are all contiguous, sharing common walls on all sides. To the NW, some stone rings (or collapsed structures) seem to share a large enclosure or corral demarcated by a single course of boulders, loosely spaced. To the NE and up the slope, there are two linear features that may be terraces. Also, down the slope there begins a possible corridor (oriented NE–SW) on the south side of the settlement, which leads to additional stone rings or collapsed structures down the slope. Significantly, all 33 sherds collected at Site 78 were uniformly dated to the Chalcolithic/Early Bronze Age. On an adjacent alluvial spur, Site 79 consists of four large stone rings, possibly circular huts or enclosures, several of which are appended to one another, and various wall alignments. At the NW edge of the site, oriented N–S across a small gully, there is a linear stone alignment which appears to be a retaining wall. Various other wall alignments appear down the slope to the NE, which seem to create corridors for navigating up the ridge towards the structures above. The entire site, where the SAAS collected few lithics and only five Chalcolithic/Early Bronze Age sherds, is extremely well-preserved. Finally, on a third alluvial, Site 80 consists of a series of rectilinear and circular stone structures (figs. 4.8–9), many of which have been damaged by clandestine excavation; some of the debris from the associated robber pits contains significant amounts of ashy soil, charred wood, and other carbonized materials. Many are also damaged due to natural causes and appear as stone tumble. Some walls, however, are apparent and reveal that several of the structures are appended to one another. Also, there are massive terrace walls on the slopes above the site. An unusually large concentration of ceramic debris lies scattered across Site 80, clearly a result of the disturbances attested above. In addition to lithic material, the SAAS collected 127 sherds from the site, which included 126 dated to the Chalcolithic/Early Bronze Age and a single sherd dated to the Late Bronze Age. This site appears to be "Wādī Yutum B," which the Jordanian-German team partially excavated in 2000 and dated to the Early Bronze Age I–II (Brückner et al. 2002: 243).

Near Wādī Yutum several additional sites where the SAAS did not collect pottery may still

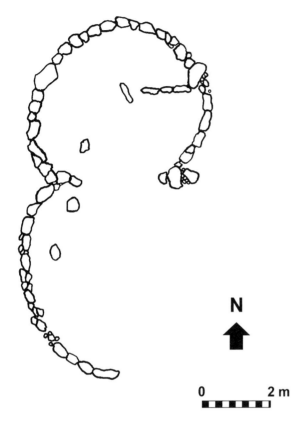

N

0   2 m

FIG. 4.8   *Plan of SAAS Site 80, Feature 1, double stone circle or enclosure.*

FIG. 4.9   *SAAS Site 80, overview of settlement in Wādī Yutum, looking southwest.*

belong to either the Chalcolithic or Chalcolithic/Early Bronze Age based on the remains of structures that seem to parallel those at nearby sites of known date. Sites 82–88 all qualify in this assessment. These sites exhibit a variety of features, which include a combination of various stone rings (Sites 82–83 and 86–88), a cairn or stone mound (Site 84), and burials (Site 85).

Further north in Area I, Site 132 is located on an old, isolated alluvial fan at the mouth of Wādī es-Sammāniya. The site is a multi-room structure characterized by various stone mounds and wall alignments. It yielded four Chalcolithic sherds and a small sample of chipped stone debris. To the east, Site 131, an isolated structure and graves, may also belong to this period but the SAAS found no pottery there, though lithics were present. Similarly, Site 130, a small enclosure far to the SW on the alluvial fan, may likewise belong to this period, although the SAAS found no pottery there either.

Site 142, on the north bank and at the mouth of Wādī el-Muhtadī, is a smelting site that consists of a large, collapsed structure. The SAAS found copper ore, copper slag, and eight Chalcolithic sherds scattered on the surface around the structure. Two nearby sites (141 and 143) may be associated with Site 142, each of which yielded evidence of metallurgical activity but no pottery. Site 141, which consists of various rock alignments and a concentration of copper slag, lies across the wadi to the south. Site 143, situated along the north bank of the wadi to the west of Site 142, consists of rock alignments and yielded copper ore and slag, and lithics.

In Area II, Site 147 is a large desert kite — the only such site recorded by the project — situated on the alluvial fan just north of Qatar village (fig. 4.10). The overall area enclosed by the kite is just under half a hectare. The walls of the kite are built solidly of granite boulders. A large circular structure is appended at the SW corner near the kite's main con-

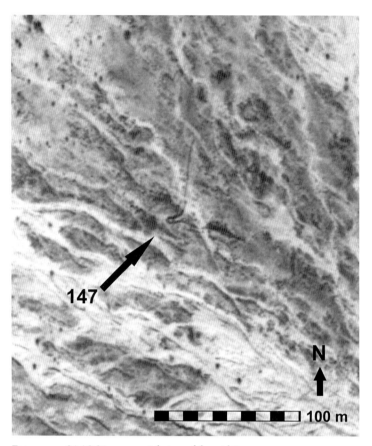

FIG. 4.10   *SAAS Site 147, aerial view of desert kite.*

vergence point, or circular catchment. Also, at the SE corner of this circular structure is a semicircular enclosure that actually joins with the main point of the kite. The SAAS collected six Chalcolithic/Early Bronze Age sherds from the site. Sites 146 and 148 nearby, where there are remains of structures but no pottery, though lithics were present at the latter, may also belong to the same period as the desert kite. This is conjectural, however.

Site 155 consists of a single stone mound, most likely a burial cairn, on an isolated hill just north of Wādī Ḍarba. The site, largely destroyed by robber trenches, yielded few lithics and four Chalcolithic/Early Bronze Age sherds near the mound. Site 154, a set of mounds or burial cairns further to the south of Site 155, may be of the same period although the SAAS found no pottery there.

Site 163 is a village site on a terraced bank of Wādī Ḥeimir. Although the SAAS collected 80 sherds dating to the Chalcolithic/Early Bronze Age, in addition to a large quantity of lithics, Site 163 will

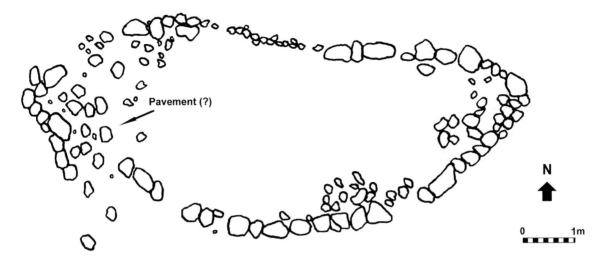

FIG. 4.11 *SAAS Site 191, indeterminate structure on small alluvial fan south of Wādī el-Quṣeib.*

be treated below in relation to the Early Bronze Age and associated with Sites 157–62.

In Area III north of Wādī Nukheila, Site 169 is an ancient, stone-paved road discovered by the SAAR in 1993 (Smith and Niemi 1994: 479; Smith 1994). It will be discussed below in relation to the Early Roman/Nabataean evidence from the survey. The SAAS found a single Chalcolithic/Early Bronze Age sherd near one segment of the road during a long transect.

The SAAS documented two artifact scatters in Area III between Wādī Nukheila and Wādī Gharandal. Site 172 is a sherd (12 Chalcolithic/Early Bronze Age and 13 Early Roman/Nabataean) and lithic scatter on the north bank of Wādī Nukheila. The SAAS collected most of the artifacts just below two bulldozer pushes that appeared recent in 1994. Also, further north, Site 178 is a pot-bust on a wadi terrace above the south bank of Wādī es-Sīq.

Site 180 is a small settlement that consists of numerous circular and rectilinear structures and an associated sherd and lithic scatter. It is located on a low spur where two small drainages merge in the first major tributary north of Wādī Gharandal. The site will be treated below as a possible Iron Age settlement. The SAAS collected only two body sherds from the site dated to the Chalcolithic/Early Bronze Age.

Site 189 lies on a low spur north of Wādī Gharandal and consists of numerous elongated graves, a rock alignment, a small circular arrange-

ment of stones that may be a grave also, and a light scatter of sherds and lithics. The latter appears set nearly flush with the ground forming some sort of pavement, with stones set slightly higher along the perimeter. Various stone piles and rock alignments characterize the other graves at the site. The SAAS collected seven Chalcolithic/Early Bronze Age sherds from the site, and the lithics collected were not diagnostic.

Located on the alluvial fan adjacent to the escarpment and south of Wādī el-Quṣeib, Site 191 is a single indeterminate structure constructed mostly of large limestone boulders with a slightly raised platform set along the interior face of the west wall (fig. 4.11). A possible entrance into the structure is set in the north wall. All 19 sherds collected at the site were dated to the Chalcolithic/Early Bronze Age.

On a wadi terrace above the north bank of Wādī el-Quṣeib, Site 199 consists of an unspecified structure, two stone rings (possibly circular huts), and a sherd and lithic scatter. There is a small hearth with recent ash deposits within the structure. There are also various oblong stone features spread out across the site, most constructed of a single course of sandstone boulders. These features all lie within a bedouin encampment with associated hearths, clearings, various rock alignments, and small stone enclosures abutting rock outcrops. There are also several items such as clothing fragments and metal objects suggesting modern reuse of the area. Among the various periods represented at the site, the SAAS collected five Chalcolithic/ Early Bronze Age sherds.

Site 203 lies on an elongated terrace above the south bank of Wādī el-Quṣeib. Various features on the terrace include stone rings or hut circles, isolated graves, miscellaneous wall alignments, and a scatter of sherds and lithics. Several wall alignments, in fact, may have served an agricultural function as retaining walls to check the erosion of the wadi terrace. Pottery from the site dated to various periods, so it is difficult to date its specific features. There were only seven Chalcolithic/Early Bronze Age sherds collected at the site, with no apparent distribution pattern. Most of the pottery was Roman/Byzantine, without further specification.

Site 204 is a cemetery with numerous graves on a terrace along the north bank of Wādī el-Quṣeib. Two additional features of the site include a stone ring and an oblong clearing. Few lithics were found and most of the few sherds from the site were Roman; the SAAS collected only one Chalcolithic/ Early Bronze Age sherd from Site 204.

Site 208 is also located on a terrace of Wādī el-Quṣeib. Since the SAAS found few lithics and only a single Chalcolithic/Early Bronze Age sherd here among other later sherds, this site will be treated below with the Early Roman/Late Roman sites.

Site 221 lies on an expansive wadi terrace along the north bank of Wādī Museimīr. The SAAS documented a total of 19 features at the site, which include bedouin encampments, stone rings or hut circles, isolated structures, graves, cairns, and a scatter of sherds and lithics. The SAAS collected a single Chalcolithic/Early Bronze Age sherd from an isolated stone ring or hut circle (Feature 8) and four sherds from a bedouin encampment (Feature 12), which probably originated from the robbed cairn nearby (Feature 11). Site 221 will be treated in more detail below with the Early Roman/Late Roman sites.

Site 226 lies on another elongated wadi terrace along the north bank of Wādī Museimīr. The site consists of an array of site types grouped into 19 features. From Feature 5, an isolated structure on the terrace, the SAAS collected nine Chalcolithic/ Early Bronze Age sherds (most from a single vessel). The enclosed area of the structure is irregular

and widens at its north end; possible storage areas abut the eastern and western sides of the enclosure. Also, from Feature 9, a circular clearing (perhaps an encampment), the SAAS collected sherds from a Chalcolithic/Early Bronze Age pot-bust where most of the pottery in the area was Early Roman/Late Roman. A few Chalcolithic/Early Bronze Age sherds were also collected in other presumed encampment areas where most of the collected pottery belonged to the Early Roman/Late Roman period. The SAAS collected lithics from across the entire terrace.

Site 234 is a group of structures on a small saddle of a steep knoll projecting from a high ridge south of Wādī Abū Barqa. The main structure is divided into two large enclosures, with two ovoid compartments, perhaps for storage, appended at the corners of the eastern part of the structure. Three other ovoid compartments are appended to the west side of the structure. Another indeterminate structure lies just south of the main structure. Also, downslope to the south is a walled enclosure, perhaps an animal pen. There are aligned terraces along the slope to the west. Perhaps due to its elevated position and effects of erosion, pottery at the site (only five Chalcolithic/Early Bronze Age and three unidentifiable [early] sherds were collected) and lithics were sparse. In addition to the structure, the presence of possible storage bins and animal enclosures suggest that this site was possibly a small farmstead. Moreover, Site 235, a group of four stone enclosures where the SAAS found no pottery, may be associated with Site 234.

On the alluvial fan south of Wādī Abū Barqa, Site 238 consists of two stone enclosures and a pot-bust. Since the SAAS found only four Chalcolithic/ Early Bronze Age sherds at the site nearest the main stone enclosure, among other later sherds, in addition to few lithics, this site will be treated below with the Late Roman/Early Byzantine sites.

Site 242 is a low-scale smelting site on a large hill NW of Wādī Abū Barqa. The site consists of several L-shaped rock alignments with a scatter of chipped stone, sherds, and copper slag. Twenty of 21 sherds collected at the site dated to the Chalcolithic/Early Bronze Age. Copper slag adhered to one of these sherds.

Site 243 lies on a projecting spur within a drainage north of Wādī Abū Barqa. The main feature consists of a series of three terraced platforms descending from the summit of the knoll. Additional terracing is evident further to the SE. Within the drainage itself is an oval enclosure with well-preserved walls. Also, on the SW face of the knoll is a well-preserved rectangular structure or tower; another ruined structure lies at the base of the bedrock knoll further to the SW. The only pottery collected at this last structure was from a pot-bust of the Byzantine period. The SAAS collected 46 Chalcolithic sherds at the main feature of the site.

The SAAS surveyed intensively the alluvial fan that extends NW from the mouth of Wādī Abū Barqa using regular transects spaced 25 m apart. By this method Chalcolithic/Early Bronze Age ceramics were found at Sites 244, 249–50, 255–58, 262–63, 265, 267, 270, and 273. Most of these sites are ephemeral and unobtrusive.

Site 244 consists of at least two graves, a stone ring, a rectilinear strip of ground cleared of large stones, and a light sherd and lithic scatter. Some large stones were set along the edges of the rectilinear strip, but there is no obvious pattern in their placement and the edges of the strip are vague and not well-defined. Most pottery at the site was near the east end of the strip. This feature is most likely the remains of a bedouin weaving strip, although there were no apparent encampment sites nearby. All pottery from the site dated to the Chalcolithic/Early Bronze Age.

There is another possible weaving strip at Site 256, where there is also a rectilinear area cleared of stones with a few larger stones scattered around the outer edge. Two stone rings nearby do not appear to have been associated with the rectilinear area. Pottery from Site 256 was predominately Chalcolithic/Early Bronze Age, in addition to some later sherds and a few lithics.

Site 249 consists of a large, isolated structure and a probable tomb, now robbed, to the west of the structure, in addition to a sherd and lithic scatter. Several small mounds of stone appear within the structure and at least one stone mound lies outside of it. Bone fragments and a single chert bead were found within the tomb. Outside the tomb, copper ore (consisting mostly of round pellets) lies scattered on the surface. Another badly damaged structure, perhaps another tomb, lies to the SW. It

appears mostly as a mound of stone tumble. At its base there is a stone retaining wall. Pottery at the site, found mostly downslope, is sparse. The SAAS collected only three Chalcolithic/Early Bronze Age sherds at the site.

Several sites (250, 255, 257, 262, 264, 270, and 273) along the same alluvial fan are mortuary in nature. Site 250 is a cemetery that consists of four low-lying stone mounds, the largest of which is badly deflated. Pottery and lithics are evenly distributed across the site — the SAAS collected exclusively Chalcolithic/Early Bronze Age pottery (11 sherds). Site 255 consists of four additional graves, two of which appear as scattered piles of stone, in addition to a light sherd (four were collected of the Chalcolithic/Early Bronze Age) and lithic scatter. Site 257 is a cemetery with three large stone mounds or burial cairns (one robbed), various smaller mounds, and stone rings. A fairly dense artifact scatter of lithics and pottery is spread evenly across the surface. Site 264 consists of three stone mounds that appear as oblong graves with no consistent orientation. The SAAS found both Early Roman/Nabataean (four sherds) and Chalcolithic/Early Bronze Age material (one sherd) at Site 264. The SAAS also found both Early Roman/Nabataean (53 sherds) and Chalcolithic/Early Bronze Age material (three sherds), in addition to lithics, at Site 262, a presumed mortuary site consisting of three cairns and a stone ring. Site 270, which yielded 18 Chalcolithic/Early Bronze Age sherds and few lithics, consists of a single stone mound or burial cairn. Finally, Site 273 is a cemetery consisting of a single large cairn and 13 graves, all oriented roughly E–W. The cairn is robbed and the SAAS found lithics, pottery, and bone fragments scattered across the surface. At Site 273 the SAAS found a single Chalcolithic/Early Bronze Age sherd and one Roman/Byzantine sherd. Sites 245, 248, 252, 259, 266, and 269, all of which appear mortuary in nature, lie on the same fan complex; at each of these sites the SAAS found no pottery, but lithics were recovered at all except Site 245.

Various encampments (Sites 263, 265, and 267) were found along the same alluvial fan; all yielded some lithics and pottery. Site 263 consists of two rectilinear areas cleared of stones, apparently foundations for tent emplacements or hut foundations

FIG. 4.12 *SAAS Site 263, Feature 1, rectilinear area cleared of stones, looking northwest.*

(fig. 4.12). In the NE corner of one of the features is a small stone mound, possibly a hearth. Modern debris lies scattered around both features. Only 24 Chalcolithic/Early Bronze Age sherds were collected at the site. Site 265 nearby may be another encampment with a stone-lined clearing. A single Chalcolithic/Early Bronze Age sherd found at the site may not be associated with the encampment. Site 267 is another encampment with large circular areas cleared of stones and debris. The SAAS found six Chalcolithic/Early Bronze Age sherds at Site 267. Also, Site 268, which may date later than the period discussed here, is another encampment nearby where the SAAS found some lithics but no pottery.

Further north along the slope of the escarpment west of Jebel el-Qā are several settlements and smaller sites of the Chalcolithic/Early Bronze Age (Sites 279–80, 286–87, 290, 294–95, 297, and 299–300). Site 279 is a small settlement spread over a large area (ca. 250 m N–S × 30 m E–W) that consists of numerous wall alignments and structures, stone rings (a few of which may be circular huts), stone mounds, and a sherd and lithic scatter. A series of wall alignments lies along the NE edge of the site. Additional stone alignments nearby may have combined to form a single large

structure. There are five or six small, figure-8 type structures or stone rings dispersed across the site, in addition to 10 more definite stone rings. There are also about 10 stone mounds or burials, at least five stones rings or hut circles, and numerous miscellaneous wall alignments. Apart from a single Roman/Byzantine sherd, all the ceramic material collected from Site 279 dated to the Chalcolithic/ Early Bronze Age.

Site 287 is another small settlement west of Jebel el-Qā spread over a large area (ca. 50 m N–S × 100 m E–W) that consists of numerous wall alignments, stone mounds, stone rings or hut circles, stone enclosures or structures, and a scatter of sherds and lithics. Two massive rectilinear enclosures, in fact, may join together to form a single large complex (fig. 4.13). Several attached, circular structures give this complex the appearance of a beehive. There is a large concentration of garnet and schist to the east (Ibrahim 1993: 65). Also, numerous other stone enclosures or structures appear with similar characteristics, but these are more scattered and disarticulated thus preventing an accurate estimation of their number. Furthermore, across the wadi to the NW is an extensive row of adjoining rectilinear and circular wall align-

FIG. 4.13   *SAAS Site 287, Feature 1, walled enclosure, looking southwest.*

ments, perhaps a residential block. Of 54 datable sherds from the site, which also included possible Neolithic and Early Roman/Nabataean, were 46 Chalcolithic/Early Bronze Age.

On the same fan complex due west of Site 287, Site 289 is smaller but exhibits similar features. The SAAS found no pottery at Site 289, however. It is likely, nonetheless, to be of the same period.

Across a narrow drainage north of Site 287, Site 294 also consists of various wall alignments, stone rings, which include a few possible hut circles, and stone mounds. Two linear wall alignments oriented N–S along the ridge lie in the northern area of the site, and a third wall alignment lies to the SE, which merges into the hillside on its east end. At least three parallel wall alignments project perpendicularly off the face of the largest wall alignment, thus forming an enclosure of sorts. These wall alignments are all too heavily disturbed to discern their specific construction. There are also six large stone rings or hut circles, some of which are appended to one other, and five smaller stone rings at the site. In addition to Chalcolithic/Early Bronze Age pottery (nine sherds), there was a large concentration of schist with garnet inclusions and garnet nuggets scattered over the site.

Furthermore, along the same slope to the east, Site 296, where the SAAS found no pottery or lithics, may be associated with Site 294, because similar structural features were documented there.

Also west of Jebel el-Qā, Site 299 is a third large settlement on the alluvial fan that extends far below and SW of Site 300 (see below) and NW of Site 294. Site 299 is also spread over a large area (60 m N–S × 45 m E–W). The site consists of a field of ca. 25 stone rings or hut circles, corral-like features (ca. three), figure-8 stone features (ca. five), and miscellaneous linear wall alignments (ca. four–five; several stone mounds at the site may in fact be collapsed structures. The corral features tend to be large, open, and circular with attached linear wall alignments. Apart from an unidentified sherd, the seven datable sherds collected from Site 299 were of the Chalcolithic/Early Bronze Age.

Near the bottom of the alluvial fan west of Jebel el-Qā, Site 280 consists of various stone rings, possibly circular huts, set next to each other, and an L-shaped stone alignment. Some of the stone rings appear as stone mounds and may be collapsed structures. Unfortunately, the site is badly damaged. The SAAS collected three Chalcolithic/Early Bronze Age sherds and a few lithics from the site.

Immediately south of Site 294, Site 286 consists of a group of stone rings, possibly hut circles, and isolated wall alignments lying on three terraced platforms. The main feature lies on the uppermost terrace. It is a curvilinear (snaking) alignment of stones. At the west edge of this alignment there are two circular stone mounds that project from its north face. Isolated wall alignments on the terrace immediately below seem to comprise enclosures. Some of the stone rings or hut circles are very well-preserved. Schist with garnet inclusions lies scattered on the slope above the site. Also, to the SE and up the slope from the main feature another series of curvilinear wall alignments join to create at least four enclosures. A single Roman/Byzantine sherd and two Chalcolithic/Early Bronze Age sherds were collected from the site.

To the west of Site 286 the SAAS found only five Chalcolithic/Early Bronze Age sherds at Site 290, which also yielded some lithics. Since the majority of the pottery here was later, this site will be treated below with the Early Roman/Nabataean sites.

Site 295 lies NW of Site 294 and is situated on four distinct terrace levels above the bed of the wadi. The site consists of numerous stone rings of varying sizes, from large to small, some of which may be circular huts. There is also one disarticulated rock alignment (wall?). The SAAS found only Chalcolithic/Early Bronze Age pottery at the site (11 sherds).

Site 297 lies on the alluvial fan SW of Site 299 and consists of two large enclosures and an associated sherd scatter. The first enclosure is partitioned internally into three separate compartments. The second enclosure, north of the first, is similar. Both have a large corral-type enclosure on their west sides and smaller compartments appended at their eastern ends. Also, abutting the first enclosure outside to the SE is a small, partitioned, rectangular area, apparently a paved platform. The only three sherds collected from the site were Chalcolithic/Early Bronze Age.

NE of Site 299, Site 300 consists of four terraces, a series of stone rings, two indeterminate structures, and a sherd and lithic scatter. The terraces are agglomerated and enclosed by very well-built walls. To the NE and across a small drainage channel are two large rectilinear structures and various

small and large stone rings — some may be circular huts. There is also a possible grave nearby. The site yielded 49 Chalcolithic/Early Bronze Age sherds, in addition to pottery of the Early Roman/Nabataean and Early Byzantine periods (plus a single unidentified sherd). Although the SAAS found no pottery at Site 301 nearby to the NW, which consists of additional stone rings of similar appearance, this site may be associated with Site 300.

West of Jebel el-Khureij in Area III, Site 304 consists of a complex of five stone rings and mounds (possibly graves), a circular enclosure, and a nearby cave. There were both Chalcolithic/Early Bronze Age and Early Roman/Nabataean sherds at the site.

Site 312 is a small settlement just south of Wādī Um Saiyāla that spans an area of 80 m N–S × 70 m E–W. The site consists of various stone mounds, stone rings or hut circles, cairns, indeterminate wall alignments, and a scatter of sherds and lithics. In the central area of the site three stone mounds and an alignment of stones in half-circles enclose an area of ca. 20 m N–S × 15 m E–W. Four additional wall alignments project inward from the perimeter and partition the enclosed area. Two of these partition walls intersect with two of the stone mounds. This enclosure lies at the west edge of a modern wadi embankment. Also, a large cairn lies to the SW, beyond which there is another stone mound with circular, structural attachments. Various other stone rings or hut circles and another cairn are present at the site. The site yielded 13 Chalcolithic/Early Bronze Age sherds, in addition to some pottery of the Early Bronze Age and the Early Roman/Nabataean period.

Site 313 is a small settlement (ca. 70 m N–S × 120 m E–W) on an alluvial fan south of Wādī Um Saiyāla. The site consists of several structures, indeterminate wall alignments, and a dense sherd scatter with some lithics. Most structures at the site are circular but at least two are rectangular. Numerous stone rings, possibly a few hut circles, and stone mounds are distributed across the site. There is also a concentration of copper ore and copper slag. The vast majority of the pottery from Site 313 was of the Chalcolithic/Early Bronze Age (101 of 106 sherds).

Site 277 is a rock-shelter along the west face of Jebel el-Khureij near the center of the 'Araba. The

Table 4.3   Early Bronze Age Sites.

Site No.	Field Site No.	No. of EB Sherds	% of Total Sherds from Site
8	21	1	7.69
58	71	5	8.33
63	74	1	1.69
158	114	36	100.00
159	113	36	100.00
162	111	39	100.00
163	110	3	3.61
203	302	3	3.66
226	281	1	0.63
243	141	26	32.50
276	133	2	5.56
311	199	7	100.00
312	196	2	2.99

rock-shelter has two main entrances lined by stone walls and forming two compartments. A small wall partitions the two compartments. Also, the overhang of the rock-shelter is completely blackened. The SAAS collected both Chalcolithic/Early Bronze Age (three sherds) and the Early Roman/Nabataean pottery (two sherds) from the site, in addition to a few lithics.

From Site 314 the SAAS collected some lithics and only two Chalcolithic/Early Bronze Age sherds. Since most artifacts were of later periods, this site will be discussed below with the Early Roman/Nabataean sites.

Similarly, since the SAAS collected only 13 Chalcolithic/Early Bronze Age sherds at Site 316 among later pottery and few lithics, this site will be discussed with the Early Roman/Late Roman sites below.

Site 317 lies on a limestone ridge at the north end of Jebel el-Khureij. The site consists of two large cairns adjacent to one another on top of the ridge and a large wall alignment on the saddle below to the east. Both cairns are robbed and one exhibits two compartments as part of its con-

struction. The wall alignment of limestone blocks extends roughly E–W across a saddle and down the slope from the robbed cairns. The wall alignment may be the structural remnants of smelting activity. The SAAS found a scatter of copper slag, lithics, and exclusively Chalcolithic/Early Bronze Age pottery (64 sherds, some with slag adhering) on the north slope below the wall.

Finally, since the SAAS collected only two Chalcolithic/Early Bronze Age sherds from Site 321 among later pottery and few lithics, this site will be discussed below with the Roman/Byzantine sites.

Early Bronze Age

The SAAS collected Early Bronze Age pottery at 13 sites: Sites 8, 58, 63, 158–59, 162–63, 203, 226, 243, 276, and 311–12 (Table 4.3). For most of these, the Early Bronze Age presence was negligible. Sites 58, 63, 163, 203, 243, and 312, for example, have been described above as Chalcolithic or Chalcolithic/Early Bronze Age sites, and many of these may have been transitional sites. Other sites, namely, Sites 203, 276, and 312 will be described below with the Roman/Byzantine or Early Roman/Nabataean period sites, because the Early Bronze Age material from them was not substantial.

Site 8 is a sherd scatter in the Radwan residential district of Aqaba that included one Early Bronze Age II–III sherd.

In the north, the SAAS recorded a unique series of Early Bronze Age sites (Sites 157–63) on high alluvial terraces in Wādī Ḥeimir (Smith and Niemi 1994: 481). All these, except Site 160, consist of many connecting oval enclosures and structures ,and all had light to dense sherd and lithic scatters.

Site 163, the westernmost in the series, is a small settlement of 12 large stone enclosures of varying size on a terraced bank of Wādī Ḥeimir. A small flagstone pavement is attached to one of the enclosures. Although the SAAS collected mostly Chalcolithic/Early Bronze Age pottery (80 sherds), in addition to three Early Bronze Age sherds from a pot-bust, the site is discussed here due to its association with Sites 157–62.

Site 162 is another small settlement on an alluvial terrace above Wādī Ḥeimir. The site consists of five stone enclosures and additional wall alignments, along with an associated lithic and sherd scatter. Most of the enclosures adjoin, and there are two circular pits with walls lined by sandstone masonry. The largest pit has been robbed. From the site the SAAS collected exclusively Early Bronze Age pottery (39 sherds).

Sites 158 and 159 lie at the junction of Wādī Ḥeimir and a small tributary and extend over an area greater than Sites 160 and 162–63. Both are settlements set on different alluvial terraces above the wadi bed and both yielded exclusively Early Bronze Age pottery (36 sherds from each site). Site 158 consists of numerous large stone enclosures and indeterminate wall alignments with an associated sherd and lithic scatter (fig. 4.14). Most of the enclosures join to form a unified network of concentric walls and stone mounds. Site 159 also consists of numerous large, stone enclosures and wall alignments with an associated sherd and lithic scatter (fig. 4.15). Also, two semicircular stone circles lie at the SW end of Site 159, and a third stone circle lies in the SE quadrant of the site that opens to the SE. A complex of contiguous and circular enclosures and additional wall alignments lie to the NW.

Site 160 is a low density lithic scatter on a narrow alluvial terrace above Wādī Ḥeimir. The site is probably associated with the Early Bronze Age settlement activity in the same area.

Sites 157 and 161 are two monolith sites on ridges south of Wādī Ḥeimir (Smith and Niemi 1994: 481). Site 157 consists of seven toppled monoliths that are all trapezoidal in segment and graded in size. The three monoliths at Site 161 are elevated on a rock platform enclosed by a terrace wall. Site 161 overlooks Site 162. Neither Site 157 nor Site 161 yielded pottery, but lithics were collected at both.

Sites 58, 63, 203, 243, and 312 have been described above among the Chalcolithic/Early Bronze Age sites. At Site 203, the SAAS found three Early Bronze Age sherds from a stone ring or hut circle. Two Early Bonze Age sherds were collected from Site 58 and one from Site 63, Ḥujeirat al-Ghuzlan. The Early Bronze Age sherds from Sites 243 and 312 derived from general collections at these sites.

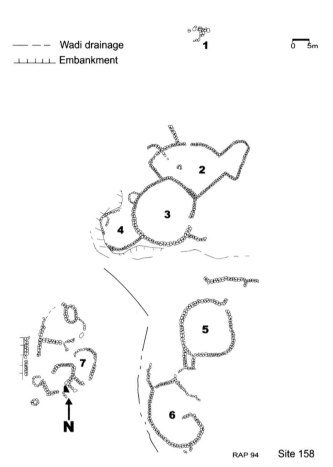

— — — Wadi drainage
⊥⊥⊥⊥⊥ Embankment

0   5m

RAP 94   Site 158

FIG. 4.14   *SAAS Site 158, plan of stone enclosures.*

Site 226, situated on an elongated wadi terrace along the north bank of Wādī Museimīr, was mentioned above among the Chalcolithic/Early Bronze Age sites. The SAAS collected a single Early Bronze Age sherd from the site.

From Site 276, located on the west face of Jebel el-Khureij, the SAAS collected several lithics but only two Early Bronze Age sherds. Most of the pottery from Site 276 was of the Early Roman/ Nabataean period and will be discussed as such below. It is possible that the early pottery from this site is to be associated with the nearby rock-shelter (Site 277).

Site 311 is a single burial on an alluvial fan SW of Wādī Um Saiyāla. The grave is robbed and sherd and bone fragments lay scattered across the site. The SAAS recovered seven sherds from the debris that may be of the Early Bronze Age II.

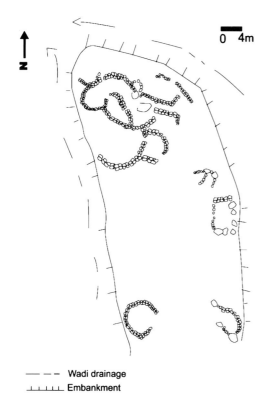

— — — Wadi drainage
⊥⊥⊥⊥⊥ Embankment

FIG. 4.15 *SAAS Site 159, plan of stone enclosures.*

Middle and Late Bronze Age

No site from the survey could be dated to the Middle Bronze Age and only one site suggests activity in the Late Bronze Age (Table 4.4). Site 80, situated on a high alluvial spur above the mouth of Wādī Yutum (fig. 4.9), was discussed above as a Chalcolithic/Early Bronze Age site. There the SAAS collected only one Late Bronze Age sherd.

Iron Age

The SAAS collected Iron Age sherds at 11 sites (Sites 14, 16, 29, 63, 72, 180, 195, 199, 206, 247, and 256; see Table 4.5). At most of these sites, however, the Iron Age material was negligible. Only one Iron Age sherd, for instance, was found at six of these sites. Most of the sites are listed and discussed in other sections.

Sites 14 and 16 are sherd scatters of dubious provenance within the urban zone of Aqaba. The SAAS collected a single sherd at each site that may belong to the Iron Age. Also, one body sherd

Table 4.4   Late Bronze Age Sites.

SITE No.	FIELD SITE No.	No. OF LB SHERDS	% OF TOTAL SHERDS FROM SITE
80	164	1	0.79

Table 4.5   Iron Age Sites.

SITE No.	FIELD SITE No.	No. OF IRON AGE SHERDS	% OF TOTAL SHERDS FROM SITE
14	11	1	1.33
16	12	1	2
29	174	186	22.57
63	74	1	1.69
72	162	1	0.50
180	321	11	84.62
195	316	4	66.67
199	309	1	3.70
206	301	1	25
247	265	43	100
256	259	6	20.69

from Site 72 may belong to the Iron Age, but this is predominately an Early Roman/Late Roman site. One sherd from Site 63, Ḥujeirat al-Ghuzlan, is Iron Age II.

Site 180 is a small settlement on a low spur where two small drainages merge in the first major tributary north of Wādī Gharandal. The site consists of at least seven circular and three rectilinear structures alongside a group of cairns, in addition to a light sherd and lithic scatter. The circular structures, perhaps hut circles, vary in size and some are eroding into the wadi. The rectilinear structures concentrate at the western end of the site. Most of the structures have been robbed, presumably for the construction of at least five large cairns at the site. Eleven sherds retrieved from the site may date to the Iron Age.

Site 195 is a contemporary bedouin encampment with evidence of earlier activity. Recent features include an animal pen, hearths, and modern debris. The interior of the animal pen is filled with dung. There are at least two hearths, which appear as circular depressions not lined with stones. Lithics and pottery lie scattered on the surface. The SAAS collected four possible Iron Age sherds at the site and a single Roman/Byzantine body sherd.

Site 199, situated on a terrace in Wādī el-Quṣeib, was described above among the Chalcolithic/Early Bronze Age sites. It yielded a single Iron Age sherd.

Also, the SAAS collected a single Iron Age sherd (Negevite?) at Site 206, a single stone ring or hut circle likewise located on a terrace in Wādī el-Quṣeib.

On the alluvial fan NW of Wādī Abū Barqa, the SAAS collected 43 Iron Age II sherds (most from a single vessel) at Site 247. The site itself consists of two rectilinear areas cleared of stones, three circular clearings (hut circles?), and a sherd and lithic scatter. The larger clearings are similar to the possible bedouin weaving strips at Sites 244 and 256 discussed above. Site 256 yielded a few lithics and six Iron Age sherds.

An important late Iron II and Persian period site, Tell el-Kheleifeh (Site 29), lies within the study area along the border between Israel and Jordan, just north of the Aqaba shoreline. The site was excavated by Glueck (1965), whose results were only recently published in final form (Pratico 1993). The SAAS did not formally survey Tell el-Kheleifeh, but the RAP staff did collect a large sample of ceramics (824 sherds) and some lithics from the surface in 1996. Of the 325 diagnostic sherds retrieved, the majority (186 sherds) dated to the Iron Age IIB/C periods (ca. 900–586 BC). In fact, the results of the surface collection closely correspond to Pratico's re-dating of the site (see Chapter 6).

Persian and Hellenistic Periods

Persian or Hellenistic sherds were found at only one site in the study area, Tell el-Kheleifeh (Site 29), discussed above as an Iron Age site (Table 4.6). From a general collection of artifacts, 20 sherds at the site were dated to the Early Persian period and four were dated to the Early Hellenistic period.

Table 4.6   Persian–Hellenistic Period Sites.

Site No.	Field Site No.	No. of Persian– Hellenistic Sherds	% of Total Sherds from Site
29	174	24	2.91

Early Roman/Nabataean

The Early Roman/Nabataean period was the best-represented among the sites documented in the survey area. A total of 88 sites (27% of all sites) yielded evidence of the Early Roman/Nabataean period (Table 4.7). From all of these the SAAS collected a total of 2545 sherds, or 33.58% of all sherds collected in the region, which included five sherds or less at 45 sites (20 of which yielded only a single sherd of this period) and 20 or more sherds at 23 sites.

Early Roman/Nabataean sites are distributed throughout the study area. These are found in Area I near Aqaba (Sites 1, 5, 7–10, 12, 14–16, 18–21, and 29), behind Jebel esh-Shahbī (Site 43), along the alluvial fan below Wādī Yutum (Sites 50, 62, 72, and 76), in the vicinity of Wādī Mulghān (Sites 107, 113, 115–16, 121, 124, and 126), and at Wādī el-Muhtadī (Sites 139, and 144–45). In Area II Early Roman/Nabataean sites are located on the slopes to the east of Siḥ Duḥayla (Sites 149–50, and 152–53), and near Wādī Nukheila (Sites 167, 169–72). In Area III, Early Roman/Nabataean sites are located near Wādī es-Sīq (Site 177), Wādī Gharandal (Sites 181, 185, and 186), in Wādī el-Quṣeib (Sites 193, 198–99, 203–4, and 207–8), Wādī Museimīr (Sites 219, 221, and 225–26), near Wādī Abū Barqa (Sites 237, 242, 257–58, 262, and 274), along the escarpment west of Jebel el-Qā (Sites 278, 283–84, 287, 290–91, and 300), near Jebel el-Khureij (Sites 274–77, 304–5, 307–8, 314, and 316), and Wādī Um Saiyāla (Sites 310, and 312–13). Further north the SAAS recorded evidence Early Roman/Nabataean activity at Wādī eṭ-Ṭayyiba(Sites 319, 321–25, and 328) and at Bir Madhkur (Site 329).

Many sites with Early Roman/Nabataean pottery do not need detailed treatment here. Most are

Table 4.7   Early Roman/Nabataean Period Sites.

Site No.	Field Site No.	No. of ER/Nab Sherds	% of Total Sherds from Site	Site No.	Field Site No.	No. of ER/Nab Sherds	% of Total Sherds from Site
1	1	4	8.89	150	330	12	30.00
5	20	2	2.94	152	136	255	97.70
7	22	1	9.09	153	135	23	17.97
8	21	7	53.85	167	146	224	100.00
9	24	3	100.00	169	101	4	44.44
10	23	1	16.67	170	109	8	100.00
12	25	1	20.00	171	108	61	100.00
14	11	1	1.33	172	107	13	52.00
15	10	5	17.24	177	326	8	27.59
16	12	20	40.00	181	102	14	16.28
18	7	7	28.00	185	323	1	33.33
19	5	2	10.00	186	151	2	15.38
20	4	4	15.39	193	314	19	73.08
21	27	1	2.63	198	310	1	25.00
29	174	3	0.36	199	309	6	22.22
31	3	3	10.71	203	302	15	18.29
43	14	1	14.29	204	305	3	33.33
50	230	3	3.53	207	298	1	20.00
62	70	2	5.71	208	299	1	25.00
72	162	24	11.94	219	295	20	31.75
76	80	1	100.00	221	291	6	16.22
107	31	3	13.64	225	289	65	37.57
113	44/45	8	7.08	226	281	66	41.51
115	47	33	100.00	237	269	4	50.00
116	46	5	100.00	242	142	1	4.76
121	91	16	100.00	257	254	1	4.76
124	90	1	20.00	262	242	53	94.64
126	89	11	100.00	264	257	4	44.44
139	127	2	7.41	274	134	38	100.00
144	103	10	100.00	275	38	344	98.00
145	104	1	100.00	276	133	27	87.10
149	331	1	33.33	277	132	2	40.00

simple sherd scatters without associated features. Sites 5, 7–10, 12, 14–16, and 18–21, for example, are sherd scatters of dubious provenance within the urban zone of Aqaba. Also in Area I, Site 31 is a scatter of 28 sherds found at the summit of Jebel esh-Shahbī, due east of Aqaba, that range in date from the Early Roman/Nabataean to Late Byzantine periods. From this vantage one has an excellent view of Aqaba, the southern end of the 'Araba valley, and the southern coastal area. Site 76, located on an old alluvial fan surface west of Wādī Yutum, consists of an artifact scatter of lithics and a single Early Roman/Nabataean sherd. Site 126 consists of a pot-bust on an old alluvial fan surface west of Wādī ez-Zibliya. In Area III, Site 172 is a sherd and lithic scatter near Wādī Nukheila which also yielded Chalcolithic/Early Bronze Age pottery. Site 177 is a sherd scatter near Wādī es-Sīq. Site 312 is a small settlement just south of Wādī Um Saiyāla where the SAAS collected lithics and 52 Early Roman/Nabataean sherds, most from a single pot-bust; the few Early Roman/Nabataean sherds from Site 50 also derived from a pot-bust.

Furthermore, many sites with Early Roman/Nabataean sherds are mortuary in nature (Sites 144–45, 149–51, 170, 193, 198, 204, 219, 257, 262, 264, 278, 310, and 314). On the alluvial fan north of Wādī el-Muhtadī there are two cemeteries (Sites 144 and 145) with at least four burials combined. The SAAS collected 10 Early Roman/Nabataean sherds at Site 144, which yielded a few lithics as well, and a single sherd of this period at Site 145. Site 170, where the SAAS collected eight Early Roman/Nabataean sherds, lies on a ridge north of Wādī Nukheila and consists of seven cairns spread over a large area (80 m N–S × 150 m E–W). Site 219 is a cemetery on a terrace of Wādī Museimīr. The site consists of 12–15 graves of varying types, which range from three large burial cairns to numerous stone rings and mounds. Although the stone rings and mounds are present throughout the site, it is difficult to define their patterns and orientation, because of deflation of the alluvial surface. At Site 219 the SAAS collected lithics and 20 Early Roman/Nabataean sherds, though most material was of later periods. Furthermore, Site 262, which consists of three cairns and a stone ring, yielded some lithics and a large number (52) of Early Roman/Nabataean

Table 4.7 (cont.)   Early Roman/Nabataean Period Sites.

Site No.	Field Site No.	No. of ER/Nab Sherds	% of Total Sherds from Site
278	224	1	100.00
283	220	2	100.00
284	221	52	100.00
287	222	5	7.81
290	205	56	91.80
291	203	9	21.43
300	207	15	21.13
304	185	16	53.33
305	184	97	100.00
307	183	72	100.00
308	235	16	32.65
310	197	1	100.00
312	196	52	77.61
313	191	1	0.94
314	234	44	65.67
316	187	5	6.49
319	152	98	96.08
321	160	3	8.82
322	154	11	100.00
323	155	1	100.00
324	156	5	83.33
325	161	37	97.37
328	158	5	71.43
329	148	452	57.58

sherds. A single Early Roman/Nabataean sherd was found both at Site 278, a burial cairn north of Wādī Abū Barqa, and at Site 310, an isolated cairn near Wādī Um Saiyāla. Sites 204, 257, and 264, which exhibit mortuary features, were discussed above with the Chalcolithic/Early Bronze Age sites.

The SAAS also recorded a series of burial cairns or tombs along the perimeter of Qā' aṭ-Ṭāba, east of

Siḫ Duḥayla (Sites 149–51). Site 149 consists of three well-preserved tombs, clearly associated with the nine tombs at Site 150 nearby. These tombs appear as stone mounds on top of internal loculi. Also at Site 150 is an isolated structure near the base of the hill. Site 151 consists of at least a dozen tombs, all apparently contemporary with those at Sites 149 and 150. Although Site 149 yielded only three sherds — one of which was of the Early Roman/Nabataean period — and Site 151 yielded none, the SAAS collected 40 sherds at Site 150, including a dozen dated to the Early Roman/Nabataean period. The other ceramics from these sites ranged in date from the Early Roman/Late Roman to the Early Byzantine period. For the most part these sites seem to be associated with the more extensive settlement activity to the north at Rujm aṭ-Ṭāba.

On an alluvial terrace in Wādī el-Quṣeib, Site 193 consists of a cemetery with at least six graves which appear as small piles of cobbles and boulders, a robbed burial cairn, and a scatter of sherds and lithics. An interior compartment of the cairn was exposed by clandestine excavation and many bone fragments lie scattered on the surface. Adjacent to the cairn was a large stone with a cross-like shape etched on it. Pottery from the site included 19 Early Roman/Nabataean sherds from a single pot-bust; the other material belonged to the Early or Late Roman period. Importantly, the graves from Site 193 seem comparable to those nearby at Site 194, where the SAAS found some lithics but no pottery.

One Early Roman/Nabataean sherd appeared at another robbed cairn in Wādī el-Quṣeib (Site 198), in addition to an Early Islamic pot-bust. The SAAS found few lithics at Site 198. West of the cairn is an unspecified stone structure, seemingly the ruins of circular hut. Near Site 198, the SAAS recorded two petroglyphs at Site 196, but the site yielded no artifacts.

Also, in the valley west of Wādī Um Saiyāla is a cemetery (Site 314) that includes at least 13 graves, one in the form of a stone ring. There is also an isolated structure to the south and an associated sherd and lithic scatter. The overall size and orientation of the graves varies considerably. The site yielded 44 Early Roman/Nabataean sherds, plus a few Chalcolithic/Early Bronze and the Early Roman/Late Roman periods sherds.

At several sites the Early Roman/Nabataean presence was negligible in relation to other periods of occupation. Many sites that yielded Early Roman/Nabataean sherds, for example, have been treated previously as Chalcolithic/Early Bronze Age sites, namely, Sites 62, 199, 242, 277, 287, 300, and 313. Sites 72, 113, 207, 208, 225, and 316 will be treated later as Early Roman/Late Roman, and Sites 139 and 203 will be treated as Roman/Byzantine. The remaining sites will be discussed roughly in order from south to north.

Site 1 lies near the shore of the Gulf of Aqaba between Tell el-Kheleifeh and Aila. It consists of two segments of decayed mudbrick walls. The nature of these wall segments is unclear. The SAAS collected four Early Roman/Nabataean sherds at the site.

Site 43, located behind Jebel esh-Shahbī, consists of three rectilinear wall foundations and at least six stone circles. The stone circles vary in size. The nature of the wall foundations and their relationship to the stone circles, if any, could not be determined. The SAAS collected a single Early Roman/Nabataean sherd and few lithics.

Sites 107 lies on the north bank of the first small tributary wadi south of Wādī Mulghān. Only two sherds from the site were of the Early Roman/Nabataean period. Because most of the pottery from this site was later, it will be discussed below with the Roman/Byzantine sites.

Sites 115 and 116 lie on a saddle near the mouth of the Wādī Mulghān gorge. Site 116 consists of a sherd scatter and a collapsed stone structure on a ridge flanking the wadi to the south. The area is heavily eroded and the structure is badly damaged. Along the eastern face of the same ridge, Site 115 consists of four structures on the slope and three terraced platforms near the base. The purpose of these structures and platforms is unknown, but they may have been agricultural, because of proximity to the drainage. The SAAS collected exclusively Early Roman/Nabataean pottery from both sites (33 sherds at Site 115 and five sherds at Site 116).

Site 121 is a bedouin campsite on the alluvial fan NW of Wādī Mulghān. The site consists of two oblong and narrow clearings with stones aligned at each end. To the south is a stone ring, a stone mound, and an oval rock alignment. The SAAS collected exclusively Early Roman/Nabataean pottery (16 sherds) at the site.

On the north branch of the Wādī Mulghān alluvial fan, Site 124 consists of poorly preserved wall alignments, perhaps once a single structure, and a light sherd and lithic scatter. What appears to be a stone-built platform lies adjacent to the westernmost wall and a similar feature is set along the easternmost wall. An apparent cemetery consisting at least five circular stone mounds lies SW of the wall alignments. The site yielded only a single Early Roman/Nabataean body sherd in addition to an Early Islamic pot-bust.

About one km north of Qāʿ aṭ-Ṭāba is a ruined structure or caravanserai (Site 153) with contemporary ruins nearby identified as Rujm aṭ-Ṭāba (Site 152) (Frank 1934: 238; Raikes 1985: 100; Khouri 1988: 129; Smith and Niemi 1994: 478–79; Smith et al. 1997: 57–58; Dolinka 2002; Dolinka et al. 2002). The structure lies west of the modern highway and it is partly buried under sand dunes encroaching from the NW. Although the SAAS was not able to record fully Site 153 in 1994, associated pottery suggests that it is contemporary with Site 152, a ruined village site east of the highway and roughly 50 m to the south. Much of Site 152 was destroyed during construction of the modern highway by removal of a large quantity of gravel from the base of the alluvial fan to line the highway bed. Further modification of the area through bulldozing activity continued as late as 1994 when the SAAS visited the area. The SAAS identified two extant structures at the site and several large mounds suggest the presence of others in the area. One of these structures at the southern end of the site appears to have been partitioned into four rooms of equal size. A cemetery of ca. 50 tombs lies on the steep slope of the alluvial fan above the village. The SAAS collected 255 Early Roman/Nabataean sherds at Site 152, including a few sherds of imported amphorae (Class 10) and Eastern Sigillata A, in addition to two Early Byzantine and one Modern sherds. Site 153 yielded 23 Early Roman/Nabataean sherds, although the bulk of the material dated to the Early Roman/Late Roman period. Dolinka's more recent and comprehensive survey of the area and more artifactual evidence suggests that the village (Site 152) was occupied continuously from the 1st

century BC to the late 2nd century AD and that the caravanserai (Site 153) post-dates the village foundation by perhaps a century. There was evidence of a limited reoccupation in the late 3rd/early 4th century (Dolinka et al. 2002: 447–48).

Located on the north bank of Wādī Nukheila, Site 167 is a small Early Roman/Nabataean period settlement (Smith and Niemi 1994: 479; Smith et al. 1997: 58, fig. 9). There is a wall alignment at the southern end of the site and a corral-type structure to the north. The NE and SE corners of the structure are well-preserved, and a possible entrance lies along the east wall. Other similar structures are visible further north. Opposite a large drainage that bounds Site 167 to the north, the SAAS recorded a petroglyph carved on a large sandstone boulder of a male ibex and what appears to be a female hunter preparing to throw a spear (Smith et al. 1997: 59, fig. 10). This rock drawing may be grouped stylistically into Emmanuel Anati's Style IV-C category, dated to between 500 BC and AD 400 (Anati 1979). The relatively large pottery sample (224 sherds) collected at the site was exclusively Early Roman/Nabataean, which included a single sherd of Eastern Sigillata A. A few lithics were also collected.

Site 171 is a large ruined structure north of Wādī Nukheila near a modern well (Smith and Niemi 1994: 481; Smith et al. 1997: 58–59, fig. 11). The existing wall alignments are difficult to trace, as they are buried in sand and stone rubble. Amidst the debris from the structure was at least one block with tool marks. Unfortunately, two large bulldozer cuts through the southern portion of the mound and two robber pits excavated in the center of the structure have nearly destroyed the site. The SAAS collected exclusively Early Roman/Nabataean pottery (61 sherds) at the site, in addition to a few lithics. This may be a watchtower that guarded the passage through Wādī Nukheila as well as N–S traffic in Wādī ʿAraba, based on proximity to the nearby ancient road (Site 169). In the foothills east and south of this site is a large cemetery of at least seven graves, some robbed.

First discovered in 1993, Site 169 is a stone-paved road situated between Wādī Nukheila and Gharandal (Smith and Niemi 1994: 479; Smith 1994; Smith et al. 1997: 59–60, fig. 12). As mentioned, a

FIG. 4.16   *SAAS Site 231, ancient road, looking northwest.*

segment of this road, which is aligned roughly N–S, lies due west of Site 171. The road stretches ca. 8 km north from the mouth of Wādī Nukheila to Gharandal and generally keeps ca. 500 m west of the foothills. The road is edged with curbstones and ranges between 3.35 and 3.74 meters wide. Although the date of the road cannot be established definitely, it may be related to the Early Roman/Nabataean settlement activity at Site 171, Gharandal (Site 181) and the fort (Site 275) in the Qaʻ as-Suʻaydiyyīn (see below). In 1998 the SAAS discovered an extension of this road, identified as Site 231, far to the north of Gharandal where it trended NW (fig. 4.16). This segment of the road is visible in intermittent stretches, while many segments are covered by sand dunes. During transects along Site 169 the SAAS collected four Early Roman/ Nabataean sherds, in addition to few sherds of the Chalcolithic/Early Bronze Age, Roman/Byzantine, and Early Islamic periods.

The spring and oasis of Gharandal (Site 181) lie in a strategic location in Wādī ʻAraba. Musil, Frank, and Glueck each explored Gharandal, though Musil sketched the only plan of the site (Musil 1907: 193–97, fig. 142; Frank 1934: 231–32; Glueck 1935: 39–40). Raikes (1985: 101) and King later visited the site (King et al. 1989: 207). The SAAR also investigated Gharandal (Smith and Niemi 1994: 482; Smith et al. 1997: 59–60). The most visible feature is the *castellum* in the floodplain west of the mouth of Wādī Gharandal (fig. 4.17). This fort is a typical *quadriburgium* with four corner towers. The fort is partially intact despite several bulldozer cuts that have damaged the south wall. The gateway cannot be discerned, but it may be along the east wall. Two other ruins lie east of the fort. A portion of a wall alignment defines the northern wall of some ruined structure—a large mounded area of rubble and fragments of mortar and plaster lie adjacent to the wall segment on its south side. Other wall alignments lie to the east which may be associated with the ruins of a low-lying water channel that approaches the fort from the east. The paucity of sherds at the site may be due to its setting amidst sand dunes and proximity to the modern road. The SAAS collected 14 Early Roman/Nabataean sherds at Gharandal, in addition to a fair amount of lithics. Most of the pottery at the site, however, was of the Roman/Byzantine period. The SAAS also found one Early Byzantine coin fragment (Obj. #504) at the site. Military occupation at Gharandal by the *cohors secunda Galatarum* is attested in ca.

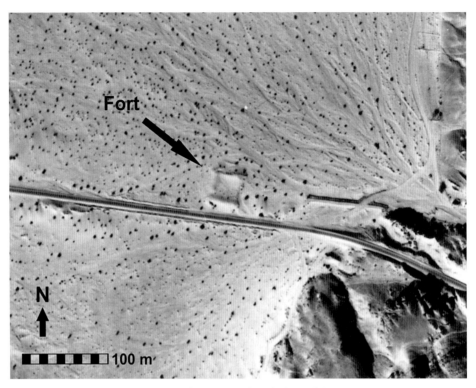

FIG. 4.17   *SAAS Site 181, aerial view of the Roman fort of Gharandal.*

AD 400 in the *Notitia Dignitatum* (*Or.* 34.44). The identity of the ancient name and garrison unit was confirmed by a Tetrarchic building inscription discovered in 2013. The site is mentioned again in AD 536 in the Beersheva Edict (Alt 1921: 8; Mayerson 1986: 148), when it was called *Ariddela* or *Arieldela*.

Site 185 lies on an alluvial terrace at a bend in a tributary wadi NE of Wādī Gharandal. The site consists of two bedouin encampments and a well-built stone structure (fig. 4.18) to the west. The encampments appear modern and lie opposite one another across a shallow drainage. The SAAS found two grinding stones at one of these encampments. The structure at the site is constructed of cut limestone blocks. Its SE wall curves toward the entrance along the east wall, and a small partition wall divides the structure internally into two compartments. There is a small barrage or terrace wall constructed across a tributary wadi elevated above the wadi terrace to the SE. The apparent intent of this barrage was to limit or prevent the flow of water as it approached the stone structure from above. The structure itself may have been for storage, but this is speculative. Also, because the SAAS collected only one Early

Roman/Nabataean sherd near the structure, its dating to this period is tentative.

Site 186 lies on a low-lying hill north of Gharandal adjacent to a modern police post. The site consists of a single wall alignment and a light scatter of lithics and sherds. Whatever structure once stood here is now buried beneath the police post. This may have been a watchtower visible from the fort at Gharandal, based on its commanding view of the valley. Pottery included two Early Roman/Nabataean sherds plus a few later pieces (Roman/Byzantine and Modern).

Site 221, which consists of various features dispersed across an alluvial terrace above Wādī Museimīr, will be discussed in more detail below with the Early Roman/Late Roman sites. At the site the SAAS collected a few lithics, one Early Roman/Nabataean sherd from a low stone mound or grave (Feature 3), and five Early Roman/Nabataean sherds from an isolated wall alignment (Feature 18), mostly buried beneath alluvial sediments.

Similarly, Site 226, situated on another alluvial terrace in Wādī Museimīr, will be discussed below with the Early Roman/Late Roman sites. The SAAS

FIG. 4.18   *SAAS Site 185, Feature 2, isolated structure, looking west.*

10 cm

FIG. 4.19   *SAAS Site 226, Feature 18, large sandstone boulder on which is depicted a petroglyph of a camel.*

recorded 19 various features at Site 226. A single Early Roman/Nabataean sherd was found near an encampment (Feature 6) cleared of large boulders and cobbles, leaving mostly a pebble pavement. Lithics extended over the entire encampment. Most Early Roman/Nabataean pottery (54 sherds), however, was found near two large boulders where

the SAAS recorded petroglyphs (Features 18 and 19; fig. 4.19).

South of Wādī Abū Barqa is Site 237, a ruined structure high on an alluvial fan overlooking a broad wadi. The ruins appear as mounded tumble of unworked boulders. The size, general shape, elevated position high above Site 238, and the excellent vantage the location affords to the west across the valley suggest it was a watchtower. There is also a segmented wall alignment nearby and a small stone structure. The SAAS collected four Early Roman/Nabataean sherds at the site, in addition to some unidentifiable (early) sherds and a few lithics.

Qā' as-Su'aydiyyīn (Site 275) is a small fort of cut limestone blocks (Smith et al. 1997: 61, fig. 13). Though the fort may have been discovered in the early 19th century (de Bertou 1839: 299; Alt 1935: 5, 7, 29), subsequent scholars overlooked it until Raikes' survey of Wādī 'Araba (Raikes 1985: 100). The SAAR also investigated the site (Smith and Niemi 1994: 482–83; Smith et al. 1997: 60–62). The fort is in a ruined state with much of its northern side stripped away by localized bulldozing activity (fig. 4.20). A large, dressed lintel stone with a *tabula ansata* (uninscribed) lies along the north wall, which suggests the location of the gateway. The SW and SE corners of the fort are visible, and

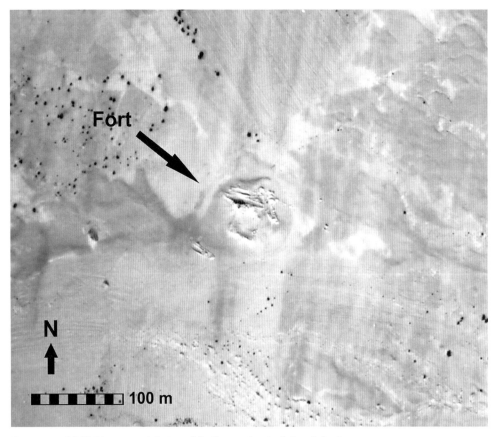

FIG. 4.20 *SAAS Site 275, aerial view of the Roman fort in Qā' as-Su'aydiyyīn.*

FIG. 4.21 *SAAS Site 274, quarried block of limestone.*

FIG. 4.22   *SAAS Site 274, fractured, discarded milestone.*

there are no towers; the large circular mound that extends beyond the NW corner probably is not a tower but a consequence of bulldozing. North of the structure is a mound of ashy soil with abundant sherds and fragments of bone, glass, and corroded metal artifacts. The vast majority of the pottery from a large surface collection at the site was of the Early Roman/Nabataean period (343 of 351 sherds from the site, or 4.54% of all sherds collected throughout the study area).

Along Jebel el-Khureij the SAAS recorded two quarries operational in the Early Roman/ Nabataean period and thus contemporary with the occupation of Qasr Qāʿ as-Suʾaydiyyīn (Site 275), from which the quarries are visible. Site 274 lies on the east face of the limestone bedrock ridge. The quarried face of the cliff is extensive and the largest platform is at the southern end. The SAAS recorded modern graffiti and two rock drawings on the face of the cliff to the north. Quarried stones extend to the east and down the slope below the terraced platform (fig. 4.21). Five fractured and discarded milestones, each anepigraphic, are among the stone debris along the slope (fig. 4.22). The quarry was probably worked by the garrison at Qasr Qāʿ as-Suʾaydiyyīn, given the proximity,

chronological evidence, and the fact that the fort was apparently built of stones quarried from this site. Site 307 is another large limestone quarry on the north and south sides of a spur projecting from Jebel el-Khureij north of Site 274. The quarried area of the ridge is less extensive here. Along the quarried terrace of Site 307 are spoil piles of cut blocks, some with extant tool marks. Two of the blocks with tool marks were reused to form a grave in the center of the northern quarried terrace. NE and below the edge of the quarried terrace is an apparent entranceway constructed of large cut blocks. Strangely, this apparent entranceway has no obvious association with any extant walls or structures. There is, however, a series of collapsed structures further to the NE and down the slope. Pottery at Site 307 concentrated around these structures. Also, at the summit of the ridge is another series of similar structures. The pottery from Site 274 (33 sherds) and Site 307 (72 sherds) was exclusively Early Roman/Nabataean. Also, both sites yielded a few lithics.

Located on the west face of Jebel el-Khureij, Site 276 consists of a square enclosure with somewhat rounded corners. Rock tumble obscures the NE and SW corners, while the NW corner is rounded and fairly well-preserved. An isolated wall alignment lies to the SW. The SAAS collected predominately Early Roman/Nabataean pottery (27 sherds) at the site, in addition to Early Bronze Age sherds and a large lithic sample, probably associated with the rock-shelter and caves above the structure (Site 277).

The SAAS collected two Early Roman/Nabataean sherds from Site 283, a large, circular enclosure on the alluvial fan to the west of Jebel el-Qā (fig. 4.23). Three small stone rings are appended to the west wall of the enclosure. The eastern edge has a linear stone alignment closing it off from the main area, where there is a well-defined entranceway with a short corridor leading into the enclosure. Behind a rectilinear compartment along the eastern edge of the enclosure, there is another appended stone ring. Further, there is a large portion of tumble in the NE corner of the main enclosure, which may suggest another appended stone ring. Large concentrations of schist flakes with a few garnet nuggets and some lithics lie scattered around the site. The site may be related to the local extraction of garnet gems.

Site 284 lies on the alluvial fan west of Jebel el-Qā. The site was initially viewed as a drainage channel, though it was later discerned to be an ancient road or pathway. Rather than being paved, the pathway had been established by clearing the stones from the alluvial surface to facilitate traffic. It winds down to the base of the alluvial fan west and below Site 287, a small settlement at the base of the ridge that yielded predominately Chalcolithic/Early Bronze Age pottery along with five Early Roman/Nabataean sherds and some lithics. Along Site 284, two-thirds of the way up the fan and in the center of the pathway, the SAAS found 52 sherds from a single Early Roman/Nabataean pot-bust. Some lithics were collected at the site as well.

Also on the alluvial fan west of Jebel el-Qā, Site 290 consists of two curvilinear wall alignments, stone rings, a possible tent encampment, and a sherd and lithic scatter. The main feature is a curvilinear wall alignment (Feature 1), now in a ruined state. Perhaps it served as part of a drainage basin for surface runoff. A second wall alignment nearby runs the same course as the main feature with which it is probably associated. A large clearing, seemingly

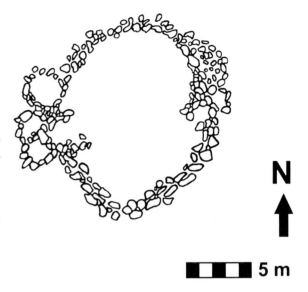

Fig. 4.23   *SAAS Site 283, large, circular enclosure.*

a tent encampment, lies to the west. A few stones are set upright along the edges of the clearing. Also, at least five stone rings lie to the north. Some sherds from Site 290 were of Chalcolithic/Early Bronze Age, though the majority (56 sherds) dated to the Early Roman/Nabataean period.

Site 291 lies on the alluvial fan north of Wādī Abū Barqa and consists of at least five stone rings or hut circles and a sherd and lithic scatter. The exact number of stone rings or hut circles is difficult to determine, as many are appended to one another and appear as figure-8 structures. The SAAS collected nine Early Roman/Nabataean sherds and a few sherds of the Roman/Byzantine period at the site, but the bulk of the ceramic material could not be identified.

Located west of Jebel el-Khureij, Site 304 consists of a complex of five stone rings and mounds (perhaps graves), a circular enclosure, and a nearby cave, in addition to a sherd and lithic scatter. The opening of the cave is partially closed off by a wall constructed of loosely packed stones. The interior of the cave shows no sign of habitation, i.e., there are no artifacts and the overhead is not blackened. The circular enclosure is built against the bottom of the cliff face NE of the cave. The stone rings, built of irregularly shaped blocks of limestone, are east of the cave. The SAAS collected 16 Early Roman/Nabataean sherds from the area. Some of the ceramic material was also of the Chalcolithic/Early Bronze Age.

Site 305, an isolated stone structure with an associated sherd and lithic scatter, also lies west of Jebel el-Khureij. The western part of the structure appears to have been disturbed by clandestine excavations, which left exposed a well-preserved wall alignment bisecting the structure on a N–S axis. The nature and function of the structure remains unclear. The SAAS collected exclusively Early Roman/Nabataean pottery at the site (97 sherds).

Site 308 consists of two isolated structures far to the west of Jebel el-Khureij. One structure is rectilinear and consists of two irregular courses of masonry on its east and west sides. Inside this feature, aligned roughly N–S, is a compartment or channel. A second structure lies to the NE. It is semicircular and comprised of several large, unworked boulders. Pottery at the site concentrates around this second structure. Pottery from the site, some unidentified, ranged in date from the Early Roman/Nabataean (16 sherds) to the Early Byzantine periods.

In order to gather comparative data, the SAAS surveyed two of the major caravanserais or forts of Wādī 'Araba north of our study area, Qasr Wādī eṭ-Ṭayyiba (Site 319) and Bir Madhkur (Site 329). Each yielded considerable amounts of Early Roman/Nabataean pottery (550 of 887 sherds from both sites or 7.26% of all sherds collected throughout the study area).

Musil, Frank, and Glueck each had visited Qasr Wādī eṭ-Ṭayyiba early in this century, followed by King et al. in 1982 (Musil 1907: 282; Frank 1934: 230, plan 22B; Glueck 1935: 37–38; King et al. 1989: 207). The qasr is a typical caravanserai. It is a rectangular structure without clear evidence of corner towers — though a large mound of stone rubble in the center of the west wall may be the remains of a collapsed tower or gateway — with a series of rooms along the interior perimeter wall surrounding a central courtyard (Smith et al. 1997: 62–63, fig. 15). Other less impressive remains in the vicinity of 'Ain eṭ-Ṭayyiba include a long, isolated wall alignment SE of the qasr and a small structure, virtually destroyed by numerous robber pits, due east of the modern well. Qasr Wādī eṭ-Ṭayyiba clearly would have served as an important way-

station on the route west through Wādī Musa bearing south. Numerous lithics were collected around the qasr, in addition to a sizeable number (98) of Early Roman/Nabataean sherds. Only a couple of pieces were later in date.

Sites 320–28 all lie in the vicinity of 'Ain eṭ-Ṭayyiba (Smith et al. 1997: 62-63). Site 327 is a lithic scatter on the south slope of a low spur east of the spring, which yielded no pottery. There were lithics but no pottery at Site 320, which consists of four stone rings or hut circles on the scree slope of the ridge east of the qasr. The stones of these features are standing upright along the perimeter. Site 326, which yielded neither pottery nor lithics, is a cemetery consisting of various stone rings and cairns. Site 321, on the other hand, consists of at least three ruined structures or hut circles and yielded three Early Roman/Nabataean sherds as well as lithics. The bulk of the ceramic material from Site 321, however, was of the Roman/Byzantine period, in addition to a few sherds of the Chalcolithic/Early Bronze Age. Site 322 consists of a small structure on a limestone ridge and a lithic and sherd scatter. The structure was built around a small pit dug into the east face of the ridge. Indeterminate wall alignments lie to the west and north. Pottery from Site 322 was exclusively of the Early Roman/Nabataean period (11 sherds). Site 323 is a small structure built of large upright boulders and smaller rock piles. A dense lithic scatter surrounds this structure, especially to the north and NW. The SAAS found only one Early Roman/Nabataean sherd at Site 323. Site 324 is a small windbreak on a knoll of a ridge east of the spring. The structure is open to the SE and of poor construction. There is a lithic scatter concentrated NW of Site 324. Pottery from Site 324 included five Early Roman/Nabataean sherds, plus one Roman/Byzantine sherd. Site 328, which yielded five Early Roman/Nabataean sherds, is another windbreak on top of a small bedrock knoll with an associated lithic scatter. Finally, Site 325 consists of a multi-room complex with an associated lithic and sherd scatter. There are two rooms to the east and two stone mounds to the west. Pottery collected at Site 325 was overwhelmingly of the Early Roman/Nabataean period.

Bir Madhkur (Site 329) lies north of where Wādī Musa, an important route from Wādī 'Araba

Fig. 4.24   *SAAS Site 184, Feature 4, remains of structure, looking east.*

to Petra, empties into Wādī ʿAraba. Frank, Glueck, and King surveyed the site (Frank 1934: 228, plan 23; Glueck 1935: 35–37, plan 6; King et al. 1989: 205). Bir Madhkur is now the focus of a multidisciplinary archaeological field project, the Bir Madhkur Project, directed by the author (Smith 2005a; 2005b; Perry 2007). The most impressive structure at Bir Madhkur is the *castellum,* now in a very ruined state. The fort is a *quadriburgium* (just over 30 × 30 m) with four corner towers. The walls are of worked limestone blocks. Within the *castellum,* rectangular mounded depressions suggest that internal structures were built against the curtain wall around a central courtyard. Though not discernible, the gateway was probably in the northern wall, now mostly destroyed by bulldozing activity and robber pits. Just to the NE is a cemetery, perhaps contemporary with the occupation of the fort in the Early Roman/Nabataean period.

SE and immediately adjacent to the fort is another structure (ca. 30 × 25 m) on the bank of a dry wadi. Glueck suggested that this was a *birkeh* and the large mound of ash just beyond its south wall might reflect local pottery production (Glueck 1935: 36). This seems unlikely, however. Visible wall alignments and linear mounds along the interior

face of the south wall suggest that internal rooms were built against the interior face of the perimeter wall. Indeed, robber pits excavated along the outer face of the east wall exposed a large quantity of ceramic artifacts and evidence of plastering on the exterior face of the wall. In addition, although the ash mound to the south contains considerable amounts of pottery, the SAAS did not find a single kiln waster in a large sample of nearly 800 sherds. The survey did recover fragments of pipes, tiles, and glass. Also, several coins found in the ash and near the robber pits included two of the 4th century AD (Objs. #19, 40). All of this evidence suggests that this structure was not a center for pottery production but rather served some other function. Perhaps it was a caravanserai, not unlikely given Bir Madhkur's prominent position along the Petra–Gaza trade route. Further similar ashy deposits immediately outside of the walls of these structures were documented at such sites as Qasr Wādī eṭ-Ṭayyiba and Qasr Qaʿ as-Suʾaydiyyīn (fig. 4.20). Alternatively, the pipes and tiles could suggest that this structure was a bath complex (Smith et al. 1997: 63–64). Numerous intersecting wall alignments and mounds, suggesting another large structure, lie west and SW of the *castellum.* This is probably

Table 4.8   Late Roman Period Sites.

Site No.	Field Site No.	No. of Late Roman Sherds	% of Total Sherds from Site
7	22	1	9.09
15	10	1	3.45
31	3	2	7.14
72	162	6	2.99
150	330	7	17.5
153	135	3	2.34
166	147	5	7.46
184	324	5	71.43
193	314	1	3.85
199	309	1	3.70
203	302	1	1.22
218	294	1	20.00
221	291	1	2.70
226	281	2	1.26
236	270	10	100.00
275	38	2	0.57
300	205	7	9.86
329	148	34	4.33
330	149	4	4.30

a domestic quarter. The SAAS found a Nabataean coin of the 1st century AD in this area (Obj. #503). Another smaller structure with evidence of at least six interior rooms lies south of the *castellum*.

Pottery from Bir Madhkur ranged from the Early Roman/Nabataean to the Late Byzantine period, though the former predominated (452 of 785 sherds were Early Roman/Nabataean).

Late Roman

The SAAS collected Late Roman pottery at 19 sites, namely, Sites 7, 15, 31, 72, 150, 153, 166, 184, 193, 199, 203, 218, 221, 226, 236, 275, 300, 329, and 330 (Table 4.8). Not all of these sites, however, will be discussed in this section. Site 199 was discussed

above among the Chalcolithic/Early Bronze Age sites and Sites 150, 153 (Rujm aṭ-Ṭāba), 193, 275 and 329 (Bir Madhkur) were discussed among the Early Roman/Nabataean sites. Site 72 will be discussed as a Early Roman/Late Roman site, Site 330 as a Roman/Byzantine site, and Site 166 as a Late Roman/Early Byzantine site.

There were few Late Roman sherds collected at the remaining sites. Sites 7 and 15 are sherd scatters in the urban zone of Aqaba, for example, and each yielded a single Late Roman sherd. The SAAS collected two Late Roman sherds from the summit of Jebel esh-Shahbī (Site 31). Also, two Late Roman sherds from Site 226 derive from a pot-bust on a terrace above Wādī Museimīr; Site 236 is another pot-bust (possibly of two vessels) with no associated features.

Site 184 is situated on a wadi terrace above an ephemeral drainage NE of Gharandal. It consists of several collapsed structures (fig. 4.24), a single stone enclosure or animal pen, and a light sherd and lithic scatter. One of the structures has been robbed and there are many sherds mixed in the debris. Also there are several stones at the site with Arabic graffiti. The SAAS collected five Late Roman sherds from Site 184, all from a pot-bust.

Site 203 consists of various features spread over an expansive alluvial terrace (84 m N–S × 141 m E–W) in Wādī el-Quṣeib. The SAAS collected a single Late Roman sherd near a stone ring or hut circle (Feature 1).

Two sites on alluvial terraces in Wādī Museimīr yielded Late Roman pottery. Site 218 consists of a small stone ring or hut circle and a pot-bust. From the site the SAAS collected a single Late Roman sherd, in addition to Early Roman/Late Roman period pottery and few lithics. Nearby, Site 221, a large site spread over an expansive alluvial terrace (95 m N–S × 245 m E–W), also yielded a single Late Roman sherd, which the SAAS found near a rectilinear structure (Feature 6).

Early Roman/Late Roman

The SAAS collected Early Roman/Late Roman sherds, without further specification, at 26 sites (Table 4.9). Not all of these sites, however, will be treated in detail in this section. Several were discussed above among the Early Roman/Nabataean sites: Sites 43, 149, 153 (Rujm aṭ-Ṭāba), 181 (Gharandal), 193, 308, and 314. Sites 4 and 177 are sherd scatters with no other associated features. The remaining sites will be treated, for the most part, from south to north.

In the embankment of the main highway leading to Aqaba are two exposed wall segments mostly buried by fluvial sediments from Wādī Yutum (Site 72). Further wall alignments are visible on the alluvial fan surface above the embankment. Although the nature and purpose of these structures remain unclear, Site 72 may relate to the ancient route to Aqaba through Wādī Yutum. Various periods are represented at the site (from the Iron Age to Modern), but the Early Roman/Late Roman ceramic material (153 of 201 sherds) predominates.

Site 113 consists of two ruined structures on a saddle between ridges above Wādī Mulghān (Smith and Niemi 1994: 475; Smith et al. 1997: 57). The largest structure, possibly a watchtower, appears as a mound of collapsed stones (fig. 4.25). Segments of the outer facing of the exterior wall are visible, but do not permit an accurate estimation of the overall size or construction of the structure. Adjacent to the south wall is evidence for later reuse of the stones, perhaps as a cemetery. The second structure lies SW of the first. Only the foundation stones of its SE and NE corners and segments along the east north walls are preserved. The remainder of the surface is littered with stones and cobbles. Also, several larger stones align along the outer edge of the NE corner. All the ceramic artifacts from the site came from the first structure, which overwhelmingly belonged to the Early Roman/Late Roman period (105 sherds) though some Early Roman/Nabataean pieces were collected there as well.

North of Gharandal Site 182 consists of several bedouin encampments dispersed across the alluvial fan, a large circular structure (fig. 4.26), which has a smaller appendage outside the SE segment of the wall, an isolated grave, and a sherd and lithic scatter. The encampments appear as linear clearings, the largest of which incorporates five stone rings. Three of these stone rings may be in fact hut circles; a possible hearth is associated with one of these features. There are three additional encampments on the same alluvial surface to the

Table 4.9   Early Roman/Late Roman Period Sites.

Site No.	Field Site No.	No. of ER/LR sherds	% of Total Sherds from Site
4	6	47	95.92
43	14	4	57.14
72	162	153	76.12
113	44/45	105	92.92
149	331	1	33.33
153	135	101	78.91
177	326	21	72.41
181	102	3	3.49
182	322	13	28.26
187	320	3	100.00
193	314	4	15.38
199	309	9	33.33
204	305	5	55.56
206	301	3	75.00
207	298	2	40.00
208	299	2	50.00
218	294	4	80.00
221	291	23	62.16
222	292	36	100.00
223	293	9	100.00
225	289	108	62.43
226	281	57	35.85
230	282	5	100.00
308	235	12	24.49
314	234	19	28.36
316	187	63	81.82

NE, where there are also at least nine other stone rings or hut circles. Most of the pottery from the site could not be identified, but the SAAS did collect 13 Early Roman/Late Roman sherds.

On an alluvial terrace in the first wadi system north of Gharandal, Site 187 consists of two

FIG. 4.25   *SAAS Site 113, Feature 1, ruined structure, perhaps a watchtower overlooking Wādī Mulghān, looking northeast.*

FIG. 4.26   *SAAS Site 182, Feature 1, large, circular structure, looking southwest.*

graves and an L-shaped wall alignment. One of the graves is oblong, whereas the other is more circular. The nature of the wall alignment could not be determined. There is also a modern bedouin encampment at the site. The three Early Roman/ Late Roman sherds from the site came from the area of the graves.

On alluvial terraces above Wādī el-Quṣeib both Sites 199 and 204 were treated above with the Chalcolithic/Early Bronze Age sites. As noted,

FIG. 4.27   *SAAS Site 207, Feature 1, large structure, perhaps domestic.*

Site 199 consists of an unspecified structure and two stone rings or hut circles. The SAAS collected nine Early Roman/Late Roman sherds at the site, seemingly associated with the stone rings or hut circles. Site 204 consists of a stone ring, possibly a hut circle, and various graves. The SAAS collected five Early Roman/Late Roman sherds from Site 204, apparently associated with the stone ring.

Site 206, a single stone ring or hut circle, is also situated in Wādī el-Quṣeib. The SAAS collected three Early Roman/Late Roman sherds from Site 206, plus one Iron Age sherd.

Site 218 is situated in Wādī Museimīr to the north and consists of a single stone ring or hut circle and a very light scatter of sherds and lithics. The SAAS collected four Early Roman/Late Roman sherds from a single pot-bust at the site, in addition to a Late Roman piece.

Site 207 is a small settlement on an alluvial terrace above Wādī el-Quṣeib. The site consists of five definite structures (perhaps domestic), two indeterminate structures, various stone mounds, stone lined pits, hearths, and an associated sherd and lithic scatter. The largest structure, which has an entrance along the SE wall, was then in use as an animal enclosure (fig. 4.27). A possible small hearth or storage area lies NW and adjacent to the

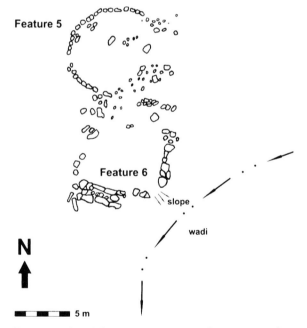

FIG. 4.28   *SAAS Site 221, Features 5 and 6, remains of an unspecified structure and a large stone enclosure.*

corner of this structure. Another structure nearby is ovoid in shape and shows no signs of modern restoration or reuse. The remaining structures are similar in shape and construction as the ovoid one. A group of hearths and stone piles lies to the south and west of the largest of these. Another structure,

FIG. 4.29 *SAAS Site 221, Feature 6, remains of an unspecified structure, looking southwest.*

smaller than all the others, is isolated at the far west end of the site. In the same area is a series of small stone-lined pits set into the ground, all about the same size. Also, three of these pits have larger, flat stones nearby, perhaps used as pit covers. Several other square soil depressions around the site may be dismantled features of this type. None appear to be hearths, however. The SAAS collected two Early Roman/Late Roman sherds at the site, in addition to a Late Roman/Early Byzantine sherd and Early Roman/Nabataean material.

Located on another alluvial terrace in Wādī el-Quṣeib, Site 208 consists of a cemetery, a possible tent encampment, a series of apparent *thamail* (shallow wells excavated in the alluvial surface to tap high levels of groundwater), two sets of rectilinear rock alignments with stones set upright (as shrines?), and sherd and lithic scatters. The cemetery consists of at least 12 graves scattered across the wadi terrace. Most are badly deflated and comprise small stone mounds of limestone and sandstone. The presumed tent encampment consists of a rectilinear clearing. Near the encampment there is a small, stone-lined pit similar to those at Site 207. The apparent *thamail* appear as circular, cleared depressions in the ground extending across the alluvial terrace. If not in fact *thamail*, these depressions may have formed naturally by ero-

sion. Finally, a rectilinear alignment of sandstone boulders lies on a spur behind the site and a second set lies to the east. The SAAS collected only four sherds at the site: two Early Roman/Late Roman, one Chalcolithic/Early Bronze Age, and one Early Roman/Nabataean.

Site 221 lies on an alluvial terrace along the north bank of Wādī Museimīr. The SAAS recorded 19 features at the site, which included bedouin encampments, stone rings or hut circles, isolated structures, graves, cairns, and a light lithic scatter that extended across most of the terrace. Feature 1 is a bedouin encampment defined by small boulders placed along the perimeter of a rectilinear enclosed area cleared of stones. There are two hearths set within this area. Additional encampments nearby were designated as Feature 12, which yielded 10 Early Roman/Late Roman sherds, and Feature 19. Feature 3, a stone mound, perhaps a grave, yielded five Early Roman/Late Roman sherds. Features 10 and 13 are also stone mounds that appear to be graves, and Feature 11 is a large, robbed cairn. Feature 4 appears to be the remains of an ancient road or cleared pathway that extends across the wadi terrace. Feature 5, where the SAAS collected a single Early Roman/Late Roman sherd and a Chalcolithic/Early Bronze Age pot-bust, is a large stone enclosure (fig. 4.28). Feature 6 (fig. 4.29) is a rectilinear unspecified structure similar to

FIG. 4.30   *SAAS Site 221, Feature 2, remains of an unspecified structure.*

Feature 2 (fig. 4.30), the ruins of another small, isolated structure. Feature 7 is a more substantial structure partitioned into two rooms by a central interior wall. Features 14 and 17 are additional structures or houses similar to Feature 6. The SAAS collected six Early Roman/Late Roman sherds from Feature 14. Features 8, 9, and 15 are stone rings, possibly hut circles. Feature 16 is a semicircular stone alignment and Feature 18 is an isolated wall alignment.

Site 222 is a cemetery on an alluvial terrace along the north bank of Wādī Museimīr. The central features consist of two large cairns and nine low mounds of stone, apparently graves with no set orientation. The graves vary in size, which suggests a mixture of adult and child burials. Roughly 2 m NW of the cemetery is a sandstone boulder with a petroglyph depicting an ibex. All of the pottery collected at the site was of the Early Roman/Late Roman period (36 sherds), most from two or three pot-busts.

Site 223 is a smelting site in Wādī Museimīr, NE of Site 222. Features include three U-shaped structures and a stone pile or grave. The SAAS found nine Early Roman/Late Roman sherds and copper slag scattered on the surface. Similar remains were documented at Site 228 (fig. 4.31) near the mouth of the wadi.

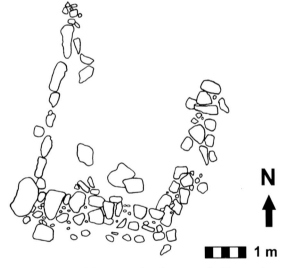

FIG. 4.31   *SAAS Site 228, isolated structure, looking northwest.*

Site 225 consists of a bedouin encampment, at least two isolated structures, an array of petroglyphs on seven sandstone boulders dispersed across an alluvial terrace in Wādī Museimīr, and sherd and lithic scatters. A grave or small burial cairn lies near the smaller structure. The petroglyphs consist of several images and Nabataean inscriptions (see Chapter 7). The former include various hunting scenes (fig. 4.32). The SAAS collected 108 Early Roman/Late Roman sherds at the

FIG. 4.32 *SAAS 225, Feature 5, rock art depicting hunting scene.*

site. The Early Roman/Nabataean period was also well-represented.

Site 226 lies on another elongated alluvial terrace along the north bank of Wādī Museimīr and is spread out over a very large area (185 m N–S × 425 m E–W). The site consists of 19 various features, which include an isolated structure, bedouin encampments, cairns, stone rings or hut circles, numerous graves, and various sherd and lithic scatters. Features 1 and 2 are small, circular clearings with small hearths in the center that show evidence of recent use. Unlike other stone rings or hut circles these features do not have stones encircling them, although rocks have been pushed to their outer edges in places. Features 3 and 9 are additional clearings, but the pottery from these features dated earlier than the Early Roman/Late Roman period. Feature 4 is a circular, low-lying mound with a small, divided stone alignment along its SW edge. Feature 5, where the SAAS found a single Early Roman/Late Roman sherd, is a rectangular structure. There is a wall at the northern end of the structure, and apparent small storage areas are set off its eastern and western sides. Features 6, 7, and 17 are bedouin encampments. Feature 8 is a stone mound, perhaps a robbed cairn, which yielded four Early Roman/Late Roman sherds.

Features 11 and 14 are also cairns, comparable to the cairn identified at Site 211 (fig. 4.33) far to the south. Feature 12 is an isolated, oblong grave. Feature 15 consists of eight stone rings, perhaps hut circles, and three possible graves. Here the SAAS collected four Early Roman/Late Roman sherds and a few more Chalcolithic/Early Bronze Age artifacts. Features 10 and 13 consist of additional stone rings or hut circles. Feature 16 is a general sherd and lithic scatter over an area that includes bedouin encampments and animal pens. The area has been disturbed, probably due to grazing and reuse over a long period of time. The SAAS collected 18 Early Roman/Late Roman sherds from Feature 16, which also yielded Chalcolithic/Early Bronze Age, Early Roman/Nabataean and Late Roman sherds. Finally, both Features 18 and 19 are petroglyphs on sandstone boulders set 10 m apart. The latter yielded 11 Early Roman/Late Roman sherds but the bulk of the pottery was of the Early Roman/Nabataean period. The SAAS also made a general collection of pottery from the alluvial terrace which ranged from the Early Bronze Age to the Early Roman/Late Roman period.

Just north of Wādī Museimīr, Site 230 consists of three stone mounds or cairns, two wall alignments, and a sherd and lithic scatter. One wall

FIG. 4.33   *SAAS Site 211, isolated cairn, looking south.*

FIG. 4.34   *SAAS Site 316, Feature 4, indeterminate, figure-8 structure that may relate to the agricultural activity in the region, looking southeast.*

alignment west of the largest cairn appears as a linear mound of stones in an L-shaped pattern. On its west side are two mounded circular features appended to the wall. The other wall alignment lies at the edge of the wadi terrace and apparently served as an enclosure. All five sherds collected were Early Roman/Late Roman.

In the ʿAraba north of Jebel el-Khureij, Site 316 consists of an indeterminate structure, various stone mounds, two wall alignments, and a sherd and lithic scatter. The stone mounds lie at the west edge of the site. One wall alignment lies north of the stone mounds, and the other, which is more curvilinear, lies to the south. Their nature

Table 4.10   Roman/Byzantine Period Sites.

Site No.	Field Site No.	No. of Roman/ Byz Sites	% of Total Sherds from Site
5	20	51	75.00
15	10	19	65.52
16	12	21	42.00
22	28	2	11.11
31	3	21	75.00
33	37	1	1.64
40	18	4	100.00
47	178	2	14.29
50	230	1	1.18
54	72	5	27.78
55	233	1	11.11
60	76	2	11.76
72	162	8	3.98
98	122	38	100.00
103	48	21	95.45
104	54	27	69.23
107	31	16	72.73
139	127	25	92.59
165	144	10	71.43
169	101	1	11.11
181	102	65	75.58
186	151	8	61.54
195	316	1	16.67
203	302	50	60.98
219	295	39	61.90
240	273	12	100.00
273	247	1	50.00
279	223	1	6.25
282	219	1	50.00
286	216	1	33.33
291	203	3	7.14
321	160	24	70.59
324	156	1	16.67
329	148	248	31.59
330	149	80	86.02

and purpose remain uncertain. A figure-8 shaped structure lies to the SE (fig. 4.34). It is built of small stones arranged in a main circle (threshing floor?) with a smaller circle appended to its SE end. There is a possible entranceway on its SE side. Pottery from Site 316 ranged from the Chalcolithic/ Early Bronze Age to the Late Byzantine/Umayyad period, though Early Roman/Late Roman pottery (63 sherds) predominated.

Roman/Byzantine

The SAAS collected Roman/Byzantine sherds at 35 sites (Table 4.10). Most of these sites have been described above. Sites 50, 54, 55, 60, 273, 279, and 286 were discussed with the Chalcolithic/Early Bronze Age sites, Sites 107, 169, 181, 186, 219, 291, 321, 324, and 329 with the Early Roman/Nabataean sites, and Site 72 among the Early Roman/Late Roman sites. Site 33 will be discussed below as an Early Islamic period site. Also, many sites where the SAAS collected Roman/Byzantine pottery are only sherd scatters and will not be treated here, namely, Sites 5, 15, 16, 22, 31, 47, 165, and 195. The remaining sites will be discussed geographically, for the most part, from south to north.

Site 40 lies on an alluvial terrace and near power lines east of Jebel esh-Shahbī. The site consists of 17 pitted burials scattered across the terrace. The burials have no uniform orientation. The SAAS collected only four sherds at the site, all Roman/Byzantine.

Site 98 lies on an alluvial fan east of a small isolated ridge between Wādī Yutum and Wādī Mulghān. The site consists of two stone mounds and numerous rock alignments. All 38 sherds from the site were exclusively Roman/Byzantine.

Site 103 lies in the center of an active drainage channel on an alluvial fan south of Wādī Mulghān. The site consists of a rectilinear structure, possibly partitioned. Most of the walls have been washed away, but the north corner has been preserved, along with part of the NE and NW walls. The SAAS collected 21 Roman/Byzantine sherds at the site.

Site 104 lies SE of Wādī Mulghān and consists of a complex of structures and wall alignments. The largest structure is elevated on the alluvial fan surface above the others, and several other wall alignments and circular stone structures are visible on the alluvial fan surface down the slope to the NE. Roman/Byzantine pottery (30 sherds) predominated at the site. Other material at Site 104 ranged in date from the Byzantine to the Early Islamic periods.

Site 107, on the north bank of the first small tributary wadi south of Wādī Mulghān, consists of various wall alignments and structures. It lies just north of Site 106 on the opposite bank of the wadi. One of the structures at Site 107 is rectilinear and lies at the eastern end of the site. A second structure to the west has a wall alignment extending from its NW corner westward, which may have formed a corner with the westernmost wall alignment at the site that stretches out from the cliff face perpendicularly to the wadi bed. Site 106 is a massive enclosure wall that wraps around a small terrace. An opening (doorway?) lies on the NE segment of the wall. While no artifacts were found at Site 106, Site 107 yielded 22 sherds, 16 of which were of the Roman/Byzantine period; the remaining sherds from Site 107 either could not be identified or were Early Roman/Nabataean or Late Byzantine.

Located on a small ridge overlooking Wādī el-Muhtadī from the south, Site 139 consists of a walled enclosure set against a cliff face and four distinct burials, two of which are small stone mounds. A modern concrete water basin lies to the south. The site yielded 25 Roman/Byzantine sherds, plus some Early Roman/Nabataean.

Site 203 lies on an alluvial terrace along the south bank of Wādī el-Quṣeib. The site spans a large area (ca. 84 m N–S × 141 m E–W), in which the SAAS recorded eight features. Features 1 and 2 are stone rings or hut circles located at the far east end of the terrace. Features 3–5 are all wall alignments. Feature 3 is a large retaining wall at the base of the slope at the south edge of the wadi terrace. Features 4 and 5 are both L-shaped retaining walls. Feature 6 consists of at least 10–20 burials of varying size and type scattered across the wadi terrace. It is difficult to determine the exact number of burials because of recent bedouin activity in the area and disturbance by erosion. Feature 7 consists of a series of soil erosion and/or water diversion check dams and walls distributed across the wadi terrace. Some walls resemble those of Features 4 and 5. Fea-

Table 4.11   Late Roman/Early Byzantine Period Sites.

Site No.	Field Site No.	No. of LR/EByz Sherds	% of Total Sherds from Site
150	330	19	47.50
166	147	58	86.57
207	298	1	20.00
238	268	17	77.27
258	251	6	100.00
329	148	18	2.29

Table 4.12   Early Byzantine Period Sites.

Site No.	Field Site No.	No. of EByz Sherds	% of Total Sherds from Site
7	22	1	9.09
14	11	1	1.33
17	8	1	3.57
31	3	1	3.57
50	230	1	1.18
52	231	2	2.67
72	162	3	1.49
150	330	2	5.00
152	136	2	0.77
166	147	4	5.97
181	102	4	4.65
199	309	4	14.81
203	302	1	1.22
219	295	2	3.17
238	268	1	4.55
300	207	6	8.45
308	235	12	24.49
316	187	1	1.30
319	152	2	1.96
329	148	28	3.57
330	149	3	3.23

ture 8 consists of a small square pattern of stones inlaid in the soil (only two stones *in situ*), similar to those found at Site 207. Pottery from the terrace ranged in date from Chalcolithic/Early Bronze to Late Byzantine, but 50 of the 82 sherds collected dated to the Roman/Byzantine period. Lithics were collected across the entire terrace as well.

Site 240 is an isolated structure, perhaps a tomb, on a sandy knoll SW of Wādī Abū Barqa. The SAAS collected exclusively Roman/Byzantine pottery (12 sherds) at the site from a single pot-bust and a few lithics.

Site 282 lies west of Jebel el-Qāʿ and consists of various unspecified structures, wall alignments, stone rings or hut circles, and stone mounds. The SAAS recorded seven features at the site. Features 1, 4, and 6 are stone rings or hut circles. Feature 2, two appended stone circles forming a figure-8 structure, lies downslope. Feature 3 is a structure that consists of a curving wall alignment and an adjacent stone ring. At the south end of the wall is another small stone ring and a short segment of another wall alignment projecting to the east. Feature 5 consists of two small stone mounds SE of Feature 1. Feature 7, an isolated rectilinear structure, lies at northern edge of the site. Site 282 yielded only one Roman/Byzantine sherd.

Site 330 consists of a small, collapsed tower and a nearby L-shaped structure. It lies 1 km east of the modern highway and opposite the former base of the Jordan Valley Authority at Bir Madhkur (Raikes 1985). The tower is largely buried in sand. Segments of the west and north walls, constructed of dressed limestone blocks, and the SW corner, are partially visible. The structure to the north has only its north and west walls exposed. To the SE, a cemetery consisting of several graves may be associated with these structures. The SAAS collected pottery ranging in date from Late Roman to Late Byzantine, but most sherds (80 of 93) dated to the Roman/Byzantine period.

Late Roman/Early Byzantine

The SAAS collected Late Roman/Early Byzantine pottery at six sites: 150, 166, 207, 238, 258, and 329 (Table 4.11). Only Site 238 will be treated here. Sites 150 and 329 were discussed above with the Early

Roman/Nabataean sites, and Site 207 was discussed above with the Early Roman/Late Roman sites. Sites 166 and 258 are merely sherd scatters and/or pot-busts.

Just south of Wādī Abū Barqa, Site 238 consists of two roughly circular stone enclosures. The largest, partially destroyed by bulldozing, is likely an animal pen. A wall extends from the west wall of the enclosure, which abuts a second wall and terminates in an upright standing stone or stele with no visible inscription. The second enclosure is smaller with a stone ring adjacent to its west side. A possible stone hearth lies to the west. Most Late Roman/Byzantine pottery (17 of 22 sherds) may have derived from a pot-bust; the Chalcolithic/Early Bronze Age and the Early Byzantine period were also represented. A similar enclosure or animal pen lies further south in Wādī Museimīr, Site 212 (fig. 4.35), at which no pottery was found.

Early Byzantine

The SAAS collected Early Byzantine pottery at 21 sites: 7, 14, 17, 31, 50, 52, 72, 150, 152, 166, 181, 199, 203, 219, 238, 300, 308, 316, 319, 329, and 330 (Table 4.12). All of these sites have been treated in previous sections. Sites 50, 52, 199, and 300 were discussed with the Chalcolithic/Early Bronze Age evidence; Sites 150, 152, 181, 219, 308, 319, and 329 with the Early Roman/Nabataean sites; and Sites 72 and 316 with the Early Roman/Late Roman evidence. Also, Sites 203 and 330 were treated above as Roman/Byzantine sites and Site 238 was discussed with the Late Roman/Early Byzantine sites. At most of these sites the number of Early Byzantine sherds was low. The remaining sites are simply sherd scatters and/or pot-busts, namely, Sites 7, 14, 17, 31, and 166.

Late Byzantine

Late Byzantine sherds were retrieved at 25 sites: 1, 5–8, 12, 14–21, 31, 35, 74, 91, 107, 110, 114, 203, 214, 329, and 330 (Table 4.13). Not all of these will be treated here. Sites 1, 107, and 329 were discussed above with the Early Roman/Nabataean sites and Sites 203 and 330 were discussed with the Roman/Byzantine sites. Sites 5–8, 12, 14–21, 31, and 74 are sherd scatters and/or pot-busts. One significant

Fig. 4.35   *SAAS Site 212, circular enclosure, looking northeast.*

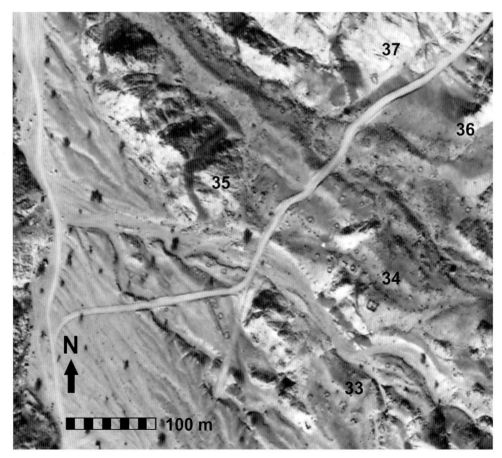

Fig. 4.36   *Aerial view of region behind Jebel esh-Shahbī where the SAAS recorded Sites 33–37.*

Table 4.13   Late Byzantine Period Sites.

Site No.	Field Site No.	No. of LByz Sherds	% of Total Sherds from Site
1	1	3	6.67
5	20	6	8.82
6	9	40	100.00
7	22	1	9.09
8	21	1	7.69
12	25	2	40.00
14	11	4	5.33
15	10	4	13.79
16	12	1	2.00
17	8	14	50.00
18	7	9	36.00
19	5	16	80.00
20	4	7	26.92
21	27	4	10.53
31	3	1	3.57
35	34	90	86.54
74	81	113	100.00
91	62	3	100.00
107	31	2	9.09
110	40	8	100.00
114	55	1	14.29
203	302	1	1.22
214	284	11	100.00
329	148	3	0.38
330	149	1	1.08

Table 4.14   Byzantine Period Sites.

Site No.	Field Site No.	No. of Byzantine Sherds	% of Total Sherds from Site
16	12	3	6
104	54	9	23.08
203	302	1	1.22
243	141	5	6.25
275	38	1	0.28

observation concerning these sherd scatters is that a larger percentage of those within the urban zone of Aqaba yielded Late Byzantine sherds. The remaining sites will be treated, for the most part, geographically from south to north.

To the east of Jebel esh-Shahbī, Site 35 is actually contiguous with Sites 33–34 and 36–37. These sites combine to cover an area of ca. 500 × 250 m (fig. 4.36). Site 35 consists of numerous structures and wall alignments. For the most part, the SAAS found few artifacts in the area. A handful of sherds collected at the site came from either pot-busts or were modern. The Late Byzantine sherds from Site 35 were found near two ruined structures.

Site 91 lies on the north slope of a ridge due north of Wādī Yutum and consists of a stone ring or hut circle. The three Late Byzantine sherds collected at the site were from a single vessel.

Site 110, a cemetery on the alluvial fan of the first tributary wadi south of Wādī Mulghān, consists of at least 16 graves. Most graves are elongated and ringed with capstones, although two appear more as circular stone mounds. The SAAS collected eight Late Byzantine sherds at the site, all from a single pot-bust.

Site 114 is another cemetery on a saddle between two ridges overlooking Wādī Mulghān. Most graves are oblong stone alignments with cleared centers, although one is circular. Two of the elongated graves have capstones. An isolated structure lies nearby. The SAAS collected one Late Byzantine sherd from Site 114.

Site 214 lies on an alluvial terrace of a tributary to Wādī Museimīr. It is a large isolated cairn virtually destroyed by clandestine excavations. There is also a petroglyph on one of the stones. The SAAS collected 11 Late Byzantine sherds from a pot-bust north of the cairn.

Byzantine

The SAAS collected Byzantine sherds at five sites: Sites 16, 104, 203, 243, and 275 (Table 4.14). All have been treated above. Site 275, the fort in Qāʿ as-

Table 4.15   Roman/Byzantine/Islamic Period Sites.

Site No.	Field Site No.	No. of R/Byz/ Islamic Sherds	% of Total Sherds from Site
14	11	45	60.00
313	191	1	0.94

Table 4.16   Late Byzantine/Umayyad Period Sites.

Site No.	Field Site No.	No. of LByz/ Umayyad Sherds	% of Total Sherds from Site
34	35	7	5.34
100	53	1	25.00
275	38	2	0.57
316	187	1	1.30

Table 4.17   Umayyad Period Sites.

Site No.	Field Site No.	No. of Umayyad Sherds	% of Total Sherds from Site
50	230	14	16.47
70	169	4	12.50

Table 4.18   Abbasid Period Sites.

Site No.	Field Site No.	No. of Abbasid Sherds	% of Total Sherds from Site
33	37	7	11.48
219	295	1	1.59

Su'aydiyyīn, was described with the Early Roman/ Nabataean sites. Sites 104 and 203 were discussed with the Roman/Byzantine period sites. Site 16 is merely a sherd scatter in the urban zone of Aqaba, and Site 243, in the foothills north of Wādī Abū Barqa, is a pot-bust at an essentially Chalcolithic site.

Roman/Byzantine/Islamic

The SAAS collected Roman/Byzantine/Islamic sherds, without further precision, at two sites: Sites 14 and 313 (Table 4.15). Site 14 is a sherd scatter in the urban zone of Aqaba. Site 313 was discussed above with the Chalcolithic/Early Bronze Age sites.

Late Byzantine/Umayyad

The SAAS collected sherds designated as Late Byzantine/Umayyad, without further precision, at four sites: Sites 34, 100, 275, and 316 (Table 4.16). Site 275, the fort in Qaʿ as-Suʾaydiyyīn, was discussed above as an Early Roman/Nabataean site and Site 316 was discussed with the Early Roman/Late Roman sites.

Site 34, lying east of Jebel esh-Shahbī, is contiguous with Sites 33 and 35–37, all of which span an

area of ca. 500 × 250 m (fig. 4.36). The site consists of numerous structures and wall alignments. The Late Byzantine/Umayyad sherds derived from a general collection across the site.

Site 100 is a single oval burial on an alluvial fan south of Wādī Mulghān. The SAAS found a single Late Byzantine/Umayyad sherd at the site.

Umayyad

The SAAS collected Umayyad sherds at two sites, namely, Sites 50 and 70 (Table 4.17). Both sites were discussed above among the Chalcolithic/ Early Bronze Age sites. Site 50 lies in the vicinity of Ḥujeirat al-Ghuzlan and 14 Umayyad sherds came from a cairn at the site. Site 70 lies near the mouth of Wādī Yutum; most Umayyad sherds from this site were from a pot-bust.

Abbasid

Abbasid pottery appeared at two sites: Sites 33 and 219 (Table 4.18). The latter, a cemetery on an alluvial terrace along the south bank of Wādī Museimīr, was treated above with the Early Roman/Nabataean sites. Site 219 yielded a single Abbasid sherd.

Site 33 is contiguous with Sites 34–37. These sites altogether cover an area of ca. 500 × 250 m and consist of numerous structures and wall alignments (fig. 4.36). The SAAS recorded 24 specific

Table 4.19   Fatimid Period Sites.

Site No.	Field Site No.	No. of Fatimid Sherds	% of Total Sherds from Site
17	8	4	14.29

Table 4.20   Fatimid/Ayyubid/Mamluk Period Sites.

Site No.	Field Site No.	No. of Fatimid/ Ayy/ Mamluk Sherds	% of Total Sherds from Site
14	11	6	8.00

Table 4.21   Early Islamic Period Sites.

Site No.	Field Site No.	No. of Early Islamic Sherds	% of Total Sherds from Site
14	11	7	9.33
33	37	25	40.98
36	68	2	4.35
44	117	5	100.00
50	230	46	54.12
58	71	1	1.67
60	76	4	23.53
63	74	2	3.39
104	54	3	7.69
124	90	4	80.00
169	101	3	33.33
198	310	3	75.00

features at Site 33. Seven Abbasid sherds from a pot-bust were collected near Feature 24, which consists of four structures. One structure is rectilinear with its entrance in the NE corner. A circular structure, similarly constructed, lies nearby. Both structures are in a ruined state. A third structure lies downslope to the east and a fourth structure lies further below. Both are relatively small. Few lithics were collected at Site 33 as well.

Fatimid and Fatimid/Ayyubid/Mamluk

The SAAS collected Fatimid sherds at one site only, Site 17 (Table 4.19). This is a sherd scatter of dubious provenance within the urban zone of Aqaba. Sherds designated as Fatimid/Ayyubid/Mamluk, without further precision, were collected at one site (Table 4.20). This is Site 14, another sherd scatter within the urban zone of Aqaba.

Early Islamic

The SAAS collected sherds designated as Early Islamic at 12 sites: Sites 14, 33, 36, 44, 50, 58, 60, 63, 104, 124, 169, and 198 (Table 4.21). Not all of these sites will be treated in detail in this section. For the most part, Islamic period pottery was meager compared to some earlier periods. All three sites in the vicinity of Ḥujeirat al-Ghuzlan just north of Aqaba (Sites 58, 60, and 63), for instance, yielded a total of only seven Early Islamic sherds compared to much larger numbers of Chalcolithic or Chalcolithic/ Early Bronze sherds. Sites 124, 169, and 198 were discussed above with the Early Roman/Nabataean sites. The Early Islamic sherds from these sites mostly came from pot-busts. Site 14 is a sherd scatter in the urban zone of Aqaba. Site 104 was discussed above with the Roman/Byzantine sites.

Sites 33 and 36 lie in a dissected drainage basin behind Jebel esh-Shahbī. As mentioned, these sites are contiguous with Sites 34–35 and 37, which together incorporate an area of ca. 500 × 250 m (fig. 4.36). Early Islamic sherds in the area tended to be sparse and many of those came from isolated pot-busts.

Site 44 lies on the slope of a ridge NE of Jebel esh-Shahbī and consists of a series of six terrace walls that cut across three small drainages. These probably facilitated some limited agricultural activity in the area. The SAAS collected five Early Islamic sherds at Site 44.

Along the Wādī Yutum alluvial fan SW of Ḥujeirat al-Ghuzlan, Site 50 has been discussed above with the Chalcolithic/Early Bronze sites. This is presumably a small settlement where the Early Islamic evidence appears mostly ephemeral, from pot-busts.

Table 4.22   Late Islamic Period Sites.

Site No.	Field Site No.	No. of Late Islamic Sherds	% of Total Sherds from Site
7	22	1	9.09
14	11	1	1.33
70	169	18	56.25

Table 4.23   Ottoman Period Sites.

Site No.	Field Site No.	No. of Ottoman Sherds	% of Total Sherds from Site
219	295	1	1.59

Late Islamic

The SAAS collected Late Islamic sherds at three sites: Sites 7, 14, and 70 (Table 4.22). Sites 7 and 14 are sherd scatters in the urban zone of Aqaba. The Late Islamic sherds from Site 70, a small settlement on an alluvial spur near the mouth of Wādī Yutum, derived from a single pot-bust.

Ottoman–Modern

The SAAS collected Ottoman and Modern period sherds at 30 sites: Sites 1, 3, 5, 7–8, 10, 14, 16, 18, 21–24, 29, 33–37, 47, 49, 52, 57, 72, 114, 152, 185, 186, 195, and 219 (Tables 4.23–24). No attempt is made here to give a full analysis of these sites because most have been discussed above in relation to other periods. The SAAS found exclusively Modern sherds at Sites 23 and 24, both sherd scatters in Aqaba.

Undetermined (Early)–Undetermined

The SAAS collected sherds designated as Undetermined (Early) at nine sites: 2, 152, 226, 234, 237, 254, 264, 267, and 319 (Table 4.25). The designation "Undetermined (Early)" means that they were judged as likely pre-classical in date. Sherds of Undetermined date were collected at 68 sites: 1, 3–4, 7–8, 10–12, 14, 16–20, 22, 29, 33–35, 37, 39, 43, 47, 50,

Table 4.24   Modern Period Sites.

Site No.	Field Site No.	No. of Modern Sherds	% of Total Sherds from Site
1	1	1	2.22
3	13	157	99.37
5	20	9	13.24
7	22	2	18.18
8	21	1	7.69
10	23	3	50.00
14	11	1	1.33
16	12	1	2.00
18	7	4	16.00
21	27	33	86.84
22	28	15	83.33
23	30	14	100.00
24	29	15	100.00
29	174	1	0.12
33	37	25	40.98
34	35	7	5.34
35	34	1	0.96
36	68	44	95.65
37	69	1	33.33
47	178	3	21.43
49	195	1	50.00
52	231	1	1.33
57	73	4	14.29
72	162	1	0.50
114	55	1	14.29
152	136	1	0.38
185	323	2	66.67
186	151	1	7.69
195	316	1	16.67

52–53, 70, 72, 103, 107, 114, 134, 137, 149, 153, 165, 182, 184, 186, 193, 197, 199, 203, 207, 221, 226, 243, 253, 256, 275–76, 282, 287, 291, 294, 299–300, 302, 308, 313–14, 316, 319, 321, 325, and 328–30 (Table 4.26). Most of

Fig. 4.37 *SAAS Site 81, isolated structure/tower overlooking Wādī Yutum, looking northwest.*

Table 4.25   Undetermined (Early) Period Sites.

Site No.	Field Site No.	No. of Undet. (Early) Sherds	% of Total Sherds from Site
62	70	14	40.00
152	136	3	1.15
226	281	1	0.63
234	272	3	37.50
237	269	4	50.00
254	237	1	100.00
264	257	4	44.44
267	245	1	14.29
319	152	1	0.98

these sites have been treated already. Only at Sites 39, 134, 137, 197, 253, and 302 did the SAAS collect exclusively unidentifiable sherds. Site 254 produced a single unidentifiable (early) sherd.

Site 39, located behind Jebel esh-Shahbī, yielded a single unidentifiable sherd. It consists of three stone mounds, perhaps burials.

On the alluvial fan NW of Wādī Mulghān, Site 134 consists of three isolated graves and yielded one unidentifiable sherd.

Site 137, between Wādī el-Muhtadī and Wādī Um Ratam in Area I, is another cemetery consisting of three isolated graves. In addition, two stone mounds lie far to the SW of the grave. The SAAS collected six unidentifiable sherds at the site.

In Wādī el-Quṣeib in Area III, Site 197 consists of four graves on an alluvial terrace. The Site yielded a single unidentifiable sherd and few lithics.

Sites 253–54 both lie on the alluvial fan NW of Wādī Abū Barqa. The former, where the SAAS collected a single unidentifiable sherd, consists of a stone ring, perhaps a grave. The latter, which yielded a single unidentifiable (early) sherd, consists of five circular clearings clustered together. The SAAS found a number of lithics and core fragments lying scattered on the surface.

Site 302 consists of three isolated stone mounds, perhaps burial cairns, on the alluvial fan NW of Jebel el-Qā. The site yielded 10 unidentifiable sherds.

Sites with No Pottery

The SAAS found no pottery at 144 of the sites surveyed. Among these, the SAAS collected lithic material at 54 sites: Sites 38, 48, 61, 66, 68–69, 123, 131, 143, 148, 157, 160–61, 164, 168, 173–75, 188, 190, 194, 201–2, 209–12, 216–17, 220, 224, 227–29, 232–33, 241, 248, 251–52, 259–61, 266, 268–69, 271–72, 303, 306, 315, 318, 320, and 327. Thus, SAAS found no artifacts whatsoever at ninety sites. These include 41 sites that are apparently mortuary in nature: Sites 41, 42, 45, 67, 71, 84–85, 87, 92, 96, 99, 101–2, 111, 117–19, 122, 125, 128–29, 133, 135, 138, 151, 154,

156, 176, 179, 192, 200, 213, 239, 245, 288, 292–93, 298, 301, 309, and 326. Strangely, 44 sites without artifacts exhibited such features as wall alignments, structures, enclosures, and/or stone rings or hut circles, along with other features that suggest more extensive human activity. These are Sites 25–28, 32, 46, 51, 64–65, 73, 75, 77, 81–83 (fig. 4.37), 86, 88–90, 93–95, 97, 105–6, 108–9, 112, 120, 127, 130, 136, 140–41, 146, 183, 205, 215, 235, 246, 281, 285, 289, and 296. Many of these sites have been discussed in earlier sections in relation to other sites where the SAAS collected pottery.

Table 4.26   Undetermined Period Sites.

Site No.	Field Site No.	No. of Undet. Sherds	% of Total Sherds from Site	Site No.	Field Site No.	No. of Undet. Sherds	% of Total Sherds from Site
1	1	35	77.78	47	178	9	64.29
3	13	1	0.63	50	230	2	2.35
4	6	2	4.08	52	231	1	1.33
7	22	4	36.36	53	232	2	50.00
8	21	3	23.08	70	169	2	6.25
10	23	2	33.33	72	162	5	2.49
11	26	0	0.00	103	48	1	4.55
12	25	2	40.00	107	31	1	4.55
14	11	8	10.67	114	55	5	71.43
16	12	3	6.00	134	93	1	100.00
17	8	9	32.14	137	124	6	100.00
18	7	5	20.00	149	331	1	33.33
19	5	8	40.00	153	135	1	0.78
20	4	9	34.62	165	144	4	28.57
22	28	1	5.56	182	322	33	71.74
29	174	1	0.12	184	324	2	28.57
33	37	3	4.92	186	151	2	15.38
34	35	117	89.31	193	314	2	7.69
35	34	13	12.50	197	311	1	100.00
37	69	2	66.67	199	309	1	3.70
39	16	1	100.00	203	302	3	3.66
43	14	2	28.57	207	198	1	20.00

Table 4.26 (cont.)   Undetermined Period Sites.

Site No.	Field Site No.	No. of Undet. Sherds	% of Total Sherds from Site	Site No.	Field Site No.	No. of Undet. Sherds	% of Total Sherds from Site
221	291	2	5.41	300	207	1	1.41
226	281	2	1.26	302	212	10	100.00
243	141	3	3.75	308	235	9	18.37
253	238	1	100.00	313	191	3	2.83
256	259	1	3.45	314	234	2	2.99
275	38	2	0.57	316	187	1	1.30
276	133	2	6.45	319	152	1	0.98
282	219	1	50.00	321	160	5	14.71
287	222	10	15.63	325	161	1	2.63
291	203	30	71.43	328	158	2	28.57
294	215	6	40.00	329	148	2	0.25
299	208	1	12.50	330	149	5	5.38

NOTES

1 I express gratitude to Dr. S. Thomas Parker for his support of this project. The 1993 archaeological reconnaissance of the southeast Wādī 'Araba was conducted under permits granted by the Department of Antiquities of Jordan and funded by an American Center of Oriental Research/USIA Fellowship. I also acknowledge the support of the Endowment for Biblical Research. Also, thanks are due to Dr. Safwan Tell, Director-General of the Department of Antiquities in 1994; Dr. Ghazi Bisheh, Director-General of the Department of Antiquities in 1996 and 1998; Ms. Sawsan Fahkri, Inspector-General of Antiquities of the Aqaba region; and to the police and military officers of the Aqaba region who assisted with the project. A special thanks is due to Dr. Pierre Bikai, Director of the American Center of Oriental Research, as well as to the staff of ACOR for their constant support and assistance. I also want to acknowledge the survey staff for each season. In 1994, this included Tina Niemi, Michelle Stevens,

and John Rucker; in 1996, Heather Walters and Carol Frey; and in 1998, Eric Lapp, Karen Kumeiga, and Michael Decker. Thanks to you all for many hot hours of productive survey in the summer sun of the 'Araba.

2 Here and throughout, though the valley is actually oriented NNE–SSW × ESE–WNW, for the sake of brevity and for ease of reading I have presented this orientation in general descriptions as N–S × E–W.

3 I exclude in this assessment 609 out of 824 sherds collected by the RAP staff from Tell el-Kheleifeh in 1996, because these were not provided with preliminary dates while in the field. In the collection, only the more diagnostic sherds were chosen for closer analysis.

4 Two problematic sherds from Site 287 may be Neolithic, without further precision. Since the bulk of the material from Site 287 dates to the Chalcolithic/Early Bronze Age, the site will be treated as such in this section.

REFERENCES

Adams, R.
1991 The Wādī Fidan Project, Jordan: 1989. *Levant* 33: 181–83.

Adams, R., and Genz, H.
1995 Excavations at Wādī Fidan 4: A Chalcolithic Village Complex in the Copper Ore District of Feinan, Southern Jordan. *PEQ* 127: 8–20.

Aharoni, Y.
1954 The Roman Road to Aila (Elath). *IEJ* 4: 9–16.
1963 Tamar and the Roads to Elath. *IEJ* 13: 30–42.

Alt, A.
1921 *Die griechischen Inschriften der Palaestina Tertia westlich der ʿAraba.* Wissenschaftliche Veröffentlichungen des deutsch-türkischen Denkmalschutz-Kommandos, ed. T. Wiegand. Berlin and Leipzig: de Gruyter.
1935 Aus der Araba, II–IV: Römische Kastelle und Strassen. *ZDPV* 58: 1–59.

Amar, Z.
1997 Gold Production in the ʿArabah Valley in the Tenth Century. *IEJ* 47: 100–103.

Anati, E.
1979 *L'Art rupestre: Negev et Sinaï.* Paris: L'Equerre.

Avner, U.
1978 Survey in the Eilat Region. *Hadashot Arkheologiyot (Archaeological Newsletter)* 67–68: 66–68.
1984 Ancient Cult Sites in the Negev and Sinai Deserts. *Tel Aviv* 11: 115–31.
1990 Ancient Agricultural Settlement and Religion in the Uvda Valley in Southern Israel. *BA* 53: 125–41.
1996 Arabah Valley. In *Archaeology in Israel*, ed. S. R. Wolff. *AJA* 100: 762–64.

Avner, U., and Magness, J.
1998 Early Islamic Settlement in the Southern Negev. *BASOR* 310: 39–57.

Avner, U., and Roll, I.
1997 Southern Arava, Roman Milestones. *Excavations and Surveys in Israel* 16: 135.

Avner, U.; Carmi, I.; and Segal, D.
1994 Neolithic to Bronze Age Settlement of the Negev and Sinai in Light of Radiocarbon Dating: A View from the Southern Negev. Pp. 265–300 in *Late Quaternary Chronology and Paleoclimates of the Eastern Mediterranean*, eds. O. Bar-Yosef and R. S. Kra. Tucson: Radiocarbon.

Bachmann, H.-G., and Hauptmann, A.
1984 Zur alten Kupfergewinnung in Fenan und Hirbet en-Nahas im Wādī ʿArabah in Südjordanien. *Der Anschnitt (Zeitschrift für Kunst und Kultur im Bergbau)* 36.4: 110–23.

Banning, E.
1988 Methodology. Pp. 13–25 in *The Wādī el Hasa Archaeological Survey 1979–1983*, ed. B. MacDonald. Waterloo: Wilfrid Laurier University.
2001 Archaeological Survey in Jordan. Pp. 685–92 in *The Archaeology of Jordan*, eds. B. MacDonald, R. Adams, and P. Bienkowski. Sheffield: Sheffield Academic.
2002 *Archaeological Survey.* Manuals in Archaeological Method, Theory, and Technique, 1. New York: Kluwer Academic/Plenum.

Barker, G. W.
1991 Approaches to Archaeological Survey. Pp. 1–9 in *Roman Landscapes: Archaeological Survey in the Mediterranean Region*, eds. G. Barker and J. Lloyd. Archaeological Monographs of the British School at Rome, 2. London: British School.

Barker, G. W., et al.
1997 The Wādī Faynan Project, Southern Jordan: A Preliminary Report on Geomorphology and Landscape Archaeology. *Levant* 29: 19–40.

1998 Environment and Land Use in the Wādī Faynan, Southern Jordan: The Second Season of Geoarchaeology and Landscape Archaeology (1997). *Levant* 30: 5–26.

1999 Environment and Land Use in the Wādī Faynan, Southern Jordan: The Third Season of Geoarchaeology and Landscape Archaeology (1998). *Levant* 31: 255–92.

2000 Archaeology and Desertification in the Wādī Faynan: The Fourth (1999) Season of the Wādī Faynan Landscape Survey. *Levant* 32: 27–52.

Bartlett, J. R.
1989 *Edom and the Edomites.* Journal for the Study of the Old Testament, Supplement Series 77. Sheffield: Sheffield Academic.

Bawden, G., and Edens, C.
1988 Tayma Painted Ware and the Hejaz Iron Age Ceramic Tradition. *Levant* 20: 197–213.

Bender, F.
1975 *Geology of the Arabian Peninsula, Jordan.* Washington, DC: U.S. Geological Survey Professional Paper 560-I.

de Bertou, Comte J.
1839 Itinéraire de la Mer Morte à Akaba par les Wadys el-Ghor, el-Arabah et el-Akabah et retour à Hebron par Pétra. *Bulletin de la Société de Géographie* 11: 274–331.

Bienkowski, P.
1995 The Edomites: The Archaeological Evidence from Transjordan. Pp. 41–92 in *You Shall Not Abhor an Edomite for He is Your Brother: Edom and Seir in History and Tradition*, ed. D. V. Edelman. Atlanta: Scholars.

2001 The Iron Age and Persian Periods in Jordan. *SHAJ* 7: 265–74.

Binford, L.
1964 A Consideration of Archaeological Research Design. *American Antiquity* 29: 425–41.

Blissenbach, E.
1954 Geology of Alluvial Fans in Semiarid Regions. *Bulletin of the Geological Society of America* 65: 175–90.

Bowsher, J.
1989 The Nabataean Army. Pp. 19–30 *The Eastern Frontier of the Roman and Byzantine Empire*, II, eds. D. H. French and C. S. Lightfoot. BAR International Series 553. Oxford: BAR.

Brown, A. G.
1997 *Alluvial Geoarchaeology: Floodplain Archaeology and Environmental Change.* Cambridge: Cambridge University.

Brückner, H.; Eichmann, R.; Herling, L.; Kallweit, H.; Kerner, S.; Khalil, L.; and Miqdadi, R.
2002 Chalcolithic and Early Bronze Age Sites near Aqaba, Jordan. Pp. 215–339 in *Ausgrabungen und Surveys im Vorderen Orient I*, ed. R. Eichmann. Orient-Archäologie, 5. Rahden: Leidorf.

Burgath, K. -P.; Hagen, D.; and Siewers, U.
1984 Geochemistry, Geology, and Primary Copper Mineralization in Wādī 'Araba, Jordan. *Geologisches Jahrbuch* 53, Reihe B: 3–53.

Cherry, J.
1983 Frogs Round the Pond: Perspectives on Current Archaeological Survey Projects in the Mediterranean Region. Pp. 375–416 in *Archaeological Survey in the Mediterranean Area*, eds. D. Keller and D. Rupp. BAR International Series 155. Oxford: BAR.

1984 Common Sense in Mediterranean Survey? *JFA* 11: 117–20.

Cohen, R.
1993a Ḥazeva, Meẓad. Pp. 593–94 in *NEAEHL*, vol. 2, ed. E. Stern. Jerusalem: Israel Exploration Society.

1993b Hellenistic, Roman, and Byzantine Sites in the Negev Hills. Pp. 1135–45 in *NEAEHL*, vol. 3, ed. E. Stern. Jerusalem: Israel Exploration Society.

1994 The Fortresses at 'En Ḥazeva. *BA* 57: 203–14.

Cohen, R., and Yisrael, Y.
1995 The Iron Age Fortresses at ʿEn Ḥaseva. *BA* 58: 223–25.
1996 ʿEn Ḥazeva – 1990–1994. *Excavations and Surveys in Israel* 15: 110–16.

Cooke, R. U., and Warren, A.
1973 *Geomorphology in Deserts.* Berkeley: University of California.

Cribb, R.
1991 *Nomads in Archaeology.* Cambridge: Cambridge University.

Dayton, J. E.
1972 Midianite and Edomite Pottery. *Proceedings of the Seminar for Arabian Studies* 5: 24– 33.

Divito, R. A.
1993 The Tell el-Kheleifeh Inscriptions. Pp. 51–63 in *Nelson Glueck's 1938–1940 Excavations at Tell el-Kheleifeh: A Reappraisal,* ed. G. Pratico. American Schools of Oriental Research Archaeological Reports 3. Atlanta: Scholars.

Dolinka, B.
2002 A Nabataean Caravanserai at Rujm Taba. *Occident & Oriens* 7.1: 19–21.
2003 *Nabataean Aila (Aqaba, Jordan) from a Ceramic Perspective.* BAR International Series 1116. Oxford: BAR.

Dolinka, B., et al.
2002 The Rujm Tāba Archaeological Project (RTAP): Preliminary Report on the 2001 Field Season. *ADAJ* 46: 429–50.

Eddy, F. W., and Wendorf, F.
1999 *An Archaeological Investigation of the Central Sinai, Egypt.* Boulder: University of Colorado.

Eichmann, R., and Khalil, L.
1998 German-Jordanian Archaeological Project in Southern Jordan: Archaeological Survey and Excavation in the Yitim and Maqaṣṣ Area 1998 (ASEYM 98). *Occident & Oriens* 3.1: 14–16.

Eichmann, R.; Khalil, L.; and Schmidt, K.
2009 Excavations at Tell Ḥujeirat al-Ghuzlan (ʿAqaba/Jordan). Excavations 1998–2005 and Stratigraphy. Pp. 17–77 in L. Khalil and K. Schmidt, eds., *Prehistoric ʿAqaba I.* Orient-Archäologie 23. Rahden: Leidorf.

Eusebius
1966 *Eusebius: Das Onomastikon der biblischen Ortnamen,* ed. E. Klostermann. Hildesheim: Olms.

Frank, F.
1934 Aus der Araba I: Reiseberichte. *ZDPV* 57: 191–280.

Fritz, V.
1994 Vorbericht über die Grabungen in Barqa el-Hetiye im Gebiet von Fenan, Wādī el-ʿAraba (Jordanien) 1990. *ZDPV* 110: 125–50.
1996 Ergebnisse einer Sondage in Khirbet en-Nahas, Wādī el-ʿAraba (Jordanien) 1990. *ZDPV* 112: 1–9.

Gilead, I.
1988 The Chalcolithic Period in the Levant. *Journal of World Prehistory* 2.4: 397–443.

Glueck, N.
1935 *Explorations in Eastern Palestine, II.* AASOR 15. New Haven: American Schools of Oriental Research.
1938a The First Campaign at Tell el-Kheleifeh. *BASOR* 71: 3–17.
1938b The Topography and History of Ezion-geber and Elath. *BASOR* 72: 2–13.
1939a *Explorations in Eastern Palestine, III.* AASOR 18–19. New Haven: American Schools of Oriental Research.
1939b The Second Campaign at Tell el-Kheleifeh (Ezion-geber: Elath). *BASOR* 75: 8–22.
1940 The Third Season at Tell el-Kheleifeh. *BASOR* 79: 2–18.
1965 Ezion-geber. *BA* 28: 70–87.

Graf, D.
1992 Nabataean Settlements and Roman Occupation in Arabia Petraea. *SHAJ* 4: 253–60.

1995   The *Via Nova Traiana* in Arabia Petraea. Pp.
        241–65 in *The Roman and Byzantine Near
        East*, ed. J. Humphrey. JRA Supplement 14.
        Ann Arbor: JRA.
2001   First Millennium AD: Roman and Byzan-
        tine Periods Landscape Archaeology and
        Settlement Patterns. *SHAJ* 7: 469–80.

Hanbury-Tenison, J. W.
1986   *The Late Chalcolithic to Early Bronze I Tran-
        sition in Palestine and Transjordan*. BAR
        International Series 311. Oxford: BAR.

Hart, S.
1987   The Edom Survey Project 1984–85: The Iron
        Age. *SHAJ* 3: 287–90.
1992   Iron Age Settlement in the Land of Edom.
        Pp. 93–98 in *Early Edom and Moab: The
        Beginning of the Iron Age in Southern Jordan*,
        ed. P. Bienkowski. Sheffield Archaeological
        Monographs 7. Sheffield: Collis.

Hauptmann, A.
1986   Archaeometallurgical and Mining-Archae-
        ological Studies in the Eastern 'Arabah,
        Feinan Area, 2nd Season. *ADAJ* 30: 415–19.

Hauptmann, A.; Heitkemper, E.; Begemann, F.;
Schmitt-Strecker, S.; and Pernicka, E.
1992   Early Copper Production at Feinan, Wādī
        'Araba, Jordan: The Composition of Ores
        and Copper. *Archaeomaterials* 6.1: 1–33.

Hauptmann, A., and Weisberger, G.
1987   Archaeometallurgical and Mining-Ar-
        chaeological Investigations in the Area of
        Feinan, Wādī 'Arabah (Jordan). *ADAJ* 31:
        419–35.
1992   Periods of Ore Exploration and Metal Pro-
        duction in the Area of Feinan, Wādī 'Araba,
        Jordan. *SHAJ* 4: 61–66.

Hauptmann, A.; Weisgerber, G.; and Knauf, E.
1985   Archäometallurgische und bergbauar-
        chäologische Untersuchungen im Gebiet
        von Feinan, Wādī 'Araba (Jordanien). *Der
        Anschnitt (Zeitschrift für Kunst und Kultur
        im Bergbau)* 37.5–6: 163–95.

Henry, D. O.
1982   The Prehistory of Southern Jordan and Re-
        lationships with the Levant. *JFA* 9.4: 417–44.
1992   Seasonal Movements of Fourth Millen-
        nium Pastoral Nomads in the Wādī Hisma,
        Southern Jordan. *SHAJ* 4: 137–43.
1995   *Prehistoric Cultural Ecology and Evolution:
        Insights from Southern Jordan*. New York:
        Plenum.

Henry, D. O.; Bauer, H.; Kerry, K.; Beaver, J.;
and White, J.
2001   Survey of Prehistoric Sites, Wādī 'Araba,
        Southern Jordan. *BASOR* 323: 1–19.

Husselman, E. M.
1971   *Papyri from Karanis*, 3rd series, E. M. Hus-
        selman, ed. Cleveland. American Philologi-
        cal Association Monograph 29, nos. 522–76.
        Atlanta: Scholars.

Ibrahim, K.
1991   *Geology of the Wādī Rahma: Map Sheet
        No. 3049 IV*, 1:50,000 Geological Mapping
        Series, Geological Bulletin No. 15. Amman:
        Geology Directorate, Geological Mapping
        Division, Natural Resources Authority.
1993   *Geology of the Wādī Gharandal: Map Sheet
        No. 3050 II*, 1:50,000 Geological Mapping
        Series, Geological Bulletin No. 24. Amman:
        Geology Directorate, Geological Mapping
        Division, Natural Resources Authority.

Ilan, O., and Sebbane, M.
1989   Copper Metallurgy, Trade and the Ur-
        banization of Southern Canaan in the
        Chalcolithic and Early Bronze Age. Pp. 139–
        62 in *L'Urbanisation de la Palestine à l'âge du
        Bronze Ancien*, ed. P. de Miroschedji. BAR
        International Series 527. Oxford: BAR.

Jobling, W. J.
1981   Preliminary Report on the Archaeological
        Survey between Ma'an and 'Aqaba, January
        to February 1980. *ADAJ* 25: 105–12.
1983   The 1982 Archaeological and Epigraphic
        Survey of the 'Aqaba–Ma'an Area of South-
        ern Jordan. *ADAJ* 27: 185–96.

Kalsbeek, J., and London, G.
1978 A Late Second Millennium B.C. Potting Puzzle. *BASOR* 232: 47–56.

Khalil, L.
1987 Preliminary Report on the 1985 Season of Excavation at al Maqaṣṣ-ʿAqaba. *ADAJ* 31: 481–83.
1988 Excavation at Magaṣṣ-ʿAqaba, 1985. *Dirasat* 15: 71–117.
1992 Some Technological Features from a Chalcolithic Site at Magaṣṣ-ʿAqaba. *SHAJ* 4: 143–48.
1995 The Second Season of Excavation at al-Maqaṣṣ-ʿAqaba 1990. *ADAJ* 39: 65–79.

Khalil, L., and Eichmann, R.,
1999 Archaeological Survey and Excavation at Wādī al-Yutum and Tall al-Magaṣṣ Area–ʿAqaba (ASEYM): A Preliminary Report on the First Season 1998. *ADAJ* 43: 501–20.
2001 Archaeological Survey and Excavation at the Wādī al-Yutum and Magaṣṣ Area – al-ʿAqaba (ASEYM): A Preliminary Report on the Second Season in 2000. *ADAJ* 45: 195–204.

Khouri, R. G.
1988 *The Antiquities of the Jordan Rift Valley.* Amman: Al Kutba.

Kind, H. D.
1965 Antike Kupfergewinnung zwischen Rotem und Totem Meer. *ZDPV* 81: 56–73.

Kindler, A.
1989 The Numismatic Finds from the Roman Fort at Yotvata. *IEJ* 39: 261–66.

King, G. R. D.; Lenzen, C. J.; Newhall, A.;
King, J. L.; Deemer, J. D.; and Rollefson, G. O.
1989 Survey of Byzantine and Islamic Sites in Jordan: Third Season Preliminary Report (1982): The Wādī ʿArabah. *ADAJ* 31: 199–215.

Knauf, E., and Lenzen, C.
1987 Edomite Copper Industry. *SHAJ* 3: 83–88.

Kozloff, B.
1981 Pastoral Nomadism in the Sinai: An Ethno-archaeological Study. *Bulletin de l'équipe écologie et anthropologie des sociétés pastorales* 8: 19–24.

Levy, T. E.; Adams, R. B.; and Shafiq, R.
1999 The Jebel Hamrat Fidan Project: Excavations at the Wādī Fidan 40 Cemetery, Jordan (1997). *Levant* 31: 293–308.

MacDonald, B.
1986 Southern Ghors and Northeast ʿAraba Archaeological Survey, Jordan, 1986. *ADAJ* 30: 407–9.
1988 *The Wādī el Hasa Archaeological Survey 1979–1983.* Waterloo: Wilfrid Laurier University.
1992 *The Southern Ghors and Northeast ʿArabah Archaeological Survey.* Sheffield Archaeological Monographs 5. Sheffield: Collis.

MacDonald, B.; Clark, G. A.; Neeley, M.;
and Adams, R.
1987 Southern Ghors and Northeast ʿAraba Archaeological Survey 1986, Jordan: A Preliminary Report. *ADAJ* 31: 391–418.

MacDonald, B.; Clark, G. A.; and Neeley, M.
1988 Southern Ghors and Northeast ʿAraba Archaeological Survey 1985 and 1986, Jordan: A Preliminary Report. *BASOR* 272: 23–45.

Mattingly, D.
1992 The Field Survey: Strategy, Methodology, and Preliminary Results. Pp. 89–120 in *Leptiminus (Lamta): A Roman Port City in Tunisia, Report No. 1*, eds. N. Ben Lazreg and D. Mattingly. JRA, Supplement 4. Ann Arbor: JRA.

Mayerson, P.
1986 The Beersheba Edict. *ZPE* 64: 141–48.

Mellaart, J.
1975 *The Neolithic of the Near East.* London: Thames and Hudson.

Meloy, J. L.
1991   Results of an Archaeological Reconnais-
       sance in West Aqaba: Evidence of the Pre-
       Islamic Settlement. *ADAJ* 35: 397–414.

Meshel, Z.
1989   A Fort at Yotvata from the Time of Diocle-
       tian. *IEJ* 39: 228–38.
1993   Yotvata. Pp. 1517–20 in *NEAEHL*, vol. 4,
       ed. E. Stern. Jerusalem: Israel Exploration
       Society.

Moore, A.
1973   The Late Neolithic in Palestine. *Levant* 5:
       36–68.

Musil, A.
1907   *Arabia Petraea*. 3 vols. Vienna: Holder.

Niemi, T., and Smith, A. M. II
1999   Initial Results of the Southeastern Wādī
       ʿAraba, Jordan Geoarchaeological Study:
       Implications for Shifts in Late Quaternary
       Aridity. *Geoarchaeology* 14.8: 791–820.

Parker, S. T.
1986   *Romans and Saracens: A History of the
       Arabian Frontier*. Winona Lake, IN: Eisen-
       brauns.
1994   The Roman ʿAqaba Project: Aila Rediscov-
       ered. *BA* 57: 172.
1996   The Roman ʿAqaba Project: The 1994 Cam-
       paign. *ADAJ* 40: 231–57.
1997a Preliminary Report on the 1994 Season
       of the Roman Aqaba Project. *BASOR* 305:
       19–44.
1997b Human Settlement at the Northern Head
       of the Gulf of al-ʿAqaba: Evidence of Site
       Migration. *SHAJ* 4: 189–93.
1998   The Roman ʿAqaba Project: The 1996 Cam-
       paign. *ADAJ* 42: 375–94.
1999   Roman ʿAqaba Project. In "Archaeology in
       Jordan," eds. P. Bikai and V. Egan. *AJA* 103:
       511–13.
2000   The Roman ʿAqaba Project: The 1997 and
       1998 Campaigns. *ADAJ* 44: 373–94.

Parr, P.
1982   Contacts between North West Arabia and
       Jordan in the Late Bronze and Iron Ages.
       SHAJ 1: 127–33.

Perry, M. A.
2007   A Preliminary Report on the Cemeteries
       of Bir Madhkur. *BASOR* 346: 79–93.

Prag, K.
2001   The Third Millennium in Jordan: A Per-
       spective, Past and Future. *SHAJ* 7: 179–90.

Pratico, G. D.
1985   Nelson Glueck's 1938–1940 Excavations at
       Tell el-Kheleifeh: A Reappraisal. *BASOR*
       259: 1–32.
1993   *Nelson Glueck's 1938–1940 Excavations at
       Tell el-Kheleifeh: A Reappraisal*. American
       Schools of Oriental Research Archaeologi-
       cal Reports 3. Atlanta: Scholars.

Raikes, T. D.
1980   Notes on Some Neolithic and Later Sites
       in Wādī ʿAraba and the Dead Sea Valley.
       Levant 12: 40–60.
1985   The Character of the Wādī ʿAraba. *SHAJ* 2:
       95–101.

Rapp, G., and Hill, C. L.
1998   *Geoarchaeology: The Earth-Science Ap-
       proach to Archaeological Interpretation*.
       New Haven: Yale University.

Rashdan, M.
1988   *The Regional Geology of the Aqaba- Wādī
       ʿAraba Area: Map Sheets 3049 III, 2949 II,
       1:50,000 Geological Mapping Series*, Geo-
       logical Bulletin No. 7. Amman: Geology
       Directorate, Geological Mapping Division,
       Natural Resources Authority.

Roll, I.
1989   A Latin Imperial Inscription from the Time
       of Diocletian Found at Yotvata. *IEJ* 39: 239–
       60.

Rosen, S.

1988a Notes on the Origins of Pastoral Nomadism: A Case Study from the Negev and Sinai. *Current Anthropology* 29: 498–506.

1988b Finding Evidence of Ancient Nomads. *Biblical Archaeology Review* 14.5: 46–53.

1992 Nomads in Archaeology: A Response to Finkelstein and Perevolotsky. *BASOR* 287: 75–85.

Rothenberg, B.

1962 Ancient Copper Industries in the Western ʿArabah. *PEQ* 94: 5–72.

1971 The ʿArabah in Roman and Byzantine Times in the Light of New Research. Pp. 211–23 in *Roman Frontier Studies 1967,* Proceedings of the 7th International Congress, ed. S. Applebaum. Tel Aviv: Tel Aviv University.

1972 *Timna: Valley of the Biblical Copper Mines.* New Aspects of Antiquity, ed. M. Wheeler. London: Thames and Hudson.

1988 *The Egyptian Mining Temple at Timna.* Researches in the ʿArabah, vol. 1. London: Institute for Archaeo-Metallurgical Studies.

1993 Timna. Pp. 1474–86 in *NEAEHL*, vol. 4, ed. E. Stern. Jerusalem: Israel Exploration Society.

1999a Archeo-Metallurgical Researches in the Southern ʿArabah 1959–1990, Part I: Late Pottery Neolithic to Early Bronze IV. *PEQ* 131: 68–89.

1999b Archeo-Metallurgical Researches in the Southern ʿArabah 1959–1990, Part II: Egyptian New Kingdom (Ramesside) to Early Islam. *PEQ* 131: 149–75.

Rothenberg, B., and Glass, J.

1992 The Beginnings and the Development of Early Metallurgy and the Settlement and Chronology of the Western ʿArabah, from the Chalcolithic Period to Early Bronze Age IV. *Levant* 24: 141–57.

Schick, R.

1995 The Settlement Pattern of Southern Jordan: The Nature of the Evidence. Pp. 133–54 in *The Byzantine and Early Islamic Near East II: Land Use and Settlement Patterns,* eds. G. R. D. King and A. Cameron. Princeton: Darwin.

Schiffer, M. B.; Sullivan, A.; and Klinger, T.

1978 The Design of Archaeological Surveys. *World Archaeology* 10: 1–28.

Seeck, O.

1876 *Notitia Dignitatum in partibus orientis occidentus,* ed. O. Seeck. Berlin: Lange.

Smith, A. M. II

1994 Southeast Wādī ʿAraba Survey. In "Archaeology in Jordan," ed. G. L. Peterman. *AJA* 98: 524.

2005a Bir Madhkur Project: A Preliminary Report on Recent Fieldwork. BASOR 340: 57–75.

2005b Pathways, Roadways, and Highways: Networks of Communication and Exchange in Wādī Araba. *NEA* 68: 180–89.

2010 *Wādī ʿAraba in Classical and Late Antiquity: An Historical Geography.* BAR International Series 2173. Oxford: Archaeopress.

Smith, A.M. II, and Niemi, T. M.

1994 Results of the Southeast ʿAraba Archaeological Reconnaissance. *ADAJ* 38: 469–83.

Smith, A.M. II; Niemi, T. M.; and Stevens, M.

1997 The Southeast ʿArabah Archaeological Survey: A Preliminary Report of the 1994 Season. *BASOR* 305: 45–71.

Whitcomb, D. S.

1994 Ayla: Art and Industry in the Islamic Port of ʿAqaba. Chicago: Oriental Institute of the University of Chicago.

Catalog of Sites

The catalog lists all 330 sites recorded by the project in numerical order by site number. The sites are numbered from south to north so that they may be more easily located on the accompanying maps. The figure numbers immediately following each site number refers to the specific map on which each site appears and in some cases, photographs or drawings of that site. The entry for each site also includes the original field site number, the modern site name (if known), the map reference on the K737 series, geographical coordinates, and reference to aerial photographs in the archive of the Royal Geographic Centre of Jordan. Additional descriptive information includes each site's approximate elevation above sea level in meters, approximate site size, a summary of all artifacts collected, and a brief site description. The "inventory rating" (a numeric value from 1 to 6) refers to the site's presumed potential for excavation. A higher inventory rating number means greater potential for excavation.

The following abbreviations are used in the catalog:

Abb	Abbasid
ARS	African Red Slip
Ay	Ayyubid
Byz	Byzantine
Chalco	Chalcolithic
EB	Early Bronze
EByz	Early Byzantine
ER	Early Roman
ESA	Eastern Sigillata A
Fat	Fatimid
Hell	Hellenistic
LR	Late Roman
LB	Late Bronze
LByz	Late Byzantine
LRRW	Late Roman Red Ware
Mam	Mamluk
Nab	Nabataean
N/A	Not applicable
Ott	Ottoman
R	Roman
TS	Terra Sigillata
UD	Undetermined
UM	Umayyad

Site No.: 1 (fig. 4.38)
Field Site No.: 1
Site Name: None
Map Reference: 3049 III, K737
Location on 1:50,000: 3269163 N / 692917 E
Elevation: 3 m
Aerial Reference No.: IGN-78-JOR 12/100 - 1298
Site Size: 55 m N–S × 20 m E–W
Inventory Rating: 1
Pottery Collected: Total = 45 (No. of Indicators: 2 / No. Saved: 7)
Pottery Registration No(s).: 377–83
Pottery Summary: 4 ER/Nab, 3 LByz, 1 Modern, 35 UD, 2 kiln wasters
Lithic Summary: N/A
Site Description: The site consists of two segments of decayed mudbrick walls situated on the beach ca. 20 m north of the shoreline. One segment measures 0.70 m wide and 0.40 m in length. The second segment, located opposite the first and separated by a sand "borrow pit," measures ca. 2 × 0.70 m. This segment is ca. 1.50–2 m higher than the first in elevation.

Site No.: 2 (fig. 4.38)
Field Site No.: 33
Site Name: None
Map Reference: 3049 III, K737
Location on 1:50,000: 3268618 N / 693901 E
Elevation: 3 m
Aerial Reference No.: IGN-78-JOR 12/100 - 1298
Site Size: 1 m N–S × 1 m E–W
Inventory Rating: 0
Pottery Collected: Total = 0 (No. of Indicators: 0

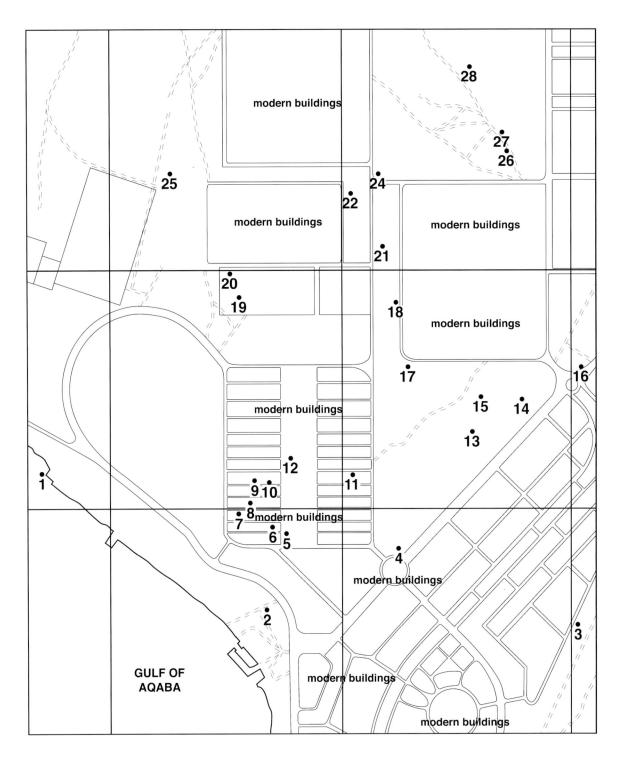

FIG. 4.38 *Aqaba Region (Region I), map 1 (Sites 1–22, 24–28).*

/ No. Saved: 0)
Pottery Registration No(s).: None
Pottery Summary: N/A
Lithic Summary: N/A
Site Description: This is a shallow wadi that cuts through the Islamic period site within Aqaba. Site recorded by Tina Niemi and S. Thomas Parker, who collected cultural remains from the baulk.

Site No.: 3 (fig. 4.38)
Field Site No.: 13
Site Name: None
Map Reference: 3049 III, K737
Location on 1:50,000: 3268555 N / 695247 E
Elevation: 73 m
Aerial Reference No.: IGN-78-JOR 12/100 - 1298
Site Size: 3 m N–S × 1 m E–W
Inventory Rating: 2
Pottery Collected: Total = 158 (No. of Indicators: 0 / No. Saved: 0)
Pottery Registration No(s).: None
Pottery Summary: 157 Modern, 1 UD
Lithic Summary: N/A
Site Description: This is a single mound or burial (1 × 3 m) and a pot-bust on an alluvial fan east of Aqaba and ca. 100 m west of railroad. The burial is oriented N–S. The pottery appears to be associated with the burial and extends ca. 3 m to the south.

Site No.: 4 (fig. 4.38)
Field Site No.: 6
Site Name: None
Map Reference: 3049 III, K737
Location on 1:50,000: 3268886 N / 694504 E
Elevation: 11 m
Aerial Reference No.: IGN-78-JOR 12/100 - 1298
Site Size: 20 m N–S × 20 m E–W
Inventory Rating: 0
Pottery Collected: Total = 49 (No. of Indicators: 1 / No. Saved: 4)
Pottery Registration No(s).: 579–82
Pottery Summary: 47 ER/LR, 2 UD
Lithic Summary: N/A
Site Description: This is a sherd scatter in an un-developed area (ca. 20 m N–S × 20 m E–W) north of a mosque.

Site No.: 5 (fig. 4.38)
Field Site No.: 20
Site Name: None
Map Reference: 3049 III, K737
Location on 1:50,000: 3268941 N / 693979 E
Elevation: 5 m
Aerial Reference No.: IGN-78-JOR 12/100 - 1298
Site Size: 30 m N–S × 12 m E–W
Inventory Rating: 0
Pottery Collected: Total = 68 (No. of Indicators: 9 / No. Saved: 0)
Pottery Registration No(s).: None
Pottery Summary: 2 ER/Nab, 51 R/Byz, 6 LByz, 9 Modern, 6 copper slag fragments
Lithic Summary: N/A
Site Description: This is a sherd scatter mixed with copper slag and kiln wasters in a vacant lot in the Radwan residential district.

Site No.: 6 (fig. 4.38)
Field Site No.: 9
Site Name: None
Map Reference: 3049 III, K737
Location on 1:50,000: 3268960 N / 693924 E
Elevation: 5 m
Aerial Reference No.: IGN-78-JOR 12/100 - 1298
Site Size: 30 m N–S × 30 m E–W
Inventory Rating: 3
Pottery Collected: Total = 40 (No. of Indicators: 34 / No. Saved: 19)
Pottery Registration No(s).: None
Pottery Summary: 40 LByz
Lithic Summary: N/A
Site Description: This is a kiln site and associated pottery dumps in and north of the "Circular Area." This site is equivalent to Meloy's Site M13 (Meloy 1991).

Site No.: 7 (fig. 4.38)
Field Site No.: 22
Site Name: None
Map Reference: 3049 III, K737
Location on 1:50,000: 3269020 N / 693768 E
Elevation: 5 m
Aerial Reference No.: IGN-78-JOR 12/100 - 1298
Site Size: 23 m N–S × 23 m E–W
Inventory Rating: 0
Pottery Collected: Total = 11 (No. of Indicators: 3

/ No. Saved: 4)
Pottery Registration No(s).: 1198–1201
Pottery Summary: 1 ER/Nab, 1 LR (LRRW/ARS), 1 EByz, 1 LByz, 1 Late Islamic, 2 Modern, 4 UD
Lithic Summary: N/A
Site Description: This is a light sherd scatter in a vacant lot in the Radwan residential district.

Site No.: 8 (fig. 4.38)
Field Site No.: 21
Site Name: None
Map Reference: 3049 III, K737
Location on 1:50,000: 3269068 N / 693817 E
Elevation: 5 m
Aerial Reference No.: IGN-78-JOR 12/100 - 1298
Site Size: 100 m N–S × 30 m E–W
Inventory Rating: 0
Pottery Collected: Total = 13 (No. of Indicators: 3 / No. Saved: 5)
Pottery Registration No(s).: 1193–97
Pottery Summary: 1 EB II–III, 7 ER/Nab, 1 LByz, 1 Modern, 3 UD
Lithic Summary: N/A
Site Description: This is a light sherd scatter in a vacant lot in the Radwan residential district.

Site No.: 9 (fig. 4.38)
Field Site No.: 24
Site Name: None
Map Reference: 3049 III, K737
Location on 1:50,000: 3269173 N / 693842 E
Elevation: 5 m
Aerial Reference No.: IGN-78-JOR 12/100 - 1298
Site Size: 25 m N–S × 50 m E–W
Inventory Rating: 0
Pottery Collected: Total = 3 (No. of Indicators: 1 / No. Saved: 0)
Pottery Registration No(s).: None
Pottery Summary: 3 ER/Nab
Lithic Summary: N/A
Site Description: This is a light sherd scatter in a vacant lot in the Radwan residential district.

Site No.: 10 (fig. 4.38)
Field Site No.: 23
Site Name: None
Map Reference: 3049 III, K737
Location on 1:50,000: 3269154 N / 693900 E

Elevation: 5 m
Aerial Reference No.: IGN-78-JOR 12/100 - 1298
Site Size: 23 m N–S × 23 m E–W
Inventory Rating: 0
Pottery Collected: Total = 6 (No. of Indicators: 3 / No. Saved: 0)
Pottery Registration No(s).: None
Pottery Summary: 1 ER/Nab, 3 Modern, 2 UD
Lithic Summary: N/A
Site Description: This is a light sherd scatter in a vacant lot in the Radwan residential district.

Site No.: 11 (fig. 4.38)
Field Site No.: 26
Site Name: None
Map Reference: 3049 III, K737
Location on 1:50,000: 3269196 N / 694270 E
Elevation: 5 m
Aerial Reference No.: IGN-78-JOR 12/100 - 1298
Site Size: 20 m N–S × 20 m E–W
Inventory Rating: 0
Pottery Collected: Total = 0 (No. of Indicators: 0 / No. Saved: 0)
Pottery Registration No(s).: None
Pottery Summary: None Collected
Lithic Summary: N/A
Site Description: This is a very light sherd scatter in a vacant lot in the Radwan residential district. No sherds were collected as these would have been unidentifiable.

Site No.: 12 (fig. 4.38)
Field Site No.: 25
Site Name: None
Map Reference: 3049 III, K737
Location on 1:50,000: 3269248 N / 693989 E
Elevation: 5 m
Aerial Reference No.: IGN-78-JOR 12/100 - 1298
Site Size: 25 m N–S × 25 m E–W
Inventory Rating: 0
Pottery Collected: Total = 5 (No. of Indicators: 2 / No. Saved: 0)
Pottery Registration No(s).: None
Pottery Summary: 1 ER/Nab, 2 LByz, 2 UD
Lithic Summary: N/A
Site Description: This is a light sherd scatter in a vacant lot in the Radwan residential district.

Site No.: 13 (fig. 4.38)
Field Site No.: 175
Site Name: Tell al-Hamra
Map Reference: 3049 III, K737
Location on 1:50,000: 3269371 N / 694785 E
Elevation: 29 m
Aerial Reference No.: IGN-78-JOR 12/100 - 1298
Site Size: 350 m N–S × 300 m E–W
Inventory Rating: 0
Pottery Collected: Total = 0 (No. of Indicators: 0 / No. Saved: 0)
Pottery Registration No(s).: None
Pottery Summary: N/A
Lithic Summary: N/A
Site Description: Based upon interviews with local residents, this site was identified through analysis of aerial photos dated 1978. Since that time a modern complex has been constructed on the site. Site is now destroyed.

Site No.: 14 (fig. 4.38)
Field Site No.: 11
Site Name: None
Map Reference: 3049 III, K737
Location on 1:50,000: 3269515 N / 694994 E
Elevation: 30 m
Aerial Reference No.: IGN-78-JOR 12/100 - 1298
Site Size: 30 m N–S × 70 m E–W
Inventory Rating: 0
Pottery Collected: Total = 75 (No. of Indicators: 27 / No. Saved: 18)
Pottery Registration No(s).: 991–1008
Pottery Summary: 1 Iron-I (?), 2 ER/Nab (1 TS-Cypriot Sigillata), 4 LByz (1 kiln waster), 45 R/Byz/Islamic, 7 Early Islamic (2 Abbasid), 6 Fatimid/Ayy/Mamluk, 1 Late Islamic, 1 Modern, 8 UD
Lithic Summary: N/A
Site Description: This is a medium density sherd scatter (3–4 sherds/m²) on mounded debris towards the north end of a vacant lot in a residential district. The area has been heavily bulldozed on two sides and much of the debris from this activity has been pushed to the north and center of the lot. This site is directly up the slope from Site 15.

Site No.: 15 (fig. 4.38)
Field Site No.: 10
Site Name: None

Map Reference: 3049 III, K737
Location on 1:50,000: 3269527 N / 694829 E
Elevation: 10 m
Aerial Reference No.: IGN-78-JOR 12/100 - 1298
Site Size: 18 m N–S × 18 m E–W
Inventory Rating: 0
Pottery Collected: Total = 29 (No. of Indicators: 7 / No. Saved: 10)
Pottery Registration No(s).: 965–74
Pottery Summary: 5 ER/Nab, 1 LR, 4 LByz, 19 R/Byz, 1 Tile
Lithic Summary: N/A
Site Description: This is a light sherd and tile scatter (ca. 3–4 sherds/m²) on an alluvial fan. The artifacts concentrate in and around small drainages cut into the fan surface. A water pipe cuts through the southern edge of the site.

Site No.: 16 (fig. 4.38)
Field Site No.: 12
Site Name: None
Map Reference: 3049 III, K737
Location on 1:50,000: 3269655 N / 695256 E
Elevation: 35 m
Aerial Reference No.: IGN-78-JOR 12/100 - 1298
Site Size: 15 m N–S × 15 m E–W
Inventory Rating: 0
Pottery Collected: Total = 50 (No. of Indicators: 24 / No. Saved: 20)
Pottery Registration No(s).: 1071–90
Pottery Summary: 1 Iron (?), 20 ER/Nab (Late Nabataean [?], 1 TS), 3 Byz (2 LRRW/ARS), 1 LByz, 21 R/Byz, 3 UD, 1 Modern
Lithic Summary: N/A
Site Description: This is a medium–large density sherd scatter (ca. 6–7 sherds/m²) immediately adjacent to the loop in the road around the "Circular Area." The artifacts may have been transported and dumped here during construction of the modern road nearby.

Site No.: 17 (fig. 4.38)
Field Site No.: 8
Site Name: None
Map Reference: 3049 III, K737
Location on 1:50,000: 3269646 N / 694496 E
Elevation: 19 m
Aerial Reference No.: IGN-78-JOR 12/100 - 1298

Site Size: 30 m N–S × 20 m E–W
Inventory Rating: 0
Pottery Collected: Total = 28 (No. of Indicators: 4 / No. Saved: 10)
Pottery Registration No(s).: 557–66
Pottery Summary: 1 EByz (LRRW/ARS), 14 LByz, 4 Fatimid (1 glazed), 9 UD
Lithic Summary: N/A
Site Description: This is a dense sherd scatter in the northwest corner of a vacant lot. The northern portion of this lot is elevated ca. 1 m above the surface of sand and gravel. Some construction debris is visible nearby.

Site No.: 18 (fig. 4.38)
Field Site No.: 7
Site Name: None
Map Reference: 3049 III, K737
Location on 1:50,000: 3269915 N / 694445 E
Elevation: 20 m
Aerial Reference No.: IGN-78-JOR 12/100 - 1298
Site Size: 15 m N–S × 15 m E–W
Inventory Rating: 0
Pottery Collected: Total = 25 (No. of Indicators: 12 / No. Saved: 7)
Pottery Registration No(s).: 529–35
Pottery Summary: 7 ER/Nab, 9 LByz (1 kiln waster), 4 Modern, 5 UD
Lithic Summary: N/A
Site Description: This is a light sherd scatter in a small depression south of a small area cleared of stones (soccer field?). The depression is ca. 0.50 m deep. The area has been extensively modified by construction work.

Site No.: 19 (fig. 4.38)
Field Site No.: 5
Site Name: None
Map Reference: 3049 III, K737
Location on 1:50,000: 3269916 N / 693751 E
Elevation: 13 m
Aerial Reference No.: IGN-78-JOR 12/100 - 1298
Site Size: 25 m N–S × 19 m E–W
Inventory Rating: 0
Pottery Collected: Total = 20 (No. of Indicators: 3 / No. Saved: 9)
Pottery Registration No(s).: 548–56
Pottery Summary: 4 ER/Nab, 7 LByz, 9 UD

Lithic Summary: N/A
Site Description: This is a light sherd scatter (ca. 1–2 sherds/m²) located east of a soccer field and ca. 50 m south of Site 19. The area has been disturbed by numerous tire tracks.

Site No.: 20 (fig. 4.38)
Field Site No.: 4
Site Name: None
Map Reference: 3049 III, K737
Location on 1:50,000: 3270026 N / 693734 E
Elevation: 13 m
Aerial Reference No.: IGN-78-JOR 12/100 - 1298
Site Size: 25 m N–S × 25 m E–W
Inventory Rating: 0
Pottery Collected: Total = 26 (No. of Indicators: 9 / No. Saved: 12)
Pottery Registration No(s).: 567–78
Pottery Summary: 2 ER/Nab, 16 LByz (8 from 1 vessel), 8 UD
Lithic Summary: N/A
Site Description: This is a sherd scatter east of a soccer field and northwest of a local school. The concentration of pottery is on a small, low-lying mound where the ground is much softer than the surrounding terrain. The area is disturbed by modern construction work.

Site No.: 21 (fig. 4.38)
Field Site No.: 27
Site Name: None
Map Reference: 3049 III, K737
Location on 1:50,000: 3270099 N / 694385 E
Elevation: 24 m
Aerial Reference No.: IGN-78-JOR 12/100 - 1298
Site Size: 20 m N–S × 38 m E–W
Inventory Rating: 0
Pottery Collected: Total = 38 (No. of Indicators: 4 / No. Saved: 0)
Pottery Registration No(s).: None
Pottery Summary: 1 ER/Nab, 4 LByz, 33 Modern
Lithic Summary: N/A
Site Description: This is a light sherd scatter behind a car wash. There is evidence here of modern dumping of debris and soil.

Site No.: 22 (fig. 4.38)
Field Site No.: 28

Site Name: None
Map Reference: 3049 III, K737
Location on 1:50,000: 3270366 N / 694226 E
Elevation: 24 m
Aerial Reference No.: IGN-78-JOR 12/100 - 1298
Site Size: 40 m N–S × 30 m E–W
Inventory Rating: 0
Pottery Collected: Total = 18 (No. of Indicators: 4 / No. Saved: 0)
Pottery Registration No(s).: None
Pottery Summary: 2 R/Byz, 15 Modern, 1 UD
Lithic Summary: N/A
Site Description: This is a light sherd scatter in the northwest corner of a vacant lot. There is some evidence here of modern dumping.

Site No.: 23
Field Site No.: 30
Site Name: None
Map Reference: 3049 III, K737
Location on 1:50,000: 3270361 N / 694621 E
Elevation: 25 m
Aerial Reference No.: IGN-78-JOR 12/100 - 1298
Site Size: 20 m N–S × 10 m E–W
Inventory Rating: 0
Pottery Collected: Total = 14 (No. of Indicators: 0 / No. Saved: 0)
Pottery Registration No(s).: None
Pottery Summary: 14 Modern
Lithic Summary: N/A
Site Description: This is a light sherd scatter in the northwest area of a modern building development.

Site No.: 24 (fig. 4.38)
Field Site No.: 29
Site Name: None
Map Reference: 3049 III, K737
Location on 1:50,000: 3270435 N / 694346 E
Elevation: 24 m
Aerial Reference No.: IGN-78-JOR 12/100 - 1298
Site Size: 20 m N–S × 20 m E–W
Inventory Rating: 0
Pottery Collected: Total = 15 (No. of Indicators: 3 / No. Saved: 0)
Pottery Registration No(s).: None
Pottery Summary: 15 Modern
Lithic Summary: N/A
Site Description: This is a light sherd scatter (ca. 1

sherd/m²) near an abandoned bus stop north of Aqaba's city center. The area is very disturbed and some dumping has occurred.

Site No.: 25 (fig. 4.38)
Field Site No.: 2
Site Name: None
Map Reference: 3049 III, K737
Location on 1:50,000: 3270464 N / 693460 E
Elevation: 18 m
Aerial Reference No.: IGN-78-JOR 12/100 - 1298
Site Size: 320 m N–S × 1 m E–W
Inventory Rating: 1
Pottery Collected: Total = 0 (No. of Indicators: 0 / No. Saved: 0)
Pottery Registration No(s).: None
Pottery Summary: N/A
Lithic Summary: N/A
Site Description: This is a linear wall alignment or embankment trending northeast–southwest. The wall is constructed with a foundation of some cut stones and cobbles, overlain with mudbricks. The foundation is ca. 2–3 m wide and is visible in only one location near the south end of the wall. The stones of the foundation measure ca. 0.20–0.30 m on a side, and some appear cut. The mudbrick wall overlying the stone foundation is ca. 0.70 m wide. The wall extends for ca. 3.20 m and trends 8 degrees northeast. Some modern buildings have been constructed on top of the wall. Possible mudbrick walls extend perpendicularly from this longer wall.

Site No.: 26 (fig. 4.38)
Field Site No.: 229
Site Name: None
Map Reference: 3049 III, K737
Location on 1:50,000: 3270553 N / 694929 E
Elevation: 36 m
Aerial Reference No.: IGN-78-JOR 12/100 - 1299
Site Size: 1 m N–S × 128 m E–W
Inventory Rating: 5
Pottery Collected: Total = 0 (No. of Indicators: 0 / No. Saved: 0)
Pottery Registration No(s).: None
Pottery Summary: N/A
Lithic Summary: N/A
Site Description: The site consists of a linear alignment of mounded stones and cobbles, ca. 0.50 m

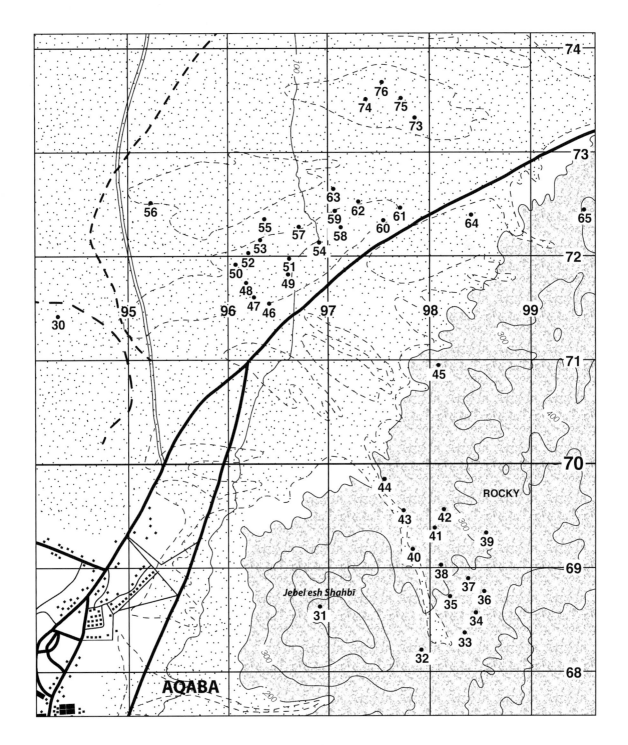

FIG. 4.39   *Aqaba Region (Region I), map 2 (Sites 30–65, 73–76).*

wide and oriented roughly E–W. It spans a distance of ca. 128 m. This is possibly a terrace wall. Further, there are numerous segments branching off it perpendicularly at somewhat regular intervals. The site is located south of Site 27. Towards its west end, the alignment breaks off for ca. 40 m before resuming. At the extreme western end of the linear mound, there is an intersection with another alignment just to the north. This latter alignment curves to the west.

Site No.: 27 (fig. 4.38)
Field Site No.: 228
Site Name: None
Map Reference: 3049 III, K737
Location on 1:50,000: 3270619 N / 694911 E
Elevation: 36 m
Aerial Reference No.: IGN-78-JOR 12/100 - 1299
Site Size: 5.50 m N–S × 100 m E–W
Inventory Rating: 2
Pottery Collected: Total = 0 (No. of Indicators: 0 / No. Saved: 0)
Pottery Registration No(s).: None
Pottery Summary: N/A
Lithic Summary: N/A
Site Description: The site consists of a series of parallel, low-lying linear cobble mounds oriented roughly northeast–southwest. The mounds are ca. 0.80 m wide and lie about 3.70 m apart (total width from outer face to outer face is 5.50 m). Outer and inner faces of the mounds are constructed of slightly larger stones than those between faces. Average stone size is no more than 0.50 m on a side. Alignments give the appearance of a possible dirt road. It is also possible, based on comparison with Site 26, that the alignments represent a form of low-lying terracing of the alluvial fan. The linear mounds measure up to 100 m in length, disrupted in the east by a modern road and in the west by recent bulldozing.

Site No.: 28 (fig. 4.38)
Field Site No.: 227
Site Name: None
Map Reference: 3049 III, K737
Location on 1:50,000: 3270891 N / 694742 E
Elevation: 40 m
Aerial Reference No.: IGN-78-JOR 12/100 - 1299

Site Size: 21.50 m N–S × 3.00 m E–W
Inventory Rating: 6
Pottery Collected: Total = 0 (No. of Indicators: 0 / No. Saved: 0)
Pottery Registration No(s).: None
Pottery Summary: N/A
Lithic Summary: N/A
Site Description: The site consists of a narrow, curvilinear feature that may be an old road segment. Not more than 3 m in width, the feature is cleared in its center and lined with small stones along its edge. It spans a distance of ca. 21 m.

Site No.: 29 (figs. 1.2, 2.8)
Field Site No.: 174
Site Name: Tell el-Kheleifeh
Map Reference: 2949 II, K737
Location on 1:50,000: 3270514 N / 691794 E
Elevation: 4 m
Site Size: 80 m N–S × 72 m E–W
Inventory Rating: 5
Pottery Collected: Total = 824 (No. of Indicators: 325 / No. Saved: 325)
Pottery Registration No(s).: 21239–564
Pottery Summary: 107 Iron IIB/C, 76 Iron IIB/Persian, 3 Iron IIC, 20 Early Persian, 4 Early Hellenistic, 3 ER/Nab, 1 Modern, 1 UD (possibly an import), 110 Negevite
Lithic Summary: Indefinite cultural-historic placement
Site Description: This is the site of Tell el-Kheleifeh just north of the Gulf of Aqaba shoreline. The SAAS did not formally survey the site, but the RAP staff did collect artifacts during a brief visit. In the pottery summary above, only the diagnostic sherds are listed. The less diagnostic body sherds were judged to date within these broad chronological parameters.

Site No.: 30 (fig. 4.39)
Field Site No.: 226
Site Name: None
Map Reference: 3049 III, K737
Location on 1:50,000: 3271580 N / 694272 E
Elevation: 36.40 m
Aerial Reference No.: IGN-78-JOR 12/100 - 1299
Site Size: 8 m N–S × 80 m E–W
Inventory Rating: 5

Pottery Collected: Total = 0 (No. of Indicators: 0
/ No. Saved: 0)
Pottery Registration No(s).: None
Pottery Summary: N/A
Lithic Summary: N/A
Site Description: The site consists of an earthen
mound situated in the northern urban district of
Aqaba and immediately adjacent to a modern road.
The mound is composed of compacted sand layers
with cobbles. Only a small portion is extant. The re-
maining portions have been destroyed by bulldoz-
ing activity. The earthen mound is ca. 2 m high and
wide. It follows a linear alignment, trending E–W.
This feature, visible in early aerial photographs of
Aqaba, may be an ancient earthwork (possibly a
diversion wall to deflect alluvial discharge). The
SAAS found no evidence to date the feature.

Site No.: 31 (fig. 4.39)
Field Site No.: 3
Site Name: None
Map Reference: 3049 III, K737
Location on 1:50,000: 3268672 N / 696940 E
Elevation: 554 m
Aerial Reference No.: IGN-78-JOR 12/100 - 1252
Site Size: 5 m N–S × 6 m E–W
Inventory Rating: 0
Pottery Collected: Total = 28 (No. of Indicators: 3
/ No. Saved: 12)
Pottery Registration No(s).: 536–47
Pottery Summary: 3 ER/Nab (1 ER lamp base), 2
LR (LRRW/ARS=Hayes Form 50/AD 240–360), 1
EByz, 21 R/Byz, 1 LByz body sherd
Lithic Summary: N/A
Site Description: The site consists of a low density
sherd scatter on the summit of Jebel esh-Shahbī. A
modern benchmark (554 m) is at the site.

Site No.: 32 (fig. 4.39)
Field Site No.: 36
Site Name: None
Map Reference: 3049 III, K737
Location on 1:50,000: 3268351 N / 697932 E
Elevation: 315 m
Aerial Reference No.: IGN-78-JOR 12/100 - 1221
Site Size: 15 m N–S × 45 m E–W
Inventory Rating: 2
Pottery Collected: Total = 0 (No. of Indicators: 0

/ No. Saved: 0)
Pottery Registration No(s).: None
Pottery Summary: N/A
Lithic Summary: N/A
Site Description: The site consists of two retaining
walls situated in the northeast foothills at the base
of Jebel esh-Shahbī. The lower wall is 24 m long
and encloses a terrace ca. 10 m wide. The wall itself
is ca. five–six courses high. The upper wall, which
stands 1–2 m high (six courses), with a width of
0.80 m, is 46 m long.

Site No.: 33 (figs. 4.36, 4.39)
Field Site No.: 37
Site Name: None
Map Reference: 3049 III, K737
Location on 1:50,000: 3268545 N / 698256 E
Elevation: 315 m
Aerial Reference No.: IGN-78-JOR 12/100 - 1221
Site Size: See below
Inventory Rating: 3
Pottery Collected: Total = 61 (No. of Indicators: 4
/ No. Saved: 17)
Pottery Registration No(s).: 2909, 3136–40, 3146–50,
3188–93
Pottery Summary: 1 R/Byz, 25 Early Islamic (4 ves-
sels), 7 Abbasid (1 glazed vessel), 25 Modern, 3 UD
Lithic Summary: Indefinite cultural-historic place-
ment
Site Description: The site is contiguous with Sites
34–37. These sites combine to cover an area of ca.
500 × 250 m. Site 33 consists of numerous structures and wall alignments. The SAAS recorded 24
distinct features. Feature 1 is an irregular, semicircular wall alignment on a bedrock ridge that opens
to the east. The wall is preserved five–six courses
high (1.10 m) and two courses wide (0.65 m). Feature 2 lies ca. 10 m to the southeast. It is a circular
structure that opens to the west and an appended
rectilinear structure on its east side. The circular
structure is 6 m in diameter, and the appended
rectilinear feature is 4 × 2.50 m and opens to the
north. Feature 2 is very similar to Site 34/Feature
7. Feature 3, an irregular wall alignment (possibly a
retaining wall), is ca. 10 m southwest of Feature 2. It
may be that Feature 3 represents a collapsed structure (similar to Feature 2), but mostly destroyed
by erosion. Feature 4 lies ca. 40 m at 330 degrees

and across a shallow drainage from Features 1–3. Feature 4 consists of two adjoining rectangular structures that measure 3 m N–S × 5 m E–W and 4 m N–S × 6 m E–W. The tumbled walls are 0.60 m wide and preserved in segments from two to three courses high. Ca. 6.50 m southeast of Feature 4, Feature 5 is a rectilinear structure measuring 6.50 m N–S × 6 m E–W and partitioned equally into inner and outer rooms. The wall preservation at Feature 5 is similar to that of Feature 4. Features 6 and 7 are situated 13 m due west of Feature 5 and across a small drainage. These structures are nearly identical to that at Feature 2. Feature 8, a small ruined structure measuring ca. 3–3.50 m on a side, lies southwest of Features 6–7 (ca. 45 m as the crow flies). Feature 9 lies ca. 36 m due south of Feature 5 and opposite an unpaved, secondary roadway. It consists of a wall alignment that extends 36 m to the southeast where it touches upon Feature 12. The wall is 0.70 m wide (two courses with rubble fill) and preserved up to 0.60 m high. A ruined structure is apparent at the northwest end of the wall alignment. Both Features 10 and 11 lie just to the northeast of the wall alignment described in Feature 9. Feature 10 is a rectilinear structure measuring 6 m N–S × 5 m E–W and open to the west. Features 11 and 12 are similar to Feature 10. Ca. 27.50 m east of Feature 11, Feature 13 is an oblong circular structure that measures ca. 5 m in diameter. Its walls are two courses wide with rubble fill (0.75m at the base) and five–six courses high. A low-lying wall alignment extends 4.75 m to the east to a small, rectangular structure dug into the bedrock, which measures 3 × 4 m. Feature 14, ca. 20 m south of Feature 13, is a poorly preserved stone enclosure measuring 6 × 4 m and open to the east, and Feature 15, a rectangular structure measuring 3 × 4 m, with walls measuring 1.20 m high and two courses wide (0.55 m). Adjacent to this structure to the north there are various wall alignments, which may be additional structures and where the SAAS found a grindstone fragment. Feature 16, ca. 193 m at 118 degrees from Feature 15, is a small, rectangular structure measuring 3.50 in diameter. Feature 16 appears to be of the same type as Feature 15 but it stands only 0.85 m high. Feature 17 is a collapsed rectilinear structure measuring 5 × 5 m with a wall alignment extending 2 m to the east. Its construc-

tion is of the same type as Feature 10. Feature 17 is 6 m southwest of Feature 16 and 13.50 m west of Feature 18, a circular structure measuring ca. 4 m in diameter and open to the southwest. The opening is 1 m wide. The walls of Feature 18 are two courses wide (0.65 m) and preserved up to three courses high. Various rectangular pits dug into the bedrock are situated to the southwest, which may have served for temporary water storage. These measure ca. 1–2 m on a side, one of which is lined with stones. Feature 19 is ca. 22 m southeast of Feature 18. Feature 19 is a circular structure that measures 5 m in diameter (of the same type as described as Feature 2). It has rectangular rooms attached to the exterior south face. Ca. 64.50 m northeast of Feature 19 lies Feature 20, a rectilinear structure on a fluvial terrace adjacent to a bedrock spur above a secondary drainage. The structure measures 4 m on a side, and it is open in the southwest corner. Its walls are two courses wide (0.60 m), although it is a single course wide (1 m) at the entrance. Various miscellaneous wall alignments lie to the northeast. Feature 21 is ca. 37 m due south of Feature 20. It is a structure that measures 4 × 5 m and appears to be of the same type as Feature 20, although it is entered from the east. Feature 22 is 20 m at 118 degrees from Feature 20. It is a circular structure that measures 4.50 m in diameter, and of basically the same type as Feature 13. Feature 23 is ca. 35 m north of Feature 13 (as the crow flies) and opposite a low ridge. Feature 23 is a large enclosure on a low fluvial terrace. The entrance appears to be in the east where massive boulders are set which measure 0.71 m on a side. The enclosure itself is 7.50 m N–S × 10 m E–W, and its walls are two courses wide (0.50 m) and no more than a single course high. Situated near the summit of the ridge above the site is Feature 24, a series of four structures of types similar to those encountered in the alluvial plain below. One structure is rectilinear measuring 4.50 N–S × 2.50 m E–W. Its entrance is set in the northeast corner. The walls are 0.50 m wide (two courses) and preserved up to 1.40 m high. A circular structure is nearby that measures 4.50 m in diameter and with walls similarly constructed. Both structures are in a ruined state. A third structure is located down the slope to the east, and a fourth structure is located further down the slope. These are both relatively small, measuring no more than 3 m in diameter, and both are largely collapsed.

Site No.: 34 (figs. 4.36, 4.39)
Field Site No.: 35
Site Name: None
Map Reference: 3049 III, K737
Location on 1:50,000: 3268647 N / 698300 E
Elevation: 315 m
Aerial Reference No.: IGN-78-JOR 12/100 - 1221
Site Size: See below
Inventory Rating: 3
Pottery Collected: Total = 131 (No. of Indicators: 23 / No. Saved: 20)
Pottery Registration No(s).: 1450–56, 1482–94
Pottery Summary: 7 LByz/Umayyad, 7 Modern, 117 UD ([LByz/Early Islamic], 13 Early Islamic = 3 Mahesh ware, ca. AD 750, 5 from 1 vessel)
Lithic Summary: N/A
Site Description: The site is contiguous with Site 33, and Sites 35–37. These sites combine to cover an area of ca. 500 × 250 m. Site 34 consists of numerous structures and wall alignments. Twenty-two distinct features were recorded here. Feature 1 is an irregular circular structure ca. 7 m in diameter. There is an adjoining rectilinear feature (5 m N–S × 2.50 m E–W) appended to the outer surface along the east wall, which opens to the south. The circular structure opens to the south as well. Its walls are ca. 0.60 m wide and 0.80 m high. Feature 2 is a circular structure ca. 4 m in diameter and with a south entrance. Its walls are two courses wide (0.80 m) and preserved up to three courses high (0.55 m). Feature 3 is a rectilinear structure measuring overall ca. 10 m N–S × 17 m E–W. The structure consists of an inner room (ca. 8 m N–S × 10 m E–W) with a ca. 1.20 m opening along the northeast wall. This leads to the outer room that measures ca. 7 m N–S × 7 m E–W. The exit from the structure is along the southeast wall of this room. The structure is built of large granite boulders, with walls that are two courses wide (0.60 m) with rubble fill and two courses high. Another wall alignment may extend from the west wall outward. Feature 4 is another irregular circular structure with a diameter of ca. 7 m. The structure opens to the west, and its walls have mostly collapsed. Abutting the outer face of the circular structure, a wall segment extends ca.

10 m to the southwest, with three additional wall alignments extending perpendicularly off of it (two of which project to the southeast by ca. 6 m [ca. 5 m and 10 m from the circular structure], and the third, ca. 6 m from the circular structure, projects ca. 6 m to the northwest). Feature 5 is a low-lying L-shaped wall alignment two courses wide (0.50 m) that once seems to have formed a 4 × 4.50 m rectangular structure. The southwest wall is destroyed, probably caused by the construction of the intrusive circular structure that is 6 m in diameter and open to the east. The walls of this circular structure are preserved up to 0.85 m high and 0.50–0.60 m wide (two courses with rubble fill). The walls seem to curve vertically which might suggest some sort of domed roof. Feature 6 is a rectangular structure measuring 3 × 3.50. Its construction is similar to Feature 3. Feature 7 is a circular structure ca. 6 m in diameter that opens to the southwest and into an adjoining square feature measuring ca. 3 m on a side. The walls of the structure are 0.40–0.50 m wide (two courses with rubble fill) and 0.60 m high (four–five courses). Feature 8 is a small rectangular structure measuring 2.50 × 2.50 m and entirely open on its southwest side. It lies 2–3 m northeast of Feature 7. Feature 9 is a square structure that measures 7 m on a side. The structure is built next to a small drainage on its southwest side and forms a terrace of sorts. Feature 10 is a square structure open on its east side and measuring 4 m on a side. Its walls are a single course wide (0.40–0.55 m) and high. Feature 11 is a small structure measuring 3 × 4 m and built of large boulders (more than 1 m on a side). Feature 12 is a circular structure measuring 5 m in diameter and open on its southeast side. Feature 13 is a circular structure that is 5.20 m in diameter and constructed similarly to Feature 12. Its walls are preserved ca. 11 courses high (1.30 m) and 0.50 m wide, and there is evidence of mud mortar along the exterior. The structure is entered through a small doorway, ca. 0.80 m wide, along the east segment of the wall. Also, there is a window feature facing W–NW in alignment with the door. Further, there is a curved wall alignment that abuts with the northeast outer face of the structure. It appears as a half-circle that is 3.50 m in diameter and projects 2.58 m from the wall. Feature 14 is similar to Feature 10. It is a rectangular structure

measuring 4 m on a side and open to the northwest. Feature 15 is a small oblong wall alignment
forming a semicircle 3 m in diameter. Feature 16 is
an L-shaped wall alignment 8 m in length. The L-
shaped extension projects from the southeast end
of the wall alignment for 3.50 m to the southwest.
Feature 17 is a circular structure 4 m in diameter
and of the same type as Feature 2 and Feature
12 described above. The structure is open to the
north. Feature 18 is another circular structure 5.30
m in diameter and of the same construction type
as Features 5 and 7 discussed above. The walls of
the structure are preserved ca. 1.20 m in high and
0.60 m wide, with a southwest entrance. Various
miscellaneous wall alignments lies southeast of
this structure. Feature 19 is a circular structure that
seems to differ from the others in that the walls
are constructed of larger boulders (0.40–1 m on a
side). The structure has a diameter of 5.25 m and
it is open to the east. At the entrance, there is what
appears to be a small apse (ca. 2 m in depth and 2
m wide). Feature 20 is a collapsed structure with
a debris mound measuring only 4 m across. The
structure may have been open to the south. Feature 21 is a large rectangular structure measuring
6.20 m N–S × 4.30 m E–W with an entrance (0.90
m wide) in the northeast corner. The walls of the
structure are preserved ca. eight courses high (1.80
m) and two courses wide (0.85 m). There is also a
niche in the interior south wall that measures 0.40
× 0.75 m (0.80 m deep and 0.55 m from the floor),
which is partially collapsed inward. Feature 22 is a
substantially larger rectangular structure measuring 24 m N–S × 18.50 E–W. The entrance into the
structure is in the north wall and measures 1.80
m wide. The structure is divided into two rooms.
The partition wall between the rooms is 9.38 m
from the entrance, which is 4.50 m wide. In the
first room, just to the east and west of the entrance,
there are elevated platforms (flat paved surfaces) on
either side of the passage through the room. These
project ca. 5.75 m from the outer walls, and their
function remains ubiquitous. The interior room is
completely empty except for a large pit excavated
in its eastern half. This feature is certainly the most
prominent at the site.

Site No.: 35 (figs. 4.36, 4.39)
Field Site No.: 34
Site Name: None
Map Reference: 3049 III, K737
Location on 1:50,000: 3268727 N / 698195 E
Elevation: 320 m
Aerial Reference No.: IGN-78-JOR 12/100 - 1221
Site Size: See below
Inventory Rating: 3
Pottery Collected: Total = 104 (No. of Indicators:
6 / No. Saved: 16)
Pottery Registration No(s).: 1434–49
Pottery Summary: 90 LByz (4 vessels), 1 Modern,
13 UD (some from a handmade bowl w/ plaster
surface, 1 handmade/painted)
Lithic Summary: N/A
Site Description: The site is contiguous with Sites
33–34 and Sites 36–37. These sites combine to cover
an area of ca. 500 × 250 m (Site 35 itself spans an
area of 72 m N–S × 60 m E–W) The site consists
of numerous structures and wall alignments. Eight
distinct features were recorded here. Feature 1 is a
rectilinear structure (ca. 5 × 5.50 m) with a cleared
center. Its walls are built of large boulders, some of
which are *in situ* in the alluvial fan surface (smaller
boulders are piled on top as a second course). The
walls of the structure have a maximum height of
0.60 m and their width ranges from 0.50 to 0.75
m. To the southeast is a smaller room opening
to the east. Feature 2 is a rectangular structure
measuring 4.50 × 5.10 m (lengthwise orientation
is NE–SW). A doorway (0.60 m wide) is set in the
southwest corner. Its walls are 0.70 m high (up to
four courses) and 0.60 m wide (two courses with
rubble fill). Also, the foundations of the walls appear buried. Feature 3 is a circular structure, with
a diameter of 4.10 m, along with an adjoining trapezoidal structure/enclosure measuring ca. 5.50 m ×
4 m. The circular structure opens to the southeast
and into the trapezoidal enclosure. The walls of
each measure ca. 0.60 m wide (two courses) and
are preserved up to two courses (ca. 0.50 m) high.
The area enclosed by the trapezoidal structure is
ca. 4 × 4.50 m. Also, the enclosure is open at its
northeast and northwest ends next to the circular
structure. At the southeast corner of the enclosure,
a wall alignment projects to the southeast for ca. 2
m before it angles to the south for another 3.50 m.

Feature 4 is another rectangular structure, which measures 3.40 × 4 m. There is an opening into the structure in the south corner. Feature 5 is a rectangular structure (4.50 × 4 m) with a center clearing dug ca. 0.40 m below the fan surface. Its walls are constructed of very large *in situ* granite boulders, some of which still have a calciferous coat. These boulders project further along the length of the north wall of the structure to the southwest with a total length of 7.70 m. There is a small platform (ca. 1 m on a side) in the west corner of this appended feature and an opening to the east. There is also an adjacent semicircular feature (ca. 2.70 × 3.50 m) constructed of very large boulders and dug below the fan surface. Feature 6 is an oval structure measuring 2 m N–S × 3 m E–W. It is constructed of large boulders on a ledge of bedrock exposed in the wadi and oriented N–S. It appears to have been recently excavated. There are two pits visibly cut into the bedrock, perhaps for burials. Feature 7 is a rectangular structure that measures 3 × 5 m and ca. 0.90 m high (five–six courses). Its walls are 0.60 m wide (with a wider base of ca. 0.75–0.80 m). These are two courses wide with rubble fill and built of large boulders and cobbles (0.20–0.40m on a side). Feature 7 opens to the southeast. Also, there are two storage areas in the south and east corners. In the northeast corner is a small stone ring, which may be the remnants of a hearth. The SAAS found a pot-bust within the structure. Feature 8 is an oblong structure measuring 3.50 × 4 m. Its walls are roughly 0.60–0.75 m wide (two courses with rubble fill) and 0.80 m high (five courses in places). A small wall segment projects 1.30 m northeast from the outer segment of the wall to the northeast, just near the entrance.

Site No.: 36 (figs. 4.36, 4.39)
Field Site No.: 68
Site Name: None
Map Reference: 3049 III, K737
Location on 1:50,000: 3268778 N / 698434 E
Elevation: 315 m
Aerial Reference No.: IGN-78-JOR 12/100 - 1221
Site Size: See Below
Inventory Rating: 3
Pottery Collected: Total = 46 (No. of Indicators: 1 / No. Saved: 2)

Pottery Registration No(s).: 3197–98
Pottery Summary: 2 Early Islamic, 44 Modern
Lithic Summary: N/A
Site Description: The site is contiguous with Sites 33–35 and Site 37. These sites combine to cover an area of ca. 500 × 250 m. Site 36 consists of an array of structures and wall alignments. Sixteen distinct features were recorded here. Feature 1 is a rectilinear wall alignment or hut foundation measuring ca. 5 m on a side. A small entrance (ca. 1 m wide) is set within the southern portion of the west wall. These walls are a single course wide (ca. 0.40 m) and preserved up to two courses high. Feature 1 lies ca. 2 m south of a large outcropping of bedrock, around which there is a large enclosure or corral. Ca. 23 m southwest of Feature 1, Feature 2 is another rectilinear wall alignment or hut foundation that consists of a single row of stones. There is a small hearth in the center of this feature. Feature 3 is an open rectangular structure 29 m and 218 degrees southwest of Feature 1. Feature 3 measures 4 × 5 m and is open to the northeast. Its walls are preserved up to two courses high and a single course wide. Feature 4, a semicircular structure abutting a large outcrop of bedrock, lies 18 m west of Feature 1. Its diameter is ca. 3–3.50 m, and there is a small entrance (1.50 m wide) to the north. Its walls are a single course wide and are preserved up to three courses high. Ca. 5.50 m southwest of Feature 4, Feature 5 is a series of two circular enclosures averaging 5 m in diameter. These resemble Feature 1 in detail. Ca. 17.50 m northwest of Feature 4, Feature 6 is a small rectilinear structure measuring 2 m N–S × 1 m E–W and with walls preserved up to three courses high and a single course wide. A similar structure (Feature 7) lies ca. 20 m to the southwest of Feature 6, but its walls are more circular. Ca. 46 m west of Feature 7, Feature 8 consists of three small wall alignments enclosing an open area of ca. 6 m N–S × 11.50 m E–W. These irregular wall alignments are preserved in some segments up to four courses high (ca. 1.20 m) and two courses wide. Feature 8 appears to be an enclosure of sorts. Feature 9, which lies ca. 60 m south–southeast of Feature 8, is a more substantial and well-preserved circular structure or enclosure. It measures 6 m in diameter, with walls preserved up to three courses high and two courses wide. An entrance (1 m wide)

is set in the northeast corner where a wall alignment extends outward 3 m (for a parallel, see Site 34/Feature 1). Ca. 5 m to the northwest, Feature 10 is another circular structure or enclosure similar to Feature 9 but without the wall alignment extending beyond the entrance. Feature 11 lies 2 m west of Feature 10. This is a poorly preserved rectilinear enclosure measuring ca. 5 × 5 m. The enclosure walls appear as a single row of large stones and rubble. Feature 12 consists of a wall alignment extending from a large granite outcropping ca. 22 m northwest of Feature 11. This may represent a single holding pen covering an area of 5 × 3 m. Feature 13 is a well-preserved circular structure ca. 18 m west of Feature 12. The walls of the structure are two courses wide and preserved up to five courses high in some places. The entrance, which is partially blocked, is from the southeast. The structure has a diameter of 5 m. Feature 14, ca. 18 m N–NE of Feature 13, is an isolated circular wall alignment with an arc measuring ca. 7 m. Feature 15, ca. 25 m north of Feature 13, is a well-constructed, stone-built rectangular structure. The structure measures 7 × 5.70 m, and there is an entrance (ca. 1 m wide) set in the northwest wall. It is built upon a terraced platform (a porch?) that extends 3 m beyond the entrance and runs parallel to the northwest wall. The height of the terraced area is ca. 0.90 m. The walls of the structure are preserved up to four courses high (0.90 m) and appear to be only a single course wide. Ca. 8 m southwest of Feature 15, Feature 16 is an oval wall alignment (ca. 4 × 2 m) extending from a large granite outcrop. The walls are up to seven courses high and a single course wide. Feature 16 probably represents another holding pen.

Site No.: 37 (figs. 4.36, 4.39)
Field Site No.: 69
Site Name: None
Map Reference: 3049 III, K737
Location on 1:50,000: 3268880 N / 698350 E
Elevation: 315 m
Aerial Reference No.: IGN-78-JOR 12/100 - 1221
Site Size: See below
Inventory Rating: 3
Pottery Collected: Total = 3 (No. of Indicators: 0 / No. Saved: 1)

Pottery Registration No(s).: 2614
Pottery Summary: 1 Modern, 2 UD
Lithic Summary: N/A
Site Description: This site is contiguous with Sites 33–36. These sites combine to cover an area of ca. 500 × 250 m. Site 37 consists of 3 distinct features. Feature 1 is an impressive structural complex. It consists of a large circular enclosure flanked by three smaller circular enclosures to the north and a fourth enclosure to the south. These open up into a larger area. The smaller enclosure at the northwest end of the structure opens to the outside. There is another entrance at the southwest end of the larger enclosure, outside of which the SAAS found a grindstone fragment. The interior of the central area measures 5 m N–S × 4 m E–W, and that of the smaller enclosures measures ca. 3 m in diameter. The walls are preserved up to six courses high and two courses thick (ca. 0.70 m). Ca. 43 m southwest of Feature 1, Feature 2 is a somewhat circular enclosure wall ca. 7 m in diameter. Feature 3 is a large, well-preserved circular structure with a curved wall extending 7 m beyond its entrance. The central enclosure is 3 m in diameter and is entered from the southwest.

Site No.: 38 (fig. 4.39)
Field Site No.: 19
Site Name: None
Map Reference: 3049 III, K737
Location on 1:50,000: 3269045 N / 698009 E
Elevation: 270 m
Aerial Reference No.: IGN-78-JOR 12/100 - 1221
Site Size: 40 m N–S × 50 m E–W
Inventory Rating: 2
Pottery Collected: Total = 0 (No. of Indicators: 0 / No. Saved: 0)
Pottery Registration No(s).: None
Pottery Summary: N/A
Lithic Summary: Indefinite cultural-historic placement
Site Description: This is a large wall that extends across a terraced alluvial spur in the middle of a large drainage east of Jebel esh-Shahbī. The wall, oriented NE–SW, measures ca. 29.50 m in length and 0.60–0.70 m wide. It follows the natural contours of the slope, and its southwest side is roughly 2 m higher than the northeast side. Two circular

installations are situated on either side of the wall at its northeast end. These circular installations or rooms abut the wall, which is preserved up to seven courses high. Wall foundations of other installations are visible on the slope above and below the main wall alignment. Also, the SAAS collected fragments of a grindstone from the site.

Site No.: 39 (fig. 4.39)
Field Site No.: 16
Site Name: None
Map Reference: 3049 III, K737
Location on 1:50,000: 3269306 N / 698459 E
Elevation: 230 m
Aerial Reference No.: IGN-78-JOR 12/100 - 1221
Site Size: 17 m N–S × 19 m E–W
Inventory Rating: 99
Pottery Collected: Total = 1 (No. of Indicators: 1 / No. Saved: 0)
Pottery Registration No(s).: None
Pottery Summary: 1 UD
Lithic Summary: N/A
Site Description: The site consists of three stone mounds, perhaps burials, on an alluvial terrace east of Jebel esh-Shahbī. Two of these are oriented E–W. The third is oriented N–S. What appears to be a stone ring or hut circle (ca. 2.50 m in diameter) is located at the far western end of the site.

Site No.: 40 (fig. 4.39)
Field Site No.: 18
Site Name: None
Map Reference: 3049 III, K737
Location on 1:50,000: 3269307 N / 697794 E
Elevation: 250 m
Aerial Reference No.: IGN-78-JOR 12/100 - 1221
Site Size: 90 m N–S × 50 m E–W
Inventory Rating: 1
Pottery Collected: Total = 4 (No. of Indicators: 1 / No. Saved: 4)
Pottery Registration No(s).: 1067–70
Pottery Summary: 4 R/Byz
Lithic Summary: N/A
Site Description: The site consists of 17 pitted burials scattered across an alluvial terrace east of Jebel esh-Shahbī. Each measures roughly 1.50 × 2 m and these are not oriented in any uniform fashion.

Site No.: 41 (fig. 4.39)
Field Site No.: 17
Site Name: None
Map Reference: 3049 III, K737
Location on 1:50,000: 3269378 N / 698030 E
Elevation: 260 m
Aerial Reference No.: IGN-78-JOR 12/100 - 1221
Site Size: 6 m N–S × 8 m E–W
Inventory Rating: 1
Pottery Collected: Total = 0 (No. of Indicators: 0 / No. Saved: 0)
Pottery Registration No(s).: None
Pottery Summary: N/A
Lithic Summary: N/A
Site Description: The site consists of two pitted burials on an alluvial terrace east of Jebel esh-Shahbī. One trends NE–SW (2.30 × 1.25 m), and the other trends roughly E–W (ca. 1.10 × 1.40 m).

Site No.: 42 (fig. 4.39)
Field Site No.: 15
Site Name: None
Map Reference: 3049 III, K737
Location on 1:50,000: 3269486 N / 698171 E
Elevation: 220 m
Aerial Reference No.: IGN-78-JOR 12/100 - 1221
Site Size: 16 m N–S × 22 m E–W
Inventory Rating: 2
Pottery Collected: Total = 0 (No. of Indicators: 0 / No. Saved: 0)
Pottery Registration No(s).: None
Pottery Summary: N/A
Lithic Summary: N/A
Site Description: The site consists of a small burial and a circular rock alignment or enclosure (ca. 7–10 m in diameter) to the west. The central area is more mounded and may be remnants of a structure, although no clear evidence exists for a wall. A possible rock alignment extends ca. 8 m to the east and connects the large mound with the burial feature. The northern edge of the site appears to be truncated by a small drainage cut.

Site No.: 43 (fig. 4.39)
Field Site No.: 14
Site Name: None
Map Reference: 3049 III, K737
Location on 1:50,000: 3269671 N / 697657 E

Elevation: 212 m
Aerial Reference No.: IGN-78-JOR 12/100 - 1221
Site Size: 40 m N–S × 40 m E–W
Inventory Rating: 2
Pottery Collected: Total = 7 (No. of Indicators: 1 / No. Saved: 4)
Pottery Registration No(s).: 1091–94
Pottery Summary: 1 ER/Nab, 4 ER/LR (3 from 1 vessel), 2 UD
Lithic Summary: Indefinite cultural-historic placement
Site Description: The site consists of three rectilinear wall foundations and up to six stone circles further to the south at the southern edge of an alluvial terrace east of Jebel esh-Shahbī. The stone circles vary in size, but these are generally 1.50–2 m × 2–2.50 m in diameter. The relationship between the wall foundations and the stone circles, if any, could not be established.

Site No.: 44 (fig. 4.39)
Field Site No.: 117
Site Name: None
Map Reference: 3049 III, K737
Location on 1:50,000: 3269860 N / 697599 E
Elevation: 200 m
Aerial Reference No.: IGN-78-JOR 12/100 - 1221
Site Size: 50 m N–S × 75 m E–W
Inventory Rating: 2
Pottery Collected: Total = 5 (No. of Indicators: 0 / No. Saved: 2)
Pottery Registration No(s).: 6657–58
Pottery Summary: 5 Early Islamic
Lithic Summary: N/A
Site Description: The site consists of a series of six terrace walls (ca. 2–3 m in length and 0.40–0.75 m high) cutting across three small drainages, which probably facilitated some limited agricultural activity in the area. Typically, the ends of the terrace walls are further up the slope than the mid-section.

Site No.: 45 (fig. 4.39)
Field Site No.: 118
Site Name: None
Map Reference: 3049 III, K737
Location on 1:50,000: 3271000 N / 698092 E
Elevation: 260 m
Aerial Reference No.: IGN-78-JOR 12/100 - 1224
Site Size: 10 m N–S × 15 m E–W

Inventory Rating: 2
Pottery Collected: Total = 0 (No. of Indicators: 0 / No. Saved: 0)
Pottery Registration No(s).: None
Pottery Summary: N/A
Lithic Summary: N/A
Site Description: The site consists of three small rock alignments, or burials, on a spur south of Wādī Yutum. These rock alignments may be associated with modern features below the site, but the evidence is not conclusive.

Site No.: 46 (fig. 4.39)
Field Site No.: 176
Site Name: None
Map Reference: 3049 III, K737
Location on 1:50,000: 3271660 N / 696439 E
Elevation: 82 m
Aerial Reference No.: IGN-78-JOR 12/100 - 1288
Site Size: 1.30 m N–S × 0.90 m E–W
Inventory Rating: 2
Pottery Collected: Total = 0 (No. of Indicators: 0 / No. Saved: 0)
Pottery Registration No(s).: None
Pottery Summary: N/A
Lithic Summary: N/A
Site Description: The site consists of a single wall alignment (ca. one course wide and five courses high). Its age is ambiguous as the feature is in close spatial proximity to modern structures. A recent trench has been dug nearby, which is oriented E–W and runs along the side of the feature. The feature does not appear in the trench cut.

Site No.: 47 (fig. 4.39)
Field Site No.: 178
Site Name: None
Map Reference: 3049III, K737
Location on 1:50,000: 3271648 N / 696225 E
Elevation: 79 m
Aerial Reference No.: IGN-78-JOR 12/100 - 1286
Site Size: 1 m N–S × 1 m E–W
Inventory Rating: 2
Pottery Collected: Total = 14 (No. of Indicators: 1 / No. Saved: 6)
Pottery Registration No(s).: 22363–68
Pottery Summary: 2 R/Byz, 3 Modern, 9 UD (4 from 1 vessel)

Lithic Summary: N/A
Site Description: This is a light sherd scatter on an alluvial fan near the mouth of Wādī Yutum. The sherds are scattered among modern debris.

Site No.: 48 (fig. 4.39)
Field Site No.: 177
Site Name: None
Map Reference: 3049 III, K737
Location on 1:50,000: 3271690 N / 696185 E
Elevation: 80 m
Aerial Reference No.: IGN-78-JOR 12/100 - 1257
Site Size: 3 m N–S × 3 m E–W
Inventory Rating: 3
Pottery Collected: Total = 0 (No. of Indicators: 0 / No. Saved: 0)
Pottery Registration No(s).: None
Pottery Summary: N/A
Lithic Summary: Indefinite cultural-historic placement
Site Description: The site consists of a circular stone mound, perhaps a large burial cairn, on an old alluvial fan surface W–SW of the mouth of Wādī Yutum. The cairn appears as a circular stone mound measuring ca. 3 m in diameter and ca. 1.20 m high.

Site No.: 49 (fig. 4.39)
Field Site No.: 195
Site Name: None
Map Reference: 3049 III, K737
Location on 1:50,000: 3271934 N / 696718 E
Elevation: 98 m
Aerial Reference No.: IGN-78-JOR 12/100 - 1257
Site Size: 11 m N–S × 11 m E–W
Inventory Rating: 3
Pottery Collected: Total = 2 (No. of Indicators: 0 / No. Saved: 1)
Pottery Registration No(s).: 22326
Pottery Summary: 1 Chalco/EB, 1 Modern
Lithic Summary: N/A
Site Description: The site, located 791 m southwest of Ḥujeirat al-Ghuzlan, consists of four linear stone alignments interconnected at right angles. These four segments were plotted using an EDM (data with project geologist) and were labeled as 195A–D. Segment 195A (oriented NE–SW) is ca. 2.50 m long. It is preserved up to a single course high and wide

(ca. 0.55 m). Segment 195B, oriented NW–SE, intersects with 195A. It is ca. 9 m long, three courses wide (1.40 m), and three courses high (0.40 m). Segment 195C, which is parallel with 195A and intersects with 195B and 195D is ca. 6 m long, one course high (0.30 m), and one course wide (0.30 m). Segment 195D, which is parallel to 195B and intersects with 195C is ca. 1.50 m long and preserved up to one course high and wide (0.30 m). These appear to represent terracing of the alluvial fan.

Site No.: 50 (fig. 4.39)
Field Site No.: 230
Site Name: None
Map Reference: 3049 III, K737
Location on 1:50,000: 3271917 N / 696093 E
Elevation: 81 m
Aerial Reference No.: IGN-78-JOR 12/100 - 1257
Site Size: 50 m N–S × 100 m E–W
Inventory Rating: 4
Pottery Collected: Total = 85 (No. of Indicators: 19 / No. Saved: 44)
Pottery Registration No(s).: 22169–71, 22225, 22308–25, 22497–500, 22278–95
Pottery Summary: 18 Chalco/EB, 3 ER/Nab (1 vessel), 1 R/Byz, 1 EByz, 14 Umayyad (1 vessel), 46 Early Islamic (possibly Umayyad), 2 UD
Lithic Summary: N/A
Site Description: The site consists of numerous wall alignments, structures, enclosures, stone mounds, and stone rings or hut circles. Feature 1 is a mounded stone alignment oriented roughly E–W at the northern edge of the site. Its length is 37 m with a width of 2 m. The height of the mound is 0.87 m. Its construction is that of stones packed together with no discernible courses and covered in alluvial sediments. Feature 2 consists of numerous rectilinear stone enclosures throughout the site that cover an area of ca. 47.40 m N–S × 24.10 m E–W. Most share common walls. The area inside each enclosure is mostly cleared of stones. Stone mounds are present within the enclosures in various places, and these seem to have no discernible pattern or particular placement. Construction of the walls of the enclosures consists of tightly packed stones a single course high and wide (0.26 m). Some of these may actually be terrace walls, and some are only semi-enclosed. Feature 3, at the southeast corner of

the site, is a linear stone mound or wall alignment for an unspecified structure. Two of the walls are aligned NE–SW, and another is aligned NW–SE. The longest is the northeast wall, which measures 5.50 m. Two corners are preserved, which set the internal dimensions at 2.70 m (northwest–southeast). The walls are 0.60 m wide (two courses), and are preserved to a height of 0.55 m (two courses in places). Construction of the walls consists of large boulders averaging 0.40 m on a side with chinking between the courses. Feature 4 denotes the presence throughout the site of stone mounds or burial cairns. They are on average 2 m in diameter and 0.28 m high. Average stone size for these cairns is 0.15 × 0.12 × 0.05 m. Feature 5 denotes the presence of numerous small stone rings or hut circles, mostly ovular, spread across the site. They measure on average ca. 3.50 × 1.50 m. Their construction is of loosely packed, unworked stones a single course high (0.15 m) and two courses wide (0.55 m). The site itself extends to the edge of the wadi terrace before terminating. The site extends further just beyond the ephemeral drainage to the northeast.

Site No.: 51 (fig. 4.39)
Field Site No.: 194
Site Name: None
Map Reference: 3049 III, K737
Location on 1:50,000: 3271934 N / 696718 E
Elevation: 96 m
Aerial Reference No.: IGN-78-JOR 12/100 - 1257
Site Size: 20 m N–S × 40 m E–W
Inventory Rating: 3
Pottery Collected: Total = 0 (No. of Indicators: 0 / No. Saved: 0)
Pottery Registration No(s).: None
Pottery Summary: N/A
Lithic Summary: N/A
Site Description: The site consists of four wall alignments. There are two wall alignments that run parallel to one another with an NW–SE orientation. The other two run parallel to each other with an NE–SW orientation. These parallel sets of walls intersect with each other to form partially rectilinear enclosures. The NW–SE segments are 16.50 m and 23.50 in length, while the NE–SW segments are 9 m and 13 m in length. The walls are preserved up to one course high and two courses wide (0.80 m).

Site No.: 52 (fig. 4.39)
Field Site No.: 231
Site Name: None
Map Reference: 3049 III, K737
Location on 1:50,000: 3272034 N / 696251 E
Elevation: 84 m
Aerial Reference No.: IGN-78-JOR 12/100 - 1257
Site Size: 43 m N–S × 60 m E–W
Inventory Rating: 5
Pottery Collected: Total = 75 (No. of Indicators: 9 / No. Saved: 20)
Pottery Registration No(s).: 22469–88
Pottery Summary: 71 Chalco/EB, 2 EByz, 1 Modern, 1 UD
Lithic Summary: Indefinite cultural-historic placement
Site Description: The site consists of terrace walls oriented E–W and possibly a water channel. There are numerous cross-walls branching off in a roughly N–S direction for ca. 20 m on each side. On top of the mounds there are visible stone (wall) alignments ca. 0.60 m wide (three courses) and ca. 0.25 m high (two courses). Near the west end of the main terrace wall there is a parallel stone alignment which may be a water channel. This feature is preserved a single course high (ca. 0.20 m) and wide (ca. 0.80 m). To the south of the main terrace wall is another possible terrace wall oriented E–W. A rectilinear enclosure is present at the west end of site. This enclosure is possibly a continuation of the terrace, with the walls oriented N–S being cross-walls. One of these has a small wall alignment branching off it which may represent another water channel.

Site No.: 53 (fig. 4.39)
Field Site No.: 232
Site Name: None
Map Reference: 3049 III, K737
Location on 1:50,000: 3272158 N / 696356 E
Elevation: 92 m
Aerial Reference No.: IGN-78-JOR 12/100 - 1256
Site Size: 14 m N–S × 15 m E–W
Inventory Rating: 4
Pottery Collected: Total = 4 (No. of Indicators: 0 / No. Saved: 4)
Pottery Registration No(s).: 22501–4
Pottery Summary: 2 Chalco/EB, 2 UD

Lithic Summary: N/A

Site Description: The site consists of a large mounded stone alignment oriented N–S (Feature 1) and three stone circles concentrated at the eastern end of site. One of these (Feature 2) has cobble and stone paving on its top. Also present in the northwest quadrant of the site is a wall alignment extending ca. 5 m N–S, which abuts into Feature 1. The alignment is preserved two courses high (0.35 m) and one course wide (0.30 m). The stone rings, perhaps circular huts, are ca. 3.50 m in diameter. Feature 1, at the western end of the site, measures 9.50 m in length. The mound is 4.30 m wide, but the actual wall alignment is on top and in the middle of tumble, which extends 1.70 m to the end of the mound. The outer west face of the wall is not visible through the tumble. The height of the mound is 0.70 m. Feature 2, ca. 8 m to east of Feature 1, is constructed in the same fashion as the other circles, but its diameter is 3.20 m. It is also filled on its interior with a mixture of cobbles and large stones to create on top an evenly paved surface. Feature 1 rests inside what may be a circular enclosure ca. 6 m long by 4 m wide (it would be appended to the middle circle), but this is problematic.

Site No.: 54 (fig. 4.39)
Field Site No.: 72
Site Name: None
Map Reference: 3049 III, K737
Location on 1:50,000: 3272280 N / 696944 E
Elevation: 102 m
Aerial Reference No.: IGN-78-JOR 12/100 - 1256
Site Size: 120 m N–S × 225 m E–W
Inventory Rating: 3
Pottery Collected: Total = 18 (No. of Indicators: 4 / No. Saved: 5)
Pottery Registration No(s).: 6484–88
Pottery Summary: 13 Chalcolithic, 5 R/Byz (1 vessel)
Lithic Summary: Indefinite cultural-historic placement
Site Description: The site consists of two large, curvilinear wall alignments running parallel to each other and separated by 1 m. Ca. 50 m to the south, one of these wall alignments joins a trapezoidal enclosure. Apart from a small stone ring within this enclosure, the enclosed area is largely cleared of stones. Also, extending ca. 225 m southwest is

what appears to be a series of stone terrace walls. The distance between terraces is ca. 15 m.

Site No.: 55 (figs. 4.7, 4.39)
Field Site No.: 233
Site Name: None
Map Reference: 3049 III, K737
Location on 1:50,000: 3272348 N / 696400 E
Elevation: 89 m
Aerial Reference No.: IGN-78-JOR 12/100 - 1256
Site Size: 4.70 m N–S × 175 m E–W
Inventory Rating: 5
Pottery Collected: Total = 9 (No. of Indicators: 2 / No. Saved: 9)
Pottery Registration No(s).: 22179–87
Pottery Summary: 8 Chalco/EB, 1 R/Byz
Lithic Summary: N/A
Site Description: The site consists of an extensive wall alignment oriented E–W and extending along the middle portion of the alluvial fan W–SW of Ḥujeirat al-Ghuzlan. The first wall segment to the east is 68 m long. After a gap of 55 m, the west segment picks up and continues 52 m. This segment is curvilinear. The wall segments appear as linear mounds of stone and alluvial deposits, with an average width of 1 m and height of 0.60 m. Both are oriented roughly N–NE by S–SW. The nature and purpose of the wall segments remain unclear. These may be remnants of some type of perimeter wall to deflect or divert water discharging from Wādī Yutum.

Site No.: 56 (fig. 4.39)
Field Site No.: 66
Site Name: Tell Maqaṣṣ
Map Reference: 3049 III, K737
Location on 1:50,000: 3272512 N / 695172 E
Elevation: 70 m
Aerial Reference No.: IGN-78-JOR 12/100 - 1286
Site Size: 50 m N–S × 75 m E–W
Inventory Rating: 9
Pottery Collected: Total = 69 (No. of Indicators: 16 / No. Saved: 22)
Pottery Registration No(s).: 2217–38
Pottery Summary: 69 Chalcolithic
Lithic Summary: Chalcolithic (see chapter 7)
Site Description: This is the Chalcolithic site of Tell Maqaṣṣ ca. 4 km north of the Gulf of Aqaba

shoreline and bisected by the modern highway. The mound itself stands nearly 6 m high. The SAAS visited the site only to collect pottery for comparative analysis.

Site No.: 57 (fig. 4.39)
Field Site No.: 73
Site Name: None
Map Reference: 3049 III, K737
Location on 1:50,000: 3272361 N / 696766 E
Elevation: 100 m
Aerial Reference No.: IGN-78-JOR 12/100 - 1256
Site Size: 100 m N–S × 170 m E–W
Inventory Rating: 3
Pottery Collected: Total = 28 (No. of Indicators: 10 / No. Saved: 10)
Pottery Registration No(s).: 6340–44, 6447–51
Pottery Summary: 24 Chalcolithic, 4 Modern
Lithic Summary: Indefinite cultural-historic placement
Site Description: This site is apparently associated with Site 63, Ḥujeirat al-Ghuzlan, based on the presence of associated artifacts and proximity. The site consists of a small tell covering an area of 15 m N–S × 22 m E–W. It is preserved up to 3 m in height. There are seven courses of stones sloping from the north side of the mound and a long wall alignment measuring 12 m E–W on top of the mound. Less substantial perpendicular walls run off of it on top of the tell. The surface is covered in rubble. The artifact density here is lower than at the nearby terrace sites (Site 54 and Site 58). Also, a smaller mound lies 260 m at 134 degrees from this larger mound. It measures ca. 12 m N–S × 9 m E–W by 8 m high, and there are possible circular wall alignments around the edge. Also, in the area southwest of the larger mound, there are a series of four long terraced wall alignments, and at least three other wall alignments. Each of these trend roughly NW–SE. The walls are two courses wide (ca. 0.75 m) with rubble fill. The westernmost wall alignment appears to have been a structure measuring ca. 4 × 5 m. The area is greatly disturbed by erosion and the encroachment of modern development.

Site No.: 58 (fig. 4.39)
Field Site No.: 71
Site Name: None

Map Reference: 3049 III, K737
Location on 1:50,000: 3272351 N / 697128 E
Elevation: 107 m
Aerial Reference No.: IGN-78-JOR 12/100 - 1256
Site Size: 110 m N–S × 140 m E–W
Inventory Rating: 3
Pottery Collected: Total = 60 (No. of Indicators: 22 / No. Saved: 18)
Pottery Registration No(s).: 6406–23
Pottery Summary: 20 Chalcolithic, 34 Chalco/EB, 5 EB, 1 Early Islamic
Lithic Summary: Indefinite cultural-historic placement
Site Description: The site consists of a series of massive wall alignments or terraces. Some of these may have joined to form several large enclosures or structures. The walls are two courses wide (ca. 0.80 m) with gravel fill. Some segments are preserved up to three courses high. Decayed mudbrick lies on top of most segments of the wall, which fans out on both sides

Site No.: 59 (fig. 4.39)
Field Site No.: 75
Site Name: None
Map Reference: 3049 III, K737
Location on 1:50,000: 3272315 N / 697000 E
Elevation: 105 m
Aerial Reference No.: IGN-78-JOR 12/100 - 1256
Site Size: 30 m N–S × 15 m E–W
Inventory Rating: 5
Pottery Collected: Total = 12 (No. of Indicators: 0 / No. Saved: 4)
Pottery Registration No(s).: 6587–90
Pottery Summary: 12 Chalco/EB
Lithic Summary: Indefinite cultural-historic placement
Site Description: The site consists of a massive stone wall (fortification/retaining wall?), which is ca. 28 m in length and oriented N–S. Large pits (excavation trenches?) have been dug before the west face of the wall revealing the foundations. The stones that make up the foundation measure ca. 0.70 × 0.50 × 0.35 m on average. The height of the wall exposed by the trenches is roughly 1.70 m, and the wall is two courses wide (ca. 1 m). Two massive, curvilinear features, ca. 4 × 5 m, project from the west face. These are separated from each

other by ca. 1.50 m. Ca. 38 m to the south there is a modern trash pit where an additional wall alignment has been exposed.

Site No.: 60 (fig. 4.39)
Field Site No.: 76
Site Name: None
Map Reference: 3049 III, K737
Location on 1:50,000: 3272421 N / 697584 E
Elevation: 123 m
Aerial Reference No.: IGN-78-JOR 12/100 - 1228
Site Size: 30 m N–S × 15 m E–W
Inventory Rating: 5
Pottery Collected: Total = 17 (No. of Indicators: 6 / No. Saved: 7)
Pottery Registration No(s).: 6692–98
Pottery Summary: 11 Chalcolithic, 2 R/Byz, 4 Early Islamic
Lithic Summary: Indefinite cultural-historic placement
Site Description: The site consists of a massive stone wall measuring ca. 20 m in length, 1.40 m wide, and 0.75 m high. The wall is two courses wide with rubble fill. A 4 m in diameter circular wall alignment is situated at the west end of the site, which appears to be constructed on a rectilinear platform. Additional rock alignments and stone mounds are present. It is difficult to determine the function of this site. Perhaps the large wall served to divert alluvial discharges from Wādī Yutum.

Site No.: 61 (fig. 4.39)
Field Site No.: 77
Site Name: None
Map Reference: 3049 III, K737
Location on 1:50,000: 3272465 N / 697667 E
Elevation: 125 m
Aerial Reference No.: IGN-78-JOR 12/100 - 1228
Site Size: 6 m N–S × 9 m E–W
Inventory Rating: 2
Pottery Collected: Total = 0 (No. of Indicators: 0 / No. Saved: 0)
Pottery Registration No(s).: None
Pottery Summary: N/A
Lithic Summary: Indefinite cultural-historic placement
Site Description: This is a stone mound or burial cairn measuring ca. 9 × 6 m and ca. 0.80 m high.

The soil on top of the mound is littered with bone fragments and some chert.

Site No.: 62 (fig. 4.39)
Field Site No.: 70
Site Name: None
Map Reference: 3049 III, K737
Location on 1:50,000: 3272552 N / 697185 E
Elevation: 114 m
Aerial Reference No.: IGN-78-JOR 12/100 - 1256
Site Size: 150 m N–S × 200 m E–W
Inventory Rating: 2
Pottery Collected: Total = 35 (No. of Indicators: 0 / No. Saved: 0)
Pottery Registration No(s).: None
Pottery Summary: 19 Chalco/EB, 2 ER/Nab (1 vessel), 14 UDE
Lithic Summary: Indefinite cultural-historic placement
Site Description: The site consists of stone rings or hut circles, a stone mound, and several wall alignments. One ring is ca. 5 m in diameter and may be associated with a rectilinear stone alignment (ca. 2 × 2 m) to the southwest. Another stone ring (ca. 2.50 × 3.50 m) lies on top of a small mound. On a bearing of 34 degrees from the stone rings at 21 m, there is a stone wall measuring ca. 10 m in length and 0.70 m wide. Also, on a bearing of 210 degrees and 42 m from the stone rings, there is a massive stone wall oriented roughly NE–SW and measuring ca. 77 m in length. This wall is ca. 1.70 m wide. Artifact distribution concentrates in the southwest area of site and north of the wall. Also at the southwest end of the site (in a bulldozed area), there is possible evidence of mudbrick from the discoloration of the disturbed soil that extends several meters from the wall. The SAAS found some copper slag at the southwest end of the wall.

Site No.: 63 (figs. 4.5, 4.39)
Field Site No.: 74
Site Name: Ḥujeirat al-Ghuzlan
Map Reference: 3049 III, K737
Location on 1:50,000: 3272644 N / 697000 E
Elevation: 110 m
Aerial Reference No.: IGN-78-JOR 12/100 - 1256
Site Size: 85 m N–S × 90 m E–W
Inventory Rating: 4

Pottery Collected: Total = 59 (No. of Indicators: 28 / No. Saved: 31)
Pottery Registration No(s).: 6429–38, 22230–50
Pottery Summary: 55 Chalco/EB, 1 EB, 1 Iron II, 2 Early Islamic
Lithic Summary: Chalcolithic (see chapter 7)
Site Description: This is the Chalcolithic or Early Bronze Age site (tell) of Ḥujeirat al-Ghuzlan situated in the floodplain of Wādī Yutum east of Tell Maqaṣṣ. The SAAS visited the site only to collect pottery for comparative analysis.

Site No.: 64 (fig. 4.39)
Field Site No.: 182
Site Name: None
Map Reference: 3049 III, K737
Location on 1:50,000: 3272378 N / 698400 E
Elevation: 155 m
Aerial Reference No.: IGN-78-JOR 12/100 - 1226
Site Size: 24 m N–S × 22 m E–W
Inventory Rating: 3
Pottery Collected: Total = 0 (No. of Indicators: 0 / No. Saved: 0)
Pottery Registration No(s).: None
Pottery Summary: N/A
Lithic Summary: N/A
Site Description: The site consists of three distinct features. Feature 1 is a small rectilinear stone structure that measures 1.90 × 1.10 m. The remains of three sides of its walls are visible. The construction is of flat rectangular stones packed together with some stone chinking. The northern half of the interior of the structure is filled with alluvial sediments, and the southern half is exposed. The south wall is preserved a single course wide and seven courses high. The extant walls are on the north, south and west sides of the structure. Feature 2 is a linear stone alignment measuring 2 m in length and preserved up to 0.43 m high (consisting of a single course of small stones). It is situated ca. 20 m south of Feature 1. Feature 3 is another linear stone alignment 0.75 m long and 0.35 m high. It is preserved up to two courses high and one course wide. It is situated ca. 20 m west of Feature 1.

Site No.: 65 (fig. 4.39)
Field Site No.: 181
Site Name: None

Map Reference: 3049 III, K737
Location on 1:50,000: 3272518 N / 699709 E
Elevation: 300 m
Aerial Reference No.: IGN-78-JOR 12/100 - 1216
Site Size: 70 m N–S × 20 m E–W
Inventory Rating: 2
Pottery Collected: Total = 0 (No. of Indicators: 0 / No. Saved: 0)
Pottery Registration No(s).: None
Pottery Summary: N/A
Lithic Summary: N/A
Site Description: The site consists of two features. Feature 1 is a rectilinear structure measuring 3.70 × 3.40 m, with walls that are three courses wide and preserved up to 10 courses high (1.65 m). Some portions of the walls are not built up, but hewn out of granite. For the most part, the walls are constructed of flat rocks, with an average stone size of 0.30 × 0.30 × 0.10 m, closely packed, with chinking. Entrance into the structure is 0.75 m wide and 1.40 m high. The structure seems to be built on top of at least two small terrace walls. Feature 2 is a circular structure that measures 1.70 m in diameter. It is on top of a higher portion of the ridge and ca. 60 m to the northwest of Feature 1. There is a narrow entrance (0.80 m) located along the south arc of the structure. This feature offers an excellent vantage point for viewing the valley.

Site No.: 66 (fig. 4.40)
Field Site No.: 173
Site Name: None
Map Reference: 3049 III, K737
Location on 1:50,000: 3272822 N / 699645 E
Elevation: 235 m
Aerial Reference No.: IGN-78-JOR 12/100 - 1216
Site Size: 6.35 m N–S × 1.50s m E–W
Inventory Rating: 2
Pottery Collected: Total = 0 (No. of Indicators: 0 / No. Saved: 0)
Pottery Registration No(s).: None
Pottery Summary: N/A
Lithic Summary: Indefinite cultural-historic placement
Site Description: The site consists of two linear wall alignments aligned N–S. The south segment is 3.40 m in length, one–two courses high, and one course wide. Average stone size is ca. 0.25 m

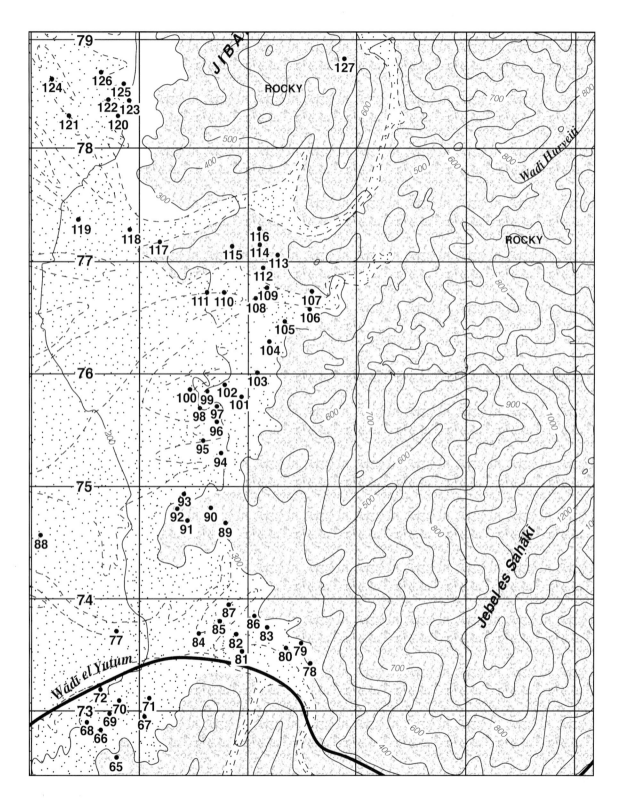

Fig. 4.40   *Aqaba Region (Region I), map 3 (Sites 65–72, 77–127).*

on a side. The stones are tightly packed together. The north segment measures 3.50 m in length, and it is preserved up to three courses high along the south end. The north end of the wall alignment has mostly tumbled. The site is located on an alluvial spur near the mouth of Wādī Yutum.

Site No.: 67 (fig. 4.40)
Field Site No.: 172
Site Name: None
Map Reference: 3049 III, K737
Location on 1:50,000: 3272945 N / 700155 E
Elevation: 220 m
Aerial Reference No.: IGN-78-JOR 12/100 - 1216
Site Size: 17 m N–S × 3 m E–W
Inventory Rating: 1
Pottery Collected: Total = 0 (No. of Indicators: 0 / No. Saved: 0)
Pottery Registration No(s).: None
Pottery Summary: N/A
Lithic Summary: N/A
Site Description: The site consists of two isolated graves on the side of low spurs near the mouth of Wādī Yutum. One grave is on the southwest side of a spur and the other is on the northeast side of the adjacent spur. The former is rectangular and measures 2 × 1.30 m. It is oriented N–S. The latter appears more elliptical and measures 2.60 × 2.30 m with roughly the same orientation as the first. A distance of 13 m separates the two graves. Both graves have been robbed.

Site No.: 68 (fig. 4.40)
Field Site No.: 171
Site Name: None
Map Reference: 3049 III, K737
Location on 1:50,000: 3272974 N / 699606 E
Elevation: 221 m
Aerial Reference No.: IGN-78-JOR 12/100 - 1216
Site Size: 10 m N–S × 2 m E–W
Inventory Rating: 0
Pottery Collected: Total = 0 (No. of Indicators: 0 / No. Saved: 0)
Pottery Registration No(s).: None
Pottery Summary: N/A
Lithic Summary: Indef. cultural-historic placement
Site Description: The site consists of a dense scatter of lithics extending down along the west face

of the slope below the railroad. Artifacts may not represent any locally stratified remains.

Site No.: 69 (fig. 4.40)
Field Site No.: 170
Site Name: None
Map Reference: 3049 III, K737
Location on 1:50,000: 3272985 N / 699752 E
Elevation: 220 m
Aerial Reference No.: IGN-78-JOR 12/100 - 1216
Site Size: 35 m N–S × 8 m E–W
Inventory Rating: 2
Pottery Collected: Total = 0 (No. of Indicators: 0 / No. Saved: 0)
Pottery Registration No(s).: None
Pottery Summary: N/A
Lithic Summary: Indef. cultural-historic placement
Site Description: The site consists of three stone rings (hut circles?) at the northern end of the site, a single stone ring or hut circle to the south, and one stone mound to the southeast. Each of the stone rings or hut circles measures ca. 2.50 m in diameter. Their walls are each a single course high and wide. Some of the stones are standing upright. Numerous lithics were found about 3 m to the north of the northernmost stone ring or hut circle. This site may be a cemetery.

Site No.: 70 (fig. 4.40)
Field Site No.: 169
Site Name: None
Map Reference: 3049 III, K737
Location on 1:50,000: 3273068 N / 699854 E
Elevation: 223 m
Aerial Reference No.: IGN-78-JOR 12/100 - 1216
Site Size: 27.70 m N–S × 37.50 m E–W
Inventory Rating: 2
Pottery Collected: Total = 32 (No. of Indicators: 2 / No. Saved: 17)
Pottery Registration No(s).: 22116–18, 22204–7, 22215–19, 22226–29, 22251
Pottery Summary: 8 Chalco/EB, 4 Umayyad (3 from 1 vessel), 18 Late Islamic (1 vessel/Gaza ware water jug), 2 UD
Lithic Summary: Indef. cultural-historic placement
Site Description: This is a small settlement where the SAAS recorded six distinct features. Feature 1 is a double stone circle or enclosure measuring

11m N–S × 6.50 m E–W, which is constructed of stones averaging ca. 0.35 m on a side. This structure is preserved up to three courses high in one area, and it is a single course wide. Both areas encircled are roughly the same size, although the eastern circle has been heavily eroded. The western circle contains two parallel inner walls projecting from the north face. These walls are small and measure 0.10 m high and wide and 1.90 m long. Situated on top of a spur 14.80 m east of Feature 1 is Feature 2, a small semicircular stone alignment measuring ca. 2.70 m in diameter. Many stones seem to have been robbed from the structure for the construction of some modern installations on the same spur. Feature 3 lies 12 m west and down the slope from Feature 2. This is a small stone ring or hut circle preserved up to three courses high and measuring 5 m N–S × 4 m E–W. A second stone ring or hut circle may have been appended to the structure but has since eroded. Feature 4 lies 9.30 m southeast of Feature 3. This is a large, semicircular structure measuring 6 m in diameter. The walls of the structure are preserved up to four courses high in some areas and one course wide. Features 5 and 6 are ca. 13.4 m southeast of Feature 4. The former is a small structure or hut circle that measures 3.20 m N–S × 3.60 m E–W. There is a linear course of boulders running in an E–W direction with a circular stone structure appended to its south face. This wall alignment, which is 2.50 m long and 2 m wide, is preserved a single course high and wide while the circular structure is preserved to at least three courses high and one–two courses wide. Feature 6 consists of a circular stone structure to the north of Feature 5 and measuring ca. 3 m in diameter. Its walls are preserved a single course high and wide.

Site No.: 71 (fig. 4.40)
Field Site No.: 180
Site Name: None
Map Reference: 3049 III, K737
Location on 1:50,000: 3273156 N / 700322 E
Elevation: 245 m
Aerial Reference No.: IGN-78-JOR 12/100 - 1216
Site Size: 2.60 m N–S × 0.25 m E–W
Inventory Rating: 2
Pottery Collected: Total = 0 (No. of Indicators: 0 / No. Saved: 0)

Pottery Registration No(s).: None
Pottery Summary: N/A
Lithic Summary: N/A
Site Description: The site consists of a single linear feature, which may be a grave. It is 2.60 m in length, up to two courses high, and one course wide. Also, it is oriented N–S.

Site No.: 72 (fig. 4.40)
Field Site No.: 162
Site Name: None
Map Reference: 3049 IV, K737
Location on 1:50,000: 3273140 N / 699698 E
Elevation: 205 m
Aerial Reference No.: IGN-78-JOR 12/100 - 1216
Site Size: 10 m N–S × 10 m E–W
Inventory Rating: 3
Pottery Collected: Total = 201 (No. of Indicators: 21 / No. Saved: 48)
Pottery Registration No(s).: 11578–89, 22327–62
Pottery Summary: 1 Iron (?), 24 ER/Nab, 153 ER/LR, 6 LR, 8 R/Byz, 3 EByz, 1 Modern, 5 UD, 2 Tiles
Lithic Summary: N/A
Site Description: The site, which is visible in the cut bank ca. 75 m east of the side road leading to Wādī Mulghān and ca. 100 m west of the railroad tracks, consists of a wall segment, four courses high, exposed in the cut bank. Another wall segment, which is ca. 1.50 m wide and two courses high, is exposed in the cut bank ca. 3 m further east. This wall would have joined the wall alignment visible on the alluvial fan surface above. Based on the exposure of the walls in the cut bank, it appears that the site is buried under ca. 0.50–0.90 m of fluvial deposits. A third wall alignment visible on the fan surface, ca. 5 m to the south, trends perpendicularly to the others. These wall alignments on the surface are two courses wide with rubble fill.

Site No.: 73 (fig. 4.39)
Field Site No.: 78
Site Name: None
Map Reference: 3049 III, K737
Location on 1:50,000: 3273367 N / 697663 E
Elevation: 130 m
Aerial Reference No.: IGN-78-JOR 12/100 - 1228
Site Size: 5 m N–S × 13 m E–W
Inventory Rating: 2

Pottery Collected: Total = 0 (No. of Indicators: 0 / No. Saved: 0)
Pottery Registration No(s).: None
Pottery Summary: N/A
Lithic Summary: N/A
Site Description: The site consists of a stone enclosure with a cleared center. The enclosure measures ca. 13 × 5 m.

Site No.: 74 (fig. 4.39)
Field Site No.: 81
Site Name: None
Map Reference: 3049 III, K737
Location on 1:50,000: 3273491 N / 697334 E
Elevation: 125 m
Aerial Reference No.: IGN-78-JOR 12/100 - 1228
Site Size: 2 m N–S × 4 m E–W
Inventory Rating: 0
Pottery Collected: Total = 113 (No. of Indicators: 8 / No. Saved: 14)
Pottery Registration No(s).: 6452–65
Pottery Summary: 113 LByz (2 vessels)
Lithic Summary: N/A
Site Description: The site consists of a pot-bust in a 4 × 2 m area south of an old drainage cut on the alluvial fan west of Wādī Yutum.

Site No.: 75 (fig. 4.39)
Field Site No.: 79
Site Name: None
Map Reference: 3049 III, K737
Location on 1:50,000: 3273562 N / 697634 E
Elevation: 125 m
Aerial Reference No.: IGN-78-JOR 12/100 - 1228
Site Size: 20 m N–S × 25 m E–W
Inventory Rating: 2
Pottery Collected: Total = 0 (No. of Indicators: 0 / No. Saved: 0)
Pottery Registration No(s).: None
Pottery Summary: N/A
Lithic Summary: N/A
Site Description: This is a rectangular structure measuring ca. 8 m on a side. The foundations are constructed of large cobbles (ca. 0.40 m on a side) with smaller stones piled on top. The interior of the structure is filled with sand. An area (5 × 2.50 m) cleared of stones is situated ca. 3 m southeast of the entrance into the structure. Also, two small

rock alignments cross small drainages west of the structure.

Site No.: 76 (fig. 4.39)
Field Site No.: 80
Site Name: None
Map Reference: 3049 III, K737
Location on 1:50,000: 3273673 N / 697430 E
Elevation: 125 m
Aerial Reference No.: IGN-78-JOR 12/100 - 1228
Site Size: 3 m N–S × 3 m E–W
Inventory Rating: 0
Pottery Collected: Total = 1 (No. of Indicators: 0 / No. Saved: 0)
Pottery Registration No(s).: None
Pottery Summary: 1 ER/Nab
Lithic Summary: Indef. cultural-historic placement
Site Description: This is a light lithic scatter (3 lithics/m²) where the SAAS found a single pottery sherd. The SAAS found these artifacts on an old cleared alluvial surface.

Site No.: 77 (fig. 4.40)
Field Site No.: 168
Site Name: None
Map Reference: 3049 III, K737
Location on 1:50,000: 3273594 N / 699789 E
Elevation: 194 m
Aerial Reference No.: IGN-78-JOR 12/100 - 1216
Site Size: 5.20 m N–S × 6 m E–W
Inventory Rating: 1
Pottery Collected: Total = 0 (No. of Indicators: 0 / No. Saved: 0)
Pottery Registration No(s).: None
Pottery Summary: N/A
Lithic Summary: N/A
Site Description: The site consists of a single circular stone structure in the wadi outwash. The walls are preserved a single course high and wide. The average stone size is 0.45 × 0.28 × 0.55 m. Within the center of the structure there are two large stones aligned E–W, and a possible entrance may exist in the east corner. The site lies adjacent to a cordoned off minefield.

Site No.: 78 (figs. 4.6, 4.40)
Field Site No.: 192
Site Name: None

Map Reference: 3049 III, K737
Location on 1:50,000: 3273420 N / 701525 E
Elevation: 295 m
Aerial Reference No.: IGN-78-JOR 12/100 - 1216
Site Size: 70 m N–S × 85 m E–W
Inventory Rating: 5
Pottery Collected: Total = 33 (No. of Indicators: 2 / No. Saved: 8)
Pottery Registration No(s).: 22489–96
Pottery Summary: 33 Chalco/EB
Lithic Summary: N/A
Site Description: This is a small settlement on a high spur above Wādī Yutum. The site consists of a complex of stone structures, including large and small stone rings and rectilinear structures. There are also apparent courtyards, large enclosures, and possible corridors providing access between structures. Beginning furthest up the slope to the northeast, there are two linear features that may be terraces ca. 8.60 m long, three courses high (ca. 0.60 m) and a single course wide (ca. 0.40 m). Ca. 4 m to the southwest there are several stone rings or hut circles constructed of tightly packed stones and preserved up to three courses high (ca. 0.60 m) and one course wide (ca. 0.30 m). The diameter of these stone rings or hut circles averages between 5 and 6 m. One contains an obvious entranceway marked by two large boulders set on either side. Its dimensions are 1.40 m high and 0.60 m wide. These stone rings or hut circles are all contiguous, sharing common walls on all sides. To the northwest, some seem to share a large enclosure or corral (7.20 × 4.50 m) demarcated by a single course of boulders, which are loosely spaced. Down the slope there begins a possible corridor (oriented NE–SW) on the south side of the settlement. This corridor is 15 m long and 3 m wide. In places it is lined with stones two–three courses high (ca. 0.60 m) and one course wide (0.30 m). At the northwest edge of the settlement, the stone rings tend to be smaller (ca. 4–5 m in diameter), though similar in construction. Some are ca. 2 m diameter. These also share common walls with no obvious room to negotiate between structures. One of these has a doorway similar to that described above. Further down the slope, some structures take on a more rectilinear aspect. There may be another corridor oriented perpendicular to the first and providing an intersection. It is 2 m

wide and oriented SE–NW. It spans a distance of ca. 5–6 m. Collapsed debris in this area is particularly dense. A courtyard (9 × 4.50 m) is shared by several circular structures here as well. Down the slope there is a large complex of smaller, contiguous stone rings or hut circles. These have mostly collapsed, but measure ca. 4–5 m in diameter. Some of the walls are preserved up to three courses high (0.50–0.60 m) and one course wide (0.30 m). There are about 15–20 of these structures. Construction in this area follows the contours of the slope. Up the slope and to the northeast structures are more often built into the hillside.

Site No.: 79 (figs. 4.6, 4.40)
Field Site No.: 193
Site Name: None
Map Reference: 3049 III, K737
Location on 1:50,000: 3273495 N / 701505 E
Elevation: 295 m
Aerial Reference No.: IGN-78-JOR 12/100 - 1216
Site Size: 30 m N–S × 50 m E–W
Inventory Rating: 4
Pottery Collected: Total = 5 (No. of Indicators: 0 / No. Saved: 4)
Pottery Registration No(s).: 22165–68
Pottery Summary: 5 Chalco/EB
Lithic Summary: Indef. cultural-historic placement
Site Description: The site consists of four large stone rings, possibly hut circles or enclosures, oriented roughly E–W and situated on a high alluvial spur overlooking Wādī Yutum. Down the slope, the westernmost stone ring or hut circle has a smaller circle appended to its east side. It is also partitioned on its east side into a separate compartment. The two middle circles, which are appended, have a smaller circle appended to their southeast sides. Size of the large circles is 6.80 m in diameter and size of the smaller circles is 3.50 m in diameter. Down the slope at the southwest edge of the site there is a figure-8 type structure situated on the edge of the ridge. It is poorly preserved (damaged caused mostly by erosion), but the doorway into the structure remains apparent and measures ca. 0.50 m wide. At the northwest edge of the site and oriented N–S across a small gully there is a linear stone alignment. It appears to be a retaining wall. It is nine courses high (1.40 m) and one course

wide (0.40 m). Construction is of tightly packed stones (average stone size is 0.25 m on a side). In the southwest area of the site is a small circular structure with its northern wall section built into the slope. The structure is constructed of boulders at the base packed with larger cobbles and topped off with flat large stones. The walls of the structure are preserved up to 10 courses high (1 m) and one course wide (0.30 m). In the northeast area of site are various linear wall alignments which seem to create corridors for navigating up the ridge towards the structures above. The entire site is extremely well-preserved. It is also in close spatial association with Site 78 (ca. 40 m to the south across the gully) and Site 80 (across another gully ca. 50 m to the north). The largest enclosure, in the middle of the site, has on its west side a small corridor projecting from its interior face. It is 1.50 m long and 0.50 m wide.

Site No.: 80 (figs. 4.6, 4.8. 4.9, 4.40)
Field Site No.: 164
Site Name: None
Map Reference: 3049 III, K737
Location on 1:50,000: 3273545 N / 701375 E
Elevation: 295 m
Aerial Reference No.: IGN-78-JOR 12/100 - 1216
Site Size: 60 m N–S × 70 m E–W
Inventory Rating: 5
Pottery Collected: Total = 127 (No. of Indicators: 13 / No. Saved: 18)
Pottery Registration No(s).: 24020–37
Pottery Summary: 126 Chalco/EB, 1 LB
Lithic Summary: Indef. cultural-historic placement
Site Description: The site consists of a series of rectilinear and circular stone structures, which average 7 m in diameter, situated on top of a high spur above Wādī Yutum. The former predominate. Generally, the structures are two courses (0.60 m) wide and three courses (0.80 m) high. The structures are badly damaged and appear mostly as stone tumble. Some walls, however, are apparent. Stone size averages 0.30 m on a side. Many structures share common walls. A geological dike bisects the site. Massive terrace walls, with standing stones six courses high, are located on the slopes above the site. Clandestine excavations, mostly small pits, have damaged the site. Some of

the debris from these pits has yielded much ashy soil, charred wood and other carbonized materials.

Site No.: 81 (figs. 4.37, 4.40)
Field Site No.: 165
Site Name: None
Map Reference: 3049 III, K737
Location on 1:50,000: 3273546 N / 700942 E
Elevation: 245 m
Aerial Reference No.: IGN-78-JOR 12/100 - 1216
Site Size: 6 m N–S × 11.70 m E–W
Inventory Rating: 3
Pottery Collected: Total = 0 (No. of Indicators: 0 / No. Saved: 0)
Pottery Registration No(s).: None
Pottery Summary: N/A
Lithic Summary: N/A
Site Description: The site consists of a rectangular structure or tower, oriented N–S, overlooking the mouth of Wādī Yutum. The stones that comprise the walls are massive — the largest measures 0.65 × 0.60 m (only the top face of the upper course is visible). The stones appear to be dressed ashlars. The eastern face of the structure measures at least ca. 6 m. A possible doorway can be seen in the middle of the south face. The west and north walls of the structure are mostly buried, indicated only by linear mounds of soil and tumble. Many of the stones of the structure have been robbed, apparently for the construction of the modern structures and entrenchments that cover the entire area.

Site No.: 82 (fig. 4.40)
Field Site No.: 167
Site Name: None
Map Reference: 3049 III, K737
Location on 1:50,000: 3273666 N / 700883 E
Elevation: 260 m
Aerial Reference No.: IGN-78-JOR 12/100 - 1216
Site Size: 5 m N–S × 63 m E–W
Inventory Rating: 2
Pottery Collected: Total = 0 (No. of Indicators: 0 / No. Saved: 0)
Pottery Registration No(s).: None
Pottery Summary: N/A
Lithic Summary: N/A
Site Description: The site consists of two figure-8 shaped stone structures on a small terrace along

the west face of a ridge extending toward Wādī Yutum. Both measure ca. 6 m N–S × 9.60 m E–W. Also, both are oriented roughly E–W, with possible entrances into the structures located in the west corners of each. The walls are preserved up to three courses high in some places, and are a single course wide (0.70 m). A space of about 10 m separates the structures. In the easternmost room of the larger structure, there is a smaller oval structure appended to the south wall. It is a single course high and wide and constructed of stones noticeably smaller than the stones of the main structure. This appendage measures 2.50 m long × 1.90 m wide. It seems likely that the whole structure functioned as a dwelling of sorts and the smaller appendage could have been an oven or storage area, or perhaps it is a secondary, intrusive grave. These structures are probably associated with the similar structure at Site 83 on the other side of the ridge. A modern trench intrudes on the site.

Site No.: 83 (fig. 4.40)
Field Site No.: 163
Site Name: None
Map Reference: 3049 III, K737
Location on 1:50,000: 3273648 N / 701107 E
Elevation: 265 m
Aerial Reference No.: IGN-78-JOR 12/100 - 1216
Site Size: 30 m N–S × 60 m E–W
Inventory Rating: 2
Pottery Collected: Total = 0 (No. of Indicators: 0 / No. Saved: 0)
Pottery Registration No(s).: None
Pottery Summary: N/A
Lithic Summary: N/A
Site Description: The site consists of seven isolated stone rings or hut circles, built mostly of granite boulders and distributed on different terraces along the ridge. On average, these measure 5 m in diameter. Average size of stones comprising standing walls is 0.60 × 0.60 × 0.40 m. The walls are mostly tumbled, but some preserved segments indicate these to be a single course wide and one–two courses in height. Some of the stone rings or hut circles exhibit entrances with one stone slab set upright on each side. Also, some join to form figure-8 type features (two of these were found). The walls of the northernmost of these abutting stone

rings or hut circles are comprised of stones spaced out instead of tightly packed. The diameter of the larger appended hut circle is roughly 10 m. Three smaller stone rings are also present, two within the eastern corners of two larger stone rings or hut circles and one appended to the interior face of the southernmost figure-8 structure. Their average size is 2 × 1.40 m. The stone rings or hut circles here may be domestic, but the larger appendage on each of the figure-8 structures probably served as corrals. Site has been slightly damaged by modern bulldozing.

Site No.: 84 (fig. 4.40)
Field Site No.: 60
Site Name: None
Map Reference: 3049 III, K737
Location on 1:50,000: 3273699 N / 700666 E
Elevation: 235 m
Aerial Reference No.: IGN-78-JOR 12/100 - 1215
Site Size: 3 m N–S × 3 m E–W
Inventory Rating: 3
Pottery Collected: Total = 0 (No. of Indicators: 0 / No. Saved: 0)
Pottery Registration No(s).: None
Pottery Summary: N/A
Lithic Summary: N/A
Site Description: This is an irregular stone mound cairn ca. 2 m in diameter and located ca. 350 m north of the highway through Wādī Yutum. Stones vary greatly in size (from 1 m to 0.20 m on a side). Two of the largest stones are set upright on either end. Cairn is in a drainage near a secondary track that winds up the alluvial fan. Site is ca. 50 m east of Site 85, and ca. 15 m lower in elevation.

Site No.: 85 (fig. 4.40)
Field Site No.: 59
Site Name: None
Map Reference: 3049 III, K737
Location on 1:50,000: 3273783 N / 700744 E
Elevation: 250 m
Aerial Reference No.: IGN-78-JOR 12/100 - 1215
Site Size: 30 m N–S × 10 m E–W
Inventory Rating: 2
Pottery Collected: Total = 0 (No. of Indicators: 0 / No. Saved: 0)
Pottery Registration No(s).: None

Pottery Summary: N/A
Lithic Summary: N/A
Site Description: The site consists of eight circular rock alignments or burials at the edge of an old/terraced alluvial fan ca. 350 m north of Wādī Yutum. These have an average diameter of 1.20 m. Some, however, are smaller with a diameter of only ca. 0.70 m. The area centered within each of the alignments has been cleared of stones.

Site No.: 86 (fig. 4.40)
Field Site No.: 166
Site Name: None
Map Reference: 3049 III, K737
Location on 1:50,000: 3273803 N / 701034 E
Elevation: 275 m
Aerial Reference No.: IGN-78-JOR 12/100 - 1216
Site Size: 62 m N–S × 12 m E–W
Inventory Rating: 2
Pottery Collected: Total = 0 (No. of Indicators: 0 / No. Saved: 0)
Pottery Registration No(s).: None
Pottery Summary: N/A
Lithic Summary: N/A
Site Description: The site consists of a set of two appended stone rings or hut circles set ca. 50 m apart. Both structures have a main stone circle ca. 3.70–4.50 m in diameter (measured from the inner face), and a second abutting circular feature that shares a common wall. The appended feature is shaped more like a teardrop. The stones, which are undressed, measure ca. 0.30 m on a side. The northernmost structure has a smaller wall alignment projecting ca. 1.10 m from the outer face of the south wall of the larger circular feature.

Site No.: 87 (fig. 4.40)
Field Site No.: 58
Site Name: None
Map Reference: 3049 III, K737
Location on 1:50,000: 3273924 N / 700912 E
Elevation: 280 m
Aerial Reference No.: IGN-78-JOR 12/100 - 1215
Site Size: 1 m N–S × 1 m E–W
Inventory Rating: 3
Pottery Collected: Total = 0 (No. of Indicators: 0 / No. Saved: 0)
Pottery Registration No(s).: None

Pottery Summary: N/A
Lithic Summary: N/A
Site Description: This is a small stone ring, less than 1 m in diameter, on an old alluvial fan surface.

Site No.: 88 (fig. 4.40)
Field Site No.: 179
Site Name: None
Map Reference: 3049 III, K737
Location on 1:50,000: 3274497 N / 698908 E
Elevation: 166 m
Aerial Reference No.: IGN-78-JOR 12/100 - 1216
Site Size: 100 m N–S × 250 m E–W
Inventory Rating: 0
Pottery Collected: Total = 0 (No. of Indicators: 0 / No. Saved: 0)
Pottery Registration No(s).: None
Pottery Summary: N/A (site destroyed)
Lithic Summary: N/A
Site Description: A large complex of (apparent) stone rings or hut circles were discovered through an analysis of aerial photos dated 1978. Since that time, bulldozer activity has destroyed the area. These stone rings or hut circles were most likely related to the Chalcolithic/Early Bronze Age settlement that extends from Tell Maqaṣṣ to the mouth of Wādī Yutum. Unfortunately, despite intensive coverage of the area, not one of the structures could be found.

Site No.: 89 (fig. 4.40)
Field Site No.: 64
Site Name: None
Map Reference: 3049 III, K737
Location on 1:50,000: 3274585 N / 700764 E
Elevation: 305 m
Aerial Reference No.: IGN-78-JOR 12/100 - 1215
Site Size: 3 m N–S × 3.50 m E–W
Inventory Rating: 3
Pottery Collected: Total = 0 (No. of Indicators: 0 / No. Saved: 0)
Pottery Registration No(s).: None
Pottery Summary: N/A
Lithic Summary: N/A
Site Description: This is a cave or rockshelter. A well-constructed stone wall (ca. 0.50 m wide and 0.60 m high) encloses the entrance, with a length of 2 m. The opening into the site is 3.50 m wide. The

height of the cave is 1.50 m, and the soil within the cave is fine and powdery with some ash.

Site No.: 90 (fig. 4.40)
Field Site No.: 63
Site Name: None
Map Reference: 3049 III, K737
Location on 1:50,000: 3274739 N / 700632 E
Elevation: 315 m
Aerial Reference No.: IGN-78-JOR 12/100 - 1215
Site Size: 20 m N–S × 20 m E–W
Inventory Rating: 4
Pottery Collected: Total = 0 (No. of Indicators: 0 / No. Saved: 0)
Pottery Registration No(s).: None
Pottery Summary: N/A
Lithic Summary: N/A
Site Description: The site consists of four stone walls, possibly a structure, constructed on a steep slope. One wall is semicircular, measuring ca. 2.30 m in diameter and 0.70 m high. Its walls are 0.30 m wide. Another is more linear and built in a drainage cut. Its walls are 0.50 m high and 0.30 m wide. A large pit is dug into the surface behind this wall. The other smaller wall alignments lie further up the slope. The purpose of these wall alignments remains unclear.

Site No.: 91 (fig. 4.40)
Field Site No.: 62
Site Name: None
Map Reference: 3049 III, K737
Location on 1:50,000: 3274784 N / 700464 E
Elevation: 295 m
Aerial Reference No.: IGN-78-JOR 12/100 - 1215
Site Size: 5 m N–S × 5 m E–W
Inventory Rating: 3
Pottery Collected: Total = 3 (No. of Indicators: 0 / No. Saved: 1)
Pottery Registration No(s).: 2610
Pottery Summary: 3 LByz (1 vessel)
Lithic Summary: N/A
Site Description: This is a stone ring or hut circle, ca. 5 m in diameter, which consists of a single row of stones set a one course high. The average stone size is 0.35 × 0.30 × 0.15 m.

Site No.: 92 (fig. 4.40)
Field Site No.: 65
Site Name: None
Map Reference: 3049 III, K737
Location on 1:50,000: 3274845 N / 700397 E
Elevation: 270 m
Aerial Reference No.: IGN-78-JOR 12/100 - 1215
Site Size: 3 m N–S × 3 m E–W
Inventory Rating: 2
Pottery Collected: Total = 0 (No. of Indicators: 0 / No. Saved: 0)
Pottery Registration No(s).: None
Pottery Summary: N/A
Lithic Summary: N/A
Site Description: This is a stone mound or cairn measuring ca. 3 m in diameter.

Site No.: 93 (fig. 4.40)
Field Site No.: 67
Site Name: None
Map Reference: 3049 III, K737
Location on 1:50,000: 3274915 N / 700401 E
Elevation: 265 m
Aerial Reference No.: IGN-78-JOR 12/100 - 1215
Site Size: 15 m N–S × 20 m E–W
Inventory Rating: 2
Pottery Collected: Total = 0 (No. of Indicators: 0 / No. Saved: 0)
Pottery Registration No(s).: None
Pottery Summary: N/A
Lithic Summary: N/A
Site Description: This is a rock alignment consisting of a single row of stones enclosing the bottom portion of a small alluvial fan in an area of 10 m N–S × 15 m E–W. The area enclosed is not cleared of stones.

Site No.: 94 (fig. 4.40)
Field Site No.: 119
Site Name: None
Map Reference: 3049 III, K737
Location on 1:50,000: 3275312 N / 700847 E
Elevation: 310 m
Aerial Reference No.: IGN-78-JOR 12/100 - 1214
Site Size: 2 m N–S × 6.50 m E–W
Inventory Rating: 3
Pottery Collected: Total = 0 (No. of Indicators: 0 / No. Saved: 0)

Pottery Registration No(s).: None
Pottery Summary: N/A
Lithic Summary: N/A
Site Description: This is a short segment of a stone wall measuring 2 m long × 0.20 m wide × 0.35 m high. Ca. 6 m further east there seems to be a similar segment of a stone wall running parallel to the first.

Site No.: 95 (fig. 4.40)
Field Site No.: 123
Site Name: None
Map Reference: 3049 III, K737
Location on 1:50,000: 3275370 N / 700629 E
Elevation: 270 m
Aerial Reference No.: IGN-78-JOR 12/100 - 1214
Site Size: 4 m N–S × 4 m E–W
Inventory Rating: 2
Pottery Collected: Total = 0 (No. of Indicators: 0 / No. Saved: 0)
Pottery Registration No(s).: None
Pottery Summary: N/A
Lithic Summary: N/A
Site Description: This is a very small cairn measuring 1 m in diameter and 1 m in high. The cairn is surrounded by a stone circle with a well-defined alignment and extends 0.65 m from the base of the cairn. The site is located on an alluvial fan ca. 100 m southeast of an isolated ridge between Wādī Yutum and Wādī Mulghān.

Site No.: 96 (fig. 4.40)
Field Site No.: 120
Site Name: None
Map Reference: 3049 III, K737
Location on 1:50,000: 3275503 N / 700705 E
Elevation: 300 m
Aerial Reference No.: IGN-78-JOR 12/100 - 1214
Site Size: 3 m N–S × 3 m E–W
Inventory Rating: 2
Pottery Collected: Total = 0 (No. of Indicators: 0 / No. Saved: 0)
Pottery Registration No(s).: None
Pottery Summary: N/A
Lithic Summary: N/A
Site Description: This is a single stone ring, perhaps a grave, with a diameter of ca. 3 m. The interior of the ring is slightly deflated by ca. 0.05 m.

Site No.: 97 (fig. 4.40)
Field Site No.: 121
Site Name: None
Map Reference: 3049 III, K737
Location on 1:50,000: 3275627 N / 700675 E
Elevation: 293 m
Aerial Reference No.: IGN-78-JOR 12/100 - 1214
Site Size: 4 m N–S × 3 m E–W
Inventory Rating: 2
Pottery Collected: Total = 0 (No. of Indicators: 0 / No. Saved: 0)
Pottery Registration No(s).: None
Pottery Summary: N/A
Lithic Summary: N/A
Site Description: This is a rockshelter formed by a large eroded boulder and open to the southeast. The opening is ca. 1.40 m high and 2 m wide. The depth of the rockshelter is 1.20 m. There is a stone wall extending forward from the opening on the southwest side. It is ca. 3 m in length, 0.30 m wide, and 0.40 m high.

Site No.: 98 (fig. 4.40)
Field Site No.: 122
Site Name: None
Map Reference: 3049 III, K737
Location on 1:50,000: 3275662 N / 700629 E
Elevation: 290 m
Aerial Reference No.: IGN-78-JOR 12/100 - 1214
Site Size: 34 m N–S × 22 m E–W
Inventory Rating: 3
Pottery Collected: Total = 38 (No. of Indicators: 0 / No. Saved: 6)
Pottery Registration No(s).: 6474–79
Pottery Summary: 38 R/Byz
Lithic Summary: N/A
Site Description: The site consists of two stone mounds (ca. 3–4 m in diameter) and numerous rock alignments. Only one of the rock alignments, ca. 14 m southwest of the stone mounds, was distinct enough to map. It is two courses wide (ca. 0.50 m), a single course high, and 5 m long. The absence of any areas cleared of stones suggests that this is probably not a campsite. The nature and purpose of this site remains undetermined.

Site No.: 99 (fig. 4.40)
Field Site No.: 52
Site Name: None
Map Reference: 3049 III, K737
Location on 1:50,000: 3275676 N / 700623 E
Elevation: 325 m
Aerial Reference No.: IGN-78-JOR 12/100 - 1214
Site Size: 1.50 m N–S × 1 m E–W
Inventory Rating: 2
Pottery Collected: Total = 0 (No. of Indicators: 0 / No. Saved: 0)
Pottery Registration No(s).: None
Pottery Summary: N/A
Lithic Summary: N/A
Site Description: This is a small stone circle or cairn (1 × 1.50 m) on top of a small granite ridge projecting up toward the alluvial fan south of Wādī Mulghān. The cairn is constructed of angular granite rocks (average stone size is 0.25 × 0.25 × 0.30 m). The center of the cairn is filled with smaller rocks. The cairn is 0.68 m high.

Site No.: 100 (fig. 4.40)
Field Site No.: 53
Site Name: None
Map Reference: 3049 III, K737
Location on 1:50,000: 3275757 N / 700485 E
Elevation: 279 m
Aerial Reference No.: IGN-78-JOR 12/100 - 1214
Site Size: 1.50 m N–S × 2 m E–W
Inventory Rating: 2
Pottery Collected: Total = 1 (No. of Indicators: 1 / No. Saved: 1)
Pottery Registration No(s).: 1478
Pottery Summary: 1 LByz/Umayyad
Lithic Summary: N/A
Site Description: The site consists of a single oval burial ca. 1.50 × 2 m on an alluvial fan south of Wādī Mulghān.

Site No.: 101 (fig. 4.40)
Field Site No.: 50
Site Name: None
Map Reference: 3049 III, K737
Location on 1:50,000: 3275769 N / 700756 E
Elevation: 315 m
Aerial Reference No.: IGN-78-JOR 12/100 - 1214
Site Size: 3 m N–S × 3 m E–W

Inventory Rating: 2
Pottery Collected: Total = 0 (No. of Indicators: 0 / No. Saved: 0)
Pottery Registration No(s).: None
Pottery Summary: N/A
Lithic Summary: N/A
Site Description: This is a circular stone mound or cairn, ca. 3 m in diameter, with a cleared center. The site is located at the center of an alluvial terrace southwest of the mouth of Wādī Mulghān.

Site No.: 102 (fig. 4.40)
Field Site No(s).: 49 & 51
Site Name: None
Map Reference: 3049 III, K737
Location on 1:50,000: 3275764 N / 700694 E
Elevation: 303 m
Aerial Reference No.: IGN-78-JOR 12/100 - 1214
Site Size: 5 m N–S × 6 m E–W
Inventory Rating: 2
Pottery Collected: Total = 0 (No. of Indicators: 0 / No. Saved: 0)
Pottery Registration No(s).: None
Pottery Summary: N/A
Lithic Summary: N/A
Site Description: This is a cemetery consisting of four stone graves on an alluvial fan between Wādī Mulghān and Wādī Yutum. Two graves are elongated, measuring ca. 1.45 × 2.40 m, and one of these has capstones. The other two are circular, measuring ca. 1 m in diameter.

Site No.: 103 (fig. 4.40)
Field Site No.: 48
Site Name: None
Map Reference: 3049 III, K737
Location on 1:50,000: 3276036 N / 701009 E
Elevation: 338 m
Aerial Reference No.: IGN-78-JOR 12/100 - 1214
Site Size: 10 m N–S × 5 m E–W
Inventory Rating: 4
Pottery Collected: Total = 22 (No. of Indicators: 4 / No. Saved: 7)
Pottery Registration No(s).: 1471–77
Pottery Summary: 21 R/Byz, 1 UD
Lithic Summary: N/A
Site Description: The site consists of a rectilinear structure (ca. 3 × 10 m), well-constructed with mas-

sive stone walls. The walls are preserved three–four courses high, 0.80 m wide (two courses with rubble fill). The site has been largely destroyed by erosion.

Site No.: 104 (fig. 4.40)
Field Site No.: 54
Site Name: None
Map Reference: 3049 III, K737
Location on 1:50,000: 3276257 N / 701115 E
Elevation: 335 m
Aerial Reference No.: IGN-78-JOR 12/100 - 1214
Site Size: 65 m N–S × 20 m E–W
Inventory Rating: 3
Pottery Collected: Total = 39 (No. of Indicators: 9 / No. Saved: 14)
Pottery Registration No(s).: 1457–70
Pottery Summary: 9 Byz (2 Amphorae=Egyptian), 27 R/Byz, 3 Early Islamic (Mahesh ware)
Lithic Summary: N/A
Site Description: The site consists of a complex of structures and wall alignments in an area of ca. 20 × 65 m on an old alluvial fan surface southeast of Wādī Mulghān. The largest structure, elevated on the fan surface above the others, measures ca. 14 m N–S × 5 m E–W. The southeast wall of the structure has largely eroded, although segments are buried under sediments washing down the fan. The same applies to the south and east corners. The walls that are visible, however, are two courses wide (ca. 0.70 m). Several other wall alignments and circular stone structures are visible on the fan surface down the slope to the northeast.

Site No.: 105 (fig. 4.40)
Field Site No.: 57
Site Name: None
Map Reference: 3049 III, K737
Location on 1:50,000: 3276370 N / 701360 E
Elevation: 250 m
Aerial Reference No.: IGN-78-JOR 12/100 - 1214
Site Size: 1 m N–S × 15 m E–W
Inventory Rating: 2
Pottery Collected: Total = 0 (No. of Indicators: 0 / No. Saved: 0)
Pottery Registration No(s).: None
Pottery Summary: N/A
Lithic Summary: N/A
Site Description: The site consists of a stone wall,

two courses wide (0.60 m) and a single course high. It is oriented NE–SW and extends for 8 m. Another wall segment (only 1.50 m in length) is visible 5 m to the east.

Site No.: 106 (fig. 4.40)
Field Site No.: 32
Site Name: None
Map Reference: 3049 III, K737
Location on 1:50,000: 3276452 N / 701630 E
Elevation: 360 m
Aerial Reference No.: IGN-78-JOR 12/100 - 1214
Site Size: 10 m N–S × 44 m E–W
Inventory Rating: 3
Pottery Collected: Total = 0 (No. of Indicators: 0 / No. Saved: 0)
Pottery Registration No(s).: None
Pottery Summary: N/A
Lithic Summary: N/A
Site Description: This is a large enclosure wall measuring ca. 0.75 m wide (two courses) and extending 44 m around a small terrace. The wall is well-constructed and possibly mortared with mud. From the eastern cliff-face, the wall extends to the west ca. 7 m to a small entrance (0.90 m wide). It then continues 15 m before curving southwest and continuing another 20 m. The area enclosed by the wall contains about five hearths which appear to be modern.

Site No.: 107 (fig. 4.40)
Field Site No.: 31
Site Name: None
Map Reference: 3049 III, K737
Location on 1:50,000: 3276590 N / 701640 E
Elevation: 360 m
Aerial Reference No.: IGN-78-JOR 12/100 - 1214
Site Size: 50 m N–S × 35 m E–W
Inventory Rating: 3
Pottery Collected: Total = 22 (No. of Indicators: 3 / No. Saved: 9)
Pottery Registration No(s).: 1202–10
Pottery Summary: 3 ER/Nab, 16 R/Byz, 2 LByz, 1 UD
Lithic Summary: N/A
Site Description: The site consists of a rectilinear structure (4 × 4 m), which has the appearance of sediment traps, a three-sided rectilinear structure

that opens to the north, and various other miscellaneous wall alignments. The foundation stones of the structures measure on average 0.80 × 0.40 m. The walls are two courses wide (ca. 0.80 m) and are aligned perpendicularly to the direction of the wadi flow. The more ephemeral looking walls (surface rock alignments) also run perpendicularly to the direction of the wadi. One wall alignment (17 m long and two courses wide) makes a corner with the three-sided structure and extends ca. 17 m to the west. One retaining wall (20 × 0.80 m) extends in the direction of the wadi. The 4 × 4 m structure trends westward about 4 m south of the north end of this wall alignment.

Site No.: 108 (fig. 4.40)
Field Site No.: 41
Site Name: None
Map Reference: 3049 III, K737
Location on 1:50,000: 3276584 N / 701040 E
Elevation: 319 m
Aerial Reference No.: IGN-78-JOR 12/100 - 1213
Site Size: 5 m N–S × 5 m E–W
Inventory Rating: 2
Pottery Collected: Total = 0 (No. of Indicators: 0 / No. Saved: 0)
Pottery Registration No(s).: None
Pottery Summary: N/A
Lithic Summary: N/A
Site Description: This is a single semicircular structure on an alluvial terrace southwest of Wādī Mulghān. The structure is 4 m in diameter and opens to the southeast. The walls are ca. 0.90 m wide and 0.70 m high. The entrance is 1.27 m wide.

Site No.: 109 (fig. 4.40)
Field Site No.: 42
Site Name: None
Map Reference: 3049 III, K737
Location on 1:50,000: 3276652 N / 701112 E
Elevation: 330 m
Aerial Reference No.: IGN-78-JOR 12/100 - 1213
Site Size: 4 m N–S × 6 m E–W
Inventory Rating: 2
Pottery Collected: Total = 0 (No. of Indicators: 0 / No. Saved: 0)
Pottery Registration No(s).: None
Pottery Summary: N/A

Lithic Summary: N/A
Site Description: This is a nomadic camp consisting of a rectangular cleared area (ca. 6 × 4 m). Lengthwise, the orientation is 248 degrees. Also, the stones cleared from the camp appear to be aligned along the perimeter of the rectangular area. Two small stone circles or hearths lie within the clearings.

Site No.: 110 (fig. 4.40)
Field Site No.: 40
Site Name: None
Map Reference: 3049 III, K737
Location on 1:50,000: 3276660 N / 700806 E
Elevation: 310 m
Aerial Reference No.: IGN-78-JOR 12/100 - 1213
Site Size: 15 m N–S × 40 m E–W
Inventory Rating: 1
Pottery Collected: Total = 8 (No. of Indicators: 0 / No. Saved: 2)
Pottery Registration No(s).: 1211–12
Pottery Summary: 8 LByz (1 vessel)
Lithic Summary: N/A
Site Description: This is a cemetery consisting of ca. 16 graves on a terraced island on an alluvial fan southwest of Wādī Mulghān. Most of the graves are elongated, measuring ca. 2 × 1 m, and oriented NW–SE (with some variance). Two of these burials are circular stone mounds measuring ca. 1 m in diameter. The elongated graves have capstones.

Site No.: 111 (fig. 4.40)
Field Site No.: 39
Site Name: None
Map Reference: 3049 III, K737
Location on 1:50,000: 3276650 N / 700648 E
Elevation: 300 m
Aerial Reference No.: IGN-78-JOR 12/100 - 1213
Site Size: 3 m N–S × 3 m E–W
Inventory Rating: 1
Pottery Collected: Total = 0 (No. of Indicators: 0 / No. Saved: 0)
Pottery Registration No(s).: None
Pottery Summary: N/A
Lithic Summary: N/A
Site Description: This is a robbed stone mound or burial on an alluvial terrace near Wādī Mulghān. Bone fragments are present in the debris surrounding the mound.

Site No.: 112 (fig. 4.40)
Field Site No.: 43
Site Name: SAAR Site 6
Map Reference: 3049 III, K737
Location on 1:50,000: 3276825 N / 701179 E
Elevation: 330 m
Aerial Reference No.: IGN-78-JOR 12/100 - 1213
Site Size: 20 m N–S × 65 m E–W
Inventory Rating: 3
Pottery Collected: Total = 0 (No. of Indicators: 0 / No. Saved: 0)
Pottery Registration No(s).: None
Pottery Summary: N/A
Lithic Summary: N/A
Site Description: The site consists of a series of nine structures on a small alluvial fan southwest of Wādī Mulghān. Four of these are open rectangular structures and the remaining are semicircular. The diameter of the semicircular structures varies between 2.50 and 3 m, while the average dimensions of the rectangular structures are 2 × 2 m (only one measures 3 × 4 m). Their walls are two courses wide (ca. 0.70 m) with rubble fill. The structures are aligned on a bearing of 258 degrees. Also, the structures that extend along the south side of the alluvial fan open to the northeast while those on the north side open to the southwest.

Site No.: 113 (figs. 4.25, 4.40)
Field Site No(s).: 44 & 45
Site Name: SAAR Site 7
Map Reference: 3049 III, K737
Location on 1:50,000: 3277060 N / 701150 E
Elevation: 320 m
Aerial Reference No.: IGN-78-JOR 12/100 - 1212
Site Size: 30 m N–S × 40 m E–W
Inventory Rating: 3
Pottery Collected: Total = 113 (No. of Indicators: 7 / No. Saved: 12)
Pottery Registration No(s).: 1217–28
Pottery Summary: 6 ER/Nab (1 TS), 2 LR, 105 ER/LR (1 ER Lamp)
Lithic Summary: N/A
Site Description: The site consists of four features. Feature 1 is a ruined structure, possibly a watchtower, which appears as a mound of collapsed stones covering an area of ca. 15 × 15 m. Segments of the outer facing of the exterior wall are visible,

but these do not allow for an accurate estimation of the overall size or construction of the feature. Adjacent to the south wall, there is evidence for later reuse of the stones, perhaps for local burials. Feature 2 is a ruined structure immediately southwest of Feature 1. Only the foundation stones of its southeast and northeast corners and segments along the east (ca. 7 m in length) and north walls are preserved. The remainder of the surface is littered with stones and cobbles. Several larger stones align along the outside edge of the northeast corner. Feature 3 is a cemetery consisting of a series of burials extending across a saddle between two ridges overlooking Wādī Mulghān. The graves measure between ca. 1 × 8 m to 2 × 1.30 m and most are oriented NW–SE. The graves are oblong stone alignments with cleared centers, although one is circular (ca. 1.30 m in diameter). Two of the oblong graves have capstones. Also, there are additional wall foundations of a structure (Feature 4) at the site that measure ca. 3.50 × 1.50 m.

Site No.: 114 (fig. 4.40)
Field Site No(s).: 55 & 56
Site Name: None
Map Reference: 3049 III, K737
Location on 1:50,000: 3277101 N / 701060 E
Elevation: 323 m
Aerial Reference No.: IGN-78-JOR 12/100 - 1212
Site Size: 15 m N–S × 45 m E–W
Inventory Rating: 2
Pottery Collected: Total = 7 (No. of Indicators: 0 / No. Saved: 3)
Pottery Registration No(s).: 1479–81
Pottery Summary: 1 LByz, 1 Modern, 5 UD
Lithic Summary: N/A
Site Description: This is a cemetery that consists of a series of burials extending along a saddle between two ridges overlooking the primary drainage of Wādī Mulghān. The graves measure between ca. 1 × 8 m to 2 × 1.30 m and most are oriented NW–SE. The graves are oblong stone alignments with cleared centers, although one is circular (ca. 1.30 m in diameter). Two of the oblong graves have capstones. Also, there are the wall foundations of a structure at the site that measure ca. 1.50 m N–S × 3.50 m E–W. The walls of the structure are two courses wide (0.75 m) and preserved a single

course high. Only the south and west walls are visible. Ca. 67 m to the south, on a low lying spur, there are two additional oblong graves.

Site No.: 115 (fig. 4.40)
Field Site No.: 47
Site Name: None
Map Reference: 3049 III, K737
Location on 1:50,000: 3277122 N / 700926 E
Elevation: 360 m
Aerial Reference No.: IGN-78-JOR 12/100 - 1212
Site Size: 16 m N–S × 30 m E–W
Inventory Rating: 2
Pottery Collected: Total = 33 (No. of Indicators: 6 / No. Saved: 11)
Pottery Registration No(s).: 1229–39
Pottery Summary: 33 ER/Nab (most from Aqaba)
Lithic Summary: N/A
Site Description: The site consists of a series of ca. four structures or installations on the southeast slope of the ridge that parallels the mouth of Wādī Mulghān. These are open-rectangular structures ca. 2.50 m wide. The orientation of the open faces for each is not uniform. Their walls are a single course wide (ca. 0.38 m) and few are more than a single course high, although one is preserved up to four courses high. There is a terraced platform on the slope below.

Site No.: 116 (fig. 4.40)
Field Site No.: 46
Site Name: None
Map Reference: 3049 III, K737
Location on 1:50,000: 3277241 N / 701010 E
Elevation: 340 m
Aerial Reference No.: IGN-78-JOR 12/100 - 1212
Site Size: 4 m N–S × 3 m E–W
Inventory Rating: 1
Pottery Collected: Total = 5 (No. of Indicators: 2 / No. Saved: 4)
Pottery Registration No(s).: 1213–16
Pottery Summary: 5 ER/Nab
Lithic Summary: N/A
Site Description: This is a light sherd scatter associated with what appears to be a small, collapsed stone structure (stone mound) at the summit of a ridge above and north of Site 113. The ruined structure measures ca. 3 m on a side.

Site No.: 117 (fig. 4.40)
Field Site No.: 82
Site Name: None
Map Reference: 3049 III, K737
Location on 1:50,000: 3277136 N / 700109 E
Elevation: 250 m
Aerial Reference No.: IGN-78-JOR 12/100 - 1211
Site Size: 3 m N–S × 13 m E–W
Inventory Rating: 2
Pottery Collected: Total = 0 (No. of Indicators: 0 / No. Saved: 0)
Pottery Registration No(s).: None
Pottery Summary: N/A
Lithic Summary: N/A
Site Description: The site consists of three burials, each measuring ca. 1–2 × 1 m, on a high alluvial terrace of Wādī Mulghān.

Site No.: 118 (fig. 4.40)
Field Site No.: 83
Site Name: None
Map Reference: 3049 III, K737
Location on 1:50,000: 3277195 N / 699968 E
Elevation: 242 m
Aerial Reference No.: IGN-78-JOR 12/100 - 1211
Site Size: 4 m N–S × 2.50 m E–W
Inventory Rating: 3
Pottery Collected: Total = 0 (No. of Indicators: 0 / No. Saved: 0)
Pottery Registration No(s).: None
Pottery Summary: N/A
Lithic Summary: N/A
Site Description: The site consists of two small stone mounds or cairns on the north bank and at the mouth of Wādī Mulghān. One measures ca. 1.50 m in diameter, while the second is more elongated and measures ca. 1.50 × 3 m.

Site No.: 119 (fig. 4.40)
Field Site No.: 84
Site Name: None
Map Reference: 3049 III, K737
Location on 1:50,000: 3277251 N / 699442 E
Elevation: 210 m
Aerial Reference No.: IGN-78-JOR 12/100 - 1235
Site Size: 1 m N–S × 2 m E–W
Inventory Rating: 3
Pottery Collected: Total = 0 (No. of Indicators: 0

/ No. Saved: 0)
Pottery Registration No(s).: None
Pottery Summary: N/A
Lithic Summary: N/A
Site Description: This is a stone mound or cairn, measuring ca. 2 × 1 m, near the mouth of Wādī Mulghān.

Site No.: 120 (figs. 4.40, 4.41)
Field Site No.: 85
Site Name: None
Map Reference: 3049 III, K737
Location on 1:50,000: 3278330 N / 699705 E
Elevation: 175 m
Aerial Reference No.: IGN-78-JOR 12/100 - 1211
Site Size: 35 m N–S × 40 m E–W
Inventory Rating: 2
Pottery Collected: Total = 0 (No. of Indicators: 0
/ No. Saved: 0)
Pottery Registration No(s).: None
Pottery Summary: N/A
Lithic Summary: N/A
Site Description: This is a campsite consisting of seven roughly circular areas cleared of stones. The diameter of the cleared areas varies from 4–5 m. A single cleared area is partially lined with a segment of a poorly constructed wall measuring ca. 2 × 0.30 m. The wall appears mostly as piled rubble. There are also five small rock piles (ca. 0.70–1 m in diameter) spread out across the area.

Site No.: 121 (figs. 4.40, 4.41)
Field Site No.: 91
Site Name: None
Map Reference: 3049 III, K737
Location on 1:50,000: 3278325 N / 699245 E
Elevation: 155 m
Aerial Reference No.: IGN-78-JOR 12/100 - 1235
Site Size: 20 m N–S × 31 m E–W
Inventory Rating: 2
Pottery Collected: Total = 16 (No. of Indicators: 4
/ No. Saved: 8)
Pottery Registration No(s).: 6625–32
Pottery Summary: 16 ER/Nab (at least 1 sherd from Aqaba)
Lithic Summary: N/A
Site Description: This appears to be a bedouin campsite on an old alluvial surface northwest of Wādī Mulghān. There are two large areas cleared

of stones that run parallel to one another and separated by 0.50 m. One measures ca. 11 × 3 m while the other measures ca. 7 × 1 m. Stones are aligned at each end of the cleared areas. To the south and on the same surface there is a stone ring (ca. 0.90 × 1.60 m), a stone mound (ca. 3 m in diameter), and an oval rock alignment that measures ca. 2.25 × 3 m.

Site No.: 122 (figs. 4.40, 4.41)
Field Site No.: 86
Site Name: None
Map Reference: 3049 III, K737
Location on 1:50,000: 3278451 N / 699714 E
Elevation: 165 m
Aerial Reference No.: IGN-78-JOR 12/100 - 1211
Site Size: 5 m N–S × 5 m E–W
Inventory Rating: 2
Pottery Collected: Total = 0 (No. of Indicators: 0
/ No. Saved: 0)
Pottery Registration No(s).: None
Pottery Summary: N/A
Lithic Summary: N/A
Site Description: This is a stone mound or burial cairn measuring ca. 5 × 5 m. It is preserved to a height of ca. 1 m. Upright stone slabs line the partially robbed interior of the cairn in a rectangular alignment measuring ca. 1.50 × 0.80 m.

Site No.: 123 (figs. 4.40, 4.41)
Field Site No.: 87
Site Name: None
Map Reference: 3049 III, K737
Location on 1:50,000: 3278583 N / 699889 E
Elevation: 195 m
Aerial Reference No.: IGN-78-JOR 12/100 - 1211
Site Size: 11 m N–S × 7 m E–W
Inventory Rating: 3
Pottery Collected: Total = 0 (No. of Indicators: 0
/ No. Saved: 0)
Pottery Registration No(s).: None
Pottery Summary: N/A
Lithic Summary: Indef. cultural-historic placement
Site Description: This is a large enclosure or corral cleared of large stones on an older alluvial surface north of Wādī ez-Zibliya and north of the Wādī Mulghān fan complex. Some of the stones along the perimeter are standing upright. The site overlooks an active drainage channel.

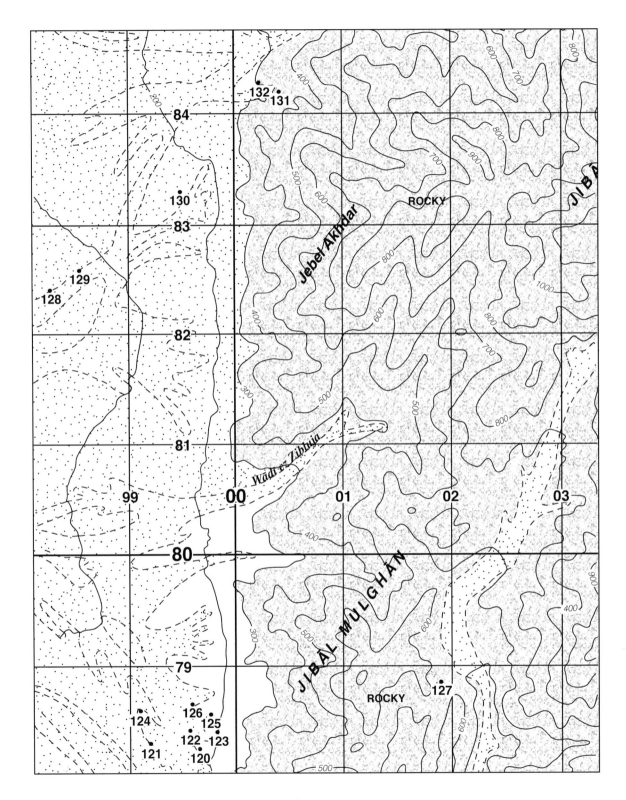

Fig. 4.41   *Aqaba Region (Region I), map 4 (Sites 120–132).*

Site No.: 124 (figs. 4.40, 4.41)
Field Site No.: 90
Site Name: None
Map Reference: 3049 III, K737
Location on 1:50,000: 3278585 N / 699141 E
Elevation: 145 m
Aerial Reference No.: IGN-78-JOR 12/100 - 1235
Site Size: 28 m N–S × 22 m E–W
Inventory Rating: 0
Pottery Collected: Total = 5 (No. of Indicators: 0 / No. Saved: 2)
Pottery Registration No(s).: 6623–24
Pottery Summary: 1 ER/Nab, 4 Early Islamic (1 vessel glazed)
Lithic Summary: Indef. cultural-historic placement
Site Description: The site consists of wall alignments, partially destroyed, that appear to have comprised a single structure measuring ca. 10 × 13 m. The walls seem to be two courses wide (0.60 m) and a single course high. Adjacent to the west wall there is what appears to be a stone platform ca. 2.50 m wide and extending beyond the wall for ca. 1.70 m. Another similar feature can be made out along the east wall. Ca. five circular stone mounds (ca. 1 m in diameter, although there is one that measures 2 m in diameter) lie southwest of the structure, perhaps representative of a cemetery.

Site No.: 125 (figs. 4.40, 4.41)
Field Site No.: 88
Site Name: None
Map Reference: 3049 III, K737
Location on 1:50,000: 3278617 N / 699833 E
Elevation: 185 m
Aerial Reference No.: IGN-78-JOR 12/100 - 1211
Site Size: 2.50 m N–S × 3.50 m E–W
Inventory Rating: 4
Pottery Collected: Total = 0 (No. of Indicators: 0 / No. Saved: 0)
Pottery Registration No(s).: None
Pottery Summary: N/A
Lithic Summary: N/A
Site Description: This is a large stone mound or cairn located in the same area as Site 122. There is a rectangular cavity at the top and within the mound lined by stones standing upright. This interior cavity measures ca. 0.25 m wide and 2.50 m long. The cairn has been robbed.

Site No.: 126 (figs. 4.40, 4.41)
Field Site No.: 89
Site Name: None
Map Reference: 3049 III, K737
Location on 1:50,000: 3278699 N / 699575 E
Elevation: 163 m
Aerial Reference No.: IGN-78-JOR 12/100 - 1211
Site Size: 5 m N–S × 3 m E–W
Inventory Rating: 0
Pottery Collected: Total = 11 (No. of Indicators: 1 / No. Saved: 5)
Pottery Registration No(s).: 6649–53
Pottery Summary: 11 ER/Nab (9 from 1 vessel)
Lithic Summary: N/A
Site Description: This is a light sherd scatter (0–2 sherds/m²) in an area of ca. 3 × 5 m on an alluvial fan surface west of the mouth of Wādī ez-Zibliya.

Site No.: 127 (figs. 4.40, 4.41)
Field Site No.: 61
Site Name: None
Map Reference: 3049 III, K737
Location on 1:50,000: 3278770 N / 701950 E
Elevation: 450 m
Aerial Reference No.: IGN-78-JOR 12/100 - 1214
Site Size: 6 m N–S × 5 m E–W
Inventory Rating: 2
Pottery Collected: Total = 0 (No. of Indicators: 0 / No. Saved: 0)
Pottery Registration No(s).: None
Pottery Summary: N/A
Lithic Summary: N/A
Site Description: This is a stone ring or hut circle, oblong in shape, measuring ca. 7 m N–S × 5 m E–W. Site is crudely constructed and situated in the center of a saddle between two peaks along a bend in Wādī Mulghān. This may be a modern feature.

Site No.: 128 (fig. 4.41)
Field Site No.: 98
Site Name: None
Map Reference: 3049 III, K737
Location on 1:50,000: 3282325 N / 698310 E
Elevation: 75 m
Aerial Reference No.: IGN-78-JOR 12/100 - 1239
Site Size: 8 m N–S × 15 m E–W
Inventory Rating: 2
Pottery Collected: Total = 0 (No. of Indicators: 0

/ No. Saved: 0)
Pottery Registration No(s).: None
Pottery Summary: N/A
Lithic Summary: N/A
Site Description: This is a small cemetery of ca.
six burials, which appear as stone piles measuring
ca. 1.50 × 1 m. There is no clear orientation to the
burials and no internal structuring is visible in the
stone piles.

Site No.: 129 (fig. 4.41)
Field Site No.: 97
Site Name: None
Map Reference: 3049 III, K737
Location on 1:50,000: 3282400 N / 698425 E
Elevation: 80 m
Aerial Reference No.: IGN-78-JOR 12/100 - 1239
Site Size: 30 m N–S × 40 m E–W
Inventory Rating: 2
Pottery Collected: Total = 0 (No. of Indicators: 0
/ No. Saved: 0)
Pottery Registration No(s).: None
Pottery Summary: N/A
Lithic Summary: N/A
Site Description: This is a cemetery consisting of
ca. 17 burials. These appear as stone piles measur-
ing on average 1 × 1.50 m. There are no observable
alignments of stone in most of these stone piles.

Site No.: 130 (fig. 4.41)
Field Site No.: 96
Site Name: None
Map Reference: 3049 III, K737
Location on 1:50,000: 3283275 N / 699530 E
Elevation: 170 m
Aerial Reference No.: IGN-78-JOR 12/100 - 1239
Site Size: 4 m N–S × 3.50 m E–W
Inventory Rating: 1
Pottery Collected: Total = 0 (No. of Indicators: 0
/ No. Saved: 0)
Pottery Registration No(s).: None
Pottery Summary: N/A
Lithic Summary: N/A
Site Description: This is a small oval enclosure (ca. 2 ×
2.50 m) on an alluvial fan surface. The enclosure opens
to the northeast. A large boulder forms the south and
west wall. The interior face of the boulder has a small
niche that has been blocked by a small cobble.

Site No.: 131 (fig. 4.41)
Field Site No.: 95
Site Name: None
Map Reference: 3049 III, K737
Location on 1:50,000: 3284150 N / 700400 E
Elevation: 330 m
Aerial Reference No.: IGN-78-JOR 12/100 - 1205
Site Size: 5 m N–S × 45 m E–W
Inventory Rating: 2
Pottery Collected: Total = 0 (No. of Indicators: 0
/ No. Saved: 0)
Pottery Registration No(s).: None
Pottery Summary: N/A
Lithic Summary: Indef. cultural-historic placement
Site Description: The site consists of three graves
and a single structure. The structure measures ca.
8.50 × 3 m with semicircular rooms opening to the
south. One of the graves is a stone mound or cairn
(3 × 2 m). A center cavity is visible on top of the
mound, which is rectangular (0.70 × 0.80 m) and
lined with upright stones. Another burial is visible
ca. 35 m west of the structure. Also, circular enclosures (water catchments?) exist in the wadi nearby.

Site No.: 132 (fig. 4.41)
Field Site No.: 94
Site Name: None
Map Reference: 3049 III, K737
Location on 1:50,000: 3284230 N / 700225 E
Elevation: 305 m
Aerial Reference No.: IGN-78-JOR 12/100 - 1205
Site Size: 16 m N–S × 96 m E–W
Inventory Rating: 2
Pottery Collected: Total = 4 (No. of Indicators: 0
/ No. Saved: 4)
Pottery Registration No(s).: 6633–36
Pottery Summary: 4 Chalcolithic
Lithic Summary: Indef. cultural-historic placement
Site Description: The site consists of several
mounds and stone alignments. The SAAS recorded
six features. Feature 1 is a stone mound measuring
4 m in diameter and 1 m high. A robbed interior
cavity (ca. 1 × 0.80 m) is visible on top of the
mound and it is lined with upright slabs of stone.
Feature 2 is an adjacent circular structure (ca. 4
× 3 m) with a curved wall extending 2 m to the
east. Feature 3, located 2 m northeast of Feature
2, is a semicircular rock alignment (ca. 3 × 1 m)

that opens to the northwest. Feature 4 is an open crescent-shaped alignment (ca. 5 × 3 m) of piled stones, perhaps an extension of Feature 3 to the northeast. Feature 5 consists of 2 distinct wall alignments, possibly a structure. These walls measure ca. 1 m in width (two courses) and run roughly parallel to one another, separated by only ca. 3 m. All of these features, which are contiguous except for Feature 5, lie in an area of ca. 18 × 18 m. They may have formed a single structure. Feature 6 is a circular stone mound 2 m in diameter, which lies 60 m from Feature 5 at 260 degrees.

Site No.: 133 (fig. 4.42)
Field Site No.: 99
Site Name: None
Map Reference: 3049 III, K737
Location on 1:50,000: 3285321 N / 699965 E
Elevation: 230 m
Aerial Reference No.: IGN-78-JOR 12/100 - 1203
Site Size: 5.50 m N–S × 2.50 m E–W
Inventory Rating: 1
Pottery Collected: Total = 0 (No. of Indicators: 0 / No. Saved: 0)
Pottery Registration No(s).: None
Pottery Summary: N/A
Lithic Summary: N/A
Site Description: This is an isolated structure (burial?) situated between two small alluvial fans near the escarpment just north of Wādī es-Sammāniya. It measures 5.50 × 2.50 m and is oriented N–S.

Site No.: 134 (fig. 4.42)
Field Site No.: 93
Site Name: None
Map Reference: 3049 III, K737
Location on 1:50,000: 3285881 N / 699138 E
Elevation: 144 m
Aerial Reference No.: IGN-78-JOR 12/100 - 1241
Site Size: 2 m N–S × 13 m E–W
Inventory Rating: 2
Pottery Collected: Total = 1 (No. of Indicators: 0 / No. Saved: 0)
Pottery Registration No(s).: None
Pottery Summary: 1 UD
Lithic Summary: Indef. cultural-historic placement
Site Description: The site consists of three graves. The first is a small, oval grave (1.40 × 1.80 m) ori-

ented E–W lengthwise. Another is situated ca. 10 m from the first and measures 2.50 × 1.70 m. This second grave is rectangular, oriented E–W, with capstones. The third is merely a small rock pile (ca. 0.50 × 0.50 m) south of the first grave, which may be a child burial.

Site No.: 135 (fig. 4.42)
Field Site No.: 92
Site Name: None
Map Reference: 3049 III, K737
Location on 1:50,000: 3286012 N / 698855 E
Elevation: 122 m
Aerial Reference No.: IGN-78-JOR 12/100 - 1241
Site Size: 10 m N–S × 58 m E–W
Inventory Rating: 2
Pottery Collected: Total = 0 (No. of Indicators: 0 / No. Saved: 0)
Pottery Registration No(s).: None
Pottery Summary: N/A
Lithic Summary: N/A
Site Description: This is a cemetery consisting of a series of 6 graves on an old alluvial fan terrace north and west of Wādī es-Sammāniya. Three of these are stone mounds (ca. 1.50 m in diameter), while the remainder are rectilinear (3.50 × 1 m) and oriented E–W lengthwise.

Site No.: 136 (fig. 4.42)
Field Site No.: 125
Site Name: None
Map Reference: 3049 III, K737
Location on 1:50,000: 3288829 N / 701254 E
Elevation: 410 m
Aerial Reference No.: IGN-78-JOR 12/100 - 1198
Site Size: 15 m N–S × 35 m E–W
Inventory Rating: 2
Pottery Collected: Total = 0 (No. of Indicators: 0 / No. Saved: 0)
Pottery Registration No(s).: None
Pottery Summary: N/A
Lithic Summary: N/A
Site Description: The site consists of two stone mounds on a steep, deflated alluvial fan. One measures ca. 3 × 2.50 m (0.80 m high) while the second, larger mound measures ca. 10 × 9 m. No internal structures could be discerned within the larger mound, which may be the remains of a tower.

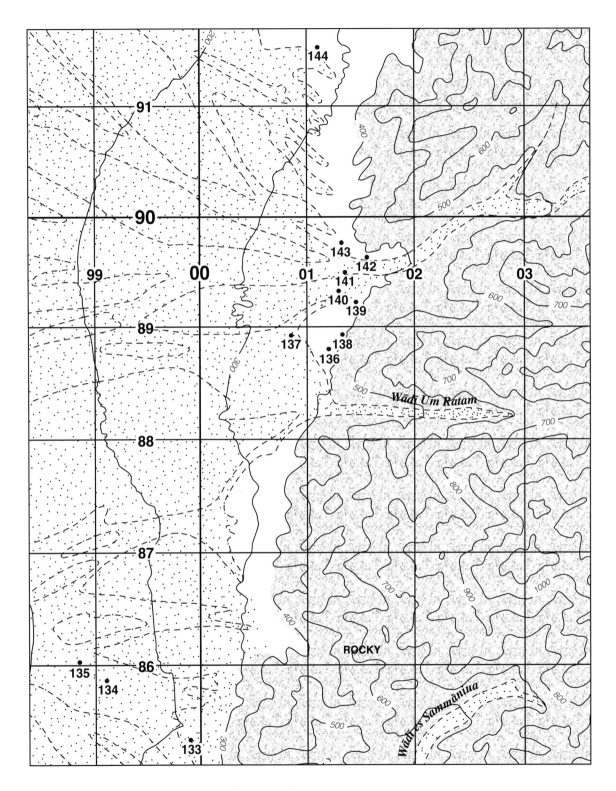

FIG. 4.42 *Aqaba Region (Region I), map 5 (Sites 133–144).*

Site No.: 137 (fig. 4.42)
Field Site No.: 124
Site Name: None
Map Reference: 3049 III, K737
Location on 1:50,000: 3288960 N / 700913 E
Elevation: 320 m
Aerial Reference No.: IGN-78-JOR 12/100 - 1198
Site Size: 57 m N–S × 20 m E–W
Inventory Rating: 2
Pottery Collected: Total = 6 (No. of Indicators: 0 / No. Saved: 0)
Pottery Registration No(s).: None
Pottery Summary: 6 UD
Lithic Summary: N/A
Site Description: This is a cemetery consisting of three graves set high on an alluvial terrace. The graves are aligned with stones, cleared in the center, with capstones at either end. These measure on average ca. 1 × 1.50 m. There orientation is E–W. Ca. 57 m southwest there are two rock mounds/ cairns (3 m in diameter) within 1 m of each other.

Site No.: 138 (fig. 4.42)
Field Site No.: 126
Site Name: None
Map Reference: 3049 III, K737
Location on 1:50,000: 3288977 N / 701373 E
Elevation: 422 m
Aerial Reference No.: IGN-78-JOR 12/100 - 1198
Site Size: 2 m N–S × 1.50 m E–W
Inventory Rating: 2
Pottery Collected: Total = 0 (No. of Indicators: 0 / No. Saved: 0)
Pottery Registration No(s).: None
Pottery Summary: N/A
Lithic Summary: N/A
Site Description: This is a single stone mound or cairn measuring 1.50 m in diameter and up to 0.50 m high.

Site No.: 139 (fig. 4.42)
Field Site No.: 127
Site Name: None
Map Reference: 3049 III, K737
Location on 1:50,000: 3289292 N / 701503 E
Elevation: 405 m
Aerial Reference No.: IGN-78-JOR 12/100 - 1198
Site Size: 12 m N–S × 18 m E–W

Inventory Rating: 2
Pottery Collected: Total = 27 (No. of Indicators: 1 / No. Saved: 8)
Pottery Registration No(s).: 6439–46
Pottery Summary: 2 ER/Nab, 25 R/Byz
Lithic Summary: N/A
Site Description: The site consists of a walled enclosure set against a cliff face, and four distinct burials, two of which are small stone mounds. The wall of the enclosure is two courses thick (0.65 m) and parallels the curve of the cliff face for ca. 8 m. The enclosure wall is built against the cliff face at the southwest end of the site. Ca. 30 m further south there is a modern concrete water basin.

Site No.: 140 (fig. 4.42)
Field Site No.: 130
Site Name: None
Map Reference: 3049 III, K737
Location on 1:50,000: 3289359 N / 701365 E
Elevation: 420 m
Aerial Reference No.: IGN-78-JOR 12/100 - 1198
Site Size: 12 m N–S × 10 m E–W
Inventory Rating: 2
Pottery Collected: Total = 0 (No. of Indicators: 0 / No. Saved: 0)
Pottery Registration No(s).: None
Pottery Summary: N/A
Lithic Summary: N/A
Site Description: This appears to be a campsite. There is an area cleared of stones measuring ca. 10 × 12 m. Within this area there is a grouping of stones that appear to be some form of pavement (ca. 2 × 1.50 m) and a stone mound (ca. 3 m in diameter).

Site No.: 141 (fig. 4.42)
Field Site No.: 131
Site Name: None
Map Reference: 3049 III, K737
Location on 1:50,000: 3289495 N / 701350 E
Elevation: 415 m
Aerial Reference No.: IGN-78-JOR 12/100 - 1198
Site Size: 20 m N–S × 50 m E–W
Inventory Rating: 2
Pottery Collected: Total = 0 (No. of Indicators: 0 / No. Saved: 0)
Pottery Registration No(s).: None

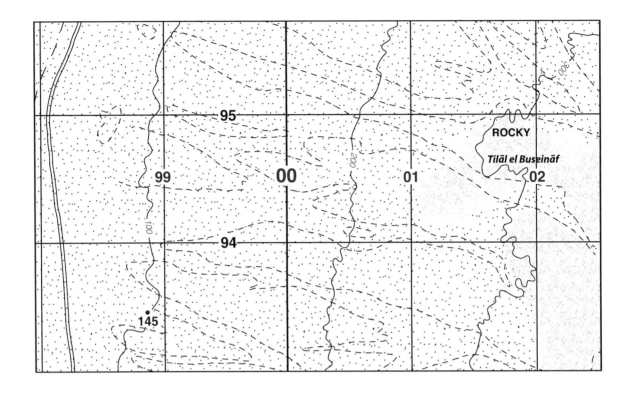

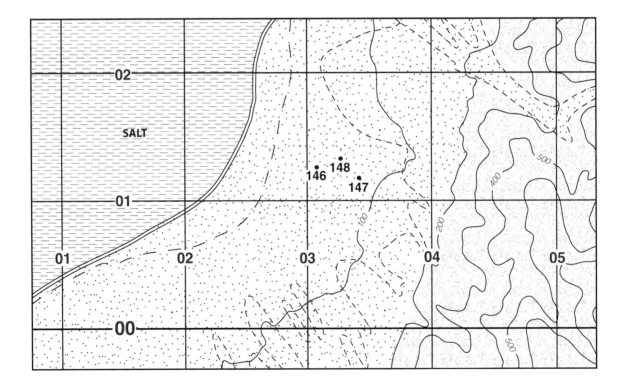

FIG. 4.43   *Darba Region (Region II). Top: map 6 (Site 145), bottom: map 7 (Sites 146–148).*

Pottery Summary: N/A

Lithic Summary: N/A

Site Description: This site consists of a rectangular rock alignment (too indistinct to regard as a wall) that measures ca. 2 × 3 m and opens to the northeast. There is some copper slag present. Also, ca. 42 m northeast is a more concentrated scatter of copper slag in an area of 9 × 28 m associated with what may be additional rock alignments. The heavier concentrations of copper slag seem to be situated on the north slope of the hill.

Site No.: 142 (fig. 4.42)

Field Site No.: 128

Site Name: None

Map Reference: 3049 III, K737

Location on 1:50,000: 3289680 N / 701490 E

Elevation: 440 m

Aerial Reference No.: IGN-78-JOR 12/100 - 1198

Site Size: 15 m N–S × 12 m E–W

Inventory Rating: 3

Pottery Collected: Total = 7 (No. of Indicators: 0 / No. Saved: 4)

Pottery Registration No(s).: 6598–6601

Pottery Summary: 7 Chalcolithic

Lithic Summary: N/A

Site Description: This is a smelting site consisting of a collapsed structure measuring ca. 8 × 10 m. The SAAS found copper ore, copper slag, and pottery scattered on the surface around the structure. The site is located on an alluvial fan above the north bank of Wādī el-Muhtadī.

Site No.: 143 (fig. 4.42)

Field Site No.: 129

Site Name: None

Map Reference: 3049 III, K737

Location on 1:50,000: 3289780 N / 701345 E

Elevation: 475 m

Aerial Reference No.: IGN-78-JOR 12/100 - 1198

Site Size: 15 m N–S × 20 m E–W

Inventory Rating: 2

Pottery Collected: Total = 0 (No. of Indicators: 0 / No. Saved: 0)

Pottery Registration No(s).: None

Pottery Summary: N/A

Lithic Summary: Indef. cultural-historic placement

Site Description: This is a smelting site with a light

concentration of lithics, copper ore, and copper slag. In the area are several miscellaneous rock alignments — most appear as single rows of stones and trending N–S. Due to the deflated and tumbled nature of the rock alignments, it is difficult to discern the shape of any structure that these may have formed. Artifacts from the site concentrate down the slope to the west.

Site No.: 144 (fig. 4.42)

Field Site No.: 103

Site Name: None

Map Reference: 3049 III, K737

Location on 1:50,000: 3291559 N / 701131 E

Elevation: 315 m

Aerial Reference No.: IGN-78-JOR 12/100 - 1197

Site Size: 50 m N–S × 89 m E–W

Inventory Rating: 2

Pottery Collected: Total = 10 (No. of Indicators: 0 / No. Saved: 0)

Pottery Registration No(s).: None

Pottery Summary: 10 ER/Nab

Lithic Summary: Indef. cultural-historic placement

Site Description: The site consists of a single grave (ca. 2 × 2 m) with capstones and oriented E–W. Four stone mounds and several additional rock alignments are apparent in the area.

Site No.: 145 (fig. 4.43)

Field Site No.: 104

Site Name: None

Map Reference: 3049 III, K737

Location on 1:50,000: 3293520 N / 698945 E

Elevation: 100 m

Aerial Reference No.: IGN-78-JOR 12/100 - 1251

Site Size: 5 m N–S × 5 m E–W

Inventory Rating: 4

Pottery Collected: Total = 1 (No. of Indicators: 0 / No. Saved: 0)

Pottery Registration No(s).: None

Pottery Summary: 1 ER/Nab

Lithic Summary: N/A

Site Description: The site consists of three burials on an old alluvial fan surface. One measures 1.35 m in diameter, another is 1.40 × 1.10 m and oriented E–W, and the third is 2.50 m in diameter with an internal cavity (ca. 0.60–0.70 m in diameter) on top.

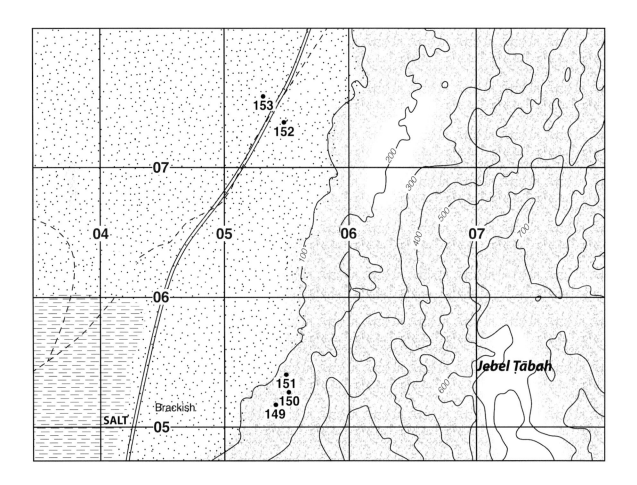

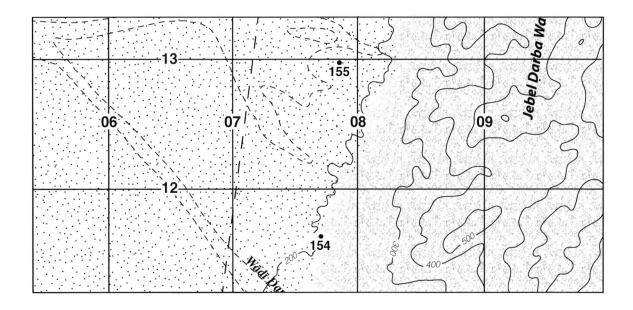

FIG. 4.44   *Darba Region (Region II). Top: map 8 (Sites 149–153), bottom: map 9 (Sites 154–155).*

Site No.: 146 (fig. 4.43)
Field Site No.: 335
Site Name: None
Map Reference: 3049 IV, K737
Location on 1:50,000: 3301265 N / 703065 E
Elevation: 58 m
Aerial Reference No.: IGN-78-JOR 12/100 - 1139
Site Size: 32 m N–S × 16 m E–W
Inventory Rating: 2
Pottery Collected: Total = 0 (No. of Indicators: 0 / No. Saved: 0)
Pottery Registration No(s).: None
Pottery Summary: N/A
Lithic Summary: N/A
Site Description: The site consists of three features. Both Features 1 and 2 (205 degrees from Feature 1) are collapsed structures, roughly circular, measuring ca. 8–8.30 m in diameter. The walls are ca. 1 m wide (two courses with rubble fill) and preserved up to two courses high. Feature 2 opens to the south. Feature 3 lies ca. 1 m to the southwest of Feature 2. It is a collapsed mound of stones measuring 7.10 × 2 m.

Site No.: 147 (figs. 4.10, 4.43)
Field Site No.: 334
Site Name: None
Map Reference: 3049 IV, K737
Location on 1:50,000: 3301285 N / 703450 E
Elevation: 78 m
Aerial Reference No.: IGN-78-JOR 12/100 - 1139
Site Size: 70 m N–S × 60 m E–W
Inventory Rating: 2
Pottery Collected: Total = 6 (No. of Indicators: 0 / No. Saved: 6)
Pottery Registration No(s).: 57576–81
Pottery Summary: 6 Chalco/EB
Lithic Summary: N/A
Site Description: This is a large desert kite, v-shaped, with the narrow angle toward the southwest. The walls are built of granite boulders ranging in size from 0.30–1.60 m on a side. At several points along the kite there are circular stone appendages against the wall. A large circular structure is appended at the southwest corner near the point of the kite. The exterior diameter of this structure at the point of the kite is 6.20 m with a wall thickness of ca. 1 m. It is preserved up to a height of 1.37 m

(seven courses). Also, at the southeast corner of this circular structure is a semicircular enclosure joining with the main point, or circular catchment, of the kite. It is preserved up to 0.60 m high (two courses). The area enclosed by this appended wall measures 4.80 × 2.3 m. The overall area enclosed by the kite is just under half a hectare.

Site No.: 148 (fig. 4.43)
Field Site No.: 333
Site Name: None
Map Reference: 3050 III, K737
Location on 1:50,000: 3301380 N / 703245 E
Elevation: 60 m
Aerial Reference No.: IGN-78-JOR 12/100 - 1139
Site Size: 60 m N–S × 100 m E–W
Inventory Rating: 2
Pottery Collected: Total = 0 (No. of Indicators: 0 / No. Saved: 0)
Pottery Registration No(s).: None
Pottery Summary: N/A
Lithic Summary: Indef. cultural-historic placement
Site Description: The site consists of two features in a boulder field near the edge of an alluvial fan just north of Qatar village. Feature 1 is a large circular structure with smaller circular structures within it. The overall diameter of the largest structure is ca. 12 m. Its walls are one course wide (0.50 m). Inside the south side of the circle is an oblong stone wall 4.78 m N–S × 5.25 m E–W. This wall is two courses wide and a single course high. Feature 2 consists of a series of 8 large stone mounds, possibly burial cairns, situated to the north and west of Feature 1. Each cairn is ca. 3 m N–S × 2.50 m E–W and constructed of large boulders measuring ca. 0.30 m on a side. None of the cairns appear to have been disturbed.

Site No.: 149 (fig. 4.44)
Field Site No.: 331
Site Name: None
Map Reference: 3050 III, K737
Location on 1:50,000: 3305035 N / 705400 E
Elevation: 130 m
Aerial Reference No.: IGN-78-JOR 12/100 - 1602
Site Size: 26 m N–S × 13.50 m E–W
Inventory Rating: 2
Pottery Collected: Total = 3 (No. of Indicators: 0 /

No. Saved: 2)
Pottery Registration No(s).: 57566–67
Pottery Summary: 1 ER/Nab, 1 ER/LR, 1 UD
Lithic Summary: N/A
Site Description: The site consists of three burial cairns or tombs which may be associated with Site 150. One tomb is oriented 241 degrees. It is rectilinear and measures 2 m N–S × 2.70 m E–W. The second tomb lies ca. 18 m to the west. It measures 4.60 m N–S × 3.90 m E–W. The slabs across the top face of the tombs are still preserved. The third tomb lies 3 m southwest from the second and measures 5.40 m N–S × 4 m E–W. The site is on a low spur on an alluvial fan overlooking Wādī ʿAraba, ca. 1000 m from the highway.

Site No.: 150 (fig. 4.44)
Field Site No.: 330
Site Name: None
Map Reference: 3050 III, K737
Location on 1:50,000: 3305125 N / 705500 E
Elevation: 130 m
Aerial Reference No.: IGN-78-JOR 12/100 - 1602
Site Size: 100 m N–S × 145 m E–W
Inventory Rating: 2
Pottery Collected: Total = 40 (No. of Indicators: 9 / No. Saved: 35)
Pottery Registration No(s).: 57568–75, 57582–608
Pottery Summary: 12 ER/Nab, 7 LR, 2 EByz, 19 LR/EByz (13=1 vessel)
Lithic Summary: N/A
Site Description: The site consists of two features. Feature 1 is an isolated structure near the base of a steep hill. The structure measures 5 m N–S × 6 m E–W. Its walls are a single course wide (0.60 m), constructed of large boulders, and preserved up to 1.20 m high. Feature 2 is a series of nine burial cairns scattered across the hill above Feature 1. The cairns are built as tombs with large flat stones covering the burial area. Most of the tombs have been robbed. The cairns measure ca. 5 m in diameter, and most are preserved up to 1.50 m high. Both the structure and the tombs appear contemporary.

Site No.: 151 (fig. 4.44)
Field Site No.: 332
Site Name: None
Map Reference: 3050 III, K737

Location on 1:50,000: 3305325 N / 705500 E
Elevation: 120 m
Aerial Reference No.: IGN-78-JOR 12/100 - 1602
Site Size: 50 m N–S × 30 m E–W
Inventory Rating: 2
Pottery Collected: Total = 0 (No. of Indicators: 0 / No. Saved: 0)
Pottery Registration No(s).: None
Pottery Summary: N/A
Lithic Summary: N/A
Site Description: The site consists of a series of burial cairns. It is difficult to determine how many cairns there are, but there may be at least 10 or 12 present. These appear similar to those at Site 150, with which they are undoubtedly associated.

Site No.: 152 (fig. 4.44)
Field Site No.: 136
Site Name: Rujm aṭ-Ṭāba – Hamlet
Map Reference: 3049 IV, K737
Location on 1:50,000: 3307335 N / 705515 E
Elevation: 48 m
Aerial Reference No.: IGN-78-JOR 12/100 - 1600
Site Size: 200 m N–S × 100 m E–W
Inventory Rating: 4
Pottery Collected: Total = 261 (No. of Indicators: 130 / No. Saved: 93)
Pottery Registration No(s).: 6699–791
Pottery Summary: 130 ER/Nab (3 handle sherds, 1 body sherd and several small fragments from a Class 10 amphora, 4 TS, some possibly LR), 125 ER/Nab bods, 2 EByz, 1 Modern, 3 UDE
Lithic Summary: N/A
Site Description: This is the village site of Rujm aṭ-Ṭāba located east of the highway and ca. 50 m to the south of Site 153. Much of the site was destroyed during construction of the modern highway when a large quantity of gravel was removed from the base of the alluvial fan to line the highway bed. Further modification of the area continues with recent bulldozing activity. The SAAS identified two extant structures and several large mounds that may indicate others in the area. One of these structures at the southern end of the site measures ca. 10 m on a side and it is partitioned into four rooms of equal size. The second structure, which lies ca. 100 m to the north, is similar in design. The walls of both structures are two courses wide and

constructed of cobbles and boulders from the fan surface. Located on the steep slope of the alluvial fan above the village, there is a cemetery of ca. 50 tombs.

Site No.: 153 (fig. 4.44)
Field Site No.: 135
Site Name: Rujm aṭ-Ṭāba – Caravanserai
Map Reference: 3049 IV, K737
Location on 1:50,000: 3307470 N / 705365 E
Elevation: 42 m
Aerial Reference No.: IGN-78-JOR 12/100 - 1600
Site Size: 25 m N–S × 25 m E–W
Inventory Rating: 4
Pottery Collected: Total = 128 (No. of Indicators: 26 / No. Saved: 26)
Pottery Registration No(s).: 22252–77
Pottery Summary: 23 ER/Nab, 101 ER/LR, 3 LR, 1 UD
Lithic Summary: N/A
Site Description: This is a ruined structure, seemingly a caravanserai, located ca. 20 m west of the highway. The structure measures ca. 21 m on a side. It is partly buried under sand dunes encroaching from the northwest. Much of the structure has been disturbed by localized bulldozing.

Site No.: 154 (fig. 4.44)
Field Site No.: 329
Site Name: None
Map Reference: 3050 III, K737
Location on 1:50,000: 3311645 N / 707675 E
Elevation: 302 m
Aerial Reference No.: IGN-78-JOR 12/100 - 1560
Site Size: 8 m N–S × 10 m E–W
Inventory Rating: 2
Pottery Collected: Total = 0 (No. of Indicators: 0 / No. Saved: 0)
Pottery Registration No(s).: None
Pottery Summary: N/A
Lithic Summary: N/A
Site Description: The site consists of two stone mounds or burial cairns on top of a low spur. Both have been vandalized. The mound to the west measures 4.50 m N–S × 6.50 m E–W and it is ca. 1 m high. It appears to be divided into two compartments, both of which have been robbed. The second mound, ca. 1 m west of the first, is 3.50 m in diameter and ca. 0.50 m high.

Site No.: 155 (fig. 4.44)
Field Site No.: 328
Site Name: None
Map Reference: 3050 III, K737
Location on 1:50,000: 3312970 N / 707865 E
Elevation: 170 m
Aerial Reference No.: IGN-78-JOR 12/100 - 1560
Site Size: 30 m N–S × 50 m E–W
Inventory Rating: 1
Pottery Collected: Total = 4 (No. of Indicators: 0 / No. Saved: 4)
Pottery Registration No(s).: 57542–45
Pottery Summary: 4 Chalco/EB
Lithic Summary: Indef. cultural-historic placement
Site Description: The site consists of a single stone mound or a burial cairn situated on an isolated hill. The mound measures ca. 3.50 m in diameter and it is preserved up to 0.80 m in height. The site is largely destroyed by robber trenches.

Site No.: 156 (fig. 4.45)
Field Site No.: 105
Site Name: None
Map Reference: 3050 III, K737
Location on 1:50,000: 3320745 N / 709142 E
Elevation: 210 m
Aerial Reference No.: IGN-78-JOR 12/100 - 1547
Site Size: 2.50 m N–S × 16 m E–W
Inventory Rating: 4
Pottery Collected: Total = 0 (No. of Indicators: 0 / No. Saved: 0)
Pottery Registration No(s).: None
Pottery Summary: N/A
Lithic Summary: N/A
Site Description: The site consists of two linear segments of a stone wall ca. 150 m south of the mouth of Wādī Nukheila on the first sand dune ridge. The first is 6 × 0.75 m, and it is somewhat curvilinear with a 0.20–0.30 m offset. The other segment (1.10 × 3.50 m) is along the north wall. This segment turns south and continues for 0.80 m. The wall is two courses wide with rubble fill. The area is heavily eroded and there is some difficulty determining more about the structure that these walls comprised.

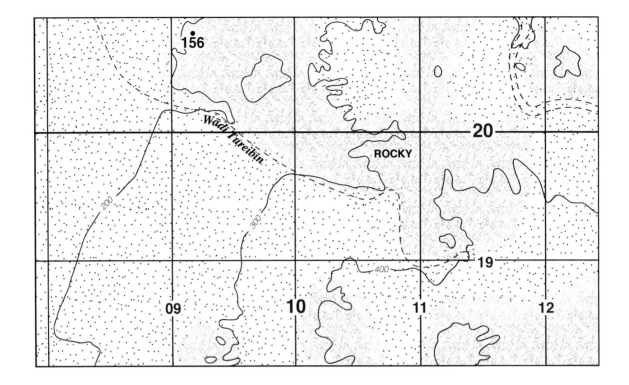

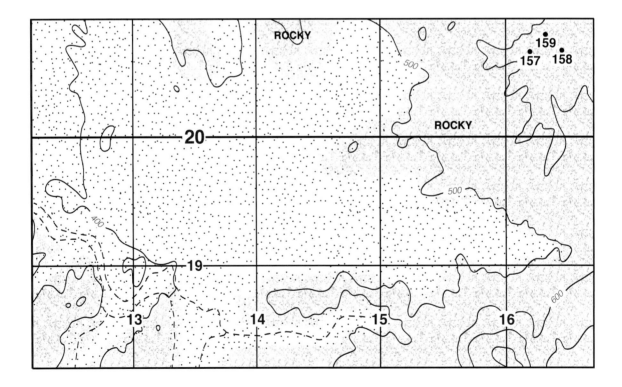

FIG. 4.45 *Darba Region (Region II). Top: map 10 (Site 156), bottom: map 11 (Sites 157–159).*

Site No.: 157 (fig. 4.45)
Field Site No.: 115
Site Name: SAAR Site 30
Map Reference: 3049 IV, K737
Location on 1:50,000: 3320675 N / 716348 E
Elevation: 470 m
Aerial Reference No.: IGN-78-JOR 12/100 - 794
Site Size: 18 m N–S × 3 m E–W
Inventory Rating: 2
Pottery Collected: Total = 0 (No. of Indicators: 0 / No. Saved: 0)
Pottery Registration No(s).: None
Pottery Summary: N/A
Lithic Summary: Indef. cultural-historic placement
Site Description: The site consists of seven toppled monoliths, graded in size and measuring on average 2 m lengthwise, 0.70 m in width, and with a thickness of 0.40 m. They are trapezoidal in section. Several robber pits have significantly disturbed the site. These were not present when Smith and Niemi discovered the site in 1993. On both sides of the row of monoliths there is what appears to be a toppled wall the top course of which is of cut granite. Alternatively, the cut granite may have been paving stones which formed a platform under the monoliths, which since have been robbed. This is suggested because there is no clear evidence for a wall foundation. These granite blocks measure ca. 0.15 × 0.25 × 0.40 m.

Site No.: 158 (figs. 4.11, 4.45)
Field Site No.: 114
Site Name: None
Map Reference: 3049 IV, K737
Location on 1:50,000: 3320710 N / 716635 E
Elevation: 455 m
Aerial Reference No.: IGN-78-JOR 12/100 - 794
Site Size: 210 m N–S × 70 m E–W
Inventory Rating: 3
Pottery Collected: Total = 36 (No. of Indicators: 2 / No. Saved: 10)
Pottery Registration No(s).: 6330–39
Pottery Summary: 36 EB (EB I–II?)
Lithic Summary: Probably Chalcolithic or later (see Chapter 5)
Site Description: This is a prehistoric settlement on an alluvial terrace above Wādī Ḥeimir. The site consists of numerous enclosures and wall align-ments with an associated sherd and lithic scatter. The SAAS recorded seven features. Feature 1, furthest to the north, is a stone mound measuring ca. 8 × 6 m. The center and west side of the mound have been robbed, exposing a small pit measuring 4 m on a side. Ca. 30 m due south of Feature 1 there lies the edge of a large complex of walls and stone mounds (Features 2–6). Feature 2 is a large, trapezoidal enclosure with an interior measuring 15 m N–S × 27.50 m E–W and with an entrance from the north. There is a square rock alignment (1.20 m on a side) in the center of the structure, one wall of which is two courses wide (all one course high). Also at the west edge of this area is a stone mound measuring ca. 5 × 4 m with a pit in the center. Feature 3 abuts with Feature 2 on its southwest side. This is another larger enclosure, which measures ca. 12 m in diameter and with walls that measure 1.50–2 m wide (two courses with rubble fill). There is an entrance into this enclosure from the east that measures 2.40 m wide. Also, a small wall alignment extends E–SE from this entrance for 4.30 m. Walls that parallel a drainage cut and extend east and west lie at the south end of Feature 3. To the west, a wall segment curves around the slope to make up another enclosure, which measures 10 × 12 m. Features 2–4 all join to form a large complex. Ca. 10 m further to the south, there is another complex (Features 5 and 6). Feature 5 is a large enclosure measuring 17 m N–S × 14 m E–W with walls that are two courses wide (1.60 m) and ca. 5 m high. The entrance into the enclosure is 2.30 m, and 5 m to the northeast beyond the entrance there is an isolated wall alignment stretching 17.50 m E–W (similar to the walls of the enclosure). In the southwest corner of the enclosure, two walls extend south to form a small trapezoidal room measuring 3 × 4 m. Ca. 5 m south of Feature 5, Feature 6 is another large enclosure, which measures 18 m N–S × 15 m E–W. The walls of this feature are somewhat indistinct and difficult to discern. There is a possible opening in the northeast. Finally, across a small drainage channel to the west of Features 5 and 6, there are numerous rock alignments (some walls apparent) and cleared areas. None of these, however, are of the same magnitude as those across the drainage, and they are generally less distinct, with only a few exceptions. Also, there are two burials at the south

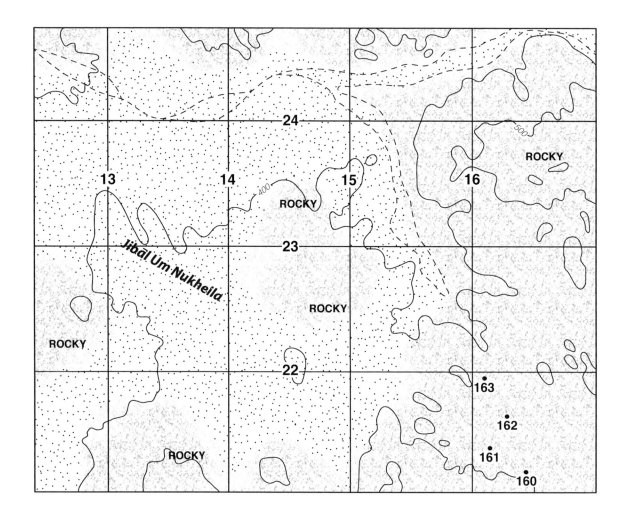

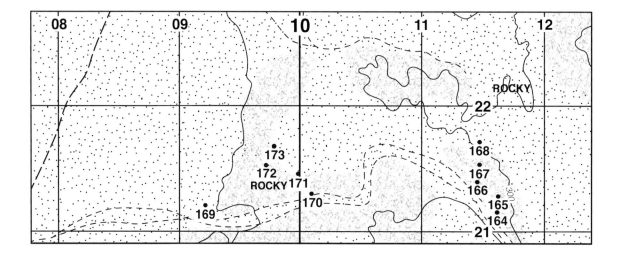

FIG. 4.46 *Gharandal Region (Region III). Top: map 12 (Sites 160–163), bottom: map 13 (Sites 164–173)*

end of the terrace. Both of these are pitted. One is a large stone mound ca. 4 m in diameter, and the other is a smaller squared feature (2.50 m on a side). Both are lined in a rectilinear fashion with rectilinear stones set upright. There are also bone fragments surrounding both pitted areas.

Site No.: 159 (figs. 4.12, 4.45)
Field Site No.: 113
Site Name: SAAR Site 29
Map Reference: 3049 IV, K737
Location on 1:50,000: 3320823 N / 716469 E
Elevation: 455 m
Aerial Reference No.: IGN-78-JOR 12/100 - 794
Site Size: 70 m N–S × 40 m E–W
Inventory Rating: 3
Pottery Collected: Total = 36 (No. of Indicators: 13 / No. Saved: 15)
Pottery Registration No(s).: 6376–90
Pottery Summary: 36 Chalco/EB (EB I–II?)
Lithic Summary: Probably Chalcolithic or later (see Chapter 5)
Site Description: This is a prehistoric settlement on an alluvial terrace above Wādī Ḥeimir. The site consists of numerous enclosures and wall alignments with an associated sherd and lithic scatter. The SAAS recorded four visible structures. At the southwest end of the site there are two semicircular stone circles measuring ca. 6 m on a side. Their walls measure 0.60 m wide (two courses with rubble fill). At the southeast end there is another stone circle measuring ca. 5 m on a side and opening to the southeast. In the northwest corner of the site is a complex of contiguous, circular enclosures and additional wall alignments that cover an area of 22 m N–S × 20 m E–W.

Site No.: 160 (fig. 4.46)
Field Site No.: 112
Site Name: None
Map Reference: 3050 III, K737
Location on 1:50,000: 3321080 N / 716346 E
Elevation: 460 m
Aerial Reference No.: IGN-78-JOR 12/100 - 1402
Site Size: 8 m N–S × 20 m E–W
Inventory Rating: 2
Pottery Collected: Total = 0 (No. of Indicators: 0 / No. Saved: 0)

Pottery Registration No(s).: None
Pottery Summary: N/A
Lithic Summary: Probably Chalcolithic or later (see Chapter 5)
Site Description: This is a lithic scatter (ca. 15 lithics/m²) on an alluvial terrace ca. 10 m above the south bank of Wādī Ḥeimir.

Site No.: 161 (fig. 4.46)
Field Site No.: 116
Site Name: SAAR Site 31
Map Reference: 3050 III, K737
Location on 1:50,000: 3321281 N / 716081 E
Elevation: 480 m
Aerial Reference No.: IGN-78-JOR 12/100 - 1402
Site Size: 20 m N–S × 9 m E–W
Inventory Rating: 3
Pottery Collected: Total = 0 (No. of Indicators: 0 / No. Saved: 0)
Pottery Registration No(s).: None
Pottery Summary: N/A
Lithic Summary: Indef. cultural-historic placement
Site Description: The site consists of three toppled monoliths on an elevated platform overlooking Site 162. There is some evidence of associated structures and perhaps a pavement underlying the monoliths. The site is situated on top of a ridge along the south bank of Wādī Ḥeimir. The first monolith is tapered and measures 1.80 m lengthwise, 0.75 m in width, and with a thickness of 0.45 m, the second measures 1.90 × 0.75 × 0.45 m (not tapered), and the third measures 1.90 × 0.60 × 0.45 m. The bases of these monoliths are set roughly in alignment, which suggests that they were in a row with their flat side facing north as they toppled to the south. Near the second monolith there is a slab of granite (0.90 × 0.90 × 0.20 m) standing upright. The platform itself is elevated and measures 20 × 9 m. Several rock piles on the platform suggest that a structure was in place there that aligned with the monoliths in the center of the ridge. A robbers pit to the west has exposed a wall of well-cut stones that measure on average ca. 0.20 × 0.20 × 0.10 m. This may be the remnants of a retaining wall.

Site No.: 162 (fig. 4.46)
Field Site No.: 111
Site Name: SAAR Site 28
Map Reference: 3050 III, K737
Location on 1:50,000: 3321603 N / 716221 E
Elevation: 440 m
Aerial Reference No.: IGN-78-JOR 12/100 - 1402
Site Size: 70 m N–S × 45 m E–W
Inventory Rating: 3
Pottery Collected: Total = 39 (No. of Indicators: 6 / No. Saved: 11)
Pottery Registration No(s).: 6597, 6659–68
Pottery Summary: 18 EB II (4 from 1 vessel), 21 EB
Lithic Summary: Probably Chalcolithic or later (see Chapter 5)
Site Description: This is a prehistoric settlement on an alluvial terrace above Wādī Ḥeimir. The site consists of five contiguous, circular enclosures and additional wall alignments, along with an associated lithic and sherd scatter. The walls of the structures measure 0.70 m wide (two courses with rubble fill) and are preserved up to four courses high in some places. Average size of stones is 0.30 × 0.25 × 0.20 m. Upright and larger boulders mark the entrances. The southernmost is the largest enclosure. Entrance into it is from the south, which has upright boulders and a path marked by two rows of cobbles leading from the south wall. There are also two semicircular features east of the entrance, which abut with the south wall. A second entrance opens to the east. On the same terrace ca. 25 m to the east there are two wells next to what appear to be robber pits. The SAAS recorded a high concentration of pottery in this area.

Site No.: 163 (fig. 4.46)
Field Site No.: 110
Site Name: None
Map Reference: 3050 III, K737
Location on 1:50,000: 3321913 N / 716070 E
Elevation: 435 m
Aerial Reference No.: IGN-78-JOR 12/100 - 1402
Site Size: 140 m N–S × 130 m E–W
Inventory Rating: 3
Pottery Collected: Total = 83 (No. of Indicators: 13 / No. Saved: 23)
Pottery Registration No(s).: 6391–405, 6466–73
Pottery Summary: 80 Chalco/EB, 3 EB (1 vessel)

Lithic Summary: Probably Chalcolithic or later (see Chapter 5)
Site Description: This is a prehistoric settlement consisting of numerous enclosures and wall alignments. The site is set on three terraced platforms above the bed of Wādī Ḥeimir. The SAAS recorded 11 distinct features. Feature 1 is a large enclosure or structure measuring 11 × 8 m with large boulders set upright at its northwest end and a small circular bin in the north corner (1 m in diameter). The walls measure 0.90–1.10 m wide (two courses), and the eastern edge of the structure is set against the cliff face. Its north wall adjoins with Feature 2, a circular platform measuring 2.50 m in diameter. Feature 3, which measures ca. 8.75 m N–S × 6 m E–W, consists of a series of semicircular enclosures made up of large boulders. Feature 4 consists of two rectilinear enclosures roughly 2–2.50 m on a side joined by a long wall on the east side measuring ca. 7.50 m. Each has an entrance flanked by large boulders. A circular rock alignment, perhaps a hearth, lies just beyond the south face of the northernmost enclosure. Feature 5 is another enclosure or structure that abuts the north face of Feature 4 and continues further north for ca. 13 m. Its width is 8 m. Feature 5 consists of a single stone alignment a single course wide (ca. 0.20 m). The south wall of the structure has eroded completely into a drainage basin. The SAAS found a basalt grinder within Feature 5. Feature 6, which measures 19 m N–S × 9 m E–W, is a continuation of Feature 5 to the northwest. Feature 7 is a large circular alignment of boulders (some set upright) measuring ca. 8 m in diameter. Most boulders are greater than 2 m on a side. Feature 8, situated on the far western edge of the second terrace, is a small figure-8 type structure that has a total length of 4 m and a width of ca. 1–2 m. Also, Features 9 and 10 are on the second terrace. Feature 9 is a large circular structure measuring 8–9 m in diameter and open to the east. Its walls are two courses wide (0.90 m) and three courses high. Feature 10 is a large oval arrangement of boulders (8 × 4 m) southeast of Feature 9. Feature 11 consists of several disarticulated wall alignments and lies on the third terrace to the west, which is elevated slightly above the first two. One wall stands three courses high at the terrace edge.

Site No.: 164 (fig. 4.46)
Field Site No.: 143
Site Name: None
Map Reference: 3050 III, K737
Location on 1:50,000: 3321045 N / 711600 E
Elevation: 290 m
Aerial Reference No.: IGN-78-JOR 12/100 - 1442
Site Size: 15 m N–S × 25 m E–W
Inventory Rating: 2
Pottery Collected: Total = 0 (No. of Indicators: 0
/ No. Saved: 0)
Pottery Registration No(s).: None
Pottery Summary: N/A
Lithic Summary: Indef. cultural-historic placement
Site Description: This is a small cemetery consist-
ing of two clearly defined burials. One is half of a
stone ring (ca. 1 m in length), and the other is a
complete ring of the same size. Additional, smaller
stone mounds in the area may be evidence for other
burials. Ca. 3.50 m west of the graves there is a rock
alignment measuring 1.50 × 2 m. A lithic scatter
extends across the site, with an artifact density of ca.
5 lithics/m² and concentrated in an area of 5 × 5 m..

Site No.: 165 (fig. 4.46)
Field Site No.: 144
Site Name: None
Map Reference: 3050 III, K737
Location on 1:50,000: 3321195 N / 711610 E
Elevation: 290 m
Aerial Reference No.: IGN-78-JOR 12/100 - 1442
Site Size: 10 m N–S × 10 m E–W
Inventory Rating: 0
Pottery Collected: Total = 14 (No. of Indicators: 1
/ No. Saved: 4)
Pottery Registration No(s).: 9592–95
Pottery Summary: 10 R/Byz (?), 4 UD
Lithic Summary: Indef. cultural-historic placement
Site Description: This is a light sherd and lithic
scatter on the upper portion of an old alluvial fan
surface.

Site No.: 166 (fig. 4.46)
Field Site No.: 147
Site Name: None
Map Reference: 3050 III, K737
Location on 1:50,000: 3321320 N / 711420 E
Elevation: 285 m

Aerial Reference No.: IGN-78-JOR 12/100 - 1442
Site Size: 45 m N–S × 20 m E–W
Inventory Rating: 1
Pottery Collected: Total = 67 (No. of Indicators: 9
/ No. Saved: 9)
Pottery Registration No(s).: 9892–900
Pottery Summary: 5 LR, 58 LR/EByz, 4 EByz
Lithic Summary: Indef. cultural-historic placement
Site Description: This is a light sherd and lithic
scatter extending across an area of ca. 45 × 20 m
located high on an alluvial fan terrace west of the
mouth of Wādī Nukheila. The surface is mostly
comprised of gravel with a few boulders.

Site No.: 167 (fig. 4.46)
Field Site No.: 146
Site Name: SAAR Site 27
Map Reference: 3050 III, K737
Location on 1:50,000: 3321430 N / 711430 E
Elevation: 290 m
Aerial Reference No.: IGN-78-JOR 12/100 - 1442
Site Size: 60 m N–S × 60 m E–W
Inventory Rating: 3
Pottery Collected: Total = 224 (No. of Indicators:
107 / No. Saved: 24)
Pottery Registration No(s).: 9744–67
Pottery Summary: 224 ER/Nab (some probably
LR, 1 TS= ESA Hayes Form 23, ca. 100 BC–AD 100)
Lithic Summary: Indef. cultural-historic placement
Site Description: This is a small settlement lo-
cated in the foothills of esh-Shera north of Wādī
Nukheila. A wall alignment, which is two courses
wide (0.80 m) and ca. 5 m long, is visible at the
southern end of the site. To the north, there is a
corral-type structure enclosing an area of ca. 6 × 8
m. The walls of this structure are two courses wide
(0.80 m) and three courses high in places. The
northeast and southeast corners are preserved, and
what may be the entrance is located along the east
wall. Another structure is visible ca. 12 m further
north. The north and west walls, which resemble
that of the structure to the south, are preserved, and
the northwest corner is curved where they join. An
additional wall alignment and possible structure
are situated further north and divided from the
southern part of the site by recent drainage cuts.
These walls are a single course wide (ca. 0.20 m)
and badly eroded. Site is bounded to the north

by a large drainage. Opposite this drainage, on a plateau that extends to the west, the SAAS found a petroglyph carved onto a large sandstone boulder (ca. 0.90 × 0.90 × 0.50 m). The image is that of a male ibex and what appears to be a female hunter preparing to throw a spear.

Site No.: 168 (fig. 4.46)
Field Site No.: 145
Site Name: None
Map Reference: 3050 III, K737
Location on 1:50,000: 3321650 N / 711430 E
Elevation: 302 m
Aerial Reference No.: IGN-78-JOR 12/100 - 1442
Site Size: 30 m N–S × 80 m E–W
Inventory Rating: 3
Pottery Collected: Total = 0 (No. of Indicators: 0 / No. Saved: 0)
Pottery Registration No(s).: None
Pottery Summary: N/A
Lithic Summary: Indef. cultural-historic placement
Site Description: This is a cemetery consisting of at least 23 burials. Some appear as stone rings (ca. 3.50 × 2 m) while others appear as stone mounds (ca. 1.50 × 0.60 m). Some of the burials have been robbed exposing a mixture of bone material.

Site No.: 169 (fig. 4.46)
Field Site No.: 101
Site Name: SAAR Site 23
Map Reference: 3050 III, K737
Location on 1:50,000: See below
Elevation: 215 m
Site Size: 9000 m N–S × 5 m E–W
Inventory Rating: 4
Pottery Collected: Total = 9 (No. of Indicators: 0 / No. Saved: 6)
Pottery Registration No(s).: 6591–96
Pottery Summary: 1 Chalco/EB, 4 ER/Nab, 1 R/Byz body sherd, 3 Early Islamic
Lithic Summary: N/A
Site Description: This is a stone-paved road following roughly a N–S alignment. A segment of this road lies due west of Site 171, blocked only by a large sand dune. The road stretches ca. 8 km north from the mouth of Wādī Nukheila to Gharandal. This road was discovered by Niemi and Smith during the 1993 reconnaissance. The road gener-

ally keeps ca. 500 m west of the escarpment and follows a straight, N–S route that is interrupted by segments buried beneath advancing sand dunes. In some areas there are short segments of the road missing. The road is edged with curbstones and has a total width of ca. 3 m. On average, the curbstones measure 0.30 × 0.40 m and are somewhat larger than the cobbles of the pavement. The curbstones and the pavement are of local granite and sedimentary wadi rocks. The only available evidence for dating the road comes from a few ceramic artifacts collected during transects along its length and not more than 50–100 m on either side. UTM coordinates for the road from south to north are 3321180 N–S / 709175 E–W to 3330960 N–S / 712460 E–W.

Site No.: 170 (fig. 4.46)
Field Site No.: 109
Site Name: None
Map Reference: 3050 III, K737
Location on 1:50,000: 3321290 N / 710003 E
Elevation: 220 m
Aerial Reference No.: IGN-78-JOR 12/100 - 1542
Site Size: 80 m N–S × 150 m E–W
Inventory Rating: 4
Pottery Collected: Total = 8 (No. of Indicators: 2 / No. Saved: 3)
Pottery Registration No(s).: 6654–56
Pottery Summary: 8 ER/Nab
Lithic Summary: N/A
Site Description: This is a cemetery consisting of at least seven stone mounds or cairns on a ridge north of Wādī Nukheila. Most of these have been robbed.

Site No.: 171 (fig. 4.46)
Field Site No.: 108
Site Name: SAAR Site 24
Map Reference: 3050 III, K737
Location on 1:50,000: 3321381 N / 709905 E
Elevation: 220 m
Aerial Reference No.: IGN-78-JOR 12/100 - 1542
Site Size: 15 m N–S × 13 m E–W
Inventory Rating: 4
Pottery Collected: Total = 61 (No. of Indicators: 8 / No. Saved: 14)
Pottery Registration No(s).: 6354–67
Pottery Summary: 61 ER/Nab (early 2nd century AD)

Lithic Summary: Indef. cultural-historic placement

Site Description: This is a large ruined structure that may have been a tower situated north of Wādī Nukheila near a modern well. The existing wall alignments are difficult to trace as they are buried in sand and stone rubble. The structure may have measured ca. 14 × 11 m, while the area encompassed by the mound of collapsed stones measures ca. 16–21 m on a side (this is difficult to determine due to its ruined state). At least one stone block was noticed with tool marks. Unfortunately, two large bulldozer cuts through the southern portion of the mound has nearly destroyed the site. Also of interest are two robber pits excavated in the center of the structure, exposing a large quantity of ashy soil and a scatter of ceramic artifacts.

Site No.: 172 (fig. 4.46)
Field Site No.: 107
Site Name: None
Map Reference: 3050 III, K737
Location on 1:50,000: 3321534 N / 709704 E
Elevation: 220 m
Aerial Reference No.: IGN-78-JOR 12/100 - 1542
Site Size: 30 m N–S × 30 m E–W
Inventory Rating: 0
Pottery Collected: Total = 25 (No. of Indicators: 5 / No. Saved: 12)
Pottery Registration No(s).: 6637–48
Pottery Summary: 12 Chalco/EB, 13 ER/Nab
Lithic Summary: Probably Chalcolithic or later (see Chapter 5)
Site Description: This is a sherd and lithic scatter in an area of ca. 30 × 30 m and 40 m southwest of Site 173. Most of the artifacts were found down the slope from two large bulldozer cuts. This disturbance is recent (as of 1994), since the area had not been modified in 1993.

Site No.: 173 (fig. 4.46)
Field Site No.: 106
Site Name: None
Map Reference: 3050 III, K737
Location on 1:50,000: 3321582 N / 709760 E
Elevation: 225 m
Aerial Reference No.: IGN-78-JOR 12/100 - 1542
Site Size: 5 m N–S × 5 m E–W
Inventory Rating: 3

Pottery Collected: Total = 0 (No. of Indicators: 0 / No. Saved: 0)
Pottery Registration No(s).: None
Pottery Summary: N/A
Lithic Summary: Indef. cultural-historic placement
Site Description: This is an oval stone mound or cairn measuring ca. 4.50 × 4 m. The interior is hollowed out. A smaller grave lies ca. 21 m to the southwest on the same hill. This grave is a ca. 2 × 2 m circular alignment of stones with a sandy interior. The site is located on small hill ca. 350 m north of Wādī Nukheila.

Site No.: 174 (fig. 4.47)
Field Site No.: 140
Site Name: None
Map Reference: 3050 III, K737
Location on 1:50,000: 3323152 N / 710090 E
Elevation: 223 m
Aerial Reference No.: IGN-78-JOR 12/100 - 1650
Site Size: 70 m N–S × 25 m E–W
Inventory Rating: 2
Pottery Collected: Total = 0 (No. of Indicators: 0 / No. Saved: 0)
Pottery Registration No(s).: None
Pottery Summary: N/A
Lithic Summary: Indef. cultural-historic placement
Site Description: This is a cemetery consisting of ca. eight stone mounds or cairns ranging in size from 2–6 m in diameter. One stone mound is oblong with capstones set upright at both ends, another is oval (3 × 1.50 m) and is oriented E–W. A circular alignment of stones ca. 6 m in diameter lies ca. 50 m due south.

Site No.: 175 (fig. 4.47)
Field Site No.: 137
Site Name: None
Map Reference: 3050 III, K737
Location on 1:50,000: 3324810 N / 710507 E
Elevation: 241 m
Aerial Reference No.: IGN-78-JOR 12/100 - 1649
Site Size: 40 m N–S × 24 m E–W
Inventory Rating: 2
Pottery Collected: Total = 0 (No. of Indicators: 0 / No. Saved: 0)
Pottery Registration No(s).: None
Pottery Summary: N/A

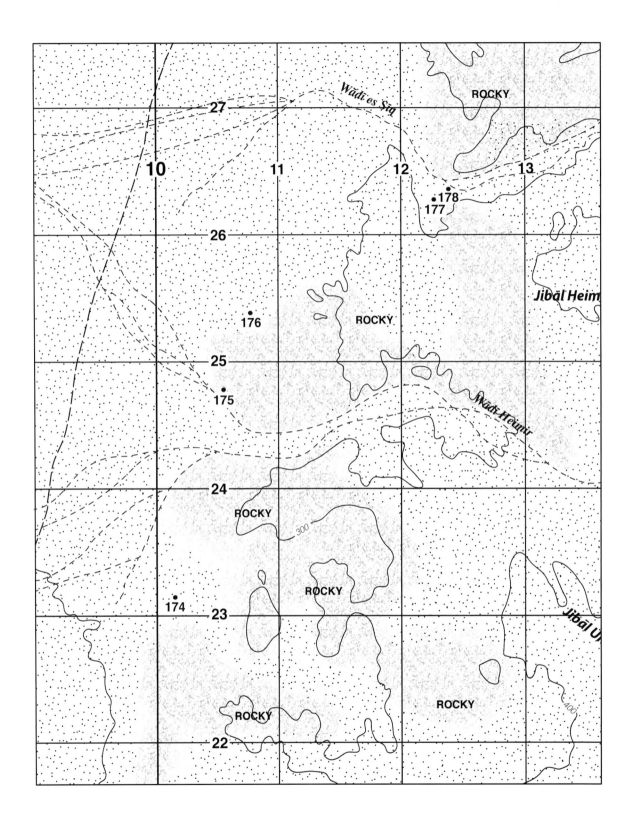

FIG. 4.47   *Gharandal Region (Region III), map 14 (Sites 174–178).*

Lithic Summary: Indef. cultural-historic placement
Site Description: This is a light lithic scatter (ca. 2 lithics/m²) on a small bedrock knob partially covered by drifting sands.

Site No.: 176 (fig. 4.47)
Field Site No.: 138
Site Name: None
Map Reference: 3050 III, K737
Location on 1:50,000: 3325376 N / 710785 E
Elevation: 245 m
Aerial Reference No.: IGN-78-JOR 12/100 - 1649
Site Size: 6 m N–S × 5 m E–W
Inventory Rating: 2
Pottery Collected: Total = 0 (No. of Indicators: 0 / No. Saved: 0)
Pottery Registration No(s).: None
Pottery Summary: N/A
Lithic Summary: N/A
Site Description: This is a stone mound or cairn measuring ca. 4.50 m in diameter. There is a wall alignment to the southwest, which is ca. 2 m in length, 0.40 m wide, and 0.40 m high. The SAAS could not determine the function of this feature. The site is located on a bedrock knoll between Wādī Ḥeimir and Wādī es-Sīq.

Site No.: 177 (fig. 4.47)
Field Site No.: 326
Site Name: None
Map Reference: 3050 III, K737
Location on 1:50,000: 3326285 N / 712320 E
Elevation: 278 m
Aerial Reference No.: IGN-78-JOR 12/100 - 1437
Site Size: 30 m N–S × 30 m E–W
Inventory Rating: 0
Pottery Collected: Total = 29 (No. of Indicators: 0 / No. Saved: 15)
Pottery Registration No(s).: 57550–64
Pottery Summary: 8 ER/Nab, 21 ER/LR
Lithic Summary: N/A
Site Description: This is an artifact scatter at the east end of an alluvial terrace. Density of the scatter is 1–5 sherds/m². No other visible features are present.

Site No.: 178 (fig. 4.47)
Field Site No.: 327
Site Name: None
Map Reference: 3050 III, K737
Location on 1:50,000: 3326335 N / 712437 E
Elevation: 278 m
Aerial Reference No.: IGN-78-JOR 12/100 - 1437
Site Size: 15 m N–S × 15 m E–W
Inventory Rating: 2
Pottery Collected: Total = 13 (No. of Indicators: 0 / No. Saved: 7)
Pottery Registration No(s).: 57534–40
Pottery Summary: 13 Chalco/EB
Lithic Summary: N/A
Site Description: This is a pot-bust on top of a wadi terrace covering an area of 15 m N–S × 15 m E–W.

Site No.: 179 (fig. 4.48)
Field Site No.: 139
Site Name: None
Map Reference: 3050 III, K737
Location on 1:50,000: 3327835 N / 711326 E
Elevation: 243 m
Aerial Reference No.: IGN-78-JOR 12/100 - 1653
Site Size: 3 m N–S × 3 m E–W
Inventory Rating: 2
Pottery Collected: Total = 0 (No. of Indicators: 0 / No. Saved: 0)
Pottery Registration No(s).: None
Pottery Summary: N/A
Lithic Summary: N/A
Site Description: This is stone mound or cairn measuring ca. 3 m in diameter. There is a very distinct ring of stones around the cairn. The site is located on a sand dune north of the mouth of Wādī es-Sīq.

Site No.: 180 (fig. 4.48)
Field Site No.: 321
Site Name: None
Map Reference: 3050 III, K737
Location on 1:50,000: 3330565 N / 713785 E
Elevation: 278 m
Aerial Reference No.: IGN-78-JOR 12/100 - 1433
Site Size: 30 m N–S × 86 m E–W
Inventory Rating: 5
Pottery Collected: Total = 13 (No. of Indicators: 2 / No. Saved: 13)
Pottery Registration No(s).: 54563–75

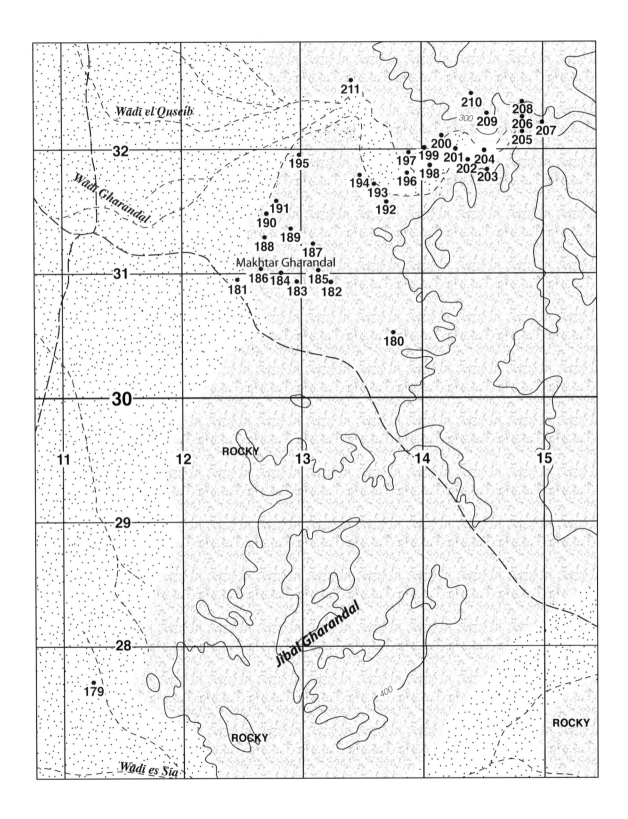

FIG. 4.48 *Gharandal Region (Region III), map 15 (Sites 179–211).*

Pottery Summary: 2 Chalco/EB, 11 Iron (?)

Lithic Summary: Indef. cultural-historic placement

Site Description: This is a small settlement consisting of ca. seven circular structures and two or three rectilinear structures. The size of the circular structures varies from 2–8 m in diameter, and these are constructed of a single course of large boulders (ca. 0.40 m on a side). Portions of some of the structures have eroded into the wadi. The rectilinear structures are similarly constructed and concentrate near the west end of the site. The best preserved measures ca. 11 × 5 m. A smaller structure measures ca. 5 × 4 m, and it is divided into two segments. Most of the structures, however, are difficult to define on account of erosion and deflation of the present surface. These also seem to have been robbed considerably for the construction of at least five large cairns, which vary in size from 4–6 m in diameter and ca. 1 m high.

Site No.: 181 (figs. 4.17, 4.48)

Field Site No.: 102

Site Name: Gharandal

Map Reference: 3050 III, K737

Location on 1:50,000: 3330960 N / 712460 E

Elevation: 215 m

Aerial Reference No.: IGN-78-JOR 12/100 - 1433

Site Size: 110 m N–S × 450 m E–W

Inventory Rating: 4

Pottery Collected: Total = 86 (No. of Indicators: 20 / No. Saved: 23)

Pottery Registration No(s).: 9588–91, 9604–7, 9787–801

Pottery Summary: 14 ER/Nab, 3 ER/LR, 65 R/Byz, 4 EByz, 1 Tile

Lithic Summary: Chalcolithic (see Chapter 7)

Site Description: The central feature is the Roman fort that measures ca. 37 m on a side with four corner towers (*quadriburgium*). The fort is almost completely buried in sand. Some internal structures seem to align against the interior curtail wall, mostly evident along the south wall. A great part of the south wall has also been disturbed by intense bulldozing activity, along with the southern portion of the western and eastern segments of where the south wall should be located. The southeast corner tower remains partially intact, which is adjacent to a bulldozer cut through the south wall.

The walls average 0.90 m wide (two–three courses) and are built mostly of cut limestone blocks. The SAAS recovered a coin (Obj. #504) of the mid-4th century AD at the site. Just east of the fort lie the ruins of another structure. There is a single definite wall alignment ca. 12 m in length and orientated E–W, with a width of 0.66 m. It is adjacent to a mounded area measuring ca. 19 m N–S × 19 m E–W and ca. 2.50 m high. The surrounding area is covered with rock rubble, and fragments of mortar and plaster. There may be additional wall alignments but they are indistinct and mostly buried under windblown sand. Further to the E–NE from this area, there is another fragmented wall alignment ca. two courses wide (0.65 m) and exposed for 1.20 m in length. Four cut limestone blocks and a single sandstone block are also visible. This may be remnants of a shallow aqueduct system that led to the fort from the spring ca. 400 m to the east. Excavations at this site, which began in 2009, recovered a Latin building inscription of the Tetrarchy that identifies the site as Arieldela and its garrison as *cohors secunda Galatarum*, as listed in the *Notitia Dignitatum* (*Or.* 34.44).

Site No.: 182 (figs. 4.26, 4.48)

Field Site No.: 322

Site Name: None

Map Reference: 3050 III, K737

Location on 1:50,000: 3330980 N / 713245 E

Elevation: 242 m

Aerial Reference No.: IGN-78-JOR 12/100 - 1433

Site Size: 57 m N–S × 76 m E–W

Inventory Rating: 2

Pottery Collected: Total = 46 (No. of Indicators: 1 / No. Saved: 29)

Pottery Registration No(s).: 54541–62, 54576–82

Pottery Summary: 13 ER/LR (8 probably from 1 vessel), 33 UD (17 from 4 vessels — 3 are wheel-made and probably date to the Iron Age or later)

Lithic Summary: Indef. cultural-historic placement

Site Description: The site consists of six features. Feature 1 is a large circular structure measuring ca. 9 m in diameter, with a smaller appended structure outside the southeast segment of the wall. Immediately north of Feature 1, Feature 2 is a small, isolated grave measuring 1.82 × 1.25 m (oriented NE–SW). Ca. 20 m east of Feature 1, Feature 3 is a nomadic campsite. There are three linear clearings measuring ca. 12 × 3 m, along with three stone rings or hut circles measuring on average 4.80 m in diameter. A possible hearth is associated with one of the stone rings. There are two smaller stone rings also present, one measuring ca. 1.50 m in diameter and another measuring 3.50 × 2 m. Features 4–6 are additional nomadic encampments on the same alluvial surface 60–100 m northeast of Feature 1. Cumulatively, there are seven larger stone rings or hut circles and two smaller stone rings present, which are similar to those at Feature 3.

Site No.: 183 (fig. 4.48)
Field Site No.: 325
Site Name: None
Map Reference: 3050 III, K737
Location on 1:50,000: 3330980 N / 712939 E
Elevation: 278 m
Aerial Reference No.: IGN-78-JOR 12/100 - 1431
Site Size: 11.50 m N–S × 6 m E–W
Inventory Rating: 2
Pottery Collected: Total = 0 (No. of Indicators: 0 / No. Saved: 0)
Pottery Registration No(s).: None
Pottery Summary: N/A
Lithic Summary: N/A
Site Description: The site consists of two isolated structures at the end of a high spur overlooking two wadi drainages. The first structure measures 3.80 m N–S × 3.50 m E–W, and its walls are ca. 0.50 m wide (two courses with gravel and cobble fill). Ca. 3.80 m to the south there is another structure measuring 4.70 m on a side, and it is constructed similarly to the first. Site may be associated with Site 184 due to proximity and similarity in construction methods.

Site No.: 184 (figs. 4.24, 4.48)
Field Site No.: 324
Site Name: None
Map Reference: 3050 III, K737
Location on 1:50,000: 3331035 N / 712867 E
Elevation: 240 m
Aerial Reference No.: IGN-78-JOR 12/100 - 1431
Site Size: 60 m N–S × 60 m E–W
Inventory Rating: 2
Pottery Collected: Total = 7 (No. of Indicators: 0 / No. Saved: 4)

Pottery Registration No(s).: 57546–49
Pottery Summary: 5 LR (1 vessel), 2 UD
Lithic Summary: Indef. cultural-historic placement
Site Description: This site, which consists of six features, is situated on a small wadi terrace above an ephemeral drainage northeast of Gharandal. Feature 3 consists of a single stone enclosure or animal pen measuring ca. 8 m in diameter. It is the farthest feature to the west on the north side of the drainage. The southern portion of the circle seems to have eroded away. The perimeter of Feature 3 is comprised of a single course of boulders and measures ca. 1 m wide. Feature 2 is the collapsed ruins of a small structure 36 m southeast of Feature 3. It measures ca. 5.20 m in diameter. Feature 1, the ruins of another structure, is 54 m southeast of Feature 3. It measures 5.80 × 5.20 m. A pit has been excavated within the south quadrant of the structure revealing a small quantity of pottery. A portion of its walls is still preserved up to a height of 0.60 m. Feature 4 is a structure located on the hillside above Feature 1, and Feature 2 is located ca. 45 m south of Feature 3. Feature 4 measures 6 × 4 m. Ca. 10 m W–SW of Feature 4, Feature 5 is a structure that is ovoid in shape and measures 4 m on a side. Feature 6 consists of a stone engraved with Arabic script. It is ca. 7 m north of Feature 5. Many other stones inscribed with Arabic script were found dispersed across the site.

Site No.: 185 (figs. 4.18, 4.48)
Field Site No.: 323
Site Name: None
Map Reference: 3050 III, K737
Location on 1:50,000: 3331050 N / 713165 E
Elevation: 238 m
Aerial Reference No.: IGN-78-JOR 12/100 - 1433
Site Size: 27 m N–S × 32 m E–W
Inventory Rating: 2
Pottery Collected: Total = 3 (No. of Indicators: 1 / No. Saved: 1)
Pottery Registration No(s).: 57541
Pottery Summary: 1 ER/Nab, 2 Modern
Lithic Summary: N/A
Site Description: The site consists of three features. Feature 1 is an encampment in a clearing that measures 12 m N–S × 32 m E–W. It is situated on a small wadi terrace and appears modern. Opposite

Feature 1, there is another encampment where the SAAS found two grinding stones. At the west end of the terrace where Feature 1 is located, Feature 2 is a solidly constructed stone structure measuring 4.18 m N–S × 4.20 m E–W. It is constructed of cut limestone blocks, with mud mortar and chinking of smaller limestone rocks. The structure is preserved up to 1.30 m high (nine courses) and its walls are two courses wide. The southeast wall curves toward the entrance along the east wall. A small partition wall oriented N–S divides the structure into two compartments. Ca. 12 m southeast of Feature 2 there is a small barrage or terrace wall constructed across a tributary wadi elevated above the wadi terrace (Feature 3). The barrage measures 5.20 × 0.40 m, and it is preserved to a height of 0.50 m. The barrage was apparently intended to limit the flow of water toward Feature 2 from above.

Site No.: 186 (fig. 4.48)
Field Site No.: 151
Site Name: None
Map Reference: 3050 III, K737
Location on 1:50,000: 3331078 N / 712750 E
Elevation: 230 m
Aerial Reference No.: IGN-78-JOR 12/100 - 1431
Site Size: 40 m N–S × 30 m E–W
Inventory Rating: 1
Pottery Collected: Total = 13 (No. of Indicators: 3 / No. Saved: 7)
Pottery Registration No(s).: 9596–9602
Pottery Summary: 2 ER/Nab, 8 R/Byz, 1 Modern, 2 UD
Lithic Summary: Indef. cultural-historic placement
Site Description: This is a wall alignment measuring ca. 6 m in length and only a single course wide. Whatever structure once stood here, it was no doubt destroyed by the construction of the modern police post. This could have been a small tower visible from the Roman fort at Gharandal.

Site No.: 187 (fig. 4.48)
Field Site No.: 320
Site Name: None
Map Reference: 3050 III, K737
Location on 1:50,000: 3331260 N / 713090 E
Elevation: 230 m
Aerial Reference No.: IGN-78-JOR 12/100 - 1431

Site Size: 15 m N–S × 38 m E–W
Inventory Rating: 2
Pottery Collected: Total = 3 (No. of Indicators: 0 / No. Saved: 3)
Pottery Registration No(s).: 54374–76
Pottery Summary: 3 ER/LR
Lithic Summary: N/A
Site Description: The site consists of three features situated in an ephemeral drainage between two spurs. Feature 1 consists of two graves. One grave is oblong and measures 2.60 × 1.40 m. It is oriented NE–SW (47 degrees). The second grave is more circular and measures 1.50 m in diameter. The SAAS found a few pottery sherds around Feature 1. Feature 2 appears to be a modern bedouin encampment with an associated hearth. Feature 3 is an L-shaped rock alignment consisting of small boulders and cobbles piled along the edge of a level surface. The walls are a single course wide and high and measure ca. 5 × 5 m.

Site No.: 188 (fig. 4.48)
Field Site No.: 100
Site Name: None
Map Reference: 3049 III, K737
Location on 1:50,000: 3331320 N / 712740 E
Elevation: 225 m
Aerial Reference No.: IGN-78-JOR 12/100 - 1431
Site Size: 50 m N–S × 100 m E–W
Inventory Rating: 3
Pottery Collected: Total = 0 (No. of Indicators: 0 / No. Saved: 0)
Pottery Registration No(s).: None
Pottery Summary: N/A
Lithic Summary: Indef. cultural-historic placement
Site Description: This is a dense lithic scatter (ca. 28–43 lithics/m²) north of Gharandal. A modern corral has been constructed at the site. Most of the lithics were concentrated east and up the slope from the corral.

Site No.: 189 (fig. 4.48)
Field Site No.: 319
Site Name: None
Map Reference: 3050 III, K737
Location on 1:50,000: 3331355 N / 712950 E
Elevation: 237 m
Aerial Reference No.: IGN-78-JOR 12/100 - 1431

Site Size: 12 m N–S × 50 m E–W
Inventory Rating: 2
Pottery Collected: Total = 7 (No. of Indicators: 1 / No. Saved: 7)
Pottery Registration No(s).: 54377–83
Pottery Summary: 7 Chalco/EB
Lithic Summary: Indef. cultural-historic placement
Site Description: The site consists of three features on a low spur north of Gharandal. Feature 1 is a circular arrangement of stones, probably a grave, set nearly flush with the ground forming some sort of pavement. It measures 1.60 m in diameter. The stones along the perimeter are set 0.10 m above the interior pavers. Feature 2 is a rock alignment located 112 degrees and ca. 30 m from Feature 1. It is a single course wide (0.60 m) and 3.20 m in length. Feature 3 is a group of several graves dispersed across the entire area of the site.

Site No.: 190 (fig. 4.48)
Field Site No.: 318
Site Name: None
Map Reference: 3050 III, K737
Location on 1:50,000: 3331540 N / 712750 E
Elevation: 230 m
Aerial Reference No.: IGN-78-JOR 12/100 - 1431
Site Size: 6.30 m N–S × 6.30 m E–W
Inventory Rating: 3
Pottery Collected: Total = 0 (No. of Indicators: 0 / No. Saved: 0)
Pottery Registration No(s).: None
Pottery Summary: N/A
Lithic Summary: Indef. cultural-historic placement
Site Description: This is a large cairn, or perhaps the ruins of a tower, that measures ca. 6.30 m in diameter and 1.10 m high. The structure is partially destroyed in the northeast quadrant, mostly by secondary robber pits. Some bone fragments are present in the disturbed remains. Nearby, modern constructions show evidence of reuse of some of the stones from the site.

Site No.: 191 (figs. 4.13, 4.48)
Field Site No.: 317
Site Name: None
Map Reference: 3050 III, K737
Location on 1:50,000: 3331585 N / 712790 E
Elevation: 222 m

Aerial Reference No.: IGN-78-JOR 12/100 - 1431
Site Size: 4.40 m N–S × 9.60 m E–W
Inventory Rating: 2
Pottery Collected: Total = 19 (No. of Indicators: 5 / No. Saved: 12)
Pottery Registration No(s).: 54245–56
Pottery Summary: 19 Chalco/EB
Lithic Summary: Indef. cultural-historic placement
Site Description: The site consists of a single, indeterminate structure on a small alluvial fan south of Wādī el-Quṣeib. It measures 4.40 m N–S × 9.60 m E–W. It is constructed mostly of uncut limestone boulders (ca. 0.40 m on a side). Along the interior face of the west wall is a slightly raised platform ca. 2.50 m across. There is a possible entrance into the structure along the north wall.

Site No.: 192 (fig. 4.48)
Field Site No.: 313
Site Name: None
Map Reference: 3050 III, K737
Location on 1:50,000: 3331645 N / 713705 E
Elevation: 261 m
Aerial Reference No.: IGN-78-JOR 12/100 - 1431
Site Size: 3.30 m N–S × 3.30 m E–W
Inventory Rating: 2
Pottery Collected: Total = 0 (No. of Indicators: 0 / No. Saved: 0)
Pottery Registration No(s).: None
Pottery Summary: N/A
Lithic Summary: N/A
Site Description: This is a single stone mound, perhaps a burial cairn, situated on a saddle above a wadi terrace that overlooks Wādī el-Quṣeib. The cairn measures 3.30 m in diameter and 0.45 m high and is in a good state of preservation.

Site No.: 193 (fig. 4.48)
Field Site No.: 314
Site Name: None
Map Reference: 3050 III, K737
Location on 1:50,000: 3331800 N / 713632 E
Elevation: 252 m
Aerial Reference No.: IGN-78-JOR 12/100 - 1431
Site Size: 50 m N–S × 20 m E–W
Inventory Rating: 2
Pottery Collected: Total = 26 (No. of Indicators: 2 / No. Saved: 8)

Pottery Registration No(s).: 54386–93
Pottery Summary: 19 ER/Nab (1 vessel), 4 ER/LR, 1 LR, 2 UD
Lithic Summary: Indef. cultural-historic placement
Site Description: This site is located on a wadi terrace along the south bank of Wādī el-Quṣeib. The site consists of three features. Feature 1 is a large stone mound, most likely a burial cairn, which has been vandalized. It measures 6.70 m in diameter and 0.92 m high. An exposed interior compartment measures 2.30 × 1 m. Numerous bone fragments are scattered around the top of the cairn. Half a meter east of the cairn is Feature 2, a large stone with a cross-like design etched on its surface. The dimensions of the stone are 0.87 m long × 0.78 m wide × 0.58 m high. Ca. 42 m at 340 degrees from Feature 1, Feature 3 is a small cemetery of at least six graves. Most of the graves appear as small piles of cobbles and boulders. One grave is oblong and measures 2.60 × 1.70 m and it is oriented E–W. Exactly 19 m at 103 degrees from Feature 1 is a rock pile with a large hole dug in it, perhaps a shallow well.

Site No.: 194 (fig. 4.48)
Field Site No.: 315
Site Name: None
Map Reference: 3050 III, K737
Location on 1:50,000: 3331825 N / 713535 E
Elevation: 250 m
Aerial Reference No.: IGN-78-JOR 12/100 - 1431
Site Size: 193 m N–S × 27 m E–W
Inventory Rating: 2
Pottery Collected: Total = 0 (No. of Indicators: 0 / No. Saved: 0)
Pottery Registration No(s).: None
Pottery Summary: N/A
Lithic Summary: Indef. cultural-historic placement
Site Description: The site consists of four features. Feature 1 is a bedouin encampment consisting of two stone fence enclosures (apparent clearings for tents) and a possible hearth (four stones set in a circle). The better preserved enclosure (8 m N–S × 5 m E–W) consists of a single course of stones with an apparent opening to the north. Feature 2 is a series of one course wide by one course high rock alignments crossing a small ephemeral drainage, which spans the eastern edge of the site.

The best preserved measures 4.30 × 0.90 m. This series of rock alignments probably managed runoff water from the surrounding hills for agricultural purposes. There appears to be recent alluvial shifts/deposits, which probably could have sustained runoff agriculture in antiquity. Around a bend to the south of the drainage are two other possible terrace walls preserved ca. 1 m in length. Feature 3 is a small stone ring or hut circle measuring 1.75 m in diameter. It appears older than the features of the encampment. Feature 4 consists of four small graves at the north end of the site. There are two distinct types of graves apparent. Two graves appear as oblong stone piles, averaging 2.20 × 1.40 m. One is oriented 360 degrees and the other is oriented 47 degrees. The other graves are more circular with a flat stone surface. One measures 1.85 m in diameter, and the other is 0.87 × 0.57 m and is oriented 100 degrees. The latter is probably an infant burial.

Site No.: 195 (fig. 4.48)
Field Site No.: 316
Site Name: None
Map Reference: 3050 III, K737
Location on 1:50,000: 3331985 N / 712975 E
Elevation: 238 m
Aerial Reference No.: IGN-78-JOR 12/100 - 1431
Site Size: 64 m N–S × 75 m E–W
Inventory Rating: 2
Pottery Collected: Total = 6 (No. of Indicators: 3 / No. Saved: 6)
Pottery Registration No(s).: 54368–73
Pottery Summary: 4 Iron (?), 1 R/Byz, 1 Modern (knob handle)
Lithic Summary: Indef. cultural-historic placement
Site Description: This is a contemporary bedouin encampment with evidence of earlier activity. Lithics and pottery are scattered across the site. Recent features include an animal pen, hearths and modern debris. The animal pen is ca. 12 × 12 m and filled with dung. There are at least two hearths, which appear as circular depressions ca. 0.70 m in diameter with no stones aligning them. Ash encircles the hearth areas.

Site No.: 196 (fig. 4.48)
Field Site No.: 312
Site Name: None
Map Reference: 3050 III, K737
Location on 1:50,000: 3331890 N / 713935 E
Elevation: 258 m
Aerial Reference No.: IGN-78-JOR 12/100 - 977
Site Size: 8 m N–S × 4 m E–W
Inventory Rating: 2
Pottery Collected: Total = 0 (No. of Indicators: 0 / No. Saved: 0)
Pottery Registration No(s).: None
Pottery Summary: N/A
Lithic Summary: N/A
Site Description: The site consists of two petroglyphs, Features 1–2, on the slope of an alluvial terrace descending into Wādī el-Quṣeib. Feature 1 depicts an ibex and an inscription on a sandstone boulder measuring ca. 1.90 m on a side. Feature 2 lies ca. 5 m north of Feature 1. It is a single petroglyph of an ibex on a sandstone boulder that measures 1.60 m on a side.

Site No.: 197 (fig. 4.48)
Field Site No.: 311
Site Name: None
Map Reference: 3050 III, K737
Location on 1:50,000: 3331910 N / 713962 E
Elevation: 260 m
Aerial Reference No.: IGN-78-JOR 12/100 - 977
Site Size: 10 m N–S × 27 m E–W
Inventory Rating: 2
Pottery Collected: Total = 1 (No. of Indicators: 0 / No. Saved: 0)
Pottery Registration No(s).: None
Pottery Summary: 1 UD
Lithic Summary: Indef. cultural-historic placement
Site Description: The site consists of four graves on a wadi terrace along the north bank of Wādī el-Quṣeib. The average size of the graves is 1.70 m N–S × 1.45 m E–W. These mainly appear as stone piles. All the graves are oriented differently. One grave had an orientation of 332 degrees. At least one grave has been vandalized. There are a number of other disarticulated rock piles that might be additional graves.

Site No.: 198 (fig. 4.48)
Field Site No.: 310
Site Name: None
Map Reference: 3050 III, K737
Location on 1:50,000: 3331915 N / 714030 E
Elevation: 270 m
Aerial Reference No.: IGN-78-JOR 12/100 - 977
Site Size: 20 m N–S × 45 m E–W
Inventory Rating: 1
Pottery Collected: Total = 4 (No. of Indicators: 0 / No. Saved: 2)
Pottery Registration No(s).: 54384–85
Pottery Summary: 1 ER/Nab, 3 Early Islamic (1 vessel)
Lithic Summary: Indef. cultural-historic placement
Site Description: The site consists of two features on an alluvial terrace above Wādī el-Quṣeib. Feature 1 is a cairn heavily disturbed by clandestine excavation. It measures ca. 3.60 m in diameter with its central area completely displaced by digging. Feature 2 lies 32 m west of Feature 1. It is an unspecified stone structure, seemingly a circular hut, 4.45 m in diameter and preserved up to 0.68 m high. The width of the walls is 0.75 m (two courses).

Site No.: 199 (fig. 4.48)
Field Site No.: 309
Site Name: None
Map Reference: 3050 III, K737
Location on 1:50,000: 3332050 N / 714135 E
Elevation: 290 m
Aerial Reference No.: IGN-78-JOR 12/100 - 977
Site Size: 112 m N–S × 493 m E–W
Inventory Rating: 2
Pottery Collected: Total = 27 (No. of Indicators: 9 / No. Saved: 23)
Pottery Registration No(s).: 54339–61
Pottery Summary: 5 Chalco/EB, 1 Iron (Negevite), 6 ER/Nab, 9 ER/LR, 1 LR, 4 EByz, 1 UD (red paint, possibly Edomite)
Lithic Summary: Indef. cultural-historic placement
Site Description: The site consists of an unspecified structure (Feature 1) set within a nomadic encampment (Feature 2) and with various oblong stone features (Feature 3) spread out across the site. Feature 1 is a structure measuring 4.60 m N–S × 5.80 m E–W. It is constructed of large boulders ranging in size from 0.30–0.90 m on a side. There is

a possible wall alignment two courses wide on the north side of the structure. In the northwest corner of the structure is a circular area enclosed by boulders measuring ca. 1.50 m in diameter. Ca. 5.70 m southwest of Feature 1 is a hearth, which measures 0.74 × 0.41 m and seems to be part of the nomadic encampment. The hearth is lined with sandstone slabs. Feature 2 is the nomadic encampment along with two stone rings, possibly circular huts. One is 4.70 m in diameter and lies at the western edge of Feature 1. The other is roughly 3.50 m in diameter, but is poorly preserved. A small hearth with recent ash deposits lies within this second stone ring. The camp covers the entire site. There are hearths, clearings, various rock alignments, and small stone enclosures abutting the rock outcrops. A number of contemporary items such as clothing fragments and metal objects suggest modern use of the site. The oblong features that comprise Feature 3 appear to be modern due to their state of preservation. They are constructed of a single course of sandstone boulders and average 2.30 × 1.10 m. Their interiors are cleared of stones.

Site No.: 200 (fig. 4.48)
Field Site No.: 308
Site Name: None
Map Reference: 3050 III, K737
Location on 1:50,000: 3332075 N / 714260 E
Elevation: 276 m
Aerial Reference No.: IGN-78-JOR 12/100 - 977
Site Size: 30 m N–S × 12 m E–W
Inventory Rating: 3
Pottery Collected: Total = 0 (No. of Indicators: 0 / No. Saved: 0)
Pottery Registration No(s).: None
Pottery Summary: N/A
Lithic Summary: N/A
Site Description: This is a cemetery consisting of 14 distinct graves, which vary in size from 2.87 × 1.20 m. to 1.34 × 0.85 m. The alignment of the graves varies perhaps suggesting that these are pre-Islamic. Each grave is oblong, built of boulders aligned along the perimeter, and filled with large cobbles and pebbles. The site lies due west of Site 201 across an ephemeral drainage.

Site No.: 201 (fig. 4.48)
Field Site No.: 307
Site Name: None
Map Reference: 3050 III, K737
Location on 1:50,000: 3332070 N / 714305 E
Elevation: 276 m
Aerial Reference No.: IGN-78-JOR 12/100 - 977
Site Size: 8 m N–S × 12 m E–W
Inventory Rating: 2
Pottery Collected: Total = 0 (No. of Indicators: 0 / No. Saved: 0)
Pottery Registration No(s).: None
Pottery Summary: N/A
Lithic Summary: Indef. cultural-historic placement
Site Description: The site consists of two burial cairns. The larger is ovoid in shape and measures 3.80 × 1.80 m, with an E–W orientation of 69 degrees. The smaller cairn measures 3.10 × 1.80 m, with an E–W orientation of 81 degrees. Around the burials are several rock scatters and stone piles which may be additional burials.

Site No.: 202 (fig. 4.48)
Field Site No.: 306
Site Name: None
Map Reference: 3050 III, K737
Location on 1:50,000: 3332040 N / 714350 E
Elevation: 275 m
Aerial Reference No.: IGN-78-JOR 12/100 - 977
Site Size: 70 m N–S × 60 m E–W
Inventory Rating: 2
Pottery Collected: Total = 0 (No. of Indicators: 0 / No. Saved: 0)
Pottery Registration No(s).: None
Pottery Summary: N/A
Lithic Summary: Indef. cultural-historic placement
Site Description: The site consists of three features. Feature 1 is a series of retaining walls, apparently to manage water for agriculture. The east side of the site consists of two parallel walls of local boulders (0.20–0.40 m on a side) and cobbles. These walls are spaced 1.56 m apart with an interior area between the walls measuring 1.02 m wide at the widest point. The walls run parallel E–W (almost exactly) for 5.20 m until cut by a tributary wadi (gully). These parallel walls likely retarded the flow of water so it did not damage crops cultivated on the surrounding terraces. Ca. 10 m west of the

gully is a series of walls, one of which measures 1 m N–S × 2.20 m E–W. Two other apparent wall alignments lie to the north. Ca. 40 m northwest of the terraces, Feature 2 is a stone circle or hut circle. It is two courses wide (0.55 m) and a single course high (ca. 0.25 m) and measures 5 m in diameter. The southwest segment of the circle is disturbed by erosion. Inside the circle is a small mound of cobbles, perhaps a hearth. Feature 3 is a robbed grave ca. 3 m north of Feature 2. What remains of this feature measures 2.10 m N–S × 1.50 E–W with a N–S orientation.

Site No.: 203 (fig. 4.48)
Field Site No.: 302
Site Name: None
Map Reference: 3050 III, K737
Location on 1:50,000: 3331940 N / 714440 E
Elevation: 270 m
Aerial Reference No.: IGN-78-JOR 12/100 - 977
Site Size: 84 m N–S × 141 m E–W
Inventory Rating: 3
Pottery Collected: Total = 82 (No. of Indicators: 15 / No. Saved: 41)
Pottery Registration No(s).: 54297–328, 54329–31, 54333–38
Pottery Summary: 7 Chalco/EB, 3 EB, 15 ER/Nab (7 from a cookpot / 1 vessel), 1 LR, 50 R/Byz, 1 Byz (amphora class 48/49), 1 EByz, 1 LByz, 3 UD
Lithic Summary: Indef. cultural-historic placement
Site Description: The site consists of at least eight features situated on a wadi terrace along the south bank of Wādī el-Quṣeib. At the eastern end of the wadi terrace, Features 1 and 2 are stone rings, probably hut circles. Feature 1 measures 2.70 m N–S × 3.20 m E–W with an interior dimension of up to 2.90 m in diameter. A possible entrance may exist along the south wall. Feature 2 is another oblong stone ring or hut circle measuring 3.80 m N–S × 3.20 m E–W and open on its south end. Stones that comprise the circle are boulder size (ca. 0.30–0.40 m on a side). The walls are preserved one course high except for the north wall, which is two courses high (ca. 0.65 m). Boulders appear mounded against the north wall. Nearer to the center of the wadi terrace, Features 3–5 are all apparent wall alignments. Feature 3 is a large retaining wall established at the base of the slope at

the south edge of the wadi terrace. The wall is built of boulders that measure ca. 0.30 m on a side. The wall extends ca. 6 m E–W. Features 4–5 are both L-shaped retaining walls. The latter measures 2.40 m N–S × 3.50 m E–W and is preserved up to three courses high (0.60 m). There is an accumulation of alluvial material in the northwest corner of this feature. Large quantities of dung within the feature indicate modern reuse as an animal pen. Feature 4 measures ca. 3.50 m N–S × 3.50 m E–W and exhibits the same characteristics as Feature 5. Feature 6 consists of numerous burials scattered across the wadi terrace, which range broadly in terms of size and type. It is difficult to determine the exact number of burials due to recent bedouin activity in the area and the disturbance caused by erosion. A good estimate is between 10 and 20 graves. Most graves appear as rock piles, although some piles are more articulated and exhibit rock alignments along their edges. A typical grave measures 2.15 m long × 0.70 m wide, with a single layer of rocks overlaid on top. Other graves appear more rounded or as small ovoid rock alignments. Feature 7 is a series of soil erosion and/or water diversion check dams and walls distributed across the wadi terrace. Some walls resemble those of Features 4–5 and usually contain concentrations of silt on the side up the slope. These features may date to different periods, without further precision. Feature 8 consists of a small square pattern of stones inlaid in the soil (only two stones *in situ*) measuring 0.34 m on a side with a depth of 0.05 m. Two other stones next to the depression are obviously part of the feature. It may be significant that the four stones are of different colors (black, tan, and two shades of red). A flat stone, possibly used to cover the feature, lay adjacent to the pit. Three other possible stone squares are within one meter of Feature 8, but appear to have been dismantled. These squares are similar to those found at Site 207. Finally, in addition to pottery and lithics at the site, was a piece of basalt (not collected) in one of the erosion control dams. The site also yielded a shell fragment and a large piece of gypsum. Many discarded articles of modern debris lie across the wadi terrace along with other evidence of recent bedouin encampments.

Site No.: 204 (fig. 4.48)
Field Site No.: 305
Site Name: None
Map Reference: 3050 III, K737
Location on 1:50,000: 3332025 N / 714485 E
Elevation: 275 m
Aerial Reference No.: IGN-78-JOR 12/100 - 977
Site Size: 31 m N–S × 119 m E–W
Inventory Rating: 2
Pottery Collected: Total = 9 (No. of Indicators: 2 / No. Saved: 6)
Pottery Registration No(s).: 54362–67
Pottery Summary: 1 Chalco/EB, 3 ER/Nab (lamp), 5 ER/LR
Lithic Summary: Indef. cultural-historic placement
Site Description: The site consists of four features. Feature 1 is a large cairn. The foundation of the cairn measures ca. 3.30 m in diameter. The boulders that form the base of the cairn are a mix of sandstone, limestone, chert, and other local stones, which average ca. 0.20 m on a side. Feature 2 lies near the cairn. It is a cleared area measuring ca. 23 × 2.30 m and oriented roughly E–W. Ca. 5 m to the east and south of Feature 2 is a small hearth with an exterior diameter of 0.80 m. Feature 3 is a semicircular arrangement of stones, perhaps a hut circle, measuring 3.60 m N–S × 2.16 m E–W and open on its east face. Feature 4 is a series of ca. 19 graves spread out across the wadi terrace. The types of graves range from rectilinear forms constructed of boulders to small stone piles of tumble.

Site No.: 205 (fig. 4.48)
Field Site No.: 300
Site Name: None
Map Reference: 3050 III, K737
Location on 1:50,000: 3332195 N / 714812 E
Elevation: 299 m
Aerial Reference No.: IGN-78-JOR 12/100 - 977
Site Size: 4.40 m N–S × 4 m E–W
Inventory Rating: 2
Pottery Collected: Total = 0 (No. of Indicators: 0 / No. Saved: 0)
Pottery Registration No(s).: None
Pottery Summary: N/A
Lithic Summary: N/A
Site Description: This is an isolated stone structure situated at the tip of a low spur with a commanding view over Wādī el-Quṣeib. The structure measures 4.40 m N–S × 4 m E–W. It may have been a small tower but this is only a plausible suggestion. The walls of the structure are preserved up to three courses high (1.20 m) and a single course wide (ca. 0.32 m). The structure comes to a point at its northwest end. The SAAS found some copper scattered outside the northwest wall.

Site No.: 206 (fig. 4.48)
Field Site No.: 301
Site Name: None
Map Reference: 3050 III, K737
Location on 1:50,000: 3332240 N / 714845 E
Elevation: 280 m
Aerial Reference No.: IGN-78-JOR 12/100 - 977
Site Size: 4.25 m N–S × 2.90 m E–W
Inventory Rating: 2
Pottery Collected: Total = 4 (No. of Indicators: 1 / No. Saved: 1)
Pottery Registration No(s).: 54332
Pottery Summary: 1 Iron (Negevite), 3 ER/LR
Lithic Summary: N/A
Site Description: The site consists of a single stone ring or hut circle on the edge of a wadi terrace along the south bank of Wādī el-Quṣeib. The largest stone of the circle is to the north and measures 1.40 m across at the top. The remaining stones of the circle average 0.45 × 0.25 × 0.20 m. The width of the perimeter is 0.40 m, appears to be two courses wide, and only one course high (up to 0.40 m). Some of the stones are set upright. The ring is oval and measures 3.10 m N–S × 2.90 m E–W. There are two possible openings into the ring, in the southwest corner and in the northeast corner. Adjacent to the large boulder in the north, there is an arrangement of small stones that may be a small storage bin set within the structure. The area enclosed by this arrangement of stones is 1.15 m N–S × 0.45 m E–W.

Site No.: 207 (figs. 4.27, 4.48)
Field Site No.: 298
Site Name: None
Map Reference: 3050 III, K737
Location on 1:50,000: 3332285 N / 714935 E
Elevation: 296 m
Aerial Reference No.: IGN-78-JOR 12/100 - 977
Site Size: 70 m N–S × 2 m E–W

Inventory Rating: 1
Pottery Collected: Total = 5 (No. of Indicators: 1 / No. Saved: 5)
Pottery Registration No(s).: 54292–96
Pottery Summary: 1 ER/Nab, 2 ER/LR, 1 LR/EByz, 1 UD
Lithic Summary: Indef. cultural-historic placement
Site Description: This is a small settlement on a wadi terrace above Wādī el-Quṣeib. The SAAS recorded 10 distinct features. Features 1–5 are all structures or perhaps houses. The largest (Feature 1) measures 5.10 m N–S × 3.50 m E–W with walls preserved up to six courses high (1 m). There is an entrance along the southeast wall. This structure is currently being utilized as an animal enclosure. To the northwest and adjacent to the corner of the structure there is an apparent hearth or storage area measuring ca. 0.50 m × 0.50 m. Feature 2 is another structure constructed of local chert and sandstone boulders. The feature is ovoid in shape and measures 3.80 m N–S × 3.20 m E–W. This feature shows no signs of modern restoration or reuse. Feature 3 is a structure which is badly disturbed by modern reuse. It measures ca. 4 m N–S × 3.80 m E–W. To the north of this structure is a possible rectilinear wall adjoining the structure on its northwest corner. This feature shows signs of use as an animal pen and is constructed of substantial boulders up to 1.20 m long. Feature 4 is an isolated structure similar to Feature 3. It is preserved up to two courses high (ca. 0.40 m) and also appears to have been used recently as an animal pen. In the same area, Feature 5 is similar to Features 1–4. Feature 6 is a group of hearths and stone piles south and west of the Features 1–5. Feature 7 is a small grave at the western end of the site. It appears as a small stone mound measuring ca. 2.10 m in diameter. Feature 8 is an isolated structure lying at the far western end of the site. It measures 2.60 m N–S × 2.50 m E–W. Foundation stones for the east wall are visible. One large boulder is built into the northwest corner which measures ca. 0.70–0.80 m on a side. Feature 9 is a small, unspecified structure with two adjacent compartments. The west compartment opens to the south. The structure measures 3.90 × 2.50 m. The compartments are roughly circular with interior dimensions of 0.80 m in diameter. Its walls are a single course wide (ca. 0.30 m) and

a single course high. Separating the two compartments are large boulders embedded in the surface. The boulders measure 0.90 m long × 0.30 m wide × 0.48 m high. Dispersed across the site, Feature 10 consists of a series of small stone-lined pits set into the ground. Three in the west end of the site have four different colored stones making up the square: red, black and two shades of gray. These pits are all about the same size, measuring ca. 0.25 m on a side. Their interiors are ca. 0.14 m on a side and 0.10 m deep. Three of the features have larger, flat stones nearby which may have been used to cover the pits. There are a number of other square soil depressions around the site which may have been dismantled features of this type. These do not appear to be hearths.

Site No.: 208 (fig. 4.48)
Field Site No.: 299
Site Name: None
Map Reference: 3050 III, K737
Location on 1:50,000: 3332320 N / 714845 E
Elevation: 297 m
Aerial Reference No.: IGN-78-JOR 12/100 - 977
Site Size: 16 m N–S × 60 m E–W
Inventory Rating: 1
Pottery Collected: Total = 4 (No. of Indicators: 1 / No. Saved: 4)
Pottery Registration No(s).: 54534–37
Pottery Summary: 1 Chalco/EB, 1 ER/Nab, 2 ER/LR
Lithic Summary: Indef. cultural-historic placement
Site Description: The site consists of five features. Feature 1 is a cemetery consisting of at least 12 graves scattered across the wadi terrace. Most are badly deflated and appear as small stone mounds of limestone and sandstone. Their average size is 2 × 1 m. Feature 2 is a series of cleared depressions in the ground—roughly oriented at 300 degrees—due possibly to erosion, or perhaps deliberately developed for water storage of surface runoff from rainfall. The area measures ca. 10 × 2 m and is bounded at some points by isolated boulder clusters. Feature 3 is a possible encampment in an area of 2.10 m N–S × 7.50 m E–W. Adjacent to Feature 3, Feature 4 is a small, stone-lined pit similar to the pits recorded as Feature 10 at Site 207. This feature is comprised of four sandstone rocks of different colors. There is a possible capstone nearby, also of

sandstone. The interior dimensions of the pit are 0.10 m on a side. Feature 5 is a rectilinear alignment of sandstone boulders set into the spur behind the site and spanning 1.80 m in length. To the east is another series of upright stones 0.60 m in length. This feature may be a possible shrine.

Site No.: 209 (fig. 4.48)
Field Site No.: 304
Site Name: None
Map Reference: 3050 III, K737
Location on 1:50,000: 3332195 N / 714550 E
Elevation: 303 m
Aerial Reference No.: IGN-78-JOR 12/100 - 977
Site Size: 10 m N–S × 7 m E–W
Inventory Rating: 2
Pottery Collected: Total = 0 (No. of Indicators: 0 / No. Saved: 0)
Pottery Registration No(s).: None
Pottery Summary: N/A
Lithic Summary: Indef. cultural-historic placement
Site Description: The site consists of three cairns. The largest measures 4.30 m in diameter and is preserved up to 1.25 m high. At the top there is a roughly cleared inner compartment measuring 1 m N–S × 0.40 m E–W. Most of the center of the cairn, however, has been disturbed by clandestine excavation. A similar but smaller cairn lies adjacent to the first. It measures 3.20 m in diameter and 0.60 m high. Ca. 30 m south of the larger cairn is a third cairn completely destroyed by clandestine excavations. The area is rich in lithic material (mostly flakes).

Site No.: 210 (fig. 4.48)
Field Site No.: 303
Site Name: None
Map Reference: 3050 III, K737
Location on 1:50,000: 3332250 N / 714525 E
Elevation: 310 m
Aerial Reference No.: IGN-78-JOR 12/100 - 977
Site Size: 4.70 m N–S × 4.70 m E–W
Inventory Rating: 2
Pottery Collected: Total = 0 (No. of Indicators: 0 / No. Saved: 0)
Pottery Registration No(s).: None
Pottery Summary: N/A
Lithic Summary: Indef. cultural-historic placement

Site Description: The site consists of a single stone mound or burial cairn roughly circular in shape and measuring 4.70 m in diameter and 0.70 m high. The cairn is built primarily of limestone and chert boulders with cobbles distributed across the top.

Site No.: 211 (figs. 4.33, 4.48)
Field Site No.: 297
Site Name: None
Map Reference: 3050 III, K737
Location on 1:50,000: 3332570 N / 713420 E
Elevation: 258 m
Aerial Reference No.: IGN-78-JOR 12/100 - 977
Site Size: 10 m N–S × 16 m E–W
Inventory Rating: 5
Pottery Collected: Total = 0 (No. of Indicators: 0 / No. Saved: 0)
Pottery Registration No(s).: None
Pottery Summary: N/A
Lithic Summary: Indef. cultural-historic placement
Site Description: The site consists of a large cairn and a small stone ring, perhaps a small grave, atop a high saddle west of a small tributary wadi emptying into Wādī el-Quṣeib. The cairn (Feature 1) measures 6.90 m in diameter. It is roughly ovoid in shape and is constructed primarily of boulders measuring 0.30 to 0.50 m on a side. The cairn is preserved to a height of 1.10 m and is free of any disturbance except minor deflation. Feature 2, a small stone circle, is 1 m in diameter and lies due east of the cairn. It consists of a single course of stones ca. 0.30 m on a side.

Site No.: 212 (figs. 4.35, 4.49)
Field Site No.: 286
Site Name: None
Map Reference: 3050 III, K737
Location on 1:50,000: 3334180 N / 714620 E
Elevation: 302 m
Aerial Reference No.: IGN-78-JOR 12/100 – 979
Site Size: 53 m N–S × 45 m E–W
Inventory Rating: 2
Pottery Collected: Total = 0 (No. of Indicators: 0 / No. Saved: 0)
Pottery Registration No(s).: None
Pottery Summary: N/A
Lithic Summary: Indef. cultural-historic placement
Site Description: The site consists of three distinct

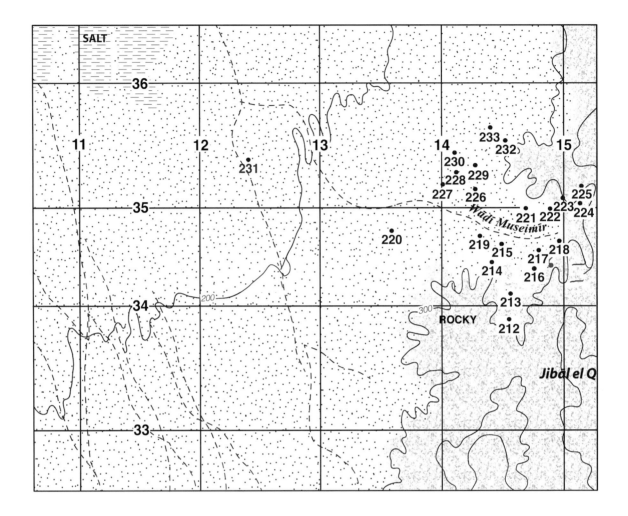

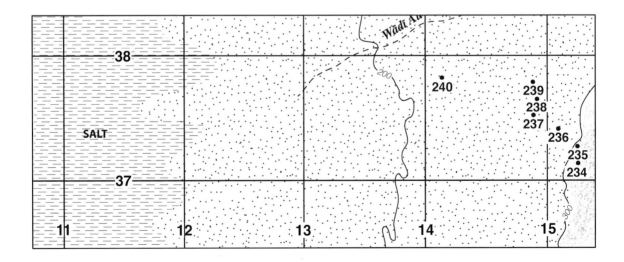

FIG. 4.49   *Gharandal Region (Region III). Top: map 16 (Sites 212–233), below: map 17 (Sites 234–240).*

features. Feature 1 is a semicircular enclosure or structure ca. 5 m in diameter. The feature is a single course of sandstone boulders that measure 0.20–0.40 m on a side. To the southeast and northwest are two wall alignments on a curve that follows the arc of the wall for ca. 4.60 m. At the northwest corner of the semicircular structure is a curvilinear wall alignment ca. 6 m in length, also constructed of a single course of sandstone boulders. Ca. 25 m southwest of Feature 1, Feature 2 is a single structure built of a single course of sandstone boulders, seemingly an animal pen. Feature 3, on a sand dune ca. 15 m southwest of Feature 1, consists of two rectilinear stone alignments that may be graves. The first lies ca. 7.20 m northeast of the second stone alignment ca. 2 m in length. The second stone alignment is ca. 2.20 m in length and is constructed of two courses of sandstone boulders and cobbles.

Site No.: 213 (figure 4.49)
Field Site No.: 285
Site Name: None
Map Reference: 3050 III, K737
Location on 1:50,000: 3334410 N / 714665 E
Elevation: 280 m
Aerial Reference No.: IGN-78-JOR 12/100 - 979
Site Size: 20 m N–S × 20 m E–W
Inventory Rating: 2
Pottery Collected: Total = 0 (No. of Indicators: 0 / No. Saved: 0)
Pottery Registration No(s).: None
Pottery Summary: N/A
Lithic Summary: N/A
Site Description: The site consists of three large cairns (perhaps burial cairns) and a single petroglyph on a sandstone boulder that measures ca. 1.60 m long × 0.90 m wide × 0.75 m high. One cairn is damaged due to robber activity. It has an interior diameter of ca. 1.90 m and an exterior diameter of 3.70 m. Another cairn appears more as an oblong stone mound 4.50 × 2.20 m and is preserved up to 0.80 m high. Ca. 20 m northwest of this second cairn lies a third cairn, roughly circular, 4.70 m in diameter and 1 m high. Several boulders had been removed from the top of the cairn.

Site No.: 214 (fig. 4.49)
Field Site No.: 284
Site Name: None
Map Reference: 3050 III, K737
Location on 1:50,000: 3334585 N / 714620 E
Elevation: 270 m
Aerial Reference No.: IGN-78-JOR 12/100 - 979
Site Size: 8 m N–S × 5.60 m E–W
Inventory Rating: 1
Pottery Collected: Total = 11 (No. of Indicators: 0 / No. Saved: 11)
Pottery Registration No(s).: 54517–27
Pottery Summary: 11 LByz (1 vessel = cookpot from central Jordan)
Lithic Summary: N/A
Site Description: This is a large, isolated cairn virtually destroyed by clandestine excavation. Although precise measurements were not possible, it is probably no more than 5–6 m in diameter). A single petroglyph is present. The SAAS collected a pot-bust ca. 20 m north of the cairn.

Site No.: 215 (fig. 4.49)
Field Site No.: 283
Site Name: None
Map Reference: 3050 III, K737
Location on 1:50,000: 3334775 N / 714585 E
Elevation: 258 m
Aerial Reference No.: IGN-78-JOR 12/100 - 979
Site Size: 2.60 m N–S × 2.90 m E–W
Inventory Rating: 2
Pottery Collected: Total = 0 (No. of Indicators: 0 / No. Saved: 0)
Pottery Registration No(s).: None
Pottery Summary: N/A
Lithic Summary: N/A
Site Description: This is a stone ring or hut circle with an interior diameter of 1.60 m and constructed of boulders that measure ca. 0.40 m on a side. There were no associated artifacts recovered, probably due to the location of the site in a highly eroded area.

Site No.: 216 (fig. 4.49)
Field Site No.: 287
Site Name: None
Map Reference: 3050 III, K737
Location on 1:50,000: 3334700 N / 714813 E

Elevation: 302 m
Aerial Reference No.: IGN-78-JOR 12/100 - 979
Site Size: 5.80 m N–S × 5.80 m E–W
Inventory Rating: 2
Pottery Collected: Total = 0 (No. of Indicators: 0 / No. Saved: 0)
Pottery Registration No(s).: None
Pottery Summary: N/A
Lithic Summary: Indef. cultural-historic placement
Site Description: This appears to be the remains of a collapsed tower measuring ca. 5.80 m in diameter and preserved to a height of at least 1 m. The feature is constructed of unworked limestone and chert boulders and cobbles measuring between 0.20–0.40 m on a side. This site is interpreted as a tower solely on the basis of the structure's size and its position on a spur commanding a view over Wādī Museimīr at the confluence of two minor drainages.

Site No.: 217 (fig. 4.49)
Field Site No.: 288
Site Name: None
Map Reference: 3050 III, K737
Location on 1:50,000: 3334775 N / 714925 E
Elevation: 284 m
Aerial Reference No.: IGN-78-JOR 12/100 - 979
Site Size: 2.20 m N–S × 2.20 m E–W
Inventory Rating: 2
Pottery Collected: Total = 0 (No. of Indicators: 0 / No. Saved: 0)
Pottery Registration No(s).: None
Pottery Summary: N/A
Lithic Summary: Indef. cultural-historic placement
Site Description: This a stone circle or grave situated at the edge of a spur overlooking the wadi. It measures 2.20 m in diameter and consists of a single course of chert and limestone cobbles and boulders that measure ca. 0.20–0.40 m on a side.

Site No.: 218 (fig. 4.49)
Field Site No.: 294
Site Name: None
Map Reference: 3050 III, K737
Location on 1:50,000: 3334905 N / 715075 E
Elevation: 277 m
Aerial Reference No.: IGN-78-JOR 12/100 - 979
Site Size: 8 m N–S × 3 m E–W

Inventory Rating: 2
Pottery Collected: Total = 5 (No. of Indicators: 1 / No. Saved: 3)
Pottery Registration No(s).: 54538–40
Pottery Summary: 4 ER/LR (1 vessel), 1 LR
Lithic Summary: Indef. cultural-historic placement
Site Description: The site consists of a single stone ring or hut circle and a few pottery sherds (mainly from a pot-bust). The site is situated on the edge of a small wadi terrace just below a small hill above Wādī Museimīr. The stone ring or hut circle measures 2.60 m in diameter and its outer wall is a single course wide (0.30 m). Two large boulders (0.80 m on a side) have been incorporated into the circle. The SAAS recorded the pot-bust ca. 8 m southwest of the stone ring.

Site No.: 219 (fig. 4.49)
Field Site No.: 295
Site Name: None
Map Reference: 3050 III, K737
Location on 1:50,000: 3334930 N / 714415 E
Elevation: 258 m
Aerial Reference No.: IGN-78-JOR 12/100 - 979
Site Size: 27 m N–S × 50 m E–W
Inventory Rating: 2
Pottery Collected: Total = 63 (No. of Indicators: 23 / No. Saved: 34)
Pottery Registration No(s).: 54483–516
Pottery Summary: 20 ER/Nab, 39 R/Byz, 2 EByz (1 vessel), 1 Abbasid, 1 Ottoman (pipe)
Lithic Summary: Indef. cultural-historic placement
Site Description: This is a cemetery located against a gravel saddle on an elevated terrace above Wādī Museimīr. It consists of between 12 and 15 graves of several different types, from three large burial cairns to numerous stone rings and stone mounds. The largest cairn 2.70 × 2.30 m. Another measures 2.70 × 1.90 m. The three cairns lie at the southwest edge of the cemetery. To the northeast is a group of miscellaneous stone piles. Some are roughly circular in shape, others are more rectilinear. Defining their patterns and orientation proved difficult, because the alluvial surface is somewhat deflated. Much pottery of several periods is strewn over the site.

Site No.: 220 (fig. 4.49)
Field Site No.: 296
Site Name: None
Map Reference: 3050 III, K737
Location on 1:50,000: 3334946 N / 713717 E
Elevation: 238 m
Aerial Reference No.: IGN-78-JOR 12/100 - 979
Site Size: 25 m N–S × 8 m E–W
Inventory Rating: 2
Pottery Collected: Total = 0 (No. of Indicators: 0 / No. Saved: 0)
Pottery Registration No(s).: None
Pottery Summary: N/A
Lithic Summary: Indef. cultural-historic placement
Site Description: The site is a large stone mound, apparently a burial cairn, measuring 4.70 m N–S × 3.60 m E–W and constructed of a mix of boulders and cobbles. The center of the cairn has been robbed out. Immediately adjacent to the southwest is stone tumble with two modern robber pits. The site lies on the south bank of a low spur above Wādī Museimīr.

Site No.: 221 (figs. 4.28, 4.29, 4.30, 4.49)
Field Site No.: 291
Site Name: None
Map Reference: 3050 III, K737
Location on 1:50,000: 3334990 N / 714755 E
Elevation: 255 m
Aerial Reference No.: IGN-78-JOR 12/100 - 979
Site Size: 95 m N–S × 245 m E–W
Inventory Rating: 3
Pottery Collected: Total = 37 (No. of Indicators: 4 / No. Saved: 35)
Pottery Registration No(s).: 54257–91
Pottery Summary: 5 Chalco/EB, 6 ER/Nab, 23 ER/LR, 1 LR (1 LRRW/ARS = Hayes form 50B [late 4th cent.]), 2 UD
Lithic Summary: Indef. cultural-historic placement
Site Description: The site consists of 19 features distributed across a wadi terrace above the north bank of Wādī Museimīr. Feature 1 is a bedouin encampment of ca. 16 m N–S × 4 m E–W. Small sandstone boulders measuring 0.20–0.30 m on a side form a roughly enclosed rectilinear area (cleared of stones) that defines the camp. Around and within this border are several elements, including two small hearths not more than 0.40 m in

diameter. Feature 2 is the ruins of a small, isolated structure measuring ca. 4.50 m N–S × 4 m E–W. The walls of the structure are two courses wide (ca. 0.80 m) and a single course high. The north wall is mostly buried. Feature 3 is a largely intact stone mound, perhaps a grave, 3.20 m N–S × 2.40 m E–W. Feature 4 is the apparent remains of an ancient road or pathway along the wadi terrace. It measures ca. 2 m wide and extends E–W for ca. 52 m. The pathway has been mostly cleared of large stones. Feature 5 is a stone enclosure ca. 7 m in diameter. The edge of the circle is a single course of sandstone boulders that measure 0.20–0.40 m on a side. Feature 6 is another unspecified structure, rectilinear in shape and measuring ca. 5 m N–S × 7 m E–W. The walls of the structure are composed of a double course of sandstone boulders (ca. 0.40 m wide). It may be that Features 5 and 6 comprise a single structure. Feature 7 is another unspecified stone structure that appears to be partitioned into two rooms by a central interior wall. This structure measures ca. 8 m N–S × 10 m E–W and its walls are two courses wide (0.40 m). Feature 8 is a stone ring or hut circle 3.30 m in diameter. Feature 9 consists of a completely enclosed circular structure ca. 2.70 m in diameter. Its walls, constructed of boulder-sized stones (0.30–0.40 m on a side), are a single course wide and three courses high. The function of the structure was undetermined. Feature 10 consists of a single grave ca. 2.30 m N–S × 1.10 m E–W. The orientation of the grave is exactly N–S. It consists of a single course of boulders heaped together. This grave is 1.70 m due west of Feature 11, a large, robbed cairn measuring 4.80 m N–S × 3.40 m E–W. The inner compartment of the cairn, exposed by the robber pits, measures 1.60 m N–S × 0.90 m E–W. The SAAS found no artifacts or bone fragments near the cairn. This cairn is situated at the western edge of Feature 12, a bedouin encampment. This encampment spans a rectilinear area measuring ca. 12 m N–S × 24 m E–W. This area encloses three roughly circular areas ringed with stones. These were probably for tent foundations. Three hearths were found within the encampment. The first hearth is rectangular (0.90 × 0.70 m) and lies ca. 3.20 m from the northwest wall. The second hearth is rectangular (1.60 × 1.10 m) and lies ca. 3 m north from the south edge of the easternmost ring feature. The third hearth lies 1 m from the east wall of the central enclosure and measures 1.20 × 1.60 m. This hearth is the most substantial, comprised of sandstone boulders ca. 0.30 m on a side. At its eastern end, Feature 12 touches Feature 13, which is an oblong stone mound, perhaps a grave. The mound (1.80 m N–S × 1.40 m E–W) rises only 0.20–0.25 m above the alluvial surface. It is comprised of large cobble-sized stones and a few boulders. Feature 14 is an unspecified structure, possibly domestic in nature. The structure measures ca. 5 m N–S × 3.30 m E–W. The thickness of the tumble of the collapsed walls is 0.90–1 m and the boulders utilized are large (ca. 60 m on a side). Feature 15 is a stone ring or hut circle 1.70 m in diameter. The walls of the circle are 0.30 m and of a single course of boulders. Feature 16, 3.30 m due east of Feature 15, is a stone semicircle 3.20 m N–S × 2.70 m E–W and opening to the east. The walls are ca. 0.30 m wide (a single course of boulder-sized stones). Feature 17 is an isolated structure, possibly domestic in nature. The walls of the structure are badly damaged, with the north face largely destroyed. These measure ca. 0.70–0.80 wide (two courses) and one course high. Feature 18 is an isolated wall alignment that measures 4.20 × 0.30 m. Only the top course of a single row of boulders is visible. Finally, Feature 19 consists of several bedouin encampments dispersed across the wadi terrace but mainly concentrated to the east. These encampments include clearings, animal pens, hearths, and modern debris strewn across the surface.

Site No.: 222 (fig. 4.49)
Field Site No.: 292
Site Name: None
Map Reference: 3050 III, K737
Location on 1:50,000: 3334990 N / 714935 E
Elevation: 280 m
Aerial Reference No.: IGN-78-JOR 12/100 - 979
Site Size: 15 m N–S × 10 m E–W
Inventory Rating: 2
Pottery Collected: Total = 36 (No. of Indicators: 0 / No. Saved: 12)
Pottery Registration No(s).: 54465–76
Pottery Summary: 36 ER/LR (most from 2–3 vessels)

Lithic Summary: N/A
Site Description: This is a cemetery on an alluvial terrace above the north bank of Wādī Museimīr. The central features consist of two large cairns and nine graves (Features 1–11), which have no uniform orientation. The best preserved cairn measures ca. 3.50 m in diameter and rises to a height of 0.70 m. The second cairn measures 4.30 m N–S × 1.90 m E–W and 0.65 m high. The graves all appear as low-lying stone mounds. Most measure no more than 2 m in length and from 1.50 to 2 m in width. The largest grave measures 3.50 × 1.90 m. The varying sizes of the graves suggest a mixture of adult and child burials. Feature 12 is a sandstone boulder with a petroglyph depicting an ibex ca. 2 m northwest of the cemetery.

Site No.: 223 (fig. 4.49)
Field Site No.: 293
Site Name: None
Map Reference: 3050 III, K737
Location on 1:50,000: 3335063 N / 715012 E
Elevation: 283 m
Aerial Reference No.: IGN-78-JOR 12/100 - 979
Site Size: 30 m N–S × 8 m E–W
Inventory Rating: 2
Pottery Collected: Total = 9 (No. of Indicators: 1 / No. Saved: 9)
Pottery Registration No(s).: 54477–82, 54531–33
Pottery Summary: 9 ER/LR (5 from 1 vessel)
Lithic Summary: Indef. cultural-historic placement
Site Description: This is a smelting site on an elevated terrace above Wādī Museimīr with four distinct features. Feature 1 is a U-shaped structure ca. 3 m on a side. It is probably associated with metal processing. The walls of the structure are two courses wide (0.45 m) with gravel fill. Ca. 20 m to the south lies Feature 2, a grave, rectilinear in form and measuring 1.70 × 1.10 m with an orientation of 129 degrees. Southwest of Feature 2, Feature 3 is a U-shaped stone enclosure of uncertain function. It measures 2.70 m N–S × 2.30 m E–W. The east face is open, just as at Feature 1. Feature 4 is another U-shaped stone enclosure, resembling both Features 1 and 3, and 8 m north of the former. It measures 2.30 m N–S × 2.60 m E–W and is also open on its east face. The SAAS found pottery, lithics, and copper slag on the surface.

Site No.: 224 (fig. 4.49)
Field Site No.: 290
Site Name: None
Map Reference: 3050 III, K737
Location on 1:50,000: 3335120 N / 715138 E
Elevation: 298 m
Aerial Reference No.: IGN-78-JOR 12/100 - 979
Site Size: 35 m N–S × 30 m E–W
Inventory Rating: 3
Pottery Collected: Total = 0 (No. of Indicators: 0 / No. Saved: 0)
Pottery Registration No(s).: None
Pottery Summary: N/A
Lithic Summary: Indef. cultural-historic placement
Site Description: The site consists of four features along an alluvial terrace above the north bank of Wādī Museimīr. Feature 1 may be an unusually large cairn or perhaps the ruins of a small tower. It measures ca. 7.50 m on a side and has a commanding view over the wadi. The feature is constructed of sandstone boulders measuring 0.20–0.50 m on a side. Its center is largely cleared of boulders and consists of a desert pavement of sand, cobbles and pebbles. The feature seems largely intact, although some disturbance may be due to deflation. Ca. 21 m southwest of Feature 1 there is a large burial cairn (Feature 2) which measures 5.20 m N–S × 6.10 m E–W. Disturbance in the center of the cairn has exposed a chamber that measures ca. 0.80 m N–S × 1.60 m E–W. At the east end is a rectangular sandstone boulder that spans the width of the excavated pit. Within the excavated area were numerous bone fragments. Feature 3 is due west of Feature 2. This is a cemetery with three graves and a single stone circle. The graves appear as stone mounds roughly oval in shape ca. 1.60 × 1 m. The easternmost grave seems more circular with a diameter of ca. 1.70 m. Appended to the westernmost grave is a stone circle, perhaps another burial, measuring ca. 1 m N–S × 1.50 m E–W. The orientation of the graves is NE–SW (58 degrees). Feature 4 consists of two petroglyphs on two sandstone boulders near Feature 2. One is ca. 5 m northwest of Feature 2 on a sandstone boulder 0.90 m long × 0.70 m wide × 0.60 m high. The other is ca. 4 m east of Feature 2 on a sandstone boulder 1.50 m long × 1 m wide × 0.75 m high.

Site No.: 225 (figs. 4.32, 4.49)
Field Site No.: 289
Site Name: None
Map Reference: 3050 III, K737
Location on 1:50,000: 3335160 N / 715193 E
Elevation: 295 m
Aerial Reference No.: IGN-78-JOR 12/100 - 979
Site Size: 33 m N–S × 30 m E–W
Inventory Rating: 2
Pottery Collected: Total = 173 (No. of Indicators: 65 / No. Saved: 71)
Pottery Registration No(s).: 54394–464
Pottery Summary: 65 ER/Nab, 108 ER/LR
Lithic Summary: Indef. cultural-historic placement
Site Description: The site consists of nine features. These include seven sandstone boulders with graffiti. Feature 1 is an unspecified structure comprised of boulders which measure up to 0.60 m on a side. The feature is rectilinear and measures 2.80 m N–S × 6.30 m E–W. At the southeast corner of Feature 1 there is a possible wall alignment ca. 2.20 m in length composed of a single course of boulders. Feature 2 is a possible grave or burial cairn lying 240 degrees southwest of Feature 1 and measuring ca. 1.60 m in diameter. The grave has been disturbed by clandestine excavation, with most of the capstones displaced and a pit exposed. The SAAS found no artifacts in the debris. Feature 3, located 170 degrees S–SE of Feature 2, is an unspecified structure. It measures 2.70 m N–S × 3.70 m E–W. This feature may be a house that is divided into two compartments by a tumble of stones (a partition wall?). Feature 4 is a petroglyph lying ca. 12 m north (10 degrees) of Feature 1. The boulder measures ca. 0.70 m on a side. A petroglyph measuring 0.68 m across and appears on one side of the sandstone boulder. Feature 5 lies 9 m at 292 degrees from Feature 1. It is another sandstone boulder measuring ca. 0.70 m on a side with petroglyphs on three of its sides. Adjacent to the boulder to the west is a possible grave, the center of which has been robbed. Feature 6 is another boulder with a petroglyph lying 29 m at 248 degrees from Feature 1. Petroglyphs appear on two faces of the boulder, which measures 1.10 m N–S × 1.40 m E–W and ca. 0.50 m high. Feature 7 lies 2.90 m northwest of Feature 6. This is another petroglyph, perhaps with script. Feature 8, located 1.70 m northwest of Feature 6,

is also a petroglyph on a sandstone boulder. The rock face measures 0.78 × 0.40 m. Feature 9 is a petroglyph on a sandstone boulder embedded in the alluvial surface. The SAAS found much pottery around Features 1, 4, and 5. Also, the SAAS noted a small quantity of malachite near Feature 1. While this is primarily an encampment, at least two isolated structures (Features 1 and 3) suggest more permanent settlement.

Site No.: 226 (figs. 4.19, 4.49)
Field Site No.: 281
Site Name: None
Map Reference: 3050 III, K737
Location on 1:50,000: 3335175 N / 715330 E
Elevation: 230 m
Aerial Reference No.: IGN-78-JOR 12/100 - 230
Site Size: 185 m N–S × 425 m E–W
Inventory Rating: 3
Pottery Collected: Total = 159 (No. of Indicators: 21 / No. Saved: 81)
Pottery Registration No(s).: 54164–244
Pottery Summary: 30 Chalco/EB (most from 2 vessel), 1 EB, 66 ER/Nab, 57 ER/LR, 2 LR (1 vessel), 1 UDE, 2 UD
Lithic Summary: Probably Chalcolithic or later (see Chapter 5)
Site Description: The site consists of 19 various features on a wadi terrace above the west bank of Wādī Museimīr. Feature 1 is a circular clearing ca. 4 m in diameter with a small hearth in the center. Some rocks encircle the hearth, which is ca. 0.90 m in diameter with evidence of recent use. The entire feature is not encircled by stones as a hut circle would be, although it does appear that rocks have been pushed to the outside edge in some places. Feature 2 is another cleared circular area ca. 5 m in diameter with a small hearth in the center. It lies at the edge of a small, ephemeral drainage and may have been partially washed away. The circular area is cleared of all large rocks and cobbles which have been pushed to the edge of the circle. Three medium sized stones form a small windbreak on one side of the hearth, 0.80 m in diameter. Feature 3 is another clearing, ovoid in shape, ca. 4.80 m N–S × 6 m E–W. Rocks partially outline the edge of the feature. These are apparently encampments of sorts. Feature 4 is a circular, low-lying mound ca. 8 m in

diameter with a small, divided, and unidentified stone alignment (1 m N–S × 0.50 m E–W) along the southwest edge. The circular mound at its highest point in the center is roughly 0.05–0.15 m higher than the edges. A small hearth associated with this feature is made of small cobbles and measures 0.60 m N–S × 0.85 m E–W. Feature 5 is a rectangular structure with a wall at the northern end and smaller storage areas off the eastern and western sides of the main area. The entire feature is ca. 9 m N–S × 11 m E–W. The main rectangular area is irregular in shape but widens to the north. The north wall (ca. 5 × 0.70 m) is preserved one course high. Along the western edge of the feature are two smaller features. The southernmost may be a portion of a wall with an apparent small, circular compartment. The northern feature is a semicircular wall alignment, perhaps a storage area. Along the eastern edge of the main feature in the north corner is a small rectangular stone alignment. Feature 6 is a bedouin encampment ca. 11 m N–S × 12 m E–W. The area has been cleared of large boulders and cobbles leaving mostly a pebble pavement. A stone-lined hearth (1 m N–S × 0.70 m E–W) is set in the western sector of the cleared area. Lithics extend over the entire encampment. Feature 7 is another large encampment measuring 10 m N–S × 8 m E–W and cleared of larger stones. A small, stone-lined hearth is embedded in the ground near the center of the clearing. The hearth measures 0.70 m N–S × 0.60 m E–W and its northwest face is open. This feature is ca. 5 m from the edge of the wadi terrace. Feature 8 is either a robbed cairn or a stone mound with a disturbed area near its south end. The mound measures 3 × 2.20 m and is ca. 0.40 m high. Feature 9 is a circular area cleared of large stones. At the northwest corner is a small, oval-shaped clearing ca. 3 × 1.50 m, which yielded a number of sherds, most apparently from the same vessel. Feature 10 is a stone ring or hut circle ca. 1.50 m in diameter. A single course of boulders ca. 0.20 m on a side form the perimeter of the feature. Ca. 1.50 northwest of Feature 10 is a linear mound of stone tumble ca. 4.50 m in length. On the west side, a single course of small boulders trends roughly N–S. Feature 11 is a roughly circular cairn ca. 4.60 m in diameter and constructed primarily of boulders 0.20–0.50 m on a side. The cairn is oriented N–S at 30 degrees. At the northeast corner of the cairn, is an area measuring ca. 1.30 m N–S × 1.80 m E–W and generally cleared of boulders. The cairn has suffered substantial damage due to erosion. Feature 12 is an isolated, oblong grave ca. 1.80 m N–S × 1.60 m E–W. There are no signs of disturbance and no artifacts were found. Feature 13 consists of two stone rings or hut circles set adjacent to each other and ca. 8 m from the edge of the wadi terrace. Each measures ca. 2 m N–S × 2.30 m E–W. The areas have been cleared of most stones and appear as rectilinear clearings with pebble and sand surfaces much lighter than the surrounding terrain. Pebble-sized chunks of charcoal are spread across the feature. Feature 14 is a cairn ca. 2.50 × 3 m and 0.80 m high. Feature 15 is a series of eight stone rings, perhaps circular huts, and three possible graves. The stone rings vary in size but are damaged and thus have no definite edges. Accordingly, most were not measured. One of the larger ones to the west appears to have a grave inside. The graves vary in size and orientation. Feature 16 is a light sherd and lithic scatter over an area that includes some nearby bedouin encampments and animal pens, some with clear modern use. The area has been disturbed, probably due to grazing and reuse over a long period of time. Feature 17 appears exactly like Feature 7, i.e. another large encampment. Its hearth is ca. 0.60 m on a side and it is open on its south face. This feature is set along the base of the ridge at the northwest edge of the site. Feature 18 is a petroglyph depicting a camel on a sandstone boulder. The boulder itself measures 1.30 m long × 1.10 m high × 0.75 m high. Feature 19 is another petroglyph on a boulder ca. 0.65 m on a side. This feature lies ca. 10 m southwest of Feature 18.

Site No.: 227 (fig. 4.49)
Field Site No.: 278
Site Name: None
Map Reference: 3050 III, K737
Location on 1:50,000: 3335340 N / 714078 E
Elevation: 260 m
Aerial Reference No.: IGN-78-JOR 12/100 - 980
Site Size: 70 m N–S × 40 m E–W
Inventory Rating: 2
Pottery Collected: Total = 0 (No. of Indicators: 0 / No. Saved: 0)

Pottery Registration No(s).: None
Pottery Summary: N/A
Lithic Summary: Indef. cultural-historic placement
Site Description: The site consists of five stone mounds or cairns on top of a spur projecting from the ridge. The southernmost mound appears to have been dismantled and a number of its stones used to form a windbreak. The original size of the mound cannot be determined. Some recent Arabic writing has been etched on a couple of rocks in the wall of the windbreak. Ca. 27 m northwest of this mound is a second mound that also appears to have been dismantled. The foundation of the mound measures 2 m N–S × 2.50 m E–W. Some modern Arabic writing is etched on one rock here. There is a third mound 6 m from this mound that has also been vandalized. Stones were tossed aside and the central portion of the mound dug out. This mound measures ca. 3 m in diameter. The fourth mound is 17 m to the northwest and has also been dismantled. No measurements were taken. The final mound is 336 degrees and 43 m from the last. It has not been vandalized as extensively as the others. It measures 1.80 m N–S × 1.60 E–W. The majority of the lithics were found near this last stone mound.

Site No.: 228 (figs. 4.31, 4.49)
Field Site No.: 279
Site Name: None
Map Reference: 3050 III, K737
Location on 1:50,000: 3335380 N / 714200 E
Elevation: 264 m
Aerial Reference No.: IGN-78-JOR 12/100 - 980
Site Size: 3.70 m N–S × 3.90 m E–W
Inventory Rating: 2
Pottery Collected: Total = 0 (No. of Indicators: 0 / No. Saved: 0)
Pottery Registration No(s).: None
Pottery Summary: N/A
Lithic Summary: Indef. cultural-historic placement
Site Description: This is an isolated structure built of unworked boulders. It is roughly circular with a diameter of ca. 3 m. The structure is open along the southeast wall, perhaps an entrance measuring 1 m wide. The site lies on a saddle overlooking a major wadi to the south and several small drainage areas and the Wādī 'Araba to the north and west. The SAAS found a single piece of copper slag at this site.

Site No.: 229 (fig. 4.49)
Field Site No.: 280
Site Name: None
Map Reference: 3050 III, K737
Location on 1:50,000: 3335445 N / 714250 E
Elevation: 262 m
Aerial Reference No.: IGN-78-JOR 12/100 - 980
Site Size: 24 m N–S × 2.20 m E–W
Inventory Rating: 2
Pottery Collected: Total = 0 (No. of Indicators: 0
/ No. Saved: 0)
Pottery Registration No(s).: None
Pottery Summary: N/A
Lithic Summary: Indef. cultural-historic placement
Site Description: The site consists of two features
on a spur overlooking a major tributary wadi. Fea-
ture 1 is a stone ring or hut circle constructed of
boulders ca. 0.20 m on a side. The circle is a single
course wide with an interior diameter of 1.60 m.
Feature 2, a roughly triangular area enclosed by two
wall alignments, is due east of Feature 1. The area
enclosed measures ca. 1.20 m wide at its thickest
point as it opens to the north. The walls are a single
course wide and built of small, unworked boulders.

Site No.: 230 (fig. 4.49)
Field Site No.: 282
Site Name: None
Map Reference: 3050 III, K737
Location on 1:50,000: 3335480 N / 714115 E
Elevation: 240 m
Aerial Reference No.: IGN-78-JOR 12/100 - 980
Site Size: 10 m N–S × 54 m E–W
Inventory Rating: 2
Pottery Collected: Total = 5 (No. of Indicators: 0 /
No. Saved: 3)
Pottery Registration No(s).: 54528–30
Pottery Summary: 5 ER/LR
Lithic Summary: Indef. cultural-historic placement
Site Description: The site consists of five features
situated along a wadi terrace oriented roughly E–W
and aligned with the wadi bed. Feature 1 is a large
cairn at the northeast end of the site. It measures
ca. 3.20 m N–S × 1.50 m E–W. Ca. 15 m to the west
of the cairn Feature 2 is an isolated wall alignment
or structure. It consists largely of mounded stones
in an L-shaped pattern. Linear concentrations
of mounded stones measure ca. 1 m wide. Two

mounded, circular features are appended to its west
side. Overall the feature measures 4.90 m N–S ×
5 m E–W. It is possible that Feature 1 joined with
this feature to form a retaining wall for an alluvial
platform. Feature 3 lies 6 m west of the south end
of Feature 2. This feature is an oblong stone mound,
perhaps a small cairn, ca. 2.70 m N–S × 1.80 E–W
and 0.50 m high. Feature 4 is an irregular stone
semicircle ca. 12 m west of Feature 3. This feature
lies at the edge of the wadi terrace and measures ca.
4.50 m N–S × 4.20 m E–W from its outer edges. The
wall of the semicircular feature consists of a single
row of boulders. Feature 5, another medium-sized
(1.20 N–S × 1 m E–W) cairn, lies on a separate wadi
terrace across a small spur, 21 m west of Feature
4. The SAAS collected a few sherds in the area
between Features 1 and 3.

Site No.: 231 (figs. 4.16, 4.49)
Field Site No.: 274
Site Name: None
Map Reference: 3050 III, K737
Location on 1:50,000: See below
Elevation: 188 m
Aerial Reference No.: IGN-78-JOR 12/100 - 1685
Site Size: 450 m N–S × 4 m E–W
Inventory Rating: 2
Pottery Collected: Total = 0 (No. of Indicators: 0
/ No. Saved: 0)
Pottery Registration No(s).: None
Pottery Summary: N/A
Lithic Summary: N/A
Site Description: This is a road, presumably ancient,
from 3.35 to 3.74 m in width and constructed of reg-
ular courses of large cobbles. The road is visible in
intermittent stretches, with other segments covered
by large and small sand dunes. Stones along the
edge of the road are slightly elevated, suggesting a
sort of curbing. This would appear to be a continuation of Site 169 (Field Site 101). UTM coordinates
for the road from south to north are 3335230 N–S /
712590 E–W to 3335675 N–S / 712375 E–W.

Site No.: 232 (fig. 4.49)
Field Site No.: 277
Site Name: Unknown
Map Reference: 3050 III, K737
Location on 1:50,000: 3335663 N / 714636 E

Elevation: 278 m
Aerial Reference No.: IGN-78-JOR 12/100 - 980
Site Size: 10 m N–S × 57 m E–W
Inventory Rating: 2
Pottery Collected: Total = 0 (No. of Indicators: 0 / No. Saved: 0)
Pottery Registration No(s).: None
Pottery Summary: N/A
Lithic Summary: Indef. cultural-historic placement
Site Description: The site consists of a stone ring or hut circle and two rectilinear clearings on top of an alluvial fan overlooking two large rockshelters. The rockshelters contain mainly modern debris and appear to be in use as goat corrals. The stone ring or hut circle measures 4.50 m N–S × 3 m E–W and lies on the alluvial fan on the north edge of a wadi bank. The circle is cleared of all large rocks. Two rectilinear areas or "strips" cleared of stones are near the stone ring. Both are aligned due E–W. The most western strip is 17 × 1–1.50 m. A few large rocks are placed along the edge, generally piled along the four corners. The second strip is 18 m east of the eastern end of the first strip. It measures 22 × 1–1.50 m. A few large rocks lie along the edge of the strip.

Site No.: 233 (fig. 4.49)
Field Site No.: 276
Site Name: None
Map Reference: 3050 III, K737
Location on 1:50,000: 3335781 N / 714520 E
Elevation: 258 m
Aerial Reference No.: IGN-78-JOR 12/100 - 980
Site Size: 1.10 m N–S × 1.10 m E–W
Inventory Rating: 5
Pottery Collected: Total = 0 (No. of Indicators: 0 / No. Saved: 0)
Pottery Registration No(s).: None
Pottery Summary: N/A
Lithic Summary: Indef. cultural-historic placement
Site Description: The site consists of two boulders inscribed with graffiti, both script and figures. One of the boulders measures ca. 1.10 m on a side. The other measures 0.30 m on a side. The site lies on an alluvial fan of Wādī Museimīr.

Site No.: 234 (fig. 4.49)
Field Site No.: 272
Site Name: None
Map Reference: 3050 III, K737
Location on 1:50,000: 3337225 N / 715187 E
Elevation: 302 m
Aerial Reference No.: IGN-78-JOR 12/100 - 983
Site Size: 80 m N–S × 48 m E–W
Inventory Rating: 5
Pottery Collected: Total = 8 (No. of Indicators: 0 / No. Saved: 8)
Pottery Registration No(s).: 51358–65
Pottery Summary: 5 Chalco/EB, 3 UDE
Lithic Summary: Indef. cultural-historic placement
Site Description: This is presumably a small farm or homestead situated on a small saddle of a steep knoll projecting west from the eastern escarpment. A large structure constructed of granite and dolomitic limestone boulders dominates the site and measures ca. 0.40–0.60 m on a side. The structure is divided into two large enclosures. One measures 5.60 m N–S × 7.50 m E–W. The other measures 5 m N–S × 8.30 m E–W. The walls are generally two courses wide (ca. 0.80 m). Appended to the corners of the eastern sector of the structure are two ovoid compartments, perhaps storage areas, each ca. 2 m in diameter. On the west side of the structure are three other appended ovoid compartments, each ca. 1.50 m in diameter. A perfectly round boulder of white limestone, 0.20 m in diameter and obviously transported to the site from the valley below, was within the structure. Ca. 5.50 m south of this structure is a smaller structure of uncertain function with an exterior diameter of 4.40 m × 4 m. Its walls are two–three courses high and 0.40–0.45 m wide. Also sloping down the hill below the structure to the south is a walled enclosure, perhaps an animal pen. A terrace wall lies west of the enclosure. It is three courses wide and ca. 0.50 m high. On the steep hillside east of the main structure is a stone wall ca. 7 m long, up to 1.50 m high, and oriented 28 degrees. The wall varies in width from two to five courses thick and is constructed of various sized stones. The northernmost segment of the wall is curved. The wall appears to be a retaining wall. Additional retaining walls of varying size lie further to the north on the slope. The area above the wall is flat and generally not more than 6 × 3

m. Also, immediately north of the main structure is a possible storage bin measuring 3.30 m N–S × 3 m E–W. It is built of large boulders up to 2 m on a side. Smaller stones were placed to enclose the area between the large boulders. The entrance is from the northeast corner.

Site No.: 235 (fig. 4.49)
Field Site No.: 271
Site Name: None
Map Reference: 3050 III, K737
Location on 1:50,000: 3337275 N / 715163 E
Elevation: 298 m
Aerial Reference No.: IGN-78-JOR 12/100 - 983
Site Size: 2 m N–S × 3 m E–W
Inventory Rating: 2
Pottery Collected: Total = 0 (No. of Indicators: 0 / No. Saved: 0)
Pottery Registration No(s).: None
Pottery Summary: N/A
Lithic Summary: N/A
Site Description: The site consists of four small stone enclosures at the base of two bedrock outcrops. At the base of the first outcrop are two enclosures, and another lies a the base of a second outcrop 4 m to the east. The western enclosures each measure ca. 2.50 × 3 m and are constructed of small boulders. The walls are preserved up to three courses high. The third enclosure measures 2.20 × 3.40 m and is of similar construction. A fourth stone enclosure lies up slope to the west and measures 2.40 × 4.20 m. The SAAS found some animal bones around these enclosures.

Site No.: 236 (fig. 4.49)
Field Site No.: 270
Site Name: None
Map Reference: 3050 III, K737
Location on 1:50,000: 3337495 N / 714030 E
Elevation: 263 m
Aerial Reference No.: IGN-78-JOR 12/100 - 983
Site Size: 4 m N–S × 2 m E–W
Inventory Rating: 0
Pottery Collected: Total = 10 (No. of Indicators: 4 / No. Saved: 2)
Pottery Registration No(s).: 51356–57
Pottery Summary: 10 LR (2 vessels)
Lithic Summary: N/A

Site Description: This is a pot-bust in an area of 4 × 2 m. The sherds belong to two different vessels.

Site No.: 237 (fig. 4.49)
Field Site No.: 269
Site Name: None
Map Reference: 3050 III, K737
Location on 1:50,000: 3337675 N / 714950 E
Elevation: 250 m
Aerial Reference No.: IGN-78-JOR 12/100 - 983
Site Size: 13 m N–S × 33 m E–W
Inventory Rating: 2
Pottery Collected: Total = 8 (No. of Indicators: 3 / No. Saved: 7)
Pottery Registration No(s).: 51345–46, 51469–73
Pottery Summary: 4 ER/Nab (2 from 1 vessel / juglet), 4 UDE
Lithic Summary: Indef. cultural-historic placement
Site Description: The site includes the ruins of a probable tower (Feature 1) situated high on an alluvial fan overlooking a broad wadi and Site 238. The ruined tower (ca. 9.40 m in diameter) consists primarily of mounded stone tumble of unworked boulders measuring ca. 0.30–0.50 m on a side. This interpretation as a tower is based on its size, general shape, and elevated position (there is excellent visibility to the west). Feature 2 is a wall alignment ca. 18 m W–SW of the tower. It is a single course wide and high and constructed of unworked boulders ca. 0.30–0.50 m on a side. The purpose of this wall alignment remains unclear. Also, 27.40 m W–SW of the tower and 5 m N–NW of Feature 2 is a square stone structure (Feature 3). It measures 2.70 m N–S × 1.90 m E–W. Three upright stones measuring ca. 0.40 m on a side remain *in situ* in the northeast corner of the structure.

Site No.: 238 (fig. 4.49)
Field Site No.: 268
Site Name: None
Map Reference: 3050 III, K737
Location on 1:50,000: 3337730 N / 714960 E
Elevation: 240 m
Aerial Reference No.: IGN-78-JOR 12/100 - 983
Site Size: 40 m N–S × 70 m E–W
Inventory Rating: 0
Pottery Collected: Total = 22 (No. of Indicators: 1 / No. Saved: 12)

Pottery Registration No(s).: 51430–33, 51461–68
Pottery Summary: 4 Chalco/EB, 17 LR/Byz, 1 EByz
Lithic Summary: Indef. cultural-historic placement
Site Description: The site consists of three features. Feature 1 is a semicircular stone enclosure 10 m in diameter. Boulders measuring from 0.20 m to 0.50 m on a side surround this enclosure on all sides but the southeast end, which seems to have been damaged by bulldozing. This feature is probably a corral or an animal pen. Associated with this feature is a wall extending from the west wall of the enclosure. Another wall, ca. 2 m in length and abutting the first wall from a general N–S direction, terminates in an upright standing stone. Feature 2 is a circular stone enclosure 5 m in diameter and similarly constructed of boulders. Adjacent to this feature on its west side is another small enclosure, also circular in shape and 2.10 m in diameter. Alluvial sediments have built up along the walls. The appended feature is probably for storage. Ca. 5.30 m to the west is a possible stone hearth with an interior measuring 1 × 0.70 m. Feature 3 consists of a pot-bust with sherds scattered over a 10 × 10 m area. This pot-bust is 39.50 m at 270 degrees from Feature 1.

Site No.: 239 (fig. 4.49)
Field Site No.: 267
Site Name: None
Map Reference: 3050 III, K737
Location on 1:50,000: 3337761 N / 714898 E
Elevation: 238 m
Aerial Reference No.: IGN-78-JOR 12/100 - 983
Site Size: 5.20 m N–S × 5.20 m E–W
Inventory Rating: 1
Pottery Collected: Total = 0 (No. of Indicators: 0 / No. Saved: 0)
Pottery Registration No(s).: None
Pottery Summary: N/A
Lithic Summary: N/A
Site Description: This is an apparent burial cairn constructed of cobbles and boulders that has been badly disturbed by clandestine excavation. One large boulder at the northwest corner of the cairn measures ca. 0.90 m on a side. The cairn itself is 5.20 m in diameter. Some bone fragments (human cranium, etc.) are mixed within the debris around the cairn. The site lies on an alluvial spur between two small drainages.

Site No.: 240 (fig. 4.49)
Field Site No.: 273
Site Name: None
Map Reference: 3050 III, K737
Location on 1:50,000: 3337871 N / 714117 E
Elevation: 209 m
Aerial Reference No.: IGN-78-JOR 12/100 - 1687
Site Size: 5 m N–S × 5 m E–W
Inventory Rating: 2
Pottery Collected: Total = 12 (No. of Indicators: 0 / No. Saved: 4)
Pottery Registration No(s).: 51366–69
Pottery Summary: 12 R/Byz (1 vessel)
Lithic Summary: Indef. cultural-historic placement
Site Description: The site consists of an isolated structure on a sandy knoll elevated slightly above the alluvial fan. The structure (3.60 m N–S × 4.30 m E–W) is constructed of boulders measuring ca. 0.50–0.60 m on a side. The north wall is preserved and appears to be three courses wide. Only the top face of the upper course is not buried in sand.

Site No.: 241 (fig. 4.50)
Field Site No.: 266
Site Name: None
Map Reference: 3050 III, K737
Location on 1:50,000: 3338650 N / 714850 E
Elevation: 240 m
Aerial Reference No.: IGN-78-JOR 12/100 - 983
Site Size: 150 m N–S × 200 m E–W
Inventory Rating: 2
Pottery Collected: Total = 0 (No. of Indicators: 0 / No. Saved: 0)
Pottery Registration No(s).: None
Pottery Summary: N/A
Lithic Summary: Indef. cultural-historic placement
Site Description: This is a dispersed lithic scatter over a small hill (a limestone outcropping) south of Wādī Abū Barqa. A small stone ring, apparently modern, is on top of the hill along with a small stone with modern Arabic script etched on its surface. Also, on the northeast side of the hill is a recently constructed stone wall lying adjacent to a flat clearing.

Site No.: 242 (fig. 4.50)
Field Site No.: 142
Site Name: SAAR Site 37

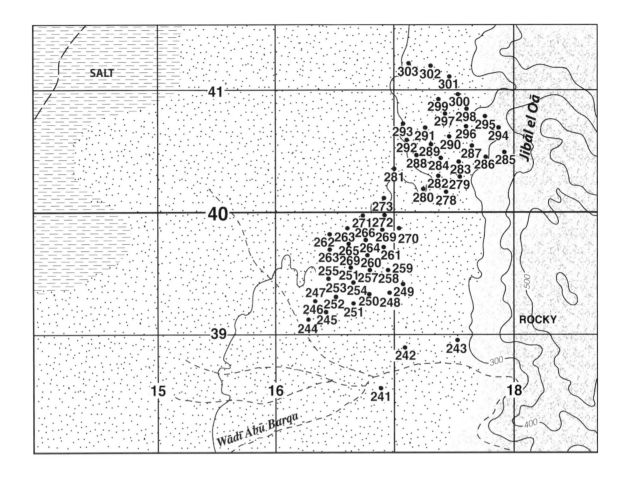

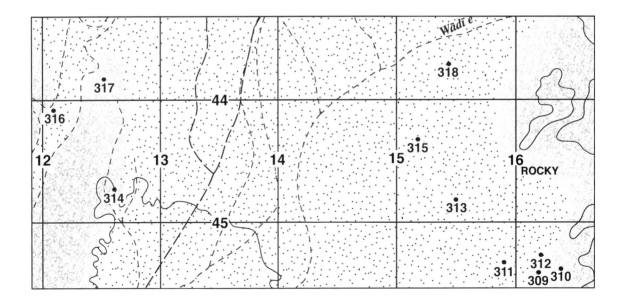

FIG. 4.50   *Gharandal Region (Region III). Top: map 18 (Sites 241–273, 278–303), bottom: map 19 (Sites 309–318).*

Map Reference: 3050 III, K737
Location on 1:50,000: 3338973 N / 715001 E
Elevation: 260 m
Aerial Reference No.: IGN-78-JOR 12/100 - 985
Site Size: 20 m N–S × 40 m E–W
Inventory Rating: 2
Pottery Collected: Total = 21 (No. of Indicators: 3 / No. Saved: 6)
Pottery Registration No(s).: 9678–83
Pottery Summary: 20 Chalcolithic (one with copper slag), 1 ER/Nab body sherd
Lithic Summary: Chalcolithic (see chapter 7)
Site Description: The site consists of numerous wall alignments with an associated sherd and lithic scatter on a gravel hill near the mouth of Wādī Abū Barqa. There are also some copper slag deposits. There is one wall of weathered limestone blocks on the west side of the hill, which is somewhat curvilinear (trends E–W, but curves 40 degrees north at the eastern end). It measures ca. 0.80 m wide (two courses), 13.50 m long, and one course high. Ca. 4 m northeast are three to five L-shaped stone alignments ca. 1–1.50 m in length.

Site No.: 243 (fig. 4.50)
Field Site No.: 141
Site Name: None
Map Reference: 3050 III, K737
Location on 1:50,000: 3339064 N / 715491 E
Elevation: 275 m
Aerial Reference No.: IGN-78-JOR 12/100 - 985
Site Size: 90 m N–S × 150 m E–W
Inventory Rating: 3
Pottery Collected: Total = 80 (No. of Indicators: 10 / No. Saved: 21)
Pottery Registration No(s).: 9586–87, 9768–74, 9864–75
Pottery Summary: 46 Chalcolithic, 23 EB, 3 EB II, 5 Byz (1 vessel), 3 UD
Lithic Summary: N/A
Site Description: This is an apparent habitation site on a projecting spur (island) in the middle of a drainage cut north of Wādī Abū Barqa. The principal features at this site are three terraced platforms descending from a 5 × 5 m vertical rock outcrop at the summit of the spur. These platforms are surrounded by walls one–two courses wide. The highest platform is ca. 1.50 × 3.50 m. After a 1 m

drop in elevation directly to the south is a second platform ca. 2.50 × 4.50 m. Following a slope to the southeast littered with rubble, and after a 4 m drop in elevation, is a third, oval-shaped, terraced platform ca. 8 × 10 m. Another 100 m farther southeast is a series of terraces descending a secondary drainage. An oval enclosure, ca. 3 × 5.50 m, with walls preserved up to 1.50 m high lies in the middle of the primary drainage. Built against the southwest face of the spur is a well-preserved rectangular structure measuring 3.40 × 8.50 m. Its walls are 0.50 m thick and preserved up to 2.20 m high in the southeast corner. Another ruined structure lies at the base of the hill to the west.

Site No.: 244 (fig. 4.50)
Field Site No.: 264
Site Name: None
Map Reference: 3050 III, K737
Location on 1:50,000: 3339305 N / 714345 E
Elevation: 202 m
Aerial Reference No.: IGN-78-JOR 12/100 - 985
Site Size: 17 m N–S × 35 m E–W
Inventory Rating: 2
Pottery Collected: Total = 14 (No. of Indicators: 0 / No. Saved: 5)
Pottery Registration No(s).: 51421–25
Pottery Summary: 14 Chalco/EB
Lithic Summary: Indef. cultural-historic placement
Site Description: The site consists of three features on top of an alluvial fan. Feature 1 is a rectilinear strip of ground cleared of large stones. Some large stones are set along the edges of the strip, but there is no obvious placement pattern and the edges of the strip are not well defined. The main rectilinear segment is 28.80 × 1.50 m, oriented lengthwise W–NW at 294 degrees. An additional, irregular segment of ground at the east end of the strip has also been cleared of large stones, is 4.80 × 2.40 m, and has a similar orientation. Feature 2 is a small semi-disarticulated stone ring comprised of a single course of small stones (average stone size ca. 0.10 m on a side). Feature 3 consists of two small piles of stone located 14 m at 350 degrees from the easternmost end of Feature 1. The eastern pile is 1.20 × 0.70 m and is oriented at 40 degrees. The western pile is 1.40 × 0.90 m and is oriented 250 degrees. Both are oblong, consist of a single course

of stones, and seem to be graves. The SAAS found most of the pottery at the east end of the strip.

Site No.: 245 (fig. 4.50)
Field Site No.: 262
Site Name: None
Map Reference: 3050 III, K737
Location on 1:50,000: 3339335 N / 714420 E
Elevation: 209 m
Aerial Reference No.: IGN-78-JOR 12/100 - 985
Site Size: 2.40 m N–S × 6 m E–W
Inventory Rating: 2
Pottery Collected: Total = 0 (No. of Indicators: 0 / No. Saved: 0)
Pottery Registration No(s).: None
Pottery Summary: N/A
Lithic Summary: N/A
Site Description: The site consists of two well-articulated graves, which appear as oblong stone rings, on the alluvial fan north of Wādī Abū Barqa. The orientation of each is 279 degrees. The smaller grave, 0.90 m from the head of the larger grave, is 1.30 m N–S × 1.60 m E–W. The larger grave to the east is 1.20 m N–S × 3.40 m E–W. Average stone size is ca. 0.76 m on a side, although there are some cobble-size stones.

Site No.: 246 (fig. 4.50)
Field Site No.: 263
Site Name: None
Map Reference: 3050 III, K737
Location on 1:50,000: 3339375 N / 714375 E
Elevation: 205 m
Aerial Reference No.: IGN-78-JOR 12/100 - 985
Site Size: 5 m N–S × 5 m E–W
Inventory Rating: 2
Pottery Collected: Total = 0 (No. of Indicators: 0 / No. Saved: 0)
Pottery Registration No(s).: None
Pottery Summary: N/A
Lithic Summary: N/A
Site Description: The site is a circular clearing ca. 5 m in diameter. The center of the feature has been cleared of cobbles and has a lighter shade than the surrounding terrain. The site appears in aerial photos as a faded circular feature.

Site No.: 247 (fig. 4.50)
Field Site No.: 265
Site Name: None
Map Reference: 3050 III, K737
Location on 1:50,000: 3339460 N / 714425 E
Elevation: 203 m
Aerial Reference No.: IGN-78-JOR 12/100 - 985
Site Size: 15 m N–S × 45 m E–W
Inventory Rating: 2
Pottery Collected: Total = 43 (No. of Indicators: 1 / No. Saved: 8)
Pottery Registration No(s).: 51370–77
Pottery Summary: 43 Iron II (most from 1 vessel)
Lithic Summary: Indef. cultural-historic placement
Site Description: The site includes two features atop the alluvial fan. Feature 1 consists of two rectilinear areas cleared of stones. Some larger stones are placed along the edges of each. The eastern strip is 19.50 × 3.10 m at the center and 2.10 m wide at each end. The western strip is 14 × 2.30 m. Three possible circular clearings (hut circles?) lie southwest of this second strip. There are no stones aligning the outer edges of these clearings, which seems unusual. The largest of the clearings measures 5.20 × 3 m.

Site No.: 248 (fig. 4.50)
Field Site No.: 256
Site Name: None
Map Reference: 3050 III, K737
Location on 1:50,000: 3339435 N / 714960 E
Elevation: 221 m
Aerial Reference No.: IGN-78-JOR 12/100 - 985
Site Size: 6.90 m N–S × 6.90 m E–W
Inventory Rating: 1
Pottery Collected: Total = 0 (No. of Indicators: 0 / No. Saved: 0)
Pottery Registration No(s).: None
Pottery Summary: N/A
Lithic Summary: Indef. cultural-historic placement
Site Description: This is a cairn 6.90 m in diameter and mounded to a height of 0.65 m. It is constructed of boulders ca. 0.40–0.50 m on a side. The site is badly deflated and shows signs of having been vandalized.

Site No.: 249 (fig. 4.50)
Field Site No.: 255
Site Name: None

Map Reference: 3050 III, K737
Location on 1:50,000: 3339440 N / 715025 E
Elevation: 220 m
Aerial Reference No.: IGN-78-JOR 12/100 - 985
Site Size: 41 m N–S × 76 m E–W
Inventory Rating: 2
Pottery Collected: Total = 3 (No. of Indicators: 1 / No. Saved: 3)
Pottery Registration No(s).: 51427–29
Pottery Summary: 3 Chalco/EB
Lithic Summary: Indef. cultural-historic placement
Site Description: The site consists of two features along a dry wadi bed. Feature 1 is a large, isolated structure ca. 27 m N–S × 15 m E–W, although the wall alignments seem mostly ambiguous. Within the confines of this structure are five stone mounds ca. 3.40 m in diameter. An oblong stone mound outside the structure measures ca. 3.40 × 2.10 m. This oblong mound is built of much larger boulders (ca. 0.75 m on a side) than those of the main structure. The easternmost mound has been robbed. It is 3.40 × 2.10 m, exactly the same size as the oblong stone mound mentioned above. These oblong features flank the structure on its east and west side. To the south, below the structure and just above the present bed of the wadi, is a possible retaining wall of boulders and spanning 5 m in length. On the eastern perimeter (northeast) of the structure a cleared area, generally circular, with a possible hut circle 2.70 m in diameter and a possible wall alignment 2.70 m in length. Feature 2, a rectilinear structure measuring 2.60 × 3.40 m, lies far to the west and may be a tomb. It is badly damaged by clandestine excavation (particularly in the center), although the lower course of the structure, built of boulders, is largely intact. There was a chert bead in the interior of the tomb along with numerous bone fragments. The solidly built walls of the tomb are 0.50 m wide. Copper ore is scattered immediately beyond the structure. Also, ca. 5 m to the southwest lies another badly damaged structure, perhaps another tomb. It appears mostly as a mound of stone tumble measuring 4.10 m N–S × 5 m E–W. Many of the boulders appear to have been flipped. At the base of this feature lies a stone retaining wall ca. 2.10 m in length. It is built of a single course of boulders and may be related to the retaining wall associated with Feature 1. There was a fairly

high density of copper ore (mostly round pellets) scattered around Feature 2. A scatter of artifacts (pottery and copper) is concentrated down slope.

Site No.: 250 (fig. 4.50)
Field Site No.: 261
Site Name: None
Map Reference: 3050 III, K737
Location on 1:50,000: 3339475 N / 714735 E
Elevation: 212 m
Aerial Reference No.: IGN-78-JOR 12/100 - 985
Site Size: 9.50 m N–S × 3.10 m E–W
Inventory Rating: 1
Pottery Collected: Total = 11 (No. of Indicators: 2 / No. Saved: 7)
Pottery Registration No(s).: 51434–40
Pottery Summary: 11 Chalco/EB
Lithic Summary: Indef. cultural-historic placement
Site Description: This is a cemetery consisting of four low-lying stone mounds interpreted as stone circles or graves. The largest, ca. 4.20 m in diameter and badly deflated, appears to be a stone circle with some larger boulders (ca. 0.40 m on a side) still in place on the southwest side. Ca. 7.30 m to the west is another badly deflated area of boulders and cobbles ca. 3.40 m in diameter. Adjacent to these is a stone mound 4.80 m in diameter and preserved 0.40 m high. This mound, though the best preserved at the site, has been robbed extensively and is deflated. The mound is comprised of boulders measuring ca. 0.40 m on a side and some cobbles. Ca. 20 m northeast of this mound is a stone semicircle 2.90 m in diameter with a heap of dirt, cobbles, and boulder in the center. The area is largely enclosed, although there are not stones along the southeast arc. Artifacts are evenly distributed across the site.

Site No.: 251 (fig. 4.50)
Field Site No.: 260
Site Name: None
Map Reference: 3050 III, K737
Location on 1:50,000: 3339490 N / 714615 E
Elevation: 209 m
Aerial Reference No.: IGN-78-JOR 12/100 - 985
Site Size: 1.40 m N–S × 24 m E–W
Inventory Rating: 2
Pottery Collected: Total = 0 (No. of Indicators: 0 / No. Saved: 0)

Pottery Registration No(s).: None
Pottery Summary: N/A
Lithic Summary: Indef. cultural-historic placement
Site Description: The site is a rectilinear area (1.40 m N–S × 24 m E–W) cleared of stones and surrounded by desert pavement. Small boulders ca. 0.30 m on a side appear in flanking pairs at the corners facing one another on the north and south side of the feature. At the east end of the feature is a group of smaller boulders facing one another. The nature of this feature remains problematic. It does not appear to be a tent emplacement. Perhaps it has cultic significance or is a direction or boundary marker. Another possibility is a "weaving" strip. The feature is oriented roughly E–W. The orientation of the line itself is 254 degrees. The direction across the width of the feature is 165 degrees.

Site No.: 252 (fig. 4.50)
Field Site No.: 239
Site Name: None
Map Reference: 3050 III, K737
Location on 1:50,000: 3339518 N / 714593 E
Elevation: 203 m
Aerial Reference No.: IGN-78-JOR 12/100 - 985
Site Size: 1.71 m N–S × 1.73 m E–W
Inventory Rating: 2
Pottery Collected: Total = 0 (No. of Indicators: 0 / No. Saved: 0)
Pottery Registration No(s).: None
Pottery Summary: N/A
Lithic Summary: Indef. cultural-historic placement
Site Description: The site is a possible grave on the side of an alluvial fan, enclosed by a rectangular alignment of stones with a cleared center. It measures 1.71 m N–S × 1.73 m E–W.

Site No.: 253 (fig. 4.50)
Field Site No.: 238
Site Name: None
Map Reference: 3050 III, K737
Location on 1:50,000: 3339530 N / 714540 E
Elevation: 203 m
Aerial Reference No.: IGN-78-JOR 12/100 - 985
Site Size: 1.10 m N–S × 0.74 m E–W
Inventory Rating: 2
Pottery Collected: Total = 1 (No. of Indicators: 0 / No. Saved: 1)

Pottery Registration No(s).: 47725
Pottery Summary: 1 UD
Lithic Summary: Indef. cultural-historic placement
Site Description: The site is a single semicircular stone circle made up of five boulders, ca. 1 m in diameter. The circle opens to the west.

Site No.: 254 (fig. 4.50)
Field Site No.: 237
Site Name: None
Map Reference: 3050 III, K737
Location on 1:50,000: 3339570 N / 714646 E
Elevation: 200 m
Aerial Reference No.: IGN-78-JOR 12/100 - 985
Site Size: 13.40 m N–S × 12.70 m E–W
Inventory Rating: 2
Pottery Collected: Total = 1 (No. of Indicators: 0 / No. Saved: 1)
Pottery Registration No(s).: 47783
Pottery Summary: 1 UDE
Lithic Summary: Indef. cultural-historic placement
Site Description: The site consists of five circular clearings clustered on top of an alluvial fan. A number of lithics and core fragments are scattered around. The circular areas are mostly cleared of stones. Surprisingly, there are no stones piled around the edge of the circular areas, yet these are interpreted as hut circles. The circular areas range from 4.30 m to 2.30 m in diameter. The other three have diameters of 2.40 m, 2.90 m, and 3.10 m. These do not appear to be tent foundations.

Site No.: 255 (fig. 4.50)
Field Site No.: 236
Site Name: None
Map Reference: 3050 III, K737
Location on 1:50,000: 3339630 N / 714465 E
Elevation: 205 m
Aerial Reference No.: IGN-78-JOR 12/100 - 985
Site Size: 15 m N–S × 15 m E–W
Inventory Rating: 2
Pottery Collected: Total = 4 (No. of Indicators: 0 / No. Saved: 4)
Pottery Registration No(s).: 51487–90
Pottery Summary: 4 Chalco/EB
Lithic Summary: Indef. cultural-historic placement
Site Description: The site consists of four graves atop an alluvial fan. The most articulated measures 2.40 m N–S × 1.20 m E–W and is mounded up to

0.50 m high. The average stone size is 0.30 m on a side. A second grave measures 1.80 m N–S × 1.20 m E–W and is roughly 0.20 m high. The other two graves are somewhat scattered piles of stone.

Site No.: 256 (fig. 4.50)
Field Site No.: 259
Site Name: None
Map Reference: 3050 III, K737
Location on 1:50,000: 3339642 N / 714550 E
Elevation: 209 m
Aerial Reference No.: IGN-78-JOR 12/100 - 985
Site Size: 17 m N–S × 15 m E–W
Inventory Rating: 2
Pottery Collected: Total = 29 (No. of Indicators: 5 / No. Saved: 21)
Pottery Registration No(s).: 51347–55, 51449–60
Pottery Summary: 22 Chalco/EB, 6 Iron, 1 UD
Lithic Summary: Indef. cultural-historic placement
Site Description: The site consists of two features on top of an alluvial fan. Feature 1 is a rectilinear area cleared of stones with a few larger stones scattered around the outer edge (with two stones at each end). The area measures 15 m × 1.10 m and it is oriented W–NW at 297 degrees. Two stone rings comprise Feature 2. One is 14.40 m north of the northeast corner of Feature 1. It measures 1.20 m in diameter. The second stone ring is 1.45 m in diameter and lies 14.40 m northeast of Feature 1. These two features do not seem to be associated. Site 255 is 265 degrees at 31 m away on the same fan complex.

Site No.: 257 (fig. 4.50)
Field Site No.: 254
Site Name: None
Map Reference: 3050 III, K737
Location on 1:50,000: 3339560 N / 714800 E
Elevation: 211 m
Aerial Reference No.: IGN-78-JOR 12/100 - 985
Site Size: 55 m N–S × 60 m E–W
Inventory Rating: 2
Pottery Collected: Total = 21 (No. of Indicators: 1 / No. Saved: 11)
Pottery Registration No(s).: 51342, 51378–87
Pottery Summary: 20 Chalco/EB, 1 ER/Nab
Lithic Summary: Probably Chalcolithic or later (see Chapter 5)

Site Description: This is a cemetery consisting of three burial cairns, several low-lying stone mounds that appear to be graves, and stone rings. The site lies along the north edge of a wadi on top of an alluvial fan, and there is an artifact scatter of lithics and pottery spread evenly across the surface. The cairns average 5 m in diameter and the best preserved is mounded up to 1.10 m high. One of these has been vandalized. Also, the stone mounds or graves vary in type. Most are circular and measure 2–2.50 m in diameter. Several are encircled by small boulders with cobble and pebbles filling the center. There are nine distinct features across the site. Feature 1 is a cairn 4.60 m in diameter and 1.10 m high. Feature 2 is a largely undisturbed cairn ca. 5 m from the edge of the wadi. Feature 3 consists of the two graves set side by side. One appears more ancient and measures ca. 2.50 m in diameter (stone circle?). The other grave, farthest east, shows evidence of recent disturbance and is possibly modern. Both graves are encircled by boulder-sized stones (ca. 0.30 m on a side) with cobbles and pebbles filling the center. Feature 4 is a rectilinear grave mounded to a height of ca. 0.47 m. Feature 5 is a stone circle with an outer course of boulders and an exterior diameter of ca. 2.10 m. The interior of the circle is cleared of boulders, with a few cobbles visible. Feature 6 is a small stone mound or cairn. The inner, exposed stones (forming a rectangle) suggest an orientation of 276 degrees N–NW. There is clandestine disturbance of the internal clay fill, particularly on the northeast side of the structure. Feature 7 is a semicircular ring structure constructed of a single course of chert and granite boulders. Both Features 8 and 9 are small stone rings.

Site No.: 258 (fig. 4.50)
Field Site No.: 251
Site Name: None
Map Reference: 3050 III, K737
Location on 1:50,000: 3339583 N / 714930 E
Elevation: 220 m
Aerial Reference No.: IGN-78-JOR 12/100 - 985
Site Size: 15 m N–S × 15 m E–W
Inventory Rating: 0
Pottery Collected: Total = 6 (No. of Indicators: 0 / No. Saved: 4)

Pottery Registration No(s).: 51491–94
Pottery Summary: 6 LR/EByz (1 vessel)
Lithic Summary: Indef. cultural-historic placement
Site Description: This is a sherd scatter or pot-bust in an area of ca. 15 × 15 m.

Site No.: 259 (fig. 4.50)
Field Site No.: 252
Site Name: None
Map Reference: 3050 III, K737
Location on 1:50,000: 3339642 N / 714975 E
Elevation: 282 m
Aerial Reference No.: IGN-78-JOR 12/100 - 985
Site Size: 6.90 m N–S × 6.50 m E–W
Inventory Rating: 1
Pottery Collected: Total = 0 (No. of Indicators: 0 / No. Saved: 0)
Pottery Registration No(s).: None
Pottery Summary: N/A
Lithic Summary: Indef. cultural-historic placement
Site Description: The site is a single stone mound or burial cairn measuring 6.90 m N–S × 6.50 m E–W and 1 m high. The center of the cairn has been robbed out with sand and bone fragments scattered along the east side. Lithics recovered were probably not associated with the cairn, but represent background noise from across the alluvial fan.

Site No.: 260 (fig. 4.50)
Field Site No.: 258
Site Name: None
Map Reference: 3050 III, K737
Location on 1:50,000: 3339685 N / 714645 E
Elevation: 208 m
Aerial Reference No.: IGN-78-JOR 12/100 - 985
Site Size: 13 m N–S × 12.50 m E–W
Inventory Rating: 2
Pottery Collected: Total = 0 (No. of Indicators: 0 / No. Saved: 0)
Pottery Registration No(s).: None
Pottery Summary: N/A
Lithic Summary: Indef. cultural-historic placement
Site Description: This is an isolated structure along the bank of a shallow wadi. It is parallel to the drainage area and has been heavily disturbed by erosion. The structure measures 13 m N–S × 12.50 m E–W. At the west end of the structure is a circular mound of boulders ca. 1.90 m in diameter.

The eastern circular area is filled with boulders. Immediately northwest of this stone mound is an area of stone tumble comprised of boulders ca. 0.30–0.40 m on a side. There is a stone circular feature 1.80 m in diameter lying ca. 5.80 m east of the stone mound. A wall trending roughly NE–SW abuts this stone circle. The wall is composed of one course of boulders ca. 8 m in length. The entire site appears as a raised platform on the edge of the wadi. It is probably a terrace structure with a possible agricultural installation utilizing seasonal runoff. The SAAS found a schist flake with garnet inclusions at the site, perhaps transported from further north in the valley.

Site No.: 261 (fig. 4.50)
Field Site No.: 253
Site Name: None
Map Reference: 3050 III, K737
Location on 1:50,000: 3339735 N / 714898 E
Elevation: 215 m
Aerial Reference No.: IGN-78-JOR 12/100 - 985
Site Size: 13 m N–S × 13.50 m E–W
Inventory Rating: 1
Pottery Collected: Total = 0 (No. of Indicators: 0 / No. Saved: 0)
Pottery Registration No(s).: None
Pottery Summary: N/A
Lithic Summary: Indef. cultural-historic placement
Site Description: The site is a rectilinear drawing or intaglio on the ground. The intaglio measures 4.34 m N × 5 m S × 4.97 m E × 5.28 m W. The orientation is 342 degrees. A lithic scatter is probably not directly associated with the site but probably represents background noise along the alluvial fan.

Site No.: 262 (fig. 4.50)
Field Site No.: 242
Site Name: None
Map Reference: 3050 III, K737
Location on 1:50,000: 3339720 N / 714575 E
Elevation: 210 m
Aerial Reference No.: IGN-78-JOR 12/100 - 985
Site Size: 12 m N–S × 64 m E–W
Inventory Rating: 2
Pottery Collected: Total = 56 (No. of Indicators: 26 / No. Saved: 33)
Pottery Registration No(s).: 51388–420

Pottery Summary: 3 Chalco/EB, 53 ER/Nab
Lithic Summary: Indef. cultural-historic placement
Site Description: The site consists of three stone mounds or cairns (perhaps graves) and a stone ring on an elevated portion of the alluvial fan. One stone mound is roughly circular and 2.20 m in diameter. Another stone mound lies 4 m west of the first and measures ca. 1.50 m N–S × 1.30 m E–W. The largest stone mound is 22 m W–NW of the others and measures 4.80 m N–S × 1.50 m E–W. This may actually be a collapsed structure. Individual blocks measure 0.40 m × 0.20 × 0.50 m. Near the first stone mound is a stone ring 1.50 m in diameter with walls 0.48 m wide.

Site No.: 263 (figs. 4.14, 4.50)
Field Site No.: 240
Site Name: None
Map Reference: 3050 III, K737
Location on 1:50,000: 3339725 N / 714500 E
Elevation: 198 m
Aerial Reference No.: IGN-78-JOR 12/100 - 985
Site Size: 44 m N–S × 35 m E–W
Inventory Rating: 1
Pottery Collected: Total = 24 (No. of Indicators: 3 / No. Saved: 14)
Pottery Registration No(s).: 47726–39
Pottery Summary: 24 Chalco/EB
Lithic Summary: Indef. cultural-historic placement
Site Description: The site consists of two features, both apparently foundations for tent emplacements or hut foundations. Feature 1 is a rectilinear area cleared of stones ca. 5.50 × 4 m. Feature 2 lies ca. 10 m northeast of Feature 1. It is another rectilinear area cleared of stone ca. 11 m N–S by 6 m E–W. In the northeast corner of Feature 2 is a small stone mound (possibly a hearth) 1 m in diameter and ca. 0.12 m high. Modern debris lies scattered around both features.

Site No.: 264 (fig. 4.50)
Field Site No.: 257
Site Name: None
Map Reference: 3050 III, K737
Location on 1:50,000: 3339740 N / 714628 E
Elevation: 211 m
Aerial Reference No.: IGN-78-JOR 12/100 - 985
Site Size: 10.30 m N–S × 5.10 m E–W

Inventory Rating: 2
Pottery Collected: Total = 9 (No. of Indicators: 1 / No. Saved: 6)
Pottery Registration No(s).: 51474–79
Pottery Summary: 1 Chalco/EB, 4 ER/Nab, 4 UDE
Lithic Summary: N/A
Site Description: The site consists of three graves along a wadi terrace. The first grave (2.90 × 1.90 m) is constructed of boulders and is badly deflated. The second grave (4.10 × 2.50 m) lies ca. 4.20 m southeast of the first and has suffered significant clandestine excavation. Modern rubbish lies scattered about. Also, the robber pits exposed an interior stone facing the grave. Ca. 25 m to the east is another grave (3.60 × 3.20 m) that is largely intact.

Site No.: 265 (fig. 4.50)
Field Site No.: 241
Site Name: None
Map Reference: 3050 III, K737
Location on 1:50,000: 3339752 N / 714523 E
Elevation: 198 m
Aerial Reference No.: IGN-78-JOR 12/100 - 985
Site Size: 7.70 m N–S × 6.20 m E–W
Inventory Rating: 1
Pottery Collected: Total = 1 (No. of Indicators: 0 / No. Saved: 1)
Pottery Registration No(s).: 47806
Pottery Summary: 1 Chalco/EB
Lithic Summary: Indef. cultural-historic placement
Site Description: This is a clearing for a tent emplacement. It is a stone-lined rectilinear area cleared of stones that measures 7.70 m N–S × 6.20 m E–W. Artifacts recovered around the site do not seem to be directly associated with the cleared area.

Site No.: 266 (fig. 4.50)
Field Site No.: 244
Site Name: None
Map Reference: 3050 III, K737
Location on 1:50,000: 3339775 N / 714663 E
Elevation: 211 m
Aerial Reference No.: IGN-78-JOR 12/100 - 985
Site Size: 2 m N–S × 1.50 m E–W
Inventory Rating: 2
Pottery Collected: Total = 0 (No. of Indicators: 0 / No. Saved: 0)
Pottery Registration No(s).: None

Pottery Summary: N/A
Lithic Summary: Indef. cultural-historic placement
Site Description: The site is a single circular clearing ca. 2 m in diameter and partially surrounded with small stones. It is probably a grave. A few lithics may be associated with the site.

Site No.: 267 (fig. 4.50)
Field Site No.: 245
Site Name: None
Map Reference: 3050 III, K737
Location on 1:50,000: 3339805 N / 714725 E
Elevation: 205 m
Aerial Reference No.: IGN-78-JOR 12/100 - 985
Site Size: 32 m N–S × 27 m E–W
Inventory Rating: 2
Pottery Collected: Total = 7 (No. of Indicators: 1 / No. Saved: 7)
Pottery Registration No(s).: 51480–86
Pottery Summary: 6 Chalco/EB, 1 UDE
Lithic Summary: Indef. cultural-historic placement
Site Description: The site consists of three features that seem to comprise a bedouin encampment. Feature 1 is a roughly semicircular area cleared of stones, 8.70 m in diameter. Large stones averaging 0.30 × 0.18 × 0.80 m border the eastern end of the area. A rectilinear linear mass of stones (ca. 1.50 m N–S × 1.40 m E–W) lies 8.10 m north of the southern boundary. Lying ca. 10 m southeast of Feature 1 and is Feature 2, a roughly circular enclosure ca. 4.80 m in diameter and bounded by stones measuring ca. 0.40 m on a side. Feature 3 lies ca. 30.40 m northwest of Feature 2. It is another large circular clearing enclosed by small stones. The surface area of this feature appears to be the oldest due to the lack of differentiation of the desert varnish on the small stones within and outside the structure. Also, this feature yielded a greater number of lithics than elsewhere. The site lies on a slightly elevated position on the alluvial fan.

Site No.: 268 (fig. 4.50)
Field Site No.: 243
Site Name: None
Map Reference: 3050 III, K737
Location on 1:50,000: 3339821 N / 714635 E
Elevation: 211 m
Aerial Reference No.: IGN-78-JOR 12/100 - 985

Site Size: 6 m N–S × 21 m E–W
Inventory Rating: 2
Pottery Collected: Total = 0 (No. of Indicators: 0 / No. Saved: 0)
Pottery Registration No(s).: None
Pottery Summary: N/A
Lithic Summary: Indef. cultural-historic placement
Site Description: This is a bedouin encampment. The main feature is a circular area cleared of stones ca. 5 m in diameter. Along the exterior of the circular area is a border of rubble with some larger unworked stones measuring ca. 0.26 × 0.10 × 0.10 m on average. A possible fire pit ca. 0.30 m in diameter lies ca. 16 m to the east. The pit consists of rocks ranging from 0.06–0.26 m on a side.

Site No.: 269 (fig. 4.50)
Field Site No.: 250
Site Name: None
Map Reference: 3050 III, K737
Location on 1:50,000: 3339861 N / 714912 E
Elevation: 205 m
Aerial Reference No.: IGN-78-JOR 12/100 - 985
Site Size: 8 m N–S × 4 m E–W
Inventory Rating: 2
Pottery Collected: Total = 0 (No. of Indicators: 0 / No. Saved: 0)
Pottery Registration No(s).: None
Pottery Summary: N/A
Lithic Summary: Indef. cultural-historic placement
Site Description: The site consists of two graves. The first is an oblong mound of stones 2.50 m N–S × 1.50 m E–W. It is oriented at 295 degrees. The second grave is 3.20 × 2.90 m with roughly the same orientation as the first. Animal burrows mark the only visible disturbance. A lithic scatter is dispersed evenly over the site.

Site No.: 270 (fig. 4.50)
Field Site No.: 249
Site Name: None
Map Reference: 3050 III, K737
Location on 1:50,000: 3339868 N / 714985 E
Elevation: 200 m
Aerial Reference No.: IGN-78-JOR 12/100 - 985
Site Size: 13 m N–S × 19 m E–W
Inventory Rating: 2
Pottery Collected: Total = 18 (No. of Indicators: 1

/ No. Saved: 8)
Pottery Registration No(s).: 51441–48
Pottery Summary: 18 Chalco/EB
Lithic Summary: Indef. cultural-historic placement
Site Description: This is a cairn measuring 3.70 m N–S × 5 m E–W and constructed mostly of boulders measuring ca. 0.35 m on a side. The boulders are mounded to a height of 0.50 m. Some stones from the cairn were probably robbed to construct small fire pits ca. 20 m down the slope to the east of the site.

Site No.: 271 (fig. 4.50)
Field Site No.: 248
Site Name: None
Map Reference: 3050 III, K737
Location on 1:50,000: 3339885 N / 714726 E
Elevation: 210 m
Aerial Reference No.: IGN-78-JOR 12/100 - 985
Site Size: 63.50 m N–S × 15 m E–W
Inventory Rating: 2
Pottery Collected: Total = 0 (No. of Indicators: 0 / No. Saved: 0)
Pottery Registration No(s).: None
Pottery Summary: N/A
Lithic Summary: Indef. cultural-historic placement
Site Description: The site consists of three circular stone structures set on a wadi terrace just above a shallow drainage. The structure furthest up the wadi measures 4.10 m N–S × 3.10 m E–W, with a height of 0.90 m. The structure consists of boulder and cobble tumble. The larger stones average 0.40 m on a side. Ca. 6 m N–NW (341 degrees) down the drainage, is a second structure, 2.30 m N–S × 3 m E–W and a single course high. The third structure is furthest down the wadi 45 m NNW (331 degrees) from the second structure and seems to be a disarticulated mound of stone tumble, 3.50 m N–S × 3.10 m E–W and 0.70 m high.

Site No.: 272 (fig. 4.50)
Field Site No.: 246
Site Name: None
Map Reference: 3050 III, K737
Location on 1:50,000: 3339951 N / 714853 E
Elevation: 210 m
Aerial Reference No.: IGN-78-JOR 12/100 - 985
Site Size: 3.20 m N–S × 3.20 m E–W

Inventory Rating: 2
Pottery Collected: Total = 0 (No. of Indicators: 0 / No. Saved: 0)
Pottery Registration No(s).: None
Pottery Summary: N/A
Lithic Summary: Indef. cultural-historic placement
Site Description: The site consists of a cleared circular area 3.20 m in diameter atop an alluvial fan. This is interpreted as a hut circle although no stones contain the circular area along the perimeter. The SAAS found a number of lithics in the area, including one core (not collected).

Site No.: 273 (fig. 4.50)
Field Site No.: 247
Site Name: None
Map Reference: 3050 III, K737
Location on 1:50,000: 3340075 N / 714860 E
Elevation: 200 m
Aerial Reference No.: IGN-78-JOR 12/100 - 985
Site Size: 27.90 m N–S × 8 m E–W
Inventory Rating: 2
Pottery Collected: Total = 2 (No. of Indicators: 0 / No. Saved: 2)
Pottery Registration No(s).: 51343–44
Pottery Summary: 1 Chalco/EB, 1 R/Byz
Lithic Summary: Indef. cultural-historic placement
Site Description: This is a cemetery consisting of a single stone mound or burial cairn and 13 graves on the edge of one side (northeast) of an alluvial fan. The cairn (5.70 × 5.15 m and 0.70 m high) has been vandalized, with lithics, pottery, and bone fragments strewn across the surface. There are at least 13 graves around the cairn. The smallest measures 1.70 × 1 m and the largest measures 2.30 × 1.80 m. All are oriented roughly E–W.

Site No.: 274 (figs. 4.21, 4.22, 4.51)
Field Site No.: 134
Site Name: SAAR Site 39
Map Reference: 3050 III, K737
Location on 1:50,000: 3339130 N / 710750 E
Elevation: 200 m
Aerial Reference No.: IGN-78-JOR 12/100 - 1664
Site Size: 170 m N–S × 20 m E–W
Inventory Rating: 2
Pottery Collected: Total = 38 (No. of Indicators: 6 / No. Saved: 13)

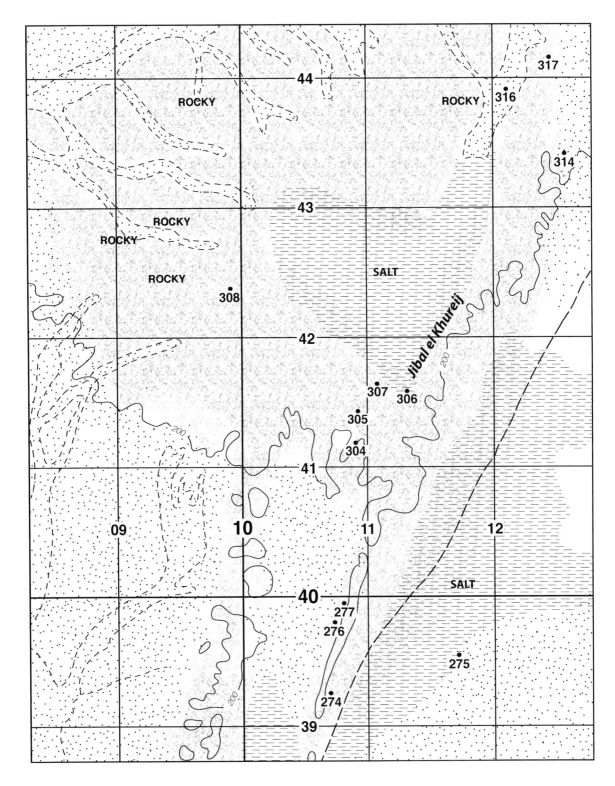

FIG. 4.51 *Gharandal Region (Region III), map 20 (Sites 274–277, 304–308, 314, 316–317).*

Pottery Registration No(s).: 6345–53, 9582–85
Pottery Summary: 33 ER/Nab
Lithic Summary: Indef. cultural-historic placement
Site Description: This is an ancient quarry on the east face of Jebel el-Khureij and visible from the fort of Qaʿ as-Suʾaydiyyīn. The ridge is composed of Cretaceous limestone. The quarry face measures ca. 154–170 m N–S with the largest platform at the south end. The SAAS found modern graffiti and two engravings on the face of the cliff to the north. Further south, quarried stones extend to the east and down the slope below the terraced platform. The quarried stones ranged in size from 0.30 × 0.30 × 0.20 m to 1.80 × 0.50 × 0.50 m. There are five fractured and discarded milestones, each anepigraphic, in the stone debris along the slope.

Site No.: 275 (figs. 4.20, 4.51)
Field Site No.: 38
Site Name: Qasr Qāʿ as-Suʾaydiyyīn
Map Reference: 3050 III, K737
Location on 1:50,000: 3339430 N / 711780 E
Elevation: 186 m
Aerial Reference No.: IGN-78-JOR 12/100 - 1687
Site Size: 45 m N–S × 45 m E–W
Inventory Rating: 3
Pottery Collected: Total = 351 (No. of Indicators: 234 / No. Saved: 251)
Pottery Registration No(s).: 80–129, 130–230, 231–306, 6669–91, 9603
Pottery Summary: 344 ER/Nab, 2 LR (possible imports from the Kerak plateau), 1 Byz, 2 LByz/Early Islamic (2 Fine Byzantine Ware), 2 UD, 1 Tile
Lithic Summary: N/A
Site Description: This is a fort in Qāʿ as-Suʾaydiyyīn. The fort is in a ruined state with much of its north side stripped away by localized bulldozing activity. The southwest and southeast corners of the fort are visible (plan in Smith et al. 1997: 61, fig. 13). The south wall measures 29 m. The length of the east wall is ca. 32.50 m, but the ill-defined northeast corner makes this measurement speculative. The exposed walls are two courses wide (ca. 0.65 m) and are largely composed of dressed limestone blocks. The structure does not appear to have corner towers, unless the large circular mound (ca. 2 m high) that extends beyond the northwest corner is a

tower. However, it is more likely a consequence of the bulldozing. Tracks from the bulldozer were still visible in 1994. The SAAS found a large, dressed lintel stone with a *tabula ansata* (uninscribed) along the north side suggesting the location of the gateway. There are other rock-cut graffiti on various blocks dispersed across the site. Disjointed wall alignments within the fort suggest some internal partitioning. There is a mound of ashy soil north of the structure with abundant sherds and a few fragments of bone, glass and corroded metal artifacts. Outlying wall alignments are visible west of the fort, but their nature remains problematic.

Site No.: 276 (fig. 4.51)
Field Site No.: 133
Site Name: None
Map Reference: 3050 III, K737
Location on 1:50,000: 3339765 N / 710840 E
Elevation: 180 m
Aerial Reference No.: IGN-78-JOR 12/100 - 985
Site Size: 25 m N–S × 25 m E–W
Inventory Rating: 2
Pottery Collected: Total = 31 (No. of Indicators: 4 / No. Saved: 8)
Pottery Registration No(s).: 6368–75
Pottery Summary: 2 EB, 27 ER/Nab, 2 UD
Lithic Summary: Probably Chalcolithic or later (see Chapter 5)
Site Description: The site consists of a square enclosure (ca. 9 × 9 m) with rounded corners situated on the west face of Jebel el-Khureij. The walls are two courses wide (ca. 0.70 m). Rock tumble obscures the northeast corner where the enclosure appears to have merged with the slope, i.e., as if the purpose here was to build an enclosed terraced platform. The northwest corner is rounded and fairly well-preserved, but the southwest corner is obscured by tumble. Another wall alignment appears ca. 12 m southwest of this southwest corner. It is a single course high, ca. 1 m thick, and up to 2 m in length. This wall is distinct from the enclosure walls to the northeast. The SAAS collected a large sample of lithics around the structure, which are probably associated with the rockshelter and caves above the site (Site 277).

Site No.: 277 (fig. 4.51)
Field Site No.: 132
Site Name: None
Map Reference: 3050 III, K737
Location on 1:50,000: 3339800 N / 710880 E
Elevation: 200 m
Aerial Reference No.: IGN-78-JOR 12/100 - 985
Site Size: 9 m N–S × 12 m E–W
Inventory Rating: 2
Pottery Collected: Total = 5 (No. of Indicators: 0 / No. Saved: 4)
Pottery Registration No(s).: 6480–83
Pottery Summary: 3 Chalco/EB, 2 ER/Nab
Lithic Summary: Indef. cultural-historic placement
Site Description: This is a rockshelter in the west face of Jebel el-Khureij. The interior of the rockshelter has two main entrances lined by stone walls. Room 1 is ca. 4 × 4 m and a small wall separates it from Room 2 to the west, ca. 3 × 4 m and less than 1 m high. Room 1 is 1.20 m high, and its ceiling is completely blackened. A third room, 1 × 1 m, lies north of Room 1 and is separated from it by a low wall.

Site No.: 278 (fig. 4.50)
Field Site No.: 224
Site Name: None
Map Reference: 3050 III, K737
Location on 1:50,000: 3340260 N / 715446 E
Elevation: 243 m
Aerial Reference No.: IGN-78-JOR 12/100 - 987
Site Size: 3 m N–S × 3 m E–W
Inventory Rating: 2
Pottery Collected: Total = 1 (No. of Indicators: 0 / No. Saved: 1)
Pottery Registration No(s).: 22468
Pottery Summary: 1 ER/Nab
Lithic Summary: N/A
Site Description: The site consists of a single stone mound or burial cairn, ca. 3 m in diameter and ca. 0.70 m high. The site lies on a low ridge north of Wādī Abū Barqa.

Site No.: 279 (fig. 4.50)
Field Site No.: 223
Site Name: None
Map Reference: 3050 III, K737
Location on 1:50,000: 3340340 N / 715450 E

Elevation: 245 m
Aerial Reference No.: IGN-78-JOR 12/100 - 987
Site Size: 250 m N–S × 30 m E–W
Inventory Rating: 3
Pottery Collected: Total = 16 (No. of Indicators: 7 / No. Saved: 12)
Pottery Registration No(s).: 22523–34
Pottery Summary: 15 Chalco/EB, 1 R/Byz
Lithic Summary: Indef. cultural-historic placement
Site Description: This is a small settlement consisting of numerous wall alignments and structures, stone rings—many may be circular huts—and stone mounds. These are grouped into six features. Feature 1, a series of linear stone alignments, lies along the northeast edge of the site. The largest segment, oriented N–S, is 9 m long. The segment perpendicular to it is oriented E–W and extends 3.50 m in length. Ca. 1 m to the east are two perpendicular segments forming a right angle. Both measure 2.30 m in length. These linear stone alignments or walls are preserved two–three courses high (1 m) and a single course wide (0.35 m). These may have formed a single structure with a possible entrance 1.50 m wide along the longer wall segment. Feature 2 denotes the presence throughout the site of five or six small figure-8 type structures or stone rings. Each has a total length of 2.70 m. These are constructed of tightly packed stones two–three courses high (0.60 m) and one course wide (0.40 m). Much like Feature 2, Feature 3 denotes the presence throughout the site of about 10 small stone rings ca. 1.80 m in diameter. The walls of these rings average 0.50 m high and 0.35 m wide. About ten small stone mounds or burials ca. 1 m in diameter and ca. 0.60 m high comprise Feature 4. Feature 5 corresponds to the five or more small stone rings or hut circles dispersed across the site. These average 3.20 m in diameter, with walls preserved up to two courses high (0.50 m) and one course wide (0.50 m). Many other miscellaneous wall alignments, similar to those of Feature 1 in terms of size were grouped as Feature 6.

Site No.: 280 (fig. 4.50)
Field Site No.: 218
Site Name: None
Map Reference: 3050 III, K737
Location on 1:50,000: 3340360 N / 715284 E

Elevation: 230 m
Aerial Reference No.: IGN-78-JOR 12/100 - 987
Site Size: 20 m N–S × 42 m E–W
Inventory Rating: 3
Pottery Collected: Total = 3 (No. of Indicators: 0 / No. Saved: 3)
Pottery Registration No(s).: 22222–24
Pottery Summary: 3 Chalco/EB
Lithic Summary: Indef. cultural-historic placement
Site Description: The site consists of four features. Features 1 and 2 are stone rings or hut circles (perhaps collapsed structures) set next to each other. Feature 1 consists of two small stone rings or hut circles appended to one other, 2 m in diameter, and oriented N–S. The feature is badly damaged, but some parts of the walls are preserved up to five courses high (0.60 m) and two courses wide (0.85 m). Just west of Feature 1 is Feature 2, a circular stone structure or hut circle ca. 2 m in diameter. It is constructed of loosely packed unworked stones with chinking, and it is preserved up to four courses high (1 m) and a single course wide (0.50 m). There is tumble both inward and outward. Ca. 10 m southwest of Feature 2 at the south end of the site is Feature 3, an L-shaped stone alignment, 3.80 m long E–W × 2.90 m N–S. It is one course high, three courses wide (0.35 × 0.90 m) and built of unworked stones tightly packed with chinking. Average stone size along the wall is 0.40 × 0.30 × 0.15 m. Feature 4, another collapsed structure 3 m in diameter, lies down the slope ca. 30 m east of Feature 1. It is preserved in places up to ca. three courses high (0.80 m) and a single course wide (0.50 m).

Site No.: 281 (fig. 4.50)
Field Site No.: 225
Site Name: None
Map Reference: 3050 III, K737
Location on 1:50,000: 3340436 N / 715024 E
Elevation: 199 m
Aerial Reference No.: IGN-78-JOR 12/100 - 987
Site Size: 10 m N–S × 4 m E–W
Inventory Rating: 3
Pottery Collected: Total = 0 (No. of Indicators: 0 / No. Saved: 0)
Pottery Registration No(s).: None
Pottery Summary: N/A

Lithic Summary: N/A
Site Description: The site consists of two stone rings or hut circles situated far to the west of Site 284. These stone rings are ca. 4 m apart. The northern ring is 1.70 m in diameter, and the southern ring is 3.20 m in diameter. They are both preserved ca. 0.50 m high and are badly damaged. Also, the southern stone ring has a circular feature 1 m in diameter appended to its north side. The walls of this circular feature measure ca. 0.50 m high and 1 m wide (0.20 m).

Site No.: 282 (fig. 4.50)
Field Site No.: 219
Site Name: None
Map Reference: 3050 III, K737
Location on 1:50,000: 3340480 N / 715321 E
Elevation: 220 m
Aerial Reference No.: IGN-78-JOR 12/100 - 987
Site Size: 35 m N–S × 20 m E–W
Inventory Rating: 3
Pottery Collected: Total = 2 (No. of Indicators: 0 / No. Saved: 2)
Pottery Registration No(s).: 22220–21
Pottery Summary: 1 R/Byz, 1 UD
Lithic Summary: N/A
Site Description: The site consists of several unspecified structures, wall alignments, stone rings or hut circles, and stone mounds. The SAAS grouped these into six features. Feature 1 is a stone ring or hut circle ca. 2 m in diameter. Its eastern segment is nearly destroyed. Otherwise the ring walls are preserved only one course high (0.45 m) and one course wide (0.50 m). 6 m south and down the slope from Feature 1 is Feature 2, which consists of two appended stone circles forming a figure-8 structure (2 × 4 m). The circles share a common wall and there is no obvious entranceway. Their construction is of packed stones preserved up to four courses high (0.90 m) and one course wide (0.40–0.50 m). The southwest side is less than 0.50 m from the north wall of Feature 3, a curving stone wall alignment and an adjacent stone ring. The wall alignment extends ca. 2.50 m E–W then turns 3.50 m N–S. At the southern end of the wall, is another small stone ring. A short segment of another wall alignment projects eastward for 4.10 m and is preserved up to four courses high (0.85

m) and one course wide (0.30–0.40m). The appended stone ring is three–four courses high (0.90 m), with the bottom course constructed of large boulders (ca. 0.50 × 0.45 × 0.30 m) with smaller stones on top (ca. 0.25 m on a side), and a single course wide (0.30–0.40 m). Feature 4 is another small stone ring or hut circle ca. 6 m southwest and down slope from Feature 2. It is ca. 2 m in diameter and a single course high (0.30 m) and wide (0.30 m). Feature 5 consists of two small stone mounds ca. 10 m apart and ca. 10 m southeast of Feature 1. These mounds average 0.90 m in diameter. 2 m north of Feature 1 is Feature 6, another small stone ring 0.90 m in diameter and a single course high and wide (0.30 m). Feature 7 lies at the north limit of the site, 12.50 m north of Feature 1. It is a small, isolated, rectilinear structure 1.50 m N–S × 2 m E–W. Its walls are of packed stones, ca. three courses high (0.40 m) and one course wide (0.50 m), with some stones slabs set upright.

Site No.: 283 (figs. 4.23, 4.50)
Field Site No.: 220
Site Name: None
Map Reference: 3050 III, K737
Location on 1:50,000: 3340481 N / 715427 E
Elevation: 230 m
Aerial Reference No.: IGN-78-JOR 12/100 - 987
Site Size: 13.30 m N–S × 12.30 m E–W
Inventory Rating: 4
Pottery Collected: Total = 2 (No. of Indicators: 0 / No. Saved: 1)
Pottery Registration No(s).: 22517–18
Pottery Summary: 2 ER/Nab
Lithic Summary: Indef. cultural-historic placement
Site Description: The site is a large, circular enclosure 13.30 m in diameter. The western and eastern limits of the enclosure open into a rectilinear area 2.80 × 3.10 m. Appended to the west wall are three small adjoining stone rings ca. 1.50–2 m in diameter and oriented N–S. The eastern edge has a linear stone alignment closing it off from the main area, where there is a well-defined entranceway with a short corridor ca. 1 m in length leading into the enclosure. Directly behind and appended to the eastern rectilinear compartment to the east is another small stone ring ca. 1.50 m in diameter. These stone rings are generally a single course high and

wide (0.20 × 0.30 m). The main central enclosure, in addition to its eastern and western rectilinear appendages, consists of a boulder base with smaller stones packed from four to five courses high in places (0.80 m). It seems to be one course wide (0.60 m), but this is unclear because the walls are badly damaged. There is also some evidence of stone chinking. Further, a large portion of tumble in the northeast corner of the main enclosure might suggest another appended stone ring, ca. 3 m in diameter. Throughout the site, the SAAS found large concentrations of schist flakes with only a few garnet nuggets.

Site No.: 284 (fig. 4.50)
Field Site No.: 221
Site Name: None
Map Reference: 3050 III, K737
Location on 1:50,000: 3340502 N / 715269 E
Elevation: 220 m
Aerial Reference No.: IGN-78-JOR 12/100 - 987
Site Size: 4.10 m N–S × 410 m E–W
Inventory Rating: 5
Pottery Collected: Total = 52 (No. of Indicators: 9 / No. Saved: 12)
Pottery Registration No(s).: 22296–307
Pottery Summary: 52 ER/Nab (1 vessel)
Lithic Summary: N/A
Site Description: This is an ancient unpaved road or pathway that winds down to the base of the alluvial fan west and below Site 287. The road is ca. 4.10 m wide. The road was established merely by clearing stones from the alluvial surface to facilitate traffic. The SAAS found a pot-bust two-thirds of the way up the fan in the center of road.

Site No.: 285 (fig. 4.50)
Field Site No.: 217
Site Name: None
Map Reference: 3050 III, K737
Location on 1:50,000: 3340500 N / 715825 E
Elevation: 290 m
Aerial Reference No.: IGN-78-JOR 12/100 - 988
Site Size: 6 m N–S × 8 m E–W
Inventory Rating: 2
Pottery Collected: Total = 0 (No. of Indicators: 0 / No. Saved: 0)
Pottery Registration No(s).: None

Pottery Summary: N/A

Lithic Summary: N/A

Site Description: The site consists of several large stones concentrated on the summit of a ridge on the south bank of a wadi, ca. 1 km north of Wādī Abū Barqa. These may have comprised a large stone hut circle. The condition of the site is poor and the alignment and size of any extant hut circle cannot be determined. The slopes below, both north and south, are littered with schist with garnet inclusions. This may have been an extraction center for garnet.

Site No.: 286 (fig. 4.50)

Field Site No.: 216

Site Name: None

Map Reference: 3050 III, K737

Location on 1:50,000: 3340560 N / 715778 E

Elevation: 260 m

Aerial Reference No.: IGN-78-JOR 12/100 - 988

Site Size: 24 m N–S × 32 m E–W

Inventory Rating: 2

Pottery Collected: Total = 3 (No. of Indicators: 0 / No. Saved: 3)

Pottery Registration No(s).: 22201–3

Pottery Summary: 2 Chalco/EB, 1 R/Byz

Lithic Summary: N/A

Site Description: The site consists of a group of stone rings or hut circles and isolated wall alignments which lie on a series of three terraced platforms. The main feature lies on the uppermost terrace. It is a curvilinear wall alignment one course high and wide (0.42 m) that covers 8 m N–S × 17 m E–W. At the western edge of the alignment are two circular stone mounds (ca. 2 m in diameter) that project from its north face. Isolated wall alignments on the terrace immediately below seem to have served as enclosures, one of which measures ca. 8 × 6 m. The stone rings or hut circles are ca. 3 m in diameter. Some are well-preserved up to three courses (ca. 0.58 m) high and a single course wide (0.30 m). Schist with garnet inclusions lies scattered on the slope above the site. Ca. 14 m southeast and up the slope from the main feature is another series of adjoining curvilinear wall alignments that create at least four enclosures in an area ca. 8 m N–S × 6 m E–W.

Site No.: 287 (figs. 4.15, 4.50)

Field Site No.: 222

Site Name: None

Map Reference: 3050 III, K737

Location on 1:50,000: 3340570 N / 715610 E

Elevation: 245 m

Aerial Reference No.: IGN-78-JOR 12/100 - 987

Site Size: 50 m N–S × 100 m E–W

Inventory Rating: 4

Pottery Collected: Total = 64 (No. of Indicators: 26 / No. Saved: 35)

Pottery Registration No(s).: 22433–67

Pottery Summary: 2 Neolithic (?), 47 Chalco/EB, 5 ER/Nab, 10 UD

Lithic Summary: Indef. cultural-historic placement

Site Description: This is a small settlement consisting of a multitude of wall alignments, stone mounds (ca. 1.50 m in diameter), stone rings or hut circles (ca. 2–3 m in diameter, with walls up to 0.60 m high and 0.60 m wide), and walled enclosures or structures (the two most prominent enclosures form distinct features). The two rectilinear enclosures (Features 1–2) are relatively large structures. Feature 1 is up the slope and south of Feature 2. The latter measures 9 m N–S × 5.50 m E–W. The south side of the enclosure is open with no evidence of any wall. The western segment of the enclosure has three segments branching off it perpendicularly ca. 1.50 m. It partitions the west side of the enclosure into three semi-enclosed areas. In the southeast corner of this structure is a stone alignment resembling a figure-8 (2.60 × 1.60 m). The larger compartment is 2 m long and the smaller projection (actually rectangular) is 0.60 × 0.70 m. Its walls are preserved two courses high in places (0.60 m). Unfortunately, it is not possible to discern any division between Feature 1 and Feature 2 and thus it is possible that both are part of one larger complex. Feature 1 also consists of a large rectangular enclosure. There are two extant segments. The first, oriented NW–SE, is 4.50 m long. The second, oriented NE–SW and cornering with the first, is 6 m long. In the northeast and southwest corners are stone mounds ca. 1.50 m in diameter and 0.50 m high. The western segment contains at least one stone alignment branching off it perpendicularly ca. 2 m to form two semi-enclosed areas. The northwest corner has a stone figure-8 structure appended to it. Both circles are ca. 3 m in diameter. The walls of Features 1 and 2 are preserved two courses wide (0.60–0.65 m) and up to four courses high (0.75 m). Also, there was a heavy concentration of garnet and schist at the east edge of the site. There are many other large walled enclosures or structures throughout the site of the same types as Feature 1 and Feature 2. These are scattered and disarticulated, preventing an accurate estimate of their number. Across the wadi to the northwest is an extensive row of adjoining rectilinear and circular wall alignments giving the appearance of a residential block.

Site No.: 288 (fig. 4.50)
Field Site No.: 202
Site Name: None
Map Reference: 3050 III, K737
Location on 1:50,000: 3340603 N / 715202 E
Elevation: 209 m
Aerial Reference No.: IGN-78-JOR 12/100 - 988
Site Size: 1.80 m N–S × 4 m E–W
Inventory Rating: 5
Pottery Collected: Total = 0 (No. of Indicators: 0 / No. Saved: 0)
Pottery Registration No(s).: None
Pottery Summary: N/A
Lithic Summary: N/A
Site Description: The site consists of a large stone mound, perhaps a grave, oriented E–W and measuring 4 × 1.80 m. Average stone size is ca. 0.30 m on a side. It is likely associated with the complex of stone circles ca. 30 m to the north (Site 291).

Site No.: 289 (fig. 4.50)
Field Site No.: 204
Site Name: None
Map Reference: 3050 III, K737
Location on 1:50,000: 3340619 N / 715278 E
Elevation: 215 m
Aerial Reference No.: IGN-78-JOR 12/100 - 988
Site Size: 30 m N–S × 15 m E–W
Inventory Rating: 3
Pottery Collected: Total = 0 (No. of Indicators: 0 / No. Saved: 0)
Pottery Registration No(s).: None
Pottery Summary: N/A
Lithic Summary: N/A

Site Description: The site consists of numerous stone mounds with associated stone rings or hut circles and curvilinear wall alignments. The SAAS recorded four distinct features at the site, each spaced ca. 5 m apart and extending from Feature 1 in the north to Feature 4 in the south. Feature 1 appears to be an ovular structure with two secondary stone mounds placed within the interior of its walls. The structure measures 3.50 × 2 m. Its southeast corner appears to have an entranceway and trends E–W. Within the structure to the west are two small stone mounds appended to each other, together measuring ca. 1.50 m diameter. They seem to be two courses high (0.90 m) and one course wide (0.60 m). Also, appended to the structure on its southwest side is a small stone ring 1.30 m in diameter. Feature 2 is a semicircular stone alignment measuring ca. 6.30 × 0.70 m. This feature is ca. 10 m southeast of Feature 1. Feature 3 is a second ovular structure similar to Feature 1. Feature 4 is a small linear stone alignment, 1.90 m long, and preserved up to two courses high (0.30 m) and two courses wide (0.40 m). A small stone mound, 1.40 m in diameter and 0.50 m high, lies south of Feature 4. There are numerous small stone rings, ca. 0.80–0.90 m in diameter and a single course high and wide, scattered across the site but not assigned separate feature numbers. There are also a few disparate stone mounds scattered across the site, ca. 1.50 m in diameter and 0.50 m high.

Site No.: 290 (fig. 4.50)
Field Site No.: 205
Site Name: None
Map Reference: 3050 III, K737
Location on 1:50,000: 3340630 N / 715432 E
Elevation: 215 m
Aerial Reference No.: IGN-78-JOR 12/100 - 988
Site Size: 40 m N–S × 60 m E–W
Inventory Rating: 3
Pottery Collected: Total = 61 (No. of Indicators: 15 / No. Saved: 26)
Pottery Registration No(s).: 22399–424
Pottery Summary: 5 Chalco/EB, 49 ER/Nab, 7 LR
Lithic Summary: Indef. cultural-historic placement
Site Description: The site consists of several features. Feature 1 is a curvilinear stone alignment on a N–S axis, 13 m N–S × 7 m E–W. There are mounds

at either end ca. 1.30 m high. No actual wall courses are evident due to collapsed debris. Also, its function is unclear; possibly it is a drainage basin for surface runoff. Ca. 15 m west of Feature 1, Feature 2 is a large area cleared of stones 20 m × 2.50 m and oriented E–W, perhaps a clearing for a tent. There are a few stones set upright along the edges of the clearing. Feature 3 lies ca. 20 m N–NE of Feature 1 and is another stone alignment 9 m long and oriented NE–SW. It seems to be on the same line as Feature 1, so they may be associated with each other. Feature 4 consists of at least five small stone rings that extend northeast and northwest between Features 1 and 3 and between Features 1 and 2. These average 2.20 m in diameter and ca. 0.52 m high. Feature 5.1 is a stone ring 3.40 m in diameter. Feature 5.2 is a smaller stone ring 1.80 m in diameter. Feature 5.1 lies 12 m south of Feature 1 and Feature 5.2 is 17 m S–SE of Feature 1. Feature 5.1 is constructed of tightly packed stones a single course high (0.40 m) and wide (0.30 m). Feature 5.2 lies 5 m west of Feature 5.1. It is constructed of packed stones, three courses (0.80 m) high and one course (0.50 m) wide.

Site No.: 291 (fig. 4.50)
Field Site No.: 203
Site Name: None
Map Reference: 3050 III, K737
Location on 1:50,000: 3340670 N / 715220 E
Elevation: 209 m
Aerial Reference No.: IGN-78-JOR 12/100 - 988
Site Size: 15 m N–S × 35 m E–W
Inventory Rating: 3
Pottery Collected: Total = 42 (No. of Indicators: 1 / No. Saved: 15)
Pottery Registration No(s).: 22575–89
Pottery Summary: 9 ER/Nab, 3 R/Byz, 30 UD
Lithic Summary: Indef. cultural-historic placement
Site Description: The site consists of at least five stone circles (the exact number is unclear as many are appended to one another and appear as figure-8 structures). Each stone circle is ca. 2 m diameter and averages 0.80 m wide (two courses) and 0.40 m high. These are set no more than 2 m apart. The best preserved stone circle has a short curvilinear stone alignment of seven stones extending 2.30 m from its southeast side. There is also a small stone

ring nearby, ca. 0.90 m in diameter, which may be remnants of a hearth. This stone ring is a single course high and wide (0.15 × 0.20 m).

Site No.: 292 (fig. 4.50)
Field Site No.: 201
Site Name: None
Map Reference: 3050 III, K737
Location on 1:50,000: 3340620 N / 715075 E
Elevation: 202 m
Aerial Reference No.: IGN-78-JOR 12/100 - 988
Site Size: 3 m N–S × 4 m E–W
Inventory Rating: 3
Pottery Collected: Total = 0 (No. of Indicators: 0 / No. Saved: 0)
Pottery Registration No(s).: None
Pottery Summary: N/A
Lithic Summary: N/A
Site Description: The site consists of a single cairn mounded ca. 1.50 m high and ca. 4.50 m in diameter. The site lies southeast of Site 293 at 118 degrees.

Site No.: 293 (fig. 4.50)
Field Site No.: 200
Site Name: None
Map Reference: 3050 III, K737
Location on 1:50,000: 3340695 N / 714990 E
Elevation: 198 m
Aerial Reference No.: IGN-78-JOR 12/100 - 988
Site Size: 5 m N–S × 2 m E–W
Inventory Rating: 2
Pottery Collected: Total = 0 (No. of Indicators: 0 / No. Saved: 0)
Pottery Registration No(s).: None
Pottery Summary: N/A
Lithic Summary: N/A
Site Description: The site consists of two stone mound burials, ca. 4 m apart. The mounds are oblong, ca. 1.20 × 0.80 m, and oriented E–W.

Site No.: 294 (fig. 4.50)
Field Site No.: 215
Site Name: None
Map Reference: 3050 III, K737
Location on 1:50,000: 3340950 N / 715725 E
Elevation: 450 m
Aerial Reference No.: IGN-78-JOR 12/100 - 988
Site Size: 65 m N–S × 30 m E–W

Inventory Rating: 3
Pottery Collected: Total = 15 (No. of Indicators: 0
/ No. Saved: 10)
Pottery Registration No(s).: 22535–44
Pottery Summary: 9 Chalco/EB, 6 UD
Lithic Summary: N/A
Site Description: The site consists of various wall
alignments, stone rings or hut circles, and stone
mounds. Feature 1 denotes three linear stone wall
alignments oriented N–S along the ridge, mostly
in the northern area of the site. One is 14 m long,
while the other is 6 m long. The latter is in the
southeast area of the site. Its principal alignment is
oriented E–W and spans ca. 7.50 m before merging
into the hillside on its eastern end. At least three
parallel wall alignments project perpendicularly ca.
2.50–3 m from the face of the principal alignment,
forming an enclosure. These wall alignments are
all too heavily disturbed to see any courses, but
the tumbled mound is ca. 1 m high. Feature 2 is
a series of stone rings or hut circles distributed
across the entire site. At least six are present, each
measuring ca. 3 m in diameter. Some are appended
to each other. For instance, there are two appended
circles at the north end of the site that abut the
bedrock slope on their eastern sides. They are
all two–three courses high (0.70 m) and a single
course wide (0.35 m). Their construction is of
loosely packed, unworked stones (average stone
size is 0.40 × 0.35 × 0.25 m). Some stone rings or
hut circles (or stone mounds) also lie further down
slope. Feature 3 consists of at least five small stone
rings, 1.80 m in diameter, three courses high (0.60
m) and one course wide (0.40 m). These are also
distributed across the entire site. Feature 4 lies at
the southern end of the site. It consists of two linear
stone alignments, possibly retaining walls, with
the longer measuring ca. 9.50 m. These walls are
up to 1.50 m high (seven courses) and 1.10 m wide.
Their construction is of wide, flat, unworked stones
packed tightly together. In this area was a massive
concentration of schist with garnet inclusions, as
well as garnet nuggets scattered across the surface.

Site No.: 295 (fig. 4.50)
Field Site No.: 214
Site Name: None
Map Reference: 3050 III, K737
Location on 1:50,000: 3340760 N / 715644 E
Elevation: 330 m
Aerial Reference No.: IGN-78-JOR 12/100 - 988
Site Size: 40 m N–S × 70 m E–W
Inventory Rating: 3
Pottery Collected: Total = 11 (No. of Indicators: 1
/ No. Saved: 10)
Pottery Registration No(s).: 22208–14, 22520–22
Pottery Summary: 11 Chalco/EB
Lithic Summary: N/A
Site Description: This site consists of various
features on four distinct terrace levels above the
wadi. Each terrace level received a distinct feature
number. Feature 1 is a linear stone mound divided
into two segments and aligned roughly N–S. The
northeast segment is 4 m long and the southwest
segment is 12 m long. These average 0.70 m high
and 0.70 m wide. Feature 2 consists of five stone
rings or hut circles. The southwest segment of
Feature 1 continues to the east of a stone ring and
abuts the adjoining one. The stone rings or hut
circles are preserved up to four courses high (0.60
m) and two courses wide (0.40 m). Their average
diameter is 2.50 m. Feature 3 is ca. 20 m up slope
(southeast) from both Feature 1 and Feature 2. This
is another series of five stone rings or hut circles
aligned along the edge of the terrace and oriented
NW–SE. Each averages ca. 3 m in diameter and is
constructed of loosely packed, angular stones with
possible chinking. The walls are better preserved
than those of Feature 2. They are 0.80 m high and
a single course wide (0.40 m). Feature 4 consists
of four large stone rings or hut circles, four smaller
ones, and a linear rock alignment (wall?), also
oriented along the terrace edge. These stone rings
resemble those below at Feature 3. The smaller
stone rings average 1.50 m in diameter, one–two
courses high (0.70 m) and two–three courses wide
(0.80 m). These are not well-preserved. Finally,
the linear rock alignment or wall measures 1.60
× 0.50 m (one course wide) and 0.40 m high. The
surfaces around Features 3 and 4 are more heavily patinated and may be older than those around
Features 1 and 2.

Site No.: 296 (fig. 4.50)
Field Site No.: 213
Site Name: None
Map Reference: 3050 III, K737
Location on 1:50,000: 3340779 N / 715566 E
Elevation: 290 m
Aerial Reference No.: IGN-78-JOR 12/100 - 988
Site Size: 30 m N–S × 50 m E–W
Inventory Rating: 3
Pottery Collected: Total = 0 (No. of Indicators: 0 / No. Saved: 0)
Pottery Registration No(s).: None
Pottery Summary: N/A
Lithic Summary: N/A
Site Description: The site is a complex of structures arranged in an oblong, rectangular orientation (E–W) on a heavily patinated alluvial terrace above the wadi. There seem to be internal partitions creating at least seven stone rings or hut circles (Feature 1), each ca. 2.50 m in diameter. To the south are two rectilinear stone alignments (Feature 2). Each is ca. 5 m long and branches off the rings. The easternmost of these alignments is curvilinear, bending to the southeast and up the slope. The walls of Feature 1 and Feature 2 are constructed of tightly packed stones approximately two courses high (0.85 m) and one course wide (0.50 m), with some variance due to the tumble. The steep slope that extends above the site to the south contains a large concentration of schist with garnet inclusions, which may explain the presence of the settlement.

Site No.: 297 (fig. 4.50)
Field Site No.: 210
Site Name: None
Map Reference: 3050 III, K737
Location on 1:50,000: 3340795 N / 715400 E
Elevation: 222 m
Aerial Reference No.: IGN-78-JOR 12/100 - 988
Site Size: 30 m N–S × 30 m E–W
Inventory Rating: 3
Pottery Collected: Total = 3 (No. of Indicators: 0 / No. Saved: 3)
Pottery Registration No(s).: 22150–52
Pottery Summary: 3 Chalco/EB
Lithic Summary: N/A
Site Description: The site consists of a large, oblong structure (Feature 1) and a large enclosure (Fea-

ture 2), both similar in appearance. Feature 1 (ca. 17 × 12.50 m) is partitioned internally into three separate compartments or enclosures. Feature 2, 14 m north of Feature 1, measures 10 × 8 m. Both features contain a large corral-type enclosure on their west sides and smaller compartments appended to the east. Each is constructed of loosely packed, unworked stones, with 0.40 m high and 0.70 m wide (two courses). The large enclosure on the west end of Feature 1 measures ca. 12.50 in diameter. Directly southeast of the enclosure is a partitioned rectangular area of 3.10 × 1.70 m, apparently a paved platform. Its west wall is shared with the enclosure. A smaller enclosure created by the partition walls, ca. 5 × 2 m, is appended to the northern part of this platform. Two additional stone circles are appended to the east. The northernmost of these is ca. 1.50 m in diameter and the southernmost is ca. 4 m in diameter.

Site No.: 298 (fig. 4.50)
Field Site No.: 209
Site Name: None
Map Reference: 3050 III, K737
Location on 1:50,000: 3340870 N / 715480 E
Elevation: 250 m
Aerial Reference No.: IGN-78-JOR 12/100 - 988
Site Size: 5 m N–S × 5 m E–W
Inventory Rating: 3
Pottery Collected: Total = 0 (No. of Indicators: 0 / No. Saved: 0)
Pottery Registration No(s).: None
Pottery Summary: N/A
Lithic Summary: N/A
Site Description: The site is a single stone mound or cairn ca. 4.50 m in diameter and is preserved ca. 1.50 m high. The SAAS found no artifacts.

Site No.: 299 (fig. 4.50)
Field Site No.: 208
Site Name: None
Map Reference: 3050 III, K737
Location on 1:50,000: 3340880 N / 715420 E
Elevation: 245 m
Aerial Reference No.: IGN-78-JOR 12/100 - 988
Site Size: 60 m N–S × 45 m E–W
Inventory Rating: 3
Pottery Collected: Total = 8 (No. of Indicators: 2 /

No. Saved: 8)
Pottery Registration No(s).: 22157–64
Pottery Summary: 7 Chalco/EB, 1 UD
Lithic Summary: N/A
Site Description: This is a large settlement on the alluvial fan extending far below and west of Site 300. The site consists of ca. 25 stone rings or hut circles, ca. three corral-like features, ca. five figure-8 stone features, and four or five miscellaneous linear wall alignments. The stone rings or hut circles, 4–5 m in diameter, are generally one course wide. Some are preserved up to four courses high. Several stone mounds in the area, which measure 3–4 m in diameter, may be collapsed structures. The figure-8 features tend to have one circular portion ca. 4 m in diameter and a more oblong part, 7–8 m in length. These share a common wall. The corrals appear as open circles 8–10 m in diameter. The largest is a complex comprised of a corral-type enclosure with attached linear wall alignments covering ca. 22 m N–S × 20 m E–W. This corral is roughly circular with an entranceway cut out. The wall segments flanking the entrance flair outward. The stones are large, averaging 0.40 × 0.35 × 0.30 m. The walls of the enclosure are one course wide and up to three courses high. On the north side, is a series of terraced, rounded stone structures. They share the corral wall and extend to the north. The average diameter for these appended structures is 6–8 m.

Site No.: 300 (fig. 4.50)
Field Site No.: 207
Site Name: None
Map Reference: 3050 III, K737
Location on 1:50,000: 3340937 N / 715431 E
Elevation: 228 m
Aerial Reference No.: IGN-78-JOR 12/100 - 988
Site Size: 40 m N–S × 80 m E–W
Inventory Rating: 4
Pottery Collected: Total = 71 (No. of Indicators: 11 / No. Saved: 24)
Pottery Registration No(s).: 22153–56, 22555–74
Pottery Summary: 49 Chalco/EB, 15 ER/Nab, 6 EByz (1 vessel), 1 UD
Lithic Summary: Indef. cultural-historic placement
Site Description: The site consists of four features. Feature 1 is a series of at least four agglomerated, rectangular terraces enclosed by well-built walls

ca. 20 m N–S × 40 m E–W. The construction of the terrace walls is of very large boulders at the base with smaller stones (average stone size is 0.45 × 0.25 × 0.25 m) forming the upper courses. The walls are badly preserved, but in places they stand at least 1.40 m high and wide. On the north side of Feature 1 is a series of at least four stone circles, also with well-built walls, preserved up to 0.90 m high, 1.20 m wide (two courses), and ca. 2 m in diameter. At least two of these are appended to each other. Feature 2 lies in the northeast sector of the site, separated from Feature 1 by a small drainage channel. Feature 2 contains both stone rings and two rectilinear structures in an area of 30 m N–S × 20 m E–W. The two rectilinear structures are up slope (southeast) from the ring complex. The better preserved of these abuts two stone rings on its north face. The stone rings are of similar construction and 1.50 m in diameter. The northwest face measures 3.20 m long, 0.70 m high (four courses), and a single course wide. The south face is 3.50 m long and similarly constructed. Some large stones standing upright are set in the northeast face. The stone rings themselves also vary in construction and size. Some utilize boulders packed with smaller cobbles. Other rings contain mostly smaller stones (average stone size 0.25 × 0.20 × 0.20 m). The rings made of smaller stones are usually smaller in size, ca. 2 m in diameter. There is also a possible grave nearby which measures 1.60 × 1.10 m. Feature 3 consists of a series of stone rings, ca. 4 m in diameter, that extend across the entire site (in addition to those just mentioned). Most of these stone rings are ca. one course high (0.35 m), although some are preserved up to three–four courses high (ca. 1.20 m) and one course wide (0.35 m). Feature 4 is to the northwest sector of the site. It is a stone circle ca. 4.50 m in diameter. It is two courses wide (0.70 m) and one course high (0.15 m). Appended to its south side is a small stone mound ca. 1.40 m in diameter and 0.60 m high. Appended to this mound on its south side is another smaller stone ring ca. 2.50 m in diameter.

Site No.: 301 (fig. 4.50)
Field Site No.: 211
Site Name: None
Map Reference: 3050 III, K737

Location on 1:50,000: 3341010 N / 715420 E
Elevation: 225 m
Aerial Reference No.: IGN-78-JOR 12/100 - 988
Site Size: 36 m N–S × 30 m E–W
Inventory Rating: 3
Pottery Collected: Total = 0 (No. of Indicators: 0
/ No. Saved: 0)
Pottery Registration No(s).: None
Pottery Summary: N/A
Lithic Summary: N/A
Site Description: The site consists of five stone rings
(burials?) and a stone semicircle. The latter is ca.
3 m long and arcs to a depth of 3 m. The walls are
preserved up to two courses high (0.60 m) and
one course wide (0.30 m). Ca. 20 m south of the
semicircle are two stone rings or graves. These are
somewhat oblong, measuring 2 × 1.20 m. Another
stone ring or burial lies ca. 8 m north of the semicircle. A fourth stone ring is ca. 10 m northwest of
the former. This site is ca. 50 m north of Site 299
and Site 300, with which it may be associated.

Site No.: 302 (fig. 4.50)
Field Site No.: 212
Site Name: None
Map Reference: 3050 III, K737
Location on 1:50,000: 3341205 N / 715275 E
Elevation: 215 m
Aerial Reference No.: IGN-78-JOR 12/100 - 988
Site Size: 14 m N–S × 8 m E–W
Inventory Rating: 3
Pottery Collected: Total = 10 (No. of Indicators: 3
/ No. Saved: 10)
Pottery Registration No(s).: 22545–54
Pottery Summary: 10 UD
Lithic Summary: N/A
Site Description: The site consists of three well-
built circular stone mounds or burial cairns set in
a row. All measure ca. 2 m high and 5 m in diam-
eter. The westernmost is ca. 4 m west of the others,
which touch one another.

Site No.: 303 (fig. 4.50)
Field Site No.: 206
Site Name: None
Map Reference: 3050 III, K737
Location on 1:50,000: 3341233 N / 715055 E
Elevation: 201 m

Aerial Reference No.: IGN-78-JOR 12/100 - 988
Site Size: 8.50 m N–S × 2.40 m E–W
Inventory Rating: 5
Pottery Collected: Total = 0 (No. of Indicators: 0
/ No. Saved: 0)
Pottery Registration No(s).: None
Pottery Summary: N/A
Lithic Summary: Indef. cultural-historic placement
Site Description: The site consists of three burial
mounds aligned roughly NE–SW. Two of the
mounds measure ca. 2 × 1.20 m and 0.30 m high.
The third mound is smaller, ca. 0.60 × 0.70 m. The
mounds are aligned in a row which trends N–S
for 8.50 m.

Site No.: 304 (fig. 4.51)
Field Site No.: 185
Site Name: None
Map Reference: 3050 III, K737
Location on 1:50,000: 3341133 N / 710865 E
Elevation: 210 m
Aerial Reference No.: IGN-78-JOR 12/100 - 1666
Site Size: 30 m N–S × 50 m E–W
Inventory Rating: 2
Pottery Collected: Total = 30 (No. of Indicators: 7
/ No. Saved: 13)
Pottery Registration No(s).: 22188–200
Pottery Summary: 14 Chalco/EB, 16 ER/Nab
Lithic Summary: Indef. cultural-historic placement
Site Description: The site consists of three distinct
features on the eastern face of a limestone ridge in
Wādī 'Araba. Feature 1 is a small cave ca. 3 × 1.75
m and 1.65 m high. Half of its opening has been
sealed off by a wall constructed of loosely packed
stones. This wall is one course wide and preserved
up to six courses high (the average stone size is 0.15
m on a side). Its interior is empty (no artifacts, no
smoke blackening on roof, etc.). Feature 2 is a small,
circular enclosure 2.70 m in diameter built against
the bottom of the cliff face. Feature 2 is ca. 10 m
northeast and 1 m lower in elevation than Feature
1. East of Features 1 and 2, Feature 3 is a complex
of five stone rings and mounds, possibly graves.
The closest is ca. 18 m to the east, the farthest is
ca. 50 m to the northeast. Each measures ca. 1.30
m in diameter. The stones are irregularly shaped
blocks of limestone that average 0.50 × 0.30 × 0.15
m. The mounds are ca. 10 m from each other. One

mound seems to have a wall extending from it 1 m to the west. The wall is one course wide and two courses high.

Site No.: 305 (fig. 4.51)
Field Site No.: 184
Site Name: None
Map Reference: 3050 III, K737
Location on 1:50,000: 3341320 N / 711010 E
Elevation: 220 m
Aerial Reference No.: IGN-78-JOR 12/100 - 1666
Site Size: 5.50 m N–S × 4.20 m E–W
Inventory Rating: 3
Pottery Collected: Total = 97 (No. of Indicators: 3 / No. Saved: 16)
Pottery Registration No(s).: 22120–35
Pottery Summary: 97 ER/Nab
Lithic Summary: Indef. cultural-historic placement
Site Description: The site consists of a nearly square stone structure 5.50 m N–S × 4.20 m E–W, constructed of loosely packed, irregularly shaped stones. Its east wall is preserved up to four courses high and one course wide. Average stone size is 0.20 m on a side. The western segment of the structure appears disturbed by clandestine excavations which exposed a possible wall alignment bisecting the structure on a N–S axis. The preserved wall is three courses high at ground level and one course wide. The nature and purpose of the structure remain unclear.

Site No.: 306 (fig. 4.51)
Field Site No.: 186
Site Name: None
Map Reference: 3050 III, K737
Location on 1:50,000: 3341501 N / 711355 E
Elevation: 235 m
Aerial Reference No.: IGN-78-JOR 12/100 - 1666
Site Size: 15 m N–S × 30 m E–W
Inventory Rating: 2
Pottery Collected: Total = 0 (No. of Indicators: 0 / No. Saved: 0)
Pottery Registration No(s).: None
Pottery Summary: N/A
Lithic Summary: Indef. cultural-historic placement
Site Description: The site consists of three features on a limestone ridge in Wādī ʿAraba. Feature 1 is a terrace wall 1 m high across a wadi. Feature 2 is a stone circle ca. 30 m down the wadi to the north-

west. This feature is 1.30 m in diameter, two–three courses high, and one course wide. Average stone size is 0.22 m on a side. Feature 3, on the south side of the wadi, is a rockshelter to the southwest (facing north). The rockshelter has a semicircular wall (with evidence of chinking) built into it, which encloses an area of 1.38 m N–S × 1.46 m E–W. The wall is preserved up to five courses high and one course wide. In some places the wall touches the roof of the rockshelter. The wadi generally trends SE–NW on the west side of Jebel el-Khureij.

Site No.: 307 (fig. 4.51)
Field Site No.: 183
Site Name: None
Map Reference: 3050 III, K737
Location on 1:50,000: 3341543 N / 711015 E
Elevation: 223 m
Aerial Reference No.: IGN-78-JOR 12/100 - 1666
Site Size: 50 m N–S × 50 m E–W
Inventory Rating: 3
Pottery Collected: Total = 72 (No. of Indicators: 6 / No. Saved: 20)
Pottery Registration No(s).: 22093–112
Pottery Summary: 72 ER/Nab
Lithic Summary: Indef. cultural-historic placement
Site Description: This is a large quarry on the north and south sides of a spur projecting from Jebel el-Khureij. The quarried platform on each side (Feature 1) measures ca. 30 m long and ca. 2 m high. Along the quarried terrace are spoil piles (two main ones, each measuring ca. 10 m in diameter and 2–3 m high), including squared blocks, some with tool marks. Two of these blocks with tool marks were reused to form a grave (Feature 3) in the center of the northern quarried terrace. This grave is rectangular (1.90 m N–S × 1.30 m E–W), with an apparent capstone at its north end measuring 0.58 × 0.45 m. The grave was once topped by a large, quarried, limestone block measuring 1.22 × 0.50 × 0.18 m. This block now lies alongside the grave, suggesting robber activity. There are no remains inside the grave, but there are faunal remains along the exterior. There is an apparent entranceway (Feature 2) ca. 10 m northeast and 2 m lower in elevation from the edge of the quarried terrace. The entrance is constructed of large, squared rectangular blocks one course high and wide. It is 0.32 m high and the

opening is 0.59 m wide. The east side consists of a single large rectangular stone with a smaller square stone to the south of it, and the west side consists of several smaller square stones packed together. Strangely, this apparent entranceway has no obvious association with any extant walls. Ca. 30 m further to the northeast and 2 m further down the slope is another series of structures (Feature 4) in a line oriented roughly N–S, which consists of four rooms, each ca. 6 m in diameter. Most of these structures appear as little more than mounds of stone tumble. The pottery concentrates around the structures. At the very summit of the ridge is another series of structures similar to those of Feature 4.

Site No.: 308 (fig. 4.51)
Field Site No.: 235
Site Name: None
Map Reference: 3050 III, K737
Location on 1:50,000: 3342214 N / 709986 E
Elevation: 220 m
Aerial Reference No.: IGN-78-JOR 12/100 - 1692
Site Size: 2.81 m N–S × 7.87 m E–W
Inventory Rating: 2
Pottery Collected: Total = 49 (No. of Indicators: 8 / No. Saved: 22)
Pottery Registration No(s).: 47784–805
Pottery Summary: 16 ER/Nab, 12 ER/LR, 12 EByz (1 vessel / cookpot), 9 UD
Lithic Summary: N/A
Site Description: The site consists of two isolated structures. The first is a stone structure, 1.40 × 1.30 m, constructed of two irregular courses of masonry on the east and west sides. Inside this feature, aligned roughly N–S, is a compartment or channel 0.29 m wide with an even stone face within. Feature 2 is ca. 2 m northeast of Feature 1. This is a semicircular stone structure 1.80 m in diameter. The semicircle is comprised of several large, unworked boulders ca. 0.40 m on a side. The SAAS recovered numerous sherds from the structure, most of which may have washed down from Feature 1 above. Ca. 10 m west of Feature 1 lies what appears to be a modern burial ca. 1.50 × 0.50 m with an E–W orientation.

Site No.: 309 (fig. 4.50)
Field Site No.: 198
Site Name: None
Map Reference: 3050 III, K737
Location on 1:50,000: 3342690 N / 716120 E
Elevation: 290 m
Aerial Reference No.: IGN-78-JOR 12/100 - 990
Site Size: 3.50 m N–S × 4 m E–W
Inventory Rating: 4
Pottery Collected: Total = 0 (No. of Indicators: 0 / No. Saved: 0)
Pottery Registration No(s).: None
Pottery Summary: N/A
Lithic Summary: N/A
Site Description: The site is an isolated stone mound or cairn on a plateau ca. 40 m northwest of Site 310 on the alluvial fan of Wādī Um Saiyāla. The cairn is of loosely packed stones averaging ca. 0.24 m on a side and preserved 0.60 m high. There is an interior compartment at the top of the mound, ca. 2 m diameter, and filled with silt. Many stones are scattered across its surface.

Site No.: 310 (fig. 4.50)
Field Site No.: 197
Site Name: None
Map Reference: 3050 III, K737
Location on 1:50,000: 3342680 N / 716320 E
Elevation: 310 m
Aerial Reference No.: IGN-78-JOR 12/100 - 990
Site Size: 5.10 m N–S × 5.10 m E–W
Inventory Rating: 5
Pottery Collected: Total = 1 (No. of Indicators: 0 / No. Saved: 1)
Pottery Registration No(s).: 22119
Pottery Summary: 1 Ottoman pipe
Lithic Summary: N/A
Site Description: The site consists is isolated cairn 5.10 m in diameter and mounded ca. 1.10 m high. It is near Sites 309 and 312 and of similar construction to those cairns.

Site No.: 311 (fig. 4.50)
Field Site No.: 199
Site Name: None
Map Reference: 3050 III, K737
Location on 1:50,000: 3342698 N / 715840 E
Elevation: 270 m

Aerial Reference No.: IGN-78-JOR 12/100 - 990
Site Size: 4 m N–S × 4 m E–W
Inventory Rating: 4
Pottery Collected: Total = 7 (No. of Indicators: 0 / No. Saved: 7)
Pottery Registration No(s).: 22172–78
Pottery Summary: 7 EB II (?)
Lithic Summary: N/A
Site Description: The site is a single burial, recently robbed, on the alluvial fan of Wādī Um Saiyāla. The stones are piled up to 1 m high and the burial is 0.20 m wide. The interior compartment of the mound, ca. 1.70 m in diameter, is filled with silt. Sherds and bone fragments lay scattered around the burial.

Site No.: 312 (fig. 4.50)
Field Site No.: 196
Site Name: None
Map Reference: 3050 III, K737
Location on 1:50,000: 3342703 N / 716173 E
Elevation: 278 m
Aerial Reference No.: IGN-78-JOR 12/100 - 990
Site Size: 80 m N–S × 70 m E–W
Inventory Rating: 5
Pottery Collected: Total = 67 (No. of Indicators: 14 / No. Saved: 26)
Pottery Registration No(s).: 22136–49, 22505–16
Pottery Summary: 13 Chalco/EB, 2 EB IVB, 52 ER/Nab (pot-bust)
Lithic Summary: Indef. cultural-historic placement
Site Description: This is a small settlement with six distinct features. Feature 1 consists of three stone mounds (the central is largest) and an alignment of stones in half-circles form a perimeter enclosing an area ca. 20 m N–S × 15 m E–W. This feature lies on the west edge of a modern wadi embankment, so it may be that the original structure was fully circular. The large central mound is 4.50 m in diameter and 1.50 m high. Trending inward from the perimeter are four additional stone alignments or walls that partition the structure into separate rooms. Two of the partition walls intersect with the two smaller stone mounds. Also, there may be interconnecting rooms around the large mound. The southeast side of the perimeter wall is built of massive standing stones, ca. 0.35 m on a side and preserved one course high and one course wide. On the northwest side the perimeter wall may have

been two–three courses wide, but this is obscured by tumble. The partition walls are similar. Finally, this main feature, on the east side of the alluvial fan, is ca. 13 m northeast of Feature 2, a large cairn 5 m in diameter and 1.50 m high. Feature 3 lies ca. 12 m southwest of Feature 2. It is a stone mound ca. 0.85 m high and 2.50 m wide with three appended stone circles on its west, northeast and southeast sides. The interior of the mound is filled with alluvial deposits and measures 0.80 m across. Appended to the southeast side of the mound is a stone circle ca. 4.10 m in diameter. Its construction is of tightly packed, large stones measuring 0.60 m high at some points and 0.80 m wide. Appended to the mound on its northeast side and connected to the southeast circle is another stone circle ca. 2.50 m in diameter. It is constructed similarly to the previous stone circle, but is only 0.45 m high and two courses wide (0.50 m). Appended to the west side of the mound is the last stone circle. It is more oblong than circular, ca. 2.50 m in diameter, and constructed in the same fashion as the northeast stone circle. Also, southwest of the mound is a large amount of tumble. Feature 4 lies ca. 5 m southeast of Feature 3. It is a stone ring 4 m in diameter, one course high, and one course wide with stones set upright. Feature 5, ca. 13 m southeast of Feature 4, is a linear stone feature constructed of massive boulders (average stone size is ca. 0.60 × 0.45 × 0.40 m) 25 m in length. Feature 6 is another large cairn ca. 45 m south of Feature 3. It is similar in construction to Feature 2.

Site No.: 313 (fig. 4.50)
Field Site No.: 191
Site Name: None
Map Reference: 3050 III, K737
Location on 1:50,000: 3343252 N / 715517 E
Elevation: 237 m
Aerial Reference No.: IGN-78-JOR 12/100 - 990
Site Size: 70 m N–S × 120 m E–W
Inventory Rating: 5
Pottery Collected: Total = 106 (No. of Indicators: 16 / No. Saved: 31)
Pottery Registration No(s).: 22369–98, 22519
Pottery Summary: 101 Chalco/EB, 1 ER/Nab, 1 R/Byz/Early Islamic, 3 UD
Lithic Summary: Indef. cultural-historic placement

Site Description: This is a small settlement of several structures and miscellaneous wall alignments on the alluvial fan below Wādī Um Saiyāla. There are multiple circular structures constructed of large, irregularly shaped stones packed tightly together. Many structures use boulders in their walls. Some walls are preserved ca. 0.60 m high and most are ca. 0.80 m wide. There is a large amount of tumble around each structure from collapsed walls. There seem to be two different types: larger structures ca. 5–6 m in diameter and smaller structures ca. 2–3 m in diameter. At least two structures are rectangular. At least one is circular with an interior partition wall dividing it into two compartments or rooms. Average stone size is 0.25 m on a side and average boulder size is 0.75 × 0.55 × 0.15 m. A complex of stone rings, many of which may be circular huts, and stone mounds comprise this site. Some of the stone mounds may be burials. Larger structures are concentrated in the western sector of the site, while mainly smaller stone circles cluster in the northeast. There is also much copper ore and copper slag at the site.

Site No.: 314 (figs. 4.50, 4.51)
Field Site No.: 234
Site Name: None
Map Reference: 3050 III, K737
Location on 1:50,000: 3343256 N / 712578 E
Elevation: 200 m
Aerial Reference No.: IGN-78-JOR 12/100 - 1692
Site Size: 39.10 m N–S × 48 m E–W
Inventory Rating: 2
Pottery Collected: Total = 67 (No. of Indicators: 7 / No. Saved: 25)
Pottery Registration No(s).: 47740–56, 47807–14
Pottery Summary: 2 Chalco/EB, 44 ER/Nab, 19 ER/LR, 2 UD
Lithic Summary: Indef. cultural-historic placement
Site Description: The site consists of a cemetery (Feature 1) and an isolated structure (Feature 2). The outline of Feature 2 is constructed of a single course of boulders and cobbles of limestone and chert. A single course of five boulders oriented 316 degrees and aligned roughly southwest seems to be an outer extension of the structure. The cemetery of 13 graves, generally appearing as piles of tumbled stones, lies to the north. Most are oblong

(ca. 1.80–2.20 m long × 1 m wide). Some graves, or grave pairs, measure ca. 4.10 × 5 m. Their orientation varies. One grave at the northwest end of the site appears as a circle of boulders (average stone size is ca. 0.35 m on a side) ca. 1.60 m in diameter. There is another grave (ca. 2.20 m in diameter) framed by circular alignment of boulders to the east. The artifacts are largely in the northeast and northwest areas of the site.

Site No.: 315 (fig. 4.50)
Field Site No.: 189
Site Name: None
Map Reference: 3050 III, K737
Location on 1:50,000: 3343682 N / 715114 E
Elevation: 220 m
Aerial Reference No.: IGN-78-JOR 12/100 - 989
Site Size: 25 m N–S × 10 m E–W
Inventory Rating: 2
Pottery Collected: Total = 0 (No. of Indicators: 0 / No. Saved: 0)
Pottery Registration No(s).: None
Pottery Summary: N/A
Lithic Summary: Indef. cultural-historic placement
Site Description: This is a cemetery consisting of at least 10 burials. Most of the burials appear as oblong stone rings (oriented E–W). The best preserved measures 3.10 m N–S × 1.40 m E–W. Other burials appear as stone mounds with no clear orientation and are much smaller in size.

Site No.: 316 (figs. 4.34, 4.50, 4.51)
Field Site No.: 187
Site Name: None
Map Reference: 3050 III, K737
Location on 1:50,000: 3343896 N / 712050 E
Elevation: 235 m
Aerial Reference No.: IGN-78-JOR 12/100 - 1692
Site Size: 45 m N–S × 35 m E–W
Inventory Rating: 3
Pottery Collected: Total = 77 (No. of Indicators: 8 / No. Saved: 26)
Pottery Registration No(s).: 47757–82
Pottery Summary: 6 Chalco/EB, 5 ER/Nab, 63 ER/LR, 1 EByz (cookpot rim), 1 LByz/Umayyad (Byzantine Fine Ware), 1 UD
Lithic Summary: Indef. cultural-historic placement
Site Description: The site consists of five features.

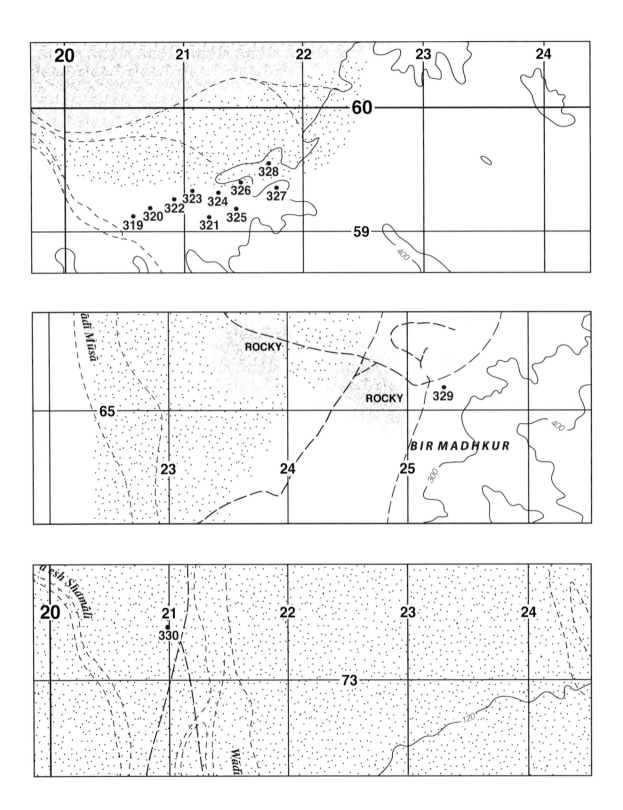

FIG. 4.52 *Gharandal Region (Region III). Top: map 21 (Sites 319–328), middle: map 22 (Site 329), bottom: map 23 (Site 330).*

Feature 1 consists of three stone mounds (ca. 4 × 3 m) spaced ca. 3 m apart along the western edge of the site. The central mound has been disturbed by clandestine excavation. Feature 2, at the north end of the site, is a linear stone alignment (trending E–W for ca. 6 m) a single course wide and high. Behind Feature 2 to the south are two small stone mounds recently robbed. Feature 3 designates the unusually dense lithic scatter that covers the entire site. Feature 4 lies ca. 10 m southeast of Feature 1. It is a figure-8 shaped structure constructed of small stones arranged in a main circle with a smaller circle appended to its southeast end. The structure (10.6 m N–S × 5.4 m E–W), which was probably agricultural (threshing floor?) has a possible entrance on its southeast side. Feature 5 is 10 m west of Feature 4 and due south of Features 1–2. Feature 5 is a curvilinear stone alignment, a single course high and wide (1.30 m), that extends 4.80 m to the southwest (average stone size is 0.23 m on a side). There is a concentration of pottery around this feature. Another linear feature, oriented N–S, lies directly east of Feature 1. This feature is similar in construction and appearance to Feature 2, but it is 10 m long. It seems that Features 1–2 make up a core area, enclosed by some sort of wall alignment, while Features 4–5 are ancillary.

Site No.: 317 (figs. 4.50, 4.51)
Field Site No.: 188
Site Name: None
Map Reference: 3050 III, K737
Location on 1:50,000: 3344150 N / 712480 E
Elevation: 250 m
Aerial Reference No.: IGN-78-JOR 12/100 - 1694
Site Size: 15 m N–S × 65 m E–W
Inventory Rating: 3
Pottery Collected: Total = 64 (No. of Indicators: 0 / No. Saved: 11)
Pottery Registration No(s).: 22113–15, 22425–32
Pottery Summary: 64 Chalco/EB (some with copper slag, 1 with possible kassiterite)
Lithic Summary: Indef. cultural-historic placement
Site Description: The site consists of three features on a limestone ridge at the northern end of Jebel el-Khureij. Features 1 and 2 are on the hilltop ca. 60 m east of Feature 3, which rests on a saddle below. Feature 1 lies ca. 3 m north of Feature 2.

Both features are circular mounds of stone tumble, although robber pits excavated into the center of each revealed clear evidence of interior walls of worked limestone blocks. Feature 1 (5 × 3 m) is in fact larger than Feature 2 (ca. 2 × 2 m). Feature 1 consists of two compartments (graves?), 2.30 × 1.60 m and 1.50 × 1.60 m. The compartments are separated by a stone wall one course high and wide and constructed of two large rectangular limestone blocks fitted closely together. The outer walls are of loosely packed stones that have been fractured at regular angles. Feature 3 is a stone wall extending roughly E–W across a saddle ca. 30 m west and 10 m down the slope from Features 1 and 2. It is ca. 0.80 m wide (two–three courses), one–two courses high, and also constructed of limestone blocks. There was a scatter of copper slag and pottery on the north slope below the wall.

Site No.: 318 (fig. 4.50)
Field Site No.: 190
Site Name: None
Map Reference: 3050 III, K737
Location on 1:50,000: 3344269 N / 715367 E
Elevation: 236 m
Aerial Reference No.: IGN-78-JOR 12/100 - 989
Site Size: 15 m N–S × 15 m E–W
Inventory Rating: 2
Pottery Collected: Total = 0 (No. of Indicators: 0 / No. Saved: 0)
Pottery Registration No(s).: None
Pottery Summary: N/A
Lithic Summary: Indef. cultural-historic placement
Site Description: The site is an oval alignment of stones (1.90 × 0.70 m.), perhaps a grave, one course high and wide. Two rock alignments run parallel through the middle of the oval, creating three compartments. A scatter of lithics extends over the entire site.

Site No.: 319 (fig. 4.52)
Field Site No.: 152
Site Name: Qasr Wādī eṭ-Ṭayyiba
Map Reference: 3050 I, K737
Location on 1:50,000: 3359080 N / 720519 E
Elevation: 230 m
Aerial Reference No.: IGN-78-JOR 12/100 - 1809
Site Size: 100 m N–S × 200 m E–W

Inventory Rating: 4

Pottery Collected: Total = 102 (No. of Indicators: 36 / No. Saved: 33)

Pottery Registration No(s).: 11327–28, 11337–42, 11350–74

Pottery Summary: 98 ER/Nab, 2 EByz, 1 UDE, 1 UD

Lithic Summary: Upper Paleolithic (see Chapter 5)

Site Description: This is the fort of Qasr Wādī eṭ-Ṭayyiba. The *qasr* is a ruined, rectangular structure ca. 24 × 23 m without clear evidence of corner towers. Its walls are ca. 1.15 m wide (two courses with rubble fill). Internal structures are aligned against the curtain walls of the structure and surround a central courtyard. Of particular interest is a large of mound of stone rubble in the center of the west wall, perhaps a collapsed tower or gateway. The north, south, and west walls of this structure seem to extend ca. 3 m beyond the outer face of the curtain wall. There are other less impressive remains in the vicinity of ʿAin eṭ-Ṭayyiba. Ca. 20 m southeast of the *qasr* is a long wall, 0.58 m wide and oriented roughly E–W, that extends in segments for ca. 61 m. Another structure, virtually destroyed by numerous robber pits and due east of the modern well, does not exceed ca. 5 × 5 m, in light of the proximity of the spoil dumps and the exposure of the southeast wall. Artifact density is thickest in this area.

Site No.: 320 (fig. 4.52)
Field Site No.: 159
Site Name: None
Map Reference: 3050 I, K737
Location on 1:50,000: 3359101 N / 720549 E
Elevation: 260 m
Aerial Reference No.: IGN-78-JOR 12/100 - 1809
Site Size: 20 m N–S × 17 m E–W
Inventory Rating: 2
Pottery Collected: Total = 0 (No. of Indicators: 0 / No. Saved: 0)
Pottery Registration No(s).: None
Pottery Summary: N/A
Lithic Summary: Indef. cultural-historic placement
Site Description: The site consists of four stone rings or hut circles on the scree slope of the ridge east of ʿAin eṭ-Ṭayyiba. These stone rings or hut circles averages ca. 3.50 m in diameter. The stones are standing upright along the perimeter. There is

a lithic scatter (ca. 0–3 lithics/m²) associated with the site.

Site No.: 321 (fig. 4.52)
Field Site No.: 160
Site Name: None
Map Reference: 3050 I, K737
Location on 1:50,000: 3359125 N / 721190 E
Elevation: 270 m
Aerial Reference No.: IGN-78-JOR 12/100 - 1814
Site Size: 30 m N–S × 100 m E–W
Inventory Rating: 2
Pottery Collected: Total = 34 (No. of Indicators: 4 / No. Saved: 8)
Pottery Registration No(s).: 11329–36
Pottery Summary: 2 Chalco/EB, 3 ER/Nab, 24 R/Byz, 5 UD
Lithic Summary: Indef. cultural-historic placement
Site Description: The site consists of at least three ruined structures or hut circles on an alluvial terrace in a wadi east of ʿAin eṭ-Ṭayyiba. The first is a roughly square structure ca. 4 × 4 m with walls one course wide (ca. 0.50–0.60 m) and the interior cleared of stones. The second structure measures ca. 3 m on a side. East of this structure is a circular alignment of upright standing stones, 1 m in diameter. The third structure is more curvilinear (ca. 6.50 × 4 m), perhaps foundations for a tent emplacement.

Site No.: 322 (fig. 4.52)
Field Site No.: 154
Site Name: None
Map Reference: 3050 I, K737
Location on 1:50,000: 3359190 N / 720950 E
Elevation: 265 m
Aerial Reference No.: IGN-78-JOR 12/100 - 1814
Site Size: 20 m N–S × 40 m E–W
Inventory Rating: 2
Pottery Collected: Total = 11 (No. of Indicators: 0 / No. Saved: 2)
Pottery Registration No(s).: 11325–26
Pottery Summary: 11 ER/Nab
Lithic Summary: Probably Chalcolithic or later (see Chapter 5)
Site Description: The site consists of a small structure on a limestone ridge and a lithic and sherd scatter of ca. 40 × 20 m. The structure, 2.50 m N–S × 5 m E–W, is constructed around a small pit dug

into the east face of the ridge. West and north of the pit there are stone walls one course wide and preserved ca. 0.60 m high.

Site No.: 323 (fig. 4.52)
Field Site No.: 155
Site Name: None
Map Reference: 3050 I, K737
Location on 1:50,000: 3359300 N / 721050 E
Elevation: 280 m
Aerial Reference No.: IGN-78-JOR 12/100 - 1814
Site Size: 15 m N–S × 10 m E–W
Inventory Rating: 2
Pottery Collected: Total = 1 (No. of Indicators: 0 / No. Saved: 0)
Pottery Registration No(s).: None
Pottery Summary: 1 ER/Nab
Lithic Summary: Indef. cultural-historic placement
Site Description: This is a small structure (2 × 2 m) built of large upright boulders and smaller rock piles. There is also a dense lithic scatter around the structure (ca. 100–200 lithics/m²), concentrated to the north and northwest. The site lies on the slope of a small saddle in the mountain range east of ʿAin eṭ-Ṭayyiba.

Site No.: 324 (fig. 4.52)
Field Site No.: 156
Site Name: None
Map Reference: 3050 I, K737
Location on 1:50,000: 3359300 N / 721275 E
Elevation: 285 m
Aerial Reference No.: IGN-78-JOR 12/100 - 1814
Site Size: 4 m N–S × 4 m E–W
Inventory Rating: 1
Pottery Collected: Total = 6 (No. of Indicators: 0 / No. Saved: 0)
Pottery Registration No(s).: None
Pottery Summary: 5 ER/Nab, 1 R/Byz
Lithic Summary: Indef. cultural-historic placement
Site Description: This is a small, poorly constructed windbreak (ca. 1 × 1.50 × 0.80 m) on a knoll of the ridge east of ʿAin eṭ-Ṭayyiba. It is built mostly of linear rock piles one–three courses wide and opens to the southeast. A lithic scatter is concentrated north and west of the structure.

Site No.: 325 (fig. 4.52)
Field Site No.: 161
Site Name: None
Map Reference: 3050 I, K737
Location on 1:50,000: 3359200 N / 721445 E
Elevation: 280 m
Aerial Reference No.: IGN-78-JOR 12/100 - 1814
Site Size: 30 m N–S × 50 m E–W
Inventory Rating: 3
Pottery Collected: Total = 38 (No. of Indicators: 4 / No. Saved: 7)
Pottery Registration No(s).: 11343–49
Pottery Summary: 37 ER/Nab, 1 UD
Lithic Summary: Probably Chalcolithic or later (see Chapter 5)
Site Description: The site consists of a multi-room complex (ca. 19 × 28 m) with an associated lithic and sherd scatter. The complex includes two rooms to the east and two stone mounds to the west. Due to its ruined nature the function of some wall alignments and mounds is difficult to determine. The largest concentration of artifacts is due west of the collapse. At the eastern edge of the site, three rooms have been dug into the base of the hill to a depth of ca. 0.10 m. One is round and the other two are more square, measuring ca. 3–4 m × 3–4 m.

Site No.: 326 (fig. 4.52)
Field Site No.: 157
Site Name: None
Map Reference: 3050 I, K737
Location on 1:50,000: 3359350 N / 721540 E
Elevation: 296 m
Aerial Reference No.: IGN-78-JOR 12/100 - 1814
Site Size: 23 m N–S × 5 m E–W
Inventory Rating: 2
Pottery Collected: Total = 0 (No. of Indicators: 0 / No. Saved: 0)
Pottery Registration No(s).: None
Pottery Summary: N/A
Lithic Summary: N/A
Site Description: This is a cemetery at least nine burials on a sloping saddle east of ʿAin eṭ-Ṭayyiba. The burials are in a linear alignment trending N–S. From the south, these include a single stone ring (ca. 2 × 2 m), a cairn (ca. 0.80 m in diameter and ca. 0.30 m high), a second stone ring (1 × 1.50 m), a second cairn (1.50 m in diameter and ca. 0.30 m

high), and five linear rock alignments that parallel the slope of the saddle. These burials are oriented E–W.

Site No.: 327 (fig. 4.52)
Field Site No.: 153
Site Name: None
Map Reference: 3050 I, K737
Location on 1:50,000: 3359340 N / 721820 E
Elevation: 235 m
Aerial Reference No.: IGN-78-JOR 12/100 - 1814
Site Size: 50 m N–S × 50 m E–W
Inventory Rating: 1
Pottery Collected: Total = 0 (No. of Indicators: 0 / No. Saved: 0)
Pottery Registration No(s).: None
Pottery Summary: N/A
Lithic Summary: Probably Chalcolithic or later (see Chapter 5)
Site Description: This is a high density lithic scatter on the southern slope of a low spur east of ʿAin eṭ-Ṭayyiba.

Site No.: 328 (fig. 4.52)
Field Site No.: 158
Site Name: None
Map Reference: 3050 I, K737
Location on 1:50,000: 3359480 N / 721750 E
Elevation: 340 m
Aerial Reference No.: IGN-78-JOR 12/100 - 1814
Site Size: 15 m N–S × 10 m E–W
Inventory Rating: 2
Pottery Collected: Total = 7 (No. of Indicators: 1 / No. Saved: 2)
Pottery Registration No(s).: 11323–24
Pottery Summary: 5 ER/Nab, 2 UD (same vessel)
Lithic Summary: Epipaleolithic (see Chapter 7)
Site Description: This is a irregularly shaped windbreak (ca. 3 × 2 m) atop a small bedrock knoll east of ʿAin eṭ-Ṭayyiba. Its walls are preserved to a height of ca. 0.40 m. There is a lithic scatter associated with the site.

Site No.: 329 (fig. 4.52)
Field Site No.: 148
Site Name: Bir Madhkur
Map Reference: 3050 I, K737
Location on 1:50,000: 3365227 N / 725342 E

Elevation: 270 m
Aerial Reference No.: IGN-78-JOR 12/100 - 555
Site Size: 140 m N–S × 220 m E–W
Inventory Rating: 4
Pottery Collected: Total = 785 (No. of Indicators: 292 / No. Saved: 192)
Pottery Registration No(s).: 9608–77, 9684–9743, 9802–63
Pottery Summary: 452 ER/Nab (3 TS, some LR), 34 LR, 28 EByz (2 LRRW/ARS), 18 R/EByz, 248 R/Byz, 3 LByz, 2 UD (imports?), 12 Tiles, 2 Bricks, 28 Pipes
Lithic Summary: N/A
Site Description: The most impressive structure at Bir Madhkur is the *castellum*, a *quadriburgium* with four corner towers measuring just over 30 × 30 m. The *castellum* is in an exceedingly collapsed state with much of the north wall destroyed by local bulldozing and robber pits. The walls, of worked limestone blocks, appear to be two courses wide (0.55–0.60 m). Within the *castellum*, rectangular mounds with depressed centers suggest internal structures against the curtain wall and around a central courtyard. The gateway into the fort could not be located but was probably in the destroyed north wall. Another structure, measuring ca. 30 × 25 m., lies on the bank of a dry wadi ca. 34 m southeast of the fort. Distinct wall alignments and linear mounds along the interior face of the south wall can be seen, suggesting rooms at least 5 × 5 m. Robber pits along the outer face of the east wall have exposed a large quantity of pottery and evidence of plastering on the exterior face of the wall. There is also a thick mound of ash to the south. The SAAS found four coins (Obj. #3, 23, 40, 41) in the ash and near the robber pits but only one was identifiable, an issue of the mid-4th century A.D. (Obj. #40). This structure may be a large bath complex. In an area of ca. 25 × 25 m west and southwest of the *castellum*, numerous intersecting wall alignments and mounds suggest a large complex of concentric structures. The nature and purpose of these constructions remains undetermined, but these may represent a domestic quarter. The SAAS recovered two more coins (Objs. #1, 503) in this area, but only one was identifiable, also of the mid-4th century A.D. (Obj. #503). Another smaller structure, situated ca. 18 m south of the *castellum*, measures ca. 18 × 10 m with roughly cut stone walls

measuring ca. 0.80 m wide and an entrance in the west wall. There is evidence of at least 6 internal rooms. Various other wall alignments lie across the site and on the ridge above the site to the northwest.

Site No.: 330 (fig. 4.52)
Field Site No.: 149
Site Name: None
Map Reference: 3050 I, K737
Location on 1:50,000: 3373425 N / 721126 E
Elevation: 110 m
Aerial Reference No.: IGN-78-JOR 12/100 - 1831
Site Size: 15 m N–S × 105 m E–W
Inventory Rating: 4
Pottery Collected: Total = 93 (No. of Indicators: 13 / No. Saved: 16)
Pottery Registration No(s).: 9876–91
Pottery Summary: 1 ER (Class 9 amphora handle), 4 LR, 80 R/Byz, 4 EByz (including 1 Class 46 amphora), 1 LByz, 4 UD
Lithic Summary: Indef. cultural-historic placement
Site Description: The site consists of a collapsed tower (ca. 5.50 × 5.50 m) and an L-shaped structure ca. 6 m to the north. The largely ruined tower is mostly buried under sand. Its west and north walls, however, are partially visible, as well as the southwest corner. Its walls are two courses wide (ca. 0.60 m) with rubble fill of dressed limestone blocks. The structure to the north has only its northern (ca. 4.20 m in length) and western (ca. 5.70 m in length) walls partially preserved. These are massive walls measuring three courses wide (ca. 1.30 m). A cemetery of ca. 13 graves lies 66 m northwest of these structures.

Site No.: N/A
Field Site No.: 275
Site Name: None
Map Reference: 3050 III, K737
Location on 1:50,000: 3339250/3339900 N / 714300/715100 E
Elevation: 220 m

Aerial Reference No.: IGN-78-JOR 12/100 - 985
Site Size: 700 m N–S × 650 m E–W
Inventory Rating: 0
Pottery Collected: Total = 0 (No. of Indicators: 0 / No. Saved: 0)
Pottery Registration No(s).: None
Pottery Summary: N/A
Lithic Summary: Indef. cultural-historic placement
Site Description: This is a dense lithic scatter across the length of an alluvial fan immediately northwest of Wādī Abū Barqa. A general collection of lithic material required a separate site number for archival purposes.

Site No.: N/A
Field Site No.: 150
Site Name: Qasr enn-Mala
Map Reference: 3050 I, K737
Location on 1:50,000: 3373191 N / 730736 E
Elevation: 400 m
Site Size: 16 m N–S × 21 m E–W
Inventory Rating: 0
Pottery Collected: Total = 16 (No. of Indicators: 0 / No. Saved: 6)
Pottery Registration No(s).: 9901–6
Pottery Summary: 1 ER/Nab, 14 ER/LR, 1 UD
Lithic Summary: N/A
Site Description: This is Qasr enn-Mala. It lies beyond the limits of Wādī ʿAraba in the foothills of the esh-Shera mountain range. The site is a rectangular structure ca. 16 × 21 m, with massive walls of dressed stone (average stone size is ca. 0.45 × 0.60 × 0.30 m) preserved up to three courses high in places. A gateway lies in the N wall and the entrance is flanked on either side by rooms. The entrance into these rooms faces an open courtyard. Constructed against the outer facing of the N wall at either end are towers, which seem to be later additions. There is a very light sherd scatter associated with this structure. Since this site lies beyond the limits of the Wādī ʿAraba, it has been excluded from the final catalog of numbered sites.

Chapter 5

Analysis and Interpretation of Lithic Assemblages Recovered from Sites in the Southeast 'Araba Archaeological Survey

by Donald O. Henry, Marni Cochrane, Cassandra Burns, and Travis Taverna

Assemblages of chipped stone artifacts were collected from the surfaces of 154 prehistoric sites that were discovered in the Southeast 'Araba Archaeological Survey (SAAS) by Smith and collaborators from 1993–1998 (Smith and Niemi 1994; Smith et al. 1997). Some 138 of these assemblages were studied in an effort to (1) establish their cultural-historic placements, (2) determine their positions in a lithic reduction stream, (3) identify the effect raw material sources may have played on site placement and reduction strategies, and (4) compare the chronologies, densities, and varieties of sites to those identified in other surveys conducted in nearby regions of southern Jordan and the Negev.

I. SAMPLE BIAS

Interpretations derived from lithic studies are largely based upon the spatial locations and the proportionate representations of various kinds of artifacts and associated attributes. Therefore, the manner in which an assemblage of artifacts is acquired and the effect of the collection procedure on the composition of artifacts may strongly influence inferences based upon spatial positions and quantitative comparisons. In light of this, it is important to identify the degree to which survey and collection strategies and depositional contexts may have biased the composition of samples collected for study. Sample bias may simply be defined as the degree to which collection samples are not truly representative of the sampled universe; e.g., the distribution of sites within a study area and the range of artifacts present on the surface of a site.

The SAAS involved both systematic and purposive strategies with the latter predominating (see Chapter 4). An intensive, systematic survey, employing pedestrian coverage following transects at 50-m intervals, was replaced after 1994 by a more specific, purposive strategy targeting structures that were identified in aerial photos. Both of these survey strategies are likely to have yielded an under-representation of Pleistocene age sites associated with prehistoric foragers. This is because such sites average ca. 150 m^2 in area and rarely display architectural features. Thus, many Pleistocene sites may have fallen between the 50-m wide spacing of the transects and few, if any, would have appeared on the aerial photos. In light of these biases, one would expect the larger Holocene age sites (e.g., Chalcolithic, Bronze Age) to be better represented because of their larger sizes and typical associations with architectural features. Of the eighteen assemblages that contained adequate numbers of artifacts (i.e., >30) for study, all were collected from sites associated with architectural features and sixteen of these are likely of Holocene age.

Sample bias at the scale of artifact collection also strongly influences the results of a lithic analysis. Collection of artifacts using a "grab sample" procedure, as followed in the SAAS, is typically biased toward larger specimens that display easily recognized formal morphologies. From the perspective of artifact classification, this procedure tends to over-represent tools and under-represent debitage and especially debris categories. The geomorphic context of the collections is likely to have further biased the artifact composition of the assemblages. Surface assemblages are exposed to sheet erosion, weathering, and edge damage from natural geologic processes, especially in colluvial settings such as the alluvial fans flanking the eastern edge of the Wādī 'Araba. Size sorting of artifacts is commonly tied to such processes and this acts to reduce the proportion of the debris category within surface assemblages. Additionally, surface weathering and associated edge damage result in an over-representation of the tool category, especially for those classes associated with informal secondary edge retouch (e.g., retouched piece, notch, and denticulate classes).

Sample size is also a potential problem and this is especially so for the collections of the SAAS. Of the 138 assemblages available for study, a mean of thirteen specimens/assemblage was recorded and only 18 assemblages contained 30 or more specimens. These 18 assemblages averaged 60 specimens per assemblage. Although sample size is a poorly-understood issue in lithic studies, traditionally 100 tools are seen as a minimum sample for analysis.

Given the patchy distribution of chert sources within the study area, an effort was made to identify raw material varieties within the assemblages and compare their proportionate representations to their spatial distributions. This kind of analytic approach often sheds light on prehistoric settlement and procurement strategies. The raw material study also was somewhat biased by the intensive patination of most artifacts. In an effort to make visual comparisons of raw material varieties, large artifacts were selected and a small flake was removed to reveal the chert below the patinated surface. The study then is biased toward the identification of chert sources for larger specimens that, in turn, tend to more strongly represent initial rather than final processing activities. This discussion of sample bias is presented to enable the reader to better evaluate the results and conclusions of the study.

II.   ANALYTIC PROTOCOL AND RESULTS

The lithic analysis involved (1) a techno-typologic classification, (2) an attribute study, and (3) a raw material analysis. Although the specific objectives of each of these components of the study differ, these components also offer a means of cross-evaluating and refining the overall interpretations of the study.

Techno-Typologic Analysis

Of the 18 assemblages that underwent detailed analysis, only six could be identified to cultural-historic taxon with some certainty based upon diagnostic artifact varieties. These included four Chalcolithic age assemblages (sites 56, 63, 181, and 242), one middle or late Epipaleolithic assemblage (Site 328), and an early Upper Paleolithic assemblage (Site 319). The other 12 assemblages lacked techno-typologic characteristics that allowed for their definite cultural-historic placement.

The techno-typologic analysis involved classifying the artifacts of each assemblage according to tool, debitage, and debris categories and the constituent artifact classes within each category (Table 5.1). The proportionate representations of the categories and classes furnish a preliminary assessment of the techno-typologic affinities of the assemblages. The analysis also offers a means of tracing each assemblage's technological reduction stream.

Table 5.1   Techno-typologic Analysis (continued on next page).

			Chalcolithic								UP		EP		Uncertain					
Site	(total)		56		63		181		242		319		328		158		159		160	
	N	%	N	%	N	%	N	%	N	%	N	%	N	%	N	%	N	%	N	%
Tools (total*)	153	14.40	3	3.90	10	12.00	7	13.00	14	13.70	12	17.40	5	9.40	4	9.10	3	5.70	2	4.80
Scrapers	68	44.40	3	100.00	8	80.00	5	71.40	5	35.70	3	25.00	1	20.00	2	50.00	1	33.30	0	0.00
Burins	0	0.00	0	0.00	0	0.00	0	0.00	0	0.00	0	0.00	0	0.00	0	0.00	0	0.00	0	0.00
Denticulates	2	1.30	0	0.00	0	0.00	0	0.00	0	0.00	0	0.00	0	0.00	0	0.00	0	0.00	0	0.00
Notches	3	2.00	0	0.00	0	0.00	0	0.00	0	0.00	0	0.00	0	0.00	0	0.00	0	0.00	2	100.00
Retouched Pieces	46	30.10	0	0.00	2	20.00	1	14.30	2	14.30	9	75.00	3	60.00	2	50.00	2	66.70	0	0.00
Borers	9	5.90	0	0.00	0	0.00	0	0.00	4	28.60	0	0.00	1	20.00	0	0.00	0	0.00	0	0.00
Proj Pts	0	0.00	0	0.00	0	0.00	0	0.00	0	0.00	0	0.00	0	0.00	0	0.00	0	0.00	0	0.00
Tab Scrapers	1	0.70	0	0.00	0	0.00	0	0.00	1	7.10	0	0.00	0	0.00	0	0.00	0	0.00	0	0.00
Massive Tools	2	1.30	0	0.00	0	0.00	1	14.30	0	0.00	0	0.00	0	0.00	0	0.00	0	0.00	0	0.00
Varia	2	1.30	0	0.00	0	0.00	0	0.00	2	14.30	0	0.00	0	0.00	0	0.00	0	0.00	0	0.00
Debitage (total*)	685	64.60	47	61.00	41	49.40	41	75.90	57	55.90	43	62.30	27	50.90	30	68.20	40	75.50	30	71.40
Cores	20	2.90	0	0.00	0	0.00	0	0.00	2	3.50	2	4.70	0	0.00	2	6.70	0	0.00	0	0.00
Flakes-Primary	23	3.40	0	0.00	4	9.80	1	2.40	2	3.50	0	0.00	0	0.00	3	10.00	0	0.00	0	0.00
Flakes-Secondary	174	25.40	11	23.40	15	36.60	10	24.40	22	38.60	9	20.90	2	7.40	9	30.00	13	32.50	4	13.30
Flakes-Tertiary	354	51.70	35	74.50	22	53.70	29	70.70	25	43.90	26	60.50	21	77.80	10	33.30	17	42.50	25	83.30
Blades-Primary	1	0.10	0	0.00	0	0.00	0	0.00	0	0.00	0	0.00	0	0.00	0	0.00	0	0.00	0	0.00
Blades-Secondary	20	2.90	1	2.10	0	0.00	0	0.00	2	3.50	1	2.30	0	0.00	3	10.00	6	15.00	0	0.00
Blades-Tertiary	36	5.30	0	0.00	0	0.00	1	2.40	4	7.00	5	11.60	3	11.10	3	10.00	4	10.00	0	0.00
CTE	10	1.50	0	0.00	0	0.00	0	0.00	0	0.00	0	0.00	1	3.70	0	0.00	0	0.00	1	3.30
Debris (total*)	222	20.90	27	35.10	32	38.60	6	11.10	31	30.40	14	20.30	21	39.60	10	22.70	10	18.90	10	23.80
Chips	95	42.80	21	77.80	9	28.10	6	100.00	6	19.40	9	64.30	15	71.40	5	50.00	5	50.00	6	60.00
Chunks	114	51.40	6	22.20	23	71.90	0	0.00	25	100.00	5	35.70	6	28.60	5	50.00	5	50.00	4	40.00
Grand Total	1060		77		83		54		102		69		53		44		53		42	

Chalcolithic Assemblages

These assemblages were principally identified by the presence of tabular scrapers, as part of the tool-kit, and the production of relatively thick, large flakes displaying large unfaceted platforms (Table 5.2).

Site 56. Of 77 chert artifacts recovered from the site, most are represented by debitage and debris. Tertiary flakes (45%) and chips (27%), followed by secondary flakes (14%) dominate the assemblage. The high proportionate representation of tertiary flakes indicates that the assemblage was derived late in a reduction sequence focused on flake production. Only three tools were recovered, consisting of a fragment of an ovoid tabular scraper and two flake scrapers.

Site 63. A sample of 83 chert artifacts was recovered, comprised mostly of chunks (28%), tertiary flakes (27%), and secondary flakes (18%). The presence of these and a smaller proportion of primary flakes indicates a broad range of reduction activities within a flake-oriented technology. The absence of cores, however, is noteworthy.

Table 5.1   Techno-typologic Analysis (continued from previous page).

Site	(total)		Uncertain 162		163		172		226		257		276		322		325		327	
	N	%	N	%	N	%	N	%	N	%	N	%	N	%	N	%	N	%	N	%
Tools (total*)	153	14.40	8	9.50	8	17.40	3	4.60	19	38.00	13	44.80	6	0.14	14	45.20	2	3.70	20	25.00
Scrapers	68	44.40	2	25.00	4	50.00	2	66.70	5	26.30	11	84.60	3	0.5	12	85.70	1	50.00	13	65.00
Burins	0	0.00	0	0.00	0	0.00	0	0.00	0	0.00	0	0.00	0	0	0	0.00	0	0.00	0	0.00
Denticulates	2	1.30	0	0.00	1	12.50	1	33.30	0	0.00	0	0.00	0	0	0	0.00	0	0.00	0	0.00
Notches	3	2.00	0	0.00	0	0.00	0	0.00	0	0.00	0	0.00	0	0	0	0.00	1	50.00	2	10.00
Retouched Pieces	46	30.10	3	37.50	3	37.50	0	0.00	13	68.40	2	15.40	2	0.33	2	14.30	0	0.00	5	25.00
Borers	9	5.90	3	37.50	0	0.00	0	0.00	1	5.30	0	0.00	0	0	0	0.00	0	0.00	0	0.00
Proj Pts	0	0.00	0	0.00	0	0.00	0	0.00	0	0.00	0	0.00	0	0	0	0.00	0	0.00	0	0.00
Tab Scrapers	1	0.70	0	0.00	0	0.00	0	0.00	0	0.00	0	0.00	0	0	0	0.00	0	0.00	0	0.00
Massive Tools	2	1.30	0	0.00	0	0.00	0	0.00	0	0.00	0	0.00	1	0.17	0	0.00	0	0.00	0	0.00
Varia	2	1.30	0	0.00	0	0.00	0	0.00	0	0.00	0	0.00	0	0	0	0.00	0	0.00	0	0.00
Debitage (total*)	685	64.60	60	71.40	37	80.40	50	76.90	31	62.00	15	51.70	32	0.73	8	25.80	49	90.70	47	58.80
Cores	20	2.90	2	3.30	5	13.50	0	0.00	0	0.00	1	6.70	5	0.16	1	12.50	0	0.00	1	2.10
Flakes-Primary	23	3.40	0	0.00	8	21.60	4	8.00	1	3.20	0	0.00	0	0	0	0.00	0	0.00	3	6.40
Flakes-Secondary	174	25.40	17	28.30	24	64.90	9	18.00	10	32.30	2	13.30	3	0.09	3	37.50	11	22.40	7	14.90
Flakes-Tertiary	354	51.70	36	60.00	0	0.00	28	56.00	17	54.80	8	53.30	14	0.44	3	37.50	38	77.60	24	51.10
Blades-Primary	1	0.10	0	0.00	0	0.00	0	0.00	1	3.20	0	0.00	0	0	0	0.00	0	0.00	0	0.00
Blades-Secondary	20	2.90	1	1.70	0	0.00	3	6.00	2	6.50	0	0.00	1	0.03	0	0.00	0	0.00	3	6.40
Blades-Tertiary	36	5.30	4	6.70	0	0.00	6	12.00	0	0.00	1	6.70	5	0.16	0	0.00	0	0.00	7	14.90
CTE	10	1.50	0	0.00	0	0.00	0	0.00	0	0.00	3	20.00	4	0.13	1	12.50	0	0.00	2	4.30
Debris (total*)	222	20.90	16	19.00	1	2.20	12	18.50	0	0.00	1	3.40	6	0.14	9	29.00	3	5.60	13	16.30
Chips	95	42.80	3	18.80	1	100.00	6	50.00	0	0.00	1	100.00	0	0	2	22.20	0	0.00	6	46.20
Chunks	114	51.40	13	81.30	0	0.00	6	50.00	0	0.00	0	0.00	6	1	7	77.80	3	100.00	7	53.80
Grand Total	1060		84		46		65		50		29		44		31		54		80	

The tool-kit is dominated by tabular scrapers (10), seven of which are ovoid and another rectangular in form. One flake scraper with continuous retouch and two retouched blades with 50% cortex on the dorsal surface were also recovered.

Site 181. Out of a total of 54 chert artifacts found at this site, the majority (80%) consists of debitage, further dominated by tertiary and secondary flakes. The assemblage appears to represent a mid- to late segment in a reduction sequence devoted to flake production.

Tools include three flake scrapers with heavy retouch, two tabular scraper fragments, and one unifacially retouched blade. Also found was a massive tool which appears to be a pick pre-form, with two apparent notches on opposing sides and faces.

Site 242. This site produced the third largest lithic assemblage, consisting of 102 artifacts. The debitage consists of a broad range of material, including cores and primary, secondary, and tertiary elements, as well as numerous chips and chunks. The two cores present have multiple striking platforms and are spherically shaped. Coupled with the presence of tools, this signifies a complete scope of the reduction stream within a technology focused on flake production.

Table 5.2 Debitage Type Frequencies.

Site	Chalcolithic				EP	UP
	56	63	181	242	328	319
Pri. Blade	3.10%	4.20%	7.70%	3.60%	0.00%	0.00%
Sec. Flake	18.80%	29.20%	34.60%	40.00%	7.70%	17.80%
Ter. Flake	75.00%	54.20%	57.70%	45.50%	80.80%	39.70%
Pri. Blade	0.00%	4.20%	0.00%	0.00%	0.00%	0.00%
Sec. Blade	3.10%	4.20%	0.00%	3.60%	0.00%	4.10%
Ter. Blade	0.00%	4.20%	0.00%	7.30%	11.50%	38.40%
N	32	24	26	55	26	98

Site	Unidentified											
	158	159	160	162	163	172	226	257	276	322	325	327
Pri. Blade	0.00%	0.00%	7.10%	3.30%	8.50%	8.20%	3.20%	0.00%	0.00%	0.00%	0.00%	6.80%
Sec. Flake	37.90%	32.50%	21.40%	38.30%	39.00%	18.40%	32.30%	18.20%	12.50%	37.50%	22.40%	15.90%
Ter. Flake	37.90%	40.00%	71.40%	53.30%	52.50%	57.10%	54.80%	72.70%	58.30%	37.50%	77.60%	54.50%
Pri. Blade	3.40%	2.50%	0.00%	0.00%	0.00%	6.10%	3.20%	0.00%	0.00%	0.00%	0.00%	0.00%
Sec. Blade	10.30%	15.00%	0.00%	0.00%	0.00%	0.00%	6.50%	0.00%	4.20%	25.00%	0.00%	6.80%
Ter. Blade	10.30%	10.00%	0.00%	5.00%	0.00%	10.20%	0.00%	9.10%	25.00%	0.00%	0.00%	15.90%
N	29	40	28	60	59	49	31	11	24	8	49	44

Fourteen tools were recovered, including two tabular scrapers. One of these was large with steep retouch, as opposed to a smaller second one. Also found were four borer/perforators formed on flakes and several retouched blocky pieces.

Epipaleolithic Assemblage

Only one assemblage contained a microlithic component indicative of the Epipaleolithic. Although no geometric microliths were recovered, the presence of microblades, both retouched and unretouched, points to the mid- or late Epipaleolithic.

Site 328. This site produced 53 artifacts of which the majority consists of debitage composed of tertiary flakes. This appears to be a flake tool technology, although field recovery methods might bias against the recovery of small blades. The site probably represents a mid- to late stage in lithic processing.

Five tools were identified, including an endscraper and a small perforator made on a flake with continuous retouch. Also found was one microblade with bifacial retouch along one margin and unifacial (obverse) retouch along the opposing margin.

Upper Paleolithic Assemblage

A single assemblage thought to be of Upper Paleolithic age was recorded. Although no truly diagnostic cultural-historic items were observed, a laminar assemblage lacking microliths can be classified only as PPNB or Upper Paleolithic. The assemblage is not consistent with a PPNB placement, given an absence of evidence of bi-directionality in core shaping as shown by cores facets and the obverse scar patterns of blades. Such indicators of bi-directionality are hallmarks of the Naviform Core Technique, the technological norm of PPNB lithic production. The blades associated with Site 319 are also relatively thick and irregular when compared to the thin, flat blades generated by the Naviform Core Technique. Finally, one might point to the relatively large, unfaceted platforms of the Site 319 assemblage as more closely resembling those of the Upper Paleolithic than PPNB.

Site 319. This assemblage consists of 69 lithic pieces. The overwhelming majority of the debitage consists of tertiary blades and flakes, in addition to twelve cores, four core-trimming elements, and several secondary blades and flakes. Although the debitage is dominated by tertiary flakes, blade production was clearly the focus of the technology, as evidenced by the presence of laminar core facets, crested blades, and blade tools.

Cores are dominated by unidirectional, single platform blade cores, but a small, exhausted, change-of-orientation and another small, exhausted opposed platform core are also recorded. Notably, core trimming elements (CTE) include three examples of crested blades that confirm that blade initiation involved this method of core shaping. The blades tend to be somewhat thick, curved, and irregular in form, bearing single, unfaceted platforms; characteristics that strongly resemble those defined for nearby Upper Paleolithic assemblages (Coinman and Henry 1995). Their scar patterns are largely unidirectional, parallel or convergent.

The tool-kit, consisting of 12 pieces, is dominated by burins, endscrapers on flakes, and retouched blades. The burins are dominated by angle and dihedral forms struck from snaps or old surfaces on blades. Three small scrapers were analyzed, all of which had invasive, heavy retouch. One of these is a carinated scraper. Two small blades with invasive backing and heavy retouch on the inverse surface were also identified. A single well-formed denticulate on a blade was also recorded.

The presence of cores, core trimming elements, and tools indicates that the assemblage was produced from lithic activities related to a full reduction stream ranging from core shaping to tool production and use.

*Assemblages of Uncertain
Cultural-Historic Affiliation*

Twelve of the eighteen assemblages that were studied failed to yield diagnostic cultural-historic evidence in the context of traditional technotypologic analyses. Although diagnostic tools or debitage were not identified in the assemblages, certain technological attributes (see next section) exhibited by the artifacts suggest Chalcolithic or perhaps even more recent affiliations.

Site 158. This site produced 44 lithic artifacts, including four tools. Tools consist of two endscrapers on flakes and two retouched blades. The debitage,

representing 70% of the assemblage, included a broad distribution of pieces, including cores and primary and secondary flakes and blades. This distribution, in addition to the presence of several chips and chunks, indicates a probable complete reduction sequence taking place at this site, with an apparent focus on flake tools.

Site 159. Fifty-three chert pieces were found at this site, again dominated by debitage (80%). Tertiary and secondary flakes comprised most of this, as well as a few secondary and tertiary blades. No cores were recovered. Three tools were found: one endscraper on a flake as well as a retouched flake and retouched blade. This appears to have been a flake tool technology representing a mid- to late reduction stage.

Site 160. Of the total 42 chert artifacts recovered, only two appear to be tools. These two are characterized by symmetrical notching on opposite margins near the proximal end. One notch (on only one tool) was formed by inverse retouch. Debitage composes 80% of this assemblage, dominated by tertiary flakes. This assemblage appears to be the result of late stage reduction in a flake tool technology.

Site 162. This assemblage consists of 84 chert specimens, including 8 tools. The tools were comprised of one blocky pick-like borer, two perforators on squarish flakes, three retouched blades, and two small endscrapers on flakes. The majority of the assemblage, however, was represented by tertiary and secondary flakes, as well as chunks. One of the cores has a single platform with only a few (6) removals, while the other core contains multiple platforms (3) with removals in varying directions. The presence of two cores combined with the absence of primary flakes indicates a reduction stage in the middle of the reduction sequence (post-primary). This assemblage appears to have a flake tool production focus.

Site 163. Forty-six chert artifacts were recovered from this site, including eight tools. These are all flake tools, including an endscraper and a denticulated flake. Most scrapers have invasive retouch and heavy marginal retouch. The debitage composes

80% of the assemblage, and includes only cores and primary and secondary flakes. These cores have 2–3 platforms and numerous removals. This, combined with the absence of tertiary elements could indicate a primary processing stage in the flake tool reduction sequence.

Site 172. Of the 65 artifacts found here, three appear to be tools represented by three flake scrapers. One of these scrapers is a denticulated endscraper on a blocky flake, one is a scraper with non-invasive retouch, and the last is a scraper with invasive retouch and heavy retouch on two margins converging at the proximal end. The debitage, composing 80% of the assemblage, is dominated by tertiary flakes (56%), also including primary and secondary flakes and secondary and tertiary blades. This assemblage appears to illustrate a long range of the reduction sequence with a flake tool technological focus.

Site 226. Of the 50 chert pieces found at this site, nineteen flake tools were found, including: one perforator on a broken flake, one bifacially retouched knife or cutting tool, one endscraper, and several other poorly-made scrapers with small, non-uniform unifacial retouch and bifacial marginal retouch. Debitage was represented by mostly tertiary and secondary flakes, although one primary flake and one primary blade were found. This site appears to have had a flake tool focus and has evidence for primary to final processing

Site 257. This site produced 29 lithic artifacts, thirteen of which were tools. Eleven flake scrapers were found, all with invasive unifacial retouch. In addition, one retouched flake and one retouched blade were recovered. The debitage consisted of one core, three core trimming elements, several tertiary flakes and blades, and a couple secondary flakes. This appears to be a flake tool technology, with evidence for post-primary reduction stages taking place at the site.

Site 276. Recovered from this site were 44 lithic artifacts, six of which were tools. These tools included three scrapers, two of which were endscrapers (one denticulated with invasive retouch) on flakes. The other two tools included a retouched flake and a

possible pick pre-form. Again the debitage composed the majority of the assemblage (70%). The debitage and debris components were comprised of an even proportion of cores and secondary and tertiary elements, along with chips and chunks. This indicates a mid- (post-primary) stage in the reduction sequence of a flake tool technology.

Site 322. Of the 31 lithic artifacts recovered from this site, thirty percent were tools, including twelve scrapers and two retouched flakes. The scrapers were made on flakes, and are small in size with invasive retouch; two endscrapers were present. The debitage recovered was minimal, but included one core, one core trimming element, and a few secondary and tertiary flakes. This appears to be a flake tool technology, with mid- to late reduction stages present at the site.

Site 325. Only two tools were contained within this assemblage, which consisted of 54 lithic pieces. The tools were one scraper with invasive retouch almost forming a notch, and one notched piece with unifacial retouch along the margins (one with inverse, one obverse). Debitage consisted entirely of tertiary and secondary flakes, lending towards a flake tool technology. This was most likely a mid- to late stage lithic processing site.

Site 327. This assemblage, consisting of 80 pieces total, produced thirteen flake scrapers in addition to two notched pieces and three retouched blades. The scrapers all have invasive unifacial retouch, including one carinated scraper. The majority of the debitage was tertiary flakes; however, one core, two core trimming elements, and several primary, secondary, and tertiary flakes and blades were found (no primary blades). This assemblage appears to be a combination flake and blade tool technology, with much of the reduction stream present at the site, from primary to final processing.

III. LITHIC ATTRIBUTE STUDY

A detailed lithic attribute study was undertaken in an effort to place the twelve assemblages that lacked culturally diagnostic tools or debitage within cultural-historic taxa based upon the presence of specific metric and technical characteristics observed on debitage. It was thought that the attributes observed for the six assemblages that were identified as to specific cultural-historic taxa could be used as reference data sets to establish the cultural-historic identities of the unknown assemblages.

Recorded Attributes

The attributes recorded in the study consisted of those associated with: (1) platform, including abraded, cortical, single facet, and multiple facet; (2) bulb type including diffuse, pronounced (without *eraillure* scar), pronounced (with *eraillure* scar), and incomplete; (3) termination type, including feather (or normal), step, hinged, and plunging; (4) compression ring noted as present/absent; and (5) lipping, also recorded as being present/absent.

Metric observations (maximum length, width, and thickness of blank, platform dimensions) were also taken for each artifact and then evaluated statistically for each assemblage. It should be noted that, while maximum measurements were taken for each artifact, individual values were averaged by site. For example, "maximum width" indicates the average of maximum width measurements taken from each site's assemblage.

The attribute profiles for each of the assemblages is described below and the data sets for the assemblages are presented in Tables 5.3–7 on pp. 304–6.

The Chalcolithic Assemblages

Site 56. Most of the platforms in the assemblage are complex, bearing multiple flake scars. However, many of the platforms in this assemblage are not complete and so could not be accurately assigned. Platforms are small on average. Of the bulbs which could be classified, most were pronounced and without *eraillure* scars. Most of the debitage terminations are feather terminations, though some terminations of other types are present. Compression rings and lipping are not common in this assemblage.

Site 63. As with the previous site, most of the platforms show multiple flake scars. This is more likely to occur later in the reduction sequence and is concurrent with the high percentage of tertiary flakes present. Platform dimensions for this site are very similar to Site 56. The striking platforms are small and the bulbs are pronounced. The majority of pronounced bulbs also bear *eraillure* scars, while slightly fewer are pronounced but lacking such scars. Most of the flake terminations at this site are feather terminations, followed closely by hinged terminations. Compression rings and lipping are not common. Debitage measurements for this site are greater, overall, than for Site 56.

Site 181. Most of the platforms show multiple flake scars, though several show only a single flake scar on the platform. Platforms are very wide on average and of moderate thickness. Unlike the previous sites, most of the bulbs are diffuse. Terminations are mostly of the feather variety. Very little evidence of compression rings or lipping is present at this site. The debitage from this site is the largest of the Chalcolithic assemblages.

Site 242. Most of the platforms bear evidence of multiple flake scars. This is in keeping with the high percentages of secondary and tertiary flakes present. The platforms are typically both wide and thick. Bulbs of percussion are mostly diffuse, though pronounced bulbs without *eraillure* scars are not uncommon. Feather terminations are the most common. The overall dimensions of these artifacts indicate that they are rather large.

Epipaleolithic Assemblage

Site 328. Though most of the platforms are broken, those that can be classified are predominantly single faceted. Platforms are small in comparison with the other sites. Most of the bulbs have been damaged, making analysis impossible. However, those bulbs that are complete are primarily either diffuse or pronounced with an *eraillure* scar. Feather terminations are most common in this assemblage. Average debitage dimensions are small as is consistent with a microlithic assemblage.

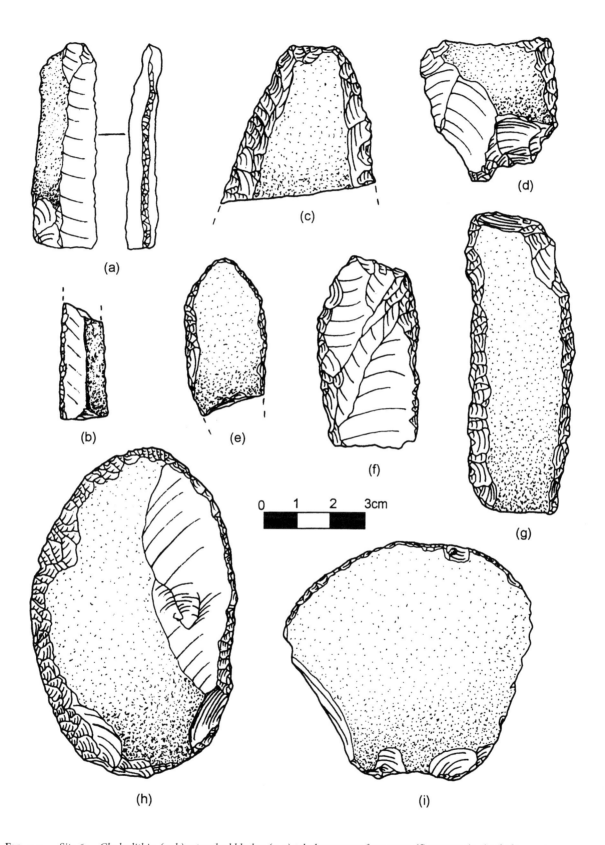

FIG. 5.1 *Site 63 – Chalcolithic. (a–b) retouched blades; (c–e) tabular scraper fragments; (f) scraper; (g–i) tabular scrapers.*

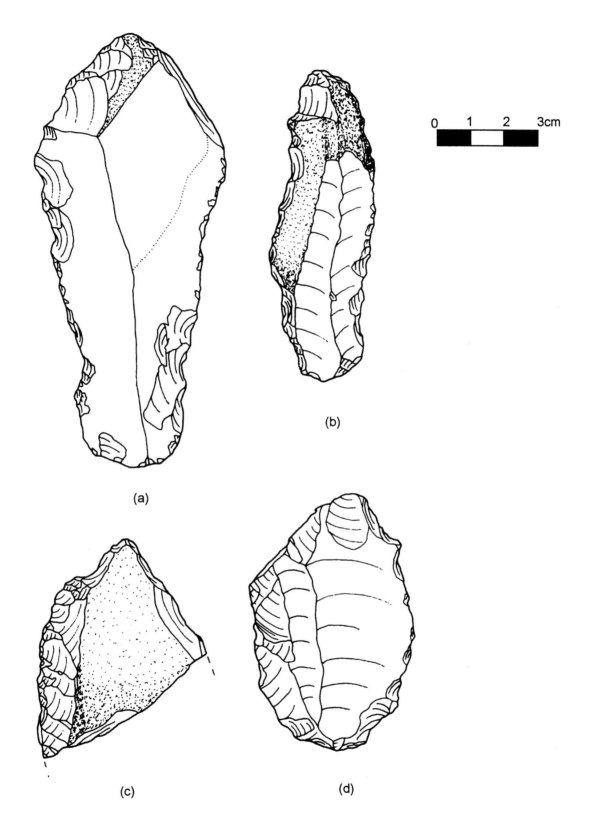

FIG. 5.2   *Site 181 – Chalcolithic. (a) pick; (b) unifacially retouched blade;(c) tabular scraper fragment; (d) flake scraper.*

Upper Paleolithic Assemblage

Site 319. Most of the platforms are complex, having multiple flake scars. Platform dimensions are rather small and bulbs of percussion are mostly diffuse. Terminations are primarily hinged, indicating habitual overloading of the platforms and most likely hard-hammer percussion. Flakes are somewhat longer than they are wide, reflecting a blade technology, and of medium thickness.

The Other Assemblages

Site 158. The most common platform types are those with multiple flake scars, followed closely by those with single flake scars. Average platform measurements for this assemblage rank near the largest of those studied. The majority of bulbs at this site are pronounced but lacking *eraillure* scars. Diffuse bulbs are also present and compose a large part of the assemblage. Feather terminations are the most common, followed by hinged terminations. Debitage dimensions, like platform dimensions, rank among the largest of any assemblage.

Site 159. Within this assemblage, platforms are wide and moderately thick. Most of the platforms bear only a single flake scar though a considerable number have multiple flake scars. Bulbs of percussion at this site are primarily diffuse, though pronounced bulbs without *eraillure* scars are also present. Feather terminations are most common. The debitage from this site is long but of moderate width and thickness.

Site 160. Platform dimensions are similar to those of Site 162 and are of moderate size. Bulbs are most commonly pronounced, though without *eraillure* scars. Pronounced bulbs with *eraillure* scars are also common. Feather terminations are dominant termination type for this assemblage, followed by hinged terminations. Debitage dimensions are quite similar to those of sites 162 and 163.

Site 162. The majority of the platforms at this site are incomplete. Of the debitage with complete platforms, most contain multiple flake scars. While the debitage type percentages of this site are nearly equal to that

of Site 163, platform dimensions are somewhat smaller. The bulbs of percussion are pronounced, both with and without *eraillure* scars. Diffuse bulbs are also present, though in a lesser amount. The remaining bulbs were incomplete and therefore could not be categorized. Terminations are primarily of the feather variety, though plunging terminations are also common. The debitage from this site ranks as the largest of those assemblages studied.

Site 163. As with most of the assemblages in this study, most of the platforms have single flake scars, though nearly as many have multiple flake scars. Platform dimensions are rather large. The majority of the bulbs are pronounced; many of these also have *eraillure* scars. Terminations are primarily of the feather type. Neither compression rings nor lipping are common in this assemblage. The debitage recovered from this site is similar in average dimensions to that of Site 162.

Site 172. Most of the platforms in the assemblage are complex, showing multiple flake scars, but platforms showing single flake scars are also relatively common. The platforms are wide and moderately thick. Most of the bulbs are diffuse. Terminations are of two main types, either hinged or feather. Compression rings and lipping, as with the other sites, are uncommon. The debitage is of a moderate size, though it ranks among the smallest of the assemblages studied.

Site 226. In this assemblage striking platforms usually have only a single flake scar and are rather large. Bulbs are pronounced; those without *eraillure* scars being more common than those with such scars. Flake terminations are mostly hinged, though feather terminations are also common. The debitage from this site could be characterized as quite large in all dimensions.

Site 257. In this assemblage platforms are, on average, complex and bear multiple flake scars. Platforms are thick, but only moderately wide. The bulbs of percussion are, also on average, pronounced but without *eraillure* scars. Feather terminations are the most common. Debitage from this site could be described as short, but moderately wide and thick.

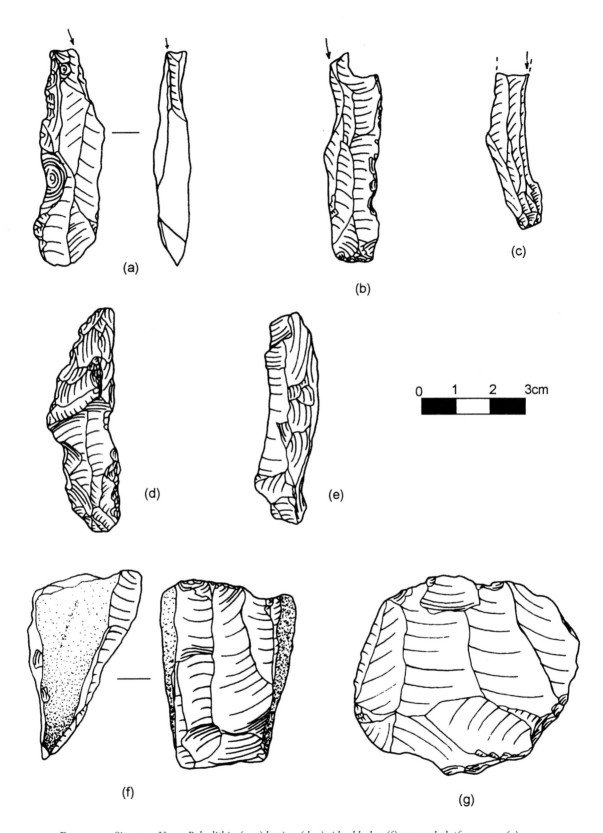

Fig. 5.3   *Site 319 – Upper Paleolithic. (a–c) burins; (d–e) ridge blades; (f) opposed platform core; (g) core.*

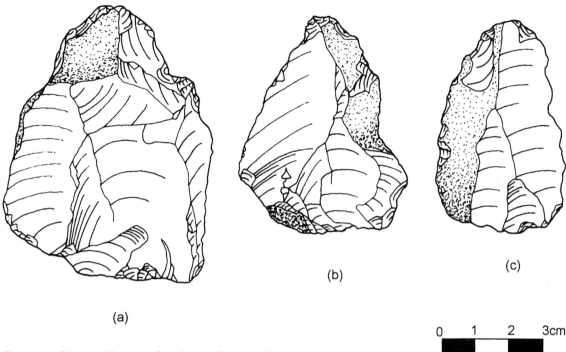

(b)

(c)

(a)

0   1   2   3cm

FIG. 5.4   *Site 226 – Uncertain date. (a) Levallois core; (b–c) Levallois flakes.*

Site 276. Site 276 is mostly composed of tertiary flakes. Most of the platforms have only a single flake scar, though flakes with multiple scars on the platforms are not uncommon. Platforms are of moderate width and thickness. Most of the complete bulbs of percussion are diffuse and terminations are mostly of the feather variety. The debitage from this site is of moderate size, though smaller than that of sites 226 and 242.

Site 327. Platforms are mostly simple in this assemblage and display only a single flake scar, though multiple flake scars are nearly as common. Platforms are a little wider than those of site 319. Most of the bulbs of percussion are diffuse. While terminations are mostly hinged, a moderate percentage of feather terminations is present. The debitage from this site is shorter and thinner than that from Site 319, though still of moderate size in comparison with that of other sites in the survey.

Site 322. The debitage from this site composed of equal amounts of primary and tertiary flakes, followed by secondary blades. Most of the platforms have multiple flake scars and are thick but only of medium width. Bulbs are mostly diffuse and terminations are predominately of the feather variety. Debitage from this site is long and thick but of moderate width.

Site 325. In this assemblage, most of the striking platforms have multiple flake scars and are of medium width and thickness. The majority of the bulbs are diffuse and the terminations are mostly of the feather variety. The debitage from this site is rather large.

Site 328. Though most of the platforms are broken, those that can be classified predominantly have single flake scars. Platforms are small, both in comparison with sites in the area and in the general survey. Most of the bulbs have been damaged, making analysis impossible. However, those bulbs that are complete are primarily either diffuse or pronounced with an eraillure scar. Feather terminations are most common in this assemblage. Average debitage dimensions are relatively small in comparison to the other assemblages.

Table 5.3   Platform Type Frequencies.

	Chalcolithic				EP	UP
Site	56	63	181	242	328	319
Abraded	8.80%	16.70%	57.50%	41.80%	19.20%	38.40%
Cortical	28.10%	20.80%	11.50%	25.50%	15.40%	19.20%
Single	15.60%	33.30%	11.50%	12.70%	19.20%	15.10%
Multiple	37.50%	29.20%	19.20%	20.00%	46.20%	27.40%
N	32	24	26	45	26	98

	Unidentified											
Site	158	159	160	162	163	172	226	257	276	322	325	327
Abraded	27.60%	40.00%	21.40%	20.00%	18.60%	42.90%	12.90%	18.20%	33.30%	0.10%	42.90%	27.30%
Cortical	37.90%	27.10%	27.50%	26.70%	39.00%	26.50%	45.20%	36.40%	20.80%	12.50%	40.80%	18.20%
Single	24.10%	24.10%	27.50%	28.30%	25.40%	22.40%	32.30%	18.20%	12.50%	12.50%	6.10%	15.90%
Multiple	10.30%	5.00%	17.90%	25.00%	16.90%	8.20%	9.70%	27.30%	33.30%	0.10%	10.20%	38.60%
N	29	36	33	61	59	49	31	14	24	2	49	44

Table 5.4   Bulb Type Frequencies.

	Chalcolithic				EP	UP
Site	56	63	181	242	328	319
Diffuse	40.60%	54.00%	42.30%	50.90%	30.70%	61.70%
Pronounced	6.30%	8.30%	11.50%	12.70%	3.80%	2.70%
Erailure	15.60%	4.20%	23.10%	18.20%	23.10%	6.80%
Incomplete	37.50%	33.30%	23.10%	18.20%	42.30%	28.80%
N	32	12	26	55	26	98

	Unidentified											
Site	158	159	160	162	163	172	226	257	276	322	325	327
Diffuse	48.20%	40.00%	53.60%	45.00%	35.60%	61.30%	32.30%	63.40%	29.10%	62.50%	55.10%	34.10%
Pronounced	17.20%	5.00%	0.00%	1.70%	5.10%	4.10%	9.70%	0.00%	37.50%	12.50%	4.10%	6.80%
Erailure	31.00%	45.00%	10.70%	13.30%	40.70%	28.60%	48.40%	9.10%	20.80%	12.50%	30.60%	25.00%
Incomplete	3.40%	10.00%	35.70%	40.00%	18.60%	6.10%	9.70%	27.30%	33.30%	12.50%	10.20%	34.10%
N	29	40	28	60	59	49	31	11	29	8	49	44

Table 5.5   Termination Type.

Site	Chalcolithic				EP	UP
	56	63	181	242	328	319
Feather	31.30%	29.20%	61.50%	45.50%	30.80%	20.50%
Step	12.50%	8.30%	15.40%	0.00%	0.00%	13.70%
Hinged	18.80%	20.80%	3.80%	18.20%	7.70%	31.50%
Plunging	6.30%	4.20%	3.80%	1.80%	3.80%	13.70%
Incomplete	31.30%	37.50%	15.40%	34.50%	57.70%	20.50%
N	32	24	26	55	26	98

Site	Unidentified											
	158	159	160	162	163	172	226	257	276	322	325	327
Feather	44.80%	40.00%	32.10%	31.70%	44.10%	34.70%	32.30%	63.60%	50.00%	62.50%	46.90%	40.90%
Step	3.40%	2.50%	10.70%	1.70%	0.00%	0.00%	0.00%	0.00%	0.00%	0.00%	0.00%	0.00%
Hinged	27.60%	22.50%	21.40%	16.70%	22.00%	36.70%	38.70%	27.30%	29.20%	25.00%	18.40%	13.60%
Plunging	10.30%	17.50%	14.30%	21.70%	16.90%	12.20%	9.70%	0.00%	8.30%	0.00%	4.10%	6.80%
Incomplete	13.80%	17.50%	21.40%	28.30%	16.90%	16.30%	9.40%	9.10%	12.50%	12.50%	30.60%	38.60%
N	29	25	28	60	59	49	31	11	24	8	49	44

Table 5.6   Compression Rings.

Site	Chalcolithic				EP	UP
	56	63	181	242	328	319
Yes	31.00%	12.50%	11.50%	10.90%	23.10%	23.30%
No	68.80%	87.50%	88.50%	89.10%	76.90%	76.70%
N	32	24	26	55	26	98

Site	Unidentified											
	158	159	160	162	163	172	226	257	276	322	325	327
Yes	31.00%	22.50%	17.90%	18.30%	25.40%	26.50%	29.00%	36.40%	20.80%	37.50%	18.40%	18.20%
No	69.00%	77.50%	82.10%	81.70%	74.60%	73.50%	71.00%	63.60%	79.20%	62.50%	81.60%	81.80%
N	29	40	29	60	59	49	31	11	24	8	49	44

Table 5.7   Lipping.

	Chalcolithic				EP	UP
Site	56	63	181	242	328	319
Yes	3.10%	4.20%	19.20%	3.60%	0.00%	6.80%
No	96.90%	95.80%	80.80%	96.40%	100%	93.20%
N	32	24	26	55	26	98

	Unidentified											
Site	158	159	160	162	163	172	226	257	276	322	325	327
Yes	0.00%	2.50%	35.70%	10.00%	1.70%	2.00%	0.00%	0.00%	0.00%	0.00%	0.00%	2.30%
No	100%	97.50%	64.30%	90.00%	98.30%	98.00%	100%	100%	100%	100%	100%	97.70%
N	29	40	28	60	59	49	26	31	24	8	49	44

IV.   DISCUSSION

A comparison of the four known Chalcolithic assemblages (Sites 56, 63, 181, and 242) with the Epipaleolithic (Site 328) and Upper Paleolithic (Site 319) ones across the five qualitative technological attributes fails to show diagnostic patterning within any of the attributes (Tables 5.3–7). The lack of patterning may result from a combination of factors including: (1) small sample sizes; (2) quite different reduction modes tied to differences in raw material availability; (3) possibly "mixed period" surface scatters; and (4) collection biases. A review of the metric attributes shows the debitage of Chalcolithic assemblages to be generally larger than that from the Upper Paleolithic or Epipaleolithic assemblages, yet there is some overlap. For example, the Chalcolithic assemblage of Site 56 yielded smaller debitage than the Upper Paleolithic Site 319. Not surprisingly, the Epipaleolithic assemblage of Site 328 yielded the smallest debitage of all assemblages studied.

The only metric attribute to display patterned co-variation with cultural-historic grouping is length/width ratio. The four Chalcolithic assemblages yield L/W ratios ranging from 0.8–1.2 in comparison to those of the Epipaleolithic (Site 328) and Upper Paleolithic assemblages (Site 319), which each yield a L/W ratio of 1.5. If we use L/W

ratio as an indicator of cultural-historic affiliation for the twelve "unknown" assemblages, the assemblages from sites 160 and 226 should be viewed as Pleistocene-aged sites, whereas the others would most likely be of Chalcolithic or later age. The assemblage of Site 322 was excluded from this analysis because of its very small sample (8 specimens).

Although there appear to be no other real indicators of Pleistocene age for the Site 160 assemblage, several specimens point to a convergent Levallois technology for the Site 226 assemblage. Moreover, this assemblage shows the highest ranking of those studied for the presence of pronounced bulbs of percussion with *eraillure* scars, a common attribute of Levantine Mousterian assemblages (Henry 1998).

Raw Material Study

In that the raw material study focused on attempting to understand the influence that variable distances to chert sources had on prehistoric lithic technology, the assemblages were segregated into five groups, or spatial clusters, based upon their locations. For each group, attention was given to distance (in km) from the nearest known chert outcropping as determined from the geological map of the area, the source (either *in situ* from outcroppings or from wadi cobbles) as determined by examination of the cortical surfaces of artifacts,

Table 5.8   Raw Material Categories.

Type	A	B	C	D
Munsell	10 Y/R 3/1 - 7/1	5 Y/R 3/1	7.5 YR 6/1	Catch-all
		7.5 YR 2/5 - 5/1	10 YR 5/1 - 7/2	
		10 YR 3/1		
Color	purple	dark brown	light to dark brown	
Inclusions	specks and banding	specks and banding	heavy banding	
Cortex	white limestone	brown limestone	tan/red/orange/white L.S.	
Patina	white	brown	tan/red/orange/white	
Luster	low-high	low-medium	non-medium	
Grain	fine-moderate	fine-moderate	fine-coarse	
Translus.	low-medium	low-medium	low-medium	
U.V.	orange	orange	orange	

and maximum size of obverse surface for the largest piece in the assemblage (cm²). The degree of patination and specific raw material types were also recorded. Three specific chert varieties were identified based upon several visual characteristics (Table 5.8).

Group 1 (Sites 56, 63, 181)

The first group of sites, all classified as Chalcolithic, is located on the extreme southeastern boundary of the Wādī 'Araba. Of these sites, the closest to a map-designated chert outcropping is Site 181, which is approximately 15.6 km from the nearest source. Site 56 is the farthest, at 18.5 km from the nearest known source. Given these distances, it is expected that the four assemblages in this group would be dominated by wadi cobbles — that is clearly not the case. Sites 56 and 181 both contain wadi cobbles and *in situ* materials, and Site 63 contains only *in situ* materials.

The abundance of *in situ* materials at these sites, despite their distance from known sources, is perhaps not so striking when one looks at the technological attributes of the assemblages. All but one of the three sites yielded both tabular scrapers and broken fragments of presumed tabular scraper

pre-forms. These tabular scrapers were made from chert Types B (primarily) and C (in only one instance). Though both of these material types appear throughout the 'Araba in the form of wadi cobbles, the abrasive limestone cortex of *in situ* material may have been preferred for its quality for enhancing grip in scraping oily substances or for use as sheep shears. Given imported *in situ* cherts are present as primary and secondary elements, it seems reasonable to assume that the tabular scrapers were manufactured on-site.

Group 2 (Sites: 158, 159, 160, 162, 163, 172)

The second group of sites is located along the southern boundary of Jibāl Um Nukheila. These sites are all much closer to known chert outcroppings than those in group one. The range for these sites from the closest chert sources is 5.2 to 6.0 km. Surprisingly, all of these sites, except Site 158 (the farthest from known chert sources), yielded only wadi cobbles. Site 158 yielded both wadi cobbles and *in situ* materials.

Technologically, these six sites all exhibit rather crude flake technologies. The tabular scraper and tabular scraper preforms are completely absent here, though end scrapers do appear. The preponderance of flakes at these sites is, perhaps, best explained by the nature of the materials. The sites in Group 1 contained exceedingly large *in situ* pieces (26.9, 73.9, 70.5, 85.6 cm² in obverse surface area), while the sites in Group 2 contained much smaller wadi cobbles (60.1, 67.6, 54.9, 67.3, 33.0, 37.0). The wadi cobbles found at these sites would have been technologically insufficient for scraper manufacture in two respects. First, they were simply too small, and second, they lacked the abrasive cortical coverage associated with *in situ* chert sources.

Group 3 (Sites: 226, 242, 257, 276)

The third group of sites is located along the extreme northeastern boundary of the Wādī ʿAraba. Sites within this group are located much closer to known chert outcroppings than those in Group 1, yet slightly farther than those in Group 2. Two of the sites (242, 276) contain exclusively *in situ* materials, with the other two sites containing both *in situ* materials and wadi cobbles.

Similar to the sites in Group 2, the sites in Group 3 lack the tabular scraper element. This is interesting in light of an abundance of *in situ* materials, which seemed to co-occur with tabular scrapers in the other site groups. Two factors, however, may explain the situation. First, the maximum size of the pieces at these sites is significantly smaller (55.4, 79.1, 57.4, 50.7 cm²) than the pieces in Group 1 and thus perhaps too small for the fabrication of tabular scrapers. Secondly, there is a much lower occurrence of chert Type B in the Group 3 assemblages and Type B was the preferred chert variety for tabular scrapers in Group 1.

Group 4 (Sites: 319, 327)

These two sites are located roughly between the Wādī ʿAraba and the Wādī Ḍarba. Their distance to known chert outcroppings is similar to the distances of sites in Groups 2 and 3. They both yielded large amounts of chert Type B *in situ* material (good for tabular scrapers); however, both sites also yielded low maximum material sizes (41.6, 50.4 cm²). Again, flakes dominated the assemblages and tabular scrapers were completely absent.

Group 5 (Sites: 322, 325, 328)

These three sites are located east of Wādī ʿAraba. Their distance to known chert outcroppings is similar to sites in Groups 2, 3 and 4, but the maximum sizes of debitage are among the smallest in the study (54.6, 31.2, 25.0 cm²). These assemblages also yielded very little of chert Type B. Not surprisingly, despite yielding predominantly *in situ* materials, the assemblages were dominated by crude flakes.

Discussion

Based on these findings, it appears as though the sites in Group 1 are outliers. They are an extraordinarily long distance from the nearest known chert sources, and they appear to have been associated with the specialized production of tabular scrapers in addition to flakes. Unfortunately, little inference can be drawn, based on the raw material characteristics of sites in the other four groups. The sites are all similar in distance from *in situ* sources, yet some contain these sources, some contain only cherts from wadi cobbles, and some contain both. Furthermore, there seems to have been no preferential selection patterns based on raw material type or size in Groups 2–5.

V.   SUMMARY AND CONCLUSIONS

Of the 138 assemblages collected for study, only 18 (13%) contained what is believed to be marginally adequate sample sizes for analysis. Traditional techno-typologic analysis and a technologic attribute study indicate that one of these is of Upper Paleolithic age (Site 319), another of Epipaleolithic age (Site 328), and two others (Sites 160 and 226) likely of Pleistocene age. Site 226 displays both techno-typologic features and technologic attributes suggestive of Levantine Mousterian affiliation. Four of the remaining fourteen sites exhibit techno-typologic characteristics (especially tabular scrapers) and technologic attributes (especially L/W ratio) pointing to Chalcolithic (or even very Late Neolithic–Early Bronze) affiliations. Other technologic indicators imply that the other ten assemblages are also of Mid–Late Holocene age.

The distribution of sites, relative to archaeological period, is strongly dominated by Chalcolithic (and perhaps Bronze Age) occurrences with only 11–22% of the sites falling in the Paleolithic. In the preliminary report of findings for the 1994 SAAS season, Smith et al. (1997:49) note that evidence for Lower Paleolithic, Upper Paleolithic, and Epipaleolithic occurrences was either absent or inconclusive. They point to some evidence of a Middle Paleolithic occupation, concentrated at sites in the northern portion of the study area, and Pre-pottery Neolithic B occupations clustered near 'Ain eṭ-Ṭayyiba (Sites 152–56 and 158–61) located north of the study area. Although specific techno-typologic signatures are not described for the Middle Paleolithic sites, PPNB point bases are attributed to Sites 152, 153, 156, and 158, and three of these are illustrated in fig. 5.4 (Smith et al. 1997:49). Although the illustrated specimens could be related to PPNB points, their fragmentary condition does not allow for the identification of specific PPNB point types (e.g., Byblos, Amuq, etc). These may, in fact, belong to later periods.

A similar pattern skewed toward mid–late Holocene occurrences was observed in a University of Tulsa study involving an intensive survey centered on three wadis overlapping the northern sector of the SAAS study (Henry et al. 2001, Henry 2006). This intensive, systematic pedestrian survey, however, did show a much greater representation of Pleistocene age sites (ca. 39%), including unambiguous Middle Paleolithic, Upper Paleolithic, and Epipaleolithic occupations associated with chronometric (¹⁴C and OSL) determinations.

The greater representation of Mid–Late Holocene occurrences in the Wādī 'Araba has been attributed to climatic shifts resulting in moister conditions during the Chalcolithic and Early Bronze Age (Niemi and Smith 1999), but conditions moister than present are also indicated by pollen and phytolith evidence from sites in the southern 'Araba radiocarbon-dated to the Epipaleolithic and Late Neolithic (Henry et al. 2001). Moreover, moister than present settings have been identified in sites located in the nearby uplands of the western Hisma, dating from the Middle Paleolithic to early Neolithic, based upon several lines of paleoenvironmental data, e.g., pollen, phytoliths, diatoms, fauna, and sediment analyses (Henry 1994, 1995, 1998, 2005, 2006; Henry et al. 2003; Henry et al. 2004). In the light of evidence for episodic moist pulses during various times in the Late Pleistocene and Holocene, the greater representation of Holocene age sites in the 'Araba likely stems from more than simply favorable conditions for settlement of the area. Geomorphic bias appears to have played a larger role in determining site densities for certain periods (Henry 2006). For example, the formation of extensive alluvial terraces and fans in the Wādī 'Araba during Chalcolithic–Bronze Age times would have resulted in burial of substantial portions of the landscape by mid/late Holocene sediments, thus obscuring earlier occupations (Niemi and Smith 1999, Henry et al. 2001, Henry 2006). The general paucity of Paleolithic sites recorded in the SAAS is likely an expression of the interplay of climatic cycles and geomorphic agencies overlain by survey biases that favored the recognition of later period sites linked to architectural features.

REFERENCES

Coinman, N. R., and Henry, D. O.
1995 The Upper Paleolithic Sites. Pp. 133–214 in *Prehistoric Cultural Ecology and Evolution: Insights from Southern Jordan,* ed. D. O. Henry. New York: Plenum.

Henry, D. O.
1994 Prehistoric Cultural Ecology in Southern Jordan. *Science* 265: 336–41.

1998 Intrasite Spatial Patterns and Behavioral Modernity: Indications from the Late Levantine Mousterian Rockshelter of Tor Faraj, Southern Jordan. Pp. 127–42 in *Neanderthals and Modern Humans in Western Asia*, eds. T. Akazawa, K. Aoki, and O. Bar-Yosef. New York: Plenum.

2005 Ayn Abū Nukhayla: Early Neolithic Adaptation to the Arid Zone. *Journal of the Israel Prehistoric Society* 35: 353–70.

2006 Cultural and Geologic Influences on Prehistoric Site Distributions in the Wādī ʿArabah. Pp. 91–101 in *Crossing the Rift: Resources, Routes, Settlement Patterns, and Interaction in the Wādī ʿArabah*. Eds. P. Bienkowski and K. Galor. Levant Supplement Series 3. Winona Lake, IN: Eisenbrauns.

Henry, D. O. (ed.)
1995 *Prehistoric Cultural Ecology and Evolution: Insights from Southern Jordan*. New York: Plenum.
2003 The *Beginnings of Human Modernity: Behavioral Organization of Neanderthals in the Southern Levant*. London: Continuum.

Henry, D. O.; Bauer, H.: Kerry, K.; Beaver, J.; and White, J.
2001 Survey of Prehistoric Sites, Wādī ʿArabah, Southern Jordan. *BASOR* 323: 1–19.

Henry, D. O.; Cordova, C.; White, J. J.; Dean, R. M.; Beaver, J. E.; Ekstrom, H.; Kadowaki, S.; McCorriston, J.; Nowell, A.; and Scott-Cummings, L.
2003 The Early Neolithic site of Ayn Abū Nukhayla, Southern Jordan. *BASOR* 330: 1–30.

Henry, D. O.; Hietala, H.; Rosen, A.; Demidenko, Y. E.; Usik, V. I.; and Armagan, T.
2004 Human Behavioral Organization in the Middle Paleolithic: Were Neanderthals Different? *American Anthropologist* 106: 17–31.

Niemi, T. M., and Smith, A. M. II
1999 Initial Results of the Southeastern Wādī ʿAraba, Jordan, Geoarchaeological Study: Implications for Shifts in Late Quaternary Aridity. *Geoarchaeology* 14(8): 791–820.

Smith, A. M. II, and Niemi, T. M.
1994 Results of the Southeast ʿAraba Archaeological Reconnaissance. *ADAJ* 38: 469–83.

Smith, A. M. II; Niemi, T. M.; and Stevens, M.
1997 The Southeast ʿAraba Archaeological Survey: A Preliminary Report of the 1994 Season. *BASOR* 305: 45–71.

Chapter 6

The Pottery from the Survey

by S. Thomas Parker

I. INTRODUCTION

This chapter aims to present an overview of the ceramics recovered by the Southeast 'Araba Archaeological Survey (hereafter SAAS), a component of the Roman Aqaba Project. As expected, ceramics were by far the most abundant type of artifact recovered by the survey and in most cases provided the main evidence for dating the various sites. In some cases the ceramics offer other evidence about the nature of a site and its relationship to the wider world. This chapter will summarize the ceramic evidence obtained by the survey and present a selection of illustrations to document the interpretations offered elsewhere in this report. It will be seen that, although the ceramic evidence is illuminating for the history of the region in several periods, the nature of this evidence leaves some major questions unresolved.

The project's regional survey recovered about 8,143 sherds *in toto* from its 330 sites. Although, as noted above, ceramics were by far the most common kind of artifact recovered by the survey, the quantity is quite small considering the number of recorded sites. Although the survey team recovered several hundred sherds from a few sites, they found no pottery at all at a significant minority of sites (n=145, or 43.9% of all sites) and most of the remainder yielded only a handful of sherds. Many of these sherds were small and badly weathered by

long exposure to the natural elements on the surface, making identification problematic. Some 1,997 of these sherds were judged diagnostic (i.e., rims, handles, and/or bases); the remainder were less diagnostic body sherds, although many of these, such as painted Nabataean fine ware, could also be identified. All sherds collected were examined in the field by the author and about 2,793 (or 34.5% of the total collected) were saved and registered for further analysis. These generally included all diagnostic sherds and a representative selection of the body sherds. In the all too frequent instances of sites that yielded only a handful of sherds, all or nearly all sherds were saved and registered. All registered sherds were returned to North Carolina State University for further analysis.

Subsequent study of the pottery was aided by several factors. First, the simultaneous excavation at Aqaba permitted much greater understanding of the local ceramic wares for the periods encountered there, i.e., from the 1st century BC to 10th century AD. Second, publication of stratified sequences of pottery from other sites in the region, such as Tell Maqass and Petra, provided more parallels for the survey material. Third, the author benefited greatly from insights offered by several scholars, such as R. Thomas Schaub for the Chalcolithic/Early Bronze Age pottery, Jeffrey Blakely for the Iron II/Persian period pottery, Roberta Tomber on the imported fine wares and amphorae of the classical periods, and Donald Whitcomb on the Early Islamic periods. Consequently, the preliminary analysis in the field was revised in some cases. I am extremely grateful to these colleagues for their insights, but naturally they are in no way responsible for the interpretations expressed here.

A selection of 168 representative sherds from eighteen sites is illustrated in this chapter. Most of these sherds derive from the better-represented periods recorded by the survey, i.e., Chalcolithic, Early Bronze, Early Roman, Late Roman, and Early Byzantine. A few sherds from the more poorly-represented periods are also included, such as Iron II, Persian, Hellenistic, and Late Islamic. Possible parallels, mostly from well-stratified contexts, are provided for many of these sherds, although there is no attempt to provide exhaustive parallels. In some cases the best parallels are from the excavation of the current project, much still unpublished but forthcoming. In these cases reference is made either to the published parallels (when available) or to the registration numbers (if unpublished).

II.   THE CERAMIC EVIDENCE FROM THE SURVEY BY PERIOD

Neolithic (ca. 8500–4500 BC)

Virtually no ceramic evidence from this period was identified from the survey. Site 287 yielded two possible Neolithic sherds, but the predominant pottery was Chalcolithic/Early Bronze.

Chalcolithic/Early Bronze Periods (ca. 4500–1950 BC)

Chalcolithic and Early Bronze pottery was frequently recovered from project sites. A total of 1,375 sherds from 72 sites were broadly dated to this period, representing 16.9% of all sherds and 21.8% of all sites. Of this total, 247 sherds were more closely dated to the Chalcolithic period and 127 sherds to the Early Bronze Age. A representative sample of 30 sherds from five different sites is illustrated here. For additional published pottery from this region in these periods, see above all the recent Jordanian-German excavations at Tell Maqaṣṣ and Tell Ḥujeirat al-Ghuzlan (near Aqaba), which

seem to span the transition from the Chalcolithic to the Early Bronze periods (Khalil, Eichmann, and Schmidt 2003; Kerner 2003). A small group of pottery from Ḥujeirat al-Ghuzlan (Site 63) is presented below (fig. 6.3:26–29).

Middle and Late Bronze (ca. 2200–1200 BC)

The survey recovered little evidence of these periods, which is typical of southern Jordan generally. Some of the so-called "Negevite Ware" has been dated as early as the Late Bronze Age. But the sherds of this distinctive ware recovered from Tell el-Kheleifeh (see below) seemingly date to the Iron Age.

Iron Age, Persian, and Hellenistic Periods (ca. 1200–63 BC)

A few Iron Age or possible Iron Age sherds were identified at a handful of surveyed sites. Sites 14, 16, 63, 72, each yielded a single such sherd. Site 247 yielded 43 Iron II sherds, but most of these appeared to derive from a single vessel. Six Iron Age sherds were recovered at Site 256. Other possible Iron Age sherds were collected at Site 180 (n=11) and at Site 195 (n=4). Sites 199 and 206 each yielded a single Negevite sherd which could date to the Iron Age.

Otherwise, the only site with significant evidence of the Iron II and Persian periods was Tell el-Kheleifeh (Site 29), which also yielded the only Hellenistic pottery recovered by the project, albeit only a handful of sherds. Although much pottery from Glueck's 1938–1940 excavation was published by Pratico (1985), the present project also collected a large ceramic sample from the surface of this site in 1996 to aid in identifying any pottery from these periods that might appear in its own excavations. As it happened, these periods were in fact totally absent from the excavations at Aqaba. Nevertheless, it seems useful to illustrate a selection of sherds from Tell el-Kheleifeh in this report, particularly since these are otherwise poorly-represented periods that immediately precede the foundation of Nabataean Aila.

Early Roman/Nabataean Period (ca. 63 BC–AD 106)

This was by far the best-documented period in terms of ceramic evidence recovered by the survey. Pottery of this period appeared at 88 of the survey sites, or 26.7% of all sites. Some 2529 sherds were dated to this period or ca. 31.1% of all sherds from the survey. In addition, a good portion of the 850 sherds more broadly dated "Early Roman/Late Roman" probably derives from this period as well. A selection of diagnostic Early Roman/Nabataean sherds from ten sites is presented here.

The pottery from this period includes some Nabataean painted and unpainted fine wares, seemingly derived from the Petra region, as well as various coarse wares, including some probably derived from Aila ("Aqaba Ware," Dolinka 2003: 79–90). Imports from farther afield included a dozen sherds of Eastern Sigillata A recovered at six sites (16, 113, 152, 167, 275, 329) scattered throughout the region and a single sherd of Cypriot Sigillata at another site (14). Single sherds from a Rhodian amphora (Peacock and Williams Class 9) and Dressel 2–4 amphora (Peacock and Williams Class 10) appeared near the caravan station of Bir Madhkur (Site 149) and at an apparent Nabataean village (Site 152), respectively.

Late Roman Period (ca. AD 106–324)

Late Roman pottery was identified at only fourteen sites and just four of these yielded five or more Late Roman sherds. However, although many fewer sherds (n=91) were identified as Late Roman compared to the previous period, this decline may be more apparent than real. First of all, many of the 850 sherds that could not be more closely dated than "Early Roman/Late Roman" may well date to this later period. This could increase the number of Late Roman sites to as many as 28 sites. Further, excavations at Petra, Aila itself, and other sites have demonstrated that the Nabataean ceramic tradition clearly continued long after the Roman annexation of Nabataea in AD 106, through the 2nd and well into the 3rd century, i.e., most of the Late Roman period. Therefore, some of the pottery dated "Early Roman/Nabataean" may actually date to the Late

Roman period, especially to the 2nd or early 3rd centuries. The actual demise of the Nabataean ceramic tradition seems to date to the late 3rd century, at least in this region. All these caveats aside, the evidence does suggest a decline in sedentary settlement in this period compared to the Early Roman/Nabataean Period. In terms of imported fine wares, some of the handful of African Red Slip sherds recovered by the survey could date as early as the 3rd century, although these probably date mostly to the Byzantine period. A selection of diagnostic Late Roman sherds from seven sites is presented here.

Early Byzantine Period (ca. AD 324–500)

Interpretation of the Byzantine period from many regional surveys in Jordan has long been hampered by failure to subdivide collected ceramics into "Early" and "Late" Byzantine," despite the fact that stratified sequences offering just such evidence have been available from central Jordan since 1973 from Tell Hesbân (Sauer 1973) and since 1987 from sites of the *Limes Arabicus* east of the Dead Sea (Parker 1987; 2006). Therefore, the present project accordingly was able to subdivide its Byzantine pottery in most cases, although a few sherds (n=22) could be identified only as generically "Byzantine." There were also a handful of imported amphora sherds which could not be closely dated but could date to the Byzantine period. These include three sherds of Gaza amphorae and five from Egyptian amphorae.

Only 72 sherds from 18 sites specifically identified as Early Byzantine were recovered by the survey, representing 0.9% of all sherds and 5.5% of all sites. Further, only three of these sites yielded five or more Early Byzantine sherds. Imported fine ware included eight sherds of African Red Slip attested at six sites (7, 17, 31, 98, 221, and 329). A selection of diagnostic Early Byzantine sherds from six sites is presented here.

Late Byzantine Period (ca. AD 500–630)

The survey recovered 305 sherds identified as Late Byzantine from 23 sites, representing 3.8% of all sherds and 7.0% of all sites. But only seven of these

Roman Aqaba Project: SAAS　　　　　　　　　　　　　　　　　　　　　**Site 275**

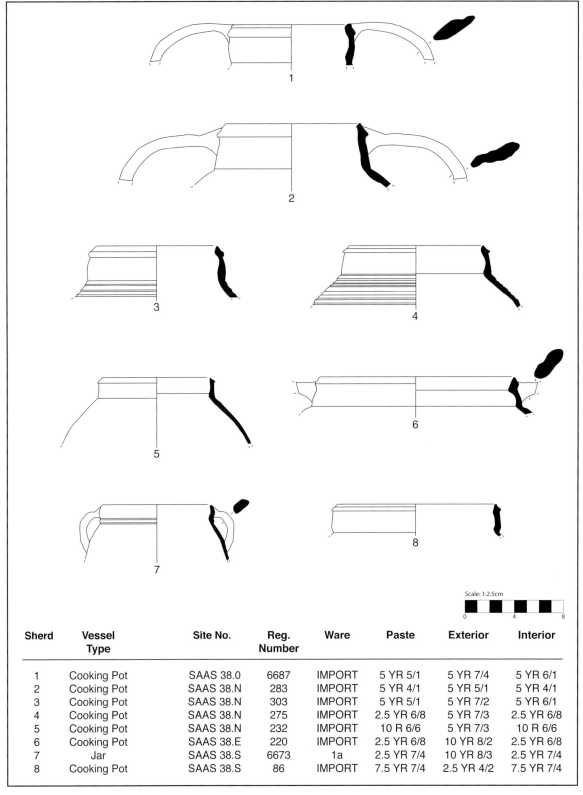

Sherd	Vessel Type	Site No.	Reg. Number	Ware	Paste	Exterior	Interior
1	Cooking Pot	SAAS 38.0	6687	IMPORT	5 YR 5/1	5 YR 7/4	5 YR 6/1
2	Cooking Pot	SAAS 38.N	283	IMPORT	5 YR 4/1	5 YR 5/1	5 YR 4/1
3	Cooking Pot	SAAS 38.N	303	IMPORT	5 YR 5/1	5 YR 7/2	5 YR 6/1
4	Cooking Pot	SAAS 38.N	275	IMPORT	2.5 YR 6/8	5 YR 7/3	2.5 YR 6/8
5	Cooking Pot	SAAS 38.N	232	IMPORT	10 R 6/6	5 YR 7/3	10 R 6/6
6	Cooking Pot	SAAS 38.E	220	IMPORT	2.5 YR 6/8	10 YR 8/2	2.5 YR 6/8
7	Jar	SAAS 38.S	6673	1a	2.5 YR 7/4	10 YR 8/3	2.5 YR 7/4
8	Cooking Pot	SAAS 38.S	86	IMPORT	7.5 YR 7/4	2.5 YR 4/2	7.5 YR 7/4

Fig. 6.1　　*Pottery from Qāʿ as-Suʾaydiyyīn (Site 275).*

sites yielded five or more Late Byzantine sherds. Because most of the fine wares mentioned were less diagnostic body sherds, some might actually date to this period, rather than to the Early Byzantine era.

Early Islamic Period (ca. AD 630–1116)

The survey recovered only 130 sherds identified as Early Islamic, including 30 Umayyad (ca. 630–750) and 18 Abbasid (ca. 750–961), from thirteen sites, representing 1.6% of all sherds and 3.9% of all sites. Only four of these sites yielded five or more Early Islamic sherds. Because some ceramic forms and wares of the Late Byzantine period continued into the beginning of the Early Islamic period, this might understate the amount of Early Islamic material present. This, for example, includes two sherds of so-called Fine Byzantine Ware from Site 275 that seems to derive from the Jerusalem area (Magness 1993: 193–201). On the other hand, since the excavations at Aqaba produced several excellent stratigraphic sequences of Early Islamic material, it seems unlikely that any significant amount of Early Islamic material recovered by the survey went unrecognized.

Late Islamic Period (ca. AD 1116–1918)

Only 41 sherds identified as Late Islamic were recovered from six sites by the survey. This included an Ottoman ceramic pipe fragment from Site 219 (Sherd 168).

III. ANALYSIS OF POTTERY FROM SPECIFIC SITES

The pottery from the survey published here is presented in the form of line drawings and descriptive tables, with some discussion in the following section. It includes 168 sherds from eighteen sites and is a representative sample of pottery from that site and period. The description accompanying each drawn sherd includes its site of origin, type of vessel (if known), the ware/fabric and the fabric color (interior, exterior surface, interior surface, and paint where present) represented by the Munsell Soil Color Charts. An Arabic number listed for some wares references fabrics produced at

Aqaba. Petrological and neutron activation analysis of Aqaba wares is presented in Parker 2013 and in a future volume of this final report. Wares listed as "IMPORT" refer to sherds not from Aqaba. For other wares see the list of abbreviations on p. xi. The Munsell color codes listed are naturally only approximations of the actual color. The analysis includes some parallels published elsewhere for comparative purposes, although there is no attempt to provide exhaustive parallels. Much of the Roman, Byzantine, and Early Islamic pottery from the survey could be compared to well-stratified ceramic sequences from the project's own excavation, partly published (Dolinka 2003) but mostly forthcoming in a subsequent volume of the final report.

Qaʿ as-Suʾaydiyyīn
(Site 275; figs. 6.1:1–6.3:23)

The pottery from this fort was mostly Early Roman/Nabataean but with some sherds from the Late Roman and Byzantine periods.

The cooking wares date from both the Early Roman/Nabataean and Late Roman period. There are several examples of the classic Nabataean closed cooking pot with a triangular rim and twin vertical strap handles (fig. 6.1:1–6). Some are of reddish ware (fig. 6.1:4–6), while others are of a darker gray fabric (fig. 6.1:1–3). Some display lightly ribbed shoulders (fig. 6.1:3–4). Such cooking pots are paralleled at many Nabataean sites, including Aqaba (Dolinka 2003: 118–19, nos. 1–3) and Petra (Murray and Ellis 1940: pls. 9:22–25, 26:39, 28:76, 30:102; Cleveland 1960: fig. 5:1; Hammond 1965: pl. 57:1; Gerber 1996: pl. 32F; Gerber 1997: fig. 7). Gerber suggests that this form dates from the mid-1st to early 2nd century AD, i.e., into the early Late Roman period. A Late Roman closed cooking pot (fig. 6.1:8) displays the typical grooved rim, offset neck, and light brown slip characteristic of this period. Parallels may be cited from el-Lejjūn (Parker 1987: figs. 100:82–83, 101:96–98; 2006: 335–36) and other sites of the *Limes Arabicus* in central Jordan (Parker 1987: figs. 94:33–35, 96:45–59), as well as from Tell Hesbân (Sauer 1973: fig. 2:45–50) and many other sites (Parker 2006: 336 for more references).

Sherd 7 represents a closed vessel of reddish ware with a white slip over its exterior surface and

Roman Aqaba Project: SAAS   **Site 275**

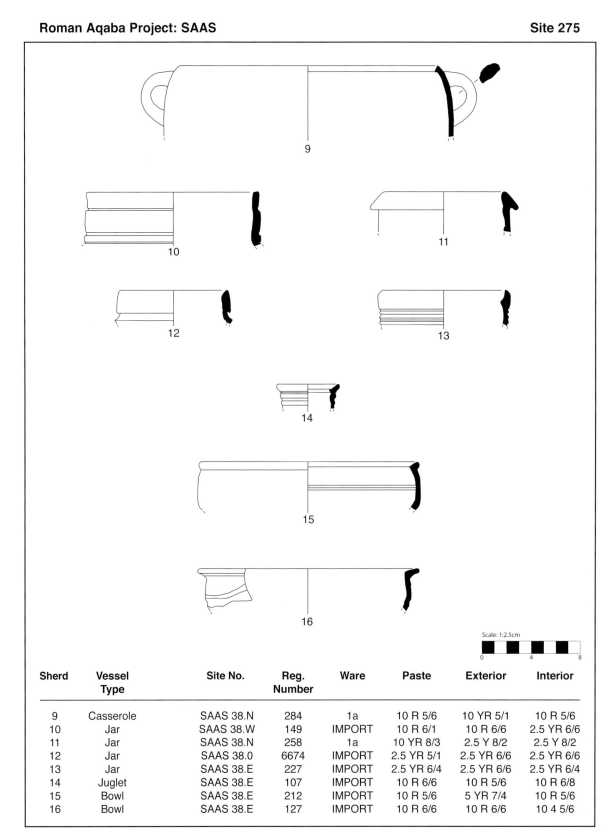

Sherd	Vessel Type	Site No.	Reg. Number	Ware	Paste	Exterior	Interior
9	Casserole	SAAS 38.N	284	1a	10 R 5/6	10 YR 5/1	10 R 5/6
10	Jar	SAAS 38.W	149	IMPORT	10 R 6/1	10 R 6/6	2.5 YR 6/6
11	Jar	SAAS 38.N	258	1a	10 YR 8/3	2.5 Y 8/2	2.5 Y 8/2
12	Jar	SAAS 38.0	6674	IMPORT	2.5 YR 5/1	2.5 YR 6/6	2.5 YR 6/6
13	Jar	SAAS 38.E	227	IMPORT	2.5 YR 6/4	2.5 YR 6/6	2.5 YR 6/4
14	Juglet	SAAS 38.E	107	IMPORT	10 R 6/6	10 R 5/6	10 R 6/8
15	Bowl	SAAS 38.E	212	IMPORT	10 R 5/6	5 YR 7/4	10 R 5/6
16	Bowl	SAAS 38.E	127	IMPORT	10 R 6/6	10 R 6/6	10 4 5/6

FIG. 6.2   *Pottery from Qāʿ as-Suʿaydiyyīn (Site 275).*

displays a triangular rim (partially obscured by the attached handle in this drawing), offset neck, and twin vertical loop handles extending from the rim to the shoulder. In short, this looks like a "miniature closed cooking pot." These are well-attested in Early Roman/Nabataean and Late Roman contexts at Aila but, like the current example, never display evidence of charring or other exposure to fire and rarely display the ribbing so characteristic of the closed cooking pots. Possible parallels may also be cited from Petra (Murry and Ellis 1940: pl. 28:77; Fellmann Brogli 1996: 256, fig. 771).

The open cooking casserole (fig. 6.2:9) is of red ware and displays a dark gray slip on its exterior side wall. The profile is incurved and displays the typical beveled rim to receive a lid. Rather than the more typical horizontal loop handles found on most casseroles, this vessel has vertical loop handles, paralleled at Petra (Fellmann Brogli 1996: 257, figs. 773–74) and Aqaba (unpublished, reg. #53459, from a 3rd-century context).

Various jugs or jars (fig. 6.2:10–14) display diverse profiles. Three (fig. 6.2:10, 12–13) are of reddish ware but exhibit dark cores; the fourth (fig. 6.2:11) is white ware with a slightly pinkish core and is paralleled at Aqaba, where it first appears in Early Roman/Nabataean contexts (unpublished, reg. #56939, from a 3rd-century context). The relatively wide-mouthed jar (fig. 6.2:10) displays several widely-spaced grooves on its neck and is paralleled at Petra (Murray and Ellis 1940: pl. 27:132–33; Gerber 2001: 360, fig. 1:26). The folded rim of another jar (fig. 6.2:12) likely dates to the Late Roman period, and a possible parallel may be cited from Petra (Gerber 2001: 360, fig. 1:19, dated 2nd or 3rd century). The fourth jar (fig. 6.2:13) displays a ribbed neck and a lip on the inner rim. The last of these vessels (fig. 6.2:14) is a jug or juglet rim of evenly-fired, fine red ware with a lightly ribbed neck.

A variety of bowls (figs. 6.2:16–6.3:23) comprises the remainder of the illustrated sherds from this site. The carinated bowls (fig. 6.2:15–6.3:18) are all of evenly-fired, finely levigated red ware. Three (figs. 6.2:15–16, 6.3:18) have flattened, elongated rims. One (fig. 6.2:16) is decorated by a single wavy line on the exterior side wall while another (fig. 6.3:18) displays the pattern of rouletting typical for this bowl and normally dated to the late 1st and early 2nd century AD. Sherd 17 is a hemispherical bowl paralleled at Oboda (Negev 1986: 74–75, nos. 555–71), Petra (Murray and Ellis 1940: pls. 8:51, 29:90; Hammond 1965: pl. 59:18; Schmid 2000: 9, fig. 60), and Aqaba (Dolinka 2003: 125, no. 14). The large bowl or krater (fig. 6.3:19) is also of red but somewhat coarser ware with a "piecrust" rim formed by finger indentations. Twin grooves were incised just below the exterior of the rim. The two closed cups (fig. 6.3:20–21) with folded rims are of similar fine ware as the carinated bowls but with thinner side walls. These closed cups are attested at a number of sites, including Petra (Fellmann Brogli 1996: 263, figs. 815–16) and Aqaba (unpublished, reg. no. #48249). Finally, two sherds (fig. 6.3:22–23) from Nabataean painted fine ware bowls complete this corpus. The pattern of dark red paint suggests both date to Schmid's Dekorphase 3a, or ca. AD 20–70 (Schmid 1996: 207, fig. 700). Although Sherd 23 lacks the fine lines normally associated with this phase, these were likely eroded away by exposure on the surface; later painted sherds lacking these fine lines, i.e., Schmid's Dekorphase 3c and 4, are invariably in dark brown or black paint, not dark red, and are of thicker and coarser ware (Schmid 1996: 209, figs. 702–4).

Site 113
(fig. 6.4:24–25)

Two Late Roman jar rims are published here from among the small number of diagnostic sherds from this site, which also included a body sherd of Eastern Sigillata A. Both rims derive from neckless bag jars with folded rims in fairly coarse gray ware. This jar is common at Aqaba in 2nd- through early 4th-century contexts (unpublished, reg. nos. #3436, #24062).

Ḥujeirat al-Ghuzlan
(Site 63; fig. 6.4:26–29)

This site has been the focus of excavation in recent years by a Jordanian-German team and is dated to the late Chalcolithic and the beginning of the Early Bronze Age (Khalil, Eichmann, and Schmidt 2003; Kerner 2003). The small corpus of sherds presented here is composed of hand-made vessels, mostly by

Roman Aqaba Project: SAAS   **Site 275**

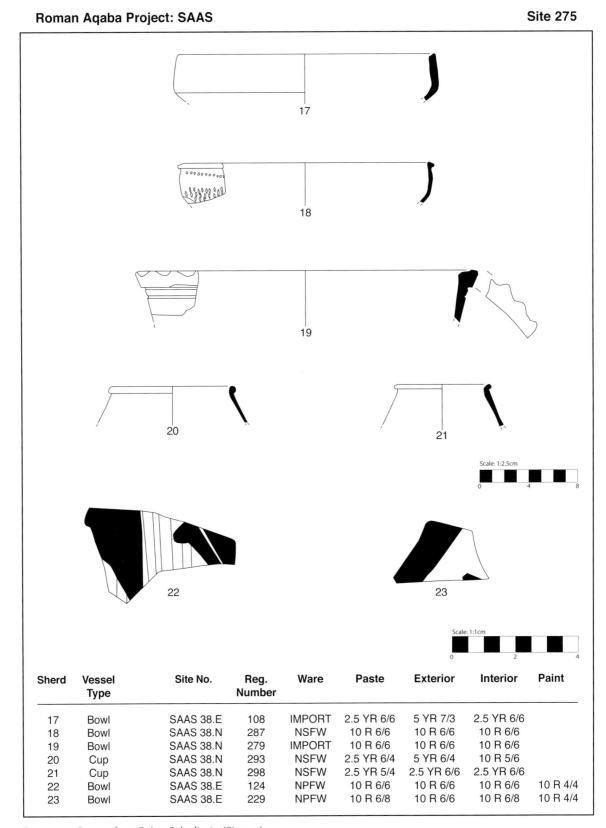

Sherd	Vessel Type	Site No.	Reg. Number	Ware	Paste	Exterior	Interior	Paint
17	Bowl	SAAS 38.E	108	IMPORT	2.5 YR 6/6	5 YR 7/3	2.5 YR 6/6	
18	Bowl	SAAS 38.N	287	NSFW	10 R 6/6	10 R 6/6	10 R 6/6	
19	Bowl	SAAS 38.N	279	IMPORT	10 R 6/6	10 R 6/6	10 R 6/6	
20	Cup	SAAS 38.N	293	NSFW	2.5 YR 6/4	5 YR 6/4	10 R 5/6	
21	Cup	SAAS 38.N	298	NSFW	2.5 YR 5/4	2.5 YR 6/6	2.5 YR 6/6	
22	Bowl	SAAS 38.E	124	NPFW	10 R 6/6	10 R 6/6	10 R 6/6	10 R 4/4
23	Bowl	SAAS 38.E	229	NPFW	10 R 6/8	10 R 6/6	10 R 6/8	10 R 4/4

FIG. 6.3   *Pottery from Qāʿ as-Suʾaydiyyīn (Site 275).*

Roman Aqaba Project: SAAS

Site 113

Site 63

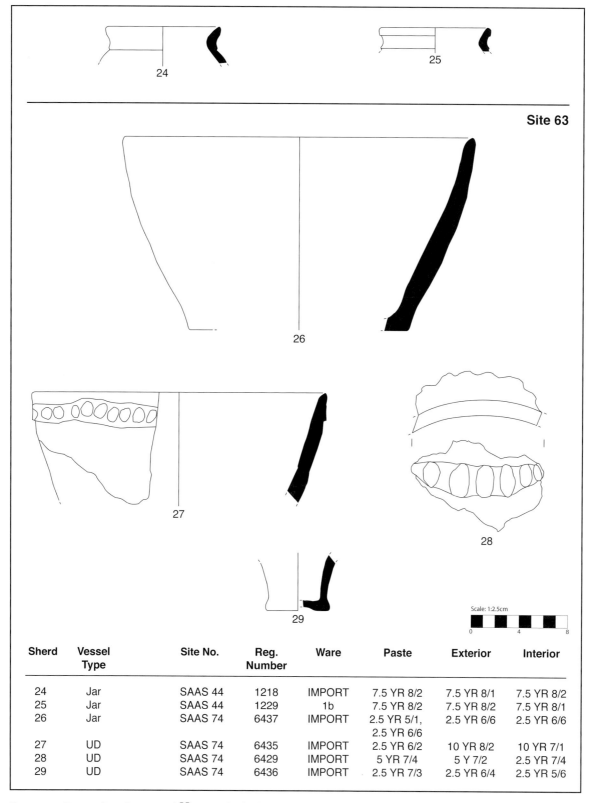

Sherd	Vessel Type	Site No.	Reg. Number	Ware	Paste	Exterior	Interior
24	Jar	SAAS 44	1218	IMPORT	7.5 YR 8/2	7.5 YR 8/1	7.5 YR 8/2
25	Jar	SAAS 44	1229	1b	7.5 YR 8/2	7.5 YR 8/2	7.5 YR 8/1
26	Jar	SAAS 74	6437	IMPORT	2.5 YR 5/1, 2.5 YR 6/6	2.5 YR 6/6	2.5 YR 6/6
27	UD	SAAS 74	6435	IMPORT	2.5 YR 6/2	10 YR 8/2	10 YR 7/1
28	UD	SAAS 74	6429	IMPORT	5 YR 7/4	5 Y 7/2	2.5 YR 7/4
29	UD	SAAS 74	6436	IMPORT	2.5 YR 7/3	2.5 YR 6/4	2.5 YR 5/6

FIG. 6.4   *Pottery from Site 113 and Ḥujeirat al-Ghuzlan (Site 63).*

Roman Aqaba Project: SAAS

Site 181

Site 163

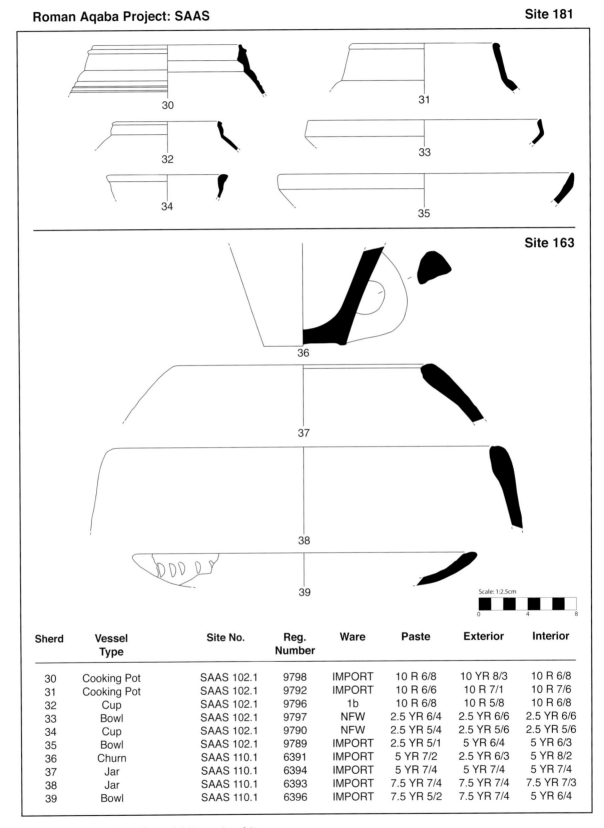

Sherd	Vessel Type	Site No.	Reg. Number	Ware	Paste	Exterior	Interior
30	Cooking Pot	SAAS 102.1	9798	IMPORT	10 R 6/8	10 YR 8/3	10 R 6/8
31	Cooking Pot	SAAS 102.1	9792	IMPORT	10 R 6/6	10 R 7/1	10 R 7/6
32	Cup	SAAS 102.1	9796	1b	10 R 6/8	10 R 5/8	10 R 6/8
33	Bowl	SAAS 102.1	9797	NFW	2.5 YR 6/4	2.5 YR 6/6	2.5 YR 6/6
34	Cup	SAAS 102.1	9790	NFW	2.5 YR 5/4	2.5 YR 5/6	2.5 YR 5/6
35	Bowl	SAAS 102.1	9789	IMPORT	2.5 YR 5/1	5 YR 6/4	5 YR 6/3
36	Churn	SAAS 110.1	6391	IMPORT	5 YR 7/2	2.5 YR 6/3	5 YR 8/2
37	Jar	SAAS 110.1	6394	IMPORT	5 YR 7/4	5 YR 7/4	5 YR 7/4
38	Jar	SAAS 110.1	6393	IMPORT	7.5 YR 7/4	7.5 YR 7/4	7.5 YR 7/3
39	Bowl	SAAS 110.1	6396	IMPORT	7.5 YR 5/2	7.5 YR 7/4	5 YR 6/4

FIG. 6.5   *Pottery from Gharandal (Site 181) and Site 163.*

coiling, of coarse ware. The fabric includes many stone inclusions, most often granite but including some mica, with voids suggesting occasional use of organic temper. One vessel (#26) is a jar with a flat base and displays a dark core. It is paralleled by excavated examples from the site (Kerner 2003: 181, fig. 19:4, 11) and may also be compared to examples from Arad in the Negev dated to EB I–II (Amiran 1978: pls. 12:19, 15:15, 16:1). Sherd 27 displays a tapered rim with band of thumb impressions applied just below the rim exterior to serve as a handle, also paralleled by excavated examples from the site (Kerner 2003: 180, fig. 18:1–8). Sherd 28 is probably from a large EB jar with a heavy band of appliqué serving as a ledge handle. Such jars have been published from the site (Kerner 2003: 180, fig. 18:9, 11) and may again be compared to examples from Arad (Amiran 1978: pl. 16:4–18, dated to EB I–II). Sherd 29 is the flat base of a small vessel, possibly coil-made and well-fired, and possibly paralleled at Arad (Amiran 1978: pl. 2:11, dated Chalcolithic).

Gharandal
(Site 181; fig. 6.5:30–35)

Excavation of this site, an important water station in Wādī ʿAraba, began in 2009 (Darby et al. 2010). Sherd 30 is the classic Early Roman/Nabataean closed cooking pot with a triangular rim and offset neck in light red ware with an exterior white slip. For published parallels see fig. 6.1:1–6 above. The closed Early Byzantine cooking pot is represented by Sherd 31, of dark red ware and a dark brown slip. The slip and slightly hooked rim are paralleled by 4th-century examples from el-Lejjūn and other sites of the *Limes Arabicus* east and southeast of the Dead Sea (Parker 1987: 535, 559, fig. 94:36–37; 571, fig. 100:84–85; 575, fig. 102:100–103; 577, fig. 103:104; Parker 2006: figs. 16.3:9, 16.18:80, 16.20:93–94, 16.31:146, 16.33:158) and from Aqaba (unpublished, reg. no. #5128). The main difference between Sherd 31 and the parallels cited above is that the former displays a somewhat inverted profile and a straight neck, rather than the more upright profile and offset neck typical of the examples from the *Limes Arabicus* sites.

Sherd 32 is another example of the closed, two-handled cup of Nabataean fine ware which looks much like a miniature cooking pot. For parallels, see fig. 6.1:7 above. Sherd 33 represents the classic carinated bowl in Nabataean fine ware, one of the most common of all Nabataean vessels. The type is generally dated from the mid-1st century BC to the 1st century AD, but with coarser and thicker descendents continuing into the 2nd and 3rd centuries. The many published parallels include examples from Petra (Murray and Ellis 1940: pl. 8:1, 71–72; Hammond 1965: pl. 59: 1–2; Schmid 2000: 8, 181–82, figs. 44–51), Khirbet edh-Dharih (Villeneuve 1990: pl. 4:3 (top); ʿAin ez-Zara (Clamer 1997: pl. 3:2), Oboda (Negev 1986: 77, no. 581), and Aqaba (Dolinka 2003: 125–26: nos. 15–16). Sherd 34 appears to be a cup, also in Nabataean fine ware, with a thickened everted rim. Finally, Sherd 35 is a shallow bowl of reddish-brown ware and a dark core. A dark brown slip has been carelessly and patchily applied to the exterior surface. The form is paralleled in Late Roman contexts at Petra (Fellmann Brogli 1996: 261, figs. 793–95).

Site 163 *(fig. 6.5:36–39)*

This settlement yielded a homogeneous ceramic sample dating entirely to the Chalcolithic and Early Bronze Age. Sherd 36 is a Chalcolithic churn with a complete vertical loop handle. Stone has been added as temper. It displays a heavy, dense slip and may be compared to examples from Arad (Amiran 1978: pl. 5:4, 6). Sherd 37 is a typical Early Bronze Age hole-mouth jar. It is coil-built of well-fired light red ware and displays fewer temper particles for this type of vessel (Kerner 2003: 180, fig. 18:12). Another possible Early Bronze Age jar is represented by Sherd 38, of dense, well-fired ware. It displays a sharply defined groove on top of the rim and some kind of exterior coating. Finally, Sherd 39 is a vessel of typical Early Bronze Age ware and is either a bowl with an upright rim (as depicted here) or another hole-mouth jar (if in fact a closed form). The exterior side wall just below the rim is decorated with lunate impressions. A parallel may be cited from Ḥujeirat al-Ghuzlan (Kerner 2003: 180, fig. 18:7)

Roman Aqaba Project: SAAS   **Site 159**

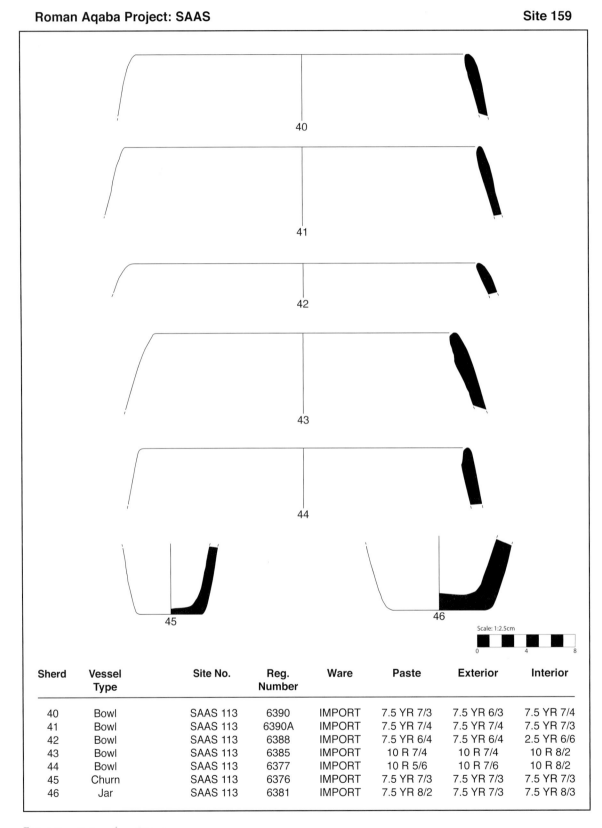

Sherd	Vessel Type	Site No.	Reg. Number	Ware	Paste	Exterior	Interior
40	Bowl	SAAS 113	6390	IMPORT	7.5 YR 7/3	7.5 YR 6/3	7.5 YR 7/4
41	Bowl	SAAS 113	6390A	IMPORT	7.5 YR 7/4	7.5 YR 7/4	7.5 YR 7/3
42	Bowl	SAAS 113	6388	IMPORT	7.5 YR 6/4	7.5 YR 6/4	2.5 YR 6/6
43	Bowl	SAAS 113	6385	IMPORT	10 R 7/4	10 R 7/4	10 R 8/2
44	Bowl	SAAS 113	6377	IMPORT	10 R 5/6	10 R 7/6	10 R 8/2
45	Churn	SAAS 113	6376	IMPORT	7.5 YR 7/3	7.5 YR 7/3	7.5 YR 7/3
46	Jar	SAAS 113	6381	IMPORT	7.5 YR 8/2	7.5 YR 7/3	7.5 YR 8/3

FIG. 6.6   *Pottery from Site 159.*

Site 159 *(fig. 6.6:40–46)*

This is another settlement that yielded exclusively Chalcolithic/Early Bronze Age pottery. Sherds 40–41 are Early Bronze Age hole-mouth bowls, both with a lime coating. Sherd 42 is a deep bowl, probably also Early Bronze Age; the fabric includes limestone probably added as temper. Sherds 43–44 are of light red ware typical of the Early Bronze Age, but Sherd 43 displays an exterior coating. The more tapered profile of Sherd 44 forms an almost vertical, upright stance. Parallels mat be cited from Ḥujeirat al-Ghuzlan (Kerner 2003: 181, fig. 19:3–4, 11). Sherd 45 is of well-fired, limestone-tempered ware with a grey coating. It may represent the base of a Chalcolithic churn but is missing the characteristic vertical loop handle. Finally, Sherd 46 is a narrow base, perhaps from a Chalcolithic jar. It is also paralleled at Ḥujeirat al-Ghuzlan (Kerner 2003: 181, fig. 19:11).

Rujm aṭ-Ṭaba
(Site 152; figs. 6.7:47–6.8:58)

This is a small hamlet associated with the adjacent caravanserai (Site 153) of the same name. The surface ceramic collection was predominately Early Roman/Nabataean (including a few body sherds of Eastern Sigillata A and imported amphorae [Dressel 2–4/Peacock and Williams Class 10]) but also included some Late Roman and a few Early Byzantine sherds.

Sherds 47 and 51 illustrate two types of jars, both of evenly-fired, coarse, light red or pink ware and covered with a dark brown slip. Sherd 47 displays a slightly hooked rim, offset neck, and deep groove at the join between the neck and shoulder. It is paralleled at Oboda (Negev 1986: 117, no. 1014). Sherd 51 is a wide-mouthed jar with a strongly everted, thickened, triangular rim.

Sherd 48 illustrates a small jar in Nabataean fine ware. It exhibits a hooked rim and short, offset neck, the latter resulting in a raised ridge about halfway down the neck exterior. It may be compared to an example from Oboda (Negev 1986: 84, no. 675).

Sherds 49–50 apparently represent the rims of large kraters, both with short necks and complex, everted rims. Both are also of the typical pinkish or light red coarse ware and are covered with a dark brown slip. Sherd 49 also displays ribbing on its shoulder. The rim profile of this vessel is paralleled at Oboda (Negev 1986: 112, nos. 980–81), although Sherd 49 lacks the incised or thumb-impressions atop the rim that decorate the vessels from Oboda.

Sherd 52 is a shallow bowl of dark red ware. It displays a rounded rim and flat base. It may be a local imitation of an African Red Slip Form 50, the latter dated from the early 3rd through late 4th century (Hayes 1972: 68–73). Somewhat similar profiles are attested from Late Roman contexts at Petra (Fellmann Brogli 1996: 261, figs. 791, 793–94) and sites of the *Limes Arabicus* (Parker 2006: fig. 16.13:56–57).

A Nabataean hemispherical bowl with a slightly incurved rim is illustrated by Sherd 53. Of fine, light red ware, it exhibits a dark core. For parallels for this bowl see fig. 6.3:17 above. Sherds 54–55 are classic Nabataean fine ware carinated bowls. Sherd 54 displays the incurved rim, while Sherd 55 exhibits a nearly upright rim. For parallels for these bowls see fig. 6.5:33 above.

Sherd 56 is the rim of an Eastern Sigillata A bowl. It is an example of Hayes Form 60A, dated to ca. AD 100–150 (Hayes 1985: 40, pl. 7:13). This form is common at Aqaba and throughout the region, including at Petra (Schneider 1996: 146, fig. 564). Sherds 57–58 represent a rim sherd and body sherd of typical Nabataean painted fine ware bowls. Both examples are Schmid's Dekorphase 3a, dated ca. AD 20–70 (Schmid 1996: 207, figs. 699–700).

Site 167 *(figs. 6.8:59–6.9:72)*

This was an Early Roman/Nabataean settlement in the foothills of esh-Shera north of Wādī Nukheila. The pottery suggests continued occupation into the Late Roman and perhaps the beginning of the Early Byzantine period.

Sherds 59–64 represent various types of closed cooking pots. Sherds 59–60 display the typical triangular rim of the Early Roman/Nabataean period. For parallels see fig. 6.1:1–6 above. Sherd 61 displays a dark core and a dark brown slip on the exterior of the vessel. The unusual profile includes a groove on the interior of the rim and a groove at

Roman Aqaba Project: SAAS   **Site 152**

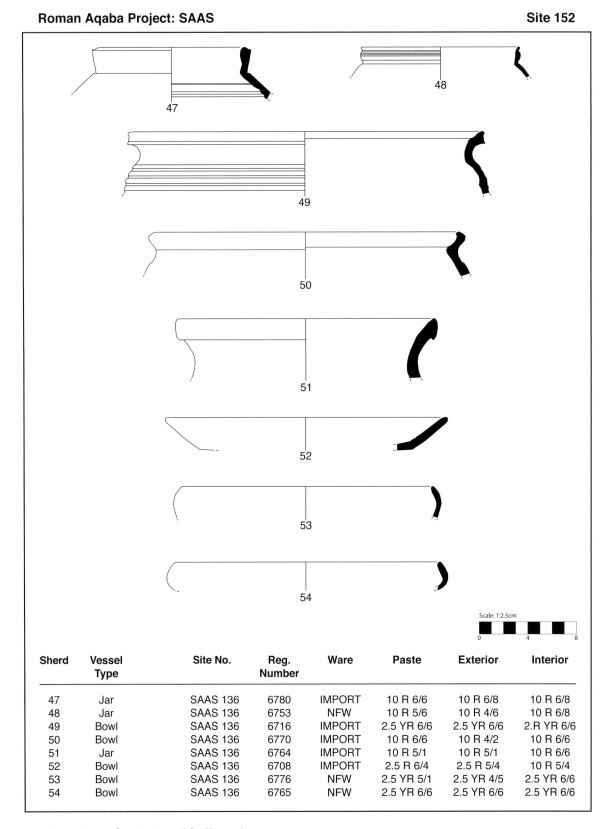

Sherd	Vessel Type	Site No.	Reg. Number	Ware	Paste	Exterior	Interior
47	Jar	SAAS 136	6780	IMPORT	10 R 6/6	10 R 6/8	10 R 6/8
48	Jar	SAAS 136	6753	NFW	10 R 5/6	10 R 4/6	10 R 6/8
49	Bowl	SAAS 136	6716	IMPORT	2.5 YR 6/6	2.5 YR 6/6	2.R YR 6/6
50	Bowl	SAAS 136	6770	IMPORT	10 R 6/6	10 R 4/2	10 R 6/6
51	Jar	SAAS 136	6764	IMPORT	10 R 5/1	10 R 5/1	10 R 6/6
52	Bowl	SAAS 136	6708	IMPORT	2.5 R 6/4	2.5 R 5/4	10 R 5/4
53	Bowl	SAAS 136	6776	NFW	2.5 YR 5/1	2.5 YR 4/5	2.5 YR 6/6
54	Bowl	SAAS 136	6765	NFW	2.5 YR 6/6	2.5 YR 6/6	2.5 YR 6/6

FIG. 6.7   *Pottery from Rujm aṭ-Ṭaba (Site 152).*

Roman Aqaba Project: SAAS **Site 152**

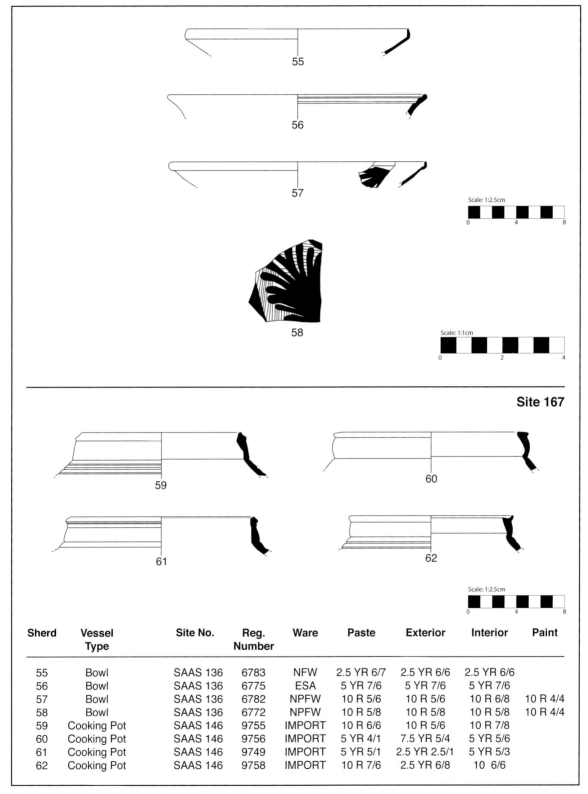

Site 167

Sherd	Vessel Type	Site No.	Reg. Number	Ware	Paste	Exterior	Interior	Paint
55	Bowl	SAAS 136	6783	NFW	2.5 YR 6/7	2.5 YR 6/6	2.5 YR 6/6	
56	Bowl	SAAS 136	6775	ESA	5 YR 7/6	5 YR 7/6	5 YR 7/6	
57	Bowl	SAAS 136	6782	NPFW	10 R 5/6	10 R 5/6	10 R 6/8	10 R 4/4
58	Bowl	SAAS 136	6772	NPFW	10 R 5/8	10 R 5/8	10 R 5/8	10 R 4/4
59	Cooking Pot	SAAS 146	9755	IMPORT	10 R 6/6	10 R 5/6	10 R 7/8	
60	Cooking Pot	SAAS 146	9756	IMPORT	5 YR 4/1	7.5 YR 5/4	5 YR 5/6	
61	Cooking Pot	SAAS 146	9749	IMPORT	5 YR 5/1	2.5 YR 2.5/1	5 YR 5/3	
62	Cooking Pot	SAAS 146	9758	IMPORT	10 R 7/6	2.5 YR 6/8	10 6/6	

FIG. 6.8 *Pottery from Rujm aṭ-Ṭaba (Site 152) and Pottery from Site 167.*

Roman Aqaba Project: SAAS　　　　　　　　　　　　　　　**Site 167**

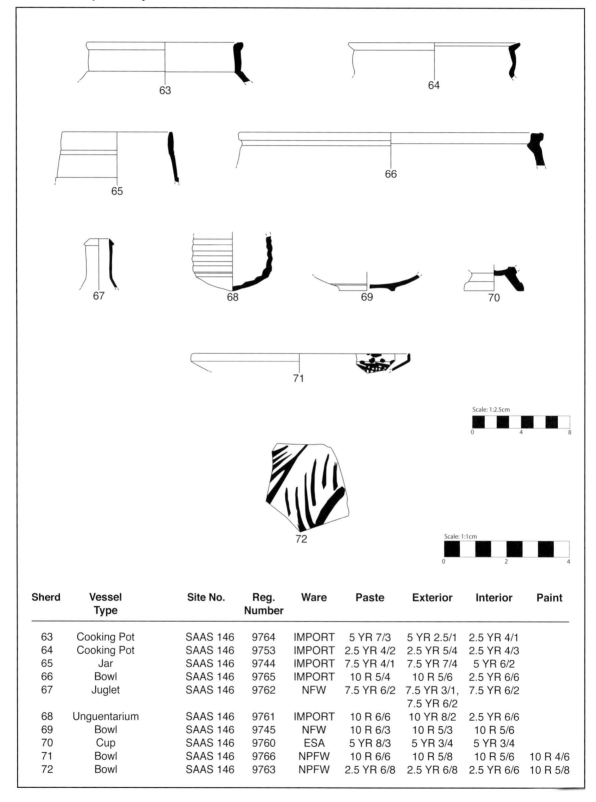

Sherd	Vessel Type	Site No.	Reg. Number	Ware	Paste	Exterior	Interior	Paint
63	Cooking Pot	SAAS 146	9764	IMPORT	5 YR 7/3	5 YR 2.5/1	2.5 YR 4/1	
64	Cooking Pot	SAAS 146	9753	IMPORT	2.5 YR 4/2	2.5 YR 5/4	2.5 YR 4/3	
65	Jar	SAAS 146	9744	IMPORT	7.5 YR 4/1	7.5 YR 7/4	5 YR 6/2	
66	Bowl	SAAS 146	9765	IMPORT	10 R 5/4	10 R 5/6	2.5 YR 6/6	
67	Juglet	SAAS 146	9762	NFW	7.5 YR 6/2	7.5 YR 3/1, 7.5 YR 6/2	7.5 YR 6/2	
68	Unguentarium	SAAS 146	9761	IMPORT	10 R 6/6	10 YR 8/2	2.5 YR 6/6	
69	Bowl	SAAS 146	9745	NFW	10 R 6/3	10 R 5/3	10 R 5/6	
70	Cup	SAAS 146	9760	ESA	5 YR 8/3	5 YR 3/4	5 YR 3/4	
71	Bowl	SAAS 146	9766	NPFW	10 R 6/6	10 R 5/8	10 R 5/6	10 R 4/6
72	Bowl	SAAS 146	9763	NPFW	2.5 YR 6/8	2.5 YR 6/8	2.5 YR 6/6	10 R 5/8

FIG. 6.9　　*Pottery from Site 167.*

the join between the neck and shoulder. Sherd 62 is of more typical light red ware but displays a shallow groove atop an elongated rim and offset neck. Parallels may be cited from a Late Roman context at Petra (Fellmann Brogli 1996: 249, figs. 755–56). Sherds 63–64 display the hooked rims and offset necks that seem to appear at the end of the Late Roman period (early 4th century). These are paralleled at sites of the *Limes Arabicus* (Parker 1987: fig. 107: 137; Parker 2006: figs. 16.42: 209–11, 16.49: 243) Amman (Zayadine 1977–78: fig. 22: 255, 311), Araq el-Emir (Brown 1984: fig. 56:111), Pella (Smith 1973: pl. 43:1294), and at Aqaba (unpublished, reg. nos. 3509, 5128).

Sherd 65 is a high-necked jar of relatively fine gray ware with a simple rounded rim, a groove under the rim exterior, and a raised ridge at the neck–shoulder join. It is paralleled at sites of the *Limes Arabicus* from Late Roman and Early Byzantine contexts (Parker 1987: figs. 98:64, 109:154–55; Parker 2006: fig. 16:18: 84) and in a Late Roman context at Aqaba (unpublished, reg. no. 83493). Similar profiles are also attested at Petra (Fellmann-Brogli 1996: 251–53, figs. 760–62), although these examples lack the raised ridge at the neck–shoulder join.

Sherd 66 is probably a krater of dark red ware that exhibits a dark core. The complex rim profile displays an interior ledge below the rim and a shallow groove atop the rim itself. A deeper groove is apparent below the rim exterior.

A high-necked juglet of fine gray ware is represented by Sherd 67. It displays a triangular rim. A possible parallel may be cited from a Late Roman context at Khirbet el-Fityān (Parker 1987: fig. 99:74).

Sherd 68 is the base of an *unguentarium*, which displays ribbing on the side wall and a slightly pointed base. It is of red ware and the exterior is covered by a tan slip. It may be compared to Johnson's Form 3 from Petra, dated to the early 1st century AD (Johnson 1990: 237, fig. 1: iii; cf. Murray and Ellis 1940: pl. 28:55).

Sherd 69 is the ring base of a Nabataean unpainted fine ware bowl. The preserved profile does not allow identifying the type of bowl.

Sherd 70 is the high ring base, probably of a cup, of Eastern Sigillata A. Unfortunately too little of the profile is preserved to assign it to a specific type.

Sherds 71–72 represent sherds from Nabataean painted fine ware bowls. Sherd 71 is a rim painted in Dekorphase 3a, dated ca. AD 20–70 (Schmid 1996: 207, figs. 699–700). Sherd 72 is a body sherd painted in Dekorphase 2b, dated ca. 30–1 BC (Schmid 1996: 205, fig. 695).

Bir Madhkur
(Site 329; figs. 6.10:73–6.14:116)

The site, a major caravan station just west of Petra in Wādī ʿAraba on the road to Gaza, yielded one of the richest collections of surface pottery from the survey, ranging from the Early Roman/Nabataean through Early Byzantine periods. Recent excavations of this site promise more important ceramic evidence (Smith 2005).

The Early Roman/Nabataean period is represented by Sherds 73–97. Sherds 73–75 represent various closed cooking pots of this period. Sherds 74–75 display the typical triangular rim. Sherd 74 exhibits a dark core while Sherd 75 is decorated with a white slip on the exterior of the vessel. For parallels, see fig. 6.1:1–6 above. Sherd 73 is of the usual red ware with the typical ribbed shoulder and vertical loop handles that are oval in section. But it displays a rather unusual rim that is more rounded in profile with two grooves under the rim exterior. Sherd 76 displays the collared rim, square in section, and incised with a shallow groove on its top that is closely paralleled by cooking pots from Aqaba (Dolinka 2003: 65, 121: no. 6). But the Aqaba examples display a more much pronounced carination at the neck–shoulder join, whereas Sherd 76 exhibits a smoother profile and may actually be a jar rather than a cooking pot. Close parallels may be cited from Petra (Murray and Ellis 1940: pl. 32: 129; Hammond 1965: pl. 58:21). Sherd 78 is the typical open cooking casserole of this period. The incurved profile displays a beveled rim to receive a lid. The ribbed exterior side wall is covered by a dark gray slip.

The closed profile of Sherd 77, perhaps a small jar, is also paralleled at Petra (Murray and Ellis 1940: pl. 26:23) and at Oboda (Negev 1986: 86, no. 697). Of typical Nabataean ware, it displays a dark core. Sherd 79 represents another small jar or perhaps a closed cooking pot of Nabataean

Roman Aqaba Project: SAAS   **Site 329** (Early Roman/ Nabataean)

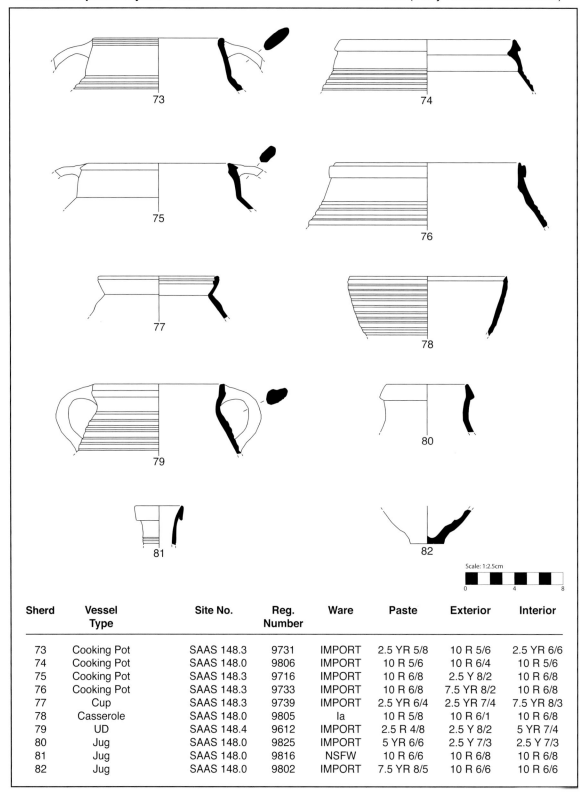

Scale: 1:2.5cm

Sherd	Vessel Type	Site No.	Reg. Number	Ware	Paste	Exterior	Interior
73	Cooking Pot	SAAS 148.3	9731	IMPORT	2.5 YR 5/8	10 R 5/6	2.5 YR 6/6
74	Cooking Pot	SAAS 148.0	9806	IMPORT	10 R 5/6	10 R 6/4	10 R 5/6
75	Cooking Pot	SAAS 148.3	9716	IMPORT	10 R 6/8	2.5 Y 8/2	10 R 6/8
76	Cooking Pot	SAAS 148.3	9733	IMPORT	10 R 6/8	7.5 YR 8/2	10 R 6/8
77	Cup	SAAS 148.3	9739	IMPORT	2.5 YR 6/4	2.5 YR 7/4	7.5 YR 8/3
78	Casserole	SAAS 148.0	9805	Ia	10 R 5/8	10 R 6/1	10 R 6/8
79	UD	SAAS 148.4	9612	IMPORT	2.5 R 4/8	2.5 Y 8/2	5 YR 7/4
80	Jug	SAAS 148.0	9825	IMPORT	5 YR 6/6	2.5 Y 7/3	2.5 Y 7/3
81	Jug	SAAS 148.0	9816	NSFW	10 R 6/6	10 R 6/8	10 R 6/8
82	Jug	SAAS 148.0	9802	IMPORT	7.5 YR 8/5	10 R 6/6	10 R 6/6

FIG. 6.10   *Pottery from Bir Madhkur (Site 329).*

Roman Aqaba Project: SAAS

Site 329 (Early Roman/ Nabataean)

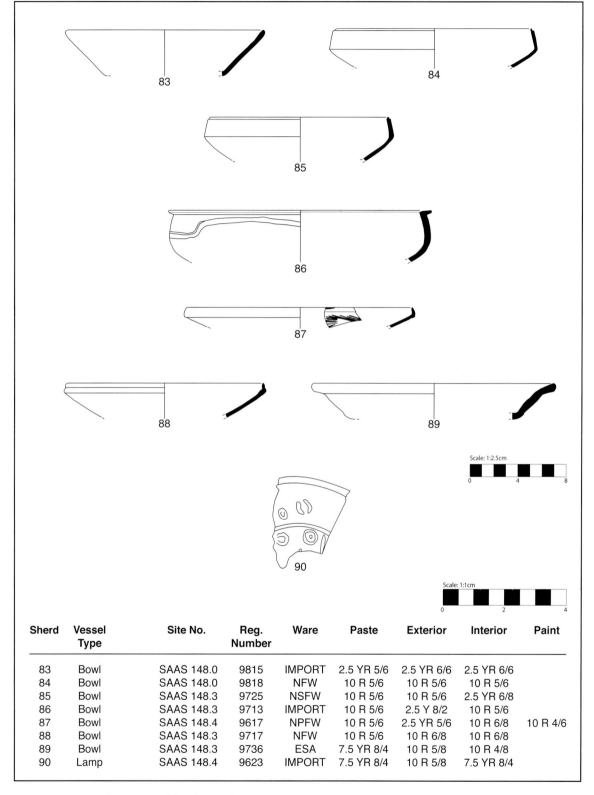

Scale: 1:2.5cm

Scale: 1:1cm

Sherd	Vessel Type	Site No.	Reg. Number	Ware	Paste	Exterior	Interior	Paint
83	Bowl	SAAS 148.0	9815	IMPORT	2.5 YR 5/6	2.5 YR 6/6	2.5 YR 6/6	
84	Bowl	SAAS 148.0	9818	NFW	10 R 5/6	10 R 5/6	10 R 5/6	
85	Bowl	SAAS 148.3	9725	NSFW	10 R 5/6	10 R 5/6	2.5 YR 6/8	
86	Bowl	SAAS 148.3	9713	IMPORT	10 R 5/6	2.5 Y 8/2	10 R 5/6	
87	Bowl	SAAS 148.4	9617	NPFW	10 R 5/6	2.5 YR 5/6	10 R 6/8	10 R 4/6
88	Bowl	SAAS 148.3	9717	NFW	10 R 5/6	10 R 6/8	10 R 6/8	
89	Bowl	SAAS 148.3	9736	ESA	7.5 YR 8/4	10 R 5/8	10 R 4/8	
90	Lamp	SAAS 148.4	9623	IMPORT	7.5 YR 8/4	10 R 5/8	7.5 YR 8/4	

FIG. 6.11 *Pottery from Bir Madhkur (Site 329).*

Roman Aqaba Project: SAAS   **Site 329** (Late Roman)

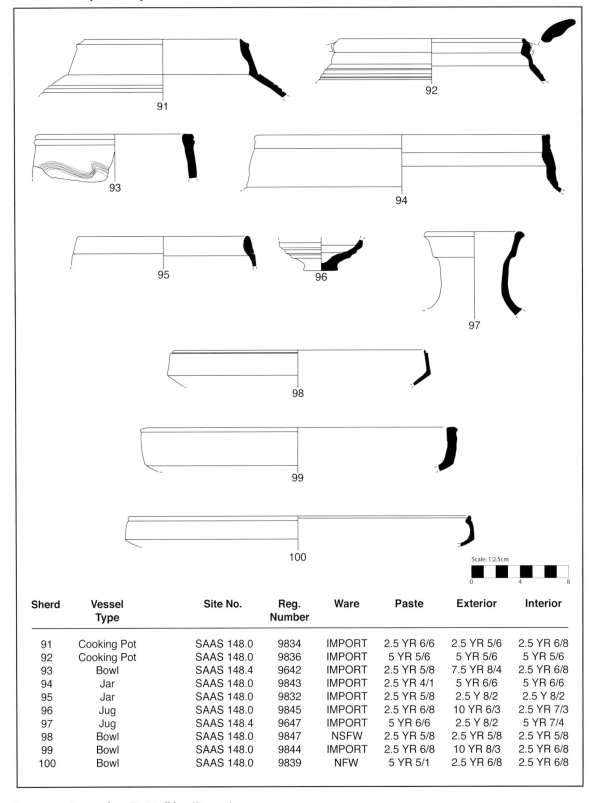

Sherd	Vessel Type	Site No.	Reg. Number	Ware	Paste	Exterior	Interior
91	Cooking Pot	SAAS 148.0	9834	IMPORT	2.5 YR 6/6	2.5 YR 5/6	2.5 YR 6/8
92	Cooking Pot	SAAS 148.0	9836	IMPORT	5 YR 5/6	5 YR 5/6	5 YR 5/6
93	Bowl	SAAS 148.4	9642	IMPORT	2.5 YR 5/8	7.5 YR 8/4	2.5 YR 6/8
94	Jar	SAAS 148.0	9843	IMPORT	2.5 YR 4/1	5 YR 6/6	5 YR 6/6
95	Jar	SAAS 148.0	9832	IMPORT	2.5 YR 5/8	2.5 Y 8/2	2.5 Y 8/2
96	Jug	SAAS 148.0	9845	IMPORT	2.5 YR 6/8	10 YR 6/3	2.5 YR 7/3
97	Jug	SAAS 148.4	9647	IMPORT	5 YR 6/6	2.5 Y 8/2	5 YR 7/4
98	Bowl	SAAS 148.0	9847	NSFW	2.5 YR 5/8	2.5 YR 5/8	2.5 YR 5/8
99	Bowl	SAAS 148.0	9844	IMPORT	2.5 YR 6/8	10 YR 8/3	2.5 YR 6/8
100	Bowl	SAAS 148.0	9839	NFW	5 YR 5/1	2.5 YR 6/8	2.5 YR 6/8

FIG. 6.12   *Pottery from Bir Madhkur (Site 329).*

coarse ware. If in fact a cooking pot, it displays no evidence of charring. A white slip is confined to the exterior surface. It exhibits an offset neck, a raised ridge around the neck, and a ribbed shoulder. Of similar ware and slip is Sherd 80, a jug with a folded, triangular rim and short neck. The form is paralleled at Petra (Murray and Ellis 1940: pl. 9: 41) and Oboda (Negev 1986: 117, no. 1017). Sherd 81 is a jug of finer ware but with a darker core. It displays an everted, folded, triangular rim with fine ribbing on its neck. The string-cut base of a small jug is represented by Sherd 82. Of red ware, it also displays a dark core. String-cut bases on such vessels are common in the Nabatean ceramic repertoire and are attested at such sites as Dhiban (Tushingham 1972: fig. 2:51) and Petra (Murray and Ellis 1940: pl. 26: 35).

Sherds 83–89 represent various bowls from the Early Roman/Nabataean period. Sherd 83 is a shallow bowl with a simple rounded rim and, apparently, a flat base. It is of relatively fine reddish-brown ware with a dark core. A thin band of white slip is visible just below the rim exterior. A possible parallel may be cited from Dhiban (Tushingham 1972: fig. 3:2). Sherds 84–85 are the classic Nabataean carinated fine ware bowls with grooved or notched rims, typically dated to the late 1st to early 2nd century AD. These bowls typically rested on a ring base, although not preserved on these examples. These two bowls lack the characteristic rouletting on the exterior side wall as attested elsewhere, including examples from Petra (Schmid 1996: 189, fig. 663) and Aqaba (unpublished, reg. #51247). Numerous parallels may be cited from various sites, including Aqaba (Dolinka 2003: 134: nos. 31–32), Petra (Murray and Ellis 1940: pls. 9:2, 4, 31:116, 118; Schmid 2000: 9, figs. 62–63), and Oboda (Negev 1986: 67, nos. 511, 513). Sherd 86, of typical Nabataean red coarse ware, is a shallow bowl with a flattened, flanged rim. It is decorated by a white slip on the exterior only and an incised wavy line along the exterior side wall. The basic form is paralleled at a number of sites, including Petra (Murray and Ellis 1940: pls. 29:96–97, 31:126) and Oboda (Negev 1986: 90, no. 746). Some published examples display twin vertical loop handles extending from the rim (e.g., Murray and Ellis 1940: pl. 31:124), although such a handle is not visible on the preserved portion of Sherd 86.

Sherd 87 is a fragment of a carinated bowl of Nabataean painted fine ware. The painted design is probably either Schmid's Dekorphase 2b or 2c, i.e., from the late 1st century BC or the early 1st century AD (Schmid 1996: 205). An example of the ubiquitous Nabataean carinated bowl of unpainted fine ware is represented by Sherd 88. It displays a groove under the rim that is paralleled at Petra (Murray and Ellis 1940: pl. 28:67, Schmid 1996: 187, figs. 656–57), Mampsis (Negev and Sivan 1977: 126, fig. 7:51), Sbaita (Crowfoot 1936: pl. I), and other sites.

Sherd 89 is an Eastern Sigillata A bowl rim. It is best classified as a Hayes Form 57, a common type throughout the region and dated to the first half of the 2nd century AD (Hayes 1985: 39). Several examples are attested at Petra (Schneider 1996: 135, 146: fig. 563), and at least eight examples were recovered at Aqaba (unpublished).

Completing this Early Roman/Nabataean group from the site is Sherd 90, a Nabataean mold-made lamp. A possible parallel may be cited from Petra (Zanoni 1996: 331, fig. 903; Grawher 2006: 297–98).

Sherds 91–107 depict sherds primarily from the Late Roman period. Sherds 91–92 are the typical closed cooking pots from the beginning of this period. They are of Nabataean red coarse ware with a thin dark core. The exterior is covered by a white slip. It displays the typical triangular but slightly grooved rim, offset neck, and groove at the join of the neck with the shoulder, which is lightly ribbed. The section of the rim of Sherd 92 is partly obscured in the drawing by a remnant of the attachment for a vertical loop handle. For parallels, see those cited for fig. 6.1:1–6 above, but especially close examples for Sherd 91 are attested at Petra (Gerber 2001: 360, fig. 1:13) and for Sherd 92 from the same site (Murray and Ellis 1940: pl. 30:102).

Sherds 93–97 represent various jugs and jars, all of coarse ware. Sherd 93 is a high-necked jar of evenly-fired, pinkish red ware decorated with a white slip over its exterior surface. Its profile displays a thickened rim, deeply grooved on the exterior. The neck below the groove is decorated by a band of wavy combing, paralleled on jars from Petra (Fellmann-Brogli 1996: 253, fig. 764). Sherd 94 is a jar or cooking pot of darker red ware with a thick dark core. Its folded, grooved rim appears rectangular in profile. Parallels may be noted from Petra (Murray

Roman Aqaba Project: SAAS   **Site 329** (Late Roman)

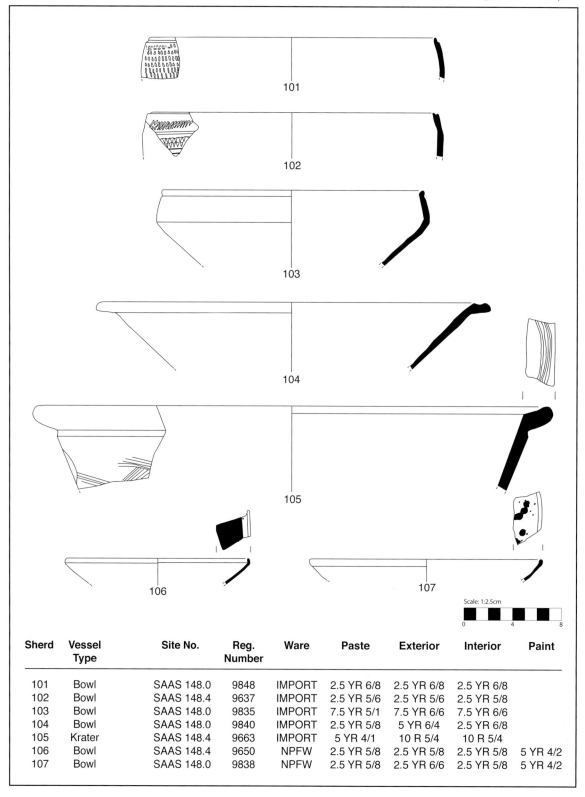

Sherd	Vessel Type	Site No.	Reg. Number	Ware	Paste	Exterior	Interior	Paint
101	Bowl	SAAS 148.0	9848	IMPORT	2.5 YR 6/8	2.5 YR 6/8	2.5 YR 6/8	
102	Bowl	SAAS 148.4	9637	IMPORT	2.5 YR 5/6	2.5 YR 5/6	2.5 YR 5/8	
103	Bowl	SAAS 148.0	9835	IMPORT	7.5 YR 5/1	7.5 YR 6/6	7.5 YR 6/6	
104	Bowl	SAAS 148.0	9840	IMPORT	2.5 YR 5/8	5 YR 6/4	2.5 YR 6/8	
105	Krater	SAAS 148.4	9663	IMPORT	5 YR 4/1	10 R 5/4	10 R 5/4	
106	Bowl	SAAS 148.4	9650	NPFW	2.5 YR 5/8	2.5 YR 5/8	2.5 YR 5/8	5 YR 4/2
107	Bowl	SAAS 148.0	9838	NPFW	2.5 YR 5/8	2.5 YR 6/6	2.5 YR 5/8	5 YR 4/2

FIG. 6.13   *Pottery from Bir Madhkur (Site 329).*

and Ellis 1940: pl. 32:129; Hammond 1965: pl. 58:21). Another jar with a folded rim and groove under the rim is depicted by Sherd 95. It is of evenly-fired coarse red ware and is decorated with a white slip on both the exterior and interior surfaces. Similar jars are attested at Petra (Fellmann-Brogli 1996: 251–53, figs. 760–62). Sherd 96 is the string-cut base of a small vessel, perhaps a small pot, jug, or juglet. The lower side walls display deep, angular ribbing. For published parallels see figs. 6.1:7 and 6.10:82 above. Sherd 97 represents a jug of pinkish coarse ware with a white slip over the exterior of the vessel. The everted rim is slightly hooked and a raised ridge is visible on the neck. Although no handle is preserved, a break in the surface of the sherd suggests that a vertical loop handle once attached to the neck at the raised ridge and probably extended to the shoulder of the vessel. A parallel may be cited from Petra (Fellmann Brogli 1996: 265, fig. 821).

Sherds 98–107 depict various open forms, mostly bowls, from the Late Roman period at this site. Sherds 98 and 100–103 represent the classic Nabataean carinated bowls of fine ware with grooved or notched rims, mostly from the beginning of this period, i.e., the early 2nd century. Some of these bowls exhibit dark cores (e.g., Sherds 100 and 103), while the others appear to be evenly fired. Two of these carinated bowls exhibit the characteristic rouletting on the exterior side wall, while the others lack this decorative feature. Parallels for the rouletted examples may be cited from Aqaba (Dolinka 2003: 134, nos. 31–32), Petra (Murray and Ellis 1940: pls. 9:2, 4, 31:116, 118; Schmid 2000: 9, figs. 62–63), and Oboda (Negev 1986: 67, nos. 511, 513), while similar bowls lacking rouletting are attested at Petra (Schmid 1996: 189, fig. 663) and Aqaba (unpublished, reg. #51247). Sherd 104 represents a large open bowl with an elongated and deeply grooved rim. Of characteristic reddish ware, it displays a white slip only on the lip and underside of its rim. The form is attested at Petra (Fellmann Brogli 1996: 260, figs. 788–89). Sherd 105 is a large bowl or krater of coarse red ware. It exhibits a thick dark core that reaches the surface of a portion of the interior of the vessel. The rim is elongated and flattened and decorated with a band of combing; additional combing is visible on the exterior side wall. There is a shallow

groove at the join between the rim and the exterior side wall. The basic form and decorative combing both atop the rim and on the exterior side wall is paralleled at Petra (Fellmann Brogli 1996: 260, fig. 790). Finally, Sherds 106–7 represent Nabataean painted fine ware bowls. Both display the very dark brown or even black paint characteristic of the late Nabataean painted tradition. Both of these sherds seemingly correspond to Schmid's Dekorphase 3c, or the first half of the 2nd century (Schmid 1996: 209, figs. 702–3) and are also paralleled at Aqaba (Dolinka 2003: 136, no. 35).

Sherds 108–16 from Bir Madhkur date primarily to the Early Byzantine period. Sherd 108 represents a typical closed cooking pot from this period. It is of dark reddish-brown ware and covered with a dark gray slip. The shoulder is ribbed. The triangular rim of the Roman period has evolved into a more rounded, grooved rim. The profile is paralleled from this period at Petra (Fellmann Brogli 1996: 244, figs. 734–35), where it appears as early as the 3rd century (Gerber 2001: 360, fig. 1:20). Sherd 109 is a jar with an incurved, folded rim and a deep groove under the rim. This form is also paralleled at Petra (Fellmann Brogli 1996: 251–52, figs. 760–61) and at Da'jāniya (Parker 2006: fig. 16.68:335). Sherd 110 may be the rim and neck of a flue pipe, possibly from the putative bath house identified at this site. The form is paralleled from 4th-century contexts at el-Lejjūn (Parker 2006: fig. 16.80:384–85). Of special importance is the rim and handle of an Egyptian amphora, depicted by Sherd 111. Of dark reddish brown ware, it corresponds to Peacock and Williams Class 53 (Peacock and Williams 1986: 206–7). This amphora is also common at Aqaba, where Egyptian amphorae predominated in the Byzantine period.

Sherds 112–15 represent various bowls from this period. Sherd 112 is a large bowl of dark red ware, covered in a gray slip. The rim is deeply grooved. Sherds 113–14 are both wide, shallow bowls of nearly identical diameter with slightly thickened, rounded rims. Both are of hard-fired, pinkish red ware and decorated with a white slip that covers the interior surface, the entire rim, and extends slightly below the exterior of the rim. Similar bowls are attested at Petra (Fellmann-Brogli 1996: 261, figs. 793–94), el-Lejjūn (Parker

Roman Aqaba Project: SAAS　　　　　　　　**Site 329** (Early Byzantine)

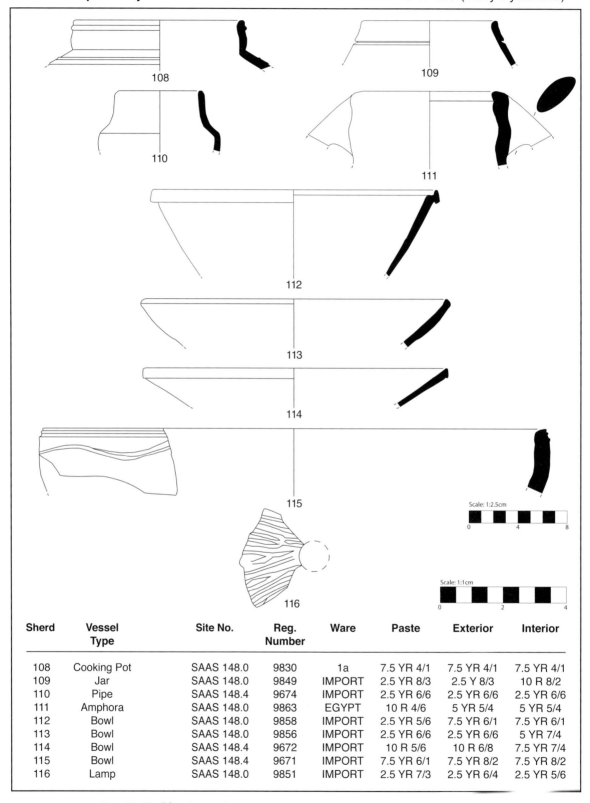

Sherd	Vessel Type	Site No.	Reg. Number	Ware	Paste	Exterior	Interior
108	Cooking Pot	SAAS 148.0	9830	1a	7.5 YR 4/1	7.5 YR 4/1	7.5 YR 4/1
109	Jar	SAAS 148.0	9849	IMPORT	2.5 YR 8/3	2.5 Y 8/3	10 R 8/2
110	Pipe	SAAS 148.4	9674	IMPORT	2.5 YR 6/6	2.5 YR 6/6	2.5 YR 6/6
111	Amphora	SAAS 148.0	9863	EGYPT	10 R 4/6	5 YR 5/4	5 YR 5/4
112	Bowl	SAAS 148.0	9858	IMPORT	2.5 YR 5/6	7.5 YR 6/1	7.5 YR 6/1
113	Bowl	SAAS 148.0	9856	IMPORT	2.5 YR 6/6	2.5 YR 6/6	5 YR 7/4
114	Bowl	SAAS 148.4	9672	IMPORT	10 R 5/6	10 R 6/8	7.5 YR 7/4
115	Bowl	SAAS 148.4	9671	IMPORT	7.5 YR 6/1	7.5 YR 8/2	7.5 YR 8/2
116	Lamp	SAAS 148.0	9851	IMPORT	2.5 YR 7/3	2.5 YR 6/4	2.5 YR 5/6

FIG. 6.14　*Pottery from Bir Madhkur (Site 329).*

2006: fig. 16.40:202), and Daʿjāniya (Parker 2006: fig. 16.68:341). The last of these vessels is Sherd 115, a large bowl of dark reddish ware exhibiting a dark core. A light gray slip covers both the interior and exterior side wall; the latter is also decorated by an incised wavy line. The rim is flattened and displays two grooves below the exterior of the rim. A somewhat similar profile, although lacking the incised wavy line, may be cited from el-Lejjūn (Parker 1987: 579, fig. 104:113). Finally, Sherd 116 is a fragment of a Byzantine mold-made lamp of pinkish ware, displaying the characteristic rays surrounding the central fill-hole (partially reconstructed in the drawing). This is a well-known type attested at many sites in central and southern Jordan, including el-Lejjūn (Parker 1987: 616, fig. 123:232–39; Parker 2006: figs. 16.72:358–61, 16.73:363, 365, 368), Petra (Zanoni 1996: 331–33, figs. 910–18, 933–34; Grawehr 2006: 345–46, figs. 504–6), and many other sites (cf. Parker 2006: 345–46 for additional parallels).

Site 330 *(fig. 6.15:117–19)*

This site includes a watchtower, other possible structures, and a cemetery. The small group of three sherds presented here dates to the Late Roman and Early Byzantine periods. Sherd 117 is the classic Late Roman closed cooking pot with a grooved rim. The light pinkish ware is covered by a light brown slip on the exterior surface only. For parallels see the discussion of Sherd 8 above. Sherd 118 is a typical Early Byzantine closed cooking pot of pinkish ware and covered by a dark brown slip only on the exterior surface. The profile displays an offset neck and hooked rim. For parallels see Sherd 31 above. A large shallow bowl of the Early Byzantine period is depicted by Sherd 119. Of light red ware, it is decorated with a white slip that covers only the rim of the vessel. For parallels see Sherds 113–14 above.

Qasr Wādī eṭ-Ṭayyiba
(Site 319; fig. 6.15:120–26)

The pottery collected from the surface of this fortlet was overwhelmingly Early Roman/Nabataean, with a few later sherds. Sherd 120 is a closed cook-

ing pot of coarse, dark red ware, rich with white mineral inclusions. The surface is covered with a dark gray slip. The vertical loop handle extends from the rim to the ribbed shoulder. There is a slight groove on the inside of the slightly bulbous rim. The morphology is paralleled by an example from Es-Sadeh (Lindner 1988:91, fig. 9:8). Sherd 121 represents either a wide-mouthed closed cooking pot or possibly a jar of the Early Roman/Nabataean period. Of typical red ware, the section exhibits a dark core. The exterior surface displays a white slip. A hooked rim rises above an offset neck. The form is paralleled at Oboda (Negev 1986: 110, no. 956), and a similar wide-mouthed vessel may be cited as a possible parallel from Petra (Murray and Ellis 1940: pl. 30:101). Sherd 122 illustrates the more typical Early Roman/Nabataean closed cooking pot with triangular rim and offset neck. For parallels, see the discussion of Sherds 1–6 above. A jug of Nabataean semi-fine ware is represented by Sherd 123. A small ledge is visible just below the interior of the rim and the neck is decorated by a shallow groove just below the exterior of the rim. The form may be compared to a jug from Petra (Schmid 2000: fig. 287).

The published ceramic corpus from this site is completed by three classic Nabataean carinated bowls of unpainted fine ware, represented by Sherds 124–26. Among the numerous parallels are examples from Petra (Murray and Ellis 1940: pl. 8:1–3, 7–22, 25:2, 29:85; Hammond 1965: pl. 59:1–13; Schmid 2000: 8, figs. 49–56) and many other sites.

Tell el-Kheleifeh
(Site 29; figs. 6.16:127–6.19:147)

This important Iron Age site, now situated ca. 500 m north of the Red Sea coast on the modern Jordanian–Israeli border, witnessed important excavations by Nelson Glueck in 1938–1940. Glueck never published a final report, leading to a re-examination and some significant reinterpretations of his material by Pratico, who published a large corpus of Glueck's pottery (Pratico 1985: 35–63). The present project collected more than 800 sherds from the surface of the site in 1996, in part as a comparative collection to aid in identification of Iron Age and Persian period pottery that might appear elsewhere

Roman Aqaba Project: SAAS   **Site 330**

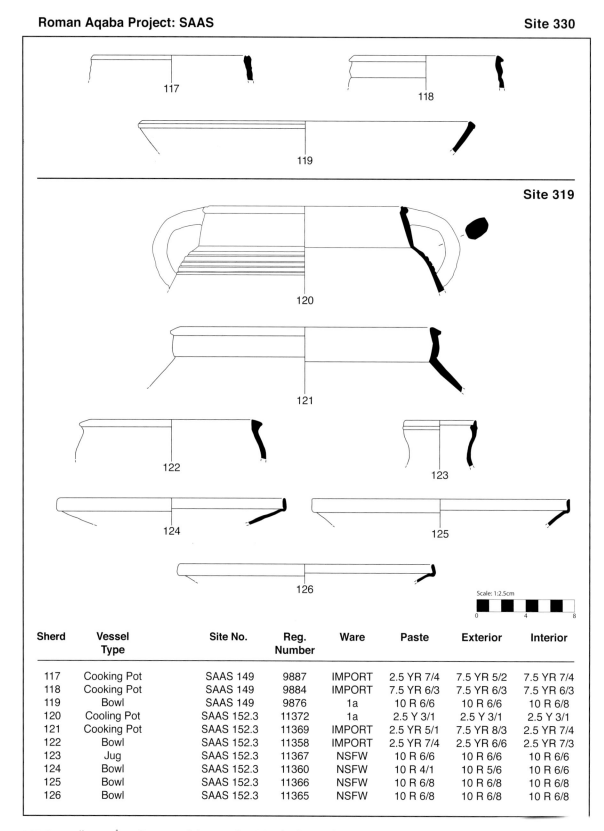

Sherd	Vessel Type	Site No.	Reg. Number	Ware	Paste	Exterior	Interior
117	Cooking Pot	SAAS 149	9887	IMPORT	2.5 YR 7/4	7.5 YR 5/2	7.5 YR 7/4
118	Cooking Pot	SAAS 149	9884	IMPORT	7.5 YR 6/3	7.5 YR 6/3	7.5 YR 6/3
119	Bowl	SAAS 149	9876	1a	10 R 6/6	10 R 6/6	10 R 6/8
120	Cooling Pot	SAAS 152.3	11372	1a	2.5 Y 3/1	2.5 Y 3/1	2.5 Y 3/1
121	Cooking Pot	SAAS 152.3	11369	IMPORT	2.5 YR 5/1	7.5 YR 8/3	2.5 YR 7/4
122	Bowl	SAAS 152.3	11358	IMPORT	2.5 YR 7/4	2.5 YR 6/6	2.5 YR 7/3
123	Jug	SAAS 152.3	11367	NSFW	10 R 6/6	10 R 6/6	10 R 6/6
124	Bowl	SAAS 152.3	11360	NSFW	10 R 4/1	10 R 5/6	10 R 6/6
125	Bowl	SAAS 152.3	11366	NSFW	10 R 6/8	10 R 6/8	10 R 6/8
126	Bowl	SAAS 152.3	11365	NSFW	10 R 6/8	10 R 6/8	10 R 6/8

FIG. 6.15   *Pottery from Site 330 and Qasr Wādī eṭ-Ṭayyiba (Site 319).*

Roman Aqaba Project: SAAS

Site 29

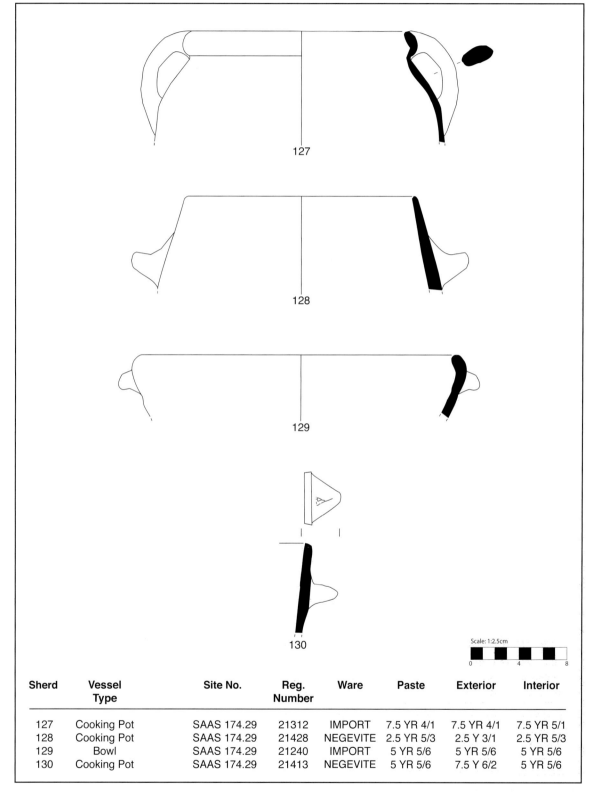

Sherd	Vessel Type	Site No.	Reg. Number	Ware	Paste	Exterior	Interior
127	Cooking Pot	SAAS 174.29	21312	IMPORT	7.5 YR 4/1	7.5 YR 4/1	7.5 YR 5/1
128	Cooking Pot	SAAS 174.29	21428	NEGEVITE	2.5 YR 5/3	2.5 Y 3/1	2.5 YR 5/3
129	Bowl	SAAS 174.29	21240	IMPORT	5 YR 5/6	5 YR 5/6	5 YR 5/6
130	Cooking Pot	SAAS 174.29	21413	NEGEVITE	5 YR 5/6	7.5 Y 6/2	5 YR 5/6

FIG. 6.16 *Pottery from Tell el-Kheleifeh (Site 29).*

Roman Aqaba Project: SAAS   **Site 29**

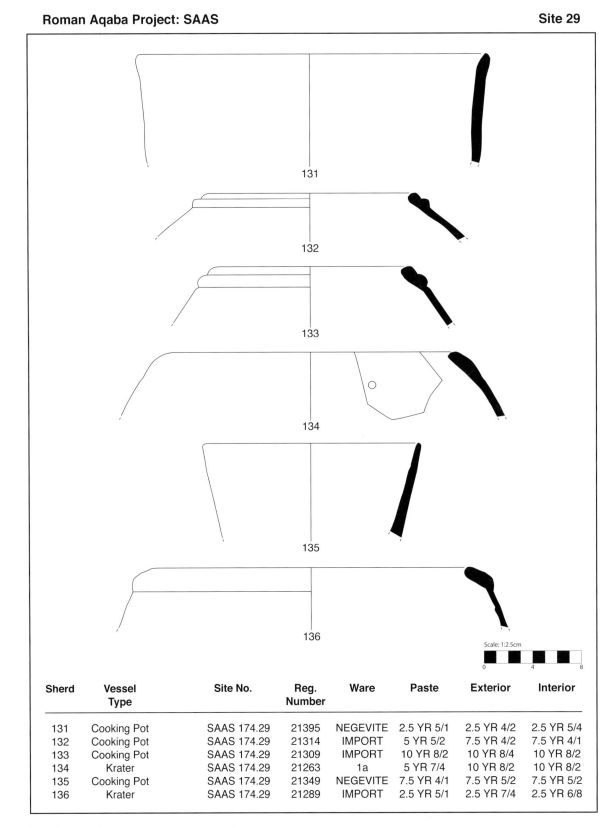

Sherd	Vessel Type	Site No.	Reg. Number	Ware	Paste	Exterior	Interior
131	Cooking Pot	SAAS 174.29	21395	NEGEVITE	2.5 YR 5/1	2.5 YR 4/2	2.5 YR 5/4
132	Cooking Pot	SAAS 174.29	21314	IMPORT	5 YR 5/2	7.5 YR 4/2	7.5 YR 4/1
133	Cooking Pot	SAAS 174.29	21309	IMPORT	10 YR 8/2	10 YR 8/4	10 YR 8/2
134	Krater	SAAS 174.29	21263	1a	5 YR 7/4	10 YR 8/2	10 YR 8/2
135	Cooking Pot	SAAS 174.29	21349	NEGEVITE	7.5 YR 4/1	7.5 YR 5/2	7.5 YR 5/2
136	Krater	SAAS 174.29	21289	IMPORT	2.5 YR 5/1	2.5 YR 7/4	2.5 YR 6/8

FIG. 6.17   *Pottery from Tell el-Kheleifeh (Site 29).*

on the survey. Thus it was rather surprising that, despite having this material in-hand, the project's own regional survey recovered almost no other Iron Age or Persian pottery. Nevertheless, it seems useful to present a small sample of the project's own surface ceramic collection from Kheleifeh. Given Pratico's previously published ceramic study, which included numerous published parallels, there is only a limited analysis of the sample presented here. A couple of fragments of Aegean amphorae (see below) suggest limited occupation continuing into the early Hellenistic period.

Sherd 127 is a closed cooking pot, most comparable to Pratico's "Grooved Rim Cooking Pot with Necks" (Pratico 1985: 39, 108, pls. 18:7–10, 19:1–4), dated on the basis of published parallels to the Iron II period and distinguishable from the more common "Edomite Cooking Pots."

Sherds 128, 130–31, 135, and 143 represent the so-called "Straight-Walled Cooking Pot" in the typical coarse hand-made "Negevite Ware." Pratico describes these as the most common type of vessel in Negevite ware at Kheleifeh (Pratico 1985: 37–38). All these vessels display a simple rounded rim. Sherds 128 and 130 include a lug handle attached to the side wall. There are clear traces of charring on the side wall below the rim of all these vessels. Close parallels may be cited for these cooking pots (Pratico 1985: 88, pl. 11:1–6, 90, pl. 12:1–10).

All the remaining pottery presented here was wheel-thrown. The more open form illustrated by Sherd 129 is red-slipped with an incurved rim and horizontal lug handles. It seems to lack close published parallels but is likely a bowl.

Sherds 132–33 depict the so-called "Edomite cooking pots," characterized by "a deeply grooved rim that is basically rectangular in section," lacking a neck, and with twin vertical loop handles. The form is paralleled primarily in central and southern Jordan and is generally dated to the late Iron II period, i.e., the 7th century BC and later (Pratico 1985: 38–39). Close parallels for these examples have previously been published from Kheleifeh (Pratico 1985: 103–9, pls. 16–18:1–6).

Sherds 134, 136, and 144 depict the rims of large kraters with incurved rims. Sherds 134 and 136 are of coarse ware and covered with a white slip. The former sherd has a simple rounded rim with a cir-

cular hole drilled through its side wall, apparently after firing. The latter has a thickened rim resulting in a raised ridge just below the rim exterior. The krater depicted by Sherd 144 differs markedly in ware, which is light red ware with a dark core and traces of a white slip. The thickened rim is almost triangular in section with a deep groove under the rim. Published parallels for Sherds 136 and 144 often include twin vertical loop handles extending from the rim down the side wall (Pratico 1985: 118–23, pls. 22–24).

Sherds 137–42 illustrate various jugs and jars. Sherd 137 appears to be a juglet fired in a reducing atmosphere, resulting in a dark gray fabric. The handle springs from the shoulder and likely extended to the rim, where traces of a handle attachment are visible (for published parallels, see Practico 1985: 141–43, pl. 30:2, 8). Sherd 138 is a jug or jar decorated with horizontal bands of dark gray paint, sometimes described as "Edomite." Pratico reported similar painted juglets among Glueck's pottery drawings, but the actual vessels could not be located (Pratico 1985: 45). He did publish other ceramic vessels with similar painted designs from the site (Practico 1985: pls. 27:10–12, 37:8–12). A wide range of vessels painted in this style has also been published from Tawilan (Hart 1995: 53–66) and other sites. Sherd 139 is a narrow-necked jar with an everted and deeply grooved rim. The pinkish ware contains large white mineral inclusions and is covered with a light red slip. Sherds 140–42 comprise a group of jars in light brown or cream ware covered with a white slip. All display thickened, slightly everted rims and a narrow groove incised near the join between the neck and shoulder. These vessels seem to lack published parallels from Kheleifeh, but similar jugs and jars are attested at Tawilan (Hart 1995: 251, fig. 28:6; 255, fig. 30:3, 14).

Sherds 145–46 represent two bowls from this site. The former sherd is of evenly-fired, light gray ware with a white slip. The open profile includes a thickened, rounded rim, a wide groove under the exterior of the rim, and a raised ridge below the groove. The latter is of pinkish ware surrounding a dark core and is also covered with a white slip. The flaring rounded rim and carinated profile is closely paralleled by published material from Kheleifeh

Roman Aqaba Project: SAAS   **Site 29**

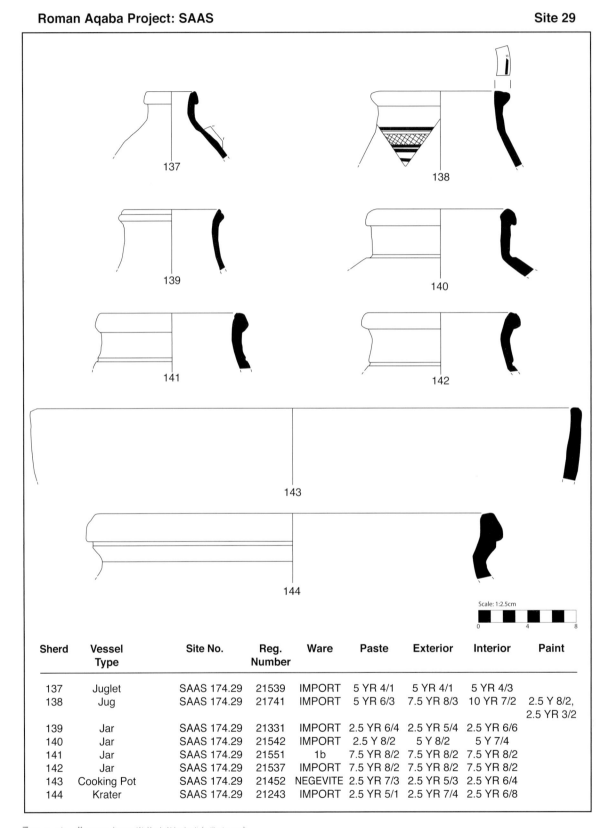

Sherd	Vessel Type	Site No.	Reg. Number	Ware	Paste	Exterior	Interior	Paint
137	Juglet	SAAS 174.29	21539	IMPORT	5 YR 4/1	5 YR 4/1	5 YR 4/3	
138	Jug	SAAS 174.29	21741	IMPORT	5 YR 6/3	7.5 YR 8/3	10 YR 7/2	2.5 Y 8/2, 2.5 YR 3/2
139	Jar	SAAS 174.29	21331	IMPORT	2.5 YR 6/4	2.5 YR 5/4	2.5 YR 6/6	
140	Jar	SAAS 174.29	21542	IMPORT	2.5 Y 8/2	5 Y 8/2	5 Y 7/4	
141	Jar	SAAS 174.29	21551	1b	7.5 YR 8/2	7.5 YR 8/2	7.5 YR 8/2	
142	Jar	SAAS 174.29	21537	IMPORT	7.5 YR 8/2	7.5 YR 8/2	7.5 YR 8/2	
143	Cooking Pot	SAAS 174.29	21452	NEGEVITE	2.5 YR 7/3	2.5 YR 5/3	2.5 YR 6/4	
144	Krater	SAAS 174.29	21243	IMPORT	2.5 YR 5/1	2.5 YR 7/4	2.5 YR 6/8	

FIG. 6.18   *Pottery from Tell el-Kheleifeh (Site 29).*

Roman Aqaba Project: SAAS   **Site 29**

Site 313

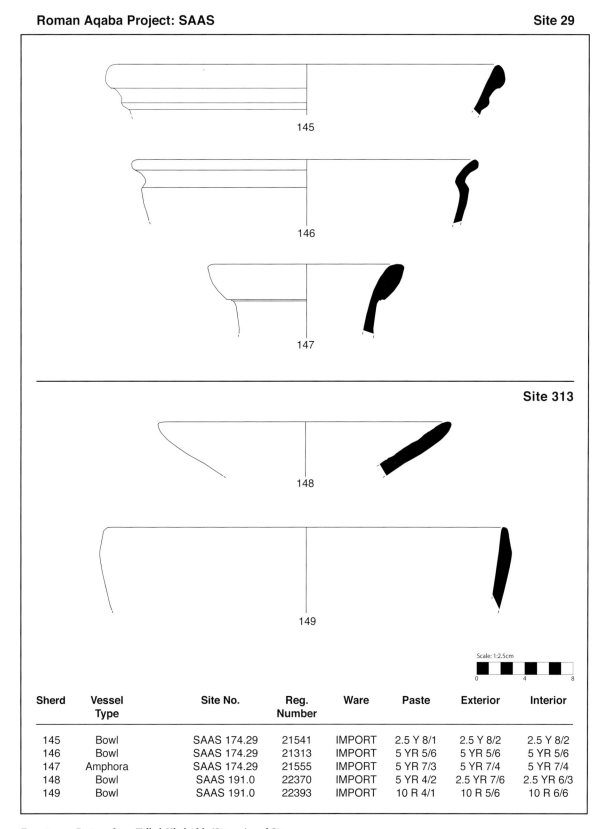

Sherd	Vessel Type	Site No.	Reg. Number	Ware	Paste	Exterior	Interior
145	Bowl	SAAS 174.29	21541	IMPORT	2.5 Y 8/1	2.5 Y 8/2	2.5 Y 8/2
146	Bowl	SAAS 174.29	21313	IMPORT	5 YR 5/6	5 YR 5/6	5 YR 5/6
147	Amphora	SAAS 174.29	21555	IMPORT	5 YR 7/3	5 YR 7/4	5 YR 7/4
148	Bowl	SAAS 191.0	22370	IMPORT	5 YR 4/2	2.5 YR 7/6	2.5 YR 6/3
149	Bowl	SAAS 191.0	22393	IMPORT	10 R 4/1	10 R 5/6	10 R 6/6

FIG. 6.19 *Pottery from Tell el-Kheleifeh (Site 29) and Site 313.*

Roman Aqaba Project: SAAS   **Site 313**

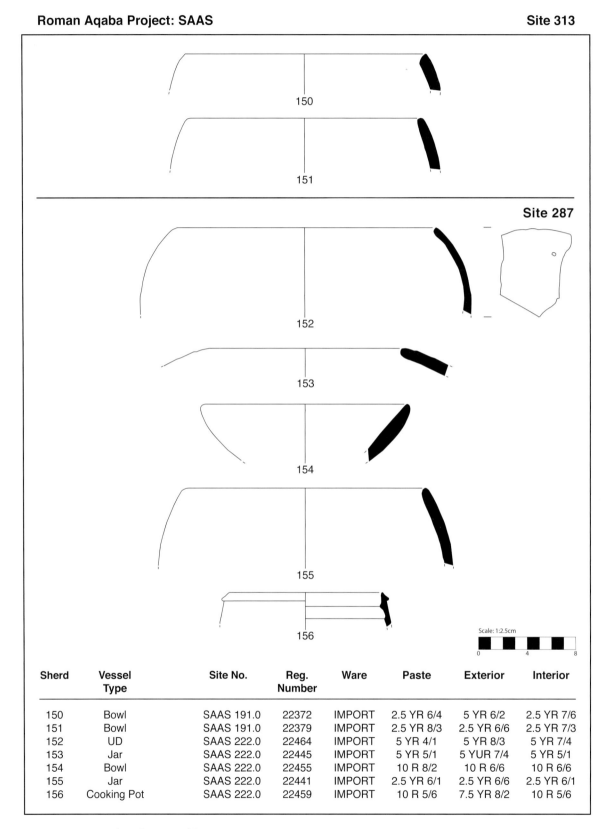

Sherd	Vessel Type	Site No.	Reg. Number	Ware	Paste	Exterior	Interior
150	Bowl	SAAS 191.0	22372	IMPORT	2.5 YR 6/4	5 YR 6/2	2.5 YR 7/6
151	Bowl	SAAS 191.0	22379	IMPORT	2.5 YR 8/3	2.5 YR 6/6	2.5 YR 7/3
152	UD	SAAS 222.0	22464	IMPORT	5 YR 4/1	5 YR 8/3	5 YR 7/4
153	Jar	SAAS 222.0	22445	IMPORT	5 YR 5/1	5 YUR 7/4	5 YR 5/1
154	Bowl	SAAS 222.0	22455	IMPORT	10 R 8/2	10 R 6/6	10 R 6/6
155	Jar	SAAS 222.0	22441	IMPORT	2.5 YR 6/1	2.5 YR 6/6	2.5 YR 6/1
156	Cooking Pot	SAAS 222.0	22459	IMPORT	10 R 5/6	7.5 YR 8/2	10 R 5/6

FIG. 6.20   *Pottery from Site 313 and Site 287.*

(Pratico 1985: 157–58, pl. 36:5–7), where such bowls have a ring base.

Finally, the rim of an Aegean amphora, possibly from Rhodes, is depicted by Sherd 147. The hard but relatively fine fabric is reddish-pink in color with a slightly darker core. The thickened rim is slightly everted. A stamped Rhodian amphora handle dated ca. 200 BC has previously been published from the site (Divito 1985: 62). The current project recovered another stamped Rhodian handle from the surface of the site in 1996, but unfortunately its Greek inscription was too worn to be deciphered.

Site 313 (figs. 6.19:148–6.20:151)

This site appears to be a small settlement, possibly associated with copper-working. The surface ceramic collection dated almost entirely to the Chalcolithic/Early Bronze Age. The small sample presented here dates entirely to these periods. All the pottery is hand-made of coarse ware with large stone inclusions and some apparent use of organic and mineral temper. Sherd 148 is the rim of an open bowl, apparently coil-built, of brown ware surrounding a dark core. Similar small bowls, although slightly deeper, are attested from Ḥujeirat al-Ghuzlan (Kerner 2003: 178, fig. 16:5–6). Sherd 149 is also a coil-built bowl of heavy, dense, dull red ware surrounding a dark core. The exterior surface is quite rough. The form is also paralleled at Ḥujeirat al-Ghuzlan (Kerner 2003: 178, fig. 16:8). Sherd 150 is also a bowl of dense ware with a gray coating on the exterior surface. Finally, Sherd 151 is a coil-built hole-mouth bowl of well-fired, dense, dull red ware; the surface is covered with a lime coating. It is also paralleled at Ḥujeirat al-Ghuzlan (Kerner 2003: 181, fig. 19:4).

Site 287 (fig. 6.20:152–56)

Similar to the preceding site, this site also appears to be a small settlement dating primarily to the Chalcolithic/Early Bronze Age. The small sample published here dates to these periods and, with one exception (Sherd 156), consists entirely of hand-made coarse ware with large stone inclusions apparently added as temper. There is also evidence of some use of organic material as temper. Sherd 152, possibly Early Bronze, is an incurved vessel of light red, well-fired ware. The small hole visible in the side wall suggests temper which has popped out during firing. Sherd 153 is possibly an Early Bronze Age hole-mouth jar of dense, well-fired, light red and buff ware. Limestone temper was possibly added to the matrix. There appears to be gray coating on the interior surface. Sherd 154 is a shallow bowl of light red, well-fired ware. It is paralleled by examples from Ḥujeirat al-Ghuzlan (Kerner 2003: 178, fig. 16:5–6). Of similar ware, but with a dark core, is Sherd 155, which displays small voids suggesting the use of organic temper. The form is also closely paralleled at Ḥujeirat al-Ghuzlan (Kerner 2003: 181, fig. 19:4).

The remaining sherd from this site is Sherd 156, an Early Roman/Nabataean closed cooking pot of typical red ware. A white slip covers the exterior surface. The vessel displays the characteristic triangular rim and offset neck. For some of the many published parallels, see the description of Sherds 1–6 above.

Site 262 (fig. 6.21:157–159)

This site yielded primarily Early Roman/Nabataean pottery, which is the date of all three sherds presented here. Sherd 157 is another example of the classic Early Roman/Nabataean closed cooking pot with triangular rim and off-set neck. The typical red ware surrounds a dark core. The exterior surface is covered with a white slip. For published parallels, see Sherds 1–6 above. Sherds 158–59 represent the classic carinated bowls of Nabataean unpainted fine ware. Both are of evenly-fired, red ware. A brown slip was applied to the exterior rim of Sherd 158, while a white slip covers the same part of Sherd 159. For published parallels, see Sherd 33 above.

Site 225 (fig. 6.21:160–163)

This multi-feature site yielded exclusively Roman period pottery, with most diagnostic sherds judged Early Roman/Nabataean, including the small group presented here. Sherds 160–61 are closed cooking pots of typical red ware and display the characteristic triangular rim and off-set neck. Both

Roman Aqaba Project: SAAS   **Site 262**

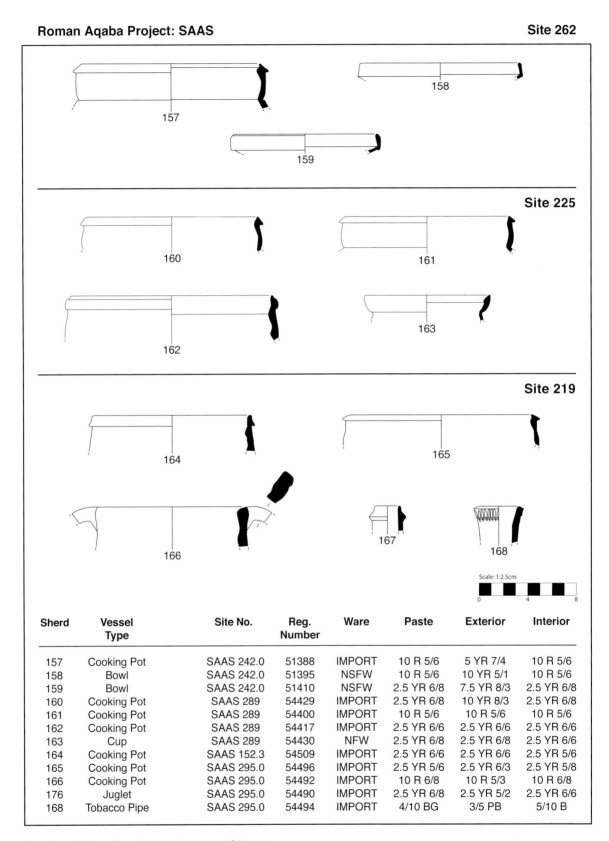

Sherd	Vessel Type	Site No.	Reg. Number	Ware	Paste	Exterior	Interior
157	Cooking Pot	SAAS 242.0	51388	IMPORT	10 R 5/6	5 YR 7/4	10 R 5/6
158	Bowl	SAAS 242.0	51395	NSFW	10 R 5/6	10 YR 5/1	10 R 5/6
159	Bowl	SAAS 242.0	51410	NSFW	2.5 YR 6/8	7.5 YR 8/3	2.5 YR 6/8
160	Cooking Pot	SAAS 289	54429	IMPORT	2.5 YR 6/8	10 YR 8/3	2.5 YR 6/8
161	Cooking Pot	SAAS 289	54400	IMPORT	10 R 5/6	10 R 5/6	10 R 5/6
162	Cooking Pot	SAAS 289	54417	IMPORT	2.5 YR 6/6	2.5 YR 6/6	2.5 YR 6/6
163	Cup	SAAS 289	54430	NFW	2.5 YR 6/8	2.5 YR 6/8	2.5 YR 6/8
164	Cooking Pot	SAAS 152.3	54509	IMPORT	2.5 YR 6/6	2.5 YR 6/6	2.5 YR 5/6
165	Cooking Pot	SAAS 295.0	54496	IMPORT	2.5 YR 5/6	2.5 YR 6/3	2.5 YR 5/8
166	Cooking Pot	SAAS 295.0	54492	IMPORT	10 R 6/8	10 R 5/3	10 R 6/8
176	Juglet	SAAS 295.0	54490	IMPORT	2.5 YR 6/8	2.5 YR 5/2	2.5 YR 6/6
168	Tobacco Pipe	SAAS 295.0	54494	IMPORT	4/10 BG	3/5 PB	5/10 B

FIG. 6.21   *Pottery from Site 262, Site 225, and Site 219.*

are covered with a white slip on their exterior surface. For published parallels, see Sherds 1–6 above. The third (Sherd 162) is either a cooking pot or jar that displays a thickened, grooved rim which is also common in this period. Among published parallels are examples from Aqaba (Dolinka 2003: 121, no. 6), Petra (Murray and Ellis 1940: pl. 32:129; Hammond 1965: pl. 58:21), and Oboda (Negev 1986: 116, no. 1012). Sherd 163 represents the rim and upper neck of a jug or perhaps a closed cup. The vessel is of fine red ware surrounding a dark core. If in fact a jug, parallels may be cited from Petra (Schmid 2000: figs. 301–2). There were also several Nabataean inscriptions dated to the 1st and/or 2nd centuries AD at this site (see Chapter 7).

Site 219 *(fig. 6.21:164–168)*

This site is a cemetery on a terrace above a wadi. The surface pottery collection was primarily Early Roman/Nabataean with a few sherds from later periods. Sherds 164 and 165 again depict the classic Nabataean closed cooking pot of red or pinkish red ware. The triangular rims rest on off-set necks. For published parallels, see Sherds 1–6 above. Sherd 166 is an Early Byzantine closed cooking pot of red ware surrounding a dark core. The exterior surface is covered with a dark brown slip characteristic of this period. The section of the vertical loop handle exhibits the beginning of the double-ridges also typical of this period. The rounded rim rises from a slightly off-set neck. Similar cooking pots are attested at el-Lejjūn (Parker 2006: figs. 16.41:207, 16.42:208, 16.49:243), Tell Hesbân (Sauer 1973: fig. 2:84–85), Amman (Zayadine 1977–78: figs. 21:334, 22:312, 314, 317), Araq el-Emir (Brown 1984: fig. 56:99–103, 108–10), and other sites. Sherd 167 is the rim and neck of a juglet, likely from the Early Roman/Nabataean period. It is a red ware with a simple rounded rim and raised ridge part way down the neck. There are vestiges of a handle attachment (not shown on the drawing) just below the raised ridge. Similar vessels may be cited from Petra (Murray and Ellis 1940: pl. 26:42; Schmid 2000: figs. 323–25). Finally, Sherd 168 is the rim of a tobacco pipe from the Ottoman period. It is of dark gray ware with incised decoration just below the rim.

REFERENCES

Amiran, R.
 1978 *Early Arad: The Chalcolitic Settlement and Early Bronze City*. Jerusalem: Israel Exploration Society.

Bignasca, A.; Fellmann Brogli, R.; Glutz, R.; Karg, S.; Keller, D.; Kolb, B.; Schneider, C.; Stucky, R.; Studer, J.; and Zanoni, I.
 1996 *Petra Ez Zantur I: Ergebnisse der Schweizerisch-Liechtensteinischen Ausgrabungen 1988–1992*. Mainz: von Zabern.

Brown, R.
 1984 The 1976 ASOR Soundings. Pp. 105–32 in *The Excavations at Araq el-Emir*, Vol. 1, ed. N. L. Lapp. *AASOR* 47. Philadelphia: American Schools of Oriental Research.

Clamer, C.
 1997 *Fouilles Archéologiques de ʿAïn Ez-Zâra/Callirrhoé: Villégiature hérodienne*. Beirut: Institut Français d'Archéologie du Proche-Orient.

Cleveland, R. L.
 1960 The Excavations of the Conway High Place (Petra) and Soundings at Khirbet Ader. *AASOR* 34/35: 55–97.

Crowfoot, G. M.
 1936 The Nabataean Ware of Sbaita. *PEFQS* 4: 14–27.

Darby, R.; Darby, E.; and Shelton, A.
 2010 The 2009 ʿAyn Gharandal Survey and Preservation Project. *ADAJ* 54: 189–201.

Divito, R. A.
1985   Tell el-Kheleifeh Inscriptions. Pp. 51–63 in *Nelson Glueck's 1938–1940 Excavations at Tell el-Kheleifeh: A Reappraisal*, ed. G. D. Pratico. American Schools of Oriental Research Archaeological Reports 3. Atlanta: Scholars.

Dolinka, B.
2003   *Nabataean Aila (Aqaba, Jordan) from a Ceramic Perspective.* BAR International Series 1116. Oxford: Archaeopress.

Erickson-Gini, T.
2010   *Nabataean Settlement and Self-Organized Economy in the Central Negev: Crisis and Renewal.* BAR International Series 2054. Oxford: Archaeopress.

Fellmann Brogli, R.
1996   Die Keramik aus den spätrömischen Bauten. Pp. 219–81 in *Petra Ez Zantur I: Ergebnisse der Schweizerisch-Liechtensteinischen Ausgrabungen 1988–1992,* ed. A. Bignasca et al. Mainz: von Zabern.

Gerber, Y.
1996   Die Entwicklung der lokalen nabatäischen Großkeramik aus Petra/Jordanien. Pp. 147–51 in *Hellenistiche und kaiserzeitliche Keramik des östlichen Mittelmeergebietes,* ed. M. Hertfort-Koch. Frankfurt: Archaeological Institute at Goethe University.
1997   The Nabataean Coarse Ware Pottery: A Sequence from the End of the Second Century BC to the Beginning of the Second Century AD. *SHAJ* 6: 407–11.
2001   Selected Ceramic Deposits. Pp. 359–66 in *The Petra Church,* eds. Z. T. Fiema, C. Kanellopoulos, T. Waliszewski, and R. Schick. Amman: American Center of Oriental Research.
2005   Late Roman Coarse Ware from Petra, Jordan: Changes in Typology and Chemical Composition. Pp. 725–36 in *Late Roman Coarse Wares, Cooking Wares and Amphorae in the Mediterranean: Archaeology*

and Archaeometry (Barcelona 14–16 March 2002), eds. J. M. Gurt i Esparraguera, J. Buxeda i Garrigos, and M. A. Cau Ontiveros. Oxford: Archaeopress.

Grawehr , M.
2006   *Petra Ez Zantur III: Ergebnisse der Schweizerisch-Liechtensteinischen Ausgrabungen.* Part 2: *Die Lampen der Grabungen auf ez-Zantur in Petra.* Terra Archaeologica V. Mainz: von Zabern.

Hammond, P. C.
1965   *The Excavation of the Main Theater at Petra, 1961–1962, Final Report.*London: Colt Archaeological Institute.

Hart, S.
1995   The Pottery. Pp. 53–66 in *Excavations at Tawilan in Southern Jordan,* eds. C.-M. Bennett and P. Bienkowski. Oxford: British Institute for Archaeology and History/ Oxford University.

Hayes, J. W.
1972   *Late Roman Pottery.* London: British School at Rome.
1985   *A Supplement to Late Roman Pottery.* London: British School at Rome.

Johnson, D. J.
1990   Nabataean Piriform Unguentaria. *ARAM* 2: 235–48.

Kerner, S.
2003   Appendix: The Pottery of Ḥujeirat al-Ghuzlan 1998 to 2003 – A First Summary. *ADAJ* 47: 175–82.

Khalil, L.; Eichmann, R.; and Schmidt, K.
2003   Archaeological Survey and Excavations at the Wādī al-Yutum and al-Magass Area – al-ʿAqaba (ASEYM): A preliminary Report on the Third and Fourth Seasons Excavations at Tell Ḥujeirat al-Ghuzlan in 2002 and 2003 Wādī al-Yutum. *ADAJ* 47: 159–83.

Lindner, M.
1988 Es-Sadeh: An Important Edomite-Nabataean Site, Preliminary Report. *ADAJ* 32: 75–100.

Magness, J.
1993 *Jerusalem Ceramic Chronology circa 200–800 CE.* Sheffield: Sheffield Academic.

Murray, M. A., and Ellis, J. C.
1940 *A Street in Petra.* London: British School of Archaeology in Egypt.

Negev, A.
1986 *The Late Hellenistic and Early Roman Pottery from Nabataean Oboda: Final Report.* Qedem 22. Jerusalem: Institute of Archaeology, Hebrew University.

Negev, A., and Sivan, R.
1977 The Pottery of the Nabataean Necropolis at Mampsis (Kurnub). *RCRF* 17/18: 108–31.

Parker, S. T.
1987 The Pottery. Pp. 525–691 in *The Roman Frontier in Central Jordan: Interim Report on the Limes Arabicus Project, 1980–1985,* ed. S. T. Parker. 2 vols. BAR International Series 340. Oxford: British Archaeological Reports.
2006 The Pottery. Pp. 329–71 in *The Roman Frontier in Central Jordan: Final Report on the Limes Arabicus Project, 1980–1989,* ed. S. T. Parker. 2 vols. Washington: Dumbarton Oaks.
2013 Coarse Ware Pottery of the First through Third Centuries at Roman Aila (modern Aqaba, Jordan). Forthcoming in *Roman Pottery in the Levant: Local Production and Regional Trade. Proceedings of the Round Table, Berlin, February 19th–20th, 2010,* eds. B. Fischer-Genz, Y. Gerber, and H. Hamel. Roman and Late Antique Mediterranean Pottery 3. Oxford: Archaeopress.

Peacock, D. P. S., and Williams, D. F.
1986 *Amphorae and the Roman Economy.* London: Longman.

Pratico, G. D.
1985 *Nelson Glueck's 1938–1940 Excavations at Tell el-Kheleifeh: A Reappraisal.* American Schools of Oriental Research Archaeological Reports 3. Atlanta: Scholars.

Sauer, J. A.
1973 *Heshbon Pottery 1971.* Andrews University Monographs 7. Berrien Springs, MI: Andrews University.

Schmid, S. G.
1996 Die Feinkeramik. Pp. 151–281 in *Petra Ez Zantur I: Ergebnisse der Schweizerisch-Liechtensteinischen Ausgrabungen 1988–1992,* ed. A. Bignasca et al. Mainz: von Zabern.
2000 Die Feinkeramik der Nabatäer. Typologie, Chronologie und kulturhistorische Hintergründe. Pp. 1–198 in *Petra – Ez Zantur II. Teil 1: Die Feinkeramik der Nabatäer. Typologie, Chronologie und kulturhistorische Hintergründe; Teil 2: Die spätantiken Wohnbauten von Ez Zantur in Petra und der Wohnhausbau in Palästina vom 4.–6. Jh. n. Chr.* Mainz: von Zabern.

Schneider, C.
1996 Die Importkeramik. Pp. 129–49 in *Petra Ez Zantur I: Ergebnisse der Schweizerisch-Liechtensteinischen Ausgrabungen 1988–1992,* ed. A. Bignasca et al. Mainz: von Zabern.

Smith, A. M., II
2005 Bir Madhkur Project: A Preliminary Report on Recent Fieldwork. *BASOR* 340: 57–75.

Smith, R. H.
1973 *Pella of the Decapolis,* Vol. I: *The 1967 Season of the College of Wooster Expedition to Pella.* Wooster, OH: College of Wooster.

Tushingham, A. D.
1972 *The Excavations at Dibon (Dhibân) in Moab: The Third Campaign 1952–1953.* Cambridge, MA: American Schools of Oriental Research.

Villeneuve, F.
  1990   The Pottery from the Oil-Factory at Khirbet
         edh-Darih (2nd Century AD): A Contribu-
         tion to the Study of the Material Culture of
         the Nabataeans. *ARAM* 2: 367–84.

Zanoni, I.
  1996   Tonlampen. Pp. 311–36 in *Petra Ez Zantur
         I: Ergebnisse der Schweizerisch-Liechten-
         steinischen Ausgrabungen 1988–1992,* ed. A.
         Bignasca et al. Mainz: von Zabern.

Zayadine, F.
  1977–78   Excavations on the Upper Citadel of
            Amman: Area A (1975 and 1977). *ADAJ* 22:
            20–56, 192–211.

Chapter 7

Nabataean Inscriptions from Wādī Museimīr in the Southeast Wādī ʿAraba

by David F. Graf

In 1994, the Roman Aqaba Project's Southeast ʿAraba Archaeological Survey (SAAS) discovered a group of Nabataean Aramaic inscriptions inside the entrance to Wādī Museimīr, just beyond its intersection with Wādī ʿAraba (Smith et al. 1997; Smith 2005; 2011; SAAS Site no. 225). Wādī Museimīr is the second major wadi system north of Gharandal, just north of Wādī el-Quṣeib (fig. 4.49, map 16). The inscriptions are engraved on sandstone boulders clustered around several small structures and some possible burial cairns, which unfortunately have been disturbed by clandestine excavations. There are also associated drawings, including an apparent hunting scene (fig. 4.32). The pottery collected from the environs was Nabataean, Early, and Late Roman (fig. 6.18). None of the inscriptions are dated, but the paleography suggests a date in the first and second centuries AD.

These seven Nabataean inscriptions are merely graffiti, but are interesting because of their location. As far as I am aware, there are no recorded Nabataean graffiti elsewhere in the southern ʿAraba. In the central ʿAraba, on the Petra–Gaza road, at Khirbet Moyat ʿAwad, some pieces of a Nabataean papyrus document were discovered on bedrock below the floor level of a building, dating from the late 1st century BC to the early 2nd century AD, based on Nabataean coins and pottery (Cohen 1993: 1139). The scraps of papyri are illegible and have never been published (pers. communication, Tali Gini-Erickson). At nearby ʿEn Raḥel, a site of similar date, excavations revealed "two camel bones bearing black-ink inscriptions in Nabataean script" (Cohen 1993: 1143). Further south in the ʿAraba, there are no attested Nabataean inscriptions, papyri, or other documents. Even Greek and Latin inscriptions are fairly rare until the Diocletianic period.[1] The Nabataean texts from Wādī Museimīr are therefore rare and important.

BOULDER I

This inscription is on a sandstone boulder about 9 m and 292 degrees from a small rectilinear structure (ca. 2.80 m N–S × 6.30 m E–W) composed of boulders about 0.6 m in length. The boulder with the inscription measures ca. 0.70 m on a side and has petroglyphs on three of its sides (fig. 7.1).

No. 1   Š'DW ŠL[M]
                   Šaʿd, Peace!

Although rock art has been superimposed on the beginning of the graffito, the initial Š of Š'DW is clear beneath the horse pecked into the rock. The name Š'DW is well-attested in Nabataean,

FIG. 7.1 *Nabataean inscription (#1) from Site 225.*

occurring throughout the Nabataean realm but particularly in North Arabia, the Sinai, and Egypt (Cantineau 1832: 152; Negev: no. 1172 with LM no. 44; al-Khraysheh 1986: 181–82). It corresponds to the Arabic name Saʿd (CIK 492, 1), which also appears frequently in theophoric names such as Arabic Saʿadallāh (CIK 497, 2) and Saʿdallāt (CIK 498, 1), i.e. "(good) luck, fortune, success of GN." See Palmyrene *S'D, S'D'L, S'DLT* (Stark 1971: 115), ENA Safaitic and Thamudic *S'D, S'D'L, S'DLT, S'DŠMS*, and ESA *S'DŠMS, S'D'TTR* (HIn 318–9). The vocalization of Nabataean names is a problem, and is offered here only as a suggestion as to how the names were pronounced (MacDonald 1999).

BOULDER II

A sandstone boulder lies ca. 29 m and 248 degrees from the small structure (fig. 7.2). It measures ca. 1.10 m N–S × 1.40 m E–W, and is ca. 0.50 high. Petroglyphs appear on two faces of the boulder. Site 289-6 = SB 21-6. Unfortunately, the surface of the

stone on the left is separated from the boulder and is lost, rendering all three inscriptions fragmentary.

No. 2   [ŠL]M NMYRW BR…..
              [Pea]ce! Numair son of….

It appears that the greeting "Peace" may have preceded the name in the graffito, but it has been defaced by later rock art. The final *–m* of *šlm* is all that seems clear now in the photograph. The name *NMRW* is also clear and appears at Petra and the Negev-Sinai region (Negev 1991: no. 736). It corresponds to Arabic *Namir*, 'the leopard' (Cantineau 1932: 120–21; cf. CIK 444, 2, *Namir*, and 440,2, *Numair*, are the corresponding Arabic names). In the Hawrān it is represented by Greek Ναμερος (Wuthnow 1930: 81). It is also well-attested in Safaitic (Harding 1971: 599) and Thamudic (King 1990: 638). The patronym is missing as a result of the loss of the surface of the stone, which cuts across the boulder in a 45 degree angle.

FIG. 7.2 *Nabataean inscriptions (#2–4) from Site 225.*

Another graffito has been engraved to the lower left of the former inscription. Traces of the letters of the name are visible, but only the first letter of the Greeting "Peace" is visible. The rest is lost.

In the lower right of the stone a third graffito is visible, but all that is clear is the initial greeting and the first name, if it is complete, since the surface of the lower left of the stone is missing.

No. 3   MLM Š[LM]
MLM, Peace!

No. 4   ŠLM ʿB[D]….
Peace! Serv[ant of]…..

The name *MLM* is followed by a *Š*, which can easily be restored as *ŠLM*, 'peace.' The name *MLM* is attested once in Nabataean at Petra (Cantineau 1932: 115; al-Khraysheh 1986: 108–9; Negev: no. 648, as *MLMW*), once in Safaitic (*HIn* 566, s.v. *MLM*), and once in Liḥyanite; cf. *MLʿM* in Safaitic (HI 562, cf. Arabic *mulāʾim*) and Thamudic E (King 1990: 628). The name *ML* also is attested several times in Thamudic E in the nearby Ḥismā desert to the south just below the Ras an-Naqab plateau (King 1990: 628, s.v. KJC 569, 573), and corresponds to Arabic *māll*, '(be rich in) flocks, wealth' (CIK 397, 1).

The name *ʿBD* ('servant') may be restored. It possibly represented either a theophoric or "basileophoric" name, but the second element is lost. It is just as possible that it represents *ʿBDʾ*, *ʿBDW*, *ʿBDY*, or *ʿBDYW* (Negev 1991: nos. 783, 798, 803, 804), or a multitude of other names (Cantineau 1932: 124–26). Even more fragmentary and illegible is the name scratched above it to the left where some letters are visible, but no reading can be ascertained.

FIG. 7.3   *Nabataean inscriptions (#5–6) from Site 225.*

BOULDER III

A sandstone boulder ca. 2.90 m NW of Boulder II (fig. 7.3).

No. 5   ŠLM 'WDW BR 'BD-MLKW
Peace! 'Awad son of Servant-of-Maliku

The name *'WDW* ('protection') is attested frequently in the Negev, Sinai, and Egypt, but not elsewhere (Cantineau 1932: 128; Negev 1991: no. 851; al-Khraysheh 1986: 136), but it is also known in Palmyrene (Stark 1971: 104). In ENA, it appears in Safaitic and Thamudic (*HIn* 447).

The patronym is an interesting addition to the "basileophoric" names composed with the names of the Nabataean kings. *'BD-MLKW* appears throughout the Nabataean realm (Negev 1991: no. 808) and also in ENA (Harding 1971: 400 lists Safaitic, and see King 1990: 577 for *'BDMK* in Thamudic E). J. T. Milik long contended that the royal name of King Malichus II (AD 40–70) should not be read as *Mlkw* in Nabataean Aramaic but rather as *Mnkw* (1981: 25; cf. Graf 2007: 128–29). It subsequently was argued that the name *'bd-Mnkw* also appeared in a number of Nabartaean texts published by Milik, Starcky,

and others, but because of the similarity of the *l* and *n* in Nabataean script, reservation was expressed by some about the reading. Now, however, the name *'bd-Mnkw* appears in a Thamudic "E" text from just east of Madaba in central Jordan (Graf and Zwettler 2004: 66) that supports Milik's observation, since the *l* and *n* are clearly different in ENA script. The theophoric nature of the Nabataean royal names in such constructions also seems possible (Graf 1994: 293–94).

Just below this inscription, there is another graffito etched in the lower right hand corner of the boulder. There may be some damage to the stone at this corner, but the reading seems clear.

No. 6   BTNW
Buṭṭān/Butaina

The name *BTNW* appears just once, at Hegra in C 306B3 (Cantineau 1932: 75; Negev 1991: no. 207; al-Khraysheh 1986: 51, for vocalization). It perhaps is represented by Βαθανιας in Greek (Wuthnow 1930: 133), but the name does not appear in ENA or Palmyrene.

FIG. 7.4 *Nabataean inscription (#7) from Site 225.*

BOULDER IV

This sandstone boulder lies 1.70 m northwest of boulder VI. The rock face measures 0.78 × 0.40 m (fig. 7.4).

No. 7 ŠLM NWPS
Peace! Naufis

The name appears to read as *NWPS*, which is new in Nabataean Aramaic, but the name NFS (Ar. *nafīs*, 'precious') is known in ENA (*HIn* 596), appearing at least a half dozen times in Safaitic and once in Taymanite (formerly 'Thamudic A'). The final letter –*s* in the name has parallels in *CIS* 220 (Hegra), *CIS* 161 (Damascus), *CIS* 183/4 (Hawran), and *CIS*

963 (Sinai), which suggests a date for this graffito in the late 1st century AD or later. The first letter of the name could be read as *Z*-, but the name *ZWPS* is unknown in Nabataean Aramaic or ENA. It seems preferable to read it as *N*-, although typically the letter is longer with a bottom curve to the left that is missing here. There are a few parallels to the letter *N* as a shorter straight line.

The location of these graffiti may be more than just the product of an isolated small Nabataean settlement. Fawzi Zayadine indicates that with the local Bedouin as guides he was able to delineate at least six routes leading west from Petra to Wādī ʿAraba. The routes to the SW are fewer and more difficult. The main one is from Gharandal in Wādī ʿAraba east to Dilagha and Tayibeh to Petra. The other is from Wādī Sabra through Wādī Abū Khusheiba, where it descends from Naqb el-Rubāʿī into Wādī ʿAraba (Zayadine 1985: 163). This route has pavement and a rock-cut path near Jebel Hārūn and a number of structures with Nabataean and Roman pottery (Ben-David 2007: 102). Since Sultan Bairbars in 1276 mentions that his ascent was from Naqb el-Rubāʿī, it is assumed that this is the route he took to Petra (Zayadine 1985: 163). This route turns from the SW directly west to head for Wādī ʿAraba. This is precisely the route that the British Colonel Jarvis took just before WWII, ascending Naqb el-Rubāʿī and entering the Wādī Abū Khusheiba, where its steep and narrow banks forced the team to abandon their cars and attempt the climb with camels and donkeys as the cliffs became sheerer and narrower. This last leg of the trek took five hours and ended with the dismounting from the stubborn animals who refused to proceed without their baggage being removed; the remainder of the journey proceeded on foot (Jarvis 1940: 143–45). These difficulties make it seem unlikely that this was the route utilized by Nabataean caravans descending to the ʿAraba. There must have been an alternative route to the SW that was easier, even if more circuitous and longer.

During the Finnish Jebel Hārūn project at Petra, an ancient road was detected running west on the north banks of Wādī al-Maḥaṭṭah for a short distance before it descended south past Rujm al-Rubaʿī and Wādī Abū Khusheiba heading south (cf. Lindner 1992b: 264–67, where there is a "spiderweb" of caravan tracks). Along this stretch the road (ca. 4.2 m wide) has periodic paving and is bordered by a curbstone wall and several small structures that appear to be guard stations or watchposts along the route, with Nabataean pottery attesting a 1st- and 2nd-century AD date (Hertrell 2002: 389–91, with fig. 4 "map"). The direction suggests that it was headed 4–5 km south to Sabra, where there was a settlement and theater (Lindner 1992a: 193, 203). According to the Finnish report, it then appears to have headed further south where it intersected and merged with a road from Ṭayibeh heading directly west to the ʿAraba, which it entered at some point north of Gharandal (Frösén and Fiema 2002: 258, map 5). This route must have afforded an easier decent to Wādī ʿAraba and in all likelihood entered the ʿAraba through Wādī Museimīr, past the structures and boulders with the inscribed Nabataean texts discussed above. The route seems to fork at various points in its western descent, so this may have been only one of several options. But, if Wādī Museimīr is one of these, it helps explain the small Nabataean settlement at this junction, which also intersects the north–south road through Wādī ʿAraba.

NOTE

1 Sartre 1993: nos. 107–14 for Phaino/Feinan further north, the Diocletianic Latin text from Yotvata (Roll 1989), and milestones of a Diocletianic road running from Yotvata north past Gharandal through the ʿAraba, perhaps headed to Phaino (Roll and Avner 2008).

REFERENCES

Abbreviations

CIS   *Corpus inscriptionum semiticarum*
ENA   Epigraphic North Arabian
ESA   Epigraphic South Arabian

Ben-David, C.
2007   The Paved Road from Petra to the ʿAraba – Commercial Nabataean or Military Roman. Pp. 101–10 in *The Late Roman Army in the Near East from Diocletian to the Arab Conquest*, ed. A. S. Lewin and P. Pellegrini. BAR International Series 1717. Oxford: Hadrian.

Cantineau, J.
1930   *Le Nabatéen,* Vol. I: *Notions générales, écriture, grammaire.* Paris: Leroux.
1932   *Le Nabatéen,* Vol. II: *Choix de textes, lexique.* Paris: Leroux.

Caskel, W.
1966   *Ǧamharat an-Nasab. Das genealogische Werk des Hišam ibn Muḥammad al-Kalbī,* vol. 2. Leiden: Brill.

Cohen R.
1993   Negev: The Persian to Byzantine Periods. Pp. 1133–45 in *NEAEHL,* vol. 3, eds. E. Stern, A. Lewinson-Gilboa, and J. Aviram. New York: Simon and Schuster.

Corpus Inscriptionum Semiticarum
1907   *Corpus inscriptionum semiticarum.* Pars II. Tomus 1–2. Paris: E. Reipublicæ Typographeo

Frank, F.
1934   Aus der ʿAraba I: Reiseberichte. *ZDPV* 57: 191–280.

Frösén, J., et al.
2001 The 1998–2000 Finnish Hārūn Project: Specialized Reports. *ADAJ* 45: 337–92.

Frösén, J., and Fiema, Z. T. (eds.)
2002 *Petra: A City Forgotten and Rediscovered.* Helsinki: Helsinki University.

Graf, D. F.
1994 The Nabataean Army and the *Cohortes Ulpiae Petraeorum.* Pp. 265–311 in *The Roman and Byzantine Army in the East*, ed. E. Dabrowa. Krakow: Uniwersytet Jagiellonski.
2007 Józef Tadeusz Milik (1922–2006): 'Nabataean Epigrapher Par Excellence.' *Polish Journal of Biblical Research* 62/2 (12): 123–30.

Graf, D. F., and Zwettler, M. J.
2004 The North Arabian "Thamudic E" Inscription from Uraynibah West. *BASOR* 335: 53–89.

Harding, G. L.
1971 *An Index and Concordance of Pre-Islamic Arabian Names and Inscriptions.* Near and Middle East Series 8. Toronto: University of Toronto.

Hertrell, E.
2001 FJHP 2000: The Ancient Road in the Survey Area. Pp. 389–91 in Frösén et al. 2001.

Jarvis, S.
1940 To Petra from the West – A Forgotten Roman Highway. *Antiquity* 14: 138–47.

Khairy, N.
1981 A New Dedicatory Nabataean Inscription from Wādī Musa. *PEQ* 113: 19–26.

al-Khraysheh, F.
1986 Die Personennamen in den nabatäischen Inschriften des *Corpus Inscriptionum Semiticarum.* Ph.D. Dissertation, Philipps-Universität Marburg/Lahn.

King, G. M. H.
1990 Early North Arabian Thamudic E. Ph.D. Dissertation, School of Oriental and African Studies, University of London.

Lindner, M.
1992a Survey of Sabra (Jordan). 1990 Preliminary Report. *ADAJ* 36: 193–216.
1992b Abū Khusheiba – A newly Described Nabataean Settlement and Caravan Station between Wādī 'Araba and Petra. *SHAJ* 4: 283–67.

Macdonald, M. C. A.
1999 Personal Names in the Nabataean Realm. *Journal of Semitic Studies* 44: 251–89.

Milik, J. T.
1981 Additional Note. Pp. 25–26 in Khairy 1981.

Negev, A.
1991 *Personal Names in the Nabataean Realm.* Qedem 32. Jerusalem: Institute of Archaeology, Hebrew University.

Niemi, T., and Smith, A. M. II
1999 Initial Results of the Southeastern Wādī 'Araba, Jordan Geoarchaeological Study: Implications for Shifts in Late Quaternary Aridity. *Geoarchaeology: An International Journal* 14/8: 791–820.

Parker, S. T.
2006 Roman Aila and the Wādī 'Araba: An Economic Relationship. Pp. 223–30 in *Crossing the Rift: Resources, Routes, Settlement Patterns and Interaction in the Wādī 'Araba,* eds. P. Bienkowski and K. Galor. Oxford: Oxbow.

Roll, I., and Avner, U.
2008 Tetrarchic Milestones Found Near Yahel in the Southern Aravah. *ZPE* 165: 267–86.

Sartre, M.
1993 *Inscriptions Greques et Latines de la Syrie* Tome XXI: *Inscriptions de la Jordanie,* Tome IV. Paris: Geuthner.

Smith, A. M. II
2005   Pathways, Roadways and Highways: Net-
       works of Communication and Exchange
       in the Wādī ʿAraba. *NEA* 68: 180–89.
2010   *Wādī ʿAraba in Classical and Late Antiquity:*
       An Historical Geography. BAR International
       Series 2173. Oxford: British Archaeological
       Reports.

Smith, A. M. II; Niemi, T.; and Stevens, M.
1997   The Southeast ʿAraba Archaeological
       Survey: A Preliminary Report of the 1994
       Season. *BASOR* 305: 45–71.

Stark, J. K.
1971   *Personal Names in Palmyrene Inscriptions.*
       Oxford: Oxford University.

Wuthnow, H.
1930   *Die semitischen Menschennamem in*
       griechischen Inschriften und Papyri des
       vorderen Orients. Leipzig: Dietrich.

Zayadine, F.
1985   Caravan Routes between Egypt and Naba-
       taea and the Voyage of Sultan Baibars to
       Petra in 1276. *SHAJ* 2: 159–74.

Chapter 8

The Hinterland of Roman Aila

by S. Thomas Parker and Andrew M. Smith II

I. INTRODUCTION

This chapter aims to synthesize the results of the regional survey, particularly in light of the evidence derived from the project's own excavation of Aqaba, as well as other relevant evidence. After acknowledging the value and limitations of the evidence collected and reviewing the environmental factors at play in the region, the discussion will proceed diachronically, focusing especially on the economic history of the classical periods, i.e., the Hellenistic through Byzantine periods.

II. THE NATURAL ENVIRONMENT: RESOURCES AND CHALLENGES

The natural environment is discussed fully in Chapter two of the present report. Smith has also published an overview in a recent monograph (Smith 2010: 1–9). Therefore, only a few salient features need rehearsal here. The southern Wādī ʿAraba is the narrowest portion of this linear valley, only 8–10 km wide. Although there is evidence of variation in climate in the prehistoric periods, all human activity in the valley since historic times has been constrained by hyper-aridity (less than 50 mm of annual precipitation) and high temperatures. One scholar has noted that "the southern Wādī ʿAraba is the driest and hottest part of both Israel

and Jordan" (Bruins 2006: 28). Rainfall occurs sporadically during the winter months, especially between November and March. This limited rainfall is also highly variable in terms of both location and amount.

The precipitation that falls on the ʿAraba and adjacent highlands feeds both groundwater and the regional drainage networks. The drainage basin of the southern ʿAraba extends 80 km from the gulf NE to Jebel Ar-Risha and Jebel el-Khureij, where the valley floor reaches an elevation of 250 m. Farther north drainage is toward the Dead Sea. Various wadis flow into Wādī ʿAraba from its flanking mountain ranges, which form a steep escarpment rising to nearly 1200 m to the east but only ca. 600 m to the west.

There are no perennial streams in the southern ʿAraba. Floods from winter storms carry sediment through steep gorges eroded into the mountains that flank the valley. Enormous alluvial fans radiate into the ʿAraba valley at the mouths of these gorges. The channels of these alluvial fans flow into four seasonal mudflats (*sabkhas*) on the valley floor. Low rainfall and high evaporation rates lead to precipitation of salts in these *sabkhas*.

Wādī ʿAraba lies in an active fault of the complex Dead Sea transform fault. Numerous earthquakes are attested in this fault system throughout historic times and greatly impacted human activity.

There is good evidence for several such events from the project's excavation at Aqaba (Thomas, Niemi and Parker 2007).

Lacking perennial rivers or streams, humans naturally exploited both wells and springs in Wādī 'Araba. The springs and wells have largely determined the location of settlements and travel routes across the region. There are several springs within the southern part of the valley. Other springs lie in the valleys within the flanking mountains, where faults and other geological structures impede subsurface flow, leading to discharge of ground water. Water could also be accessed via wells in the sabkhas, although this water tends to be brackish. There is no evidence in the immediate vicinity of Aqaba for diversion of drainage into reservoirs for irrigation or domestic use. Wells were apparently sufficient for these purposes. But there is clear evidence of various walls and channels that diverted floodwater away from settlements, at least within recent historical times. There is substantial evidence of a large-scale system of structures to channel, impound, and redirect water to agricultural fields in the late Chalcolithic and beginning of the Early Bronze Age around Tell Ḥujeirat al-Ghuzlan (Niemi and Smith 1999; Brückner et al. 2002; Heemeier et al. 2009). In the Early Islamic period, there was an elaborate system of underground tunnels, vertical shafts, and irrigation channels (qanats or foggara) to water agricultural fields in the mudflats west of the Tāba sabkha (Avner and Magness 1998).

Apart from its precious water, the southern 'Araba also offered other natural resources, including a variety of stone, metals, soils, flora, and fauna.

As Niemi notes in Chapter 2, several sources of stone were locally available for construction and other purposes, as revealed by the project's excavation. Especially important were several types of igneous rocks, as well as sandstone, siltstone, and limestone. The most common stones used to construct Roman and Byzantine Aila were granites and crystalline dike rocks outcropping locally in the eastern mountains. But this locally exposed granitic bedrock on the east side of the valley is difficult to quarry and shape. Much rarer are sandstones, which outcrop no closer than ca. 10 km from Aqaba. Sedimentary rock quarries lie 10 km west of Aqaba (Avner and Magness 1998). Limestone could be also

obtained from several locations within the 'Araba, including just north of the Wādī el-Muhtadī fan and from Jebel el-Khureij and Jebel Ar-Risha, where outcrops in the middle of the valley display clear evidence of quarrying in antiquity. Chert, used for tools, also was readily available in the region.

Other types of rock were imported from much greater distances. Basalt, for example, was commonly used at Aila for querns, mortars, and pestles, but there is no local source in the Aqaba region. Outcrops of basalt are attested north of Ma'an and northward along the plateau east of the rift valley and the Dead Sea, 50 km SE of Quweira, in the mountains along the west shore of the Gulf of Aqaba and farther afield. The soft chlorite and graphite schist ("steatite") vessels, employed for cooking and other purposes at Aila, apparently were imported from the Hejaz in NW Saudi Arabia (Grubisha 2000).

Undoubtedly the most important natural resource for human exploitation in Wādī 'Araba in historic times is copper. The closest source to Aqaba is the Timna region, ca. 20 km north of Aqaba on the west side of the valley. There are additional sources of copper along the east side of the valley in Wādī Abū Khusheiba and Wādī Faynan, 90 and 125 km NE of Aqaba, respectively. The copper ore is associated with iron at Timna and with manganese at Faynan. There is extensive evidence of copper mining and processing in these districts as early as the Chalcolithic period and of intensive exploitation in the Roman era (Rothenberg 1972; 1988; 1999a; 1999b; Hauptmann and Wiesberger 1987; 1992; Hauptmann 2006; 2007; Barker, Gilbertson, and Mattingly 2007). The presence of copper ore and copper slag recovered from various stratigraphic contexts at Aila suggests the importation and at least small-scale copper processing on site in several periods.

The possibility of gold-mining in the region, attested by various literary sources, is more problematic, as discussed by Niemi in Chapter 2. She cites several sources in southern Jordan but also notes uncertainty about their exploitation in antiquity. However, various lines of evidence do suggest gold production in the Early Islamic period in a wadi NW of Aqaba (Avner and Magness 1998; Meshel 2006).

Other resources available in the region and attested from archaeological contexts at Aqaba include gypsum, bitumen, sulfur, and salt. Four different types of raw gypsum, used to make plaster and mixed in cement or mortar, appeared in most RAP excavation areas. Gypsum appears in Wādī ʿAraba in the Gharandal area, in Wādī Abū Barqa (RAP Site 302), in the Tāba *sabkha,* and around the Dead Sea. Most gypsum samples recovered at Aila are satinspar, found west of Jebel Muhtadī, 25 km north of Aqaba, in outcrops near Gharandal, and farther afield. The RAP excavations also yielded several bitumen (asphalt or pitch) samples likely from the Dead Sea, where it was harvested by the Nabataeans (Hammond 1959). Bitumen was used as a sealant for waterproofing, as an ingredient in medicines, in agriculture, and was exported to Egypt for embalming (Nissenbaum 1993). The Dead Sea was also a likely source of sulfur, used in antiquity in medicines, fumigation, and bleaching cloth. Three sulfur samples were collected by RAP. Finally, the region offered several sources of halite (salt), including the Dead Sea, several *sabkhas* in Wādī ʿAraba, or by simple evaporation of water from the Red Sea.

Various types of soils are found in the ʿAraba valley. There is a close relationship among the local soils, geomorphology, hydrology, and vegetation (Bruins 2006: 39–40). The soils of the Aqaba fan are typical of those developed on coarse parent materials (sands and gravels) in a hyperarid environment. Niemi's analysis in Chapter 2 shows that these alluvial fan soils are very porous and have limited agricultural potential because of their low natural fertility and free draining nature.

The natural vegetation of the southern valley is dominated by species that can tolerate the hyper-aridity and extreme temperature variations, including shrubs such as chenopods (e.g., jointed anabis, *Anabasis articulata*) and trees such as acacia and tamarisk. It is notable that carbonized remains of these plants appeared in several stratified contexts at Aqaba, suggesting their importation as fuel (Parker 2000: 378; 2002: 422; 2006: 228).

Wild fauna offered a potential human resource through hunting, especially in the prehistoric periods. The range of species present in the southern ʿAraba is suggested by faunal remains recovered at Aqaba from Early Roman through Early Islamic

contexts. A few bones of gazelle, ostrich, birds, and ostrich eggshells suggest occasional hunting, but wild terrestrial fauna clearly made no significant contribution to the diet or economy of Roman Aila. This is in strong contrast to marine resources such as fish and shellfish, which served as major food resources throughout Aila's history.

The southern valley also offered areas for grazing domestic livestock, especially on a seasonal basis. Ethnographic evidence from the 17th through 19th centuries suggests that the ʿAraba was a contested region among nomadic tribes in part due to the seasonal foliage available during winter and spring (van der Steen 2006: 249; Bailey 2006). Analysis of faunal remains from excavated contexts at Aila suggests the regular and sustained importation of sheep and goats "on the hoof" from surrounding areas, presumably including Wādī ʿAraba (Parker 2006: 228–29).

Although much of the valley is obviously ill-suited for agriculture, there are small areas that evidence cultivation in antiquity. Farmers in the Chalcolithic period constructed dams across the surface of the Aqaba fan that slowed runoff to permit more infiltration of water into the underlying soils. It also encouraged deposition of suspended sediment in the runoff behind the dams. Farther north, as noted above, there is evidence of irrigation agriculture in several portions of the valley (Smith 2010: 7). Botanical evidence from the project's excavation of Aqaba itself suggests the possibility of local agricultural production, particularly of barley (pers. comm. Jennifer Ramsay; to be published subsequently).

The ubiquity of mudbrick architecture and evidence for sustained ceramic production throughout the history of Aila underscores the importance of natural sources of clay. The superstructure of most buildings excavated in Aila was of poured mud or coursed mudbrick. The prevalence of mudbrick implies a lack of easily-hewn rocks in the immediate vicinity. Local pottery production is evidenced by stratified kiln wasters and ceramic slag throughout Aila's history. Thus, clay to supply local ceramic production must have been available if not abundant. Niemi in Chapter 2 identifies several potential local clay sources around the Aqaba region and in southern Wādī ʿAraba, including clay beds south of Aqaba, the *sabkhas* in Wādī ʿAraba, and deposits from Wādī Yutum and other drainages.

Stratigraphic sections in RAP excavation Area N and in backhoe Trench BH 21, ca. 500 m from the shoreline, revealed natural deposition of thin-bedded mud and possible reservoir clean-out mud piles. In Area N the mud layers appeared to be modified by human activity, with a pile of cut blocks of mud adjacent to pits apparently dug into the mud layer. The top of a clay layer in Trench BH 21 also showed evidence of having been cut and removed. Early Roman/Nabataean potsherds were associated with this activity. Subsequent analysis suggests that these deposits were more likely exploited for material to make mudbrick rather than pottery, as originally suggested (Parker 1998: 378; 2000: 375).

In short, despite the harsh nature of Wādī ʿAraba, particularly its southern sector, the valley nevertheless offered a rich array of resources to sustain local human populations, supply the economy of the city of Aila on its southern border, and, at least in some periods, export to the wider Mediterranean world.

III. PREVIOUS RESEARCH AND THE NATURE OF THE EVIDENCE

Given the almost complete absence of documentary sources (apart from Aqaba itself) specific to the southern Wādī ʿAraba, the archaeological evidence is obviously paramount. Smith notes in Chapter 4 that 19th- and early 20th-century western travelers largely bypassed the region, although a few did offer some valuable ethnographic observations. He then summarizes the meager amount of previous archaeological research in the region both in the above chapter and in a recently published monograph (Smith 2010). Since the conclusion of the RAP survey in 1998, the region has witnessed some new archaeological excavations and surveys. The most notable for the classical periods are the excavations of the Late Roman fortlet at Yotvata on the western side of the valley (Avner, Davies, and Magness 2004; 2005; Davies and Magness 2006; 2007; 2008; 2011), Smith's own continuation of excavation of Bir Madhkur and survey of its environs (Smith 2005), Dolinka's survey of Rujm aṭ-Ṭāba (Dolinka 2006b), and the more recent excavation of the

Late Roman fortlet of ʿAin Gharandal (Darby et al. 2010). Understandably, all the evidence currently available from these projects is only preliminary but will be exploited in the following discussion. It is gratifying to see these new excavations take the field, as they promise a new era of research in the southern valley.

Finally, the strengths and limitations of currently available evidence must be summarized before offering any historical synthesis. As Smith notes in Chapter 4, SAAS did not intensively and exhaustively survey the entire SE ʿAraba. The project survey was constrained by limited human and financial resources, time, terrain, and political factors. Its methodology also adapted to address the radically different landscapes of the region and evolved over time in light of such factors as acquisition of aerial photographic coverage between the first and second seasons and actual results from the field. There are undoubtedly more archaeological sites to be discovered in this region. Further, as both Niemi and Henry et al. observe elsewhere in this report, geomorphological factors, such as fluvial deposition, likely have partially obscured or even completely covered some archaeological sites in the valley. Nevertheless, the project survey likely produced a fairly representative sample of the archaeological resources from the historical periods in the southeastern valley.

IV. A HISTORY OF THE SOUTHEAST WĀDĪ ʿARABA

The distribution of sites in the SE ʿAraba appears to be related directly to proximity to local resources, such as water or minerals, or in areas that facilitate travel or transport, such as wādī systems. This distribution is largely that of site clusters near local resources, although some sites — generally more ephemeral ones — are more isolated. This may reflect geomorphological bias, perhaps even related to climatic conditions in antiquity, because most sites throughout the study area seem more transitory, especially those more distant from important resources. What follows is an assessment of the site data that highlights any patterns or relationships of significance in terms of settlement activity in the region. This discussion deals primarily with the proto-historical and historical periods, from the Chalcolithic to the Islamic period, with cursory treatment of the Paleolithic and Neolithic periods.

The Prehistoric Periods

As Henry et al. note in Chapter 5, the evidence collected by the present project relative to the prehistoric periods must be treated with great caution. The survey produced some evidence of the presence of Paleolithic peoples in the region, but this cannot in any way be regarded as a representative sample. Nevertheless, Henry observes that the density of both Paleolithic and Neolithic sites in both the southern Wādī 'Araba and the valley in general is relatively low, particularly compared to the subsequent Chalcolithic and Early Bronze Age periods. He suggests that this density is best explained by "a combination of prehistoric settlement strategy and geomorphic bias," i.e., that Paleolithic and Neolithic sites were buried under later sediments (Henry 2006: 99).

The absence of nearly any Late Neolithic pottery in the study area could also be due to a recognition problem, lack of visible sites, or a combination of both, although a possible Neolithic presence is suggested by two problematic sherds from Site 287. The fact that several Late Neolithic sites have been recorded near Eilat (Avner, Carmi, and Segal 1994) suggests that sites belonging to this period may still be discovered (Mellaart 1975; Moore 1973). Also, in the foothills of the 'Araba between Wādī Nukheila and Wādī Ḥeimir, Henry et al. (2001: 10–11) documented a substantial Late Neolithic site with abundant lithics but no pottery, which suggests that more sites may be discovered by more intensive survey of the region, especially in the north. Interestingly, their findings suggest a moister regional climate for the Late Neolithic period than that of today. A wetter climate has also been postulated for the Chalcolithic and Early Bronze Age (Niemi and Smith 1999), when settlement in Wādī 'Araba intensified.

Chalcolithic and Early Bronze Age

There is considerable evidence of human activity during the Chalcolithic and Early Bronze Age throughout the study area. Sites cluster along the Wādī Yutum alluvial fan north of Aqaba at Tell Maqaṣṣ and Ḥujeirat al-Ghuzlan, along the north bank of Wādī Yutum itself, near Wādī Gharandal, in Wādī el-Queib, Wādī Museimīr, and along the escarpment south and north of Wādī Abū Barqa. The SAAS also recorded Chalcolithic or Chalcolithic/Early Bronze Age sites, although in less concentrated numbers, near Wādī es-Sammāniya, Wādī el-Muhtadī, Sīḫ Duḥayla, Wādī Ḍarba, Wādī Nukheila, Jebel el-Khureij, in Wādī Ḥeimir, to the south of Wādī es-Sīq, and near Wādī Um Saiyāla and Qasr Wādī eṭ-Ṭayyiba.

There is some evidence of copper smelting in the Chalcolithic or Chalcolithic/Early Bronze Age at Wādī el-Muhtadī, Wādī el-Queib, and Wādī Abū Barqa. There must be further investigation to determine how this activity relates to the settlement activity and mining industry in the Faynan region further north (Bachmann and Hauptmann 1984; Hauptmann 1986; Hauptmann, Weisgerber, and Knauf 1985; Hauptmann and Weisgerber 1987; Hauptmann et al. 1992; Barker et al. 1997; 1998; 1999; 2000), or to that of Timna to the SW (Rothenberg 1962; 1999a; 1999b). It is also unclear whether the copper found at sites in the study area derived from the Timna or from the Faynan districts (Burgath, Hagen, and Siewers 1984; Ilan and Sebbane 1989; Hauptman 2006).

Further mineral extraction is evident in the Chalcolithic or Chalcolithic/Early Bronze Age along the escarpment north of Wādī Abū Barqa, where there is an outcropping of schist with garnet inclusions (Ibrahim 1993: 65). The SAAS found garnet nuggets or schist with garnet inclusions at Sites 260, 283, 285–87, 294, and 296. Site 283 (fig. 4.23) may in fact date to the Early Roman/Nabataean period and Sites 287, 294, and 296 are all small settlements. Chalcolithic/Early Bronze Age pottery predominated at Site 287 and was the only datable pottery from Site 294. Site 296 yielded no artifacts. How the garnet mined or gathered from the area was used (e.g., as an ornamental stone) cannot be determined, since there seems to be no excavated contexts in the region where the material has surfaced.

The relationship between the Chalcolithic or Chalcolithic/Early Bronze Age sites from the northern and southern sectors of the study area and the relationship between these sites with other Chalcolithic settlements in the Levant remains problematic (cf. Hanbury-Tenison 1986; Avner, Carmi, and Segal 1994; Prag 2001). Tell Maqaṣṣ and Ḥujeirat al-Ghuzlan certainly represent a shift (at least from the preceding Neolithic period) toward larger settlements based on irrigation agriculture, in contrast to the more ephemeral settlements further north in the valley, where pastoralism may have been a more common means of subsistence. There is, for example, a general lack of agricultural features in the north, though large sites with architectural features may still suggest some subsistence activity based on horticulture. Unfortunately, the patterns of economy and settlement for the Chalcolithic period or the Chalcolithic/Early Bronze Age are not well-understood (Henry 1995: 354–55). The relationship between transitory and more settled activity in the valley, to the extent that this was based on geomorphological variables and climatic conditions, should be examined more thoroughly (Henry et al. 2001; Barker et al. 2000). Thus, without some excavation of the sites in the north, both architectural sites and transitory ones, and more closely datable artifacts on which to base analyses, no chronological sequencing of the Chalcolithic or Chalcolithic/Early Bronze Age data can be attempted that might determine the contemporaneity and interrelationships of sites throughout the study area, much less draw comparisons or contrasts with sites immediately outside the study area. For example, it may be safe to conclude that the majority of the Chalcolithic or Chalcolithic/Early Bronze Age sites from the project reflect "Timnian" occupational patterns in which settlement was primarily in small, ephemeral hamlets and seasonal camps—such as those found in the desert of Sinai (Kozloff 1981; Eddy and Wendorf 1999) and in southern Jordan (Henry 1982; 1992; 1995: 353–54)—and subsistence activity was based largely on nomadic pastoralism. The sites north of Aqaba, however, would seem anomalous in this assessment, because Tell Maqaṣṣ and Ḥujeirat al-Ghuzlan, in addition to sites in their vicinity, closely resemble "Ghassulian" occupational patterns, which are characterized by more permanent settlement activity and subsistence based less on

pastoralism than on horticulture (Gilead 1988). Further investigation is necessary to determine whether one or the other pattern was more or less intrusive to the region and the extent to which either pattern grew from natural responses to the environment, in particular climatic conditions.

Only a few sites yielded clear evidence of the Early Bronze Age. These were in Wādī Ḥeimir, where Sites 158–59 and 162–63 appear to be settlements and Sites 157 and 161 perhaps are of cultic significance, and immediately north of Aqaba. But this limited evidence is probably due more to difficulties distinguishing clear divisions between Early Bronze Age and Late Chalcolithic material culture (Avner 1978: 66–68). The ceramic and chipped stone assemblages collected from sites near Aqaba, for instance, suggest occupation in both periods, and the recent Jordanian-German excavations in Wādī Yutum have confirmed an Early Bronze Age presence at the sites there. Smith et al. (1997: 52) emphasized the relatively large number of tabular chert scraper knives and fragments found at sites in the vicinity of Ḥujeirat al-Ghuzlan, in addition to a backed retouched and truncated sickle blade, glossed on both edges, recovered from Site 54. Such evidence indeed suggests that occupation in the region continued from the Chalcolithic into the Early Bronze Age. However, because of the paucity of published regional assemblages, analyses of lithic and pottery data from the region are at an early stage and not entirely reliable for distinguishing between Late Chalcolithic and Early Bronze Age settlement activity (Brückner et al. 2002: 248–49).

Middle Bronze and Late Bronze Age

No pottery from the survey could be identified as Middle Bronze Age, and the Late Bronze Age is represented only at one site by a single sherd. This general picture is mirrored in the NE Wādī ʿAraba (MacDonald 1992: 71) and in the valley in general (Bienkowski 2006: 13). There is a limited Late Bronze Age presence at sites to the west and south, however. There is evidence of so-called "Midianite" pottery or "Qurayya painted ware" throughout the region and beyond. It is attested in NW Arabia, at sites in Wādī ʿAraba, and in the northern Negev. It is attested at Yotvata, Timna, Tell el-Kheleifeh, and on the island of Jezirat Faraun in the Gulf of Aqaba (Rothenberg 1972: 180–202; 1988: 93–94, figs. 4–13; Dayton 1972; Kalsbeek and London 1978; Parr 1982; Rothenberg and Glass 1983; Bawden and Edens 1988; Pratico 1993: 49–50). It is usually dated to the 13th and 12th and perhaps 11th centuries BC, although Bienkowski has argued for continued use in southern Jordan into the 9th century based on radiocarbon dating. Midianite pottery is limited to a few sherds at Yotvata and Jezirat Faraun and may be interpreted largely as transient activity. The same is probably true of the few Midianite sherds from Tell el-Kheleifeh, which lack any reliable stratigraphic context (Pratico 1993: 50). The Midianite presence is far more extensive at Timna, however, and related to the Egyptian mining expeditions between the 14th and 12th centuries BC (Rothenberg 1988: 270–78). In contrast, the SAAS found no Midianite pottery in the study area.

Negevite pottery, a coarse handmade ware, is generally regarded as contemporary with Midianite wares. This pottery, however, cannot be used as a close chronological indicator, since it spans from at least the 13th to 6th centuries BC (Pratico 1993: 35–38). The SAAS collected pottery resembling Negevite ware at a few of the Chalcolithic/Early Bronze Age sites in the valley just north of Aqaba, but especially at Tell el-Kheleifeh. This may suggest that these sites were reoccupied in later periods. As a coarse handmade ware, however, this pottery should not be regarded as indicative of any specific period, since handmade pottery production continues today with strikingly similar results. This is particularly true if this pottery is analyzed solely based on typological indications of ware and/or fabric and/or form. Perhaps these handmade wares are more indicative of a particular lifestyle in areas where individuals and/or communities shifted between nomadic and sedentary modes of existence.

The Iron Age and Persian Period

The Iron Age is sparsely represented in the survey area and in the southern Wādī 'Araba generally. A few Iron I Age sites are attested on the western side of the valley, some associated with the copper mines around Timna. Yet, as noted in a recent synthesis, there is also an apparent absence of Iron II sites thus far on the western side of the southern valley (Bienkowski 2006: 14). Glueck's excavation of Tell el-Kheleifeh on the coast NW of Aqaba originally concluded that occupation began in the 10th century BC. But Pratico's study of the pottery suggests occupation from the 8th to 4th centuries BC (Pratico 1993: 71–72). This agrees with our own pottery collection from the site and the 1999 soundings by M.-L. Mussell, unfortunately largely unpublished before her untimely death (Mussell 2000). Also, Site 180, a settlement near Wādī Gharandal, yielded 11 possible Iron Age sherds. For the most part, the Iron Age is negligible elsewhere, although some sherds of undetermined age may date to this period. Evidence from Hart's survey on the plateau (Hart 1987: 287; 1992) and Jobling's survey to the east (Jobling 1981; 1983), when compared to evidence from gathered by the SAAS, suggests that the region was sparsely settled by sedentary peoples in the early Iron Age (12th through 10th centuries BC). This may explain the Iron Age material at the rather ephemeral sites near Wādī Abū Barqa (Sites 247 and 256), where enigmatic clearings were identified as bedouin weaving strips. Iron Age sites were more numerous in northern parts of our study area (Hart 1992; MacDonald 1992: 73–81; Fritz 1994; Cohen 1994; Cohen and Yisrael 1995; 1996; Levy 2009; Levy et al. 1999; 2003; 2004).

A major external factor on Wādī 'Araba in this period was the rise of trade routes, above all for incense, connecting the southern Arabian Peninsula and the Mediterranean. This development, it is usually argued, is associated with the domestication of the camel as a vehicle for long-distance transport (Zarins 1989). Reconstructions of the overland route usually pass through Wādī 'Araba, but its origins have been variously dated from as early as the 13th/12th centuries to as late as the 7th century BC (Albright 1970; Groom 1981; Finkelstein 1988; 1995; Retsö 1991). A more recent analysis connects the rise of the incense route with continued Egyptian exploitation of the Timna copper mines in the 13th/12th centuries (Jasmin 2006).

Although some scholars have argued for an earlier date, the Edomites had emerged with a distinct settled culture no later than the 8th century BC (Hart 1987: 287; Knauf and Lenzen 1987; Bienkowski 1995; Levy et al. 2004). The northern head of the Gulf of Aqaba is described in the biblical tradition as being disputed and controlled in different periods by both Edomites and Judaeans (Bartlett 1989; Bienkowski 2001). Pratico emphasizes Edomite influence in his analysis of wheelmade pottery from Tell el-Kheleifeh, which serves as a basis for his 8th- to 4th-century BC date for the site. Architectural parallels, meanwhile, link Tell el-Kheleifeh with other Judaean Iron Age sites in the Negev, some as early as the 10th century BC (Pratico 1993: 71–73). Still unresolved is this disparity between the late Iron Age date of the pottery from Tell el-Kheleifeh and the earlier dates suggested by the architecture.

Apart from Tell el-Kheleifeh, the SAAS recorded no Persian or Hellenistic period sites, which may suggest another gap in sedentary occupation in the area from at least the 5th to the early 2nd centuries BC. Even the Hellenistic and Persian material at Tell el-Kheleifeh does not suggest substantial settlement activity. Limited activity, however, is suggested epigraphically (Divito 1993: 51–63). Of interest is the discovery of a stamped Rhodian jar handle from Tell el-Kheleifeh dated to ca. 200 BC (Divito 1993: 62); the RAP staff collected a similar sherd at Tell el-Kheleifeh in 1996. Further north, there was Hellenistic occupation at Moyat 'Awad in the western 'Araba, and MacDonald identified seven sites (3.8% of all sites) from this period during his survey of the southern Ghor and northeast 'Araba (MacDonald 1992: 83–95; Cohen 1993b). Yet these were the poorest-represented periods among MacDonald's sites. Nevertheless, it may be that some pottery from the SAAS identified as Early Roman/Nabataean actually belongs to the Late Hellenistic period.

Hellenistic and Early Roman/Nabataean

Diodorus Siculus, writing in the 1st century BC but relying on earlier Hellenistic sources, provides a description of the region and its inhabitants in the 4th century BC. The Nabataeans, according to Diodorus, "live in the open air, claiming as native land a wilderness that has neither rivers nor abundant springs … and it is their custom neither to plant grain, set out any fruit-bearing tree, use wine, nor construct any house; and if anyone is found acting contrary to this, death is his penalty" (19.94; cf. Diodorus 2.48–49). Again according to Diodorus (3.43.3), the Nabataeans in the Hellenistic period inhabited many villages along the coast of the Gulf of Aqaba, raised livestock, and engaged in naval piracy. There seems to be some contradiction here, since one passage infers that the Nabataeans were nomads and the latter mentions them living in villages. One might conclude that the Nabataeans included both sedentary and nomadic elements, a phenomenon well-attested in later and in better documented periods in the region. Assuming the reliability of Diodorus' depiction, then, at least some portion of the Nabataeans were nomads who survived in part by an ability to secure and manage water resources in the desert. This raises an important question: what sort of imprint on the archaeological landscape might we expect from nomads? We should recognize that groups pursuing "nomadic" subsistence strategies do leave evidence of their activities, mostly in the form of campsites, which tend to be well-preserved in desert regions (Rosen 1988a; 1988b; 1992; Cribb 1991). Thus some sites documented by the SAAS which yielded no artifacts but apparent evidence of pastoralist activities may belong to this period.

A recent synthesis of the Negev during the Hellenistic period suggests that the Nabataean presence in this region was largely limited to securing passage of the caravan traffic from Petra across the northern Wādī 'Araba and the Negev en route to Gaza. They constructed a series of small forts along the Petra–Gaza route that protected and serviced this traffic in the 3rd and 2nd centuries BC (Erickson-Gini 2006: 157–60).

By the late 1st century BC, the situation had seemingly changed. The Nabataeans had become sedentary (Strabo, *Geography* 16.4.21–26). This settlement activity in our study area may be apparent at the village of Rujm aṭ-Ṭāba and at many other minor sites with architectural features. For example, the SAAS collected Early Roman/Nabataean sherds at 88 sites, some of which may have been inhabited in the 1st centuries BC/AD. However, it is not possible in most cases, based on the few closely datable surface sherds, to determine whether a site is pre- or post-Roman annexation (AD 106). Furthermore, the presence of

Nabataean pottery does not necessarily suggest that the entire population of these sites was sedentary. Though it is true that nomadic or semi-nomadic (or semi-sedentary) peoples are difficult to discern archaeologically because of such factors as mobility and use of perishable items, their presence, as noted, is not altogether lost in the archaeological landscape. Perhaps there are residual traces of their activities in the many cemeteries, cairns, or isolated graves distributed throughout the study area, particularly in areas remote from sedentary sites. It is also not self-evident that nomadic or semi-nomadic peoples abstain entirely from the use of non-perishable items such as pottery, or that they themselves never engage in the production of crude pottery. Several sites, for example, with Nabataean pottery were ephemeral in nature and included encampments.

The Nabataean period was by far the best-represented period in terms of ceramic evidence recovered by the survey. Nabataean pottery appeared at 89 survey sites, or 27.0% of all sites, which yielded 31.1% of all sherds collected by the survey. Nabataean sites are distributed throughout the study region. These range from transitory sites, such as encampments, to more permanent villages or fortified settlements that show signs of agricultural activity. Unfortunately, we cannot be more precise about the chronological distribution of the evidence in terms of forms of subsistence activity. It is notable however that, among the sites that yielded closely datable Nabataean pottery, the earliest dates to the late 1st century BC (Schmid's Dekorphase 2b), with most dating to the 1st century AD (Schmid's Dekorphase 3a–3b; Schmid 1996; 2000). In short, the picture of Nabataean sedentary settlement in the SE Wādī 'Araba accords fairly well with that in the Negev as proposed by Erickson-Gini.

Further Nabataean presence in the region is attested by a group of seven Nabataean Aramaic inscriptions near the intersection of Wādī Museimīr and Wādī 'Araba. The inscriptions cluster around several small structures and possible burial cairns (Site 289). The associated pottery at this site was Nabataean and Late Roman. Graf in Chapter 7 notes that the paleography of the inscriptions suggests a date in the 1st or 2nd century AD. Although

merely graffiti, these are significant as the first recorded Nabataean inscriptions in the southern 'Araba.

It is indeed likely that, from at least the late 1st century BC, pastoralists and agriculturalists comingled in the region, perhaps as long as a central authority guaranteed regional security. The development of a Nabataean standing army probably facilitated stability in the region, though we know too little of the makeup of these forces or their deployment (Bowsher 1989; Graf 1994). Perhaps these forces account for the Nabataean presence at the major defensive outposts of the valley, including Gharandal (fig. 4.17) and Bir Madhkur in our area, in addition to several other important sites to the north and west (MacDonald 1992: 86–89; Cohen 1993a; 1993b; 1994; Meshel 1993). These sites served a dual purpose of guarding local resources, especially water, and monitoring traffic in the valley.

It is not clear to what extent the Nabataeans exploited the rich copper resources of the valley. Although Hauptmann and Weisgerber (1992) have dated the principal period of copper extraction and processing during the classical era at Faynan to the 2nd to 4th centuries AD, i.e., after the Roman annexation, others have argued for at least limited Nabataean smelting (Mattingly et al. 2007a: 293; Grattan et al. 2007).

Generally, the Nabataean occupation of the region is viewed in the context of their role as middle-men in the incense trade with South Arabia. Imported amphorae from this period appeared at Rujm aṭ-Ṭāba (Site 152), which yielded sherds of Class 10/Dressel 2–4 amphorae (Peacock 1986: 105–6) and Site 330, which produced a handle of a Class 9, or Rhodian, amphora (Peacock 1986: 102–4). The fortified settlements in the 'Araba thus guarded the trade passing from Petra or Aila en route to ports along the Mediterranean coast or to the cities of the north, though goods would also have been shipped to Aila or Petra as well for export (Dolinka 2003: 91–97; Graf 1992).

Aila was a Nabataean foundation in the late 1st century BC. Parker has suggested that Aila was founded as a response to the threat to Nabataean commercial interests posed by new or revitalized ports on the Egyptian Red Sea coast after the Roman conquest of Egypt in 30 BC. These Egyptian ports began to divert the eastern commercial traffic away from the traditional caravan route across the Arabian Peninsula and perhaps even sea trade via the Nabataean port of Leuke Kome. Thus the Nabataeans wanted a new port to extend the sea lanes as far north as possible on the Arabian side of the Red Sea (Parker 2009a).

The foundation of Aila should also be considered in light of other regional developments in this period. Erickson-Gini has argued that in the late 1st century BC the Nabataeans developed a network of roads and caravan stations along a previously little-used route across the Ramon Crater between Petra and Gaza. This was a more direct route than the earlier Hellenistic route, which crossed the Negev farther north. Further, she suggests, this period witnessed the first extensive Nabataean settlement in the Negev in general. Such settlement intensified in the 1st century AD, with the establishment of large agricultural villages such as Oboda, Mampsis, Rehovot, Nessana, and Sobota (Erikson-Gini 2006: 160–63). Thus, as seen above, it is notable that the closely datable Nabataean sites from the SE ʿAraba also date to this period. Petra itself witnessed the development of a perfume industry, a value-added product derived from processing imported incense. Johnson has argued that this industry appeared in precisely this period, i.e., the late 1st century BC (Johnson 1987; 1990). The receptacles of this product, Nabataean ceramic unguentaria, begin appearing at this time in the archaeological record at many sites, including Aila, as testimony to the widespread trade of this product.

The Nabataean settlement of Humayma (Avara), about midway between Aila and Petra in the northern Hisma on the route later formalized by the *Via Nova Traiana*, also was apparently founded in this period. Although the excavators suggest its foundation under either Aretas III (ca. 85–62 BC) or Aretas IV (9 BC–AD 40; Oleson 2010: 50–53), the ceramics from the site published to date clearly suggest the latter reign as the more likely possibility. In particular, there seems to be no evidence at Humayma of the earliest Nabataean painted fine ware pottery (Dekorphase 1, ca. 150–50 BC) but abundant evidence for later periods, especially Dekorphase 3a (ca. AD 20–70; Schmid 1996; 2000). Given the recent development of

a reasonably tight Nabataean ceramic typology, especially for the fine wares, it should be profitable to re-examine surface ceramic collections from other sites in southern Jordan to date more closely the beginnings of Nabataean sedentary settlement. At this point one can only suspect that such intensification of sedentary settlement of the rural landscape in southern Jordan also began in the late 1st century BC.

Whatever the precise date of their foundation, the numerous Nabataean/Early Roman sites in the SE ʿAraba yielded significant quantities of Nabataean fine wares, likely imported from Petra. Some of the coarse wares from survey sites derived from Aila (Dolinka 2003: 79–90). This implies some level of commercial contact with both cities in this period. A handful of sigillata sherds (mostly Eastern Sigillata A) recovered at seven sites scattered over the region reflect imports from even farther afield. It is unclear whether such fine ware sherds imply importation for local consumption or merely accidental breakage of such goods in transit between the major urban centers. Excavation of Aila, for example, yielded over 2,000 fragments of Eastern Sigillata A.

Late Roman

Scholars continue to debate the causes of the Roman annexation of Nabataea in AD 106. The diversity of opinion is in large part due to the paucity of primary sources. Earlier notions of a relatively peaceful transition to direct Roman rule have been challenged by emerging archaeological evidence, which may suggest serious Nabataean resistance to the annexation. This is obviously not the forum to rehearse this issue (for a convenient summary, cf. Parker 2009c), but evidence from Aila itself suggests some discontinuity of occupation in three Nabataean domestic areas (Areas B, M, and O) excavated on the northern fringes of the site. All three domestic complexes were temporarily abandoned around the turn of the 2nd century, but then were soon reoccupied later in the same century (Parker 2003: 321–24, 331–32; Retzleff 2003). Evidence of destruction and then abandonment around this period is also attested farther south in Area J. An earthquake, which also seems to have affected the region at the beginning of the 2nd century, may have been an additional factor or even serve as an alternative explanation to human agency (Thomas, Niemi, and Parker 2007; Parker 2009c).

The evidence recovered from the project's survey sheds little light on this issue. Significantly fewer sites (n=19) yielded evidence of Late Roman occupation compared to the preceding Early Roman/Nabataean period. But, as discussed in the chapter on the pottery from the survey, such evidence should be interpreted cautiously. First, many of the more broadly dated "Early Roman/Late Roman" sherds may well date to the later period. This could increase the number of Late Roman sites to as many as 28. Further, the Nabataean ceramic tradition clearly continued long after the Roman annexation, i.e., through the 2nd and well into the 3rd century; effectively, most of the Late Roman period. Therefore, some pottery dated "Early Roman/Nabataean" could in fact date to the Late Roman period, especially to the 2nd century. Several sites did yield Nabataean painted fine ware sherds of Schmid's Dekorphase 3c, or ca. AD 100–150. All these caveats aside, the evidence does suggest a decline in sedentary settlement in this period compared to the Early Roman/Nabataean Period.

Aila itself gained greater prominence following the Roman annexation of Nabataea in AD 106 as the southern terminus of the *Via Nova Traiana,* the highway that linked Aila with Bostra in Syria (Graf 1995). It may be significant that the dated milestones of this road suggest that the segment extending north from Aila was completed first, in AD 111, while more northerly segments were not finished until up to three years later. A secondary network of roads presumably existed in the 'Araba at that time as well, both to facilitate N–S traffic along the length of the valley and E–W traffic across the valley (Aharoni 1954; 1963; cf. Rothenberg 1971). Sites 169 and 231 (fig. 4.16) may both be interpreted as possible remains of such a network. Also, segments of an ancient road and a cache of sandstone milestones have been identified in the western 'Araba north of Yotvata, but these date from AD 293 to 324 (Avner 1996; Avner and Roll 1997) and are thus contemporary with a Tetrarchic inscription from Yotvata itself (Roll 1989). This road in fact may have followed an earlier, well-

established course, perhaps even passing through 'En Defiya ('Ain Defiya) where the remains of a road station, founded in the Early Roman/Nabataean period but clearly occupied into the 2nd and 3rd centuries, have been excavated (Cohen 1993b; Dolinka 2006a; Smith 2010: 28–29). Directly related to the development of the 'Araba's road system are Site 274 and possibly Site 307. These are both ancient quarries. The SAAS found five fragmentary anepigraphic milestones at Site 274 (fig. 4.22), and the quarrying activity at the site most likely relates to construction of the Roman fort in Qā' as-Su'aydiyyīn (Site 275; fig. 4.20; Smith 2010: 34–36). Most of the pottery collected at the fort dates to the 2nd century, suggesting that the Romans built the fort shortly after the annexation. A papyrus from Karanis of AD 107, just after the annexation, documents stone-cutting by Roman legionaries in Arabia (Husselman 1971: 8.466). Occupation at the fort in Qā' as-Su'aydiyyīn and the quarrying at Site 274, however, do not seem to continue much beyond the 2nd century, though this would need to be confirmed by excavation. In addition, the SAAS documented numerous towers, or possible towers, in the study area that may have safeguarded some of the routes through the valley. This includes Site 81 (fig. 4.37), which overlooks the mouth of the Wādī Yutum, in addition to Sites 113, 136, 171, 186, 190, 205, 216, 224, 237, and 330. Sites 113, 171, 186, and 237 all yielded Early Roman/Nabataean pottery; Sites 81, 136, 190, 205, 216, and 224 yielded no pottery; and the ceramics from Site 330 ranged in date from Early Roman to Late Byzantine.

Aila itself has yielded much evidence during the Late Roman period to suggest continued economic vitality, perhaps after a brief decline immediately following the Roman annexation. In addition to completion of the *Via Nova Traiana,* mentioned above, the reopening of the Nile–Red Sea canal in the same period allowed for direct access to Egypt by an all-water route, although probably only on a seasonal basis (Parker 2009b). This may explain the dramatic increase in this period of Egyptian amphorae, which begin to surpass those from Gaza as the most abundant imported amphorae at Aila, and the first appearance of Egyptian Red Slip pottery in the 3rd century. Nevertheless, Aila undoubtedly continued to exploit Wādī 'Araba in this period. Recent research suggests that this was the most intensive period of copper mining at Faynan. Aila itself has yielded copper ore, copper slag, and hundreds of copper and copper alloy artifacts (Parker 1998: 389). The city also probably continued to import fuel, food, and other resources from the 'Araba and exported marine products, dates, and transshipped goods from the Red Sea littoral northward via the 'Araba.

Early Byzantine

Only 18 sites yielded Early Byzantine pottery, representing 5.5% of all sites and roughly equivalent to the number of Late Roman sites. Several small settlements were abandoned, seemingly by the end of the Late Roman period, which include Sites 113, 152–53 (Rujm aṭ-Ṭāba), 208, 225, the fort in Qaʿ as-Suʾaydiyyīn (Site 275; fig. 4.20), and Qaṣr Wādī eṭ-Ṭayyiba (Site 319), in addition to those sites recorded in the vicinity of Ain eṭ-Ṭayyiba (Sites 320–28). This is mirrored in the west at 'En Defiya (Dolinka 2006a), Bir Menua, and 'En Rael (Cohen 1993b). There are also fewer sites from the later periods recorded within the immediate hinterland of Aqaba. Some exceptions include Sites 72 and 106–7, which show no break in settlement between these periods. These sites could be interpreted as agricultural, while additional agricultural activity near Wādī Mulghān in the later Roman and Byzantine periods may be evidenced at Sites 103–4 and further north in the valley at Sites 139 and 203.

The turn of the 4th century also witnessed a major administrative change, as Wādī 'Araba along with the Negev and southern Jordan were transferred from the province of Arabia to Palestine. Palestine itself was then partitioned later in the 4th century, with the 'Araba assigned to *Palaestina Salutaris* (later styled *Palaestina Tertia*). As was typical elsewhere, provincial authority was divided between a civilian governor, or *praeses,* and a military governor, or *dux.*

Continued trade through the region is suggested by imported fine ware (African Red Slip) attested at six SAAS sites (7, 17, 31, 98, 221, and 329) and a few imported amphora sherds from the Gaza region and Egypt (Sites 104, 203, 329). These could not be closely dated but may be Byzantine.

While the hinterland of Roman Aila may have experienced a decline in settled population from the Early Roman/Nabataean to the Early Byzantine period, the urban population must have increased significantly by the end of the 3rd century. Eusebius (*Onomasticon* 6.17–20; 8.1–3) informs us of the transfer of *Legio X Fretensis* from Jerusalem to Aila by this time, when it was the base of the prefect of this legion (*Notitia Dignitatum Or.* 34.30). There may have been some connection between the transfer of the legion to Aila and the apparent abandonment of some of the smaller defensive outposts and watchtowers in the valley (e.g., Sites 81, 113, 153, 171, 224, 237, 275, and 319), but our sources are silent on any such circumstances. Perhaps security conditions predicated such shifts in settlement patterns. Occupation at larger settlements such as Gharandal (fig. 4.17) and Bir Madhkur in the east, and Yotvata and Ḥazeva in the west, nevertheless, continued into the Early Byzantine period, although a decline in settlement at this time seems evident at 'En Defiya and Moyat 'Awad in the western 'Araba (Meshel 1989; Cohen 1993b; 1994; Roll 1989; Kindler 1989; cf. discussion by Graf 2001). This is hardly surprising, since these sites continued to safeguard a key resource of the valley: water.

The *Notitia Dignitatum* places several military units in the valley in the late 4th century under the *dux Palaestinae* (*Or.* 34). In addition to the legion at Aila, mentioned above, many scholars identify sites and thus units listed in this document with nine sites in the 'Araba, including two units of *equites sagittarii indigenae* (*N.D. Or.* 34.26, 29), three *alae* (*N.D. Or.* 32, 34, 36), and four *cohortes* (*N.D. Or.* 38, 42–44; cf. Smith 2010: 112, plus the second unit of *equites sagittarii indigenae,* based at Zoara,). These units, combined with *Legio X Fretensis* at Aila, represented a substantial military commitment to control the valley. These were strung out along both sides of the valley, generally at key water sources and/or where major E–W routes crossed the valley. The dated milestones from the western 'Araba of 293–324 and the Tetrarchic inscription from Yotvata have already been cited above, plus the newly discovered Tetrarchic military inscription from Gharandal. All this suggests that these arrangements date back to reign of Diocletian (284–305), who clearly was responsible for a major strengthening of the entire southeastern frontier (Parker 2009d).

A major unresolved question is how long the copper industry continued in the valley. It was certainly vigorous in the 4th century, as attested by various literary sources and archaeological evidence. Byzantine ecclesiastical sources continue to mention the site through the 5th and into the 6th century (Smith 2010: 25–28), but Hauptmann suggests that copper production ended at Faynan ca. 500 (Hauptmann et al. 1992: 8).

Aila itself was clearly flourishing throughout the Byzantine period. A major monumental structure, interpreted as an early church, was erected around the turn of the 4th century (Parker 2003: 324–26). Some intra-site migration is observable in the 4th century, however, as the northern domestic areas were abandoned in favor of settlement farther south. In the late 4th or early 5th century, the city was fortified (or possibly refortified) by a stone curtain wall with projecting towers (Parker 2003: 326–29). Significant levels of commerce at Aila are suggested by large numbers of imported amphorae, especially from Egypt and Gaza but also from a variety of other Mediterranean sources, and imported fine wares, especially African Red Slip. Above all is the appearance ca. 400 of the Aila amphorae, produced in huge numbers in the city itself. Although there is some evidence for export of these containers northwards, as they are attested for example at Humayma and Petra, it is notable that the SAAS produced not a single sherd of these Aila amphorae. It thus seems clear that the primary market for this traffic was southwards by sea along the Red Sea littoral (Parker 2009b).

Late Byzantine and Early Islamic

In the hinterland of Aila and elsewhere in the SE ʿAraba, there are few Late Byzantine and Early Islamic period sites. The survey recovered 305 sherds identified as Late Byzantine from 23 sites, (7.0% of all sites). The survey recovered Early Islamic pottery, including 30 Umayyad (ca. 630–750) and 18 Abassid (ca. 750–961) sherds, from thirteen sites (3.9% of all sites). Because some ceramic forms and wares of the Late Byzantine period continued into the Early Islamic period, this might understate

the amount of Early Islamic material present. On the other hand, since the excavations at Aqaba produced several excellent stratigraphic sequences of Early Islamic material, it seems unlikely that any significant amount of Early Islamic material recovered by the survey went unrecognized. This could reflect a significant decline in the regional population from the 6th century (Schick 1995). When Aila capitulated to the Muslims in 630, for example, Yuḥanna ibn Ruʾba, the official negotiating the terms at distant Tabuk, agreed to pay a one dinar poll tax per adult, a total of 300 dinars (for a discussion of sources, see Schick 1995: 151–54). If this sum is accurate, there would appear to have been a drop in the population of Aila itself between ca. 300, when the *Legio X Fretensis* was transferred to the city, and 630. Perhaps the demobilization of the legion, possibly ca. 530 (Parker 1986: 151–54), affected the city's demographics. In contrast, it may also be that Yuḥanna intentionally understated Aila's population in order to keep the tax low. Interestingly, the treaty specifically guaranteed protection of Aila's trade by land and sea, which suggests that the city continued in the 7th century to serve as a commercial nexus of regional importance — thus the routes through Wādī ʿAraba probably remained in use. Furthermore, evidence from the RAP excavations underscores Aila's prosperity in the Late Byzantine and Early Islamic periods (Parker 1997a; 1998; 2000), though this contrasts with the evidence from the survey of the immediate countryside, which shows the gradual abandonment of rural sites in these periods.

This evidence may also be viewed in light of the Beersheba Edict, an (apparently) 6th-century inscription that lists a number of sites (mostly in *Palaestina Tertia*) and amounts to be collected and/ or paid in *solidi*. The fragmentary nature of the text has led to widely divergent interpretations. A recent reinterpretation, based in part on the discovery of a new fragment of the inscription at Beersheba, includes a useful survey of previous scholarship on the issue (Di Segni 2004). Di Segni suggests that the text lists amounts to be paid by local soldiers and civilians as a special tax to fund facilities and services for pilgrims traveling through the region. Whatever interpretation is accepted, the text clearly lists several settlements usually identified with toponyms in Wādī ʿAraba, including several with garrisons, but with few if any in the SE ʿAraba.

This picture of few archaeological sites recorded in the SE ʿAraba of the Late Byzantine or Early Islamic period, interestingly, contrasts with evidence from the SW ʿAraba that shows a sharp increase in regional settlement activity in the Early Islamic period (Avner and Magness 1998; Whitcomb 2006). It is not clear why such a shift in settlement activity to the west seems apparent in the archaeological record. Perhaps it is due to a recognition problem, but this would seem unlikely in light of all the comparative data from Aqaba itself (Parker 2000; Whitcomb 1994). The SAAS, nonetheless, recorded some sites of the Early Islamic periods, which allows for a limited discussion. The Early Islamic activity documented behind Jebel esh-Shahbī, for instance, may have related to the collection of raw materials for local glass production, or perhaps may have been connected with the gold production documented in

the 10th century in the SW ʿAraba (Amar 1997). In order to substantiate either supposition, however, further investigation would be necessary.

Late Islamic

The SAAS recovered pottery identified as Late Islamic at only four sites or only 1.2% of all sites. This picture is confirmed, at least for the 18th and 19th centuries, by Western travelers, who reported primarily the presence of nomadic tribes in Wādī ʿAraba on a seasonal basis (van der Steen 2006; Bailey 2006). The only conclusion that we can draw is that this portion of the valley was sparsely settled in terms of sedentary folk in the Late Islamic period. In fact, much of both the Early and Late Islamic period evidence suggests nomadic transhumance more than settlement. Aqaba itself, of course, was little more than a sleepy fishing village and seasonal stop for the Haj by the Ottoman period.

REFERENCES

Aharoni, Y.
1954   The Roman Road to Aila (Elath). *IEJ* 4: 9–16.
1963   Tamar and the Roads to Elath. *IEJ* 13: 30–42.

Albright, W. F.
1970   Midianite Donkey Caravans. Pp. 197–205 in *Translating and Understanding the Old Testament: Essays in Honor of Herbert G. May,* eds. H. T. Frank and W. L. Reed. Nashville, TN: Abingdon.

Amar, Z.
1997   Gold Production in the ʿAraba Valley in the 10th Century. *IEJ* 47: 100–103.

Avner, U.
1978   Survey in the Eilat Region. *Hadashot Arkheologiyot (Archaeological Newsletter)* 67–68: 66–68.
1996   ʿAraba Valley. In "Archaeology in Israel," ed. S. R. Wolff. *AJA* 100: 762–64.

Avner, U.; Carmi, I.; and Segal, D.
1994   Neolithic to Bronze Age Settlement of the Negev and Sinai in Light of Radiocarbon Dating: A View from the Southern Negev. Pp. 265–300 in *Late Quaternary Chronology and Paleoclimates of the Eastern Mediterranean,* eds. O. Bar-Yosef and R. S. Kra. Tucson, AZ: Radiocarbon.

Avner, U.; Davies, G.; and Magness, J.
2004   The Roman Fort at Yotvata: Interim Report (2003). *JRA* 17: 405–12.
2005   The Roman Fort at Yotvata, 2004. *IEJ* 55: 227–30.

Avner, U., and Magness, J.
1998   Early Islamic Settlement in the Southern Negev. *BASOR* 310: 39–57.

Avner, U., and Roll, I.
1997   Southern ʿArava, Roman Milestones. *Excavations and Surveys in Israel* 16: 135.

Bachmann, H.-G., and Hauptmann, A.
1984   Zur alten Kupfergewinnung in Fenan und Hirbet en-Nahas im Wādī ʻAraba in Südjordanien. *Der Anschnitt (Zeitschrift für Kunst und Kultur im Bergbau)* 36.4: 110–23.

Bailey, C.
2006   Relations between Bedouin Tribes on Opposite Sides of the Wādī ʻAraba, 1600–1950. Pp. 251–58 in *Crossing the Rift. Resources, Routes, Settlement Patterns and Interaction in the Wādī ʻAraba,* eds. P. Bienkowski and K. Galor. Levant Supplementary Series 3. Oxford: Oxbow.

Barker, G. W.
2002   A Tale of Two Deserts: Contrasting Desertification Histories on Rome's Desert Frontiers. *World Archaeology* 33.3: 488–507.

Barker, G. W., et al.
1997   The Wādī Faynan Project, Southern Jordan: A Preliminary Report on Geomorphology and Landscape Archaeology. *Levant* 29: 19–40.
1998   Environment and Land Use in the Wādī Faynan, Southern Jordan: The Second Season of Geoarchaeology and Landscape Archaeology (1997). *Levant* 30: 5–26.
1999   Environment and Land Use in the Wādī Faynan, Southern Jordan: The Third Season of Geoarchaeology and Landscape Archaeology (1998). *Levant* 31: 255–92.
2000   Archaeology and Desertification in the Wādī Faynan: The Fourth (1999) Season of the Wādī Faynan Landscape Survey. *Levant* 32: 27–52.

Barker, G. W.; Gilbertson, D.; and Mattingly, D. (eds.)
2007   *Archaeology and Desertification: The Wādī Faynan Landscape Survey, Southern Jordan.* Oxford: Oxbow.

Bartlett, J. R.
1989   *Edom and the Edomites.* Journal for the Study of the Old Testament Supplement Series 77. Sheffield: Sheffield Academic.

Bawden, G., and Edens, C.
1988   Tayma Painted Ware and the Hejaz Iron Age Ceramic Tradition. *Levant* 20: 197–213.

Bienkowski, P.
1995   The Edomites: The Archaeological Evidence from Transjordan. Pp. 41–92 in *You Shall Not Abhor an Edomite for He is Your Brother: Edom and Seir in History and Tradition,* ed. D. V. Edelman. Atlanta: Scholars.
2001   The Iron Age and Persian Periods in Jordan. *SHAJ* 7: 265–74.
2006   The Wādī ʻAraba: Meanings in a Contested Landscape. Pp. 7–28 in *Crossing the Rift. Resources, Routes, Settlement Patterns and Interaction in the Wādī ʻAraba,* eds. P. Bienkowski and K. Galor. Levant Supplementary Series 3. Oxford: Oxbow.

Bienkowski, P. and Galor, K. (eds.)
2006   *Crossing the Rift. Resources, Routes, Settlement Patterns and Interaction in the Wādī ʻAraba.* Levant Supplementary Series 3. Oxford: Oxbow.

Bowsher, J.
1989   The Nabataean Army. Pp. 19–30 in *The Eastern Frontier of the Roman and Byzantine Empire,* II, eds. D. H. French and C. S. Lightfoot. BAR International Series 553. Oxford: British Archaeological Reports.

Brückner, H.,
2002   Chalcolithic and Early Bronze Age Sites near Aqaba, Jordan. Pp. 215–339 in *Ausgrabungen und Surveys im Vorderen Orient I,* ed. R. Eichmann. Orient-Archäologie 5. Rahden: Leidorf.

Bruins, H. J.
2006   Desert Environment and Geoarchaeology of the Wādī ʻAraba. Pp. 29–43 in *Crossing the Rift. Resources, Routes, Settlement Patterns and Interaction in the Wādī ʻAraba,* eds. P. Bienkowski and K. Galor. Levant Supplementary Series 3. Oxford: Oxbow.

Burgath, K.-P.; Hagen, D.; and Siewers, U.
1984   Geochemistry, Geology, and Primary Copper Mineralization in Wādī ʿAraba, Jordan. *Geologisches Jahrbuch* 53, Reihe B: 3–53.

Cohen, R.
1993a   Ḥaẓeva, Meẓad. Pp. 593–94 in *NEAEHL*, vol. 2, ed. E. Stern. Jerusalem: Israel Exploration Society.
1993b   Hellenistic, Roman, and Byzantine Sites in the Negev Hills. Pp. 1135–45 in *NEAEHL*, vol. 3, ed. E. Stern. Jerusalem: Israel Exploration Society.
1994   The Fortresses at ʿEn Ḥaẓeva. *BA* 57: 203–14.

Cohen, R., and Yisrael, Y.
1995   The Iron Age Fortresses at ʿEn Ḥaseva. *BA* 58: 223–25.
1996   ʿEnḤaẓeva – 1990–1994. *Excavations and Surveys in Israel* 15: 110–16.

Cribb, R.
1991   *Nomads in Archaeology.* Cambridge: Cambridge University.

Darby, R.; Darby, E.; and Shelton, A.
2010   The 2009 ʿAyn Gharandal Survey and Preservation Project. *ADAJ* 54: 189–201.

Davies, G., and Magness, J.
2006   The Roman Fort at Yotvata, 2005. *IEJ* 56: 105–10.
2007   The Roman Fort at Yotvata, 2006. *IEJ* 57: 106–14.
2008   The Roman Fort at Yotvata, 2007. *IEJ* 58: 103–12.
2011   The Roman Fort at Yotvata: A Foundation under Valens? *JRA* 24: 469–80.

Dayton, J. E.
1972   Midianite and Edomite Pottery. *Proceedings of the Seminar for Arabian Studies* 5: 24–33.

Diodorus Siculus
1933–67 *Library of History.* 12 vols. in the Loeb Classical Library. Trans. C. H. Oldfather et al. Cambridge, MA: Harvard University.

Divito, R. A.
1993   The Tell el-Kheleifeh Inscriptions. Pp. 51–63 in *Nelson Glueck's 1938-1940 Excavations at Tell el-Kheleifeh: A Reappraisal,* ed. G. Pratico. American Schools of Oriental Research Archaeological Reports 3. Atlanta: Scholars.

Di Segni, L.
2004   The Beersheba Tax Edict Reconsidered in the Light of a Newly Discovered Fragment. *Scripta Classica Israelica* 23: 131–58.

Dolinka, B. J.
2003   *Nabataean Aila (Aqaba, Jordan) from a Ceramic Perspective.* BAR International Series 1116. Oxford: British Archaeological Reports.
2006a   ARABIA ADQUISITA? Ceramic Evidence for Nabataean Cultural Continuity during the Antonine and Severan Periods: The Aqaba Ware from Horvat Dafit. Ph.D. diss., University of Liverpool.
2006b   The Rujm Ṭāba Archaeological Project (RTAP): Results of the 2001 Survey and Reconnaissance. Pp. 195–214 in *Crossing the Rift. Resources, Routes, Settlement Patterns and Interaction in the Wādī ʿAraba,* eds. P. Bienkowski and K. Galor. Levant Supplementary Series 3. Oxford: Oxbow.

Eddy, F. W., and Wendorf, F.
1999   *An Archaeological Investigation of the Central Sinai, Egypt.* Boulder, CO: University of Colorado.

Erickson-Gini, T.
2006   'Down to the Sea:' Nabataean Colonization in the Negev Highlands. Pp. 157–66 in *Crossing the Rift. Resources, Routes, Settlement Patterns and Interaction in the Wādī ʿAraba,* eds. P. Bienkowski and K. Galor. Levant Supplementary Series 3. Oxford: Oxbow.
2010   *Nabataean Settlement and Self-organized Economy in the Central Negev: Crisis and Renewal.* BAR International Series 2054. Oxford: Archaeopress.

Eusebius
1904 *Onomasticon der Biblischen Ortsnamen.* Ed.
      E. Klostermann. Leipzig: Hinrichs.

Finkelstein, I.
1988 Arabian Trade and Socio-Political Condi-
      tions in the Negev in the Twelfth–Eleventh
      Centuries BCE. *JNES* 47.4: 241–52.
1995 *Living on the Fringe: The Archaeology and
      History of the Negev, Sinai, and Neighboring
      Regions in the Bronze and Iron Ages.* Mono-
      graphs in Mediterranean Archaeology 6.
      Sheffield: Sheffield Academic.

Fritz, V.
1994 Vorbericht über die Grabungen in Barqa
      el-Hetiye im Gebiet von Fenan, Wādī el-
      ʿAraba (Jordanien) 1990. *ZDPV* 110: 125–50.

Gilead, I.
1988 The Chalcolithic Period in the Levant.
      Journal of World Prehistory 2.4: 397–443.

Graf, D. F.
1992 Nabataean Settlements and Roman Occu-
      pation in Arabia Petraea. *SHAJ* 4: 253–60.
1994 The Nabataean Army and the *Cohortes
      Ulpiae Petraeorum.* Pp. 265–311 in *The Ro-
      man and Byzantine Army in the East,* ed. E.
      Dabrowa. Cracow: Jagiellonian University.
1995 The *Via Nova Traiana* in *Arabia Petraea.* Pp.
      241–65 in *The Roman and Byzantine Near
      East,* ed. J. Humphrey. JRA Supplement 14.
      Ann Arbor, MI: JRA.
2001 First Millennium AD: Roman and Byzan-
      tine Periods Landscape Archaeology and
      Settlement Patterns. *SHAJ* 7: 469–80.

Grattan, J. P.; Gilberston, D. D.; and Hunt, C. O.
2007 The Local and Global Dimensions of
      Metalliferous Pollution Derived from a
      Reconstruction of an Eight Thousand Year
      Record of Copper Smelting and Mining at
      a Desert-Mountain Frontier in Southern
      Jordan. *JAS* 34.1: 83–110.

Groom, N.
1981 *Frankincense and Myrrh: A Study of the
      Arabian Incense Trade.* New York: Longman.

Grubisha, D.
2000 An Analysis of the Steatite Artifacts from
      the Archaeological Site of Aila, Jordan.
      M.A. thesis, University of Wisconsin at
      Milwaukee.

Hammond, P. C.
1959 The Nabataean Bitumen Industry at the
      Dead Sea. *BA* 22: 40–48.

Hanbury-Tenison, J. W.
1986 *The Late Chalcolithic to Early Bronze I Tran-
      sition in Palestine and Transjordan.* BAR
      International Series 311. Oxford: British
      Archaeological Reports.

Hart, S.
1987 The Edom Survey Project 1984–85: The Iron
      Age. *SHAJ* 3: 287–90.
1992 Iron Age Settlement in the Land of Edom.
      Pp. 93–98 in *Early Edom and Moab: The
      Beginning of the Iron Age in Southern Jordan,*
      ed. P. Bienkowski. Sheffield Archaeological
      Monographs 7. Sheffield: Collis.

Hauptmann, A.
1986 Archaeometallurgical and Mining-Ar-
      chaeological Studies in the Eastern ʿAraba,
      Feinan Area, 2nd Season. *ADAJ* 30: 415–19.
2006 Mining Archaeology and Archaeometallur-
      gy in the Wādī ʿAraba: The Mining Districts
      of Faynan and Timna. Pp. 125–33 in *Cross-
      ing the Rift. Resources, Routes, Settlement
      Patterns and Interaction in the Wādī ʿAraba,*
      eds. P. Bienkowski and K. Galor. Levant
      Supplementary Series 3. Oxford: Oxbow.
2007 *The Archaeometallurgy of Copper: Evidence
      from Faynan, Jordan.* Berlin: Springer.

Hauptmann, A., et al.
1992 Early Copper Production at Feinan, Wādī
      ʿAraba, Jordan: The Composition of Ores
      and Copper. *Archaeomaterials* 6.1: 1–33.

Hauptmann, A., and Weisgerber, G.
1987 Archaeometallurgical and Mining-Archae-
ological Investigations in the Area of Feinan,
Wādī ʿAraba (Jordan). *ADAJ* 31: 419–35.
1992 Periods of Ore Exploration and Metal Production in the Area of Feinan, Wādī ʿAraba,
Jordan. *SHAJ* 4: 61–66.

Hauptmann, A.; Weisgerber, G.; and Knauf, E.
1985 Archäometallurgische und Bergbauar-
chäologische Untersuchungen im Gebiet
von Feinan, Wādī Araba (Jordanien). *Der
Anschnitt (Zeitschrift für Kunst und Kultur
im Bergbau)* 37.5–6: 163–95.

Heemeier, B.; Rauen, A.; Waldhör, M.;
and Grottker, M.
2009 Water Management at Tell Ḥujeirat al-
Ghuzlan. Pp. 247–71 in *Prehistoric ʿAqaba
I*, eds. L. Khalil and K. Schmidt, Orient-
Archäologie, 23. Rahden: Leidorf.

Henry, D. O.
1982 The Prehistory of Southern Jordan and Relationships with the Levant. *JFA* 9.4: 417–44.
1992 Seasonal Movements of Fourth Millennium Pastoral Nomads in the Wādī Hisma,
Southern Jordan. *SHAJ* 4: 137–43.
1995 *Prehistoric Cultural Ecology and Evolution:
Insights from Southern Jordan.* New York:
Plenum.
2006 Cultural and Geological Influences on Prehistoric Site Distribution in the Wādī ʿAraba. Pp. 91–101 in *Crossing the Rift. Resources,
Routes, Settlement Patterns and Interaction
in the Wādī ʿAraba,* eds. P. Bienkowski and
K. Galor. Levant Supplementary Series 3.
Oxford: Oxbow.

Henry, D. O.; Bauer, H.; Kerry, K.; Beaver, J.;
and White, J.
2001 Survey of Prehistoric Sites, Wādī ʿAraba,
Southern Jordan. *BASOR* 323: 1–19.

Husselman, E. M. (ed.)
1971 *Papyri from Karanis,* 3rd series, ed. E.M.
Husselman. Cleveland. American Philo-

logical Association Monograph 29, nos.
522–76. Atlanta: Scholars.

Ibrahim, K.
1993 *Geology of the Wādī Gharandal: Map Sheet
No. 3050 II,* 1:50,000 Geological Mapping
Series, Geological Bulletin No. 24. Amman:
Geology Directorate, Geological Mapping
Division, Natural Resources Authority.

Ilan, O., and Sebbane, M.
1989 Copper Metallurgy, Trade and the Ur-
banization of Southern Canaan in the
Chalcolithic and Early Bronze Age. Pp. 139–
62 in *L'Urbanisation de la Palestine à l'âge du
Bronze Ancien,* ed. P. de Miroschedji. BAR
International Series 527. Oxford: British
Archaeological Reports.

Jasmin, M.
2006 The Emergence and First Development of
the Arabian Trade across the Wādī ʿAraba.
Pp. 143–50 in *Crossing the Rift. Resources,
Routes, Settlement Patterns and Interaction
in the Wādī ʿAraba,* eds. P. Bienkowski and
K. Galor. Levant Supplementary Series 3.
Oxford: Oxbow.

Jobling, W. J.
1981 Preliminary Report on the Archaeological
Survey between Maʿan and ʿAqaba, January
to February 1980. *ADAJ* 25: 105–12.
1983 The 1982 Archaeological and Epigraphic
Survey of the ʿAqaba–Maʿan Area of Southern Jordan. *ADAJ* 27: 185–96.

Johnson, D. J.
1987 Nabataean Trade: Intensification and Culture Change. Ph.D. diss. University of Utah.
1990 Nabataean Piriform Unguentaria. *Aram*
2.1–2: 235–48.

Kalsbeek, J., and London, G.
1978 A Late Second Millennium B.C. Potting
Puzzle. *BASOR* 232: 47–56.

Kindler, A.
1989   The Numismatic Finds from the Roman Fort at Yotvata. *IEJ* 39: 261–66.

Knauf, E., and Lenzen, C.
1987   Edomite Copper Industry. *SHAJ* 3: 83–88.

Kozloff, B.
1981   Pastoral Nomadism in the Sinai: An Ethno-archaeological Study. *Bulletin de l'Équipe Écologie et Anthropologie des Sociétés Pastorales* 8: 19–24.

Levy, T. E.
2009   Pastoral Nomads and Iron Age Metal Production in Ancient Edom. Pp. 147–77 in *Nomads, Tribes, and the State in the Ancient Near East: Cross-disciplinary Perspectives,* ed. J. Szuchman. Chicago: Oriental Institute of the University of Chicago.

Levy, T. E.; Adams, R. B.; Anderson, J. D.; Najjar, M.; Smith, N.; Arbel, Y.; Soderbaum, L.; and Muniz, M.
2003   An Iron Age Landscape in the Edomite Lowlands: Archaeological Surveys along the Wādī al-Guwayb and Wādī el-Jariyeh, Jabal Hamrat Fidan, Jordan. *ADAJ* 47: 247–77.

Levy, T. E.; Adams, R. B.; and Shafiq, R.
1999   The Jebel Hamrat Fidan Project: Excavations at the Wādī Fidan 40 Cemetery, Jordan (1997). *Levant* 31: 293–308.

Levy, T. E; Adams, R. B.; Najjar, M.; Hauptmann, A.; Anderson, J. D.; Brandl, B.; Robinson, M. A.; and Higham, T.
2004   Reassessing the Chronology of Biblical Edom: New Excavations and 14C Dates from Khirbat en-Nahas (Jordan). *Antiquity* 78: 863–76.

MacDonald, B.
1992   *The Southern Ghors and Northeast 'Araba Archaeological Survey.* Sheffield Archaeological Monographs 5. Sheffield: Collis.

Mattingly, D.; Newson, P.; Grattan, J.; Tomber, R.; Barker, G.; Gilbertson, D.; and Hunt , C.
2007a The Making of Early States: The Iron Age and Nabataean Periods. Pp. 271–303 in *Archaeology and Desertification: The Wādī Faynan Landscape Survey, Southern Jordan,* eds. G. W. Barker, D. Gilbertson, and D. Mattingly. Oxford: Oxbow.

Mattingly, D.; Newson, P.; Creighton, O.; Tomber, R.; Grattan, J.; Hunt, C.; Gilbertson, D.; el-Rishi, H.; and Pyatt, B.
2007b A Landscape of Imperial Power: Roman and Byzantine Phaino. Pp. 305–48 in *Archaeology and Desertification: The Wādī Faynan Landscape Survey, Southern Jordan,* eds. G. W. Barker, D. Gilbertson, and D. Mattingly. Oxford: Oxbow.

Mellaart, J.
1975   *The Neolithic of the Near East.* London: Thames and Hudson.

Meshel, Z.
1989   A Fort at Yotvata from the Time of Diocletian. *IEJ* 39: 228–38.
1993   Yotvata. Pp. 1517–20 in *NEAEHL*, vol. 4, ed. E. Stern. Jerusalem: Israel Exploration Society.
2006   Were there Gold Mines in the Eastern 'Araba? Pp. 231–38 in *Crossing the Rift. Resources, Routes, Settlement Patterns and Interaction in the Wādī 'Araba,* eds. P. Bienkowski and K. Galor. Levant Supplementary Series 3. Oxford: Oxbow.

Moore, A.
1973   The Late Neolithic in Palestine. *Levant* 5: 36–68.

Mussell, M.-L.
2000   Tell el-Kheleifeh. *AJA* 104: 577–78.

Niemi, T. M., and Smith A. M., II
1999   Initial Results from the Southeastern Wādī 'Araba, Jordan Geoarchaeological Study: Implications for Shifts in Late Quarternary Aridity. *Geoarchaeology* 14.8: 791–820.

Nissenbaum, A.
1993 The Dead Sea – An economic Resource for 10,000 years. *Hydrobiologia* 267: 127–41.

Oleson, J. P.
2010 *Humayma Excavation Project, 1: Resources, History, and the Water Supply System.* ASOR Archaeological Reports 15. Boston, MA: American Schools of Oriental Research.

Parker, S. T.
1986 *Romans and Saracens: A History of the Arabian Frontier.* Winona Lake, IN: Eisenbrauns.
1998 The Roman 'Aqaba Project: The 1996 Campaign. *ADAJ* 42: 375–94.
2000 The Roman 'Aqaba Project: The 1997 and 1998 Campaigns. *ADAJ* 44: 373–94.
2002 The Roman 'Aqaba Project: The 2000 Campaign. *ADAJ* 46: 409–28.
2003 The Roman 'Aqaba Project: The 2002 Campaign. *ADAJ* 47: 321–33.
2006 Roman Aila and Wādī 'Araba: An Economic Relationship. Pp. 227–34 in *Crossing the Rift. Resources, Routes, Settlement Patterns and Interaction in the Wādī 'Araba,* eds. P. Bienkowski and K. Galor. Levant Supplementary Series 3. Oxford: Oxbow.
2009a The Foundation of Aila: A Nabataean Port on the Red Sea. *SHAJ* 10: 685–90.
2009b The Roman Port of Aila: Economic Connections with the Red Sea Littoral. Pp. 79–84 in *Red Sea IV: Connected Hinterlands.* Society for Arabian Studies Monographs. BAR International Series 2052: Oxford: British Archaeological Reports.
2009c *Arabia Adquisita:* The Roman Annexation of Arabia Reconsidered. Pp. 1585–92 in *Limes XX: Roman Frontier Studies.* XXth International Congress of Roman Frontier Studies, eds. A. Morillo, N. Hanel, and E. Martín. 3 vols. Madrid: Consejo Superior de Investigaciones Científicas.
2009d The Roman Frontier in Southern Arabia: A Synthesis of Recent Research. Pp. 142–152 in *The Army and Frontiers of Rome: Papers offered to David Breeze on the Occasion of his Sixth-fifth Birthday and his Retirement from Historic Scotland,* ed. W. S. Hanson. JRA Supplementary Series 74. Portsmouth, RI: JRA.

Parr, P.
1982 Contacts between North West Arabia and Jordan in the Late Bronze and Iron Ages. *SHAJ* 1: 127–33.

Peacock, D. P. S., and Williams, D. F.
1986 *Amphorae and the Roman Economy: An Introductory Guide.* New York: Longman.

Prag, K.
2001 The Third Millennium in Jordan: A Perspective, Past and Future. *SHAJ* 7: 179–90.

Pratico, G. D.
1993 *Nelson Glueck's 1938–1940 Excavations at Tell el-Kheleifeh: A Reappraisal.* ASOR Archaeological Reports 3. Atlanta: Scholars.

Retsö, J.
1991 The Domestication of the Camel and the Establishment of the Frankincense Road from South Arabia. *Orientalia Suecana* 40: 187–219.

Retzleff, A.
2003 A Nabataean/Roman Domestic Complex at the Red Sea Port of Aila. *BASOR* 331: 45–65.

Roll, I.
1989 A Latin Imperial Inscription from the Time of Diocletian Found at Yotvata. *IEJ* 39: 239–60.

Rosen, S.
1988a Notes on the Origins of Pastoral Nomadism: A Case Study from the Negev and Sinai. *Current Anthropology* 29: 498–506.
1988b Finding Evidence of Ancient Nomads. *Biblical Archaeology Review* 14.5: 46–53.
1992 Nomads in Archaeology: A Response to Finkelstein and Perevolotsky. *BASOR* 287: 75–85.

Rothenberg, B.

1962   Ancient Copper Industries in the Western
        'Araba. *PEQ* 94: 5–72.

1971   The 'Araba in Roman and Byzantine Times
        in the Light of New Research. Pp. 211–23 in
        Roman Frontier Studies 1967, Proceedings
        of the 7th International Congress, ed. S.
        Applebaum. Tel Aviv: Tel Aviv University.

1972   *Timna: Valley of the Biblical Copper Mines.*
        London: Thames and Hudson.

1988   *The Egyptian Mining Temple at Timna.* Re-
        searches in the 'Araba, 1. London: Institute
        for Archaeo-Metallurgical Studies.

1999a   Archeo-Metallurgical Researches in the
        Southern 'Araba 1959–1990, Part I: Late
        Pottery Neolithic to Early Bronze IV. *PEQ*
        131: 68–89.

1999b   Archeo-Metallurgical Researches in the
        Southern 'Araba 1959–1990, Part II: Egyp-
        tian New Kingdom (Ramesside) to Early
        Islam. *PEQ* 131: 149–75.

Rothenberg, B., and Glass, J.

1992   The Beginnings and the Development of
        Early Metallurgy and the Settlement and
        Chronology of the Western 'Araba, from
        the Chalcolithic Period to Early Bronze
        Age IV. *Levant* 24: 141–57.

Schick, R.

1995   The Settlement Pattern of Southern Jordan:
        The Nature of the Evidence. Pp. 133–54 in
        *The Byzantine and Early Islamic Near East
        II: Land Use and Settlement Patterns,* eds.
        G. R. D. King and A. Cameron. Princeton,
        NJ: Darwin.

Schmid, S. G.

1996   Die Feinkeramik. Pp. 151–281 in Petra Ez
        Zantur I: Ergebnisse der Schweizerisch-
        Liechtensteinischen Ausgrabungen 1988–
        1992. Mainz: von Zabern.

2000   *Petra – Ez Zantur II.* Teil 1: *Die Feinkeramik
        der Nabatäer. Typologie, Chronologie und
        kulturhistorische Hintergründe.* Mainz: von
        Zabern.

Smith, A. M., II

2005   Bir Madhkur Project: A Preliminary Report
        on Recent Fieldwork. *BASOR* 340: 57–75.

2010   *Wādī 'Araba in Classical and Late Antiquity:
        An Historical Geography.* BAR Internation-
        al Series 2173. Oxford: British Archaeologi-
        cal Reports.

Smith, A.M. II; Niemi, T. M.; and Stevens, M.

1997   The Southeast 'Araba Archaeological
        Survey: A Preliminary Report of the 1994
        Season. *BASOR* 305: 45–71.

Strabo

1930   *Geography.* 8 vols. in the Loeb Classical
        Library. Trans. H. L. Jones. Cambridge, MA:
        Harvard University.

Thomas, R.; Niemi, T. M.; and Parker, S. T.

2007   Structural Damage from Earthquakes in the
        2nd-9th Century A.D. at the Archaeologi-
        cal Site of Aila in Aqaba, Jordan. *BASOR*
        346: 59–77.

van der Steen, E.

2006   Nineteenth-century Travelers in the Wādī
        'Araba. Pp. 243–50 in *Crossing the Rift.
        Resources, Routes, Settlement Patterns
        and Interaction in the Wādī 'Araba,* eds. P.
        Bienkowski and K. Galor. Levant Supple-
        mentary Series 3. Oxford: Oxbow.

Whitcomb, D. S.

1994   *Ayla: Art and Industry in the Islamic Port
        of Aqaba.* Chicago: University of Chicago.

2006   Land Behind Aqaba: the Wādī 'Araba dur-
        ing the Early Islamic Period. Pp. 239–42 in
        *Crossing the Rift. Resources, Routes, Settlement
        Patterns and Interaction in the Wādī 'Araba,*
        eds. P. Bienkowski and K. Galor. Levant
        Supplementary Series 3. Oxford: Oxbow.

Zarins, J.

1989   Pastoralism in Southwest Asia: The Second
        Millennium BC. Pp. 127–55 in *The Walking
        Larder: Patterns of Domestication, Pastoral-
        ism, and Predation,* ed. J. Clutton-Brock. One
        World Archaeology 2. London: Unwin Hyman.

Index